To Henry,
with affection,
Bob and Stan
chicago
11/6/92

WITHOUT CONSENT OR CONTRACT
Conditions of Slave Life and the Transition to Freedom
Technical Papers (Volume II)

WITHOUT CONSENT OR CONTRACT
The Rise and Fall of American Slavery

Conditions of Slave Life and the Transition to Freedom:
Technical Papers, Volume II

edited by

Robert William Fogel
and Stanley L. Engerman

With contributions by

Stephen C. Crawford, Stanley L. Engerman, Robert W. Fogel, Claudia
Goldin, A. Meredith John, Charles Kahn, Herbert S. Klein, Laurence J.
Kotlikoff, Robert A. Margo, Pedro C. de Mello, Joseph D. Reid, Jr.,
Anton J. Rupert, Ralph Shlomowitz, Richard H. Steckel, James
Trussell, and Steven B. Webb

W. W. NORTON & COMPANY · NEW YORK · LONDON

Printed in the United States of America.

The text of this book is composed in Bodoni Book, with the display set in Betan Medium Agency and Bold Condensed. Composition and manufacturing by the Haddon Craftsmen, Inc.

First Edition

Library of Congress Cataloging-in-Publication Data
Without consent or contract. Technical papers : the rise and fall of American slavery / edited by
  Robert W. Fogel and Stanley L. Engerman; with contributions by Stanley L. Engerman . . . [et al.].
  — 1st ed.
      p.   cm.
   Supplement to: Without consent or contract / Robert William Fogel.
   Includes bibliographies and indexes.
   Contents: v. 1. Markets and production — v. 2. Conditions of slave life and the transition to
freedom.
      1. Slavery—United States—History.   2. Slavery—United States—Econometric models.
3. Slavery—Economic aspects—United States.   I. Fogel, Robert William.   II. Engerman, Stanley
L.   III. Fogel, Robert William. Without consent or contract.
E441.F63   1989 Suppl. 2
306.3′62′0973—dc20   89-8571

ISBN 0-393-02792-9

W.W. Norton & Company, Inc., 500 Fifth Avenue, New York, N.Y. 10110
W.W. Norton & Company, Ltd., 10 Coptic Street, London WC1A 1PU

1 2 3 4 5 6 7 8 9 0

To

Lionel W. McKenzie
Richard N. Rosett
Henry Rosovsky
W. Allen Wallis

For their constant encouragement

Contents

Publisher's Note   ix
Conventions Followed in Referencing   xi
General Introduction   xv

PART IV. SLAVE DEMOGRAPHY

Introduction   367

17. Children and Choice: A Comparative Analysis of Slave and White Fertility in the Antebellum South   *Richard H. Steckel*   369
18. Slave Mortality: Analysis of Evidence from Plantation Records   *Richard H. Steckel*   393
19. Logistic Models of Slave Child Mortality in Trinidad   *A. Meredith John*   413
20. The Age of Slaves at Menarche and Their First Birth   *James Trussell and Richard H. Steckel*   435
21. The Slave Breeding Thesis   *Robert W. Fogel and Stanley L. Engerman*   455
22. Factors in Mortality in the French Slave Trade in the Eighteenth Century   *Herbert S. Klein and Stanley L. Engerman*   473

PART V. MATERIAL ASPECTS OF SLAVE LIFE

Introduction   487

23. Work, Disease, and Diet in the Health and Mortality of American Slaves   *Richard H. Steckel*   489
24. The Nutrition and Health of Slaves and Antebellum Southern Whites   *Robert A. Margo and Richard H. Steckel*   508
25. A Linear-Programming Solution to the Slave Diet   *Charles Kahn*   522
26. Punishments and Rewards   *Stephen C. Crawford*   536
27. An Agency Approach to Slave Punishments and Awards   *Charles Kahn*   551

PART VI. The Transition to Freedom

Introduction   569

28. Saints or Cynics: A Statistical Analysis of Parliament's Decision for Emancipation in 1833   *Steven B. Webb*   571

29. Philanthropy at Bargain Prices: Notes on the Economics of Gradual Emancipation   *Robert W. Fogel and Stanley L. Engerman*   587

30. The Manumission of Slaves in New Orleans, 1827–1846   *Laurence J. Kotlikoff and Anton J. Rupert*   606

31. The Economics of Emancipation   *Claudia Goldin*   614

32. Expectation of Abolition and Sanguinity of Coffee Planters in Brazil, 1871–1881   *Pedro C. de Mello*   629

33. Sharecropping as an Understandable Market Response: The Postbellum South   *Joseph D. Reid, Jr.*   647

34. "Bound" or "Free"? Black Labor in Cotton and Sugar Cane Farming, 1865–1880   *Ralph Shlomowitz*   665

Appendix: Contents of Companion Volumes   B1

Acknowledgments   B7

References   B9

Unpublished Memorandums   B31

Additional Works on Slavery and Related Topics by the Contributors   B33

About the Contributors   B39

Index   B43

Publisher's Note

This is one of three volumes that provide the technical foundations to the interpretive volume of *Without Consent or Contract: The Rise and Fall of American Slavery*. This volume contains papers #17–#34. Its companion, *Markets and Production: Technical Papers,* contains papers #1–#16. The papers are a selection of the principal papers produced by collaborators in a research project on the economics of slavery that began in 1965.

Papers that were previously published have been revised to take account of new research, but many of the papers are published here for the first time. The full canon of research on slavery and related topics by the contributors is listed at the end of this volume. Each volume of *Technical Papers* contains a full set of references and an index.

Conventions Followed in Referencing

In cross-reference to companion volumes of *Without Consent or Contract,* titles are abbreviated to *RF* for the interpretive volume, *EM* for *Evidence and Methods,* and *TP* for either of the volumes of *Technical Papers;* the number of the page, chapter, note, or paper cited immediately follows the abbreviation. For the titles that correspond to these reference numbers, see the Appendix to this volume.

WITHOUT CONSENT OR CONTRACT

Conditions of Slave Life and the Transition to Freedom
Technical Papers (Volume II)

General Introduction

The papers collected in the two volumes of *Technical Papers* are the outgrowth of a loosely structured inquiry into the economics and demography of slavery. The project began inadvertently, largely as the by-product of a decision to edit a collection of essays on the cliometric contribution to the interpretation of American economic history (Fogel and Engerman 1971a). In this connection, we planned a series of review essays, several of which dealt with the economics of slavery and its aftermath (Engerman 1966, 1967, 1971b; Fogel and Engerman 1971b and 1971c). We consider these review essays, which were written mainly between 1965 and 1968, to be the start of the project, although it was not actually formalized until 1968.

The project remained loosely structured until its close, not only because that style conformed to our concept of how collaborative social-scientific research should be undertaken, but also because there were more first-rate issues to be addressed than we could cope with and because some of the most fruitful initiatives arose spontaneously, often as unanticipated by-products of other endeavors. The evolution of our work on the manifests of slaves shipped interregionally on coastwise vessels is a case in point. We originally collected a large sample of these documents because of the light they might shed on patterns in the interregional slave trade. We did not appreciate the value of the information on height recorded in the manifests until several years later, when James Trussell and J. M. Tanner educated us on the uses of anthropometric data as indicators of nutritional status and health. That discovery led to some of the most important papers on demographic and health issues that emanated from our project (see papers #19, #20, #23, and #24, in this volume).

In other cases, new research projects were initiated by papers submitted for the fulfillment of a course requirement or as dissertation proposals. We had, for example, given little thought to the economics of slavery in the cities until Claudia D. Goldin proposed the analysis set forth in #7, in *TP*, Vol. I, or to the way in which markets for indentured servants operated until David W. Galenson began work on the problem (see papers #1 and #2, in *TP*, Vol. I). Similarly, it was the interest of Laurence J. Kotlikoff and Sebastian E. Pinera in the theory of international trade that led them to apply the general equilibrium models employed in that field to the analysis of the Old South's stake in the interregional slave trade (see paper #6, in *TP*, Vol. I).

The loose structure also promoted diversity of opinion within the group and permitted investigators to pursue their own preliminary hypotheses about particular aspects of slave economies and demographic systems. The principal glue that held the project together was a shared investment in the discovery of data sets relevant to the study of slavery, the retrieval and transformation of these data sets into machine-readable form, and the application of the statistical and behavioral models of the social sciences to the analysis of the information contained in these data.

Many issues were addressed by more than one investigator. It was not uncommon for different investigators to obtain different results, sometimes because the questions were addressed to different data sets and, hence, reflected different aspects of a complex whole and sometimes because different analytical techniques produced different results even when applied to the same data set. And when differences in findings could not be satisfactorily resolved, the studies still provided useful information about the range of uncertainty that surrounded the issues and about the sensitivity of results to plausible alternative methods of analysis. Such unresolved issues, some large, some small, have not been swept under the table. They are reflected in the contributions to this volume and are more fully explored in the companion volume subtitled *Evidence and Methods.*

The direction of the project was influenced by external factors, one of which was the upsurge of research on slavery and black history generally, which covered issues far beyond those that we directly encompassed. Nevertheless, discoveries in such fields as cultural, political, and religious history suggested numerous new approaches to the problems on which we were working and influenced the interpretation of our findings, just as the work on the economics of slavery influenced the other fields. We also benefited from the development of new statistical methods, the plunging costs of data processing, advances in economic and demographic models, and new discoveries in the biomedical area—all of which made it possible to tackle issues in the 1980s that were beyond contemplation or prohibitively expensive in the 1970s.

The direction of the project was also influenced by the rich and insightful criticisms of *Time on the Cross,* two books intended to report and interpret the initial (and to us, quite startling) provisional findings tossed up about a third of the way through the project. Whether these criticisms were made by colleagues outside of the project, by research assistants within it, or by colleagues and students who later contributed to the project, all of the criticisms were helpful in developing a new research agenda that guided our work since 1975. The new agenda was also an evolving agenda, because it consisted of subprojects underway or proposed before the publication of *Time on the Cross,* of new projects added as a consequence of the debate, and of still other projects suggested by new discoveries both inside and outside of our group.

The debate over *Time on the Cross* set off a new, more intense round of research into the three questions that had been at the center of cliometric work on slavery before 1974 and that were also central topics in *Time on the Cross:* the profitability and economic viability of slavery, the rate of southern economic growth between 1840 and 1880 and the factors which influenced it, and the relative productivity of slave and free agriculture. Not only was there a searching reexamination of the conceptual bases for many of the earlier computations, but many aspects of the operation of slave markets and antebellum agriculture, commerce, and manufacturing were more deeply probed than ever before. New bodies of relevant data were uncovered, which made it possible to estimate variables and parameters about aspects of the slave economy that previously had to be left to conjecture. Our contribution to this set of issues is represented by the papers in *TP*, Vol. I as well as by a number of the entries in the companion volume, *Evidence and Methods*. Although the new work has not dramatically revised the basic estimates of profitability, the rate of southern economic growth, or the relative productivity of slave agriculture that were reported before 1975, it has produced a far more detailed and textured picture of the slave economy and of the forces that influenced its development.

The most dramatic new cliometric findings since 1974 have to do with the health and demography of slave populations, which were still infant subjects when we dealt with them in *Time on the Cross*. No other field of slavery research has grown more explosively than these have, and the sophistication of the investigators in demography, nutrition, and general biomedical knowledge has grown apace. The analysis of immense bodies of demographic and anthropometric data for slave populations in the United States, the British West Indies, Cuba, Brazil, and various ethnic groups in Africa became feasible as the cost of data processing declined. These developments produced better explanations of both the high fertility rates of U.S. slaves and of the differences between their fertility rates and those of the slave populations in the Caribbean and South America. It turns out that most of what appeared to be international differences in slave fertility rates are actually differences in mortality rates, because mortality was very poorly measured. Papers representative of our work on these topics will be found in Parts IV and V, in this volume.

Another important new direction in research after 1974 involved the study of emancipation processes and postemancipation societies. Papers dealing with these questions (see Part VI, in this volume) span not only economic and political issues but also involve consideration of the conflicting aspirations of ex-slaves and of planters—of mentalité. Getting at such issues involves as much ingenuity in archival research as work on vital rates or the measurement of productivity.

The papers included in *Technical Papers*, Vols. I and II are only a fraction of the technical investigations undertaken by collaborators in the project. The total output has included twelve dissertations, eleven books, scores of published papers, and numerous unpublished research memorandums. Those unpublished memorandums that are available for distribution are listed at the back of this volume, and will be sent to interested scholars on request for the cost of reproducing and shipping them. Copies of tapes containing the principal data sets employed in this project have been deposited with the Inter-University Consortium for Political and Social

Research at the University of Michigan, which maintains an international lending library of computer tapes. Scholars desiring copies of these tapes should contact the consortium.

ROBERT WILLIAM FOGEL
STANLEY L. ENGERMAN

PART FOUR
SLAVE DEMOGRAPHY

Introduction

Issues related to the demography of slave populations, in the United States and elsewhere, have long been a source of controversy, both during the slave era and, subsequently, among scholars dealing with slavery. Charges of deliberately working slaves to death, of encouraging "slave breeding," and of other deliberate interferences with fertility were part of the abolitionist critique of slavery. Alternatively, the very high rate of natural increase of the U.S. slave population, a pattern sharply in contrast with the rates of decrease of the slave population in the West Indies, had been used to argue for a more favorable material treatment of U.S. slaves. At issue in these debates, in addition to the arguments about the inferences to be drawn concerning the nature of planter motivation, is the nature and autonomy of choices made, particularly in regard to family and fertility, by the slaves themselves within the plantation setting.

The papers in Part IV draw on a number of different antebellum sources, including the U.S. census records, probate and plantation records, and the manifests listing slaves (by age, height, and gender) shipped in the coastal trade after 1808. For the study of Trinidad, the detailed slave registrations imposed by the British after 1813 are a rich source of data, and the study of the French slave trade is based on reports of captains of slave ships and related sources in French archives.

Richard H. Steckel's first article, based on census data for whites and plantation and probate records for slaves, compares and contrasts the circumstances of the high fertility of both populations in the nineteenth-century South, focusing on ages of birth of first and last children, child spacing, and the percentage of females who bore children. Steckel then uses plantation records to analyze the patterns of mortality of the slave population, pointing to differences by size of plantation, crops grown, and other factors. A. Meredith John uses the registration reports for Trinidad as the basis for reestimating child mortality by sophisticated demographic procedures to obtain a more refined set of estimates of child mortality. This calculation is important in providing greater understanding of the distinctly different demographic patterns of the U.S. slave population and those of slaves elsewhere in the Americas.

The next two essays deal with questions of U.S. slave demography that have important implications for the study of slave culture and behavioral patterns. By using data from the coastal shipping manifests to obtain estimates of the age of

367

menarche of slave females and using the probate and plantation records to estimate the ages of slave females at the birth of their first child, James Trussell and Richard H. Steckel are able to point to the difference in time between these events and to discuss the questions this finding raises for arguments concerning slave cultural beliefs and planter interference with slave fertility to encourage higher rates of reproduction. Robert W. Fogel and Stanley L. Engerman provide some specific tests of the "slave breeding hypothesis"—the argument that there was a deliberate interference with slave female fertility patterns—using primarily demographic information from the Parker-Gallman sample of southern agriculture in 1860, in addition to other census data, to study variations in slave fertility over time as well as the patterns of differences attributable to socioeconomic characteristics in 1860. Herbert S. Klein and Stanley L. Engerman use French slave-trading records to examine mortality rates of slaves and crew in the "middle passage" from Africa to the New World in the eighteenth century. With data from individual voyages, they analyze the impact of voyage length, degree of shipboard crowding, and port of departure on the pattern of mortality rates and their changes over time.

SEVENTEEN

Children and Choice: A Comparative Analysis of Slave and White Fertility in the Antebellum South

Richard H. Steckel

INTRODUCTION

The U.S. population grew rapidly during the nineteenth century. Between 1810 and 1860 the average annual rates of growth of the slave and of the white population were about 2.4 percent.[1] The U.S. rates were high compared to other slave populations in the Western Hemisphere and to contemporary European populations. Elsewhere in the Western Hemisphere slave deaths exceeded births and the colonies depended heavily on imports to maintain or increase their populations.[2] Between 1800 and 1850 Europe and Russia were growing at about 0.7 percent and world population was growing at about 0.5 percent per annum.[3]

The similarities and contrasts in demographic behavior and in social and economic conditions across these populations suggest several intriguing topics for research. This paper focuses on one of them: the measurement and comparative analysis of slave and southern white fertility. The comparative approach provides a useful context in which whites are used as a backdrop for devising and testing hypotheses about slave behavior. Although research has been done on slave fertility (Zelnick 1966; Farley 1965, 1970; Eblen 1972, 1974), the results are based on census data, apply to the entire slave population, and have limited value for understanding individual behavior. Studies of antebellum white fertility often rely on aggregate data and/or focus on the North (Yasuba 1962; Easterlin 1971, 1976a, 1976b; Smith 1972, 1973; Forster and Tucker 1972; Leet 1976; Easterlin et al. 1978; Vinovskis 1979). The insights of this paper depend on previously unused data and on new ways of analyzing data for individual slaves and southern whites.

The salient patterns of fertility are conveniently measured by a child-woman ratio. The ratio is sometimes called a measure of effective fertility because the numerator includes only surviving births. The measure can be influenced by infant and early childhood mortality as well as the mortality of women of childbearing age, completeness of registration, and migration, but studies show that the child-woman ratio is highly correlated with direct measures of fertility (Bogue and Palmore 1964; Tuchfeld et al. 1974; Tucker 1974). The ratio is employed here both because direct measures are not readily available and because this measure can be easily calculated for a wide variety of geographic units in census years from 1800 to 1860. It should be noted, however, that small differences in the ratio may not reflect genuine differences in fertility behavior.

The decline in the ratios is a conspicuous pattern in Table 17.1. The ratio for whites declined slowly at first, then more rapidly during the 1840s, declining by 26 percent from 1800 to 1860.[4] Between 1820 and 1830 the ratio for slaves was approximately constant and then gradually fell 12 percent by 1860. The ratios for both populations declined more in the West.

Although the time trends were similar for slaves and whites, the regional patterns differed. The ratio for slaves was higher in the East, whereas the opposite pattern existed for whites. Among slaves the regional differences were small at first and then widened to 7 percent by 1860. While among slaves the regions had initially similar ratios and then grew apart, among whites the regions were initially disparate and then became more alike. In addition, the ratio for whites was 6 to 10 percent higher than the ratio for slaves between 1820 and 1840 and the ratios were approximately equal by 1850.

Explanations for the pattern in the child-woman ratios are sought at demographic and at socioeconomic levels.[5] The demographic analysis relies on a measure called the synthetic total fertility rate. This measure has four components or determinants: age at first birth, age at last surviving birth, surviving child spacing, and the proportion of women who eventually have surviving children.

The data base for this paper includes plantation records, probate records, census manuscript schedules for free persons in 1860, and the 1860 published census. The plantation records include 77 large plantations located in forty-two counties and eight southern states. These records include plantations involved in the production of all of the major southern staples and cover the period from 1739 to 1865. The probate records are from forty counties in Georgia, Louisiana, and Virginia, and consist of 540 plantations of various sizes that list slaves by families. The plantations are located in counties that specialized in growing all the major southern staples and cover the period from 1801 to 1865. Four random samples of households from a random sample of thirty southern counties in 1860, all drawn from the manuscript census, provide information about whites. The data in three of these samples were combined to provide estimates of demographic statistics at the county level and the fourth sample furnishes information on the demographic and socioeconomic behavior of individuals. An additional sample of fifty-seven counties, drawn from the published census, provides county-level data for whites and slaves. Detailed discussions of the data and their limitations can be found in Steckel (1985).

The next section discusses child-woman ratios at the county level. Later sections

Table 17.1. Number of Children under Ten per Thousand Women Aged 15–49 among Whites and Slaves in the East, the West, and Total, by Census Year, 1800–1860

Census Year[a]	Whites			Slaves		
	East[b]	West[c]	Total	East[b]	West[c]	Total
1800	1,615	2,104	1,687	—	—	—
1810	1,579	1,983	1,683	—	—	—
1820	1,518	1,859	1,635	1,490	1,457	1,482
1830	1,430	1,785	1,571	1,499	1,460	1,486
1840	1,421	1,704	1,556	1,434	1,370	1,406
1850	1,257	1,435	1,353	1,396	1,314	1,354
1860	1,203	1,374	1,303	1,369	1,278	1,318

[a]The age distributions required to calculate the ratios in 1800, 1810, and 1820 were obtained by interpolation. The procedure is discussed in Steckel (1985), 3–4.
[b]Includes Delaware, the District of Columbia, Georgia, Maryland, North Carolina, South Carolina, and Virginia.
[c]Includes Alabama (after 1810), Arkansas (after 1810), Florida (after 1820), Kentucky, Louisiana (after 1820), Mississippi, Missouri (after 1800), Tennessee, and Texas (after 1840).

Sources: U.S. Census Office (1802, 1811, 1821, 1832, 1841, 1853, 1864b).

discuss the synthetic total fertility rate, evidence on components of the synthetic total fertility rate, the probability that a woman has a surviving child, age at last surviving birth, surviving child spacing, the regional differential, and the time trend. Conclusions are presented in the last section.

CHILD-WOMAN RATIOS AT THE COUNTY LEVEL

Although the similar time trends in child-woman ratios for slaves and whites may be a coincidence, the pattern suggests that common factors may have influenced fertility in these populations. The fact that the ratio for whites was higher prior to 1850 and the regional contrast, however, suggest that differential factors must have been involved.

The role of regional factors can be investigated further by disaggregation. Using a sample of fifty-seven southern counties drawn from the 1860 census, the child-woman ratio of slaves was regressed on the child-woman ratio of whites.[6] The regression shows that no statistically significant relationship exists between these variables; R-square is only 0.02.

The low correlation confirms that county-specific determinants of fertility must have differed or that common determinants operated at different levels. While this conclusion is interesting, the analysis does not reveal the determinants involved. This paper now turns to the components of the synthetic total fertility rate, which is better suited to this analysis of determinants.

A SYNTHETIC TOTAL FERTILITY RATE

A total fertility rate, R, is defined by the following equation:

$$R = \left(\frac{L - F}{S} + 1 \right) \beta \tag{1}$$

where L is average age at last birth, F is average age at first birth, S is the average child-spacing interval, and β is the proportion of women who eventually have children. The expression in parentheses is the total fertility rate for women who had at least one child. Multiplication of this expression by β converts the measure to the total fertility rate for all women. The meaning of R depends on the method of estimating the variables on the right-hand side of the equation. To obtain a true total fertility rate one needs the values of L, F, S, and β in the fertility schedule pertaining to a particular time period. Unfortunately these measures are not available and can only be estimated approximately. I call the value of R obtained from approximations of L, F, S, and β a "synthetic" total fertility rate. In the discussion that follows the symbol R denotes the synthetic total fertility rate and TFR designates the true total fertility rate.

As explained below, the calculated R is biased downward relative to TFR because of the nature of the available data. Nevertheless, the construction of R and the examination of the factors that cause it to vary over space and time are useful exercises. The measure R is highly correlated with the child-woman ratio (CW), which suggests that R remains a useful device in explaining variation in that ratio, despite the fact that it and its components are measured with error.

Although biases in the components imply that R < TFR, the extent of bias varies from component to component. In the case of F, there is a procedure which removes the principal biases inherent in the method of calculation heretofore employed in studies of slave demography. The estimation of F by subtracting the age of the oldest surviving child from the age of the mother suffers from downward biases introduced by adult mortality, population growth, and truncation error—all of which stem from the use of cross-sectional samples. On the other hand, an upward bias is introduced because of the absence of children who did not survive to be counted in the cross section. These biases can be largely eliminated by calculating F as "the singulate mean age at first birth," which turns on the proportions of women without surviving children in the standard five-year age groups (Trussell and Steckel #20, in this volume).

Unfortunately, no such simple solution is available for the measurement of L, which is calculated by subtracting the age of the youngest surviving child from the age of the mother for the cohort of women aged forty-five to fifty-four at the time of enumeration. The biases inherent in this procedure vary with the body of data that is employed. Use of the 1860 census manuscript schedules for whites probably biases L slightly downward as a measure of age at last birth. The same procedure applied to slaves using probate data probably biases L upward.[7]

The measure S is calculated for women aged fifteen to forty-nine with at least two surviving children. The spacing interval between surviving children is, of course, a function of the mortality rate, and will be greater than the spacing interval between births by an amount that will vary with the mortality rate. Estimates of the average birth interval and the underenumeration of deaths on plantations that systematically recorded deaths indicate that use of cross-sectional data from probate records makes S too high by about 56 percent.[8] The effect, holding other variables constant, is to bias R downward relative to TFR by slightly less than 30 percent,[9] although the magnitude of the error will vary from one body of data to another. This is not the only difficulty stemming from the use of census and probate data. Ages of mothers and children are only available to the nearest year. With the large samples that are available this should cause little problem, however, since one would expect the errors in exact age to approximately cancel in calculating the child-spacing mean. Calculations are limited to women below age forty-nine because reproductive activity is usually complete by this age. Spacing information on children is available for some women older than forty-nine years, but using the data risks additional contamination due to death and departure of children from the household.

The proportion of women ever bearing children is estimated by the proportion of women with surviving children in the age group thirty-five to thirty-nine. This figure underestimates the true β for two reasons. A few women no doubt had first births above age thirty-nine and a few with births before that age lost all their children through death or departure from the household before the enumeration.

The higher the cutoff age the smaller is the first source of bias and the larger is the second. Age thirty-nine is selected as the upper limit because the proportions with no surviving children rise slightly in the southern white census data above this age, suggesting that the second source of bias becomes the larger of the two. For this reason the age group thirty-five to thirty-nine is also the oldest group used to compute the singulate mean age at first birth.

The synthetic total fertility rate is suggested as an analytical device that has the advantages that it can easily be estimated from cross-sectional data and it decomposes changes in fertility into elements which have decision-making counterparts. Age at first birth closely corresponds to the decision of when to marry or cohabitate and β reflects the decision of whether to marry or cohabit.[10] The values of L and S reflect contraceptive efforts (if any), breast-feeding practices, nutrition, attitudes about the regularity of intercourse, and, if data on surviving children are used, child death rates.

Although the relationship between R and the child-woman ratio might be determined algebraically, this route would be tedious and the results would be too cumbersome for convenient use. Instead, the relationship is estimated empirically. The results for the southern white data are shown in equation 2:

$$R = 0.3472 + 0.004173CW$$
$$(0.8737)\ (13.71) \tag{2}$$

where N = 30, R-square = 0.870, CW represents the number of children under ten per thousand women aged fifteen to forty-nine in the county, and R is estimated by the means suggested above; t-values are shown in parentheses. The fit is extremely good.

EVIDENCE ON THE COMPONENTS OF R

QUALITY OF SLAVE DATA

Tables 17.2, 17.3, and 17.4 give information on demographic characteristics arranged by data source, region, and plantation size. The first task is to evaluate the representativeness and consistency of evidence in the slave samples. This is accomplished by comparing sample and population values of the child-woman ratio and by comparing the computed and predicted values of synthetic total fertility. The computed value of R is that value implied by estimates of its components, whereas the predicted value is that value implied by the child-woman ratio and equation 2.

The ratios for slaves approximate the values for the population. The time trend in Table 17.1 suggests that the ratio of 1,395 for the probate data approximately equals the value which prevailed for the slave population in the early 1840s. The plantation record value of 1,300 is lower than the ratio during any antebellum census year. This result is consistent with the fact that the plantations in this sample are quite large and the observation that fertility declined with plantation size.

Table 17.2. Demographic Characteristics by Region for Whites and Slaves

Group	Symbol	East Value	East N	East Standard Deviation	West Value	West N	West Standard Deviation	Total Value	Total N	Total Standard Deviation
Whites, 1860, Census	L	38.7	716	4.95	38.9	1,056	5.01	38.8	1,772	4.98
	F	23.5	—	—	22.4	—	—	22.7	—	—
	S	2.83	2,150	1.68	2.71	3,455	1.53	2.76	5,605	1.59
	β	0.787	975	—	0.857	1,357	—	0.828	2,332	—
	R	5.01	—	—	6.07	—	—	5.66	—	—
	CW	1,203	—	—	1,374	—	—	1,303	—	—
	Predicted R	5.37	—	—	6.08	—	—	5.78	—	—
Slaves, Probate Data	L	39.2	26	7.27	41.3	61	4.61	40.7	87	5.62
	F	21.0	—	—	20.3	—	—	20.6	—	—
	S	2.92	1,685	1.77	2.91	1,189	1.68	2.92	2,874	1.73
	β	0.873	181	—	0.843	172	—	0.858	353	—
	R	6.31	—	—	6.93	—	—	6.76	—	—
	CW	1,411	—	—	1,381	1,363	—	1,395	2,651	—
	Predicted R	6.24	—	—	6.11	—	—	6.17	—	—
Surviving Slaves, Plantation Record Data	L	—	—	—	—	—	—	38.4	52	6.24
	F	—	—	—	—	—	—	21.4	—	—
	S	3.29	224	2.11	3.21	535	2.19	3.23	759	2.17
	β	—	—	—	—	—	—	0.798	84	—
	R	—	—	—	—	—	—	5.00	—	—
	CW	—	—	—	—	—	—	1,300	653	—
	Predicted R	—	—	—	—	—	—	5.77	—	—

Table 17.3. Probate Data, Demographic Characteristics by Plantation Size (Measured by Slaves)

	Size 1-24			Size 25-74			Size 75+		
Symbol[a]	Value	N	Standard Deviation	Value	N	Standard Deviation	Value	N	Standard Deviation
L	41.2	34	4.73	40.6	30	4.74	39.9	23	7.49
F	19.8	—	—	20.8	—	—	21.6	—	—
S	2.82	1,106	1.69	2.91	1,066	1.72	3.06	702	1.82
β	0.886	114	—	0.868	129	—	0.818	110	—
R	7.61	—	—	6.77	—	—	5.71	—	—
CW	1,692	870[b]	—	1,491	953[b]	—	1,143	828[b]	—
Predicted R	7.41	—	—	6.57	—	—	5.12	—	—

[a]Defined in connection with equations 1 and 2.
[b]Number of women aged fifteen to forty-nine.

Table 17.4. Probate Data, Demographic Characteristics for Virginia and Georgia and Louisiana

Symbol[a]	For Virginia			For Georgia and Louisiana		
	Value	N	Standard Deviation	Value	N	Standard Deviation
L	42.8	11	2.79	40.3	76	5.85
F	20.5	—	—	20.6	—	—
S	2.78	1,022	1.61	2.99	1,852	1.80
β	0.916	95	—	0.837	258	—
R	8.26	—	—	6.35	—	—
CW	1,820	645[b]	—	1,329	2,006[b]	—
Predicted R	7.94	—	—	5.89	—	—

[a]Defined in connection with equations 1 and 2.
[b]Number of women aged fifteen to forty-nine.

The regional values of the probate data ratios approximate the population values which prevailed in the early 1840s. The regional difference in the sample is not quite as large as in the population, possibly because the sample for the East is based on plantations in only thirty-five counties in Virginia and Georgia and the sample for the West is based on plantations in only five counties in Louisiana. Furthermore, variables in addition to region influence the results.

In the probate data the computed R differs by region in direct opposition to that of the child-woman ratio. It is also puzzling that the predicted values of synthetic total fertility are below the computed values for all groups of slaves in the probate sample shown in Tables 17.2, 17.3, and 17.4.[11] The predicted value does not differ uniformly from the computed value. For example, the difference is relatively small for the probate data slaves in the East and relatively large for probate data slaves in the West. The pattern of differences between predicted and computed values may provide clues useful for determining the source or sources of error.

One would expect to find some differences between the computed and the predicted values because the equation does not explain all of the variation between variables. Table 17.5 shows, for various population groups, the approximate probability of obtaining a difference at least as large as the one observed under the hypothesis that equation 2 is the appropriate relationship between the variables. The differences are quite unlikely for the following groups: probate data slaves in the West (Louisiana), surviving slaves in the plantation record data, all slaves in the probate data, and slaves in the probate data on plantations larger than seventy-five.

An alternative explanation for the discrepancies between the computed and the predicted values of R is the recording practices embodied in the probate data. Older children were often listed apart from their mother, particularly on large plantations and on holdings in the West.[12] Many women aged forty-five to fifty-four who had their last child at a young age therefore appear to be childless and are excluded from the sample. Selectivity in the sample biases L and the computed value of R upward.

Although age at surviving last birth is biased upward by recording practices

Table 17.5. Approximate Probability That the Absolute Value of the Computed R Minus the Predicted R Is at Least as Large as the Observed Difference

Group	Computed R	Predicted R	Absolute Value of Computed − Predicted	Approximate Probability
Whites, 1860 Census, East	5.01	5.37	0.36	0.40
Whites, 1860 Census, West	6.07	6.08	0.01	0.98
Whites, 1860 Census, Total	5.66	5.78	0.22	0.77
Slaves, Probate Data, East	6.31	6.24	0.07	0.87
Slaves, Probate Data, West	6.93	6.11	0.82	0.06
Slaves, Probate Data, Total	6.76	6.17	0.59	0.17
Surviving Slaves, Plantation Record Data	5.00	5.77	0.77	0.07
Slaves, Probate Data, Plantation Size 1–24	7.61	7.41	0.20	0.64
Slaves, Probate Data, Plantation Size 25–74	6.77	6.57	0.20	0.63
Slaves, Probate Data, Plantation Size 75+	5.71	5.12	0.59	0.17
Slaves, Probate Data, Virginia	8.26	7.94	0.32	0.47
Slaves, Probate Data, Georgia and Louisiana	6.35	5.89	0.46	0.27

Table 17.6. Inferred and Sample Values of Age at Surviving Last Birth for Various Groups of Probate Record Data

Groups	Inferred	Sample
East	39.0	39.2
West	38.5	41.3
Total	38.7	40.7
Plantation Size 1–24	40.6	41.2
Plantation Size 25–74	39.9	40.6
Plantation Size 75+	37.7	39.9
Virginia	41.8	42.8
Georgia and Louisiana	38.7	40.3

Source: The sample values are from Tables 17.2, 17.3, and 17.4.

there is sufficient information available from child-woman ratios to estimate the bias attributable to recording practices. The estimating procedure assumes that all of the error is attributable to L. Equation 2 and the child-woman ratio imply a value for R, and given information about the other components of R, one can then solve equation 1 for L. Table 17.6 shows the inferred and the sample values. The differences are particularly large for slaves in the West and for holdings with seventy-five or more slaves.

Table 17.5 suggests that surviving slaves in the plantation record data do not have the pattern of upward bias in age at surviving last birth found in the probate data. The average age of the oldest surviving child for women aged forty-five to fifty-four and the proportion with at least one surviving child are quite high for these plantation record slaves. Furthermore, the predicted value of R is above the computed value, the opposite direction implied by upward bias in age at surviving last birth.

The spacing interval for slaves in the plantation record data is quite high relative to the estimate from probate data, which suggests that the upward bias in the calculated R may be related to spacing. The bias in S is probably associated with recording practices. No attempt was made to correct for second (or higher) slave marriages for men in the plantation record data. These marriages are difficult to detect because slave husbands who lived on other plantations are not listed with the family. The plantation records of surviving slaves therefore contain an upward bias in surviving child spacing attributable to a gap in the spacing of children related by a second marriage. Applying the technique used for L, the inferred value of S is 2.73 years.

DIFFERENCES IN R

The data in Table 17.7 explain the percentage difference in R in terms of the components of R for nine comparisons of population groups. The relative importance of each component is determined from the expression for the percentage change in R, dR/R. Equation 3 shows that the percentage change is a weighted average of the percentage changes of the components:

$$\frac{dR}{R} = \frac{L}{L-S+F} \cdot \frac{dL}{L} - \frac{F}{L-F+S} \cdot \frac{dF}{F} - \frac{(L-F)}{L-F+S} \cdot \frac{dS}{S} + \frac{d\beta}{\beta} \quad (3)$$

Calculations are based on the inferred values of L given in Table 17.6.

The results in Table 17.7 suggest several hypotheses about demographic and socioeconomic behavior. There is great diversity in the importance of the components in explaining the differences in the synthetic total fertility rate. Those comparisons involving the larger percentage differences are usually the most interesting because they involve a greater range of behavior. The various components do not always have the same sign in explaining a given difference, and consequently the extent of diversity is sometimes masked by the size of the percentage differences.

Table 17.7 shows that age at last surviving birth played an important role in determining differences in fertility. Since family limitation was presumably not widespread in these populations, the result suggests that factors other than birth control probably had an important impact on age at last birth. The role of remarriage is discussed later in this paper.

The comparison in row 1 shows that F, S, and β largely explain the difference between whites and slaves. The effect of S is negative because it operates against the difference in R, i.e., slave fertility was higher despite a larger spacing interval. Relatively high slave fertility is attributable to F and β; L is about equal for the two groups, but it should not be concluded that they have similar values for the same reason or reasons.

The difference in R in row 2 is too small to warrant investigation as a genuine difference in behavior. The comparison in row 3 shows that most of the regional difference in white fertility is explained by when and whether women married.

Among slaves the largest regional differential is given in the comparison in row 5. Most of this difference is attributable to differences in L and β.

Rows 7 through 9 reveal the importance of declining age at last surviving birth as plantation size increases; F and β also play important supporting roles. All of the components operate to lower slave fertility on larger sized plantations.

THE TIME TREND

The slave data are not sufficiently numerous nor are they distributed in a way that permit useful comparisons over time. Most of the slave data are concentrated toward the end of the antebellum period. Similarly, all the white data relate to one year, so no direct comparisons over time are possible. Nevertheless the available results can be utilized in a way that sheds light on demographic change over time.

Table 17.8 shows the values of the components of R for whites under the assumption that all of the change in R (and therefore in the child-woman ratio) from 1800 to 1860 is attributable to a given component. The results shed light on the role of each component in explaining the time trend. The value for each component was obtained by solving equation 1 for the component and then substituting the predicted value of R (from equation 2) in 1800 and the observed values of the other components in 1860 into the equation. The value of 44.6 for L is impossibly high. European demographers have found that age at last birth is approximately 40 years for women with completed families in populations that do not practice family limita-

Table 17.7. Explanation of the Percentage Difference in Synthetic Total Fertility Rates[a]

	Group	R	Absolute Difference in R	Percentage Difference in R	R	Percentage Difference Attributable to				
						L	F	S	β	Total
(1)	Whites, 1860 Census	5.66	0.51	8.6	6.17	−6	120	−55	41	100
(2)	Whites, 1860 Census	5.66	0.11	1.9	5.77	−108	352	49	−193	100
(3)	Whites, 1860 Census, East	5.01	1.06	19.1	6.07	6	31	19	44	100
(4)	Slaves, Probate Data, East	6.24	−0.13	−2.1	6.11	106	−148	−13	155	100
(5)	Slaves, Probate Data, Georgia and Louisiana	7.94	−2.05	−29.6	5.89	46	2	21	31	100
(6)	Slaves, Probate Data	6.17	−0.40	−6.7	5.77	22	57	−85	106	100
(7)	Slaves, Probate Data, Size 1–24	7.41	−0.84	−12.0	6.57	25	36	22	17	100
(8)	Slaves, Probate Data, Size 25–74	6.57	−1.45	−24.8	5.12	43	16	17	24	100
(9)	Slaves, Probate Data, Size 1–24	7.41	−2.29	−36.6	5.12	37	23	19	22	100

Note: Group labels for the comparison column (R, second): Surviving Slaves, Plantation Records (2); Whites, 1860 Census, West (3); Slaves, Probate Data, West (4); Slaves, Probate Data, Virginia (5); Surviving Slaves, Plantation Records (6); Slaves, Probate Data, Size 25–74 (7); Slaves, Probate Data, Size 75+ (8); Slaves, Probate Data, Size 75+ (9).

[a] The calculations for slaves are based on inferred values of L given in Table 17.6, the inferred value of S (plantation records only), and on predicted values of R.

Table 17.8. Values of Predicted R and the Components of R for Whites under the Presumption That All of the Change in R from 1800 to 1860 Is Attributable to a Single Component

Symbol	Value
Predicted R	7.39
L	44.6
F	16.9
S	2.03
β	1.08

Source: Calculated from Table 17.2 using equations 1 and 2.

tion (Henry 1956, 87–93; Wrigley 1966). If 40 years is an upper bound on L, then a decline in age at last birth through family limitation or any other means could explain no more than about 21 percent in the decline in R.

It is unlikely that a rise in S explains all of the decline in R for whites, although it could have played an important supporting role. S is about 21 percent higher than the interval between births (see note 8, of this paper). Dividing 2.03 by 1.21 gives an interval of about 20.1 months. This value is not biologically impossible, but is extraordinarily low by historical standards. The very fertile French-Canadian population of the seventeenth and eighteenth centuries had an average spacing interval of 23.3 months between live births (Henripin 1954, 84). If the interval between surviving children implied by the French-Canadian data ($2.35 = (23.3 \times 1.21)/12$) is taken as a lower bound for whites in 1800, then a rise in S could explain no more than about 49 percent of the decline in R.

Because some women are sterile, an upper limit on β is about 0.95 (Eaton and Mayer 1953, 236; Smith 1960, 111; Goubert 1968, 595). Since some women fail to marry and no children survive in some marriages, a realistic upper limit for β is about 0.92. If 0.92 is the upper limit, then a fall in β could explain at most about 37 percent of the decline in R for whites.

Reasonable limits on changes in the components of R suggest that changes in marriage behavior contributed to the decline in white fertility. Since L and S together explain no more than 70 percent, when and whether women married accounts for a minimum of 30 percent of the decline in R.

The technique discussed above has little value when applied to the slave data because the observed values for L, F, S, and β are based on data prior to the end of the antebellum period. Furthermore, the child-woman ratio for slaves cannot be calculated prior to 1820, so the range of time and probably the range in value of this ratio are smaller for slaves than whites.

THE PROBABILITY THAT A WOMAN HAS A SURVIVING CHILD

THE APPROACH

Most slaves and whites probably followed a regimen of natural fertility. It appears that differences in and changes over time in fertility are explained more by the frequency with which women had any children and the age at which childbearing began, rather than control of births after the start of childbearing. The comparative analysis examines all components of R, but the central role of when and whether a woman had a child in these populations suggests that F and β should be given particular attention. Since F and β are calculated from proportions of women with surviving children, these two components are treated together.

Table 17.9 shows the proportions of women with surviving children and the singulate mean age at first birth. Age at first birth for slaves, estimated from probate data, was 2.1 years lower than age at first birth for whites; when estimates were based on plantation records, that for slaves was 1.3 years lower than for whites. Earlier childbearing among slaves is also revealed by the proportions of women with surviving children in different age groups. In the age group fifteen to nineteen slaves were two to three times more likely than whites to have a surviving child. The slave proportions are also higher in the next age group, but thereafter the results are mixed and depend upon the subgroups compared. Slaves on large plantations were least likely to have had a surviving child.

Analysis of white fertility (Steckel 1980a, 1985) reveals the positive influence of wealth on the probability that a woman of a given age had a surviving child. Wealth is a factor which enables a prospective couple to establish a household. Some wealth is not binding in the sense that it was a necessary condition for family formation, but those with some wealth had a greater probability of establishing a household. Since owners provided the food, clothing, and shelter necessary for family formation, slaves' efforts were in effect, "subsidized" in family-formation decisions—a "subsidy" paid for by the overall exploitation of the slave labor force. In the absence of parental help, whites had to acquire the necessary wealth through a process of saving. Because loans were generally unavailable to whites for purposes of family formation, the economic independence of whites relative to slaves probably delayed family formation.

Since owners provided food, clothing, and shelter to slaves, one might ask why age at first birth was not lower than the one observed. The typical slave woman was capable of childbearing by approximately age fifteen (Trussell and Steckel #20, in this volume), and owners therefore sacrificed some reproductive potential by inducing, or allowing, childbearing to be as late as it was. Why did owners permit operation below maximum reproduction capacity? One of the difficulties with the slave breeding argument is its narrow focus on the direct costs and benefits of producing children as the relevant criteria in decision making. Direct costs such as mother's time lost from work and maintenance costs of the children as well as the direct benefit of the value of child were no doubt relevant, but these variables may have been only contributing factors. Slave men and women probably had free choice in the selection of available partners (Steckel 1985). Marriage at young ages under conditions of free choice may have produced costly (in terms of foregone output) unstable relationships. It is probably not accidental that slaves usually needed the permission of their owner, or owners, to marry. Through this device owners may have increased age of marriage above what it would have been in the absence of control. Owners may have discouraged, and slaves may have avoided, early marriage because the children born soon after these marriages had a high risk

Table 17.9. Singulate Mean Age at First Birth and Proportions of Women with Surviving Children by Five-Year Age Groups for Various Population Groups

Group	15–19		20–24		25–29		30–34		35–39		Singulate Mean
	Proportion	N	Proportion	N	Proportion	N	Proportion	N	Proportion	N	
Whites, 1860 Census, East	0.046	1,988	0.387	1,706	0.660	1,369	0.724	1,107	0.787	975	23.5
Whites, 1860 Census, West	0.093	2,907	0.499	2,744	0.732	2,178	0.844	1,776	0.857	1,357	22.4
Whites, 1860 Census, Total	0.074	4,895	0.456	4,450	0.705	3,547	0.798	2,883	0.828	2,332	22.7
Slaves, Probate Data, East	0.203	330	0.636	247	0.792	212	0.819	193	0.873	181	21.0
Slaves, Probate Data, West	0.232	332	0.654	292	0.768	233	0.825	200	0.843	172	20.3
Slaves, Probate Data, Total	0.218	662	0.646	539	0.780	445	0.822	393	0.858	353	20.6
Surviving Slaves, Plantation Record Data, Total	0.136	125	0.571	112	0.732	123	0.726	95	0.798	84	21.4
Slaves, Probate Data, Size 1–24	0.258	233	0.707	184	0.848	151	0.877	154	0.886	114	19.8
Slaves, Probate Data, Size 25–74	0.237	245	0.617	196	0.768	164	0.835	127	0.868	129	20.8
Slaves, Probate Data, Size 75+	0.141	184	0.610	159	0.715	130	0.732	112	0.818	110	21.6
Slaves, Probate Data, Virginia	0.221	172	0.702	131	0.852	108	0.882	93	0.916	95	20.5
Slaves, Probate Data, Georgia and Louisiana	0.216	490	0.627	408	0.757	337	0.803	300	0.837	258	20.6

of death. Analysis of plantation records indicates that the expected probability of infant death was 50 percent higher for births to mothers under age twenty compared to births among older women (Steckel #18, in this volume).

The proportions of women with surviving children in the age group thirty-five to thirty-nine are underestimates of the proportion of women who eventually marry. A very small proportion of women married after age forty. Reliable estimates of this behavior are not available, but it probably did not exceed 1 or 2 percent of all women. Some couples who marry cannot have children, but this proportion is probably not above 0.05 in well-nourished populations. Finally, about 6 percent of these women lost all children through death (Steckel 1985, 242–243). The sum of the downward biases is probably less than 12 percentage points and it is reasonably safe to conclude that a portion of women in both populations did not marry. Due to uncertainties about infant mortality rates for slaves and whites, it is not known whether the proportion who eventually married was higher among whites or slaves.

Even if the proportions who eventually married were equal in the two populations, one cannot conclude that the same determinants operating at the same level were involved. Although one might expect relatively more slaves to marry because family formation was "subsidized," slaves apparently operated under constraints of partner availability that were not common among whites. A dummy variable representing whether a women had a surviving child was regressed on a constant and age. In a logistic function specification of the relationship, the constant specifies the earliest age at which women had children and the coefficient of the age variable measures the rate at which women had first children thereafter. The coefficient of the age variable is lower for slaves than whites. This result is consistent with greater difficulty among slaves in finding a partner. Slaves on small holdings usually had to marry someone on another plantation, but possibilities were limited by distance. Slaves on large holdings may have had greater choices on the plantation, but the costs in terms of distance implied by the size of the farm limited possibilities for marrying off the plantation (Steckel 1985, 226–230).

AGE AT LAST SURVIVING BIRTH

It cannot be strongly argued that age at last surviving birth was lower among slaves than whites, because sufficient data are lacking for slaves. The evidence that is available suggests that childbearing ended earlier among slaves. The high age at last surviving birth indicates that whites did not practice family limitation to an important extent. This argument has less force when applied to slaves, particularly those who lived on large plantations. In contrast to whites, slaves had little economic incentive to limit births. The low age at last surviving birth and lack of incentive to limit births suggest that remarriage behavior may have been a factor. Analysis of plantation records that list the names of both parents for each birth shows that there was some changing of partners when families were small, but slave women soon settled into stable unions. Beyond the first few births, women had children almost exclusively with one man. The rate of partner change among these women was substantially lower than expected based upon death of husbands if all widows remarried (Steckel 1985). Consequently some women in their late twenties and thirties lived as widows and did not bear children.

The explanation for different remarriage patterns is not entirely clear, although one factor may have been support for the family. White widows with children probably sought another spouse as a means of providing for themselves and the children, whereas the owner's support eliminated this motive for slave widows. A second factor could have been differential mortality. Higher male mortality rates among slaves compared to whites would have generated a relative excess of slave widows and a lower age at last birth even if the remarriage rates were the same for both groups of women.

CHILD SPACING

The synthetic total fertility rate was relatively higher for slaves (as estimated from probate data) compared to whites, despite a longer surviving child-spacing interval.[13] The difference in the intervals is statistically significant at less than 0.005 and represents an important behavioral difference between these populations.

Several factors may influence surviving spacing intervals including rates of child survival, nutrition levels, rates of pregnancy wastage, duration of lactation, and frequency of intercourse during lactation. As noted earlier, the child death rates of slaves were approximately double those of whites. Information that is available on slave and white heights provides an index of nutrition and health. These data suggest that adults in both populations had reasonably nutritious diets (Margo and Steckel 1983, #24, in this volume; Steckel 1986c). The scanty evidence available on breast-feeding practices suggests that work in the fields reduced daytime breast-feedings among slave women and the overall breast-feeding to one year or less, whereas the correspondence and journals of nineteenth-century southern white women reveal an average duration of 13.5 months (McMillan 1985; Steckel #23, in this volume; Steckel 1986c). We lack quantitative information on rates of pregnancy wastage and frequency of intercourse during lactation.

The data in Table 17.10 on spacing between surviving children by birth order can provide insight into slave-white differences. Comparison of the totals for each population indicates that the interval for slaves exceeded that for whites up to births 4–5. Only the difference for births 1–2 is statistically significant, however. This finding suggests that factors specific to birth order may explain the difference. Statistical tests for differences across subgroups suggest no systematic patterns.

Two factors may have contributed to higher intervals at low birth orders, particularly between the first two births. First, slaves had children earlier than whites. Table 17.9 shows that about three times as many slaves as whites had surviving children in the age group fifteen to nineteen, and the proportion was also higher for slaves in the age group twenty to twenty-four. Analysis of slave data indicates that infant mortality was about 56 percent higher for births to women aged fifteen to nineteen compared to older women (Steckel #18, in this volume). Lower rates of

Table 17.10. Surviving Child-Spacing Intervals by Birth Order for Various Population Groups

Birth Order Group	1–2			2–3			3–4			4–5			5–6			6–7 or higher		
	$\overline{X}$	s	N	$\overline{X}$	s	N	$\overline{X}$	s	N	$\overline{X}$	s	N	$\overline{X}$	s	N	$\overline{X}$	s	N
Probate, Total	3.17	2.04	1,125	2.89	1.63	750	2.71	1.42	457	2.64	1.30	276	2.59	1.46	150	2.43	1.00	116
Probate, East	3.21	2.13	558	2.95	1.74	428	2.77	1.51	286	2.63	1.30	192	2.67	1.53	120	2.49	1.04	101
Probate, West	3.14	1.94	567	2.81	1.47	322	2.63	1.25	171	2.67	1.31	84	2.27	1.06	30	2.07	0.57	15
Probate, Size 1–24	3.07	2.01	426	2.69	1.47	290	2.80	1.58	183	2.59	1.15	105	2.39	1.26	61	2.63	1.24	41
Probate, Size 25–74	3.18	2.01	406	3.03	1.69	278	2.54	1.26	165	2.50	1.21	108	2.80	1.70	59	2.28	0.80	50
Probate, Size 75+	3.31	2.12	293	3.00	1.74	182	2.83	1.33	109	2.97	1.59	63	2.60	1.28	30	2.40	0.85	25
Whites, Total	2.84	1.68	304	2.72	1.71	211	2.60	1.58	157	2.46	1.43	112	2.77	1.60	74	2.44	1.24	79
Whites, East	3.11	1.88	106	2.61	1.40	70	2.71	1.54	58	2.54	1.37	39	2.65	1.38	26	2.63	1.60	27
Whites, West	2.69	1.55	198	2.77	1.85	141	2.54	1.61	99	2.42	1.46	73	2.83	1.72	48	2.35	1.01	52

Sources: Manuscript schedules of the 1860 census and 540 probate data plantations.

infant survival for children born to young mothers would have lengthened the measured interval for low birth orders (even though the actual interval between live births is shortened by infant mortality). Second, analysis of slave partner changes between various pairs of births indicates that most changes occurred when women were young, particularly between their first two births (Steckel 1985, Ch. 5). Loss of a husband through death or separation reduced the frequency of childbearing. The average interval to the second birth in a pair is 28.4 months (N = 437) in couples where the same father was listed for the children and 40.7 months (N = 23) where the fathers of the children differed (Steckel 1985, Ch. 5). Unfortunately, I do not have comparable data for whites. It has been observed, however, that marriages where the partners are young tend to be unstable. Therefore, early childbearing among slaves may also have contributed to the spacing pattern by birth order.

THE REGIONAL DIFFERENTIAL

The discussion in the second section of this paper indicated that child-woman ratios of slaves and whites were poorly correlated at the county level. Regression of the slave ratio on the white ratio and a constant produced an R-square of only 0.02. If a dummy variable representing residence in the West is added to the regression as an explanatory variable, the coefficient of the variable is -134.4 and is statistically significant at 0.05. Compared to the East, residence in the West reduced the ratio for slaves relative to whites. Thus, for example, if a county in the East and a county in the West had equal ratios for whites, one would expect the ratio for slaves in the western county to have been 134.4 units less than the ratio for slaves in the eastern county.

The differential effect of region on slaves and whites may have been related to migration. The child-woman ratio among slave migrants between 1850 and 1860 was about 583,[14] which is about 44 percent of the ratio for the entire slave population in 1860. The child-woman ratio among white migrants is not known, but the ratio in counties organized just before their first inclusion in a census is high. These counties probably contained a high proportion of recent migrants and the census provides some insight into their fertility. One must be cautious, however, because some children were no doubt born after the move. Nineteen counties were organized in Arkansas, Louisiana, and Texas one or two years prior to their inclusion in the census of 1840 or 1850. The ratio in these counties was higher than the ratio for the South in the respective census year. The foregoing suggests that the ratio of slave migrants was substantially below that of white migrants.[15]

The probable effects of migration are clearer if the dummy variable representing states in the West is changed to a dummy variable representing states that were net importers of slaves. This regression is

$$CWS = 712.3 + 0.5407CWW - 262.1Rimp$$
$$(2.934) \quad (2.736) \qquad (4.092) \hspace{3cm} (4)$$

where N = 57, R-square = 0.254, CWS and CWW are the ratios for slaves and whites respectively, and Rimp is the dummy variable defined above. T-values are shown in parentheses. The dummy variable explains a large and statistically significant difference in the child-woman ratios. Note that the coefficient of CWW is positive and statistically significant but that the explanatory power of the regression is still reasonably low. The positive coefficient for CWW may reflect factors such as climate that may have had similar effects on mortality in each population.

A starting point for understanding the difference between slave and white migration is to ask why the child-woman ratio of slave migrants is so much less than the child-woman ratio for the entire slave population. One economic justification is that transport costs were approximately equal for children and adults, but since adults were more valuable it was more profitable to ship predominately adult slaves. In addition, transportation of slave children may have been unprofitable because death rates of child migrants were higher than those of adults.

THE TIME TREND

The determinants of the decline in the child-woman ratio over time were probably quite different for slaves than for whites. The analysis of slave fertility in this paper and detailed analysis elsewhere (Steckel 1985) indicate that fertility declined with plantation size and was relatively higher in areas that produced tobacco. The growth in plantation size during the antebellum period could have explained as much as 50 percent of the decline in the ratio for slaves. The diminished importance of tobacco may explain approximately one-third of the decline.

The redistribution of wealth could have been an important factor underlying the decline in white fertility. Analysis of fertility at the household level indicates that individuals with no wealth had a substantially lower probability of having a child. The pattern of redistribution over time at the aggregate level is not known, but redistribution could have explained much of the decline (Steckel 1980a, 1985).

CONCLUSIONS

Comparative analysis helps to identify determinants of fertility among slaves and southern whites. Both populations operated essentially under regimens of natural fertility. Childbearing began at an early age (compared to Europeans) and after the first child, births tended to arrive at regular intervals unless the process was interrupted by separation or by death of the husband.

Although lack of family limitation was common to these groups, the socioeconomic forces behind the family formation process were quite different. The economic independence of white families implied that marriage was usually delayed until sufficient resources were amassed to support a family. "Subsidy" by the owner enabled slaves to begin families at an earlier age. Although slaves were able to begin the process earlier, their partner choices were restricted relative to whites, and search for an acceptable partner may have delayed family formation for some slaves. While a significant group of slaves never found partners, lack of wealth may have prevented marriage for a significant group of whites.

After the start of childbearing, the frequency of births was somewhat lower for slaves compared to whites. Arrangement of the intervals by birth order indicates that slaves were concentrated at low birth orders. Early childbearing could have lengthened measured slave birth intervals (as opposed to intervals between live births) relative to whites via high infant mortality rates for births to young mothers and by higher separation rates for young couples.

The average age at which childbearing ended may have been lower for slaves. Slave widows may have had difficulty finding new partners, and because the family was supported by the owner, slaves may have had less economic incentive than whites to remarry.

High fertility of white relative to slave migrants contributed to contrasting regional fertility patterns. The migration patterns may have been related to econo-mies of scale in frontier activities and relatively high transport costs for children.

The time trend in slave fertility was related to growth in plantation size and the decline of tobacco in southern agriculture. Redistribution of wealth could have contributed to the decline in white fertility.[16]

NOTES

1. Calculated from data reported in U.S. Bureau of the Census* (1909), 132, and using the formula $P_1/P_0 = e^{rN}$, where P_1 is the 1860 slave population, P_0 is the 1810 slave population, $N = 50$, and r is the annual rate of growth. The rate of increase for whites is discussed in Potter (1965), 631–679.
2. Rates for other slave populations in the Western Hemisphere are given by Eblen (1975), 211–247, Curtin (1969), and Roberts (1957).
3. The figures are the Carr-Saunders estimates reported in Glass and Grebenik (1965), 58.
4. All percentage differences in this section are calculated using the average of the two figures as the base.
5. Additional details concerning the data and methods used in this paper can be found in Steckel (1980a, 1985).
6. Sampling procedures are discussed in Steckel (1985).
7. The estimates of biases to L are not all in the same direction. For whites the biases are (1) death of the youngest child or a block of younger children biases L downward, (2) including women as young as age forty-five biases L upward because some births that occurred after age forty-five are omitted, (3) because all children of some women left home before the enumeration, some women appear to be childless and are excluded from the sample. This last phenomenon biases L upward because the women probably had their last birth at a young age. The three biases were simulated using sensitiv-ity analysis for relevant parameters where necessary. The first bias is probably 1.2 to 2.2 years, the second is probably 0.1 to 0.5 years, and the third is about 0.3 years. Thus the net bias is downward approximately 0.4 to 1.8 years.

   The value of L estimated from probate data suffers from the three biases discussed above, plus a fourth bias attributable to probate-recording practices whereby older children of women aged forty-five to fifty-four were frequently not listed with their mothers. Therefore, many women aged forty-five to fifty-four who had their last birth at a young age appear to be childless. An indirect procedure, discussed later in the paper, indicates that the fourth bias is upward by approximately 2 years. If the biases estimated for whites are applied to slaves, the net bias in L estimated from probate data is biased upward approximately 0.2 to 1.6 years.
8. The average interval between surviving births is too large primarily because the denominator used

*Prior to 1900, the government agency that issued census documents was called the U.S. Census Office. All references after 1900 are to the U.S. Bureau of the Census.

in this measure fails to incorporate nonsurviving births that occurred between the oldest and the youngest surviving child. The measure is also defective because it excludes births that occurred after the youngest or before the oldest surviving child, but correction for these omissions is difficult because it depends upon unobserved ages at first and last birth. Only the correction for losses of births between the oldest and the youngest surviving child is considered here. An estimate of the interval between live births was reached through simulation using information on mortality rates, the distribution of the ages of the youngest and the oldest surviving children in the family, and trial values of the interval between live births. The distribution of the ages of youngest and oldest surviving children and a trial value of the live birth interval imply a number of live births, which when diminished according to the mortality schedule, imply an interval between surviving births. Values of the live birth interval were tried in sequence until equality between the implied and the observed interval between surviving births was reached. The formula for the implied interval between surviving births is

$$
\frac{\displaystyle\sum_{i=0}^{n-1}\sum_{j=i+1}^{n}(j-i)\,N_{ij}}{\displaystyle\sum_{i=0}^{n-1}\sum_{j=i+1}^{n}\left[\left(\frac{j-i}{s}\cdot N_{ij}\cdot P_{ij}\right)-N_{ij}\right]+N_{ij}}
$$

where s is the trial value of the live birth interval, j denotes the age of the oldest surviving child, i is the age of the youngest surviving child, N_{ij} is the number of families with youngest surviving child aged i and oldest surviving child aged j, P_{ij} represents the average of the probabilities of non-survival from birth to age k where $k = i + 1, \ldots j - 1$, and n is the age of the oldest surviving child in the sample.

Given estimates of slave mortality from Steckel (1986c) and data on surviving slaves from probate records, the estimated interval between surviving births was 1.87 years or 22.4 months, which is 1.05 years or 12.6 months below the observed interval between surviving births of 2.92 years reported in Table 17.2. A similar calculation for southern whites based on the average of the Model West logit life tables of Haines and Avery (1980), 88, yields an estimated interval between live births of 2.28 years (or 27.4 months) compared with 2.76 years reported in Table 17.2.

9. Equation 1 shows that the elasticity of R with respect to S is $-(L - F)/(L - F + S)$, which is slightly less than 1 in absolute value. The decline in the birth interval from 2.92 to 1.87 increases the calculated value of R from 6.18 to 9.16.

10. Marriage is a legal concept that was well defined in white society. As applied to slaves, the term "marriage" refers to cohabitation that was socially recognized but not defined or enforced by law. The term is applied to whites and slaves with the understanding that it has a different meaning in each society.

11. Plantations from Georgia and Louisiana are grouped together because the sample from Georgia is rather small. In addition, the child-woman ratios in the samples from these states are approximately equal.

12. See Steckel (1985), Table 30.

13. This discussion relies on probate data because of uncertainty about the spacing interval in the plantation record data.

14. Calculated from net migration figures in Sutch (1975a). The ratio in a sample of slaves transported by ship from the 1820s to the 1850s is 578. This sample is discussed in Steckel (1979).

15. Migration could have made an important contribution to the regional difference, particularly for slaves. In 1850, the annual outmigration rates from the East and the annual inmigration rate into the West were about 1 percent for slaves (migration data are available in Fogel and Engerman 1974a, 1:46). The child-woman ratio in a region, CW, can be represented as a weighted average:

$$
CW = (1 - a)CW_1 + aCW_2
$$

where a is a weight, CW_1 is the ratio for the resident population and CW_2 is the ratio for migrants. In 1850, CW was 1,396 in the East. Net migration figures in Sutch (1975a) and slave manifests discussed by Steckel (1979) indicate that CW_2 was about 583. If a is 0.01, then CW_1 is 1,404.2, which implies that the ratio in the East was made approximately $1,404.2 - 1,396 = 8.2$ units higher by outmigration in one year. A similar analysis shows that the ratio in the West was made about 7.4 units lower by inmigration. Since the regional difference was 82 units in 1850, about 19 percent $= (8.2 + 7.4)/82$ of the regional discrepancy is explained by migration. Note that this technique assumes that the migrant population adjusted to its new surroundings in one year, i.e., the child-woman ratio of the previous year's migrants equaled the ratio in the West as a whole. If the process of adjustment took longer (shorter) then the technique underestimates (overestimates) the role of migration.

Prior to 1850 migration rates were higher and the regional difference in the ratios was smaller. In 1830, for example, most of the regional difference in child-woman ratios is explained by the technique discussed above.

The role of migration in the regional difference for whites is difficult to estimate because the child-woman ratio of white migrants is not known. Migration probably explains a smaller percentage of the regional difference for whites, however, because the ratio for white migrants was closer to the ratio for the resident population and because the regional discrepancy for whites was larger than for slaves.

16. The research was supported by NSF grants GS-3262, GS-27262, and SOC 76-002; by the National Institute of Mental Health; by the Rockefeller Foundation through a grant to the University of Chicago for the Study of Economics of Population and Family Decision Making; and by Ohio State University.

EIGHTEEN

Slave Mortality: Analysis of Evidence from Plantation Records*

Richard H. Steckel

INTRODUCTION

Since the inception of slavery in North America the free population has been concerned with the mortality of the slave population. Slaveowners were concerned with mortality for purposes of estimating the profitability of slave investments. Opponents of slavery and the slave trade used actual and presumed slave mortality experience as arguments for abolishing the system. Death rates were viewed as a measure of demographic performance that reflected, and were in part determined by, such factors as diet, physical treatment, and the quality of medical care and housing—all under the control of the slaveowners. Consequently, information on deaths was used as a standard for evaluating the severity of the slave system and for assessing regional and international differences in slavery. In the postbellum period, scholars researched and debated various issues in slave mortality. The modern discussion includes issues in the levels and determinants of slave mortality, but research has concentrated on levels, possibly due to inadequate data for extensive research on determinants of mortality.

Studies of slave mortality have frequently relied on census data and mortality estimation techniques. Sydnor (1930) estimated the life expectancy of Mississippi slaves at age twenty. Evans (1962) derived a set of age-specific death rates using 1850 census data combined with an adjustment for underenumeration of deaths based on Jacobson's 1850 life table for whites. Farley (1970, 1965) used stable population analysis, model life tables and a census survival procedure for obtaining various estimates of slave life expectancy at birth. Eblen (1972) argued that the slave mortality experience is approximately represented by the Coale and Demeny

*Reprinted with revisions and additions, and with permission from *Social Science History* 3(1970):86–114.

model W5 life table and in another paper (1974) developed an analysis based on methodology in the United Nations study *The Concept of a Stable Population.*

These studies yield a wide range of results. Estimates of life expectancy at birth range from 27.8 to 38.1 years.[1] Furthermore, the results apply to the entire slave population and have limited value for analyzing factors that influenced slave mortality.[2]

Postell (1951) approached slave health and mortality from the plantation level. He relied extensively on plantation records to develop an impression of plantation health conditions. The records were also used to calculate rates of morbidity, birth, and infant mortality, but there was no statistical analysis of the rates.

Contributions to the study of slave mortality have been part of an effort by scholars to understand mortality in North America prior to the twentieth century. Issues that have concerned historical demographers include the time trend in mortality rates, regional differences in mortality rates, and mortality rate differentials between blacks and whites.[3] The sketchy evidence which is available (see Walsh and Menard 1974, Morgan 1975, Rutman and Rutman 1976, Smith 1978) suggests that mortality rates in the South were very high during the early colonial period and that conditions improved sometime during the 1700s. Lockridge (1966) and Vinovskis (1972) suggest mortality rates in Massachusetts may have been relatively low and stable for nearly two centuries prior to the Civil War. Several studies (Thompson and Whelpton 1933; Yasuba 1962; Meeker 1972, 1976; Easterlin 1977) have argued or challenged that nineteenth-century mortality rates were relatively constant up to about 1800. *Time on the Cross* (Fogel and Engerman 1974a) and the ensuing debate (Vinovskis 1975, Sutch 1976) focused attention on antebellum life expectancies of blacks, whites, the North, and the South.

The objective of this paper is to investigate slave mortality using a data base of plantation records. The records are employed to estimate mortality rates and to obtain a statistical analysis of some determinants of mortality. The possibility of underreporting of death is considered in selecting and analyzing the records.

The data consist of slave lists on eleven large plantations that spanned a period of eighty years. Three main crops and four states are represented in this sample. One should be cautious in attempting to extrapolate results from these data to the entire slave population: The number of plantations is small and little is known about the influence of plantation characteristics on mortality.

THE DATA

Most southern planters kept a variety of business records, such as financial ledgers, planting and harvesting accounts, livestock and slaughter records, food and clothing allotments to slaves, inventories of slaves and equipment, lists of slave births and deaths, and business accounts with slaves. As part of a research project on slave demography, an intensive search of southern archives was undertaken to acquire a sample of demographic records.[4] To date, the lists containing useful demographic information from seventy-seven plantations have been assembled and prepared in machine-readable form.

The slave lists may be described as cross sections or time series. The cross sections are inventories that vary in detail, ranging from a simple list of the names of the working-age slaves or taxable slaves on the plantation at a given date to elaborate lists that include the name, sex, age or date of birth and perhaps the value of each slave. The birth list is the most common source of time-series data. Such lists usually include the name of a slave child; the sex; and the month, day, and year of birth; however, since sex is sometimes omitted and cannot always be reliably inferred from the name and some children are unnamed, an analysis by sex is not undertaken here. Children who died in early infancy were sometimes unnamed. Occasionally other parts of an entry, such as day of birth, are missing. The birth lists are usually arranged in chronological order. Generally, the births to all mothers on a plantation are arranged in the same list, although in some cases the lists are subdivided by families.

Death lists are also a source of time-series data. These lists were sometimes made an integral part of the birth list with another column added for date of death. Some owners maintained a separate death list, usually arranged in chronological order, so that by matching names with a birth list or inventory list, one can infer ages at death and mortality rates.

The range of completeness of death information is very great. A few plantations have no death information whatsoever and many have a partial death list where the information appears to have been sporadically recorded; death is sometimes indicated by an "X" or by a "dead" notation only. Fifty-seven of the seventy-seven plantations have a birth list, and of these thirty-one have a partial or incomplete death list. Eleven plantations have lists for which deaths were systematically recorded and there is no apparent underreporting of the incidence and date of death. These eleven plantation lists are distinguished by the absence of "X" or "dead" notations. The infant mortality rates on these plantations are plausibly high and range from 176 to 392 per thousand live births. These eleven plantations are described in Table 18.1 and form the data base for the mortality analysis in this paper. Each of the eleven lists probably contains some underreporting of births and infant deaths, especially where death occurred immediately after birth. The extent of this underreporting probably was in the range of 20 to 40 percent of all live births for reasons discussed elsewhere (see Steckel #23, in this volume, and the sources cited therein). This paper investigates mortality patterns in births and deaths that owners reported.

The plantation record data set is useful for constructing several demographic statistics, including age of the mother at childbirth, child-spacing intervals, and the seasonal pattern of births and deaths. The ideal type of information for construction of these statistics is a birth history of each slave woman; but information recorded in the form of a birth history is available for only a few women in the sample. Complete or partial birth histories can be constructed for many slave women by matching names. This and related problems are discussed elsewhere by Steckel (1977, 34–50).

Table 18.1. Description of Plantation Records Containing Systematic Evidence on Slave Mortality

	Title of Collection	Archival Location[a]	Name of Plantation	Geographic Location	Main Crop(s)	Approximate Average Number of Slaves	Approximate Dates of Information
(1)	John and Keating S. Ball Papers	SHC	Comingtee	Berkeley District, South Carolina	Rice	215	1803–1833
(2)	John and Keating S. Ball Papers	SHC	Stokely	Berkeley District, South Carolina	Rice	105	1805–1833
(3)	Ball Family	USC	Comingtee	Berkeley District, South Carolina	Cotton	210	1786–1825
(4)	Peter Gaillard Plantation Records	SHC[b] SCHS		Orangeburg District, South Carolina	Cotton	75	1840–1863
(5)	Samuel Porcher Gaillard	USC	Orange Grove	Sumter District, South Carolina	Cotton	210	1786–1825
(6)	Accounts of Good Hope Plantation	SCHS	Good Hope	Orangeburg District, South Carolina	Cotton	65	1835–1856
(7)	James H. Hammond	USC		Edgefield District, South Carolina	Cotton	150	1832–1863
(8)	Mackay and Stiles Family Papers	SHC	Orange	Chatham County, Georgia	Rice/ Cotton	85	1814–1860
(9)	Samuel McCutcheon	LSU		St. Charles Parish, Louisiana	Sugar	165	1832–1861
(10)	William J. Minor and Family Papers	LSU	Southdown	Terrebonne Parish, Louisiana	Sugar	230	1849–1864
(11)	Henry Watson, Jr.	Duke		Green County, Alabama	Cotton	90	1843–1860

[a]Duke = Duke University Library, Durham, North Carolina; LSU = Louisiana State University, Baton Rouge, Louisiana; SCHS = South Carolina Historical Society, Charleston; SHC = Southern Historical Collection, University of North Carolina, Chapel Hill; USC = South Caroliniana Library, University of South Carolina, Columbia.
[b]Microfilm.

AGE-SPECIFIC MORTALITY RATES

The birth and death lists can be used to calculate age-specific mortality rates. Age-specific mortality rates are commonly estimated from vital registration and census enumeration data. The techniques used with vital registration data produce very little useful information when applied to the plantation records because age distributions are frequently not available or are usually available for only one or two dates and because the enumerated deaths may apply to only a portion of the plantation population. Deaths were frequently recorded as part of the birth list and under these circumstances the population for which mortality rates can be calculated consists of slaves listed as a birth.

Age-specific mortality rates were calculated by single years of age and then grouped by the age categories of zero, one to four, five to nine, and so forth. Age at death was calculated as the age implied by the dates of birth and death. The number at risk at age x was calculated as the number of live births that could have lived to age $x + 1$ during the recording period less the number who did not survive to age x.[5] The procedure generates cumulative errors in the number at risk at successive ages if death is underreported. This influence is discussed in more detail below. The procedure is equivalent to that used in preparing mortality rates for a given birth cohort, and the experiences of a number of cohorts are blended together. The number of cohorts available is determined by the duration for which births and deaths were recorded. A twenty-five-year recording period yields twenty-four cohorts for calculating infant mortality, twenty-three cohorts for calculating mortality at age one, and so forth. The number of cohorts is one less than the number of years of data because the last birth cohort can not be used. Births during the last year of recording are not subject to a full year at risk in the sense that deaths occurring after the end of the recording period would not be enumerated. The number at risk at successive ages declines not only from mortality but also because the number of cohorts available diminishes.

The results are shown in the last two rows of Table 18.2. The mortality rates stop with the age group twenty to twenty-four due to the limited duration of the recording periods. The value of N represents the number at risk at each age shown.

Before discussing the age pattern of mortality it is useful to mention that the pattern may reflect special features of the sample. In 1860 one-half of the slaves

Table 18.2. Age-Specific Mortality Rates from Plantation Records

Age	Mortality Rate	Level West	N
0	233.14	6	2,372
1	201.22	3.3	1,787
5	54.44	4	1,141
10	37.40	5.5	744
15	34.96	9	435
20	29.70	10	244

Source: Plantation records described in Table 18.1.

lived on plantations consisting of fewer than approximately twenty-five slaves, whereas the plantations described in Table 18.1 were much larger.[6] The regression analysis indicates that the probability of death tended to increase with plantation size. Several plantations in the sample were located in areas that probably had relatively high death rates. Rice plantations are overrepresented in the sample relative to the population, and the regressions show that the probability of death was higher on rice plantations.[7] Tobacco plantations are not included in the sample. This crop was frequently grown in upland areas, where mortality rates probably were lower.

The changing mix of plantation characteristics may influence the age pattern of mortality. The mix changes due to variations in plantation size and in the duration of the recording period. Large plantations with long recording periods have the most observations. Consequently the mix of plantation characteristics varies across age groups. Some plantations are not represented in the oldest age groups.

One might suspect that the age pattern of mortality is related to underreporting. Perhaps infant deaths were underreported so that the number at risk at successive ages is overstated. One difficulty with an underreporting of death argument as a simple explanation of the age pattern of mortality is that mortality rates in the age groups one to four and five to nine are very high. If infant deaths were under-reported and the number at risk at older ages was overstated, then the rates in the age groups one to four and five to nine would be even higher. The death rates in these age groups are already so high that underreporting does not appear to have been important, at least at these ages.

The calculated level of infant mortality may be related to underreporting of births and infant deaths. Owners may have failed to record either event, particularly if death occurred soon after birth. This type of underreporting does not exaggerate the number at risk at older ages. Underreporting is considered further in a later section of this paper.

Because slaves lived in North America one may be tempted to compare the age pattern of mortality with that found in the model West life tables (Coale and Demeny 1966). Infant mortality exceeds mortality in the age group one to four by approximately 54 to 59 percent in W4 through W7 of the model tables. While difficulties with reporting may exist in the plantation record data, it is not appropriate to conclude that they do exist based on comparisons with the model West tables. The model West tables are based primarily on twentieth-century data drawn largely from Western countries. Public health measures (particularly in the area of water supply), improved living standards, and advances in medical technology may have altered the age patterns of mortality from those that prevailed during the first part of the nineteenth century. Kiple and Kiple (1977a) argue that diet, the African environmental heritage, and the North American climate combined to generate high levels of child mortality among slaves. Those who survived beyond early childhood may have had low mortality rates because those who were not well suited to the diet and climate of North America were eliminated early in life.

Relatively high mortality in the age group one to four may be attributable in part to the termination of breast-feeding. Breast-fed infants tend to experience lower mortality rates than artificially fed infants.[8] The advantages of breast milk are that it is nutritionally ideal, provides some immunity, and is clean. Upon weaning, slave children probably encountered a less-favorable diet and less-sanitary conditions in manual feeding. These conditions produce higher death rates.

The limited information available on the subject indicates that slave children were breast-fed about one year.[9] One might then expect a concentration of deaths shortly after age one. Table 18.3 shows that over 25 percent of the deaths among children who died from age one to four occurred thirteen to sixteen months after birth. The frequency of death fell sharply after sixteen months and then declined gradually thereafter. These figures suggest that weaning played a role and that other important factors were involved in relatively high mortality for the age group one to four.

It may be useful to speculate about a life table for slaves in the plantation record sample. A life table was selected among those available in Coale and Demeny (1966) according to the best "fit" with the mortality rates shown in Table 18.2. The best fit was determined by minimizing the mean-squared difference in the mortality rates. The mean-squared difference was lowest for S6; S7 was a close second and N6 was a distant third. The expectation of life at birth in the South table is 32.5 years for females and 31.6 for males in level 6, and 35.0 for females and 33.9 for males in level 7. The results are reasonably close to estimates found by other scholars and cited earlier. It should be emphasized that the estimated life expectancies are speculative because no information is available for slaves at older ages and because of potential problems with the plantation record data.

MORTALITY RATES BY TIME PERIOD

Table 18.4 shows mortality rates by time period for infants and children aged one to four and five to fourteen. Insufficient data are available for calculating mortality by time period for those who survived beyond age fourteen. The table shows that mortality rates tended to be highest from the 1820s to the 1840s. The rates for infants and children aged one to four declined after the 1820s, whereas the rate for children aged five to fourteen reached a peak during the 1840s.

One should be cautious in investigating the time pattern of mortality because of

Table 18.3. Relative Frequency of Deaths Thirteen to Fifty-Nine Months after Birth among Children Who Died between Ages One and Four

Months after Birth	Percent
13–16	25.1
17–20	15.1
21–24	13.6
25–28	9.7
29–32	7.2
33–36	6.1
37–59	23.3
N	279

Source: Plantation records described in Table 18.1.

Table 18.4. Mortality Rates of Infants and Children by Time Period

Time Period	Infants		Children 1–4		Children 5–14	
	N	Mortality Rate	N	Mortality Rate	N	Mortality Rate
1786–1799	113	319	59	153	14	0
1800–1809	197	223	124	105	54	74
1810–1819	289	197	206	131	138	29
1820–1829	263	259	192	266	91	110
1830–1839	217	254	113	265	28	143
1840–1849	415	251	218	239	91	154
1850–1863	878	215	551	176	146	68
1786–1863	2,372	233	1,463	191	562	82

Note: The mortality rates of infants and children represent the number of deaths of those aged x to $x + n$ per thousand of those who survive to age x.
Source: Plantation records described in Table 18.1.

the possible role of underreporting, the changing mix of characteristics of women having children, and the changing mix of plantation characteristics. These considerations are explored further in the next two sections.

The bulge in mortality rates from the 1820s to the 1840s may have been related to increased mobility of the population. Mobility was made easier by a transportation network of canals, railways, and steamboats created during this period. Fogel and Engerman (1974a, 1:46) estimate that 835,000 slaves moved from exporting to importing states in the seven decades from 1790 to 1860. Nearly 60 percent of the total moved between 1820 and 1850. Slaves moved long distances were exposed to new epidemiological environments that probably resulted in higher death rates for a period of one to two years after the move.[10] Slaves who resided in the importing regions were exposed to new varieties of disease, to which they had low resistance, brought by slaves and whites from the exporting areas. Substantial migration occurred after 1850, but the effects on mortality may have been less severe because the disease environment within the South became more homogeneous as a consequence of earlier migration.

Epidemics may have contributed to the time pattern of mortality. Cholera was prevalent in the southern United States during the 1830s and 1840s (see Rosenberg 1962). The South was particularly hard hit in 1833.

UNDERREPORTING OF BIRTHS AND INFANT DEATHS

The problem of underreporting is approached through two techniques. The first relies on the proportion of infant deaths that occur soon after birth. The second is based on distributions of the intervals between successive confinements. An alternative approach to the underreporting problem, which is discussed in Steckel #23, in this volume, and in Steckel 1986a and 1986c, makes use of the relationship among stature in early childhood, birth weight, and neonatal mortality.

The course of infant mortality over time provides a basis for investigating underreporting using the first method. An inspection of Table 18.4 shows that with the exception of the decades of 1800–1809 and 1810–1819, infant mortality declined gradually from the late 1700s to the Civil War. The results from 1800 to 1819 are particularly low and may be related to underreporting.

The proportion of infant deaths that occurred soon after birth provides a crude criterion by which underreporting of births and infant deaths can be measured. Wrigley (1977, 283) reports that roughly one-half of all infant deaths occur within the first month of life. Table 18.5 shows the results of one method of applying this criterion. The table shows the proportions who died within twenty-eight days of birth, as well as an adjustment of the infant death rate based on minimum proportions of 0.40, 0.50, and 0.60. The adjustment consists of estimating the number of births and infant deaths not reported if the minimum proportion prevailed, and then recalculation of the infant death rate. For example, there were 197 births reported in 1800–1809 and 0.97 of those that died within the first year died within twenty-eight days. If 0.40 actually died within twenty-eight days, then $(0.297D + X)/(D + X) = 0.40$ is the relevant relationship where D is the observed number of infant deaths and X is the number of deaths (and births) not recorded. Since $D = 0.223 \times 197 = 44$, it follows that $X = 8$ and the adjusted infant mortality rate is $(44 + 8)/(197 + 8) = 254$ per thousand. There is no adjustment from 1786 to 1799 for proportions 0.40 and 0.50 because the proportions for these years are above the minimum.

The level of infant mortality is very much open to question using this method of adjustment. The adjustment is particularly crude because the proportion of deaths that occur within twenty-eight days of birth is probably influenced by variables that

Table 18.5. Proportion of Infant Deaths Occurring within Twenty-Eight Days of Birth and Adjusted Infant Death Rates by Time Period

Time Period	Proportion of Infant Deaths Occurring within 28 Days of Birth	Infant Death Rate if Proportion Is at Least 0.40	Infant Death Rate if Proportion Is at Least 0.50	Infant Death Rate if Proportion Is at Least 0.60
1786–1799	0.528	319	319	347
1800–1809	0.297	254	288	338
1810–1819	0.212	244	280	328
1820–1829	0.429	259	286	334
1830–1839	0.190	316	357	411
1840–1849	0.277	287	325	377
1850–1863	0.303	242	276	323
1786–1863	0.311	259	295	344

Note: The proportion of infant deaths occurring within twenty-eight days of birth is calculated only for those births and deaths for which month, day, and year of the events are given. This subset includes 438 of the 553 deaths implied by columns two and three of the last row of Table 18.4.
Source: Plantation records described in Table 18.1.

affect the level of mortality. Its primary value is detecting time periods of gross underenumeration. The periods 1810–1819 and 1830–1839 seem to fall into this category. The adjustments do not change the result of a period of declining infant mortality, although the timing of the decline is affected.

An alternative method of adjusting the results is deletion of plantations. Table 18.6 shows the proportion of infant deaths that occurred within twenty-eight days of birth on each plantation. The proportions range from 0.146 to 0.667. The lowest four are quite low and are distinguished by a gap between them and the next highest proportion. The gap and the low proportions for this group suggest that underreporting existed in these lists.

The procedure cannot be usefully applied to subsections of most of the remaining lists because the sample sizes are too small. The Gaillard list (row 4 in Table 18.1) has the largest number of observations and a period of questionable reliability in reporting. On this plantation the infant mortality rate was only 104 per 1,000 from 1810 through 1819. During the same time period there were 14 infant deaths and only 1 of these occurred within twenty-eight days of birth. If the true proportion was 0.4, the probability of obtaining 1 or less in 14 infant deaths is less than 0.01. This result strongly suggests the possibility of underenumeration during this period.

Table 18.7 shows infant mortality by time period for the seven plantations with a proportion of infant deaths occurring within twenty-eight days of birth in excess of 0.30. The period 1810–1819 for the Gaillard plantation (row 4) is also omitted from the sample. This method of adjustment also produces a downward trend in infant mortality.

The regression analysis in subsequent sections uses the proportion of infant deaths that occurred within twenty-eight days of birth as a measure of underreporting. Owners who were faithful in recording births and infant deaths were probably diligent in recording deaths at older ages. Furthermore, underenumeration of infant deaths biases mortality rates downward at older ages. Consequently, the pro-

Table 18.6. Proportion of Infant Deaths That Occurred within Twenty-Eight Days of Birth by Plantation

Plantation (row in Table 18.1)	Proportion
Ball (2)	0.667
Watson (11)	0.577
Minor (10)	0.500
Ball (1)	0.426
Good Hope (6)	0.421
Gaillard (4)	0.326[a]
Ball (3)	0.302
Gaillard (5)	0.188
Mackay and Stiles (8)	0.158
Hammond (7)	0.157
McCutcheon (9)	0.146

[a]The proportion is 0.468 if the period 1810–1819 is omitted.
Source: Plantation records described in Table 18.1.

Table 18.7. Infant Death Rates by Time Period on Plantations in Which the Proportion of Infant Deaths That Occurred within Twenty-Eight Days of Birth Is at Least 0.300

Time Period	Number of Births	Infant Death Rate per Thousand
1786–1799	113	319
1800–1809	197	223
1810–1819	134	291
1820–1829	225	276
1830–1839	69	275
1840–1849	135	252
1850–1863	154	249
1786–1863	1,327	261

Source: Plantation records described in Table 18.1.

portion is used as a measure of the completeness of enumeration during infancy and at older ages.

Henry (1968) proposed a method for measuring the underreporting of infant deaths based on comparison of the distributions of intervals between confinements. Since lactation prevents or delays the return of ovulation in a sizable fraction of women, the interval between confinements depends on the fate of the first child in the interval. For the purpose of analysis the intervals are arranged into three groups: (1) the first child lived until age one, (2) the first child died before age one, and (3) the fate of the first child is unknown.[11] In the absence of underreporting of infant deaths the distributions 1 and 3 are drawn from the same population. If there is underreporting of infant deaths then a portion of births of unknown fate died before age one and distribution 3 consists of a weighted average of distributions 1 and 2. The appropriate weighting factor can be estimated by choosing weights which minimize chi-square. In this procedure the expected (or theoretical) frequency is a weighted average of the frequencies in distributions 1 and 2 and the observed frequency is given by distribution 3.

Table 18.8 shows the appropriate distributions for slaves.[12] Distribution 3 is nearly identical to distribution 1, indicating that underreporting of infant deaths was infrequent. The calculations which minimize chi-square reveal that distribution 3 consists of 99 percent of distribution 1 and 1 percent of distribution 2. One percent of the intervals in distribution 3 (approximately five intervals) are intervals of distribution 2. Consequently the estimated level of underreporting of infant deaths equals $5/(5 + 308) = 1.6$ percent. This result suggests that slave lists described in Table 18.1 are a reliable source of death information.

REGRESSION ANALYSIS OF MORTALITY

The discussion in previous sections suggested that mortality varied by time period. This section explores the possible influence of time period as well as main crop,

Table 18.8. Distribution of the Interval between Successive Confinements According to the Fate of the First Child in the Interval

Interval (months)	Distribution		
	1	2	3
Under 15	0.017	0.253	0.020
15–20	0.091	0.364	0.091
21–26	0.337	0.188	0.354
27–32	0.298	0.078	0.291
33–38	0.139	0.059	0.136
39–44	0.035	0.029	0.033
51–56	0.017	0.003	0.018
N	483	308	508

Source: Plantation records described in Table 18.1.

plantation size, and age of the mother (for infants). The variables used in the regression analysis are defined in the Appendix to this paper. All independent variables are defined as a series of dummy variables so that non-linear relations may be detected and estimated. All regressions in this section are based on individual data. The mortality of infants, children aged one to four, and children aged five to fourteen are analyzed in this section.

The dependent variables in this section are dichotomous, with value equal to 1 if death occurred, and 0 otherwise.[13] Estimation of a relation with a dichotomous dependent variable using the ordinary least squares linear probability model can involve serious difficulties, including predictions that lie outside the unit interval, sensitivity of the fitted relationship to the location of the explanatory variables, inapplicability of the usual tests of significance for the estimated coefficients, and a multiple R-square that does not have a clear meaning. The maximum likelihood logistic probability model overcomes these difficulties.[14]

The maximum likelihood estimation uses a model of the form

$$P = \frac{1}{1 + \exp\left[-\left(a + \sum_{i=1}^{n} \beta_i X_i\right)\right]} \tag{1}$$

where P is probability of death, a is a constant, the β_i are parameters, the X_i are independent variables, and n is the number of independent variables in addition to the constant. The relations in this section were also estimated using an ordinary least squares program, and despite the potential for a disparity in results the two methods of estimation usually yield approximately the same implications for behavior.

The regression results are shown in Tables 18.9 through 18.11. The values of $\partial P/\partial X_i$ shown in each table are the partial derivatives of the probability function P with respect to the independent variable X_i evaluated at the means of the independent variables. The effect on the dependent variable of a unit change in an independent variable is given by $\partial P/\partial X_i$. The value of $-2 \log \lambda$ shown in the footnote to each table is a measure of the statistical significance of the regression. The term λ is the likelihood ratio and equals the value of the likelihood function obtained when all parameter values are set equal to zero, divided by the value of the likelihood function obtained under the maintained hypothesis. The variable $-2 \log \lambda$ has a chi-square distribution with as many degrees of freedom as parameter values set equal to zero, which is twelve in the case of Table 18.9. The value of 35.9 in Table 18.9 shows that the estimated relation is highly significant.

The independent variables eligible for inclusion in each regression were plantation size (Size 100–199, and so forth), main crop (Mixed, and so forth), and time period (Time 1800–1809, for example). The proportion of infant deaths on the plantation that occurred within twenty-eight days of birth (Prop 0–28), was also included as a measure of the completeness of enumeration. Studies have shown (United Nations 1954, 6–8) that infant mortality is a U-shaped function of the age of the mother, and dummy variables representing mother's age (Mother 29–24, and so forth) were included as independent variables in the analysis of infant mortality.[15] All relevant independent variables were eligible in regressions estimated by an OLS stepwise procedure.[16] The independent variables with t-values less than 1 were excluded. The retained variables were used in estimation with the maximum likelihood procedure, and the results are shown in Tables 18.9, 18.10, and 18.11. As an alternative procedure all eligible variables were included in the maximum likelihood procedure and the variables with t-values less than 1 were deleted. This procedure generated results similar to those obtained by the OLS stepwise procedures.

Features of interest in Tables 18.9, 18.10, and 18.11 are time patterns of mortality that differ from those in Table 18.4. The downward trends among infants, children aged one to four, and children aged five to fourteen evident in Table 18.4 do not appear in the time period coefficients. When controlling for other variables, the probability of infant death was at a minimum from 1810 to 1819 and then rose to a peak during the 1840s. The probability of death of children aged one to four was elevated from 1820 to 1849 and dropped of slightly thereafter. The probability of death of children aged five to fourteen was at a minimum from 1810 to 1819 and was elevated from 1830 to 1849.

Variations in the distribution of mother's age at childbirth may contribute to the differences in the time pattern of infant mortality shown in Tables 18.4 and 18.9. The mother's age coefficients in Table 18.9 show that infant deaths were highest among young mothers.[17] If other independent variables are evaluated at their sample means, the expected probability of infant death was 34.6 percent for births to mothers under age twenty compared to about 22.2 percent for births among older women. During the early years of the recording period on a plantation the age composition of mothers was heavily weighted by young women and over time the distribution of ages became weighted more toward older women.

Changes in the plantation size and main crop mix of the sample may also have contributed to the divergence in results between Table 18.4 and Tables 18.9, 18.10, and 18.11. For example, the probability of death was relatively high on rice plantations and observations from these plantations were relatively numerous during the early decades of the 1800s.

The variable Prop 0–28 fails to enter the regressions reported in Tables 18.9

Table 18.9. Regression of a Dichotomous Variable Representing an Infant Death on Mother's Age, Plantation Size, Main Crop, and Time Period

Variable	Coefficient	$\partial P/\partial X_i$	Asymptotic t-Value	Sample Mean
Const	−1.0458	—	4.557	—
Mother 20–24	−0.6594	−0.1204	2.731	0.2937
Mother 25–29	−0.5400	−0.09860	2.079	0.2188
Mother 30–34	−0.6004	−0.1096	2.117	0.1665
Mother 35–39	−0.6828	−0.1247	2.007	0.0963
Mother 40+	−0.6222	−0.1136	1.583	0.0595
Size 100–199	0.5948	0.1086	1.620	0.0535
Size 200+	0.2308	0.04213	1.254	0.5493
Rice	0.4782	0.08730	1.420	0.0809
Time 1810–1819	−0.8652	−0.1580	1.138	0.0238
Time 1820–1829	−0.5660	−0.1033	1.221	0.0523
Time 1830–1839	0.6722	0.1227	2.591	0.1070
Time 1840–1849	0.7596	0.1387	3.912	0.2509

Note: Dependent Variable = Infant; N = 841; −2 log λ = 35.9.
Source: Plantation records described in Table 18.1.

Table 18.10. Regression of a Dichotomous Variable Representing the Death of a Child Aged One to Four Years on Plantation Size, Main Crop, Time Period, and the Proportion of Infant Deaths That Occurred within Twenty-Eight Days of Birth

Variable	Coefficient	$\partial P/\partial X_i$	Asymptotic t-Value	Sample Mean
Const	−2.0678	—	5.987	—
Size 200+	0.4046	0.06002	2.192	0.5995
Mixed	0.2604	0.03863	0.9506	0.1105
Rice	0.2818	0.04178	1.361	0.2174
Sugar	−0.4312	−0.06396	1.957	0.1764
Time 1820–1829	0.9082	0.1347	3.788	0.1312
Time 1830–1839	1.0392	0.1542	3.590	0.0772
Time 1840–1849	1.0068	0.1493	3.931	0.1490
Time 1850–1859	0.5926	0.08791	2.822	0.3766
Prop 0–28	−0.8318	−0.1234	1.371	0.3217

Note: Dependent Variable = Chil 1–4; N = 1,463; −2 log λ = 46.1.
Source: Plantation records described in Table 18.1.

Table 18.11. Regression of a Dichotomous Variable Representing the Death of a Child Aged Five to Fourteen Years on Main Crop and Time Period

Variable	Coefficient	$\partial P/\partial X_i$	Asymptotic t-Value	Sample Mean
Const	−2.0800	—	10.15	—
Rice	0.9954	0.06215	2.498	0.2064
Time 1820–1829	−1.0874	−0.06789	1.996	0.2456
Time 1830–1839	1.0098	0.06304	1.665	0.0498
Time 1840–1849	1.0968	0.06848	2.737	0.1619

Note: Dependent Variable = Chil 5–14; N = 562; −2 log λ = 18.9.
Source: Plantation records described in Table 18.1.

and 18.11 and the coefficient has an unexpected sign in Table 18.10. Prop 0–28 may not be a good indicator of the completeness of enumeration because it is heavily influenced by other factors. It is also possible that underenumeration was not a serious problem. The negative coefficient in Table 18.10 may reflect selectivity in those who survive to age one. On plantations where Prop 0–28 was high, unhealthy children may have tended to die very early in life rather than at ages one to four. A similar process of selectivity could have existed within the first year of life.

Among the main crop dummies, rice is consistently associated with a high probability of death. Compared with other crops, the expected probability of death in rice cultivation was 41 percent higher among infants, 26 percent higher among children aged one to four, and 28.7 percent higher among children aged five to fourteen if other independent variables shown in Tables 18.9 through 18.11 are evaluated at their sample means. One might suspect that the disease environment along the rice coasts of Georgia and South Carolina is responsible for this finding. The climate of sugar production in the lower Mississippi Valley was similar to that where rice was produced, yet sugar does not register as a crop associated with a high probability of death. Among children aged one to four the probability of death was lowest on sugar plantations. Slight variations in climate may have played an important role in affecting mortality. It is also possible that features of rice cultivation, such as standing water that produced disease-transmitting insects, contributed to high mortality rates in rice growing areas.

The plantations in the sample are very large relative to the median for the slave population, so one cannot obtain extensive information about the influence of plantation size on mortality. The results for young children agree with Higman's (1976) finding for Jamaican slaves that mortality rates tend to increase with plantation size. Relative to plantations with under 100 slaves, the expected probability of infant death was 55 percent higher among plantations of size 100 to 199 and 19 percent higher among plantations larger than 200 if other independent variables are evaluated at their sample means. Children aged one to four had a 40 percent higher expected probability of death on plantations larger than 200 relative to smaller sizes. Plantation size did not systematically influence the probability of death on plantations larger than 200 relative to smaller sizes. Plantation size did not systematically influence the probability of death of children aged five to fourteen. Since slaves on large plantations frequently had access to hospitals and medical care, one might expect the probability to decline with size; however, many early nineteenth-century medical practices no doubt increased the probability of death. Furthermore the numbers on large plantations probably increased the chances that someone nearby harbored a communicable disease. Very large plantations may have had greater contact with disease environments outside the plantation and, therefore, realized greater chances of importing disease. The possible influence of outside contact on mortality might be studied further on those plantations where records of slave purchases are available. Comparisons of mortality rates before and after purchases may provide some insight into this issue.

THE SEASONAL PATTERN OF DEATH

The seasonal pattern of death provides insights into determinants of mortality. Through this apparatus a variety of variables that may influence mortality, such as location, size, and crop, are held constant and one captures the influence of seasonal factors on mortality.

Table 18.12 shows the seasonal pattern of death for infants, for children aged one to four, and for persons aged five and over, fifteen to twenty-nine, and over fifty. Table 18.13 provides the results of some chi-square tests involving the distributions shown in Table 18.12. Since a high proportion of infant deaths occur soon after birth, it is not surprising that the seasonal patterns of birth and infant death are significantly different at only 0.62. The coefficient of correlation between the seasonal patterns of birth and death is 0.70. There is no systematic relation between the seasonal patterns of conception and death.

The patterns of non-infants in Table 18.12 have large seasonal variation. For example, in the group aged one to four the number of deaths during the peak summer months was nearly five times greater than the minimum established during the winter. This general pattern tends to prevail among the older age groups as well and is the reverse of the pattern for the United States in modern times (see Rosenwaike 1966). The reversal is no doubt associated with a dramatic change in the types of disease that bring about death. Diseases such as malaria, yellow fever, typhoid, hookworm, and parasitic infections flourished during the warm summer months in the antebellum South, but are not important killers today. The reversal may also be related to a shift to industrial employment. Unlike industry, seasonal work in agriculture requires periods of intense labor that may have contributed to

Table 18.12. The Seasonal Pattern of Slave Deaths by Age Group of the Deceased

Month	Infants	1–4	5+	15–49	50+
January	0.0723	0.0314	0.0547	0.0549	0.0574
February	0.0774	0.0533	0.0925	0.0947	0.0631
March	0.0585	0.0515	0.0888	0.0707	0.1244
April	0.0871	0.0591	0.0941	0.0649	0.1088
May	0.0878	0.0600	0.0706	0.0785	0.0670
June	0.0960	0.0739	0.0871	0.1298	0.0692
July	0.0964	0.1458	0.1048	0.1020	0.0862
August	0.1084	0.1487	0.1207	0.1099	0.1627
September	0.0911	0.1536	0.0800	0.0974	0.0296
October	0.0706	0.0886	0.0592	0.0864	0.0670
November	0.0701	0.0768	0.0565	0.0243	0.0594
December	0.0843	0.0572	0.0911	0.0864	0.1053
N	570	344	431	124	103

Note: The seasonal pattern for those aged five to fourteen cannot be extracted from the last three columns because the exact age at death is not known for a portion of those aged over five. The distributions have been adjusted for the number of days in each month.
Source: Plantation records described in Table 18.1.

some deaths. Nearly 30 percent of the deaths among slaves aged fifteen to forty-nine occurred during the harvest months of August, September, and October.

The chi-square tests shown in Table 18.13 reveal some interesting differences across age groups.[18] One of the more interesting results is that the distributions for children aged one to four and persons aged over five are significantly different; the extent of seasonal variation is smaller among those over five years old. The distribution of those aged over fifty has multiple peaks. This feature is not found in the other distributions, but it may be in part a consequence of the small sample size. The distribution of those aged fifteen to forty-nine is not significantly different from a random (flat) distribution.

One must be cautious in attributing causes to the seasonal patterns. The distributions may capture the influence of a variety of factors, including weather, work routine, diet, and exposure to communicable diseases from outside the plantation. Furthermore, the distributions may exaggerate the importance of season on mortality rates through inventory effects. Seasons that were particularly harsh may have depleted the stock of slaves who were weak and therefore susceptible to death in subsequent months; however, the high incidence of tropical diseases in the South suggests that variations in weather probably played a major role.

SUMMARY AND CONCLUSIONS

This study analyzed evidence on slave mortality available from eleven slave lists maintained by owners of large plantations. Collectively the plantations span the period from 1786 to 1864. Sufficient data are available to calculate mortality rates for infants, children, and young adults. Mortality rates were relatively high among young children. Among the model life tables provided by Coale and Demeny, the age pattern of slave mortality most closely resembles that of the South populations. Underreporting of births and infant deaths, a changing mix of characteristics in the sample, improved living standards and medical care, diet, the African environmental heritage, the North American climate, and breast-feeding patterns may have affected the age pattern of mortality.

Table 18.13. Results of Some Chi-Square Tests Involving the Distributions in Table 18.12

Comparison	Chi-Square	Significant at
Infants and Births	9.031	0.62
1–4 and 5+	32.962	0.005
1–4 and 15–49	17.776	0.09
1–4 and 50+	25.957	0.01
15–49 and 50+	13.231	0.29
1–4 and Random	81.177	0.005
5+ and Random	22.765	0.025
15–49 and Random	12.580	0.33
50+ and Random	17.720	0.10

Source: Plantation records described in Table 18.1.

Mortality rates calculated for infants, children aged one to four, and children aged five to fourteen were relatively high during the period from 1820 to 1850. The results do not appear to be substantially influenced by underreporting. The time pattern of mortality rates may have been related to encounters with new disease environments resulting from increased mobility of the southern population. In a regression analysis of mortality that includes variables representing main crop, plantation size, and mother's age (for infants), time period dummies show a fluctuating pattern with elevations during the middle of the antebellum period. The time period dummies may capture genuine time period effects as well as omitted but relevant plantation characteristics.

The regressions indicate that the expected probability of infant death was 56 percent higher among births to women under age twenty. The expected probability of death was substantially higher on rice plantations and tended to increase with plantation size among infants and children aged one to four. The effect of rice may reflect climate and special features of rice cultivation. Very large plantations may have facilitated the spread of disease.

Deaths among children aged one to four were heavily concentrated in the summer months and deaths among slaves aged fifteen to forty-nine tended to be concentrated during the summer. The seasonal patterns probably reflect the seasonal prevalence of infectious diseases and may also capture variations in the diet and work routine.

APPENDIX: DEFINITION OF VARIABLES

Mother 15–19* = 1 if mother under age twenty, 0 otherwise.

Mother 20–24 = 1 if mother aged twenty to twenty-four, 0 otherwise.

Mother 25–29 = 1 if mother aged twenty-five to twenty-nine, 0 otherwise.

Mother 30–34 = 1 if mother aged thirty to thirty-four, 0 otherwise.

Mother 35–39 = 1 if mother aged thirty-five to thirty-nine, 0 otherwise.

Mother 40+ = 1 if mother aged over forty, 0 otherwise.

Size 1–99* = 1 if plantation under size 100, 0 otherwise.

Size 100–199 = 1 if plantation of size 100–199, 0 otherwise.

Size 200–299 = 1 if plantation of size 200+, 0 otherwise.

Cotton* = 1 if main crop is cotton, 0 otherwise.

Mixed = 1 if engaged in mixed farming, 0 otherwise.

Rice = 1 if main crop is rice, 0 otherwise.

Sugar = 1 if main crop is sugar, 0 otherwise.

Time 1786–1799* = 1 if 1786–1799, 0 otherwise.

Time 1800–1809 = 1 if 1800–1809, 0 otherwise.

Time 1810–1819 = 1 if 1810–1819, 0 otherwise.

Time 1820–1829 = 1 if 1820–1829, 0 otherwise.

Time 1830–1839 = 1 if 1830–1839, 0 otherwise.

Time 1840–1849 = 1 if 1840–1849, 0 otherwise.

*These independent variables were excluded from the regressions.

Time 1850+ = 1 if 1850+, 0 otherwise.

Prop 0–28 = Proportion of infant deaths that occurred within twenty-eight days of birth

Infant = 1 if live birth died within one year, 0 otherwise.

Chil 1–4 = 1 if child who survived to age one died before age five, 0 otherwise.

Chil 5–14 = 1 if child who survived to age five died before age fifteen, 0 otherwise.

Const = Constant.

NOTES

1. Both estimates are for females. The estimate of 27.8 years if from Farley (1970), 67, and the estimate of 38.1 years is from Evans (1962), 212.
2. Sydnor's estimates apply to Mississippi slaves.
3. Useful summary discussions of these issues can be found in Fogel et al. (1978), Vinovskis (1978), and Easterlin (1977).
4. A more detailed description of the records can be found in Steckel (1977), 19–50.
5. The lists denote some stillbirths, but the definition applied and completeness of coverage are difficult to assess. The number at risk reflects slave sales that were denoted in the lists. How complete the enumeration of sales was is not known and it should be observed that underenumeration of sales results in an overstatement of the number at risk. The mortality rates shown in Table 18.2 were high for young children, suggesting that if underenumeration of sales existed, it was probably not important at young ages. The rates at older ages could be biased downward by a failure to record sales.
6. Median plantation size at the state level was calculated by linear interpolation (where necessary) of the distribution of slaveholdings reported in the 1860 census. The average for the South is weighted by the slave population of each state.
7. According to the 1850 census, slaves in the plantation agricultural sector were distributed among the main crops as follows: cotton, 73 percent; tobacco, 14 percent; sugar, 6 percent; rice, 5 percent; hemp, 2 percent (U.S. Census Office 1854, 94).
8. The advantages of breast-feeding diminish as sanitation and the nutritional quality of substitute foods improve. This subject, and a higher incidence of mortality following weaning, are discussed by Knodel and Kinter (1977). See also Woodbury (1925) and Cantrelle and Leridon (1971).
9. Lactation practices on a slave plantation are discussed in Hammond (1844). In the plantations in Table 18.1 the mean interval between recorded births was 30.5 months (N = 1,176) and the median was 26.8 months. Since lactation has a contraceptive effect it is doubtful that breast-feeding continued much longer than a year on average.
10. Migration, disease environments, and mortality are discussed by Curtin (1968).
11. In the event of multiple confinements the groups become (1) at least one child lived until age one, (2) all the children died before age one, and (3) the fate of at least one child is unknown.
12. Inventory lists or disposition lists on three plantations and age at death information established that certain slaves lived beyond their first birthday. Slaves for whom survival beyond age one could not be established were used for distribution 3. Since the final interval tends to be large, Henry (1968) recommends that final intervals be excluded. Truncation of recording implies that final intervals cannot be established in many families. Consequently, the last interval in each sequence of births was omitted.
13. For example, the variable equals 1 if a child survived to age five but died before age fifteen. The variable equals 0 if a child who survived to age five also survived to age fifteen. The only children included in the sample are those whose experience is observable during the age span five to fifteen. Similar considerations apply to the analysis of mortality in other age groups.
14. A discussion of the effects of the linear probability model with a binary dependent variable can be found in Nerlove and Press (1973), 3–9. The maximum likelihood logistic probability model

employed in this section is discussed in the above report. The computer program used in estimation was originally written by K. Maurer and R. Olsen and modified by Linda Shaffer. Houston Stokes converted the program to IBM 370 use and made it available to me.

15. Infant mortality rates are also U-shaped as a function of birth order. Since mother's age and birth order are positively correlated, the former variable probably captures much of the separate effects of birth order.

16. The stepwise procedure is discussed in Draper and Smith (1966), 171–172.

17. The singulate mean age at first birth for slaves was 20.6 years in a sample of probate records and 21.4 years in a sample of plantation records. Relatively high infant mortality rates from childbirth at young ages may have discouraged slaves and slaveowners from early marriage. Slave age at first birth is discussed in Steckel (1977).

18. A chi-square test is appropriate only if all theoretical frequencies are sufficiently high. Some tests involving slaves aged fifteen to forty-nine or over fifty may be questionable in this regard. However, grouping the data by classes of two months each does not substantially change the test results shown in Table 18.13.

NINETEEN

Logistic Models of Slave Child Mortality in Trinidad

A. Meredith John

In 1811, the British abolitionists adopted a new tactic in their bitter battle to end slavery in British colonies, a battle that had been fought in newspapers, at public meetings, and in Parliament for nearly a quarter of a century. Prior to 1811, the abolitionists had achieved some, though limited, success in their campaign: In 1806, Parliament passed an act abolishing the transatlantic slave trade and, a short time later, abolished the slave trade among the British Caribbean colonies as well (Davis 1975,443; Eltis 1972).

Behind many of the actions of the abolitionists lay the firm belief that any rational and moral person, when faced with the facts and horror of slavery, would have no option but to support its abolition (Walvin 1982, 53). Thus many of the activities of the abolitionists were aimed at publicizing the plight of the slaves in the British colonies. To this end, the African Institution, a London abolitionist society, resolved in 1811 that a sympathetic member of the House of Commons, Dr. William Wilberforce, should introduce a resolution in Parliament calling for a bill requiring the registration of slaves in the British West Indian colonies. Ostensibly, the motivation for slave registration was simple: The annual enumeration of the slave population would serve as a check on illegal intercolony traffic in slaves. There was, however, another less obvious product of a registration system which accounted for the fate of each slave at regular intervals: The registration scheme would provide cold, hard, data on the mortality and fertility of the Caribbean slave population. This, the abolitionists believed, would strengthen their case to the point that the abolition of slavery would be inevitable (Murray 1965, 77–79).

The slave registration act was stalled by the Secretary of State for War and Colonies Lord Liverpool, who was anxious to avoid a parliamentary confrontation with the abolitionists. Instead, Lord Liverpool offered the promise of an order-in-council requiring the registration of slaves in Trinidad, a recently acquired British colony which did not yet have its own legislative assembly. The order was drafted by James Stephen, a leading abolitionist, who tailored the specifications of the registration order to suit the purposes of the African Institution. The order for the

413

registration of the Trinidadian slaves was published in London on March 26, 1812 (C.O. 295/28).

At the time of the initial slave registration, Trinidad was very much a frontier colony, with less than 10 percent of its land under cultivation. The first significant immigration to the island began in 1783, when the Spanish government issued a *cedula de población,* calling for settlers, both free and slave, for Trinidad (Millette 1970, 7). Fourteen years later the British captured Trinidad from the Spanish; the colony was formally ceded to Britain in 1802.

At the time of the British acquisition of Trinidad, the population consisted of 2,261 free whites, 5,276 free colored, 1,232 Arawak Indians, and 19,709 slaves (Mallet [1797] 1964). Most of the free whites were Spanish or French; few people, either slave or free, had been born in Trinidad.

The initial registration of the slaves in Trinidad took place, for the most part, in March 1813. For each slave, the slaveowners were to report given name and surname; color; occupation; age; height; birthplace if the slave had been born in the Caribbean or, if not, the country or district in Africa from which the slave had been shipped; distinguishing marks; and relationship to other family members with whom the slave lived. The incentive for registering all one's slaves was strong: Any slave found to be unregistered would be deemed free (C.O. 295/28). A total of 17,087 plantation slaves were registered in Trinidad in 1813; of these, 4,295 were children less than fifteen years old.

The order called for periodic revision of the registers at which time any changes in the status of each slave was noted: birth, death, manumission, sale, or desertion. The first update of the Trinidadian slave registers took place in January 1815, 1.75 years following the initial registration of slaves.

INFANT AND CHILD MORTALITY AMONG THE SLAVES

In his journal, M. G. Lewis, a Caribbean planter, cited the case of a slave woman on his plantation who had borne ten children, only one of whom had survived, and of another slave who had produced twelve children, of whom only two reached adolescence. On his plantation, mothers of four, five, and six children frequently had no surviving children. Many planters offered cash rewards to mothers who raised a child successfully to his first birthday; some offered rewards to the attending midwife as well (Patterson 1967, 101).

The practices reported among some slaves regarding childbirth were inimical to infant survival. The umbilical cord was tied with a burned rag and not examined for nine days. The child was kept in the same clothes for the first nine days of his life and was given to a wet nurse; his mother began to nurse him on the tenth day. Often a newborn was not entered into plantation records unless he had survived his first two weeks (Brathwaite 1981, 7; Patterson 1967, 154–155).

Perhaps the most important single killer of newborn slaves was neonatal tetanus: One physician claimed that nearly one-quarter of slave infants died in the first two weeks of this cause (Collins [1811] 1971, 139). Higman found that among the slaves in Jamaica, the major reported cause of infant mortality was tetanus. In addition to tetanus, the principal causes of death listed for slave children were bowel disorders, putrid sore throat, colic, whooping cough, measles, smallpox, yaws, and malnutrition (Higman 1976, 120).

Maternal factors were perceived as being important determinants of infant and child mortality. One writer claimed that those estates with the highest per capita agricultural production experienced the highest infant and child mortality rates because mothers did not have time to care for their children (Patterson 1967, 154). Higman noted that the perceptions of nineteenth-century writers was that creole mothers (mothers born in the Caribbean) were more conscientious in their child rearing than were African mothers (mothers born in Africa), who tended to neglect their children (Higman 1976, 120). Patterson posited that the children of household servants fared better than the children of field-workers since the former were often raised with the white children (Patterson 1967, 154).

Infectious diseases were rife and lethal in the young slave population; both measles and smallpox took a heavy toll in lives. Some owners attempted to innoculate their slaves, infants included, against smallpox by making a small incision in the arm of the slave and implanting a piece of cotton thread which had been drawn through the ripe pustules of an infected slave. Although adults rarely died as a result of the innoculation, the operation was known to be risky for children "from four years and under" (Collins [1811] 1971, 277). Slaves themselves tried to innoculate their children against yaws, a highly contagious bacterial skin disease prevalent in tropical countries and which, if not fatal, often resulted in malformed bones and joints (Higman 1976, 114).

The exposure of the child to infectious diseases was, to some degree, influenced by the characteristics of the plantation, particularly the size of the plantation and the crop grown there. Larger plantations were more conducive to the rapid spread of infectious diseases; however, to the extent that larger plantations were self-contained units and so required little contact with individuals from other plantations, there would be reduced opportunity for the spread of infectious disease from one plantation to another. The exceptions were provisions plantations, which grew foodstuffs to sell elsewhere on Trinidad: The provisions plantations were subject to a constant flow of outside visitors. Larger plantations were likely to have their own provisioning grounds, thus limiting the contact of these slaves to the outside world and perhaps ensuring them a more ample and nutritious food supply.

The disease environment could, potentially, vary with the crop grown on the plantation. For example, in much of the Caribbean, coffee tended to be grown in dry hilly areas while sugar was grown in swampy coastal areas. In Trinidad, however, there was little geographic variation in plantations since, as a result of poor transportation, plantations tended to be established along the coast, irrespective of the crop grown (Mallet [1797] 1964; Joseph [1838] 1970).

A more subtle aspect of the environment in which the slaves lived stemmed from the attitude of the slaveowners toward their slaves. It has been suggested that Catholic slaveowners were more humane in their treatment of slaves than were Protestant owners: The difference reflected their underlying perceptions of slaves

(Tannenbaum 1946). To the Catholics, slaves were human beings, albeit of a very inferior sort, but who nonetheless had fundamental rights as human beings. To the Protestants, slaves were merely property.

LOGISTIC MODELS OF MORTALITY

The plantation slave registers do not give the age at death of those slaves who died in the period between March 1813 and January 1815; the only information given is whether or not the slave died during the 1.75 year interval. The most appropriate models of slave mortality given these data are binary response models, such as logit or probit models. In this study, logistic regression models are employed in the analysis of period slave mortality, or more specifically, in estimating the probability of surviving through the interregistration period or dying in the interregistration interval.

THE DEPENDENCE OF MORTALITY UPON AGE

It is obvious that an individual's probability of surviving through any time period is a function of his age: Young children and old adults have higher probabilities of dying than do young adults. Unfortunately, however, the relationship between mortality and age is not simple: There is no closed form expression which adequately specifies the relationship between mortality and age. While one might achieve reasonable accuracy in describing the $_nq_x$ function by, say, a fourth-order polynomial in age, the coefficients of the higher order age terms have no obvious and intuitive demographic interpretation.

The problem of expressing the dependence of mortality upon the individual's age in a statistical model can be resolved by employing an empirical rather than analytical function of age in the models. Specifically, rather than including a polynomial in age as an explanatory variable in a model describing the probability of death of an individual aged x, the probability of surviving to age x, $p(x)$, taken from an appropriate life table, can be used to express the form of the dependence of mortality upon age. Next, a relationship between two life tables, first noted by Brass, can be invoked: In many cases, the logit of one life table can be expressed as a linear function of the logit of another life table (Brass et al. 1967, 127–128). The logit of a function of a random variable, $f(x)$, is defined as:

$$\text{logit } f(x) = \ln\left[\frac{1 - f(x)}{f(x)}\right] \tag{1}$$

In this case, the random variable is the probability of surviving to age x, denoted by $p(x)$ and derived from the life table survival function as $l(x)/l(0)$. If $p(x)$ is the probability of surviving to age x, then $(1 - p(x))$ is the probability of dying at some age less than x, and the logit of $p(x)$ is the natural logarithm of the ratio of the probability of dying before age x to the probability of surviving to at least age x:

$$\text{logit } p(x) = \ln\left[\frac{1 - p(x)}{p(x)}\right] \tag{2}$$

The logit of the probability of surviving to age x in one life table can be expressed as a linear function of the logit of the probability of surviving to the same age in another life table:

$$\ln\left[\frac{1-p(x)}{p(x)}\right] = \alpha + \beta \cdot \ln\left[\frac{1-p_s(x)}{p_s(x)}\right] \tag{3}$$

where the subscript s denotes a standard life table. The parameters of this relationship can be estimated by ordinary least squares if it is assumed that a normal error term ϵ_i is added to the right-hand side of equation 3.

The coefficients in the Brass model have simple interpretations. The intercept parameter, α, denotes the "level" of mortality prevailing in the life table; variations in α generate a set of nested survival functions. The parameter β governs the slope of the generated survival function, or more formally, denotes the relationship between adult and child mortality. Thus, variations in β generate a set of survival functions which intersect at age a^*, which is the mean of the mean ages of the survival functions.

The Brass logit relation among life tables is based on the observation that the logit of the probability of surviving from birth to age x in one life table is a linear function of the corresponding logit in another life table. It can be shown, however, that the relationship is far more general: The logit of the probability of surviving from exact age x to exact age $(x + n)$ in one life table is a linear function of the corresponding logit in another life table; x need not be zero in order for the relationship to hold. Furthermore, the relationship holds for survivorship probabilities between age groups rather than exact ages. Thus for the plantation slave data, the logit of the probability of surviving from complete age x to complete age $x + 1.75$ can be expressed as a linear function of the corresponding logit in a standard life table (John 1988).

There remains the question of the choice of an appropriate standard life table. Using the Coale and Demeny model life tables, Brass et al. demonstrated that the most appropriate standard from which to recover a known life table via the logit relationship is a standard which has an age pattern of mortality similar to that of the table to be generated. Similarly, it can be shown that the most appropriate standard for generating the probability of surviving from age x to age $x + n$ is a standard life table with an age pattern of mortality similar to that believed to exist in the life table being estimated (John 1988).

AN ALTERNATIVE APPROACH TO THE LOGIT RELATIONSHIP

Another way of formulating the relationship between the logits of two life tables is embodied in a logistic regression model, in which the dependent (response) variable for each individual is binary: $y_i = 1$ if individual i survives from age x to $x + n$ and 0 if individual i dies between ages x and $x + n$. Then Y_i, which is the probability that an individual will survive from age x to $x + n$, is given by

$$E(y_i) = Y_i = \Pr(y_i = 1) \tag{4}$$

where $0 \leq Y_i \leq 1$.

Binary response models originated in the testing of the tolerance of individuals to drugs. Hence these models are also known as dose-response models; the response of an individual to a given dose is either survival or death. The ability of an individual to withstand a particular dose is termed his "tolerance," which is randomly distributed over individuals: Some have high tolerance while others do not. In the case of the slaves, the question is not their tolerance to a drug, but rather their tolerance to environmental insult and personal characteristics.

Let θ denote the individual's tolerance, or his ability to withstand his environment. The variable θ is distributed over the population as $f(\theta)$. Let X_i be the logit of an underlying standard mortality schedule. Then, for individual i, aged x:

$$X_i = \ln\left[\frac{1 - p_s(x)}{p_s(x)}\right] \tag{5}$$

The parameter β is an appropriate coefficient of the logit term. If $\theta < X_i'\beta$, then the individual dies ($y_i = 0$); if $\theta > = X_i'\beta$, then the individual survives ($y_i = 1$). It follows that

$$\Pr(y_i = 1) = E(y_i) = Y_i = \Pr(\theta < X_i'\beta) = 1 - F(X_i'\beta) \tag{6}$$

If it is assumed that the distribution of tolerance, $f(\theta)$, is logistic, then

$$\Pr(y_i = 1) = Y_i = \frac{1}{1 + e^{-(\alpha + \beta X_i)}} \tag{7}$$

The parameters α and β behave in exactly the same manner as in the case of the linear regression of the logit of one life table against the logit of another life table. In particular, if the standard life table provides a perfect description of the mortality pattern in the observed population, then α would be 0 and β would be -1.0.

THE ADDITION OF COVARIATES

It may be that an individual's probability of surviving from age x to $x + n$ deviates in some systematic way from the populationwide probability of surviving through the age interval. In other words, there may exist heterogenity in the population: The probability of surviving from age x to $x + n$ may be a function of other factors in addition to age. For example, an individual's probability of surviving from age x to $x + n$ may depend not only upon age (in the form of the life table probability of surviving), but also upon his personal and environmental characteristics, such as his occupation.

Let X_i be the logit of the life table probability of surviving for individual i, aged x. Let Z_i be an ($n \times 1$) vector of covariates believed to influence the individual's chances of survival. If

$$\theta_i < X_i'\beta + Z_i'\gamma \tag{8}$$

then the individual dies ($y_i = 0$) while if

$$\theta_i \geq X_i'\beta + Z_i'\gamma \tag{9}$$

the individual survives $(y_i = 1)$. It follows that

$$\Pr(y_i = 1) = \frac{1}{1 + e^{-(\alpha + X_i\beta + Z_i\gamma)}} \tag{10}$$

AN EXAMPLE

As an illustration of the sort of model described above, consider a male child aged x at the time of the 1813 slave registration. For this slave we define the following variables:

$y_i =$ 1 if the slave survived the 1.75 year interregistration period; 0 if he died.

YAGE $=$ the logit of the probability of surviving from age x to age $x + 1.75$ in the male slave population life table.

CROP $=$ a series of dummy variables for the principal crop on the slave's plantation.

ORPHAN $=$ 1 if the child is not living with his mother; 0 otherwise.

OC $=$ 1 if owner is Catholic; 0 otherwise.

Then the logistic model is

$$\Pr(\text{survive}) = \frac{1}{1 + e^{-(\alpha + \beta \cdot \text{YAGE}_i + \gamma_1' \text{CROP}_i + \gamma_2' \text{OC}_i + \gamma_3 \text{ORPHAN}_i)}} \tag{11}$$

If the covariates have no effect upon the individual's probability of surviving, and if the population life table explains the individual's probability of surviving well, then the parameter estimates should be:

$$\hat{\alpha}, \hat{\gamma}_1', \hat{\gamma}_2', \hat{\gamma}_3 = 0 \tag{12}$$

where $\hat{\beta} = -1.0$. It has been shown elsewhere that the parameter estimates are robust to the choice of the standard mortality schedule: Even if the life table estimated for the population is not absolutely correct, the logistic regression model will nonetheless yield reliable parameter estimates (Trussell and Preston 1982, 18).

HYPOTHESIS TESTING

The significance of individual parameter estimates, β_j, can be investigated by testing the null hypothesis $H_0: \beta_j = 0$. The random variable,

$$\left[\hat{\beta}_j / \hat{\sigma}_{\beta_j}\right]^2$$

has a chi-square distribution with 1 degree of freedom. At the 0.05 level of significance, the critical value for the chi-square distribution with 1 degree of freedom is 3.84. Thus if the test statistic

$$\left[\hat{\beta}_j / \hat{\sigma}_{\beta_j}\right]^2$$

is greater than 3.84, the null hypothesis is rejected and it is concluded that the coefficient β_j is significantly different from zero. In the tables to follow (19.3–19.10), the probability associated with each parameter estimate is the probability that the test statistic will be so large if the true value of β_j is zero. Thus the smaller this probability, the higher the confidence that the parameter estimate is significantly different than zero.

Tests of the joint significance of several parameters are done using the log-likelihood ratio test. For example, suppose that the slave population contains N_A orphan boys and N_B non-orphaned boys, for a total of $N = N_A + N_B$ boys. The hypothesis to be tested is that, overall, mortality of orphan boys differs from that of boys with living mothers. Formally:

$$\gamma' = [(k - 2) \times 1]$$
$$H_0: \alpha_A, \beta_A, \gamma'_A = \alpha_B, \beta_B, \gamma'_B$$
$$H_1: \alpha_A, \beta_A, \gamma'_A \neq \alpha_B, \beta_B, \gamma'_B \tag{13}$$

Thus three models must be estimated: all boys ($N_A + N_B - k$ degrees of freedom), orphaned boys ($N_A - k$ degrees of freedom) and non-orphaned ($N_B - k$ degrees of freedom).

In the test of the null hypothesis of equal coefficients for orphans and non-orphans, the restricted model is the model containing all boys; it is restricted since the coefficients for both orphan and non-orphan boys are restricted to the same value. The likelihood function for the restricted model is

$$L_0 = L_0 \left(y | \hat{\alpha}_0, \hat{\beta}_0, \hat{\gamma}'_0\right) \tag{14}$$

Under the alternative hypothesis, the parameters of the unrestricted model are estimated separately for orphans and non-orphans; the likelihood function is

$$L_1 = L_A(y | \hat{\alpha}_A, \hat{\beta}_A, \hat{\gamma}'_A) \cdot L_B(y | \hat{\alpha}_B, \hat{\beta}_B, \hat{\gamma}'_B) \tag{15}$$

Thus the asymptotic likelihood ratio test statistic is

$$-2 \ln A = -2 \ln (L_0 / L_1) = -2 \ln \{\ln (L_0) - [\ln (L_A) - \ln (L_B)]\} \tag{16}$$

which is distributed as chi-square with $(N_A + N_B - k) - (N_A - k + N_B - k)$ $= k$ degrees of freedom.

INTERPRETATION OF THE PARAMETER ESTIMATES

The interpretation of the parameter estimates from logistic regression models is not simple. The coefficients do not behave in the same manner as in linear regression, in which the coefficients indicate the proportionate change in the dependent variable per unit change in the explanatory variable. Nor can the coefficients in a logistic model be interpreted as the relative risk of an event occurring in the presence or absence of a characteristic, as they can be in a hazards model.

In a logistic model, a positive parameter estimate indicates that the probability of surviving will increase as the value of the covariate increases. A negative parameter estimate indicates that the probability of surviving will decrease as the covariate increases. The larger the absolute value of the coefficient, the greater will be its impact upon the probability of surviving. However, the actual magnitude of the impact depends upon the values of the other covariates.

Consider the following example, in which the parameter estimates are all significantly different from zero. Let the life table probability of surviving the interregistration interval be 0.98; its logit is thus -3.892. ORPHAN and PROVISION are binary categorical variables. The estimated model is

$$\text{Pr(survive)} = \frac{1}{1 + e^{-[-0.008 + (-0.969)(-3.892) + (-0.818)\text{ORPH} + (1.154)\text{PROV}]}} \quad (16)$$

The estimated probability of surviving can be calculated for the four possible combinations of ORPHAN and PROVISION:

	ORPHAN		Relative
	0	1	Risk
PROVISION			
0	0.977	0.950	1.028
1	0.931	0.857	1.086
Relative Risk	1.049	1.108	

The effect of being an orphan is deleterious: On both provisions and non-provisions plantations, orphans are less likely to survive the interregistration interval than are non-orphans. On non-provisions plantations, non-orphans are 1.028 times more likely to survive than are orphans, while on provisions plantations, the relative risk of surviving is 1.086. Thus the effect on survival probabilities of being an orphan varies with the value of the other covariates describing the child: Being an orphan had more effect on children living on provisions plantations than on children living on other plantations. It follows, therefore, that the effect of a given covariate must be evaluated at a fixed level of the other covariates, such as at the means of the other covariates, or at values describing a typical observation.

MODELS OF SLAVE MORTALITY

The mortality experience of the Trinidad plantation slave children can be explored using logistic regression models of the individual slave child's probability of surviving the 1813–1815 interregistration period in an attempt to answer such questions as whether or not children on sugar plantations suffered higher mortality than did those on other types of plantation, whether or not slave mortality varied with the child's occupation, and whether or not family dissolution had a deleterious effect on children.

DESCRIPTION OF COVARIATES

The dependent variable was assigned the value 1 if the child was present in both the 1813 and 1815 registrations, which implied that he had survived the period and had remained on his original plantation. The dependent variable took the value 0 if the slave died during the interregistration period. Slaves who were not present in the registration in 1815 due to sale, manumission or any other reason were excluded from the analysis since, in logistic regression models, there is no mechanism for dealing with censored observations.

The standard survival functions used to express the dependence of mortality on age were taken from the life tables fit to the slave data. Thus two standard survival functions were employed: one for boys and one for girls. The variable actually employed in the models was the logit of the life table probability of surviving from age x to age $x + 1.75$:

$$YAGE(x) = \ln\left[\frac{1 - {}_{1.75}S_x}{{}_{1.75}S_x}\right] \tag{17}$$

where

$$_{1.75}S_x = \frac{{}_1L_x + 1.75}{{}_1L_x} \tag{18}$$

For example, for a ten-year-old boy, the variable YAGE took the value:

$$YAGE\,(10) = \ln\left[\frac{1 - {}_{1.75}S_{10}}{{}_{1.75}S_x}\right] \tag{19}$$

where ${}_{1.75}S_{10}$ is a function of the Trinidad male life table.

Plantation size was coded as the number of slaves reported in the plantation's slave return; the square of the number of slaves was also used to investigate a possible non-linear relationship between plantation size and slave survival. The variable for owner's religion was based upon the owner's reported nationality: French and Spanish owners were deemed Roman Catholic while British owners were not.

The slave height data were coded in two ways. The first was as a continuous variable, HT, reported in inches. The second was a set of categorical variable: SHORT, AVG, and TALL. Among children, the classification was based upon both age and height: For example, a ten-year-old boy was coded SHORT if he were among the shortest 20 percent of the ten-year-old boys in the population. Individuals recorded as less than 18 inches tall or more than 86 inches tall were discarded from the sample.

A description of the slave's occupation was entered in the 1813 registration; several hundred different occupations were recorded. The reported occupations were grouped into six broad occupational categories: no job, field, domestic, skilled, head slave, and outside non-field labor. Occupations among children may have been underreported since it is possible that, in order to avoid charges of cruelty or abuse, owners failed to report that very young children were already working. Whether or not this deliberate misreporting occurred, and the extent of the resulting misclassification, cannot be ascertained.

The main crop of the plantation was indicated by a set of categorical crop variables: SUGAR, COFFEE, COTTON, COCOA, and PROVISIONS. If a plantation grew more than one crop, then each of the appropriate categorical variables took the value 1. Hence, a plantation could appear in more than one crop category. A few plantations, such as the single plantation growing guinea grass, took the value zero in all crop categories.

Children who were not registered in the same households as their putative mothers were given the value 1 for the categorical variable ORPHAN. The name of this variable is somewhat misleading since the category included some children who were living in their father's household (but not with a mother), and excluded some children who were sharing a household with an adult woman who was not their biological mother. Hence, a more appropriate title for this variable would be "apparently motherless."

The emphasis on identifying those children living with their mothers stems from questions about the effect of maternal characteristics on child survival. For the children who appeared to be living with their mothers, maternal height was coded in the form described above, but without reference to age: SHORT, AVG, and TALL. Maternal occupation was also coded in the manner previously described. Maternal age at the child's birth was calculated as mother's reported age in 1813 less the child's reported age in 1813.

REGRESSION RESULTS

Suppose that there was no heterogeneity in the slave population with respect to mortality: A slave's chance of surviving was a function only of his age, and not of his environment. If the survival function used in the regressions described well the mortality experience of the slaves, then, with the exception of the variable representing the standard mortality schedule, the estimated coefficients should all be 0, and the coefficient of the standard schedule should be -1.0.

Four sets of models were estimated for slave children: For boys and girls separately, models were created for all children and for those children living with mothers (Tables 19.1 and 19.2). For children living with their mothers, direct maternal effects were represented by a variable denoting whether or not the mother was creole, a variable for the mother's reported age at the birth of the child, a pair of categorical variables for mother's height, and a set of categorical variables for mother's occupation. The nutritional status of the child was represented by the child's height, coded as a pair of dummy variables: SHORT and TALL. The nutritional status of nursing infants may have been affected by the nutritional status of their mothers, which in turn may have been a function of the mother's occupation. Children who worked as domestic servants may have had access to more or better food than other children, whereas children who worked in the field might have been undernourished since their caloric requirements were greater than those of other children. The exposure of the child to infections and infestations was, to some degree, influenced by characteristics of the plantation, particularly the size of the plantation and the crops grown. The religion or nationality of the plantation owner might well influence the manner in which the slaves were used, with Roman Catholic owners more benign in their treatment of slaves.

In early childhood (ages zero to four), boys were much more sensitive to their environments than were girls (Tables 19.3 and 19.4). For a young boy, the probability of surviving fell with increasing plantation size, perhaps because plantation size was associated with increased exposure to infectious pathogens. The religion of

Table 19.1. Means for Children Matched with Mothers

N	All Girls 0–14 1,607	Girls 0–4 790	Girls 5–14 817	All Boys 0–14 1,572	Boys 0–4 769	Boys 5–14 803	Definition
SURV	0.916	0.866	0.964	0.933	0.893	0.971	Equals 1 if child survived interregistration period
SIZE	77.27	76.29	78.22	76.06	74.74	77.32	Number of slaves on plantation
SIZE^2	9,407	9,445	9,370	9,311	9,207	9,411	Number of slaves, squared
RC	0.514	0.515	0.514	0.504	0.492	0.515	Equals 1 if owner is Roman Catholic
TALL	0.217	0.246	0.188	0.179	0.180	0.178	Equals 1 if child is in tallest 20 percent by age
SHORT	0.211	0.231	0.191	0.230	0.224	0.235	Equals 1 if child is in shortest 20 percent by age
Child's Occupation							
NOJOB	0.719	0.977	0.470	0.700	0.967	0.444	Equals 1 if child has no job
OUTSIDE	0.006	0.001	0.010	0.073	0.001	0.143	Equals 1 if child has outside job, other than field work
FIELD	0.133	0.015	0.250	0.142	0.021	0.257	Equals 1 if child is a field-worker
DOS	0.140	0.006	0.270	0.084	0.010	0.154	Equals 1 if child is a domestic servant
Crops							
SUGAR	0.721	0.705	0.735	0.738	0.729	0.747	Equals 1 if a sugar plantation
COFFEE	0.115	0.122	0.107	0.101	0.101	0.101	Equals 1 if a coffee plantation
COTTON	0.065	0.054	0.076	0.051	0.049	0.052	Equals 1 if a cotton plantation
COCOA	0.121	0.129	0.114	0.129	0.144	0.115	Equals 1 if a cocoa plantation
PROV	0.060	0.056	0.064	0.048	0.052	0.046	Equals 1 if a provisions plantation
Maternal Characteristics							
MTALL	0.252	0.237	0.266	0.258	0.244	0.272	Equals 1 mother is in tallest 20 percent of women
MSHORT	0.212	0.213	0.211	0.207	0.205	0.209	Equals 1 mother is in shortest 20 percent of women
MAAB	26.86	27.14	26.58	26.54	26.93	26.16	Mother's age at birth
MFIRM	0.008	0.001	0.010	0.008	0.006	0.011	Equals 1 if mother is infirm
MOUTSIDE	0.005	0.003	0.007	0	0	0	Equals 1 if mother has outside job
MFIELD	0.828	0.851	0.806	0.841	0.860	0.822	Equals 1 if mother is a field-worker
MDOS	0.149	0.139	0.159	0.138	0.126	0.148	Equals 1 if mother is a domestic servant
MNOJOB	0.006	0.003	0.009	0.011	0.006	0.015	Equals 1 if mother has no job
CREMOM	0.253	0.232	0.273	0.231	0.219	0.242	Equals 1 if mother is creole

Table 19.2. Means for All Children

N	Boys		Girls	
	5–14 1,115	0–4 844	5–14 1,099	0–4 866
SURV	0.97	0.89	0.96	0.86
RC	0.53	0.49	0.54	0.52
SIZE	74.68	75.65	75.44	75.76
SIZE^2	9,044	9,503	9,084	9,766
ORPHAN	0.26	0.08	0.24	0.08
TALL	0.18	0.19	0.19	0.24
SHORT	0.24	0.22	0.19	0.24
Child's Occupation				
NOJOB	0.40	0.96	0.44	0.97
FIELD	0.28	0.02	0.26	0.02
DOS	0.18	0.01	0.29	0
OUTSIDE	0.15	0.01	0.01	0.01
Crops				
SUGAR	0.73	0.73	0.70	0.70
COFFEE	0.12	0.09	0.12	0.13
COTTON	0.06	0.05	0.08	0.05
COCOA	0.12	0.14	0.13	0.13
PROVISIONS	0.05	0.05	0.07	0.06

the owner did not seem to influence the child's survival, which in retrospect is hardly surprising: The differences in the owners' treatment of slaves may have been manifested primarily in the way in which slaves were worked, which would affect adults rather than children.

The nutritional status of the young boys, as reflected in their heights, was an important determinant of their survival: Boys who were tall for their age had a greater chance of surviving than did boys who were short. The mortality of boys was not affected by mother's occupation or mother's birthplace, suggesting that there was very little systematic variation in the type of care that mothers could or would give their children. The survival of boys was unaffected by reported maternal height, but survival rose with increasing maternal age at the boy's birth. (A squared term in maternal age was not significantly different from zero at the 10 percent level.)

Boys who lived on provisions plantations fared less well than did their counterparts on other plantations. As suggested earlier, these boys may have been exposed to many more infectious diseases because of the large numbers of callers at such plantations buying provisions.

The mortality of older boys (ages five to fourteen) appears to have been determined largely by age rather than environmental or personal characteristics. The insignificance of maternal effects is not surprising for older boys, since maternal effects are, in general, important for younger rather than older children. The unimportance of the boy's job and of the crop of the plantation is, at first glance, surprising given that more than half the older boys work, but the pattern is exactly

Table 19.3. Boys Matched with Mothers: All Covariates

	0–14		0–4		5–14	
	β	Probability	β	Probability	β	Probability
INT	-0.362	0.63	-0.063	0.94	-6.564	0.07
YAGE	-0.969	0.84[a]	-0.794	0.34[a]	-2.945	0.08[a]
SIZE	-0.013	0.07	-0.019	0.03	0.012	0.41
SIZE^2	5.0×10^{-5}	0.11	7.6×10^{-5}	0.05	-4.9×10^{-5}	0.40
RC	0.296	0.20	0.211	0.42	0.588	0.26
TALL	1.098	0.01	0.918	0.04	1.665	0.11
SHORT	-0.475	0.03	-0.591	0.02	-0.215	0.65
NOJOB	—		—		—	
OUTSIDE	0.251	0.74	—		-0.221	0.79
FIELD	-0.161	0.70	—		-0.185	0.74
DOS	-0.221	0.69	—		1.444	0.28
SUGAR	0.129	0.78	0.223	0.67	-0.524	0.62
COFFEE	0.073	0.86	0.233	0.65	-0.688	0.48
COTTON	—		—		—	
COCOA	-0.137	0.74	-0.133	0.78	-0.483	0.59
PROVISIONS	-0.773	0.14	-1.076	0.07	—	
MTALL	-0.042	0.87	0.097	0.74	-0.448	0.37
MSHORT	0.204	0.47	0.301	0.36	-0.187	0.74
MAAB	0.040	0.03	0.048	0.03	0.009	0.77
MDOS	0.476	0.21	0.298	0.47	0.874	0.40
CREMOM	0.197	0.48	0.149	0.63	0.557	0.40
$-2 \ln\Lambda$	678.08		477.44		180.29	

[a]H_0: B(YAGE) = -1.0.

Table 19.4. Boys Matched with Mothers: Age Only

	0–14		0–4		5–14	
	β	Probability	β	Probability	β	Probability
INT	0.546	0.04	0.858	0.02	−5.636	0.07
YAGE	−0.892	0.37	−0.699	0.14	−2.858	0.07
−2 ln Λ	712.71		510.07		196.64	

Notes: H_0: B(YAGE) = −1.0. Effect of covariates: H_0: variables other than YAGE do not add significant explanatory power to the model:

	χ^2	df	Probability
(i)	712.71 − 678.08 = 34.63	17	0.01
(ii)	510.07 − 477.44 = 32.63	14	0.00
(iii)	196.64 − 180.29 = 16.35	17	0.50

the same as for adult creole males: Job and crop are not significant determinants of mortality.

Young girls were much less sensitive to their environments than were their male counterparts (Tables 19.5 and 19.6). The only factors which influenced a young girl's mortality were maternal age at birth and the girl's height: The probability of survival rose with maternal age at birth, and fell if the girl were short. The young girl's chances of survival were unaffected by other maternal factors and by plantation characteristics. Among the older girls, those who were short for their age were more likely to die than were other girls; the shortness may reflect chronic undernutrition at early childhood ages.

The insensitivity of older children to their environments, relative to younger children, reflects in part a selection process: The less robust individuals die in early childhood, leaving only the stronger children who are less sensitive to environmental insult. The insensitivity of girls to their environments, relative to boys, is a common, but not well understood, feature of sex differences in mortality.

Was the dissolution of slave families, through sale or death, detrimental to the survival prospects of children? In particular, were children who were not living with their mothers less likely to survive than were children who were living in the maternal household? Individually, maternal factors other than mother's age at birth appeared not to influence the chances of infant and child survival. As a group, the maternal characteristics did not add significantly to the explanatory power of the models of survival (Tables 19.7 and 19.8). It is possible, however, that there existed some maternal effect not captured by mother's age, occupation, height, and birthplace. To test this, the models of childhood mortality were reestimated for all children, whether or not they were living with their mothers; the presence or absence of mothers was indicated by the variable ORPHAN (Tables 19.9 and 19.10).

The absence of his mother adversely affected a boy's probability of survival, irrespective of his age, although the effect was slightly more pronounced for younger boys. Girls, on the other hand, seemed not to suffer greater mortality if their mothers were absent, again reflecting the relative insensitivity of the girls to their environments.

Table 19.5. Girls Matched with Mothers: All Covariates.

	0–14		0–4		5–14	
	β	Probability	β	Probability	β	Probability
INT	0.200	0.76	−0.354	0.67	2.831	0.26
YAGE	−0.953	0.74[a]	−0.991	0.96[a]	−0.512	0.52[a]
SIZE	−0.006	0.29	−0.005	0.48	−0.014	0.34
SIZE^2	9.0×10^{-6}	0.71	-4.8×10^{-7}	0.98	5.2×10^{-5}	0.40
RC	0.232	0.26	0.295	0.23	0.093	0.82
TALL	−0.115	0.63	0.270	0.31	0.878	0.24
SHORT	−0.478	0.03	−0.423	0.11	−0.707	0.09
NOJOB	—	—	—	—	—	—
FIELD	0.356	0.44	—	—	0.091	0.89
DOS	−0.149	0.72	—	—	−0.262	0.60
SUGAR	−0.107	0.80	−0.049	0.92	−0.154	0.84
COFFEE	−0.617	0.11	−0.423	0.37	−1.163	0.10
COTTON	—	—	—	—	—	—
COCOA	0.203	0.59	0.282	0.54	0.334	0.63
PROVISIONS	−0.555	0.26	−0.792	0.18	0.500	0.67
MTALL	0.272	0.25	0.006	0.98	1.082	0.09
MSHORT	0.093	0.70	0.169	0.56	−0.262	0.57
MAAB	0.017	0.25	0.034	0.06	−0.021	0.42
MDOS	−0.188	0.51	−0.384	0.23	0.338	0.59
CREMOM	0.343	0.16	0.331	0.23	0.509	0.33
−2 ln Λ	823.25		573.52		231.99	

[a] H_0: $\beta(\text{YAGE}) = -1.0$.

Table 19.6. Girls Matched with Mothers: Age Only

	0–14		0–4		5–14	
	β	Probability	β	Probability	β	Probability
INT	0.101	0.70	0.175	0.63	1.087	0.60
YAGE	−0.964	0.75	−0.913	0.67	−0.674	0.61
−2 ln Λ	847.27		597.66		249.26	

Notes: H_0: B(YAGE) = −1.0. H_0: variables other than YAGE do not add significant explanatory power to the model:

		χ^2	df	Probability
(i)	847.27 − 823.25 =	24.02	16	0.09
(ii)	596.66 − 573.52 =	24.14	14	0.04
(iii)	247.26 − 231.99 =	17.27	16	0.37

AN ILLUSTRATION

Consider a two-year-old boy who lived on a cotton plantation with seventy-five slaves owned by a Protestant owner. The boy was of average height, as was his mother who was born in Africa; she was a field-worker and was twenty-seven years old when her son was born. If all the covariate coefficients were significantly different from zero, then his probability of surviving the interregistration period would be 0.8521. If he were tall, his chances of survival would increase to 0.9352, and if he were short, his chances of survival would fall to 0.7614. If he were of average height, but living on a provisions plantation, the probability that he would survive would be 0.6627. Finally, if there were several factors working against him simultaneously, such as being short, living on a provisions plantation, and having a mother who was twenty years old when he was born, his estimated probability of survival would be 0.4386.

SUMMARY

When the available data on mortality is limited—in particular, when the actual date of death is not known, and the only available information is whether or not an individual survived to the end of a given time period—logistic models of mortality can used to estimate a survival function for the population. Logistic models of survivorship have two distinct advantages. First, the dependence of survivorship upon age can be incorporated into the model by taking advantage of the relationship between the logits of the survival functions of two life tables and employing the logit of the probability of surviving from age x to $x + n$ from a standard life table as an age-dependent covariate in the logistic regression. Second, heterogeneity in survivorship can be considered by using both discrete and continuous covariates in the regression models; the coefficients of the covariates express deviations from the standard life table associated with each covariate.

There are two disadvantages to the use of logistic models of survivorship. First, there is no way to use censored observations in the regression models; if an individual is lost to the survey before his death or the end of the survey period, then he must be excluded from the analysis. Second, the parameter estimates from logistic

Table 19.7. Boys Matched with Mothers: Maternal Variables Excluded

	0–14		0–4		5–14	
	β	Probability	β	Probability	β	Probability
INT	0.86	0.10	1.447	0.02	-6.486	0.06
YAGE	-0.964	0.80	-0.767	0.28	-3.016	0.06
SIZE	-0.013	0.08	-0.018	0.03	0.010	0.49
SIZE^2	4.8×10^{-5}	0.12	7.3×10^{-5}	0.05	-4.3×10^{-5}	0.46
RC	0.316	0.16	0.218	0.40	0.616	0.24
TALL	1.074	0.01	0.891	0.05	1.701	0.10
SHORT	-0.531	0.02	-0.636	0.01	-0.204	0.67
NOJOB	—	—	—	—	—	—
OUTSIDE	—	—	—	—	—	—
FIELD	-0.244	0.56	—	—	-0.293	0.59
DOS	-0.204	0.71	—	—	1.193	0.26
SUGAR	0.091	0.84	0.158	0.76	-0.469	0.64
COFFEE	0.094	0.82	0.263	0.61	-0.718	0.44
COTTON	—	—	—	—	—	—
COCOA	-0.171	0.68	-0.204	0.66	-0.466	.59
PROVISIONS	-0.797	0.13	-1.152	0.05	—	—
-2 ln Λ	685.64		483.89		183.18	

Notes: H$_0$: B(YAGE) = -1.0. H$_0$: maternal characteristics do not add significant explanatory power to the model:

	χ^2	df	Probability
(i) 685.64 – 678.08 =	7.56	5	0.18
(ii) 483.89 – 477.44 =	5.56	5	0.35
(iii) 183.18 – 180.29 =	2.89	5	0.72

Table 19.8. Girls Matched with Mothers: Maternal Variables Excluded

	0–14		0–4		5–14	
	β	Probability	β	Probability	β	Probability
INT	0.771	0.12	0.656	0.29	2.015	0.39
YAGE	−0.930	0.62	−0.924	0.71	−0.627	0.61
SIZE	−0.006	0.33	−0.004	0.19	−0.014	0.34
SIZE^2	6.8×10^{-6}	0.78	-4.0×10^{-6}	0.88	5.3×10^{-6}	0.40
RC	0.245	0.24	0.315	0.19	0.068	0.87
TALL	−0.114	0.63	−0.272	0.30	0.923	0.22
SHORT	−0.461	0.04	−0.397	0.13	−0.661	0.11
NOJOB	—	—	—	—	—	—
FIELD	0.381	0.41	—	—	−0.025	0.96
DOS	−0.085	0.84	—	—	−0.152	0.76
SUGAR	−0.075	0.86	−0.019	0.97	0.025	0.97
COFFEE	−0.578	0.13	−0.393	0.39	−1.018	0.14
COTTON	—	—	—	—	—	—
COCOA	0.123	0.75	0.212	0.64	0.200	0.77
PROVISIONS	−0.501	0.31	−0.662	0.25	0.542	0.63
−2 ln Λ	828.50		579.78		239.53	

Notes: H_0: $\beta(\text{YAGE}) = -1.0$. H_0: maternal characteristics do not add significant explanatory power to the model:

	χ^2		df	Probability
(i)	828.50 − 823.25	= 5.25	5	0.38
(ii)	579.78 − 573.52	= 6.26	5	0.28
(iii)	239.53 − 231.99	= 7.54	5	0.18

Table 19.9. All Children

	Boys, 5–14		Boys, 0–4		Girls, 5–14		Girls, 0–4	
	β	Probability	β	Probability	β	Probability	β	Probability
INT	−2.856	0.20	1.421	0.02	4.051	0.04	0.826	0.16
YAGE	−1.911	0.19[a]	−0.820	0.37[a]	0.050	0.07[a]	−0.869	0.50[a]
RC	0.649	0.10	0.183	0.44	0.088	0.80	0.325	0.15
SIZE	0.007	0.50	−0.019	0.02	−0.002	0.84	−0.007	0.34
SIZE^2	-3.7×10^{-5}	0.39	7.3×10^{-5}	0.02	1.0×10^{-5}	0.83	8.8×10^{-6}	0.73
ORPHAN	−0.767	0.04	−0.818	0.03	−0.175	0.63	−0.358	0.32
TALL	1.392	0.06	0.446	0.20	0.849	0.17	−0.130	0.60
SHORT	−0.191	0.61	−0.628	0.01	−0.909	0.006	−0.270	0.27
NOJOB	—	—	—	—	—	—	—	—
FIELD	−0.200	0.65	—	—	0.462	0.32	—	—
DOS	0.517	0.43	—	—	0.029	0.94	—	—
OUTSIDE	−0.274	0.64	—	—	—	—	—	—
SUGAR	−0.515	0.52	0.125	0.80	−0.646	0.30	−0.138	0.78
COFFEE	0.042	0.95	0.345	0.50	−0.710	0.18	−0.449	0.32
COTTON								
COCOA	−0.072	0.92	−0.091	0.84	−0.068	0.90	0.226	0.61
PROVISIONS	−0.489	0.60	−1.154	0.04	0.713	0.52	−0.897	0.09
−2 ln Λ	305.00		549.22		354.23		653.37	

[a] H_0: $\beta(\text{YAGE}) = -1.0$.

Table 19.10. All Children: Age Only

	Boys, 5–14		Boys, 0–4		Girls, 5–14		Girls, 0–4	
	β	Probability	β	Probability	β	Probability	β	Probability
INT	−1.493	0.41	0.805	0.02	2.629	0.11	0.23	0.51
YAGE	−1.469	0.41	−0.694	0.61	−0.172	0.10	−0.856	0.44
$-2 \ln \Lambda$	323.96		576.20		362.90		672.01	

Notes: H_0: $B(YAGE) = -1.0$. H_0: variables other than YAGE do not add significant explanatory power to the model:

		χ^2	df	Probability
(i)	323.96 − 305.00 =	18.96	13	0.12
(ii)	576.20 − 549.22 =	26.98	10	0.
(iii)	362.90 − 345.23 =	17.67	12	0.12
(iv)	672.01 − 653.37 =	18.64	10	0.05

regression models are not easy to interpret. Covariates can be ranked by the relative magnitude of the estimated effect: A covariate with an estimated coefficient of 0.50 will have a greater impact on increasing the probability of survivorship during an interval than will a covariate with an estimated coefficient of 0.10. However, the actual magnitude of the effect of a covariate depends upon the values of the other covariates describing the interval. Thus one cannot say, for example, that being an orphan causes a 4 percent decrease in the probability of surviving; the degree of the effect of being an orphan depends upon the other characteristics of the child and his environment.

Young boys appear to have been more sensitive to their environments than were young girls: The probability of surviving the interregistration interval varied with environmental and personal characteristics for boys more so than for girls. The dissolution of slave families, particularly the separation of children from their mothers, seemed to adversely affect the boys but not the girls. The relative robustness of the girls to their environment is consistent both with other studies of slave mortality and with the general literature on sex differences in survivorship.

TWENTY

The Age of Slaves at Menarche and Their First Birth[*]

James Trussell and Richard H. Steckel

One of the main areas of controversy generated by the conclusions of Fogel and Engerman as reported in *Time on the Cross* (1974) involves the degree of intrusion into the sexual behavior of slaves by their owners. They assert that the evidence indicates that slave women did not bear children as soon as they were physiologically capable. This finding, in turn, casts doubt on the common assumption that slaveowners deliberately manipulated the reproductive behavior of female slaves in order to increase their stock of slaves for sale or their own use. Criticisms have been leveled at both the methodology and the interpretation of Fogel and Engerman. In this paper we analyze the biases inherent in their methodological procedure, propose a new method of estimation that avoids these biases, and comment on the substantive issue of whether reproductive behavior was substantially manipulated.

We consider only the extent of a particular type of manipulation that is admittedly defined in a very narrow way. Beyond question, some slaveowners did manipulate the fertility of their slaves (Yetman 1970, 34–92, 288, 307–308; Botkin 1945, 140; Frazier 1966, 53–54; Olmsted [1861] 1953, 46 n. 2; Bancroft [1931] 1959, 68, 74, 76–77; Kemble 1961, 94–96). Undoubtedly such manipulation was psychologically and physically significant to the individual woman and her family. We are concerned here with whether such manipulation resulted specifically in an early start to the reproductive career *and* whether it was extensive enough to have a significant aggregate demographic impact. Other possible forms of manipulation, such as deliberately delaying the first birth on the grounds that good husbandry would avoid early mating, will not be considered. In applying a technique of estimation that is well known to demographers we hope not only to advance the substantive discussion of a particular issue, but also to demonstrate its flexibility and potential usefulness to economic and social historians.

[*]Reprinted from *The Journal of Interdisciplinary History*, 8(1978):477–505, with revisions and with permission of the editors of *The Journal of Interdisciplinary History* and The MIT Press, Cambridge, MA. © 1978 by The Massachusetts Institute of Technology and the editors of *The Journal of Interdisciplinary History*.

THE PROCEDURE OF FOGEL AND ENGERMAN

The authors had access to probate data that listed the ages of a female slave and her children, if there were children living with her.[1] They simply subtracted the age of the eldest child from the age of the mother to obtain an estimate of the age of the woman at her first birth.[2] Then the mean age at first birth was computed in the usual manner. Their procedure has several biases, only two of which have been recognized by either the writers or their critics. Before examining them it is necessary first to recognize clearly just what we seek to measure, since one of the primary reasons for confusion in the debate derives from imprecise specification of this measure.

FERTILITY SCHEDULES

It is clear that the statistics that we seek to estimate should measure fertility behavior alone. The statistic—in our case the mean—should not reflect demographic processes, such as mortality or past fertility, that are extraneous to our present enquiry. Demographers have long recognized that only one distribution possesses the property of being a function solely of reproductive behavior—the schedule of age-specific fertility rates.

The mean that we seek to measure is the mean of a particular fertility schedule that we call the age-specific schedule of *first* births, computed from accurate vital registration data by dividing the first births to women at each age by the number of women at each age. This division yields the probability of having a first birth at each age. By centering these observations on the midpoints of each age interval and connecting these points with a curve, we can present the age-specific first-birth schedule graphically as in Figure 20.1. Two points are worth noting. Since the procedure of computing the first-birth schedule involves only surviving women, its shape, and therefore its mean, are unaffected by mortality. Furthermore, computation of such schedules of first births, as well as of marriages or all births, is unaffected by the rate of growth of a population. In summary, such schedules are independent of the underlying age distribution of the population.

Unfortunately, registration of slave births, and indeed of births in general, was non-existent in the mid-nineteenth century. Therefore, some other method must be employed for finding the mean of the first-birth distribution. Fogel and Engerman employed one such method, but it is replete with biases.

ADULT MORTALITY: DOWNWARD BIAS

Let us consider a population with a simple fertility schedule to illustrate the downward bias exerted by mortality. Suppose that one-third of the women reaching age fifteen; one-third, age twenty; and one-third, age twenty-five have a first birth on their respective birthdays (see Table 20.1). Further, let us assume that each year

Figure 20.1. The effect of mortality and growth on the distribution of first births. The distributions pictured here were deliberately not normalized to sum to 1 so that the differences in the patterns could be more easily seen.

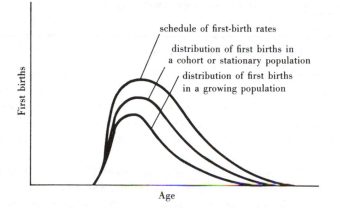

ninety women experience their fifteenth birthday; sixty, their twentieth; and thirty, their twenty-fifth. Thirty women die between their fifteenth and twentieth birthdays and between their twentieth and twenty-fifth. The mean age of the first-birth schedule is clearly 20 years; but since mortality increasingly takes its toll fewer women are alive to give birth at later ages. Therefore by counting the *number* of women instead of the *proportion* who have a first birth at each age, the schedule is tilted and its mean is shifted downward. The distribution obtained in this manner is the distribution of first births in a cohort of women or, alternatively, in a stationary (non-growing) population. The particular distribution in Table 20.1 has a mean of 18.33 instead of 20.

GROWTH: DOWNWARD BIAS

A growing population adds a further downward bias to the mortality bias. Note that in the previous example the population was not growing, since each year the same number of women reached their fifteenth, twentieth, and twenty-fifth birthdays as the year before. Of course more women could have reached, say, age seventy each year due to falling adult mortality, so that the whole population would be growing, but such growth *beyond* the age range of fertility would not affect estimation of the mean. If the population were growing instead, as was undoubtedly true of the slave

Table 20.1. The Effect of Mortality on the Estimated Mean Age at First Birth

Age of Woman	First-Birth Rate	Number of Women	Number Having First Birth
15	1/3	90	30
20	1/3	60	20
25	1/3	30	10

Source: Figures reflected constructed examples.

population, then the age distribution might be 120, 70, and 30 instead of 90, 60, and 30. In this case the observed mean, using the same first-birth schedule as before, would be 17.95 instead of 20. The effect on the first-birth distribution of both growth and adult mortality is shown graphically in Figure 20.1.

TRUNCATION: DOWNWARD BIAS

Another source of bias inherent in the Fogel-Engerman procedure is that the experience of younger women is overrepresented. Women who are twenty cannot have had a first birth at age thirty-two but women aged thirty-two can have had a first birth at age twenty. Such a bias can best be demonstrated by an example, in which we eliminate growth and mortality in order to isolate the truncation bias due to a cross-sectional sample of women.

In Table 20.2 we see that ninety women experienced a birth at age fifteen: thirty of those now aged fifteen, thirty now aged twenty, and thirty more now aged twenty-five. Similarly, sixty women experienced a first birth at age twenty and thirty, at age twenty-five. If we considered only women aged twenty-five we would have calculated the correct mean—20—since these women have all borne their first child. By including women aged fifteen and twenty in the sample, however, we bias the mean downward to 18.33 years since their early experience, but not their experience that has yet to occur, is included. Such truncation bias crops up frequently with sample surveys and even experienced demographers have missed its sometimes subtle forms. If the Fogel-Engerman procedure is used on the growing population described in the section above, truncation bias reduces the estimated mean from 17.95 to 17.29. Therefore, in our simple example the three sources of error combined produce an estimated mean which is biased downward by 2.7 years.

CHILDHOOD MORTALITY AND SALES: UPWARD BIAS

Both Fogel and Engerman and their critics most consistently recognize the upward bias caused by the nature of the data. The age of a woman at first birth cannot be computed directly from certain of the records, such as the probate inventories, since we have no information on children who were born and died before the information

Table 20.2. The Effect of the Sampling Frame on the Estimated Mean Age at First Birth

Age of Woman	First-Birth Rate	Number of Women	Number of Women in the Population Who Ever Reached Each Age	Number Who Experienced Birth at Each Age
15	1/3	90	270	90
20	1/3	90	180	60
25	1/3	90	90	30

Source: See Table 20.1.

was recorded. Since some first-born children must have died before being recorded, and the probability of this occurrence rises monotonically (never going down) with the duration of time since the first birth, then on average the age of women at first birth will be overstated and the mean of the distribution will be biased upward. Furthermore, any occurrence, such as a sale, that results in the first-born child's having been omitted from the records accentuates this bias; under the usual method of computing the age at first birth, death and omission are equivalent. It should be emphasized that the source of this bias lies in the data themselves. It might at first appear that the information we seek—the age of a woman at first birth—cannot therefore be retrieved. Fortunately, we are not in such a bad position, but discussion of how such reconstitution is accomplished will be postponed until later. Now, let us assume that we do know the age of the woman at the birth of her first child and return to the biases of the procedure of estimation.

TOWARD AN UNBIASED ESTIMATION PROCEDURE

Even when the data are not faulty the standard method of computing the mean introduces three sources of downward bias that can be summarized as follows. Both population growth and adult mortality ensure that the *number* of younger women will be overrepresented. By using a cross section of women to obtain the age at first birth of all women and then computing the mean in the usual way, the fertility experience of young women is overrepresented since young women who will bear their first child after the date of the survey do not have their events counted. The reasoning behind the assertion above—that the summary statistic of interest is the mean of the first-birth schedule—should now be clear. Statistics such as the mean age at first birth are meaningful only insofar as we can understand that they are large or small. Whether such numbers are large or small is determined by comparison with other populations. In making such a comparison we want to isolate fertility behavior. Specifically, we do not want to compare measures that are influenced by the age structure, which in turn is governed by past mortality and fertility (and migration). The first-birth schedule is unaffected by such extraneous processes, and measures of its location, such as the mean or the median, are the statistics of interest.

Fogel and Engerman recognized the biases due to population growth and childhood mortality and, to compensate, made an *ad hoc* adjustment to their computed mean. Their corrections are reasonable, but the large number of assumptions underlying them have inevitably caused debate. Addressing methodology, rather than the substantive results, this debate is unfortunate since an unbiased estimation procedure exists and is well-known to demographers in another context.

Long ago, Hajnal (1953) set out to compare the mean age at first marriage of various populations. Wishing to avoid the impact of the age distribution, he used the mean of the first-marriage schedule as his measure of location. He interpreted the first-marriage schedule as the schedule of first marriages that would be observed in an artificial cohort that experienced no mortality or migration, and called the mean age at first marriage of such a cohort the "singulate" mean. The singulate mean (or mean of the nuptiality schedule) is now widely used by demographers both as a summary measure and as a parameter entering models designed to estimate other demographic parameters from incomplete or inaccurate data.

Next Hajnal showed that the singulate mean could be estimated from just the marital-status distribution of the population. Specifically, from a classification of the population by standard five-year age groups into single, married, widowed, and divorced, one can construct the proportion of women (or men) in each age group who are ever married (married and widowed and divorced divided by the total) or its complement, which is easier to compute, the proportion never married (single divided by total). By integrating by parts the familiar formula for the calculation of the singulate mean age of marriage, Hajnal devised a formula involving only the proportions never married by five-year age groups. (The steps for computing the singulate mean and an example are provided in the Appendix to this paper.) As he also shows, this formula is unbiased provided that the mortality (and migration) schedules of single and ever-married persons are the same. In fact we know that they are not, but it has been shown that the bias resulting from the small differences that do exist is negligible.

Hajnal presented two examples to illustrate this point. For Ireland in 1941, explicit recognition of differential mortality lowers the mean age for males from 32.60 to 32.11; for women the corresponding figures are 28.71 and 28.64. A less extreme example is provided by Sweden in 1935; introducing differential mortality lowers the male mean by 0.15 years and the female mean by only 0.07 years. It is interesting to note that the singulate mean is trivially upward biased in the two examples given by Hajnal. This result is not accidental; it occurs because single persons experience less favorable mortality than do ever-married persons. The converse, which is easy to prove simply by reversing the patterns of mortality given in both the illustrations and the mathematical Appendix to this paper, will be important for our use of the procedure: If single persons experienced more favorable mortality than ever-married persons, then the singulate mean would be biased downward.

The mathematical proofs underlying the previous assertions are all contained in an appendix to Hajnal's original article, but a simple verbal argument showing that the three biases are eliminated may be helpful. First it should be clear that by using *proportions* in each age group the adult mortality and growth biases are eliminated. The impact of the age distribution *within* five-year age groups is still present, but its numerical effect is trivial both absolutely and in relation to the age distribution impact over the entire age range on the Fogel and Engerman estimate.

Remember that the schedule of first marriages is estimated by dividing first marriages to people aged x by the number of persons aged x in a given year. By extending the age groups to a length of five years we obtain the average first-marriage rate per year over each of the five years of age. Empirically, the biases generated by extending the age groupings from one to five years, and thereby including some age distribution effect, are truly negligible. If single and ever-married people experience the same mortality, the proportion of people ever-married in each five-year age grouping will be the same as the average cumulated first-marriage schedule in the same-age interval. Finally, by using the cumulated first-married schedules (i.e., the proportion ever married), truncation bias is thereby avoided since the weight given to a group of women aged x rises with the age of the women. The formula explicitly recognizes that women aged thirty can only have been married at ages below thirty.

The singulate mean age of marriage is easy to compute and requires only an age and marital distribution of the population. It has been used by historical demographers to analyze the effect of nuptiality on fertility. It should also prove valuable to economic historians interested in analyzing the relationship between nuptiality and economic variables.

EXTENSION TO THE SINGULATE MEAN OF THE FIRST-BIRTH SCHEDULE

The extension of the methodology of computing the singulate mean to fertility is immediate. All one needs is a breakdown of the proportion of women with no children ever borne by five-year age groups. Unfortunately the data on slaves in the probate listings or in plantation records will only provide us with a breakdown of women with no *surviving* children by five-year age groups. By comparing the means computed from children ever born and children surviving for a number of populations with both sets of tabulations, however, we see that their difference is negligible. As Table 20.3 shows, the largest difference is only 0.20 years and the average difference is only 0.35 years. These countries represent a range of rates of population growth and of (infant) mortality experience so that we can be reasonably certain that the singulate mean age at first birth computed from surviving children only is an accurate estimate of the singulate mean computed from children ever born.

The reason for the striking lack of difference between the two means might at first seem surprising, but it follows readily from the empirical finding that the proportion of women with children surviving is roughly a constant proportion of the proportion of women who have ever borne children. Expressed in a different way, the proportion of women whose children have *all* died is rather constant over age.

It should also be noted that by truncating the formula at age forty instead of, say, age fifty, the resulting mean is a somewhat downward biased estimate of the singulate mean of the entire birth schedule. The numerical bias is small however, since few first births occur after age forty. There is a practical reason, as well, for truncating at age forty. The series of proportions of women with no children ever borne becomes erratic after age forty in each of the countries listed in Table 20.3. This phenomenon is not restricted to these countries alone and has been widely noted elsewhere. One reason for the rise in proportions with no children after age forty might be that women report themselves as having had no children if they have grown up and left home. A small group of women who had few children early and omit children no longer at home would generate the observed rise.

Although the Hajnal procedure overcomes one of the deficiencies of the data in

Table 20.3. The Singulate Mean Age at First Birth below the Age of Forty Computed by the Hajnal Formula

Country	From Children Ever Born	From Children Surviving	Difference	Estimated Probability of Dying before Age 2, $q_2{}^a$
Yugoslavia, 1971[b]	22.41	22.42	0.01	0.060
El Salvador, 1971[b]	20.57	20.69	0.12	0.141
Dominican Republic, 1970[b]	20.99	21.01	0.02	0.136
Nepal, 1971[b]	21.87	21.88	0.01	0.136
Jordan, 1972[c]	20.58	20.57	−0.01	0.082
Cambodia, 1962[d]	22.23	22.40	0.17	0.128
Solomon Islands, 1970[e]	22.64	22.68	0.04	0.095
New Hebrides, 1967[f]	21.32	21.30	−0.02	0.134
Fiji, 1956[h]	20.58	20.63	0.05	0.115
Fiji, 1966[g]	21.55	21.60	0.05	0.083
Western Samoa, 1956[i]	21.93	22.00	0.07	0.117
Western Samoa, 1961[i]	21.79	21.85	0.05	0.096
Western Samoa, 1966[l]	21.63	21.70	0.07	0.117
Bermuda, 1960[i]	21.22	21.23	0.01	0.019
Seychelles, 1960[i]	20.81	20.78	−0.03	0.081
Seychelles, 1971[l]	21.19	21.15	−0.04	0.095
Senegal, 1960[i]	19.29	19.49	0.20	0.245
Gilbert and Ellice Islands, 1968[k]	21.29	21.35	0.06	0.141
Gilbert and Ellice Islands, 1973[j]	21.99	21.96	−0.02	0.114
Rhodesia, 1969[l]	20.54	20.66	0.13	0.131
Tanzania, 1967[l]	18.77	18.74	−0.02	0.197
Costa Rica, 1973[l]	22.39	22.44	0.04	0.080
Bahrain, 1971[l]	21.15	21.02	−0.14	0.089

[a] Estimated from Trussell (1975)
[b] United Nations (1974).
[c] Jordan (1972).
[d] Siampos (1968).
[e] British Solomon Islands (1970).
[f] New Hebrides (1968).
[g] Fiji (1968).
[h] Fiji (1958).
[i] United Nations (1964).
[j] Gilbert and Ellice Islands Colony (1975).
[k] Gilbert and Ellice Islands Colony (1970).
[l] United Nations (1976).

the probate records—births that were unrecorded due to death—is it affected by the absence of older children who were sold or who left the maternal household for any other reason? The older the mother, the higher is the probability that her oldest living child will not be recorded in the probates. Consequently, if the usual method of computing mean age at first birth is employed, this deficiency in the data source will introduce an upward bias. What can be said about the direction and magnitude of the bias when the Hajnal formula is employed?

Counterintuitive as it may seem, under the Hajnal formula, the separation of children from the maternal household introduces a downward bias in the mean age at first birth. This difference in the direction of the bias is not so surprising when it is recalled that the singulate mean will be affected by the non-recording of live children only if *all* of a woman's children have left her household. Since the average interval between births was quite short, and since it was relatively rare for children to be separated from their mothers before they reached age ten, women whose children have all left their households will not be misclassified as childless until relatively late in their childbearing period. Moreover, such misclassification will increase with age.[3] Table 20.4 shows that the earlier the age at which such misclassification begins, and the more rapid the rise in the misclassification of women, the larger the downward bias. Note also that when there is such misclassification of women, truncation at age forty reduces the downward bias.

The precision of the Hajnal technique on marriage data is due to the virtual absence of differential mortality between the single and the ever married. In adopting the procedure for estimating the mean age of the first-birth schedule we have implicitly assumed no differential mortality between those who have never and those who have ever borne children. Since maternal mortality is significant, this assumption is patently invalid. Note, however, that the resulting estimate of the mean will be biased *downward* because the direction of the differential is opposite that in the nuptiality formulation. Since childless women experience more favorable mortality than those who have ever borne a child, the Hajnal formula produces a mean that is lower than the true mean of the first-birth schedule.

THE MEAN AGE AT FIRST BIRTH OF FEMALE SLAVES

Data from plantation records and probate records were used to calculate the observed proportion of women with no children by standard age groups.[4] The plantation record sample consists of thirty-four large plantations in which children could

Table 20.4 The Effect on the Singulate Mean of Misclassification of Women Because All of Their Children Have Left the Maternal Household

Age	Assumed True Schedule	Proportion of Females without Children	
		Misclassification Becomes Significant Beginning at Age 35	Misclassification Begins Earlier Beginning at Age 25 and Rises More Rapidly
10–14	1.00	1.00	1.00
15–19	0.75	0.75	0.75
20–24	0.40	0.40	0.40
25–29	0.32	0.32	0.34
30–34	0.26	0.26	0.31
35–39	0.20	0.21	0.30
40–44	0.16	0.18	0.32
45–49	0.15	0.24	0.38
Singulate Mean Age, Truncated at Age 45	21.9	20.4	17.5
Singulate Mean Age, Truncated at Age 40	21.3	21.0	19.0

Source: See Table 20.1.

be matched with mothers through birth histories or an enumeration of the slaves by families. The probate data sample has 540 plantations of various sizes in which slave women are listed with their surviving children.

The proportions childless and the singulate mean ages at first birth are listed in Table 20.5. We see that they are higher for the plantation record sample. A major factor responsible for the differences is probably the plantation size distributions of the two samples. The average plantation size is about 108 slaves for the plantation record sample and about 23 slaves for the probate data. A second consideration that may be related to the differences is the distribution of the two samples over time. The plantation record findings are heavily concentrated in the period after 1850, whereas the probate data are more evenly spread over the antebellum period. Since slave fertility declined during the antebellum period, one might expect this phenomenon to register in the form of delayed childbearing and a higher singulate mean age at first birth in the plantation records. A third factor may be an artifact of the data. If birth histories from the plantation records more completely match children with their mothers, then, *ceteris paribus,* the singulate mean will be higher. Both samples represent the major crops and regions of the South. Since the probate data are more representative of the antebellum slave population we conclude that the better estimate of mean age at first birth is the probate data figure of 20.6 years.

Proportions childless taken directly from both sets of data show a rise in the age group forty to forty-four which, as discussed above, we believe to be erroneous. In order to approximate more closely what the real situation is likely to be, we have assumed that the proportion childless at ages forty to forty-four is the same as the proportion in the group thirty-five to thirty-nine. If we had assumed that it was smaller than in the age group thirty-five to thirty-nine, the estimated mean would, of course, have been higher.

In the third row of Table 20.5, the proportions of white southern women who were childless in 1860 and their resulting singulate mean age at first birth are listed. These proportions were obtained by drawing a random sample of households from the 1860 census schedules. Slave women, on the average, had their first child about two years earlier than southern white women. For the sake of comparison, data obtained from the 1970 U.S. census are listed in rows 4 and 5 of Table 20.5. It can be seen that black women today bear their first child approximately two years earlier than do white women. The average black woman, therefore, both today and a century ago, started her reproductive career at a *relatively* earlier age.

The difference between the singulate mean and the Fogel and Engerman estimate of 22.5 years could be due either to the method of computation or to differences in the data base. To test the source of the discrepancy we used their procedure on the probate sample; the resulting mean was 22.3 years. We conclude, therefore, that the difference between the estimates is indeed due to the method of calculation.

DID SLAVE CHILDBEARING START EARLY OR LATE?

Whether the singulate mean age of first childbearing of slaves is early or late can only be judged in relation to its closeness to the mean age at which childbearing is

Table 20.5. Proportions of Women Childless by Standard Age Groups

		10–14	15–19	20–24	25–29	30–34	35–39	40–44	Singulate Mean
Slaves	Plantation Records[b]	1.0	0.812	0.426	0.260	0.215	0.182	(0.182)[a]	21.0
	Number	163	165	148	131	135	99	—	
Slaves	Probate Records[b]	0.998	0.782	0.354	0.220	0.178	0.142	(0.142)	20.6
	Number	655	662	539	445	393	353	—	
White, Southern	1860 Census[b]	(1.0)	0.926	0.544	0.295	0.202	0.172	(0.172)	22.7
	Number		4,895	4,450	3,547	2,883	2,332	—	
White, 1970	Census[c]	(1.0)	0.934	0.578	0.240	0.134	0.114	(0.114)	23.1
Black, 1970	Census[c]	(1.0)	0.802	0.382	0.196	0.136	0.131	(0.131)	20.7

[a]The figures in parentheses were not supplied in the original sources; they were estimated by the authors.
[b]Steckel (1985).
[c]U.S. Bureau of the Census (1973), Tables 8 and 65.

physiologically or biologically possible. An observed mean age of twenty would be late if childbearing could begin at twelve but early if childbearing could only commence at twenty. The mean age at which childbearing can begin depends upon two factors: the mean age at menarche and the duration of the period of adolescent sterility following menarche. These two factors may not be independent (Frisch 1975); the period of adolescent sterility may be shortened if menarche is early. The term "adolescent sterility" is unfortunate, since not all women are sterile following menarche. Some cycles are anovulatory and others display a short luteal phase (the time from ovulation to the onset of menses) and are therefore probably not capable of supporting pregnancy. Indeed, Doring found that in the age group twelve to fourteen, 60 percent of cycles were anovulatory while another 30 percent had a shortened luteal phase (Doring 1969). In what is usually thought of as the prime reproductive ages from twenty-one to twenty-five years the corresponding figures were 13 percent and 26 percent respectively. The incidence of complete cycles did not reach a maximum until the age groups twenty-six to thirty (83 percent) and thirty-one to thirty-five (84 percent). Similarly, Vollman (1967) found that following menarche 45 percent of the cycles were anovulatory and another 44 percent were associated with short luteal phases. In contrast, between the ages of twenty-two and forty-four an average of only 2 percent of cycles were anovulatory; short luteal phases did not disappear with increased age but comprised a rather constant 15 percent of all cycles in healthy adult women.

Fecundability is defined as the monthly probability that conception will occur in a population that is not lactating or practicing contraception (Gini 1924). There is mounting evidence that fecundability conforms to Henry's (1965) hypothesis: Fecundability is zero until age a, rises until age b where it remains rather constant until age c when it begins to fall to zero again at some age d. Most estimates of fecundability for newly married women lie in the range 0.2 to 0.3.[5] The inverse of fecundability gives an estimate of the mean waiting time to conception in a population with a constant probability of becoming pregnant each month. If we weight the fecundability of newly married women (0.25) by the ratio of incidence of complete cycles (10 percent) following menarche (twelve to fourteen years), to the incidence of complete cycles (61 percent) following marriage (twenty-one to twenty-five years), we obtain a conservatively small estimate of fecundability following menarche of 0.041. The estimate is conservative because it will be assumed to the constant average fecundability for several years following menarche; a conservatively high estimate of the mean waiting time of 24.4 months is obtained. That this estimate of the mean waiting time to conception is high can be demonstrated by comparison with Jain's (1969) estimate of the mean delay between marriage and first conception in a group of Taiwanese women in which those pregnant before marriage were excluded. The mean delay falls from a high of 13.4 months for those married at ages twelve to fifteen to 7.2 months for those married at age twenty.

If only 85 percent of pregnancies end in births, if spontaneous abortions occur at 3 months' gestation, and if the period of postpartum amenorrhea associated with a spontaneous abortion is two months, then on average the waiting time to the first birth would be $[24.4/0.85 + 5(0.15/0.85) + 9] = 38.6$ months or about 3 years.[6] The assumption that fecundability remains constant at 0.04 almost certainly produces an overestimate of the mean waiting time before the first birth. Talwar (1965) found that the median waiting time declined from 2.71 to 0.92 years for Indian women married at ages thirteen and nineteen respectively. From ages thirteen to twenty-two (the highest reported age) the median waiting time never exceeded three years in a population rarely exposed to the risk of pregnancy before marriage. Most marriages took place shortly after menarche, although some preceded it. Menarche in the population that Talwar studied occurred after about age fourteen; the median waiting time following marriage at age fourteen was only 1.96 years.[7] Talwar estimates that in this sample of Indian women the proportion not fecund drops from a high of 98 percent at age eleven to 65 percent, 40 percent, and 20 percent at ages fourteen, fifteen, and sixteen respectively; our assumption of constant low fecundability therefore biases the estimated mean waiting time upward. To be on the safe side, in order to place an upper bound on the estimate let us assume, however, that the mean waiting time is indeed three years; a more reasonable estimate would be 2–2.5 years.

Among samples of populations around the world, a large variation exists in the ages of menarche reported in the literature from a low of 12.4 years among the Chinese to a high of 18.4 and 18.6 among girls of the Lumi and Bundi peoples in New Guinea; selected findings are reported in Table 20.6.[8]

Many factors have been found to be associated with age of menarche such as fatness in adolescence, physique, health status, and month of the year (Johnston 1974). Menarche is probably partly determined by genetics since the correlation between ages at menarche decreases steadily as the genetic similarity decreases (Hiernaux 1968). Race and climate may also control age at menarche (Roberts 1969; Bojlen and Bentzon 1968). In addition Roberts and Dann (1967) have shown that the age of menarche is positively associated with both the number of siblings and birth order when social class is held constant; they found a delay of 0.15 years per sibling and an advance of 0.19 years per birth rank. Rather large urban-rural and social class influences have been noted as well (Bai and Vijayalakshmi 1973; Burrell et al. 1961; Kralj-Cercek 1956; Prabhakar et al. 1972; Madhavan 1965; Wilson and Sutherland 1950).

The best-established factor, undoubtedly operating through many of the environmental factors noted above, is nutrition. Severe malnutrition unquestionably delays menarche. Tanner has linked the historical trend toward earlier age at menarche to increased standards of nutrition. Bojlen and Bentzon have noted that this trend is absent in Eskimos whose nutritional level has also remained trendless over the same period (Dreizen et al. 1967; Ellis 1945; LaPorte 1946; Tanner 1965, 1973b; Bojlen and Bentzon 1968). On the basis of observations in Slovenia in 1956, Kralj-Cercek postulated that age of menarche is related to the protein content, and especially the amount of meat in the diet, but his determination of the age of menarche is open to question.[9]

In discussing the trend toward earlier physical maturation Tanner (1965, 59) argued that "it seems likely to be due to an influence which starts early in life. The best guess might be that better infant feeding, and particularly giving infants more

Table 20.6. Estimates of the Mean Age at Menarche from Selected Populations

Population	Mean	Comments
Black, South Africa[a]		Economically badly off
Not Poor	15.00	
Poor	15.40	
White, Alabama, United States[b]		
Malnourished	14.45	
Well-Nourished	12.43	
Nigerian Schoolgirls[c]	14.07	High economic status
Andhra Pradesh, India[d]		
High Socioeconomic Group	13.11	
Middle Socioeconomic Group	13.27	
Low Socioeconomic Group	13.35	
India[e]		
Madras, Urban	12.76	
Madras, Rural	14.16	
Kerala, Urban	13.24	
Kerala, Rural	14.42	
New Guinea[f]		
Bundi, All	18.10	Malnourished
Bundi, Chimbu	17.60	Malnourished
Bundi, Non-Chimbu	18.60	Malnourished
Kaiapit	15.60	
Megiar	15.50	
Chimbu	17.50	
Lumi	18.40	Malnourished
London Schoolgirls[g]	13.02	Indicates end of trend; no change between 1959 and 1966–1967
U.S. College Women[h]	13.10	Indicates end of trend; no change between mothers and daughters
Ceylon[i]		
Urban	12.84	
Rural	14.39	

[a]Burrell et al. (1961).
[b]Dreizen et al. (1967).
[c]Tanner and O'Keeffe (1962).
[d]Bai and Vijayalakshmi (1973).
[e]Madhavan (1965).
[f]Malcolm (1970), 51–55.
[g]Tanner (1973a).
[h]Damon (1974).
[i]Wilson and Sutherland (1950).

protein early in life, is more responsible than any other aspect of nutrition." However, diet throughout childhood, as well as exposure to disease, appear to be important influences on the age of menarche.[10] In spite of the numerous references in the literature on menarche to the possible role of protein, no link has been definitely established; indeed there is considerable debate about the relative roles of calories, protein, and fat.[11]

Without direct data on the age of menarche, estimation of the mean age at menarche of slaves would be subject to a large degree of error, since menarche appears to be controlled by the interaction of many factors. Even in the absence of direct data, however, an upper bound can be established with confidence. Given the influence of diet and the reported nutritional level of the slave diet (Fogel and Engerman 1974a, 1:109–115; Sutch 1975b, 359–396), especially the estimated per capita consumption of 8 ounces of meat and over 4,000 calories a day, it is very unlikely that the mean age at menarche exceeded sixteen. Sixteen years should be an upper bound since all populations reported in modern literature with means above sixteen suffer from severe malnutrition; a more likely estimate would be fifteen.

Fortunately, another body of data, heretofore ignored, confirms that menarche in slaves occurred at an age that must be considered early by the historical standards listed by Tanner (1962, 143–155). Growth is a process marked by the passage of events that occur in a well-defined order: the development of teeth, the appearance of pubic hair, and the spurt in growth, measured by height or weight gain, during adolescence. Particularly important is the observation that menarche occurs soon after the peak of the adolescent growth spurt (Frisch and Revelle 1969). The length of time between the age of peak growth spurt and menarche differs among populations. Data cited by Tanner and Eveleth (1975) show mean delays of 1.0 and 1.5 years for surveyed groups from Hong Kong and London respectively (Tanner et al. 1976). A later London survey found a mean decay of 1.33 years. Frisch and Revelle found that the delay increased from 0.86 years in the earliest to 1.3 years in the latest menarche groups among women drawn from three American longitudinal growth studies conducted from 1930 through 1950. Cycles II and III of the Health Examination Study conducted by the National Center for Health Statistics indicate that the average difference for American women is currently 1 year.[12] Although variability among populations does exist, the time between peak height spurt and menarche is not long; for at least those populations that mature rather early we can safely conclude that menarche occurs within 2 years after the peak height spurt.[13] Choosing a delay of 2 years provides us with a conservatively high estimate of the mean age at menarche.

The previous discussion, although interesting, would be useless unless a body of data showing heights by age existed. Fortunately, through a legislative fluke, a vast quantity of height data is readily available. Section 9 of the Bill for the Abolition of the Slave Trade, passed on March 2, 1807, directed that the captain of any ship of 40 or more tons transporting any slave from any port in the United States to any other place within the jurisdiction of the United States had to compile duplicate manifests that specified the slave's name, sex, age, and height. The purpose of Section 9 was to prevent smuggling; this section, and Section 8, which prohibited the transport of slaves for sale in ships smaller than 40 tons, were repealed in 1864 when coastwise slave trade was prohibited forever. A large collection of manifests completed in accordance with this act is now deposited in the National Archives (Record Group 36); more than 40,000 slaves are enumerated, together with their ages and heights.[14] The proportion of slaves who were transported for the purpose of sale is unknown.

We have analyzed a sample of these data. The results, pictured in Figure 20.2,

Figure 20.2. Height velocity for female slaves.

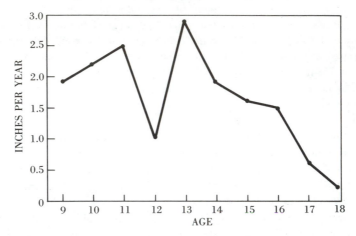

derived from Table 20.7, are encouraging. The growth curve looks very reasonable in both the pattern of the mean heights by age and the deviations around the pattern.[15] It could be argued that the mean height curve looks reasonable because ages were assigned by the recorder on the basis of height. It is hardly possible that such a rule would have preserved a variation around the mean at each age which looks normal. The behavior of both standard deviations and means indicates that although both height and age may have been recorded with error, the errors did not significantly distort the age-height profile.

One might object that slaves being shipped constitute a selected population that is far from a random sample of all slaves. The nature of such selection is not clear, however. The best case for selectivity could be made if all slaves had been shipped for sale. We know that this assumption is not true, but let us examine the nature of the bias that would result in order to determine whether the possibly non-random population is an important issue. If all slaves were intended for sale, then, based on

Table 20.7. Heights in Inches by Age for Female Slaves

Age	Number	Mean	Standard Deviation
8	73	46.3	4.71
9	87	48.2	4.02
10	90	50.4	4.42
11	75	52.9	3.12
12	134	53.9	4.05
13	113	56.7	4.06
14	164	58.6	3.47
15	200	60.2	3.12
16	321	61.7	2.41
17	284	62.3	2.41
18	392	62.7	2.60

Source: Shipping manifests in the National Archives (Record Group 36).

the used-car analogy it could be plausibly argued that slaves sold would tend to be "lemons": less healthy or smaller. On the other hand, there is some economic justification for the counterargument that only larger, more healthy slaves would be shipped for sale, based upon the observation that only high-grade commodities tend to be exported whereas a variety of grades is usually available in the region of production. The explanation frequently offered for this phenomenon is that fixed transport costs for all grades imply that higher quality commodities have a relatively higher price at the point of destination. Consequently it is only profitable to ship the higher grades.

Suppose, then, that slaves who were shipped were selected because they were either taller or shorter than the average slave of the same age. From Table 20.8 we see that if only slave women whose height was above average (i.e., those in the 75th or 90th centile) were picked, then the estimate of the age of peak velocity would be identical to that of the average (50th centile) woman. On the other hand, if only lemons—those of below average height—were chosen, then the resulting estimate of the age at peak velocity would be higher than that of the average slave woman. In either case, the estimated age would not be lower than the true age. We conclude, therefore, that the question of the selectivity of the population is unlikely to be an important one insofar as estimation of the age at peak velocity is concerned.

From Figure 20.2 we see that female slaves experienced a well-defined spurt that is centered on age thirteen. We therefore conclude that menarche occurred at age fifteen, assuming a conservative delay of two years, and probably occurred earlier.

Combining the estimates of mean age at menarche and waiting time until the first birth, we see that if slaveowners successfully manipulated the fertility of slave women by causing them to bear as soon as possible, then the observed mean age at first birth should not have exceeded $15 + 3 = 18$ years. Since the observed mean is in fact 20.6 or some 2.6 years later, we must conclude that slave women did not bear children at the earliest possible age. More reasonable estimates of the mean ages of menarche and waiting time until the first birth indicate that successful manipulation would have led to an observed mean age of first childbearing of from 16.5 to 17 years; such an estimate only reinforces our conclusion.

Table 20.8. Annual Velocity in Centimeters for Females Who Are of below-Average, Average, and above-Average Height Calculated from Cross-Sectional Data

Age	Centile				
	10th	25th	50th	75th	90th
From 9.0 to 10.0	5.4	5.5	5.8	6.0	6.2
10.0 to 11.0	5.4	5.9	6.3	6.8	7.1
11.0 to 12.0	4.9	6.2	6.6	7.0	7.5
12.0 to 13.0	7.1	6.7	6.2	5.8	5.3
13.0 to 14.0	4.7	4.4	4.1	3.7	3.4
14.0 to 15.0	2.5	2.6	2.1	1.9	1.7
Point Estimate of Peak	12.5	12.5	11.5	11.5	11.5

Source: Calculated from Tanner et al. (1966), Table III-B.

We have emphasized methodology. Our conclusions are tentative, although we doubt that bigger samples will reverse our findings.[16] We trust that they will focus attention on several important questions that remain to be answered. Did slaveowners *try* to manipulate fertility, or less extremely, did they try to create conditions favorable to the realization of maximum reproductive potential? If they did not, what were their reasons? If they did try, why was there a rather long delay between the attainment of reproductive capacity and the first birth and why did so many females remain childless?[17]

APPENDIX: CALCULATION OF THE SINGULATE MEAN AGE AT FIRST BIRTH

The technique devised by Hajnal is presented below. In the original article mathematical appendixes facilitate the interpretation of the results. Here we only list the steps involved. The figures in brackets result from applying each step to the probate record data listed in Table 20.5.

1. Add the proportions childless from the age group ten to fourteen up to and including the age group thirty-five to thirty-nine and multiply the result by 5.0. [(0.998 + 0.782 + 0.354 + 0.220 + 0.178 + 0.142) × 5 = 2.674 × 5 = 13.37]
2. Add 10.0. [13.37 + 10 = 23.37]
3. Average the proportions for the age groups thirty-five to thirty-nine and forty to forty-four. [(0.142 + 0.142) × 0.5 = 0.142]
4. Multiply the result of step 3 by 40.0 and subtract from step 2. [23.37 − (0.142 × 40) = 23.37 − 5.68 = 17.69]
5. Subtract the result of step 3 from 1.0. [1.0 − 0.142 = 0.858]
6. Divide the result of step 4 by the result of step 5. [17.69 ÷ 0.858 = 20.6]
7. The result of step 6 is the singulate mean age at the first birth of those who bear a child before age forty.

The extension to an upper age limit of forty-five or fifty is immediate.

NOTES

1. For a description of the data see Fogel and Engerman (1975).
2. In the probate records, there is no guarantee that the children listed with the women were actually their own. The magnitude of the effect of adoption on their procedure of estimation is likely to be small, however. The sign of the possible bias, *ignoring the other biases listed below,* is unambiguously negative; for unless the eldest child were an adopted child, the procedure would be unbiased. Adoption, however, was apparently rare among slaves. Sutch (1975b), 409–410, has estimated that only about 1 percent of slave children under the age of thirteen were orphans. A more sophisticated technique of estimation involving model fertility and mortality schedules shows that even if the expectation of life of slaves had been only thirty years, the proportion of orphans under age thirteen would have been 0.008. Using data from over 1,400 plantations retrieved from the ex-slave narratives, Crawford (1980) found that slightly over 90 percent of children under age thirteen lived with at least one natural parent. Virtually all of the remainder lived in a cabin with either other children or young adults (6 percent) or in the master's household (3 percent). Among children aged thirteen

to seventeen, 84 percent of the males and 65 percent of the females lived with at least one of their natural parents.

3. This point may be made more clearly through an example. Consider a population with no mortality for which a listing of women with their children still living at home is compiled. On the sole criterion of whether children are listed the woman will be classified as either a mother or a non-mother. Virtually every woman aged fifteen to nineteen who has ever borne a child will be correctly classified as a mother. On the other hand, many women aged sixty to sixty-five will be misclassified as non-mothers because their children no longer live at home. The proportion misclassified therefore rises monotonically with the age of the woman since the average age of children, and particularly the age of the youngest child (who is likely to be the last to leave the nest) rises monotonically with the age of their mothers. Such a process has the effect of progressively flattening the ogive of the distribution of women who have ever borne children. A flattening of the ogive produces a concentration of the distribution toward younger ages. The effect, therefore, is identical to the effect of mortality on the Fogel-Engerman procedure; it is graphically represented in Figure 20.1. The effect of adoption on the procedure of estimation is even smaller than its effect on the Fogel-Engerman procedure, which we have already concluded is small. The Hajnal estimate will be unaffected as long as an adopted child is not the only child listed with the mother. The sign of the potential bias resulting from adoption is indeterminate.

4. A detailed description of the data and procedures is available in Steckel (1985).

5. For a detailed review of the literature on estimating fecundability and a summary of the estimates see Menken (1975).

6. The first term in the equation arises because everyone must wait 24.4 months for a conception leading to a live birth, 0.15 must wait an additional 24.4 months to conceive one prior spontaneous abortion, 0.15^2 must wait an additional 24.4 months to conceive a second prior spontaneous abortion, etc. This infinite series reduces to 24.4/0.85. The second term arises because each spontaneous abortion has a gestation length of 3 months and a period of postpartum amenorrhea of 2 months, and the expected number of spontaneous abortions is $0.15 + 15^2 + 0.15^3 + \ldots = 0.15/0.85$. The third term arises because each live birth conception is followed by a gestation period of 9 months.

7. The mean was approximately 2.6 years.

8. Tanner (1973a), 95–96 and Malcolm (1970), 51–55. The mean age at menarche is best calculated by the status quo method. Numbers of women are asked whether or not they have menstruated and those who have menstruated are tabulated by age. The mean and variance of the age at menarche distribution are then estimated by probit analysis, described in Finney (1952), or by logit analysis, first used in this context by Burrell et al. (1961). Most of the studies reported here have used probit analysis on status quo observations. Note that the mean could be calculated by the Hajnal scheme as well. Historical estimates of the mean age at menarche in Norway, Germany, Finland, and Sweden, which form the basis for the belief in a long-term downward trend presented, for example, in Tanner (1962), 143–155, were calculated by the much less reliable procedure of recollected age and may therefore be substantially in error. The populations studied, moreover, may not have been representative (see Tanner 1965). Evidence for a downward trend, based on probits fitted to data in the twentieth century, is rather conclusive; but whether the mean age fell during the nineteenth century is questionable. For a complete discussion, see Brundtland and Walle (1976).

9. Burrell et al. (1961) found that among South African black schoolgirls, the poor, who received much less protein than the non-poor, had a higher age of menarche. Also noting the possible role of protein: Wilson and Sutherland (1960), Wark and Malcolm (1969), and Malcolm (1969) suggested the differences in mean age at menarche and growth rates among the Kaiapit people and the Bundi and Lumi peoples in New Guinea may be due to differential protein intake.

10. See Tanner (1990) for his most recent views on secular trends in menarche. Cf. Tanner (1981a, 1981b) and his earlier studies (1962, 1975).

11. Many nutritionists have recently denigrated the independent role of protein in malnutrition. More often the problem is one of insufficient calories. Adding protein without improving the quantity of the diet will accomplish little; but, increasing caloric intake may well increase protein intake. For a full discussion see Joy and Payne (1975). Rose Frisch and her colleagues have developed over the

past several years a precise theory of control of menarche. They have shown that there is a minimum relative fatness of the female body necessary for the onset and maintenance of menstrual cycles (see Frisch and McArthur 1974). Experimental work with rats on high-fat and low-fat diets showed that the high-fat diet rats had estrus significantly earlier than the low-fat diet rats. Fat was substituted isocalorically for carbohydrate in these experiments (Frisch et al. 1975). The data suggest that "An increase in the amount of calories from fat in the diets of developed countries in the last century may have contributed to the secular trend to an earlier age of menarche" (1975, 4174).

12. A discussion of the estimation of the time of peak velocity in height can be found in National Center for Health Statistics (1973b), 70–72, App. II. The report of age at menarche for the same group of women is contained in National Center for Health Statistics (1973a), 2.

13. We have deliberately allowed for a margin of error in the estimation of the delay between peak velocity and menarche by assuming a lag of 2 years. In each of the studies cited above, the mean age at menarche was estimated from the status quo method by fitting logits or probits to the proportion of women menstruating at each age. Because the underlying distributions (either the normal or logistic) are continuous, the point estimate of the mean can be confidently accepted. In several studies, however, estimates of the peak velocity were taken as the midpoint of the year in which the greatest increment in height occurred. The point estimate of the mode, therefore, is constrained by the way in which the data are organized; if yearly intervals are used, then the only candidates for the mode occur also at yearly intervals. This defect can be corrected by fitting a curve to the set of points representing the mean height attained at each age. The age at which the derivative of this curve reaches its maximum is then the point estimate of the mode. There are many choices of fitting procedures. We chose to fit a 7th degree polynomial through 8 points; the points were chosen so that the interval between the 4th and 5th points coincided with the year of peak growth. Our estimate based on yearly data for the United States differs from the "best" estimate of the National Center of Health Statistics (based on half-year intervals) by only 0.02 year. A similar calculation using slave data places the mode at 13.2 years. Accepting the 1-year delay currently experienced by Americans, the mean age at menarche of slaves would have been 14.2 years. Our estimate of 15.0 allows for the possibility that the delay might have been longer. We do not, however, believe that a longer interval is likely, for it was only 1.1 years in a population with a much later growth spurt, peaking at age 14.5, reported by Malcolm (1969); if the polynomial fit is used, the delay is only 0.9 years.

14. For a full description of the history of the act and of the extant manifests, see Wesley (1942).

15. As long ago as 1939, Shuttleworth (1939), 51, noted that "the variability [of height] increases to a maximum value of 7.552 centimeters at age 13.5, closely coincident with their age at maximum growth, and then declines to 6.949 centimeters at age 18.5." Many subsequent studies have found the same relation between variation in attained height and velocity; for the latest U.S. data see National Center for Health Statistics (1970), 22, and National Center for Health Statistics (1973a), 35.

16. The sample of slave heights by age is being substantially enlarged in order to permit construction of age and height profiles by decade for each decade 1810–1819 through 1850–1859. The results of this investigation will be reported at a later date.

17. The proportion that actually remained childless is not as large as the proportion given in Table 20.5, since a larger proportion of women have no living children (or no children living with them) than the proportion never to have borne a child. The difference between the two lies probably in the neighborhood of 0.05. This estimate is based upon the differences listed in Table 20.3.

TWENTY-ONE

The Slave Breeding Thesis

Robert W. Fogel and Stanley L. Engerman

T he most vigorous and persuasive exposition of the slave breeding thesis is that set forth by Richard Sutch in two essays published in 1975 and in a third essay jointly authored with Herbert Gutman (Gutman and Sutch 1976a). Sutch (1975b, 411–412) defines slave breeding

> as any practice of the slave master intended to cause the fertility of the slave population to be higher than it would have been in the absence of such interference. So defined, "breeding" includes the use of "reward" for childbearing, the encouragement of early marriage and short lactation periods, and the provision of both pre- and postnatal medical care, as well as practices more reprehensible to modern sensibilities.

Sutch goes on to argue that slave fertility rates during the late antebellum era were as high as they were because slaveowners manipulated the sexual behavior of slaves in order to push their fertility rates as close to the biological limit as possible. The incentive for manipulation was the rapid upward movement in slave prices, which he characterizes as "a provocation to slave breeding" (Sutch 1975b, 411). It was the dehumanizing nature of slavery that, according to Sutch, made the manipulation of the sexual behavior of slaves possible.

While Sutch defined slave breeding to include all measures by planters that served to promote fertility, including provision of medical care and nutritious diets, he strongly suggests that it is "barnyard" practices which were central to slave breeding. Because slave plantations were "profit maximizing agricultural enterprises," he argues, and because of "the pressures of the competitive system," the typical slaveowner came "to regard his slaves solely as capital assets no different in kind from acres of land, from farming implements, or from work animals" (Sutch 1975a, 173). Imbued with such an outlook many planters willingly seized whatever mechanism was available to them for increasing fertility. Sutch holds that the manipulation of the sex ratio was an effective instrument for such purposes and that the effect of a slave breeding policy was to induce a positive correlation between fertility and the ratio of women to men. A positive correlation is to be expected, he continues, because a slave breeder did "not need to have one man for each woman. He could have each man impregnate many women" (Sutch 1975a, 191).

Sutch (1975a, 195) put forward three pieces of evidence that provide, in his view, "circumstantial evidence . . . strong enough to conclude that many slaveowners in the American South systematically bred slaves for sale." These are (1) a marked positive correlation between his fertility index and the ratio of females to males, (2) a "marital" fertility rate in the slave-exporting states so high that it exceeded the marital fertility rate among Cocos Island women aged twenty to twenty-four by nearly 20 percent, and hence approached "the extremes of individual experience" (Sutch 1975a, 194), and (3) the identification of forty-seven slave farms with ratios of women to men that have less than one chance in ten of having occurred due to purely random factors and that had a "marital" fertility rate in excess of that found for Cocos Island women in the age category twenty to twenty-four.

In each of these instances the measures of fertility that Sutch used departed from those conventionally used by demographers. In his demonstrations of a positive correlation between fertility and the ratio of females to males, for example, Sutch did not use the conventional child-woman ratio (C/W), which he calls "female fertility," but the ratio of children to adults $[C/(W + M)]$, which he refers to as both "adult fertility" and "child productivity" (see Table 21.1 for the definition of the variables). He justifies this switch in measures on the grounds that the usual measure is inappropriate for a slave-breeding economy."The appropriate index," he writes, "for measuring the impact of a sharply unequal sex balance on the economic return of the slave holder is the ratio of children to *adults* of both sexes" (Sutch 1975b, 413). On the basis of this assertion Sutch presented a table, which is reproduced here as Table 21.2, and argued that the positive correlations between the inverse of the sex ratio (W/M) and adult fertility $[C/(W + M)]$ (cf. columns 1, 2, and 3 of Table 21.2) provided support for the proposition that slave breeders were manipulating the ratio of women to men in order to raise fertility. He acknowledged that the fertility of women (C/W) was negatively correlated with an increase of the inverse of the sex ratio (W/M) (cf. columns 1, 4, and 5 of Table 21.2), but did not view this as contradictory evidence.

Sutch's references to the ratio $C/(W + M)$ are ambiguous. He sometimes treats it as an index of fertility and sometimes as an index of productivity (cf. Sutch 1975a, 192–193; Sutch 1975b, 413; Gutman and Sutch 1976, 155). Use of this ratio as a measure of fertility is not out of the question since it is reasonably well correlated with the conventional child-woman ratio, although, of course, it yields values that are lower than the conventional measure. A regression between the two ratios yielded

$$\frac{C}{W + M} = 0.758 + \underset{(58.685)}{0.483} \frac{C}{W} \tag{1}$$

where R-square $= 0.61$ and the figure in parentheses is the t-value. But if the objective is to explain why the U.S. slave population had as high a crude birth rate as it did, it is difficult to see why one should prefer Sutch's measure to the conventional one. Sutch's measure is merely the conventional child-woman ratio multi-

Table 21.1. Definitions of Symbols Employed in the Equations and Tables

Symbol	Definition
C	Number of children of a defined age.
W	Number of women of a defined age.
M	Number of men of a defined age.
γ	the elasticity of C/W with respect to M/W.
R	W/M, the inverse of the sex ratio.
P_{fk}	Price of a female slave, aged k.
R_t	Net income derived from a female slave in year t through her work in the fields.
λ_t	Probability that a slave will survive from age k to age t.
B	Zero-age price of a slave.
ϕ_t	Probability of giving birth during the tth year for married women.
r	Internal rate of return or discount rate.
$\overset{*}{\lambda}$	Rate of decline of λ.
$\overset{*}{\phi}$	Rate of decline of ϕ.
α	Proportion of a year's work time in the fields that a female loses due to pregnancy and confinement.
H_{f20}	Annual hire rate on a twenty-year-old female who will devote the full year to field work.
t	Subscript designating age.
k	Age of a slave at the point of decision regarding fertility policy.
f	Subscript designating females.

Table 21.2. Sutch's Estimates of "Productivity" and Fertility Rates on Farms with Five or More Women, Parker-Gallman Sample, 1860

(1) Sex Ratio, Women per Man	Ratio of Children (0–14) to Adults (15–44)		Number of Children per Thousand Years of Prime Fertility Experience		Number of Farms with Five or More Women	
	(2) Selling States	(3) Buying States	(4) Selling States	(5) Buying States	(6) Selling States	(7) Buying States
$R > 3.0^a$	1.37	0.85	233.6	122.4	19	11
$2.0 < R \leq 3.0$	1.36	1.09	245.1	222.2	22	18
$1.5 < R \leq 2.0$	1.27	1.07	275.1	229.2	42	42
$1.1 < R \leq 1.5$	1.14	0.97	248.1	233.3	66	86
$1.0 < R \leq 1.1$	1.01	0.88	232.6	209.6	36	44
$R < 1.0$	0.99	0.81	276.0	239.8	63	132

[a] Includes farms with no men.
Source: Sutch (1975a), 193.

plied by the share of the adult population that is female $(C/W) \times [W/(W + M)] = C/(W + M)$.

Sutch insists that for a slave economy his measure is the correct one and that it contains information about the effect of the sex ratio on fertility that is not contained in the conventional child-woman ratio. Indeed, he contends that the negative correlation between $C/(W + M)$ and M/W sustains the slave breeding hypothesis. Since C/W is positively correlated with *both* M/W and $C/(W + M)$, the negative correlation between $C/(W + M)$ and M/W is indeed peculiar. Sutch dismisses this paradox by arguing that female fertility C/W decreased with the inverse of the sex ratio W/M because both venereal diseases and resistance to slave breeding *increased* with the inverse of the sex ratio. Sutch offers no evidence to sustain these conjectures, but even if they were true, they would be an explanation for why slave breeding practices reduced rather than increased fertility. While the conjectures might be relevant for the Jamaican case, where we need to explain a relatively low crude birth rate, they are not relevant to an explanation of the high crude birth rates that characterized American slaves.

Sutch's defense of the use of $C/(W + M)$ is more economic than demographic. He suggests that what was important to a slave breeder was not whether manipulation of the sex ratio increased the fertility of females but whether it increased the productivity of his operation, and productivity, he asserts, is measured by children per adult. "The number of children per woman might decline at high women-to-men ratios," he writes, "but yet the number of children produced per a given investment in adults could continue to increase" (Sutch 1975b, 413). It should be noticed that this defense of the unorthodox fertility measure involves the redefinition of slave breeding. Slave breeding is no longer the maximization of fertility but the maximization of output of children per unit of invested resource. Slave breeding may now lower fertility, and hence income from the sales of children. By economizing on the number of males devoted to the slave breeding process, however, labor is released for production in the field, increasing the total income per dollar of invested resource.

Sutch's argument thus embraces not one but two theories of slave breeding—an explicit theory and an implicit one. The explicit theory, set forth at the outset of his first essay on the subject (1975a) and repeated in his subsequent essays (1975b and 1976), holds that slave breeders were persons who manipulated the sex ratio and other variables to increase births. This is, of course, the traditional view of slave breeding. The second theory, implicit in the defence of his unorthodox measure, is that slave breeders were persons who manipulated the sex ratio to economize on the labor of men in the "production" of children. While the manipulation might reduce the total number of births, it would increase the output of conventional products by an amount that would be more than enough to compensate for the decrease in births. Interesting and novel as is Sutch's implicit theory of slave breeding, we do not pursue it here, since it is our objective to explain why fertility was high, not why it was low.[1]

The issue that must be faced here is more traditional. It is whether the conventional fertility ratio C/W or Sutch's ratio $C/(W + M)$ should be regressed against the sex ratio to test the hypothesis that masters could increase the number of births by lowering the sex ratio (raising the ratio of females to males). No long chain of reasoning is needed to demonstrate the relevance of the conventional fertility ratio. The proof follows directly from the statement of the "production function" for children. If that production function is homogeneous of degree one (cf. *EM*, #50) we may write

$$C = Wg\left(\frac{M}{W}\right) \qquad (2)$$

Dividing both sides of equation 2 by W, yields

$$\frac{C}{W} = g\left(\frac{M}{W}\right) \tag{3}$$

Consequently if, as Sutch believes, masters could increase births by lowering the sex ratio, one should find a negative correlation between the *conventional* child-woman ratio and the sex ratio.

Equation 3 was run on Sutch's data source, the Parker-Gallman sample, in loglinear, linear, and quadratic forms, at both the farm and county levels. The results are shown in Table 21.3. In all cases the sign of the correlation between the fertility ratio and the sex ratio is positive.[2] Lowering the sex ratio thus reduced fertility, not increased it, as Sutch contends. Moreover, the quadratic equations show that the relationship is positive not only for values of the sex ratio below one, but also for values above one. Indeed variations in the sex ratio had a greater impact on fertility when M/W was greater than one than when it was less than one. This suggests that the impact of the sex ratio was not only on the age-specific "marital" fertility schedule, but also on such variables as age of women at the birth of their first child, the proportion of women who ever bore a child, the proportion of widows who remarried, and the length of the interval between marriages.[3]

We are still left with the puzzle as to why Sutch's adult fertility index is negatively correlated with the sex ratio, when the correlation between C/W and M/W is positive. Does this reversal in sign support Sutch's claim that his measure contains information about the impact of the sex ratio on fertility that is not already captured by a regression of C/W on M/W? It can be demonstrated that all of the information about the effect of the sex ratio on fertility is already contained in the regression of C/W on M/W, and that the reversal in sign obtained from a regression of $C/(W + M)$ on M/W is a statistical artifact having no behavioral significance. Indeed, the negative correlation between $C/(W + M)$ and M/W by itself does not even warrant the inference that the sex ratio affects fertility, since it can be shown that $C/(W + M)$ and M/W will be negatively correlated even when variations in the sex ratio have no affect on fertility.

Consider the case where the relationship between C/W and M/W may be approximated by a loglinear function, as in

$$\frac{C}{W} = A\left(\frac{M}{W}\right)^{\gamma} \tag{4}$$

where A = the intercept, and γ = the elasticity of C/W with respect to M/W. Multiplying both sides of equation 4 by $W/(W + M)$ and rearranging terms yields

$$\frac{C}{M + W} = A\left(\frac{M}{W}\right)^{\gamma}\left(1 + \frac{M}{W}\right)^{-1} \tag{5}$$

The effect of the multiplication is to make the sign of the correlation in equation 5 a function of γ and M/W. Evaluation of the first derivative of equation 5 reveals that the condition for the correlation to be negative (or for the correlation between $C/(W + M)$ and W/M to be positive) is

Table 21.3. Regressions Relating C/W and M/W Fitted to Data on Slave Plantations in the Parker-Gallman Sample

Dependent Variables	Constant	Coefficients of Independent Variables (figures in parentheses are t-values)				Number of Observations	R-Square
		M/W	$(M/W)^2$	Regional Dummy (equals 1 for West)	$\ln (M/W)$		
Farms as Units of Observation							
(1) C/W	0.6659 (26.461)	0.1797 (9.108)	—	—	—	2,169	0.0369
(2) C/W	0.7182 (24.546)	0.0763 (2.138)	0.0275 (3.479)	—	—	2,169	0.0422
(3) C/W	0.7435 (20.938)	0.0777 (2.178)	0.0273 (3.449)	−0.0437 (−1.258)	—	2,169	0.0429
(4) $\ln (C/W)$	−0.0907 (−7.800)	—	—	—	0.2498 (11.619)	2,169	0.0586
(5) $\ln (C/W)$	−0.0597 (−3.242)	—	—	−0.0514 (−2.166)	0.2516 (11.704)	2,169	0.0607
Counties as Units of Observation							
(6) C/W	0.5504 (12.357)	0.2720 (7.259)	—	—	—	359	0.1286
(7) C/W	0.5440 (8.322)	0.2816 (3.441)	−0.0026 (−0.133)	—	—	359	0.1286
(8) C/W	0.5433 (7.562)	0.2817 (3.435)	−0.0026 (−0.134)	0.0011 (0.025)	—	359	0.1286
(9) $\ln (C/W)$	−0.2536 (−10.917)	—	—	—	0.2087 (4.060)	359	0.0441
(10) $\ln (C/W)$	−0.2583 (−6.813)	—	—	0.0076 (0.158)	0.2084 (4.045)	359	0.0442

$$\frac{W}{M} < \frac{1-\gamma}{\gamma} \quad \text{or} \quad \frac{M}{W} > \frac{\gamma}{1-\gamma} \tag{6}$$

The regression of equation 4 on Sutch's data source, the Parker-Gallman sample, at the farm level indicates that $\gamma = 0.25$ and that it is significantly different from both 1 and 0 (see Table 21.3, rows 4 and 5). The condition in equation 6 is thus $W/M < 3.0$, which implies that column 1 of Table 21.2. should be positively correlated with columns 2 and 3 throughout the range that these columns show a positive correlation. It also implies the reversal in sign in the category $R = (W/M) > 3$ (the average value of R in that category is 14.5). Thus both the positive correlation between C/W and M/W and the negative correlation of $C/(W + M)$ and W/M imply, in this case, exactly the same behavior: Namely, that fertility was decreased by raising the female to male ratio.

The reversal in sign does not depend on the loglinear specification of equation 4. It can also come about in the linear case as well as with any higher order polynomial. The point is that multiplication of C/W by $W/(W + M)$ can cause a reversal in sign merely because the first term is positively correlated with M/W and the second term is negatively correlated with it. The condition for reversal of sign in the linear case can be derived as follows:

$$\frac{C}{W} = \alpha + \beta\left(\frac{M}{W}\right) \tag{7}$$

$$\frac{W}{M + W} = \frac{1}{1 + \frac{M}{W}} \tag{8}$$

with $\beta > 0$. Then

$$\left(\frac{W}{M + W}\right)\left(\frac{C}{W}\right) = \frac{C}{M + W} = \frac{\alpha + \beta\left(\frac{M}{W}\right)}{1 + \frac{M}{W}} \tag{9}$$

and

$$\frac{d\left(\frac{C}{M + W}\right)}{d\left(\frac{M}{W}\right)} = \frac{\beta - \alpha}{\left(1 + \frac{M}{W}\right)^2} \tag{10}$$

Since $1 + (M/W)$ can only take positive values, the sign of equation 10 depends on the values of α and β; $C/(W + M)$ and M/W will be negatively correlated if $\alpha > \beta$, and positively correlated if $\alpha < \beta$. The implication of equation 10 is that the substitution of Sutch's measure for the conventional child-woman ratio will reverse the sign of the correlation with C/W when the influence of the sex ratio on fertility is positive but relatively small. Indeed, the reversal in sign would also have to take place if $\beta = 0$. But $\beta = 0$ means that the sex ratio has no effect on fertility. In this case Sutch's measure would be negatively correlated with the sex ratio and quite significant, not because masters practiced slave breeding but only because C/W was multiplied by an identity with a negative slope. In actual fact the value of β, as determined from the Parker-Gallman sample, is positive but small relative to α ($\beta = 0.180$, $\alpha = 0.666$) and significantly different from both 0 and α at the 0.001 level. The implication is exactly the same as that indicated in the loglinear case. Both the positive correlation between C/W and M/W, and the negative correlation between $C/(W + M)$ and M/W, imply exactly the same behavior: Fertility was reduced by raising the female-to-male ratio.[4]

It is the use of an unorthodox measure that also led Sutch to the conclusion that the "marital" fertility rate of slaves approached "the extremes of individual experience." What Sutch calls a "marital" fertility rate is merely an unorthodox child-woman ratio: namely, the ratio of children one to fourteen to *either* women or men aged fifteen to forty-four, whichever is *lower*. Since it was quite common for marital partners to live on different farms, especially on farms with less than fifteen slaves,[5] Sutch's measure leads to the conclusion that slave women were much more fertile than they actually were.[6] Indeed, if we use a standard fertility ratio, the number of children zero to four divided by the number of women twenty to forty-four, the fertility of slave women in the Parker-Gallman sample turns out to be far from the biological limit.

Table 21.4 shows that while the fertility of slave women in the Parker-Gallman sample was high relative to that of white women in most regions of the United States in 1860, it was well below the fertility of U.S. white women in 1810. The proximate explanation for the relatively high fertility of slave women in 1860 is not that it was pushed to biological capacity but that it did not decline as rapidly after 1810 as did the fertility of white women. We will return to this question again. For the present, we wish merely to emphasize that the fertility rate of slave women in 1860 was well below biological capacity. Table 21.4 shows that it was 59 percent of the fertility rate achieved by white women in the West North Central region in 1810 and just 64 percent of the level of Cocos Island women.

Sutch's assertion that he was able to identify forty-seven "breeding farms" in the Parker-Gallman sample also rests on an unorthodox measure of fertility. He argues that it is reasonable to assume that any slave farm that meets two conditions is a slave breeding farm. These are (1) "the farm must have a ratio of women to men in the 15–44 age group so large as to occur less than 10 percent of the time by chance if men and women were distributed randomly" and (2) the "marital" fertility rate, as defined by Sutch,[7] must exceed 375 per thousand—a figure which, he argues, ensures that the fertility rate on these farms will exceed the peak age-specific fertility rates of the Cocos Island women. The application of the first condition yielded a total of eighty-seven farms (3 percent of the slave farms in the Parker-Gallman sample). The application of the second condition reduced the number to forty-seven farms.

Table 21.5 reports on our attempt to replicate Sutch's experiment. While we

Table 21.4. A Comparison of the Child-Women Ratios of Slave Women in the Parker-Gallman Sample with Those of Other Populations

	Population or Sample	Number of Children under 5 per 1,000 Women Aged 20–44
(1)	Parker-Gallman Sample	1,056
	U.S. White Women, 1810	
(2)	All Regions	1,290
(3)	New England	1,052
(4)	Middle Atlantic	1,289
(5)	East North Central	1,702
(6)	West North Central	1,801
(7)	South Atlantic	1,325
(8)	East South Central	1,700
(9)	West South Central	1,383
	U.S. White Women, 1860	
(10)	All Regions	886
(11)	New England	622
(12)	Middle Atlantic	767
(13)	East North Central	999
(14)	West North Central	1,105
(15)	South Atlantic	918
(16)	East South Central	1,039
(17)	West South Central	1,084
(18)	Cocos Island Women, 1947	1,647

Sources: Row 1, all slave farms in the Parker-Gallman tape with at least one slave woman aged twenty to twenty-four. *Rows 2–17*, U.S. Bureau of the Census (1975), I:54. *Row 18*, Smith (1960), 102.

Table 21.5. Children under Five per 1,000 Females Aged Fifteen to Forty-Four on Various Subcategories of Slave Farms in the Parker-Gallman Sample (figures in parenthesis are 95 percent confidence intervals)

	Subsample	Children under 5 per 1,000 Females Aged 15–44
(1)	Sutch's 47 "Breeding" Farms	757 ($\pm$ 97)
(2)	All 102 Farms That Meet Sutch's Restriction on the Ratio of Females to Males	614 ($\pm$ 62)
(3)	All Slave Farms in the Slave-Exporting States That Are "Non-Breeding" Farms	872 ($\pm$ 45)
(4)	All Slave Farms in the Slave-Importing States That Are "Non-Breeding" Farms	889 ($\pm$ 51)
(5)	All "Non-Breeding" Farms in the 40 Counties from Which Sutch Drew His "Breeding" Farms	895 ($\pm$ 86)

Note: In rows 3–5, non-breeding farms are defined as those which fail Sutch's restriction on the sex ratio.
Source: The Parker-Gallman tape.

were able to identify his 47 farms and calculate standard child-woman ratios, our application of the first restriction yielded not 87 but 102 farms. Table 21.5 shows that the "non-breeding" farms in both the slave-exporting and slave-importing states had fertility ratios that were 15 to 17 percent higher than those of Sutch's 47 "breeding" farms. And it was only Sutch's second restriction, which removed 55 farms with child-woman ratios below the average of the original 102, that brought the child-woman ratio up to 757 per thousand. The 102 farms that met Sutch's restriction with respect to the sex ratio had child-woman ratios that were between 30 and 31 percent below those that failed to meet the restriction.[8]

THE ECONOMIC BASIS OF THE SLAVE BREEDING HYPOTHESIS

So far we have considered only the demographic case for the slave breeding hypothesis. We have seen that each of the demographic criterion set forth by Sutch contradicts rather than sustains the hypothesis that the high fertility rate of slaves can be explained by the deliberate manipulation of the sex ratio by planters. But Sutch's argument is, at its core, an economic argument. Indeed it is an extreme version of a proposition that some social scientists consider to be quite plausible; namely, that fertility is largely controlled by a small number of narrowly defined economic variables.

Whatever reservations one might have about the validity of this proposition as an explanation of the fertility behavior of free populations today, in the slave case such an economic argument appears to make more sense. Sutch argues that slave fertility was completely controlled by masters who based their decisions with respect to slave fertility purely on the price of slaves, increasing their "production" of slaves whenever this price increased. Nor was market compulsion to practice slave breeding confined to a few extremists. Since Sutch holds that *each* newborn slave was worth 15 percent of the peak-age price of a female (1975b, 415–416), and given the highly competitive nature of slave agriculture, the pressure was pervasive (Sutch 1975a, 173–175). There is not only an intuitive plausibility to this argument; there also appears to be prima facie support for it in the upward secular movement of both the slave population and slave prices between 1810 and 1860. Even more impressive support for a link between economic and demographic variables emerges from the analysis of the relationship between rates of change in both slave prices and slave population. As is indicated in Figure 21.1, these variables are inversely related to each other. Goldin (1976) has shown this inverse relationship implies an aggregate elasticity of demand for slaves of about 0.1, which is significantly different from both 0 and 1. Her regressions on each of ten urban cities as well as her pooled cross-sectional and time-series regression produced estimates of an urban elasticity of demand for slaves in the neighborhood of 1 (cf. Table 21.6). Consequently, the inverse correlation between rates of change in population and prices is much more marked in the urban case than it is for the total population (see curve for Charleston in Figure 21.1).

Figure 21.1. A comparison of the rate of change in the slave population with the rate of change in slave prices.

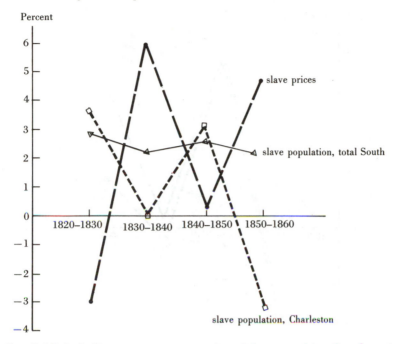

But Goldin's findings are more supportive of the proposition that the price of slaves responded to fluctuations in their supply rather than for the slave breeding hypothesis per se. The slave breeding hypothesis holds that masters increased slave fertility when prices rose. If that hypothesis is correct, one should expect a positive correlation between the rates of change in slave prices and population, rather than the negative correlation shown in Figure 21.1. Indeed, as Figure 21.2 shows, the rates of change in slave prices and fertility were, in fact, uncorrelated. It might be thought that absence of the expected correlation stems from a misspecification on Sutch's part. It could be argued that the policies of masters with respect to fertility were determined not by the prices of slaves alone, but by the relationship between the prices of slaves and the cost of breeding them—that is, by the profitability of slave breeding. Since the principal element of cost is the cost of the mother's time, the profitability of breeding, and hence fertility, should fluctuate with the price-to-

Table 21.6. Goldin's Estimates of Demand Elasticities for Slaves by Various Aggregates

Aggregates	Estimated Elasticity	Standard Error	Degrees of Freedom
All South (rural plus urban)	0.077	0.012	2
4 Old South Cities	0.607	0.214	14
2 New South Cities	0.072	0.550	6
4 Border State Cities	1.326	0.435	14

Sources: Goldin, (#7, in *TP*, Vol. I), Table 7.5 and equation 17.

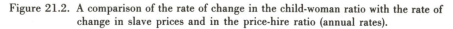

Figure 21.2. A comparison of the rate of change in the child-woman ratio with the rate of change in slave prices and in the price-hire ratio (annual rates).

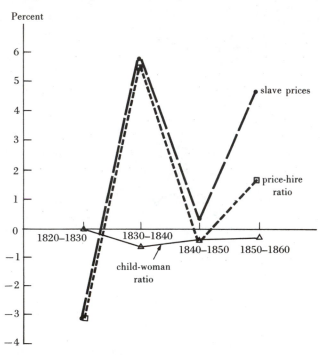

hire ratio. But as Figure 21.2 shows, the rate of change in fertility is also uncorrelated with the rate of change in the price-to-hire ratio.

The absence of a correlation between prices and fertility suggests that the inverse correlation between rates of change in prices and population was probably due to fluctuations in mortality. Since the development of time series on mortality rates in the antebellum South is still in an early stage, any conclusion on this issue must be treated as provisional. However, the currently available data on the fluctuations in the stature and mortality rates of both blacks and whites during the antebellum era is consistent with such a conclusion (see #19, #23, #24, in this volume; Fogel et al. 1978; Fogel and Engerman 1979; and the sources cited in these references). The similarity of the fluctuations in stature and mortality of both blacks and whites suggests that these fluctuations were inherent in the epidemiology of the antebellum South. If that is correct, then the inverse correlation between the rate of change in slave prices and population would be explained by fluctuations in mortality exogenous to the slave populations, to which the slave economic system responded with adjustments in price.

Despite the absence of support for the slave breeding hypothesis in the demographic data or in the relationship between the demographic data and slave prices, the appeal of the hypothesis remains. If the master was a rational, calculating capitalist, one would think that he should have been in the business of manipulating fertility. How can one explain the failure of such an individual to engage in slave breeding? To get at this question we have to confront the implicit premise on which the slave breeding hypothesis rests: that offspring were a major source of the income realized from an investment in slaves. The premise can be assessed by making use of equation 11.

$$P_{fk} = \sum_{t=k}^{n} \frac{R_t \lambda_t}{(1+r)^{t-k}} + B\Sigma \frac{\phi_t \lambda_t}{(1+r)^{t-k}} \tag{11}$$

where P_{fk} is the price of a female slave aged k, R_t is the net income derived from a female slave in year t through her work in the fields, λ_t is the probability that a slave will survive from year k to age t, B is the zero-age price of a slave, Φ_t is the probability of giving birth in the tth year of life for married women, r is the internal rate of return or discount rate, t is the subscript designating age, k is the age of the slave at the point of decision regarding fertility policy, and f is a subscript designating females. The first right-hand term of equation 11 is the value of the field work capacity of a female at age k, and for convenience we designate that term by V_c. The second right-hand term is the value of the childbearing capacity of a female at age k.

In equation 12 we consider the case of a female aged twenty, and for convenience, use the continuous rather than the discrete form for the value of the child-bearing capacity. Hence

$$P_{f20} - V_c = \phi_{20}B \int_0^{25} e^{-(\overset{*}{\lambda} + \overset{*}{\phi} + r)t}dt =$$

$$\frac{\phi_{20}B}{\overset{*}{\lambda} + \overset{*}{\phi} + r}[e^{-(\overset{*}{\lambda} + \overset{*}{\phi} + r)(0)} - e^{-(\overset{*}{\lambda} + \overset{*}{\phi} + r)(25)}] \tag{12}$$

where $\overset{*}{\lambda}$ = the rate of decline of λ and $\overset{*}{\Phi}$ = the rate of decline of ϕ. Substituting the values of the variables shown in Table 21.7 we obtain

$$P_{f20} - V_c = \frac{0.5B}{0.166}[e^{-(0.166)(0)} - e^{-(0.166)(25)}] = 2.965B \tag{13}$$

Since $B \approx 0.05P_{f20}$, it follows that the value of the childbearing capacity is $2.956B = 0.148P_{f20}$ or approximately 15 percent of the value of a woman at age twenty.[9] Since a twenty-year-old female slave was worth about \$620 in the Old South in 1850, about \$92 was due to her childbearing capacity and about \$528 due to her capacity as a field laborer.

We can pose the further question: When would it have paid a slave breeder to reduce the total fertility of a twenty-year-old female slave by delaying the age of first birth by one year?[10] If the birth of the first child was delayed by one year, the value of the childbearing capacity would decline from $0.148P_{f20}$ to

$$\frac{0.5B}{0.166}[e^{-(0.166)(1)} - e^{-(0.166)(25)}] = 0.125P_{f20} \tag{14}$$

Table 21.7. Estimates of Variables Used in Computing the Value of the Childbearing Capacity of a Female Slave at Age 20

Variable	Value	Sources and Notes
ϕ_{20}	0.5	Marital fertility rates in non-contraceptive societies during ages 20–24. Cf. Henripin (1954); Henry (1965); Smith (1977), Table 1; United Nations (1967), 24; Wrigley (1966), 116–123.
$\overset{*}{\phi}$	0.051	The average annual rate of decay in ϕ over ages 22.5–42.5. United Nations (1967), 24.
$\overset{*}{\lambda}$	0.015	The average annual rate of decline in $\ell\,(x)$ schedule between ages 20 and 45 in the Coale and Demeny model life table W6f.
r	0.10	The internal rate of return on an investment in male slaves over the period 1840–1860. Fogel and Engerman (1974a), 2:78.
P_{f20}	\$620	The approximate average price of a female at age 20 in the Old South about 1850. Fogel and Engerman (1974a), 1:76.
B/P_{f20}	0.05	The approximate ratio of the price of a zero-aged child to the price of a female at age twenty. Fogel and Engerman (1974a), 1:76. Sutch has disputed this figure, arguing that the correct ratio is 0.15. See note 9 of this paper for a discussion of the issue.

Consequently, the condition for a slave breeder to seek to delay a first birth by one year is

$$(0.148 - 0.125)P_{f20} < \alpha H_{f20} \tag{15}$$

or

$$\frac{P_{f20}}{H_{f20}} < 43.5\alpha \tag{16}$$

where α = the proportion of a year's work time in the fields that a female loses due to pregnancy and confinement and H_{f20} = the annual hire rate on a twenty-year-old female who will devote the full year to field work. Equation 16 is a threshold function for interfering with existing fertility patterns and it is plotted in Figure 21.3.[11] Each point in the unshaded area is a combination of values of P_f/H_f and α that might have been observed. The bounds of the unshaded area are determined by the attained values of P_f/H_f and have been drawn to reflect the observed range of variation of the price-hire ratio in the Old South during 1830–1860, which was between 9.03 and 6.37 (Evans 1962, 216). Masters who were on the threshold line at a given initial price-hire ratio and α would have had an incentive to alter the prevailing age at first birth unless either the price-hire ratio changed or if α changed. Masters not initially on the threshold line were out of equilibrium even at the initial price. They would have had an incentive to alter either age at first birth or α even if the price-hire ratio had not changed. It should be noted that optimal level of α is independent of the price-hire ratio, but depends only on the cost of reducing the level of α. Among the costs that are relevant here are deleterious effects on the health of the mother or child, and resistance to changes in accustomed confinement periods. Whatever the level of the price-hire ratio, masters should have sought the minimum α consistent with these costs.

Figure 21.3. Boundaries for manipulating age of first birth of slave mothers, if masters
closely followed the price-hire ratio. The boundaries of response are determined by the variation in the price-hire ratio. The boundaries shown here
reflect the range of variation of P/H for prime-aged males as computed from
Evans's data for the Old South between 1830 and 1860.

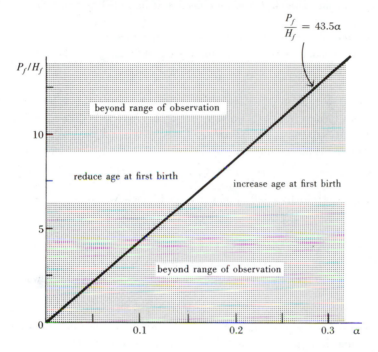

If α was close to its optimal level, the incentive to alter fertility would have
arisen principally from fluctuations in the price-hire ratio. Since this ratio varied
not only randomly but showed distinct trends over time, shouldn't one have observed trends in fertility that paralleled trends in the price-hire ratio? The answer
depends on how successful masters were in their attempts to manipulate fertility.
Such a correlation would appear if most masters were able to more or less adjust
fertility to conform to optimal conditions. But if most masters encountered considerable difficulty in attempts to manipulate fertility, they could have found themselves perpetually off the threshold line without ever achieving any substantial
movement toward it. The failure of fertility to respond to the price-hire ratio suggests that would-be slave breeders were either unsuccessful or exercised a limited
degree of influence over fertility, so that the effect of their manipulations were
protracted over periods of time that were longer than the duration of the cycle in the
price-hire ratio. In such a world the apparent absence of correlation between the
change in the price-hire ratio and in the child-woman ratio could be explained by a
combination of a weak correlation and an extremely complicated phasing of the
relationship between the change in P_f/H_f and in C/W.

Sutch (1975a, 173) argues that the economics of slavery compelled masters to
manipulate slave fertility and that abstention from such practices were "a luxury

only a few could afford." Just how expensive was this luxury? Consider a slave-owner in 1850 who was initially located on the threshold function, so that he had no incentive to reduce or increase the age of first birth. Suppose that there was a fall of 10 percent in the price of slaves without a corresponding decline in the annual hire rate. By how much would his income decline if he failed to delay the age of first birth by one year?

Since the slaveowner was initially on the threshold function, the loss in child income due to a one-year delay was initially equal to the gain in field income:

$$(0.148 - 0.125)P_{f20} = 0.023P_{f20} = \alpha H_{f20} \tag{17}$$

After the 10 percent drop in slave prices, a one-year delay in first birth would still increase his income from field work by αH_{f20}, but his loss in "child" income would be only $(0.023)(0.9)P_{f20} = 0.9\alpha H_{f20}$. Consequently, failure to reduce fertility would reduce his potential income by

$$\alpha H_{f20} - 0.9\alpha H_{f20} = 0.1\alpha H_{f20} \tag{18}$$

If the P_{f20} was initially \$620, from equation 17 we have

$$0.1\alpha H_{f20} = (0.1)(0.023)(\$620) = \$1.43 \tag{19}$$

as his gain from delaying the first birth of an eligible woman. If we assume that the planters could delay first births among all women who had not yet borne a child, the master's gain per slave of all ages and both sexes on his farm would be

$$(\$1.43)(0.0477) = \$0.068 \tag{20}$$

where 0.0477 is the proportion of all slaves (males plus females) on a farm with a representative age and sex distribution, who had not yet become pregnant but who would eventually have at least one live birth.[12] The profit that a master earned per slave on a farm that was representative with respect to age and sex distribution is equal to approximately \$42.[13] Consequently the percentage loss in profit from failing to delay first births by one year is approximately $(\$0.068)(100) \div \$42 = 0.16$ percent. If the master's rate of profit was originally 10 percent, failure to delay the age of the first birth by one year would reduce his rate of profit to 9.98 percent $(10 \times 0.998 = 9.98)$.[14]

This result is robust to alternative estimates of critical parameters. If, for example, we reduced the initial rate of profit from 10 to 8 percent, the failure to delay births by one year would still lead to the same percentage reduction in the profit rate (to two significant places). The same result would be obtained if Φ was reduced from 0.051 to 0.031. If we accepted Sutch's contention that the birthright was equal to 15 percent of the peak-age price,[15] the reduction in the profit rate would be 0.50 percent (from 10 to 9.95). If we considered the case of a 50 percent fall in the price-hire ratio, the reduction in the profit rate would be 0.8 percent (from 10 to 9.92). If we made all four changes simultaneously, the reduction in a master's profit rate from failing to delay births by one year would be 2.4 percent (from 8.00 to 7.81).

In other words, the profit to be gained or lost from manipulating the age of first birth to increase fertility is so small it gets lost in the error term. But to be lured even by that small increment to profit, the master would have to believe that he could precisely calculate the optimal fertility rate at time t with respect to a payoff that would not be realized until $t + 15$ or $t + 20$, since it was not until slaves reached age fifteen or over that they would be sold. He would also have to have enormous faith in the price-hire ratio at time t as a predictor of that ratio at time $t + 15$. And he would have to believe that the slaves just did not care how they were manipulated, that a woman who wanted to get married immediately would offer no resistance to a one-year delay in the date. If she or her mate became sullen and resentful, just a slow walk out to the field each morning would be enough to wipe out the master's gain from delaying the date of marriage.

NOTES

1. See *EM* #50, for a model for a two-product firm and an exploration of its implications. That paper shows that the ratio $C/(W + M)$ is irrelevant to the issue of efficiency in the production of children or the conventional product.
2. In the county regressions (rows 7 and 8 of Table 21.3), the sign on the quadratic term is negative but not statistically significant. Even if it were treated as statistically significant, the sign of the correlation would be positive for $0 < M/W < 54$, which covers the entire range of observation.
3. The influence of these variables is discussed by Steckel, #18, in this volume.
4. A linear or non-linear regression of $C/(W + M)$ on M/W could lead to a different sign than that obtained from similar regressions between C/W and M/W, merely because of a correlation between the error term and the independent variables due to a misspecification of the model. The reversal in sign to which Sutch alludes did not involve a misapplication of the ordinary least squares model, since it appears when the relevant variables are simply arrayed, as in Table 21.1.
5. Crawford has found that on plantations with one to fifteen slaves, at least 28 percent of the children were reared in households in which their fathers were owned by different masters than their mothers (*RF*, 147–153; *EM*, #51; Crawford 1980).
6. The bias is further exacerbated by Sutch's restriction of his sample to farms that had at least one slave woman aged fifteen to forty-four without a corresponding restriction on men.
7. The measure of "marital" fertility employed by Sutch here is different from the one he employed to demonstrate that females were at the biological limit of fertility. It is the ratio of children under fifteen to the number of *males* age fifteen or over, multiplied by the ratio of the number of females fifteen to forty-four to the equivalent prime-fertility years lived by women aged fifteen to forty-four. Sutch converted calendar years into equivalent prime-fertility years on the basis of the age-specific fertility schedule of the Cocos Island women, with the fertility rate at ages twenty to twenty-four set equal to 1 (cf. Sutch 1975a, 188–89, 193).
8. It might be thought that Sutch used the condition

$$1 - \sum_{x=0}^{k} \frac{n!}{x!\,(n-x)!} p^x (1-p)^{n-x} \leq 0.10 \text{ (for } n \geq 4)$$

to determine plantations with excessively high ratios of females to males, where n = the number of slaves aged fifteen to forty-four on a plantation, x = the number of females aged fifteen to forty-four on a plantation, and p = the proportion of all slaves in the South aged fifteen to forty-four who were female. Instead he computed the probability of each point in each distribution for $x > n - x$. Any point meeting this condition for which the probability was <0.1 was taken to be a "slave breeding" ratio. Of course the probability of a given point in a distribution of $x/(n-x)$ will diminish as n increases. If the distributions had been defined on a continuous scale, every point in the distributions would have had a probability of zero. For a discrete distribution in which $n = 65$, even $x(n - x) = 33/32$ has a probability < 0.1. That is why the sex ratios on Sutch's large slave farms are so close to 0.5. The imbalance in sex ratios comes from mainly his second condition and his use of males rather than females in the denominator of his fertility ratio.

9. The zero-age price of children cannot, of course, be observed. However, it was estimated by fitting a sixth degree polynomial, which indicated that the zero-age price was about 0.04 of the peak-age price of males, with a slightly higher ratio for females (cf. Fogel and Engerman 1974a, 1:72, 2:86).

Sutch (1975b, 415–416; Gutman and Sutch 1976a, 158–159) has disputed the result. Noticing that the fitted line fell slightly below what appeared to him as the average of the scatter of prices at ages 0.5, 1.5 and 2.5 (cf. Fogel and Engerman 1974a, 1:72, Fig. 16), he argued that if the line had been correctly fitted, the intercept would have been 0.15. But this conjecture is quite wrong. Various fits, including curves falling slightly above these three observations, yielded zero-age prices varying between 0.03 and 0.07 of the peak-age price. There is no reasonable fitting procedure that will yield Sutch's figure of 0.15. Rather than using a fitted line one could estimate the discounted-present value of the average relative prices at age 0.5 or 1.5, which were 0.06 and 0.10 respectively. If we extrapolate the last figure back to age 0, discounting for deaths (see *EM*, #23) between ages 0 and 1.5 as well as for the rate of return, the zero-age price is 0.05. This last figure is, of course, a bit too high since no allowance was made for maintenance costs between age 0 and age 1.5 (cf. *EM*, #49).

Sutch also argues that these early-age prices are biased downward because the appraisers must have based their estimates on the relatively few prices of children sold without mothers. "Since the absence of an infant's mother would greatly increase the risk of death, it would likely depress the value of the child" (Sutch 1975b, 415). Children sold separately were, of course, not the only basis for assessing the prices of infants and other young children. Since many women aged 20, 21, etc. were sold both with an infant child and without one, the market was constantly assessing the value of a child. It is possible to recover these values by running regressions on the prices of mothers sold with children, making the price a function of the ages of the mothers, with dummy variables for the prices of children at given ages. This procedure, applied both to probate records and the invoices of slave sales in New Orleans, yields price relatives quite similar to those indicated by appraisers. Sutch's conjecture that infants and young children sold separately had lower prices is also incorrect. The New Orleans data indicate that their prices were higher, probably because the transactions costs were a larger percentage of the final price for children sold separately than with their mothers. Sutch is correct in his belief that very few infants were sold separately. At New Orleans 99 percent of the sales at this age were with mothers (cf. Kotlikoff, #3, in *TP*, Vol. I; *EM*, #34).

10. "Slaveowners should have found it both good business *and* at least acceptable morality to encourage marriage at a young age. This would make available to women more time during their lives to bear children and thus increase the size of the completed family" (Gutman and Sutch 1976a, 139).

11. The argument that follows is based on an assumed fall in slave prices, but it is equally applicable to a rise in slave prices. If prices rise, the threshold function would give the condition for a planter to seek to advance age of first birth by one year. Equations 12–16 would then yield the loss to a planter who failed to advance age of first birth by one year.

12. Computed from the distribution of first births in Trussell and Steckel (#20, in this volume) and the distribution of the population in Coale and Demeny's W6f, for $R = 25.00$.

13. Computed from age-earnings profile and the age distribution of slaves in the Parker-Gallman sample (cf. Fogel and Engerman 1974a, 1:76, 2:80–83).

14. If, on "slave breeding" farms, the proportion of the population that was eligible for a delay of first birth was 0.0954, failure to delay first births would reduce the profit rate from 10 to 9.97.

15. Cf. note 8.

TWENTY-TWO

Factors in Mortality in the French Slave Trade in the Eighteenth Century*

Herbert S. Klein and Stanley L. Engerman

A s the history of the Atlantic slave trade is becoming better known, traditional historiography on the subject has been systematically reexamined. Not only have the estimates of the numbers shipped from Africa and of the relative role of the different trading nations been reinterpreted in the light of new quantitative evidence, but the questions of the magnitude and determination of slave mortality are first coming under serious scrutiny.[1] While it remains evident that slave mortality in the transoceanic crossing, the so-called middle passage, was quite high by the standards of sedentary populations, normally being at levels characteristic of epidemic periods in Europe, they were certainly below estimates frequently presented in the historical literature. These discussions often placed mortality at between one-fourth and one-half of the slaves shipped.[2] Moreover the rates of mortality of slaves in voyage were not markedly different from those of the crew on the vessels on which they were shipped, and were also comparable with the experience of troop and convict shipments from Europe in the same period.[3]

The usual arguments as to the cause of the rate of slave mortality put forward by contemporary critiques and subsequent historians of the trade, was that deliberate overcrowding and inhuman conditions aboard the slavers were the prime causes of this high mortality.[4] The classic example of the slave ship *Brookes*, a Liverpool-based slave ship of the 1780s and 1790s which is familiar for its diagrams of slave accommodations, is presented as an illustration of this overcrowding situation. But just as the mortality estimates have been revised on the basis of new quantitative data for the eighteenth and nineteenth centuries (with an average of 10–15 percent in the former century and less than 10 percent on all trades in the latter) these same data offer new insights into the question of the causal factors which influenced this rate of mortality. In addition to this apparent downward trend in slave mortality

*Reprinted, in translation and with revisions, with permission from *Annales, économies, sociétés, civilisations* 31 (1976):1213–1224.

over the course of the eighteenth and nineteenth centuries, it is also important to
recognize the extreme diversity in the experience of slave ships even in any one
year. In the attempt to understand the reasons for the decline in the mortality
among slaves shipped to America, analysis of the factors related to differentials in
slave mortality, such as length of voyage and degree of crowding, is useful. In
addition, such understanding is central to any study of the economics and demography of the slave trade.

In this short study our intention is to evaluate the role of several frequently
discussed factors in the determination of mortality on slave ships. Of particular
concern are measures of crowding (such as the number of slaves per ton), the
African sources of supply, and the carrying capacity of vessels, as well as the length
of time the slaves were involved in internal transit to African ports, the time
between arrival at port and ship's departure, and the length of the voyage from
Africa to the New World. Unfortunately in the materials used here, the data relating to those aspects of the time in transit between capture and arrival in the New
World are not available, although we are able to make some analysis of the effects
of voyage length based upon material used in another study.

The basic source for this study is a survey of the eighteenth-century Nantes
slave trade generated by Rinchon in both published and manuscript form.[5] This is a
listing of over 1,300 French slave ships which sailed from Nantes between 1697
and 1793 of which 794 have complete data for the period 1712–1777 available.[6]
While the Rinchon lists have come under criticism in recent years from French
scholars and do have errors and deficiencies, they are nevertheless the best available data on this vital trade and they represent the most complete sample from the
eighteenth-century French slave trade.[7] While it is probable that current research
will lead to a great expansion of the number and quality of available data, we
believe that the general trends indicated in the present materials will prove to be
valid for all subsequent additions to the Nantes listings of Rinchon. The French
data are unique among the presently available statistics for the Atlantic slave trade
in several respects. They present complete data for these ships, not only on the data
of sailings from France, the ship's tonnage, the number of slaves carried, and
African port of exit, but also important information on the mortality experience of
the slaves in the transatlantic crossing and on the mortality patterns of the crew.
The following analysis will use these data to examine some of the determinants and
correlates of the mortality of slaves.

As is evident from Figure 22.1, the annual average mortality experience per
slave ship which departed from Nantes for the period between 1712 and 1777
shows both the sharp year to year fluctuations in slave mortality as well as the mild
downward trend in the rate of mortality over the century.[8] This long-term reduction
was not due to shifts in African ports of departure or to marked variation in ship's
tonnage or carrying rates. A similar decline characterized the mortality experience
of the crews, and the determinants of these declining rates remains an issue for
further examination.[9] Looking at the distribution of mortality by ships (Figure
22.2), indicates both the wide range of experience over the trade as well as the

occurrence, although infrequent, of the very high mortality which as been pointed to in the literature. It is not that no ships experienced high mortality, but rather that this was not typical of the middle passage. Note also that the median mortality rate of about 10 percent was below the mean experience.

In trying to analyze the determinants of this mortality pattern, we used an index of overcrowding, the number of slaves shipped per ton of vessel. It was anticipated, given the debates on so-called tight packing, that mortality would be highest where the number of slaves per ton was greatest. As seen in Table 22.1, such a pattern did not occur. Rather the mortality rate seemed to be independent of the number

Figure 22.1. Average annual slave mortality, by ships, 1712–1777.

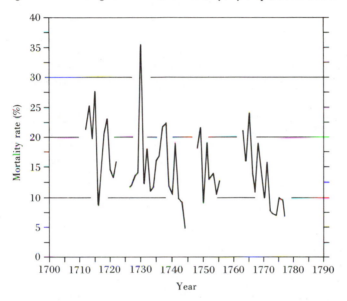

Figure 22.2. Distribution of slave mortality rates, by number of ships.

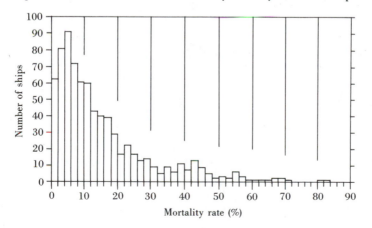

Table 22.1. Average Slave Mortality per Ship, by Slaves per Ton per Ship

Range of Slaves per Ton	Average Mortality (percent)	Number of Ships
Less Than 0.88	19.2	16
0.88–1.389	15.1	70
1.39–1.639	16.8	51
1.64–1.889	13.3	98
1.89–2.139	15.7	120
2.14–2.389	15.1	117
2.39–2.639	12.6	98
2.64–2.889	13.6	83
2.89–3.139	17.4	45
3.14–3.389	17.0	38
Above 3.39	15.6	27
Total	14.9	763

shipped per ton.[10] Of course, in general, slave ships carried more individuals per ton than did other vessels. But within the range carried, the degree of crowding did not seem to affect mortality.

There is, however, some difficulty in the relationship between the measured slaves per ton and the degree of crowding suggested by the material in Table 22.2. For it seems that the numbers of slaves per ton was highest on vessels of 100–149 tons, falling quite markedly on ships of greater tonnage. As shown by Table 22.3

Table 22.2. Average Slaves per Ton per Ship, by Ship's Tonnage

Tonnage	Average Slaves per Ton	Number of Ships
Less Than 100	2.36	173
100–149	2.43	157
150–199	2.31	180
200–249	2.11	128
250–299	1.84	75
300–349	1.50	29
Above 350	1.30	21
Total	2.21	763

Table 22.3. Average Slave Mortality per Ship, by Ship's Tonnage

Tonnage	Average Mortality (percent)	Number of Ships
Less Than 100	14.5	173
100–149	13.7	157
150–199	17.2	180
200–249	13.7	128
250–299	14.6	75
300–349	18.6	29
Above 350	12.1	21
Total	14.9	763

these smaller vessels had high mortality experience.[11] The reason for the negative relationship between slaves per ton and tonnage is not clear: The British slave-tonnage regulation law of 1788, which assigned specified slave per ton ratios, permitted a higher ratio of slaves per ton for smaller vessels.[12] Given this relationship, the most appropriate test of the crowding argument and its impact on slave mortality could be to examine the relationship within a given tonnage group, between the number of slaves per ton and mortality rate. This comparison is shown in Table 22.4, which indicates that the extent of crowding on ships of a given size did not appear to affect the mortality. Thus the best indication at present is that, within the range observed, the degree of crowding, in itself, did not significantly affect mortality. Most ships fell within the range of 1.39–2.88 slaves carried per ton, a range which includes the maximum allowed by both English and Portuguese regulations.[13] The relatively narrow range, and the limited effect upon mortality, suggests that economic considerations may have been the important determinant of the degree of crowding, considerations which no doubt were then reflected in the codes regulating the trade.[14]

Regression analysis based on the 763 ships similarly points to this interpretation. The correlations are poor, neither tonnage nor slaves per ton by themselves accounting for even 1 percent of the variation in mortality rates. Moreover, as shown by the following multiple regression, where M is mortality rate, T is tonnage, and SPT slaves per ton, both together still fail to account for 1 percent of the variation (standard errors in parentheses)

$$M = 16.25 - 0.0024T - 0.4253SPT$$
$$ (0.0071) \quad (0.8060)$$

where R-square $= 0.0039$. The explanatory power of the regression is increased somewhat (to R-square $= 0.0086$) when allowance is made for differences in port of departure. Ships from West Africa, other things being equal, have a mortality rate about 3 percentage points above that of ships departing from Angola.

It is important to note, also, as shown in Table 22.5, that the ships with high slave mortality were also ships with the heaviest mortality of the crew.[15] The data indicate also that overall mortality of the crew exceeded that of the slaves. At present it is difficult to separate out where the crew deaths did occur on the full voyage, whether prior to arrival in in Africa, during the period of purchase of slaves while on the African coast, or on the voyage itself. But the positive relationship between slave mortality during voyage and crew mortality suggests the possible importance of similar factors in mortality.[16] Apparently, the determinants of slave mortality, as affected by disease and by provisioning, had a similar impact upon the sailors in the crew as well.[17] As noted above, one of the important aspects of the middle passage was not available in the Nantes data, and that is the length of time at sea. It is to be expected that this would have an important effect on mortality. In the simplest case, of course, the longer the voyage the greater the period of risk and the higher the number of deaths expected. However, there are more important aspects to the relationship between mortality and voyage length. Given the finite

Table 22.4. Average Slave Mortality per Ship, by Tonnage and Slaves per Ton (number of ships in parentheses)

Ship's Tonnage	Slaves Per Ton											Totals
	< 0.88	0.89–1.38	1.39–1.63	1.64–1.88	1.89–2.13	2.14–2.38	2.39–2.63	2.64–2.88	2.89–3.13	3.14–3.38	3.39 >	
1–99	26.1 (4)	13.6 (14)	23.2 (11)	14.5 (16)	11.2 (17)	14.6 (25)	8.8 (26)	9.9 (22)	22.5 (16)	14.7 (11)	20.9 (11)	14.5 (173)
100–149	1.4 (1)	15.6 (10)	17.0 (7)	17.9 (14)	17.4 (19)	12.5 (29)	12.4 (18)	10.0 (19)	10.6 (15)	16.2 (12)	12.1 (13)	13.7 (157)
150–199	26.3 (3)	9.2 (12)	20.0 (9)	17.8 (13)	18.4 (26)	15.3 (31)	17.1 (27)	18.5 (32)	19.3 (12)	19.0 (13)	6.2 (2)	17.2 (180)
200–249	11.3 (1)	22.4 (6)	14.0 (6)	8.0 (20)	13.2 (41)	16.1 (23)	12.9 (20)	13.0 (6)	15.2 (2)	21.0 (2)	44.1 (1)	13.7 (128)
250–299	35.8 (2)	10.9 (10)	9.7 (8)	11.2 (23)	21.3 (13)	21.2 (9)	10.1 (6)	11.9 (4)	—	—	—	14.6 (75)
300–349	38.3 (1)	22.2 (11)	13.4 (7)	17.3 (6)	18.4 (3)	—	2.9 (1)	—	—	—	—	18.6 (29)
350–399	5.1 (2)	13.6 (1)	21.5 (2)	10.3 (2)	13.6 (1)	—	—	—	—	—	—	12.6 (8)
400–449	0.3 (1)	15.7 (3)	1.7 (1)	11.6 (4)	—	—	—	—	—	—	—	10.6 (9)
450 and Over	1.3 (1)	18.4 (3)	—	—	—	—	—	—	—	—	—	14.1 (4)
Totals	19.2 (16)	15.1 (70)	16.8 (51)	13.3 (98)	15.7 (120)	15.1 (117)	12.6 (98)	13.6 (83)	17.4 (45)	17.0 (38)	15.6 (27)	14.8 (763)

Table 22.5. Average Crew Mortality per Ship, by Slave Mortality per Ship

Range of Slave Mortality (Percent)	Average Crew Mortality (Percent)	Number of Ships
0.1–1.99	13.3	47
2.0–3.99	11.7	55
4.0–5.99	13.7	51
6.0–7.99	16.7	39
8.0–9.99	18.0	42
10.0–11.99	19.6	28
12.0–13.99	17.4	24
14.0–15.99	20.8	19
16.0–19.99	19.3	32
20.0–29.99	26.8	49
30.0–39.99	19.9	22
40.0–49.99	28.9	19
Greater Than 50.0	32.5	12
Total	18.3	439

capacity of ships, there would be limitations upon the amount of provisions of food and water to be carried. The longer the time at sea, therefore, the more likely that shortage of provisions might occur. Similarly, given the possibilities for spoilage of water and food, as well as the incubation period for diseases, the longer the voyage the greater would be the expected death rate. Materials collected for the Brazilian and Portuguese slave trade to Brazil in the nineteenth century do provide some clue as to the effect of voyage length on slave mortality. A study of 386 ships delivering slaves to Brazil in the period 1825–1830, discussed in greater detail elsewhere (Klein and Engerman 1975), provides data which permit this examination. As can be seen from the following regression, slave mortality rates were positively correlated with time at sea. Where M is the mortality rate of slaves and D is the number of days at sea, the regression shows that:

$$M = -4.7 + 0.28D$$
$$(0.02)$$

where R-square $= 0.330$. Thus about 33 percent of the variance of mortality is explained by the length of the voyage, with the explanatory power of the regression increased somewhat (by 3 percentage points) when the African port of exit is considered. All other things being equal, this result suggests that for every day at sea there was an increase of about one slave death aboard the vessel. There is also a reasonably significant difference shown between the various African ports. For example, there was a spread of 2.9 percentage points per sailing between the Congo and the other major West African ports (3.3 percent to 6.2 percent). It is unclear whether this was due to conditions at the given ports which affected health conditions, whether it is to be accounted for by the interior distance traveled by the slaves to reach the port, or whether various ports obtained their slaves from different disease areas, which meant that slaves were moving into new disease environments, creating more hazardous health conditions. Moreover, as seen in Table 22.6, the relationship between time at sea and mortality rates was heavily influenced by the difference between expected sailing time and actual voyage time. For shipments from Congo and Angola, where average sailing time was thirty-three days, a marked increase in mortality is seen in ships sailing over fifty days, whereas for Mozambique departures, where sailing time averaged sixty-one days, a sharp increase occurred for voyages of over seventy days. These patterns indicate the great importance of unexpectedly long sailing times on mortality, suggesting the role of provisioning rules and practices in explaining mortality. It should be noted that the Portuguese death rates of 1825–1830 are considerably below those of eighteenth-century Nantes slavers, a continuation of the declining trend noted in all slave trades in the late eighteenth and early nineteenth centuries.[18] Nevertheless it would be expected that those factors which influenced the relationship between mortality and sailing time would also have held in the earlier period.

The preceding analysis has cast doubt on the overcrowding argument as used to explain high slave mortality in the middle passage. As noted earlier, the slave ships did carry more people than did other vessels, but within the observed range of variation, there seemed no relationship between slaves carried per ton and mortality. The reasons for the relatively limited variation in slaves carried per ton might be explained by economic considerations, which precluded the desirability of excessive crowding which might have led to substantial increases in mortality. In that case, where excessive crowding led to higher mortality, economic profits might be less than would be observed if ships had a more limited number of slaves and a lower mortality experience. Thus to show that within a range there was no effect of crowding upon mortality, does not necessarily mean both that there were no economic limits on the number of slaves carried, or that there was an obvious correlation between profitability and crowding.

Another possible constraint on slaves carried is suggested by the importance of the effect of sailing time on mortality. For, based on expected voyage length, the magnitude of provisions desired would absorb a substantial part of the carrying capacity of the ship. Given that certain minimal daily needs of food and water were required to maintain slave health and to reduce susceptibility to disease, there were clearly demands for space for this purpose. For example, both French and British contemporary commentators suggest that the minimum water requirements for slaves was 3 pints per day. This meant that a minimum requirement for a fifty-day voyage of a slave ship carrying 300 slaves would have been 5,625 gallons. Yet this was a bare minimum, for water spoilage was a constant threat, and it was common to take double the amount needed. Thus the oft-cited slave ship *Brookes* carried 34,000 gallons of water for its 600 slaves and forty-five sailors for a trip lasting forty-nine days. This doubling of the minimum requirement seems to have been the norm, as seen in several other ships described by the British officials in the 1780s. The *Brookes* also carried some 7 tons of yams, 20 tons of rice and dried beans, 2 tons of bread and other assorted foodstuffs.[19] If Rinchon's calculations of the space required for provisions in the hold of the *Brookes* are accepted as accurate, then it

Table 22.6. Relationship between Rates of Mortality on Ships Bound for Brazil and Length of Voyages Undertaken between 1825 and 1830

Length of Voyage in Days	Number of Ships Originating in			Rates of Mortality (%)			Total	
	Congo	Angola	Mozambique	Congo	Angola	Mozambique	Ships	Mortality (%)
20–29	34	51	—	2.9	4.7	—	85	4.0
30–39	65	107	—	3.2	6.3	—	172	5.2
40–49	14	21	12	3.1	6.2	6.4	47	5.3
50–59	2	4	30	8.6	14.5	8.3	36	9.1
60–69	2	1	20	11.1	21.5	10.3	23	10.9
70–79	—	—	15	—	—	20.1	15	20.1
80–89	—	—	7	—	—	23.1	7	23.1
More than 90	—	—	1	—	—	34.9	1	34.9

Source: Klein and Engerman (1975), 381–398.

appears that provisions and spare sails and maintenance equipment for the ship occupied as much space as the slaves.[20] Thus any increase in the number of the slaves put aboard would be at the expense of provisioning and storage space. The constraint here, it should be noted, was on space, and not on costs. For the bulk of the foodstuffs consumed by the Africans in the crossing were purchased on the African coast, with rice and yams serving as staples in the diet. The costs for these foods and for the water, represented less than 5 percent of the total costs of outfitting the vessels and therefore offered little financial restraint on adding extra food.[21]

In analyzing the cause of death in both the eighteenth-century French and British trades, it is evident that the primary killer was dysentery, then yellow fever and other unexplained "fevers," followed by communicable diseases such as measles and smallpox.[22] Given the relationship between food consumption and health conditions and the importance of amebic dysentery as a cause of slave deaths, then problems of sanitation and the maintenance of clean food and water were central to the reduction of mortality at sea. The importance of provisioning rules based upon expected sailing time is seen by the varying patterns shown by the different African ports of exit. For example, if the rate of spoilage of water was simply based upon time at sea then all slave vessels should have suffered correspondingly similar rates of mortality after a common length of time at sea. But as we have seen in Table 22.6, this was not the case. Equally, it is difficult to immediately comprehend the relationship between food spoilage and the increasing incidence of slave mortality. What does appear certain, is that long voyages usually ended with both slaves and crew going on reduced rations, with subsequent increases in scurvy and related diseases. This would seem to support the idea that similar rules of provisioning operated in all trades, with captains provisioning for expected sailing times, plus some allowance for the possibility of longer voyages. But beyond some allowance for increased time at sea, provisioning would absorb too much space, and it was when this allowed time was exceeded that the increasing risk of spoilage and unhealthy sanitary conditions meant sharply increased death rates for the slaves and the crew. It should be stressed that, occasionally, the sudden appearance of communicable disease distorted this problem. But of these diseases, the only one which seems to have been extremely difficult to control and which resulted in high deaths when developed was measles.[23] The incidence of smallpox should have been declining over the period since French and British captains were already routinely inoculating their slaves by the second half of the eighteenth century.

The analyses we have attempted in this paper have been a test of the thesis of overcrowding and its relationship to slave mortality. We have argued from the Rinchon compilations that the number of slaves per ton did not significantly influence the rate of slave mortality. This does not mean that extraordinary overcrowding would not lead to large-scale deaths, but that the pattern of housing slaves aboard ship did not lead to the occurrence of such densities at which such a correlation between overcrowding and mortality could have occurred. From the parallel analysis of the Portuguese data we have pointed out that time at sea was more systematically related to slave mortality than the other variables which we have examined. We are currently in the process of developing a similar data set for the British slave trade in the 1790s for which all the relevant variables can be gathered together for one trade. Also it is hoped that our analysis can be more fully tested as the relevant information on tonnage, time at sea, and the nature of slave deaths emerge from the manuscript materials in the relevant French archives.

NOTES

1. See for this new material Curtin's original (1969) and up-dated articles (1975). On the new evidence of mortality, aside from the chapter on this subject in Curtin, see Klein (1969); Klein and Engerman (1975); Green-Pedersen (1973); and Anstey (1975), 414–415.

2. For a survey of this traditional literature, see Klein (1969), 533–534.

3. British troops sent from England to the West Indies in the late eighteenth century suffered a mortality of 11 percent in the crossing for some twelve ships which on average carried 703 troops per vessel from England (United Kingdom, House of Lords 1792). On convict and other mortality see Klein and Engerman (1975).

4. The most systematic presentation of this argument is contained in Mannix and Cowley (1962), 105–106.

5. The published lists of Nantes slave ships from 1748 to 1792 are found in Rinchon (1938), 1:248–301. We are indebted to Professor Philip Curtin for the use of his codebook and punched data set of these materials. The unpublished collection of recordings of Nantes slave ships which Rinchon made for the period 1697–1747 are to be found in *Le Centre de recherches sur l'histoire de la France Atlantique* (Nantes), Fonds Rinchon, Boîtes 10 à 12. These materials were made available to us in xerox form by Robert Stein of York University in Toronto.

6. The Rinchon manuscript listing contains some 400 voyages from which 45 were eliminated either because of incomplete recordings or because the figures gave zero mortality rates. The printed list starts in 1748 and contains 910 ships, of which only 428 were retained for the same reasons. Finally in dealing with crew mortality there is a further reduction because of the frequent lack of such data. Within the period 1711–1777 there are years in which no sailings whatsoever were reported. While slave mortality data are available for a few years in the late 1780s and 1790s, we have decided not to include these data. Although an extremely active trade existed after 1784, with the annual number of ships being higher between 1785 and 1792 than before (see Meyer 1960), changes in legislation on colonial shipping in 1785 create problems with the tonnage data. It has been argued that this new legislation possibly brought new types of ship into the slave trade (see Everaert 1963, 54–55).

7. The late Professor Jean Mettas in a personal communication (October 7, 1974) argued that Rinchon made errors of judgment on identifying African ports and seriously overestimated the Senegambia ports and underestimated the Guinean ones. We have therefore combined these two zones into one large West Africa category. He also stated that Rinchon made many simple arithmetic errors, which do appear in the printed, though not the manuscript, recordings. Until his recent and untimely death, Professor Mettas was engaged in a major reanalysis of the French Atlantic slave trade and had begun to explore the trade of other ports besides Nantes (see his 1973 paper). At the same time Professor Serge Daget has been generating a major new data set on the nineteenth-century slave trade of France (see Daget 1971, 1973).

8. The particularly high mortality suffered by slaves in the year 1730 was largely due to the fact that four of the twelve ships had death rates of 60 percent and above.

9. Average crew mortality on 439 ships which had data for both the crew and slave mortality was 18.3 percent. When the large sample of ships which had crew mortality data (with or without slave mortality information) was analyzed, the crew mortality was slightly lower than this figure, but still higher than the slave mortality rate.

10. The simple correlation between slaves per ton and slave mortality is −0.0158.
11. The correlation of slaves per ton with tonnage is −0.3767; and of slave mortality with tonnage is −0.0052.
12. See United Kingdom, House of Lords (1788).
13. *Ibid.* For the Portuguese data which varied from between two to three slaves per ton depending on construction, see Klein (1972), 902, n. 12.
14. While it is correct that the expected mortality experience in transit would affect the prices paid for slaves in Africa, after purchase it was economically desirable for captains to achieve a low mortality rate. Thus, as discussed below, excessive crowding would not have been a profitable arrangement.
15. The correlation is 0.3769.
16. The regression is

$$\text{Crew Mort} = 13.18 + 0.3718M$$
$$(0.0437)$$

where R-square = 0.1421. Strictly interpreted this is consistent with about 70 percent of the mortality of the crew occurring at times other than the middle passage, and about 30 percent during the middle passage. Unfortunately, in the Rinchon compilation the time of crew deaths is not indicated.
17. A limited sample from British surgeons reports in the 1790s indicates that except for occupational injuries, sailors tended to suffer from many of the same diseases as slaves. See United Kingdom, House of Lords (1799).
18. The cause for this decline is difficult to isolate. There was, for example, improvement in ships' speed with the introduction of copper sheathing, which was more rapidly introduced into the British slave trade than any other naval trades (see Rees 1971). There was also the systematic introduction by the 1760s and 1770s in all trades of inoculation against smallpox. See for example Rinchon (1964), 188, which shows Van Alstein innoculating slaves by the 1760s. The slave captain William Sherwood also reported innoculating slaves on a voyage in 1777 (see United Kingdom 1790, 495). At this point it is difficult to assess what effect the various factors had on overall slave mortality decline.
19. United Kingdom (1788), 1–3.
20. See Rinchon's (1964), 44–45, diagrammatic presentation and calculations.
21. The Nantes slave ship *Reine de France*, of 150 tons and a forty-seven–man crew, transported 404 slaves from Guinea to St. Domingue in 1744. For this trip it purchased on the African coast 13,000 pounds of fresh foods including rice, chickens, and goats, for the approximate cost in trading goods of 2,500 livres. This represented the approximate purchase cost of nine slaves in Africa. This same 2,500 livres figure represented under 2 percent of the total value of goods carried by the *Reine* from France to purchase slaves and ivory on the coast (Rinchon 1964, 84–85).
22. The few published ships' logs constantly cite the "flux," or dysentery, as the single greatest malady suffered. In calculating the cause of death of the slaves shipped by Captain John Newton from Sierra Leone to Antigua in 1751–1752, seventeen of twenty-four deaths were listed as due to the "flux," with two more listed as "fever and flux." Some of the flux deaths occurred several weeks after initial contagion, while the bouts of dysentery seemed to come in cycles (Martin and Spurrell 1962, 29ff; also see Falconbridge 1788, 25). The captain of the French slave ship *L'Economie* reported that the majority of slaves who were buried at sea were killed by dysentery.
23. See for example United Kingdom (1790), 493–494.

PART FIVE

MATERIAL ASPECTS OF SLAVE LIFE

Introduction

The evaluation of the material aspects of slave life is an issue that formed an important part of the abolitionist attack on slavery as well as the proslavery defense in the antebellum period. And, as with other issues in the papers included in this volume, the discussion of material aspects has continued to be a source of controversy among scholars concerned with the slave experience. The impact that the gains to the planter from reducing costs and increasing revenues could have had on slave diet and working conditions, and the development of a structure of incentives for slaves that included some positive rewards as well as the negative punishments permissible only under slavery, were central features in determining the conditions of slave life, and they greatly influenced patterns of slave production and reproduction. Some of the topics discussed in Part IV relate to the material aspects of slave life, and those in Part V go beyond demographic concerns to deal with the frequently debated issues of slave diet, work routines, health, and rewards and punishments. All have implications for understanding both the conditions under which slaves lived their own lives and the beliefs and behavior of the southern planter class.

Some of the articles in Part V are by researchers who apply economic and theoretical analyses to data collected by colleagues and others are by researchers whose studies are based on new data collected from plantation records, shipping manifests, military records, and the post–Civil War amnesty request forms of white Southerners. In addition to these sources, an important body of interviews with ex-slaves collected by the Works Progress Administration (WPA) in the 1930s has been utilized, which describes the ex-slaves' perceptions of the operations of plantations, of planter behavior, of material treatment, of the systems of punishment and reward in the antebellum period, and of their own lives. This source, unique to the United States, provides the slaves with a voice in the description of many aspects of southern life.

Richard H. Steckel, utilizing primarily plantation records and coastal shipping manifests, examines the patterns of physical growth and achieved heights of the slave population, as well as their mortality experience. These are important indications of how the slaves were fed and worked as well as how diet and work influenced slaves' health and physical development. With Robert A. Margo, Steckel utilizes a number of different sources that provide data on height by age for southern whites to provide comparisons of physical development with that of the black slave population and to place the relative material treatment of slaves, particularly in regard to health and nutrition, within a broader perspective. In the first of his two papers, Charles Kahn applies a linear-programming approach to the estimated food requirements of the slaves to obtain an estimate of the least-cost diet to compare with the costs of the slave diets presented previously by Fogel and Engerman and by Richard Sutch. His intent is both to examine the nature of the planter response to differing relative prices and to determine if the planters did reduce the diet of slaves to a sheer subsistence level. Stephen C. Crawford uses the ex-slaves' discussions of punishments and rewards in the WPA narratives to analyze their perceptions of this aspect of the slave experience and of the various features of plantation life that influenced the nature and frequency of the punishment of slaves. These ex-slave descriptions provide an essential understanding of day-to-day life on the plantation, of the master-slave interaction, and the nature of the slave adjustment to and influence on their conditions of life. In his second paper, Kahn builds on the analysis in the paper by Crawford. He draws on recent economic theory concerning the behavior of principals and agents to examine the choices made by planters in determining the system of rewards and punishments on the plantation, using descriptive information drawn from the testimony of ex-slaves.

TWENTY-THREE

Work, Disease, and Diet in the Health and Mortality of American Slaves

Richard H. Steckel

The economic and demographic analysis of slavery has been a prolific and re-warding field of historical research in recent decades. Progress has been made on the profitability, viability, and efficiency of slavery, and new findings have emerged on the flows and losses in the Atlantic slave trade, on the levels and determinants of fertility and mortality, and on related areas of the slave family, slave culture, and the political movement to abolish the institution. New methods of analyzing tradi-tional sources, and especially newly exploited data sources, have contributed to the vigor of the field. Much work has been cast in comparative terms, with other populations in the Western Hemisphere and the free population serving as back-drops for study of American slavery.

The issue of health arose during the antebellum era when abolitionists charged that slaves were neglected and abused while proslavery writers maintained that owners took good care of their chattel. The issues of the antebellum debate have endured during the twentieth century, however, because little persuasive evidence for either side was uncovered during the nineteenth century. Such evidence is important for appraising the harshness of slavery and for understanding the condi-tion of blacks upon emancipation and therefore the course of postwar economic and social development.

This paper discusses recent findings on levels and causes of slave mortality, the most notable development being the perception that infants and children had ex-traordinarily poor health.[1] Recognizing that many deaths would have occurred because medical technology was primitive during the antebellum era, the question of levels is formulated in terms of the excess mortality of slaves. Table 23.1 shows that most of the excess losses were concentrated before age five. Notably, the slave infant mortality rate was about 17 percentage points above the rate for the entire antebellum population of the United States.

Carelessness, neglect, and infanticide have been recurrent themes in the litera-ture on the causes of infant mortality. More recently prenatal care and sudden

Table 23.1. Mortality Rates Per Thousand for Slaves and the Antebellum Population

Age	Slaves	Entire United States
0	350	179
1–4	201	93
5–9	54	28
10–14	37	19
15–19	35	28
20–24	30	39

Sources: Age zero, slaves, Steckel (1986c), n. 5, 17; slaves aged one and above, Steckel (#18, in this volume), 397; United States, Haines and Avery (1980), 88; average of Model West and logit tables.

infant death syndrome; environmental variables such as main crop, region, and time period; and diet, climate, work, the disease environment, and adaptations to African conditions have been linked with slave health (see, for example, Fogel and Engerman 1974a; Sutch 1975a, 1976; Savitt 1978; Kiple and Kiple 1977a; Steckel 1979, #18, in this volume, 1986a, 1986b, 1986c; Kiple and King 1981; Campbell 1984). This paper examines mortality data from plantation records and height data from slave manifests to appraise these possible explanatory factors.

The discussion of health and mortality is arranged by age. Infant mortality is divided into neonatal (birth to one month) and postneonatal (second month to one year) components on the grounds that circumstances during pregnancy primarily determined stillbirths and other losses soon after birth whereas later infant deaths often had diverse causes associated with breast-feeding practices, diet, and other aspects of infant care. Although the period from age one to maturity is discussed as a unit, the years from late childhood to early adolescence were a crucial watershed in slave health.

This paper shows that patterns of disease and diet, and especially work, expressed by season of the year and by main crop were important influences on newborn health. Attenuated breast-feeding practices and a poor diet aggravated the health of older infants. Important improvements in health began to occur around age ten when slaves entered the labor force and received a better diet. Adverse conditions of the 1820s and 1830s and early childbearing also contributed to excess mortality.

DATA SOURCES

Plantation owners maintained a variety of business records, including planting and harvesting accounts, financial ledgers, inventories of slaves and equipment, food and clothing allotments, and lists of births and deaths. An extensive search of southern archives identified over thirty birth lists for which the deaths were frequently recorded. Of these, eleven large plantations had substantially complete death lists as characterized by regular chronological entries and the absence of "X" or "dead" notations. The recorded infant mortality rates on these units were plausible and ranged from 176 to 392 per thousand live births. However, the shares of neonatal deaths among all infant deaths were implausibly low on some units, which suggests that some early deaths and the corresponding births were not recorded. The plantations ranged in size from 65 to 230 slaves; collectively they grew cotton, rice, and sugar; and operated in South Carolina, Georgia, Alabama, and Louisiana from the 1780s to the early 1860s (additional discussion of these records is available in Steckel #18, in this volume, 1985).

Heights are relevant for the study of health because growth and illness or mortality are opposite sides of the same coin; infections retard growth and children whose growth is retarded tend to have higher mortality rates.[2] Stature is a measure of net nutrition (or nutritional status), which is determined by actual diet minus claims on the diet made by physical activity, disease, and maintenance. Slaves were measured as a by-product of legislation designed to prevent smuggling after the Atlantic slave trade was outlawed beginning in 1808. The coastwise trade in the United States continued as a monitored activity in which ship captains recorded heights, ages, and other characteristics on manifests as part of an identification scheme designed to prove that slaves entering American ports originated within the country (Wesley 1942). The data for this study (National Archives, Record Group 36) consist of 10,562 manifests and 50,606 slaves originating largely from Atlantic coast ports and transported primarily from 1820 to 1860 (see Steckel 1986c).

DEATHS BEFORE THE END OF THE FIRST MONTH

There is a high positive correlation between birth weights and heights in early childhood among poor populations in developing countries. This evidence and information on the health and prenatal condition of slave women suggest that very low birth weights were a major cause of high mortality rates of slaves in early infancy. Specifically, the majority of slave newborns probably weighed less than 2,500 g, or 5.5 pounds and neonatal mortality rates were at least 150 and possibly as high as 250 per thousand (Steckel 1986a).[3] Moreover, the share of stillbirths among all births may have been in the range of 10 to 15 percent.

Studies of fetal development and birth weights show that the following factors are systematically associated with stillbirths and neonatal deaths: general malnutrition of the mother; specific dietary deficiencies of the mother; maternal and fetal infections; work during pregnancy, especially effort that requires standing; ingestion of toxic substances such as alcohol and tobacco; small stature of the mother; and possibly genetic factors.[4] Although information is lacking to incorporate maternal height, toxic substances, and genetic factors into an analysis of mortality data in plantation records, a tentative appraisal of relative importance suggests that the first four factors on the list, and especially work, disease, and diet, were major contributors (Steckel 1986a).

The probability of early death was investigated using a logit regression model in which mother's age, plantation size, year of birth, and month of birth were independent variables (Steckel 1986c). Seasonal rhythms varied by main crop and the only crop type that had enough observations for seasonal analysis was cotton (five farms). As a way of appraising the importance of the underreporting of mortality, those farms on which the recorded share of neonatal deaths among all infant deaths was at least 30 percent (three farms) were also analyzed separately. The most striking finding is shown in Table 23.2.[5] Although noticeable differences existed in particular months depending on the data base, the overall results show a concentration of early deaths in February to April and a second smaller concentration in September to November. The average probability per month in February to April and September to November was 280–390 percent higher (depending on the data source) than the average probability in other months. These results suggest that an important share of the excess infant mortality might be explained by seasonal rhythms.

Seasonal patterns of health related to weather, work, and diet have been documented for agricultural populations in developing countries (Hytten and Leitch 1971, 452–454), and it is reasonable to investigate the possible role of these factors for slaves. Studies of fetal growth under unfavorable conditions show that the outcome of pregnancy depends upon the extent, timing, and duration of deprivation (National Research Council 1970; Stein et al. 1975, Chs. 10, 12; esp. Moore 1983, 247–251). Specifically, rates of neonatal mortality, and particularly stillbirths, were highest among pregnancies conceived in famine or exposed to famine during the first trimester only. Undernutrition during the last trimester alone did not elevate stillbirths, but reduced birthweight and increased neonatal mortality. Thus, high rates of stillbirths signify deprivation at or near conception.

What were the seasonal rhythms in the cultivation of cotton?[6] In regard to work, ordinarily the period from Christmas through New Year's Day was a holiday or slack season. The remainder of January was ordinarily a light month for work because inclement weather and lack of daylight discouraged or prevented field work. By late January or early February the ground was prepared for the planting season of March and April. The preparation and planting season was particularily strenuous because the tasks were physically demanding, little help could be obtained from the old and the young, and owners pressed work at an intense pace to meet deadlines for successful planting of the crop. A brief lay-by period followed

Table 23.2. The Probability of Death within One Calendar Month of Birth by Month of Birth and Data Source[a]

Month of Birth	Rate Greater Than 0.30	All Plantations
January	0.116	0.179
February	0.221	0.471
March	0.692	0.488
April	0.335	0.375
May and June	0.197	0.222
July and August	0.054	0.154
September	0.464	0.310
October	0.342	0.220
November	0.380	0.351
December	0.265	0.230

[a]Probability per month of 30.4 days.
Source: Steckel (1986c), Table 2.

planting, and the hoeing season, in which the cotton was thinned and weeded, continued through June or early July. The next lay-by period extended from the remainder of July until the harvest began in mid or late August. Although many hours were devoted to the harvest, the work was physically less demanding and the pace easier than preparation and planting, and the effort was distributed over more workers.

Evidence on work effort by pregnant slave women and modern studies of women's work and birth outcomes suggest that a decline in nutritional status associated with work may have been important to high rates of stillbirths and neonatal mortality. Plantation manuals, daily work records, and other sources show that women's work was arduous and that pregnant women had little reduction in work loads before the fifth month (Campbell 1984; Jones 1985, 16–17). Table 23.3 shows that women continued to work in some capacity almost until delivery, at least during seasonal peaks in the demand for labor. Although modern studies of work and birth outcomes suggest that work may reduce birthweights by 100 to 350 g (Tafari et al. 1980; Naeye and Peters 1982; Ashby 1915, 62) and that neonatal mortality rates were about twice as high among black women who continued working beyond two weeks before confinement (Rochester 1923, 119), it should be recognized that work effort in these studies was probably modest by standards of slaves. Low birth weights attributable to demanding work is a familiar problem in many developing countries and many antenatal programs now stress the benefits of less work for pregnant women (Ashworth 1982, 20).

Fetal infections and maternal illnesses such as respiratory and gastrointestinal infections and malaria are common sources of intrauterine growth retardation in developing countries (Urrutia et al. 1975). African women infected with *Plasmodium falciparum* malaria, for example, had newborns weighing 263 g below those born to non-infected mothers (Jelliffe 1968). Monthly patterns of illness and mortality suggest that infections were prevalent during the summer and early autumn in the antebellum South. Mortality rates for slave adults were highest during June, July, and August, and these months accounted for 34.2 percent of all deaths for the age group fifteen to forty-nine (Steckel #18, in this volume, 408). Southern observers noted that the "sickly season" occurred in August and September (Editor 1851, 84).

Table 23.3. Daily Cotton-Picking Rates before and after Birth

Time Period	Rate (lb)[a]	Percent
9–12 Weeks before	73.2	83.4
5–8 Weeks before	69.2	78.8
1–4 Weeks before	67.0	76.3
Week of Birth and Week after	31.3	35.6
2–3 Weeks after	8.6	9.8
4–7 Weeks after	58.9	67.1
8–11 Weeks after	80.6	91.8
Other Weeks	87.8	100.0

[a]Assumes the woman was twenty-five years old.
Source: Calculated from Metzer (#10, *TP*, Vol. I), 202.

Seasonal fluctuations in diet probably contributed to seasonal patterns of early losses but the available evidence suggests that fluctuations in other factors were much more important for health. Nominally the diet was probably best from mid-summer, when fresh vegetables were available, through early winter, when the slaughter of livestock began. If fluctuations in diet were primarily responsible for the seasonal patterns, then losses would have been greatest during the spring and approximately six to eight months thereafter. The low rates of loss in December and January create difficulties for an approach that emphasizes the diet.

Evidence presented in Table 23.4 is useful for constructing a reasonable assessment of causal factors among work, disease, and diet. Given that deprivation near the time of conception causes high rates of stillbirths whereas neonatal deaths are caused largely by deprivation near conception or near delivery, the high rates of stillbirths during November and December suggest that net nutritional deprivation was greatest during the preparation and planting season.[7] The adverse effects of work during the harvest and diseases of the "sickly season" may have more than offset any improvements in the diet because stillbirth rates were also elevated during the late winter and early spring. The lack of stillbirths in September and October, combined with the high neonatal mortality rates during these months, point to deprivation shortly before delivery at this time of year as an important, adverse ingredient in newborn health.

Slaveowners often attributed "smothering" deaths of seemingly healthy infants to careless mothers who rolled on infants while sleeping and some historians have argued that some deaths soon after birth were examples of infanticide by mothers who did not want their children reared as slaves (Johnson 1981). The analysis of seasonal patterns of early mortality and the information that sudden infant death syndrome often has causes stemming from deprivation during the fetal period (Naeye 1980; Valdes-Dapena 1980) is consistent with the argument that many of these deaths were examples of the syndrome (Savitt 1978, 122–127).

It was explained earlier that observations are lacking for a regression analysis of seasonal patterns in crops other than cotton. However, if all plantations are included and main crops other than cotton are added to the list of explanatory variables, then rice and to a lesser extent sugar emerge as high mortality crops. The

Table 23.4. Mortality Rates per Thousand by Month of Birth and Days after Birth

Month of Birth	Stillbirths	Days from Birth to Death				Number of Stillbirths Plus Births
		0–1	2–6	7–29	0–29[a]	
January, May, June, July	0	8	21	24	52	387
February, March, April	18	36	19	43	95	224
August, September, October	3	10	23	36	67	314
November, December	31	21	16	11	48	194
All Months	10	17	21	30	64	1,119

[a]The rows do not sum to the figure in this column because the number at risk changed from one age group to the next. For example, those who survived day one formed the group at risk in days two to six.
Source: Steckel (1986c).

expected loss was 23.3 percent in cotton but 47.2 percent in rice ($t = 3.66$) and 35.0 percent ($t = 1.78$) on sugar farms. Malaria and other diseases prevalent in coastal counties may have contributed to illness during pregnancy and, therefore, to high rates of loss in rice and sugar compared with cotton (none of the cotton plantations in the sample was located in a coastal county). Yet rice and sugar were produced in similar, swampy localities and losses in rice exceeded those in sugar. Work routines may explain the difference. Sugar and cotton were punctuated by heavy labor demands and lay-by periods but rice had a seasonal sequence of labor demands that was relatively moderate and uniform and capable of being performed by women. Therefore the typical woman on a rice farm may have exerted more effort during pregnancy and fewer newborns may have escaped the adverse consequences of this work.

POSTNEONATAL MORTALITY

The postneonatal mortality rate calculated from plantation records was 162 per thousand, which was roughly two-thirds more than the rate for the free population.[8] Since low birth weight increases the risk of mortality beyond the neonatal period (Fitzhardinge and Steven 1972; Christianson et al. 1981; McCormick 1985), prenatal developments explain part of the excess postneonatal mortality. However, the chances of survival for the remainder of the first year depend heavily on diet, disease, and care, and in this category breast-feeding patterns and food supplements are the leading candidates for understanding the high rates of loss. The nature and timing of food supplements were important to health because breast milk is clean, nutritionally ideal, and provides some immunity (Knodel and Kinter 1977; Wray 1978), but supplements such as pap and gruel that were common during the nineteenth century were nutritionally poor, especially in protein, and were frequently contaminated or served in contaminated utensils (Wickes 1953). Under these conditions attenuated breast-feeding increased the risk of illness and mortality.[9]

The scanty evidence available on breast-feeding patterns suggests that whites frequently continued for more than one year while slaves may have nursed for less than one year.[10] Moreover, plantation work records and instructions to overseers indicate that supplements probably began within two to three months following birth. Rates of cotton picking, shown in Table 23.3, exceeded two-thirds of normal in weeks four to seven after delivery and were nearly 92 percent of normal in weeks eight to eleven after delivery. The achievement of near-normal levels by eight to eleven weeks and of normal levels thereafter suggests that little work time was lost for breast-feeding after the second month following delivery. Plantation owner James Hammond rated "sucklers" as half-hands for one month after going out and as three-quarter hands thereafter (Tucker 1958, 363).

Patterns of postneonatal mortality were investigated using a logit regression model that included plantation size, time period, main crop, mother's age, month of birth, and gender as independent variables (Steckel 1986c). The most interesting findings pertain to time period, plantation size, and main crop. The probability of postneonatal death was systematically lowest (under 100 per thousand) before 1825 and climbed to approximately 250 per thousand by the late 1830s and then fell to roughly 120 per thousand by the late 1850s. The profile cannot be explained by changes in the completeness of enumeration as measured by the recorded share of infant deaths occurring within twenty-eight days of birth. The profile is probably not a fluke because deaths of older slave children followed a similar pattern and the heights of slave children declined during the 1830s and began to recover during the 1840s (Steckel 1979, 377). Increasing rates of migration that spread communicable disease may have contributed to the pattern. However, migration rates were also high during the 1850s and this simple explanation cannot account for the decline in mortality rates unless the disease environment eventually became more homogeneous as a result of previous migration. Cotton prices were low near the peak in the mortality rates and owners may have invested less in slave health during these years. In addition, cholera was prevalent in the South during the 1830s and 1840s (Rosenberg 1962). The findings that heights of northern whites declined among those born during the late 1820s and the 1830s (Margo and Steckel 1983; Komlos 1987) and that life expectation at age ten calculated from genealogies declined by five years during the same time period (Fogel 1986, 41) suggests that causes may not have been unique to the South. Whatever the causes that may be found for the time pattern, the focus of Vinovskis (1972), Meeker (1972; 1976), Easterlin (1977), and others on identification and explanation of long-term trends has missed the aspect of cycles or fluctuations in health.

The expected probability of postneonatal infant death was 8.4 percent on units of 75 slaves and 13.8 percent on units of 200 slaves. The increase in deaths with size could have been caused by greater numbers and higher density, which promoted the spread of disease, but size had no systematic influence on early infant losses. Because women's productivity in the fields was greater on large units (*RF*, 76), breast-feeding and other time spent on child care were relatively more expensive to owners of working mothers on these units. Unfortunately the data available do not permit separate measures of the importance of care versus the disease environment for children. The adverse effect of size on survival agrees with Higman's (1984) findings for Jamaican slaves.

Postneonatal mortality rates were systematically lower in sugar agriculture compared with other types of farm. The expected rate of loss was 14.9 percent on cotton plantations but only 6.6 percent if sugar was the main crop. This finding suggests that the poor reputations of the crop and the areas in which it was grown may be undeserved, at least for this age group in the United States. The work routine in sugar often required heavy labor for ditching and plowing, which may have freed women's time for postnatal care (Gray [1933] 1958, 2:749–751). Breast-feeding may have been abbreviated during the sugar harvest, but labor demands for women could have been relatively even and low during the rest of the year such that breast-feeding was encouraged.

The average age at first birth was 22.7 years among antebellum southern whites and about 2 years less among slaves recorded in probate records (Steckel 1985,

103). Since infant mortality rates were relatively high for children born to young mothers, one can measure the effect of earlier childbearing among slaves on the chances of survival. The actual birth rates of slaves and whites below age 20 are unknown, but the percent of women listed with a surviving child was about three times higher among slaves compared to whites in the age group 15–19 (Steckel 1985, 116). If the percent with surviving children is used as an index of relative birth rates, then the reduction in slave losses can be estimated by changing the weights on age coefficients in regressions of neonatal and postneonatal mortality. These calculations suggest that slave infant mortality rates would have been 4.7 to 5.8 percent lower if slaves had the same age pattern of early childbearing as whites (Steckel 1986c, 451).

CHILDHOOD TO MATURITY

Table 23.5 displays estimated heights by sex from childhood to maturity.[11] The estimated velocity profiles closely resemble the pattern characteristic of modern growth studies (see Eveleth and Tanner 1976). The estimates decline uniformly for several years after age 4.5, reaching a preadolescent minimum around age 9.5 in females and age 10.5 in males. The adolescent growth spurt is clearly visible in both sexes, and growth continued on average into the late teens or early twenties. In accordance with modern studies, slave girls matured more rapidly than the boys.

The nutritional requirements for growth increase substantially during adolescence, and growth may be retarded at these ages depending upon the nature and extent of deprivation during adolescence and during earlier years. Thus the age at which the peak of the adolescent growth spurt is reached is a useful index of health and nutrition. Recent studies of well-nourished populations place these values in the range of 11.5–12.0 years among girls and 13.0–14.0 years among boys (Eveleth and Tanner 1976, 165). Point estimates for slaves obtained from the smoothing procedure are 13.27 years for girls and 14.75 years for boys, and consequently adolescent growth among slaves was retarded by 1–1.5 years compared with modern standards.

The events of growth usually proceed in a well-defined sequence. A sequence that has implications for historical and economic questions is the fact that menarche in girls usually occurs within 1–1.5 years following the peak of the adolescent growth spurt. The point estimate of 13.27 years for girls affirms the conclusion reached in earlier work on a smaller sample that female slaves could have given birth by approximately age 17–17.5 on average (Trussell and Steckel #20, in this volume). The average age at first birth among slave women was about 19.8 to 21.6 years, depending upon plantation size (Steckel 1982; 1985). Since it is likely that slaves did not practice family limitation, these data suggest that most slave girls abstained for a period of time after they were sexually mature.

The last column of data for each sex gives the centiles of modern height standards achieved by slaves (calculations are discussed in Steckel 1986b).[12] As children the slaves were roughly 5–5.5 inches below modern standards but the gap

Table 23.5. Estimated Slave Heights Compared with Modern Standards

	Males			Females		
Age	Estimated Slave Height	Velocity[a]	Centile of Modern	Estimated Slave Height	Velocity[a]	Centile of Modern
4.5	35.70	2.85	0.2	35.90	2.77	0.5
5.5	38.42	2.62	0.4	38.53	2.51	0.9
6.5	40.93	2.41	0.7	40.93	2.29	1.3
7.5	43.26	2.24	1.0	43.12	2.11	1.5
8.5	45.42	2.10	1.3	45.16	1.98	1.6
9.5	47.47	2.00	1.4	47.12	1.93	1.5
10.5	49.45	1.96	1.9	49.06	1.99	1.4
11.5	51.42	1.99	2.4	51.13	2.16	1.8
12.5	53.44	2.08	2.9	53.39	2.38	1.2
13.5	55.59	2.21	3.1	55.84	2.46	0.8
14.5	57.85	2.31	2.2	58.18	2.16	1.6
15.5	60.15	2.26	1.2	60.04	1.53	5.8
16.5	62.29	1.97	1.2	61.24	0.90	13.4
17.5	64.04	1.51	3.8	61.91	0.46	20.0
18.5	65.30	1.02	9.2	62.24	0.22	24.5
19.5	66.11	0.63	15.4	62.39	0.10	26.8
20.5	66.59	0.36	20.0	62.46	0.05	27.8
21.5	66.86	0.20	23.3	62.49	0.02	28.1
Adult	67.17	—	27.1	62.51	—	28.4

[a]Value of the first derivative of the Preece-Baines function at exact age shown. This is an "instantaneous" measure of velocity.
Source: Steckel (1986b), 730–731.

exceeded 6 inches during early adolescence and then declined to about 1.6 inches for adult males and 1.4 inches for adult females. The height of the typical slave child would trigger alarm in a modern pediatrician's office. At age 4.5 boys on average reached only centile 0.2 and girls attained only 0.5. Progress was slow for many years thereafter. Upward movement through the centiles, or catch-up growth, occurred after age 4.5 but the first centile of modern standards was not reached until age 6.5 in females and age 7.5 in males. The apparent reversal, or downward slide through the centiles, that occurred following age 11.5 in girls and age 13.5 in boys is largely attributable to the fact that the adolescent growth spurt begins one to two years earlier in the standard population. Sustained catch-up growth took place after age 13.5 in girls and about age 16.5 in boys, and by adulthood males reached centile 27.1 and females reached 28.4.

Comparisons with populations measured during the eighteenth and nineteenth centuries and with poor populations of the twentieth century reveal that growth was extraordinarily retarded among slave children and that the extent of recovery from growth depression was remarkable, if not unprecedented. Table 23.6 shows the centiles of modern height standards reached by various historical populations in Europe, the United States, and the Caribbean. Three features of the comparisons are notable (these features also hold for a much larger set of comparisons given in Steckel 1986b; 1987). First, American slave children were the smallest in the table, although the advantages over Trinidad slaves and German peasants were slight. Second, American slaves had the largest recovery from growth depression between childhood and maturity, measured in terms of closing the gap in inches below modern standards.[13] Third, American slaves climbed upward through the centiles between ages 10.5 and 13.5 while other populations declined or showed almost no improvement at these ages.

The most extensive compilation of height data for developing countries is contained in Eveleth and Tanner (1976). Comparisons with this source show that young slave children fell among or below the poorest populations. At age three, for example, children from urban areas of Bangladesh attained centile 0.3 as males and centile 0.4 as females, and those from the slums of Lagos, Nigeria, reached centile 12.1 as males and centile 6.4 as females. It is clear that American slaves had an exceptionally poor start in life.

Developing countries that had relatively small children also had relatively small teenagers and adults. A regression of height relative to modern standards at older ages on height relative to modern standards at young ages gives a sense of the extent to which slaves were different. The following equation was estimated:

$$LRHTA = -0.0138 + 0.8575 LRHTC$$
$$(-1.17) \qquad (5.61)$$

where N = 39, R-square = 0.46, $LRHTA$ is the natural log of relative height as adults or older teenagers (ages sixteen through eighteen) and $LRHTC$ is the natural

Table 23.6. Centiles of Modern Standards Achieved by Various Populations by Age, Males

Age	Stuttgart, Aristocrats 1772–1794	Germany, Peasants 1790s	Trinidad, Creole Slaves 1813	England, Factory Workers 1833	Boston, American Parents, 1875
4.5	—	—	0.4	—	—
5.5	—	—	0.6	—	14.0
6.5	—	2.7	0.8	—	15.6
7.5	—	2.1	0.8	—	15.8
8.5	16.5	1.6	0.8	—	15.2
9.5	12.2	1.1	0.8	1.8	13.8
10.5	10.2	0.9	0.9	1.9	13.8
11.5	8.6	0.8	0.9	1.8	13.3
12.5	7.8	0.7	0.9	1.5	13.8
13.5	7.2	0.6	0.8	1.1	14.4
14.5	5.4	0.3	0.4	0.7	13.4
15.5	3.5	0.1	0.09	0.4	11.5
16.5	3.6	0.1	0.04	0.5	12.3
17.5	7.1	0.6	0.2	0.8	18.0
18.5	11.7	1.7	0.6	1.1	23.0
19.5	15.1	—	2.3	—	—
20.5	17.0	—	2.9	—	—
Adult	18.7	4.4[a]	3.8	1.3[a]	28.2[a]

[a]Predicted from data through age eighteen.
Source: Steckel (1987).

log of relative height as children (ages three through eight); t-statistics are given in parentheses.[14]

Whether slaves fit the pattern for developing countries can be assessed by substituting the relative height of slave children into the equation. At age 4 slaves attained 87.4 percent of modern standards (average for males and females), which implies an estimated relative height as adults of 87.9 percent of modern standards. An 80 percent confidence interval for the predicted value of relative adult height is (81.7 percent, 94.5 percent). Yet slaves reached 95.1 percent of standard height at age 17.5 and 96.2 percent of standard height at age 18.5. In contrast with the case of American slaves, the conditions that retarded growth for children in developing countries tended to persist throughout the growing years.

The pattern of slave growth is so unusual that it is important to consider whether the results are credible. The Appendix to this paper (available on request from the author) discusses questions of accuracy of measurements and representativeness of the sample and argues that it is probably safe to take the data at ages three and above at face value. Moreover, medical evidence shows that humans and animals have a remarkable power to recover depending upon the timing, source, duration, and intensity of the insult and especially the circumstances after the period of deprivation (Tanner 1978, 46–47). However, consumption of toxic substances, such as alcohol and tobacco, during pregnancy may permanently stunt a child's growth.

It was noted earlier that heights are a measure of net nutrition, that is, actual diet minus claims on the diet made by illness, physical effort, and maintenance. There is little direct evidence on illness by age but the mortality data in Table 23.1 suggest that sickness decreased during childhood. Slave mortality rates declined sharply after age five, and fell below ten per thousand after age six (based on data for individual years of age).

It is unlikely that work made an important claim on the diet before late childhood. Interviews of ex-slaves indicate that the transition to the adult labor force was gradual and may have begun in some instances as early as age six or seven (Crawford 1980). On average slave children did not produce enough to more than cover their maintenance costs until about age ten (Fogel and Engerman 1974a, 1:76). If judgments about the decline in sickness with age and lack of work effort are correct, the conclusion that the diet remained poor during childhood is inescapable.

Independent evidence suggests that the childhood diet was poor. Slaveowners frequently discussed the care and feeding of slaves in southern agricultural journals. It is clear that deliberations focused on working slaves. One planter stated that "a negro deprived of a meat diet is not able to endure the labor that those can perform who are liberally supplied with it" (Breeden 1980, 94). Others usually stated allowances of meat, corn, and other foods in terms of working or laboring hands (Breeden 1980, 92–109). If children were mentioned at all, they usually received "proportionally less," which probably meant "proportional to work effort." The allocations were frequently made to families and the vagueness or lack of specifics about non-workers conveys no information about actual consumption by children. Meat was scarce—a half a pound of pork per day was a typical recommended ration for a worker—and was probably regarded as a luxury. Parents and other workers in the family may have claimed meat and other nutritional foods at the expense of children. This behavior has occurred repeatedly during hard times within developing countries (Bongaarts and Cain 1982). The emphasis by owners on the labor force could have given legitimacy to reallocation within the family, especially during hard times.

The descriptive literature contains evidence of malnutrition among children. Slaveowners discussed the shiny bodies and plump bellies of their young slaves and some travelers interpreted the glistening ribs of pudgy youngsters as signs of good health. These are signs of malnutrition, especially a protein deficiency (Kiple and Kiple 1977a, 289).

Table 23.1 shows that slave mortality rates declined little after age seven. If the mortality rates are accepted as an index of illness, then diet and physical exertion were the major variables affecting the growth profile during and after late child-hood. Table 23.4 makes clear that most of the absolute difference between slave heights and modern standards was made up during the late adolescent and post-adolescent period,[15] but the foundations for this achievement were laid by a strong adolescent growth spurt. It was noted earlier that slaves experienced catch-up growth after age ten while other populations declined or showed almost no improvement. Comparisons with the Bundi of New Guinea—the shortest population ever studied by auxologists (scientists who study physical growth)—also suggests that relative improvement for slaves occurred beginning in late childhood (Steckel 1986c, 734–735). Other things being equal, net nutrition should have deteriorated for slaves at the ages when they began hard work around age ten. The point is that other things were not equal; there must have been an improvement in the diet more than offsetting the additional requirements of physical activity, thereby allowing a small amount of catch-up growth. The emphasis by slaveowners on meat for workers is consistent with this pattern.

SLAVERY AND HEALTH

Did the pursuit of profits under slavery contribute to the poor health of children? In attempting to answer this question it is important to consider forces that were substantially outside slaveowners' power and understanding; a poor disease environment in the South, biological adaptations to African conditions, and ignorance of appropriate nutrition and causes of disease fall into this category. Although evidence on the disease environment is scanty, it is reasonable to conjecture that the South's semi-tropical climate would have caused higher rates of illness and mortality compared with the North. The decline in adult heights from the border to the lower coastal states of the South is consistent with this hypothesis (Margo and Steckel 1983, #24, in this volume). To the extent that conditions were worse in the South, the use of data for the entire country in Table 23.1 misses the point; one should compare slaves with southern whites. On the other hand, southern whites were taller than northern whites at the time of the American Revolution and their height advantage, as measured by southern amnesty records and muster rolls of northern whites who fought in the Civil War, persisted during the mid-nineteenth century (Sokoloff and Villaflor 1982; Margo and Steckel 1983, #24, in this volume). Since adults and the corresponding children in free populations tend to reach roughly the same centile of modern height standards (Steckel 1986c, 1987), the evidence on adult heights suggests that southern white children had relatively good health, i.e., the relatively poor health of slave children cannot be attributed principally to a harsh disease environment in the South. Yet study of the growth profile of slaves from childhood to maturity has shown that comparisons of adult heights alone can be misleading and so actual resolution of the issue awaits mortality records, height data, or other evidence on southern white children.

Kiple and Kiple (1977a) employed information on nutrition-related diseases, accounts by southern physicians, and census data on causes of death to argue that the poor health of slave children was substantially attributable to biological adaptations to African conditions that clashed with conditions in North America. This argument cannot be tested directly with height and mortality data, but the remarkable growth recovery during and after adolescence shows that people of African descent could achieve reasonably good health in North America. Because slaves did not reach modern standards as adults, the height data are consistent with the hypothesis that biological adaptations influenced health. However, the extent of the recovery creates difficulties for the view that biological adaptations were primarily responsible for the poor health of children.[16]

There is little doubt that ignorance contributed to high infant and child mortality rates during the antebellum period. These rates fell dramatically during the late 1800s and early 1900s with the acceptance and refinement of the germ theory of disease, the development of sanitation systems and better personal hygiene, and improved understanding of prenatal and postnatal care. Yet mortality rates of slave infants and children were approximately double those for the free population. How did slaveowners reach decisions on the care and feeding of slaves? Even though owners lacked the rudiments of scientific understanding of nutrition and health, knowledge about desirable feeding practices and work habits could have accumulated through a long process of trial, error, observation, and adjustment. By the late antebellum period planters had considerable experience with the institution of slavery. Is it possible, for example, that owners had discovered through trial and error that feeding meat to children was unprofitable? The unusual growth profile of slaves enhances the prospects for this line of reasoning. Moreover, planters were experienced at feeding livestock and had reasons to suspect a connection between diet and growth.

Feeding meat to slave children can be thought of as an investment in which net income was negative during the early years of the investment period because meat was costly and children did not work. However, children who had adequate nutrition were taller and stronger when they began working. The rate of return on this investment was calculated by estimating the expected value of additional output (including that following from lower mortality rates) from workers who attained modern height standards based on the value of slaves by height. Annual outlays per child necessary to cover the nutritional deficit ranged from $3.80 at age one to $5.90 at age nine.[17] The estimated rate of return on this investment was negative; the present value of expected outlays exceeded the present value of expected returns (Steckel 1986b). Thus it was profitable to exclude meat from the diet of slave children. Calculations in this vein also suggest that attenuated breast-feeding was profitable (Steckel 1986c) and that hard work during pregnancy may have been profitable.[18] Fundamentally, forced labor under slavery raised women's productivity in the fields and the high value of their time led to prenatal and postnatal practices that were detrimental to health. The remarkable ability of humans to recover physically from deprivation before adolescence and the cost of a good diet contributed to decisions that prolonged poor health during childhood. Planters were informed best about the additional output or savings in costs realized by hard work during pregnancy, attenuated breast-feeding routines, and meat rations for workers only, but ignorance led planters to underestimate the adverse consequences of these actions, which exacerbated poor health.

IMPLICATIONS

The health and diet of American slaves has been extensively debated in recent years. Robert Fogel and Stanley Engerman (1974a) used the disappearance method to estimate food consumption for adults as the difference between food production and non-slave utilization on large southern farms located at least 50 miles from a city and argued that the diet was substantial calorically and exceeded recommended levels of the chief nutrients. Richard Sutch (1975b, 1976) criticized the Fogel and Engerman estimates as too generous, especially for important nutrients, but concluded that without question the diet was sufficient to maintain the slave's body weight and general health. The data and methods of this study shed light on three aspects of the debate. First, the finding of dramatic catch-up growth supports the Fogel-Engerman position that working slaves were well fed. Second, Fogel and Engerman invoked, and critics generally accepted, the assumption in the disappearance method that children and adults had approximately the same nutritional status. The unusual growth profile of slaves shows that this assumption effectively overfed the children and underfed the workers. Third, since no scholar had suggested that nutrition was generally poor, the finding that children were substantially malnourished indicates that children were generally overlooked in the literature on health.[19]

Because perceptions of the slave diet have been reasonably favorable, the implications of malnutrition during childhood have been largely unexplored. Research on the economic and social history of blacks in the postbellum South, for example, has recognized the effects of slavery on literacy and skills and has incorporated discrimination after the war, but poor nutrition during childhood may also have been relevant (Higgs 1977; Ransom and Sutch 1977; Margo 1986). Studies of child development show that moderate but chronic nutritional deprivation during early childhood temporarily retards the acquisition of motor skills and permanently stunts mental development (Chavez and Martinez 1982; Brozek and Schurch 1984). Poor nutrition during slavery may have impeded the economic progress of blacks after the war.

If investments in good nutrition for slave children had low rates of return, why did free populations tend to invest relatively more in the growth of young children? One explanation hinges on the importance of nutrition in early childhood to cognitive development; planters may have valued only the physical development of raw labor whereas free populations also valued mental development because it promoted success in a competitive market environment. Another is altruism. Slaveowners may have cared relatively little for slave children, but free parents were willing to transfer resources toward their own children.

Whatever the reasons for the relatively poor health of slave children, it is clear that certain conceptions of slave childhood should be redrawn. Genovese (1974, 404–405), for example, portrays these ages as "protected years" that provided a "foundation of physical health" and that childhood was a "time to grow physically" and to "parry the most brutal features of [their] bondage." Instead, poor nutrition restricted exploration and play and retarded growth. Slave children may have sought to escape childhood and to join the labor force because of the nutritional rewards.

If slaveowners used food to promote the work ethic, it may have been done partly at the expense of the slave family, insofar as it reduced interaction between children and working-age slaves. Workers generally had breakfast and lunch in the fields and may well have eaten after the children during the evening. Discussions of eating arrangements suggest that children were often fed separately (Genovese 1974, 507; Breeden 1980, 281–288). Working adults may have had relatively little time to spend with young children on a regular basis. Under these conditions grandparents or other older slaves may have played the most important role in socializing young slave children. Former slaves who gravitated toward nuclear families after emancipation may have been poorly equipped through lack of experience to train young children.

The personality of slaves and resistance to slavery have been widely debated in the literature. Stanley Elkins (1976, 82), for example, portrayed the typical slave as "Sambo," who was "docile," "humble," and "childlike." Bauer and Bauer (1942) maintained that slaves were lazy and irresponsible while Stampp (1956, 97–109) envisaged slaves retaliating against bondage by slow and careless work and damage to property. Fogel and Engerman (1974a, 1:147, 231) argued that most slaves were diligent and responsible workers who identified with their owner's interests. This literature generally ignores the possible role of nutrition on behavior, yet there is considerable evidence that nutrition influences personality development. Moderately malnourished children are apathetic, emotionally withdrawn, less aggressive, and more dependent (Chavez and Martinez 1982; Brozek and Schurch 1984). The finding that slave children were poorly nourished should be integrated into research on the slave personality.

The high rates of infant and child losses may seem implausible given the known high rate of natural increase of American slaves. The apparent contradiction can be explained by high fertility rates and by the finding that age patterns of slave mortality did not fit those distilled from free populations of the West.[20] High fertility was achieved because new pregnancies quickly replaced losses from still-births and neonatal deaths while attenuated breast-feeding increased the chances of conception among women whose newborns survived beyond early infancy.[21]

The conclusion that breast-feeding patterns were attenuated is important for the debate over the extent, sources, and goals of slave cultural evolution in the Western Hemisphere. Unlike the United States, a high volume of imports to the Caribbean constantly renewed African customs and, consistent with those customs, breast-feeding in the sugar colonies continued in some form for about two years after birth (Klein and Engerman 1978; Handler and Corruccini 1986). The available evidence shows that the duration was much shorter among slaves in the United States and was abbreviated compared with upper-class southern whites. Thus the goals of change were not to imbue slaves with southern ideals and clearly slaves were not the source of change. Instead, the example of breast-feeding indicates that planters reckoned with the high value of women's time in formulating rules and regulations that shaped cultural practices. The extent to which slaves were able to impose costs and deny profits by successfully resisting changes desired by owners or by success-fully initiating changes unwanted by owners is a measure of the autonomy of slave culture. In this regard it would be interesting to know the extent to which long intervals of breast-feeding in the sugar colonies were driven by an accommodation to prior beliefs or by a low value of women's time in sugar cultivation.

NOTES

1. More complete discussions of these findings are available in Steckel (1986a, 1986b, 1986c, 1987). The most substantial change in perceptions of slave health in recent decades has occurred in the area of infant and early childhood mortality. Before reaching the level reported in Table 23.1, estimates of the infant mortality rate have climbed from 152.6 per thousand (Postell 1951, 158) to 182.7 (Evans 1962, 212), 274 to 302 (Farley 1970), and 246 to 275 (Eblen 1972, 1974).

2. There is a synergy between malnutrition and infection. Infections reduce appetite and impede nutrient absorption and utilization, and malnourished children are more susceptible to illness (see Scrimshaw 1975; Chavez and Martinez 1982; Martorell 1980). Friedman (1982) shows that small slaves in Trinidad had relatively higher death rates.

3. A point estimate for the neonatal mortality rate is 227 per thousand (Steckel 1986c, n. 17). The actual figure for the antebellum free population is unknown, but the share of neonatal deaths among infant deaths ranges from 35 to 70 percent across countries that have infant mortality rates in excess of 10 percent (Bouvier and van der Tak 1976; Mata 1978; Ashworth 1982). If the actual figure was 50 percent for the antebellum free population then neonatal mortality rates for slaves was about two and one-half times as high for slaves compared with the free population (Steckel 1986c, n. 39).

4. General references in this area include Hytten and Leitch (1971), Tanner (1978), Hurley (1980), Hytten and Chamberlain (1980), and Naeye and Tafari (1983).

5. Lack of deaths required that births be combined in May and June and in July and August.

6. See, for example, Riley (1909), Davis (1943), Stephenson (1936), Covert (1912), and Gray ([1933] 1958).

7. Stillbirths and neonatal deaths tend to be preterm and may have an average gestation period of roughly seven to eight months. Attempts to pinpoint times of deprivation by counting months is at

best approximate given the small sample sizes for stillbirths and neonatal deaths. Based on a chi-square test of homogeneity the pattern of stillbirths is significantly different from a random (flat) pattern at 0.005.

8. See note 3 above and Steckel (1986c), n. 39. In this paper the number at risk for calculating the postneonatal mortality rate is the number who survived the neonatal period.

9. The adverse effects of very short breast-feeding practices on health were observed in parts of nineteenth-century Finland, where mortality rates of 124 to 201 per thousand were sustained for the period one to six months following birth (Lithell 1981, 185).

10. McMillen (1985), 344, finds a range of 6 to 22 and an average of 13.5 months based upon the journals and correspondence of southern white women (N = 16). Recommendations for slaves were 9 months (Affleck 1851, 435) to one year (Hammond 1844).

11. The raw data, which are published in Steckel (1987), were smoothed to obtain more accurate estimates of the true mean heights and to obtain point estimates of useful measures such as the age at peak height velocity during adolescence. The smoothing procedure utilized Preece-Baines Model 1 (Preece and Baines 1978).

12. The modern standards used in calculating the centiles are based on British children (Tanner et al. 1966), but other standards for well-nourished children from Europe, European descent, and African descent would give similar results (see Eveleth and Tanner 1976, App.). The National Center for Health Statistics (1977) has published standards (whites and blacks combined) frequently used in North America and these exceed the British standards for males, for example, by 0.7 cm at age 10.0 and by 2.1 cm as adults. Among females the excess of the North American standards is 1.9 cm at age 10.0 and 1.5 cm as adults. Use of the British standards therefore slightly understates the absolute level of deprivation compared with North American standards.

    Persons of African descent mature slightly earlier than Europeans and persons of European descent (Eveleth and Tanner 1976, 225–226), yet adult heights are nearly identical [black males attain 174.5 cm, on average at age 17.5, while white males attain 175.8; among females at 17.5 the average heights are 162.0 (blacks) and 162.8 (whites); see National Center for Health Statistics (1973)]. Therefore, standards based on Europeans or substantially on persons of European descent slightly understate the contrast in health between slave children and slave adults.

13. It was noted earlier that ingestion of toxic substances during pregnancy may permanently stunt a child's growth. Consumption of rum during pregnancy may have contributed to the lack of recovery among slaves in the Caribbean compared with the United States.

14. It would be desirable to have measurements throughout the growing years, but studies generally focused on an age block within the growing years and so the youngest and the oldest ages within the block were used for the regression. Studies lacking measurements below age nine or above age fifteen were ignored. The regression includes only those populations that attained no more than 98 percent of modern height standards as children. The modern standards are from Tanner et al. (1966).

15. Calculations involving average height differences between survivors and non-survivors show that less than 1 percent of the height gain toward modern standards during and after adolescence can be explained by selectivity with respect to survivors (see Steckel 1986c, n. 33).

16. It is possible that measured recovery was promoted in part by selective mortality of slaves who adapted poorly to conditions in North America.

17. Protein and calorie deficits often occur together, at least in developing countries, but the investment problem was cast in terms of a protein deficit because growth is sensitive to protein inadequacy, protein was relatively expensive, and owners recommended that little meat be fed to children.

18. Annual net earnings of slave women were about $70 during their childbearing years and the value of a slave infant was about $50 (Fogel and Engerman 1974a, 1:76, 82). A difficulty in measuring the profitability of hard work is the lack of information on the trade-off between work during pregnancy and infant health, and so the calculations below are merely suggestive. Suppose that reduced work loads could have reduced infant mortality rates by 20 percentage points (to a level approximately equal to that in the free population). Assuming that a woman had one child on average every two years, then the expected annual gain from less work would have been about $5 = ($50 × 0.20)/2. Yet it is doubtful that a reduction in work loads that would have cost on

average $5 per year (corresponding to an average reduction in work effort of about 7.1 percent = 5/70) would have been sufficient to reduce infant mortality rates by 20 percentage points. This point is reinforced by the finding that much of the strain on fetal development occurred during seasonal peaks when labor was particularily valuable (see *EM*, #49, for a more elaborate computation and an alternative interpretation).

To the extent that owners did not understand the connection between prenatal care and infant health and attributed infant mortality to other factors, they would have been led to underestimate the benefits of less work during pregnancy and to have required more work. How much owners might have reduced work loads during pregnancy, increased breast-feeding, and furnished meat to children if they had more reliable information on the benefits to health is unknown. The calculations suggest, however, that the assumption of ignorance is not required to explain poor health. The available evidence indicates that owners had little economic incentive to experiment with methods to improve infant health through less work or to promote child health through extended breast-feeding and a protein-adequate diet.

19. Kiple and Kiple (1977a) drew attention to the poor health of slave children.
20. Age patterns of mortality are discussed in Coale and Demeny (1983).
21. Movement from a regimen of regular and exclusive breast-feeding to one of partial breast-feeding and supplements may have an importance influence on fertility by reducing the production of the hormone prolactin (see Habicht et al. 1985).

TWENTY-FOUR

The Nutrition and Health of Slaves and Antebellum Southern Whites

Robert A. Margo
and
Richard H. Steckel

INTRODUCTION

Until recently, historians seeking to compare the nutritional experiences of the American slave and southern white populations have relied extensively on traditional sources such as plantation account books, agricultural and medical journals, diaries, the manuscript censuses of agriculture and population, and the ex-slave narratives (Gray [1933] 1958, Hilliard 1972; Fogel and Engerman 1974a; Sutch 1975b; Savitt 1978). Physiologists, anthropologists, and nutritionists have demonstrated, however, that sensitive and reliable indexes of the average nutritional status of a population may be constructed from anthropometric data. This paper analyzes height-by-age data for slaves and southern whites taken from two Civil War sources: the muster rolls of the U.S. Colored Troops and the Confederate amnesty records, both of which provide information on males in late adolescence through adulthood. The amnesty records are particularly valuable because other nineteenth-century sources are sparse for the South. In particular, the Confederate Army did not record heights. Regression analysis is used to explore the variation in height across different groups in the slave and southern white populations and over time.

The paper is part of a larger project that uses height-by-age data to study secular trends in nutritional status in the United States and Western Europe since 1750. Detailed discussions of the methodology of this line of investigation and some of the principal findings to date are contained in Steckel (#23, in this volume, 1986a, 1986b), Fogel et al. (1982), Fogel et al. (1983), and Margo and Steckel (1983).

EX-SLAVE RECRUITS

This section analyzes height-by-age data drawn from the muster rolls of the black regiments serving in the Union Army from 1863 to 1865. The sample was originally collected by John Olson, and has been reduced for our purposes by excluding soldiers born or enlisted in the free states.[1] Unfortunately, the rolls do not identify free blacks at enlistment, but this procedure eliminates the most likely cases. We also make use of the aggregate statistics of the sample of ex-slave recruits collected by Gould ([1869] 1969). Because very few recruits were age seventeen and under, we restrict our attention to soldiers aged eighteen to forty-nine. The final data base contains 7,599 observations.

Table 24.1 records the mean and standard deviation of height at each age and a comparison with modern British height standards.[2] Based on the 98 percent criterion, ex-slave recruits reached adult height around age nineteen, approximately one year later than northern whites during the antebellum period (Margo and Steckel 1983), and three years later than modern British males (Tanner et al. 1966). The absolute increment in height from eighteen to age twenty-two was 1.4 to 1.5 inches, compared to 1.0 inches for modern British males from age sixteen to nineteen. At age eighteen, the mean height was at the 9th to 10th British centile, while at maturity, the mean height was at the 25th British centile. Thus growth among ex-slave recruits was attenuated, and catch-up substantial in late adolescence.

Table 24.2 reports regressions of adult (ages twenty-three to forty-nine) and young adult (ages eighteen to twenty-two) heights on dummy variables indicating age (for young adults), occupation, complexion, migrant status, place of birth, year of enlistment, and year of birth (for adults). The regression on adult height extends our earlier work (Margo and Steckel 1982) by employing a more refined dummy variable classification for place and year of birth, and by controlling for year of enlistment. Because the regressions for adults do not differ substantively from our earlier findings, the discussion focuses primarily on young adults. We also report a regression for a subset of the young adult sample in which three continuous,

Table 24.1. Mean Height by Age of Ex-Slave Recruits

	Gould Sample			Olson Sample			
Age	N	Mean (Inches)	Centile of Modern	N	Mean (Inches)	Standard Deviation	Centile of Modern
18	4,016	65.6	10.0	1,033	65.3	2.4	9.0
19	2,889	66.1	13.1	637	66.3	2.5	14.7
20	2,533	66.6	17.6	762	66.6	2.5	17.6
21	2,433	66.8	19.8	638	66.9	2.5	21.2
22	2,119	67.1	24.5	625	66.7	2.5	18.9
23–34	11,018	67.1	24.5	2,953	67.2	2.6	24.8
23–49				3,904	67.2	2.7	24.8

Sources: Gould ([1869] 1969) 147, Table XXI; Olson sample of ex-slave recruits; and calculated from Tanner et al. (1966).

county-level variables were matched to each observation, using the information on the recruit's county of birth and census data for 1860. These variables are MSH, median slave holding (a size such that exactly one-half of the slaves lived on larger units); STAPLE, the value of staple crop production (rice, cotton, sugar, and tobacco) in the total value of agricultural output; and PSURB, the fraction of male slaves residing in urban areas (population exceeding 2,500). These variables measure the effects of plantation size, crop mix, and urbanization on the heights of pre-adults; see Margo and Steckel (1982) for a similar analysis of adult ex-slave recruits. Because it is difficult to identify local or regional influences on health from the heights of those who moved long distances while growing up, the sample is restricted to non-migrants (that is, recruits enlisting in the same state in which they were born). This restriction eliminated all but seventeen of the young adult recruits born in Louisiana, Maryland, North Carolina, and Virginia, and these observations were also excluded due to insufficient numbers.

Civilian occupation had a small influence on young adult height. Among recruits aged eighteen to twenty-two, domestics and the semi-skilled were approximately 0.2 to 0.4 inches shorter than skilled recruits, and the sizes of the differentials were slightly larger among adults. Since movement into non-field occupations often did not occur until later in the slave life cycle (Fogel and Engerman 1974a), relative productivity differentials associated with physical strength probably account for the patterns observed among adults. Taller, stronger slaves would have a comparative advantage as field hands and in skilled tasks (Metzer, #10, *TP*, Vol. I; Friedman 1982).[3]

The theory of heterosis (Tanner 1978) suggests that height might be positively related to light skin color, and some scholars (for example, Genovese 1974) have argued that light-skinned slaves were better treated. The results indicate a small but significant positive association between height and light skin color among adults, consistent with both theories, but the effect was insignificant among young adults.

Data on place of enlistment can be used to study the relationship between migration and slave height. On the one hand, migrants might have been taller if planters selected the strongest and healthiest slaves when moving to a new area. The necessity of adjusting to a new disease environment, and possibly a short-run reduction in living standards, however, might induce a negative association between migration and height. The results show that migrants were taller on average than non-migrants, but the effect was very small and statistically insignificant. We note, however, that our data do not distinguish between true migration and wartime dislocation.

Slave heights varied across place of birth. Relative to those born in Kentucky or Tennessee, young adult recruits born in the upper South Atlantic states (Maryland, Virginia, and North Carolina), Louisiana, and especially South Carolina, were significantly shorter. A similar regional pattern existed among adult recruits, except that those born in Arkansas or Missouri were significantly taller (0.5 inches).

Data on year of enlistment measure the effect of changing wartime conditions (see Margo, #9, *TP*, Vol. I) on the distribution of height among ex-slave recruits.

Table 24.2. Height Regressions: Ex-Slave Recruits

	Regression Number		
Variable	(1) Adults (Ages 23–49)	(2) Pre-Adults (Ages 18–22)	(3) Pre-Adults, Non-Migrants
Constant	67.22	66.91	67.13
	(445.60)	(472.56)	(284.94)
Age			
18	—	−1.46	−1.43
		(11.76)	(8.38)
19	—	−0.44	−0.46
		(3.23)	(2.52)
20	—	−0.03	0.05
		(0.21)	(0.27)
21	—	0.14	0.22
		(1.01)	(1.22)
Occupation			
Domestic Servant	−0.37	−0.19	−0.34
	(1.47)	(0.99)	(1.21)
Semi-Skilled	−0.53	−0.17	−0.29
	(1.62)	(0.56)	(0.80)
Skilled	−0.06	0.23	0.25
	(0.30)	(0.94)	(0.82)
Light Skin	0.37	0.15	0.15
	(2.51)	(1.09)	(0.73)
Migrant Across			
State Lines	0.05	0.03	—
	(0.40)	(0.29)	
Place of Birth			
Alabama or Mississippi	−0.26	−0.19	−0.41
	(1.70)	(1.36)	(1.30)
Florida or Georgia	−0.08	0.16	−0.70
	(0.34)	(0.74)	(1.73)
Arkansas or Missouri	0.51	0.19	−0.17
	(2.96)	(1.39)	(0.33)
Maryland, Virginia, or North Carolina	−0.24	−0.38	—
	(1.55)	(1.97)	
Louisiana	−0.39	−0.82	—
	(1.20)	(2.32)	
South Carolina	−0.92	−1.22	−2.01
	(4.21)	(5.87)	(4.62)
Year of Enlistment			
1864	−0.09	−0.03	−0.21
	(0.78)	(0.30)	(1.08)
1865	0.02	0.08	0.75
	(0.11)	(0.42)	(1.98)
Year of Birth			
Before 1820	0.04	—	—
	(0.18)		
1820–1824	0.41	—	—
	(2.20)		
1825–1829	0.35	—	—

Table 24.2 (continued)

	Regression Number		
Variable	(1) Adults (Ages 23–49)	(2) Pre-Adults (Ages 18–22)	(3) Pre-Adults, Non-Migrants
	(2.23)		
1830–1834	0.47	—	—
	(3.20)		
1835–1839	0.12	—	—
	(0.96)		
MSH	—	—	−1.06
			(2.42)
STAPLE	—	—	0.46
			(1.20)
PSURB	—	—	−0.09
			(0.27)
N	3,652	3,593	2,068
R̄-Square	0.02	0.10	0.12

Notes: Columns 1 and 3: the intercept refers to a dark-skinned field hand born between 1840 and 1844 in Kentucky or Tennessee and enlisting in the same state in which he was born in 1863; column 2: the intercept refers to dark-skinned field hand age twenty-two, born in Kentucky or Tennessee, and enlisting in the same state in which he was born in 1863. Absolute value of t-statistics in parentheses.
Source: Olson sample of ex-slave recruits.

The results indicate that recruits at all ages enlisting in 1863 or 1865 were slightly taller than those enlisting in 1864, but neither effect was statistically significant. Adult recruits born between 1820 and 1834 were significantly taller than those born before 1820 or after 1835, consistent with our earlier findings (Margo and Steckel 1982).[4]

Turning to the results for young adult non-migrants (Table 24.2, column 3), the three additional variables (MSH, STAPLE, and PSURB) are jointly significant at the 10 percent level. Perhaps the most important finding is the significant negative association between median slave holding and young adult height, significant at the 2 percent level. The estimate implies that ex-slave recruits from very large plantations (over 100 slaves), other variables held constant at their sample means, would reach only the 8th British centile by their twenty-second birthday. Our earlier work on adult recruits (Margo and Steckel 1982) found a smaller negative effect of plantation size, suggesting that continued growth through the early to mid-twenties may have been a mitigating factor. The height disadvantage on large plantations may reflect the intense work regime characteristic of large plantations, a poorer diet (Crawford 1980, 114), or a more virulent disease environment (Steckel, #18, in this volume, 1986c; Savitt 1978).

Evidently specialization in staple crops had no significant effect on young adult height once plantation size was controlled for. Urbanization was negatively related to pre-adult height, consistent with harsher environmental conditions in cities, but the effect was statistically insignificant. Finally, note that the significantly shorter heights observed among the South Carolina natives does not disappear when the additional variables are introduced into the regression. Without additional information, it is difficult to account for the South Carolina effect, or it may be that county-level census data are inadequate for capturing the factors behind the regional variation in height. As we show in the next section, however, white South Carolina natives were also short, suggesting that our finding is not a statistical artifact, but the result of a set of environmental conditions less conducive to physical growth than in other areas of the South.

AMNESTY RECORDS

ORIGINS OF THE DATA

Very early during the Civil War, Congress took the practical position that a large number and variety of offenses against the U.S. government did not constitute treason. Through a series of laws, Congress established penalties of fines, imprisonment, disfranchisement, loss of the right to perform legal contracts, and confiscation of property for many acts of rebellion (Dorris 1953). Congress also approved legislation that could mitigate these penalties and the penalty imposed for treason. The thirteenth section of the Confiscation Act (July 17, 1862) authorized the president to extend pardon or amnesty to any persons who may have participated in the rebellion.

On December 8, 1863, President Lincoln announced a plan of amnesty and reconstruction. The essence of the proclamation was that all persons, with certain exceptions, who participated in the rebellion were granted a full pardon with restoration of all rights of property, "except as to slaves and in property cases where rights of third parties shall have intervened, and upon the condition that every such person shall take and subscribe an oath." The exceptions were (1) civil or diplomatic agents of the Confederacy, (2) persons who left judicial stations under the United States to aid the rebellion, (3) military or naval officers of the Confederacy above the rank of colonel in the army and lieutenant in the navy, (4) all who left seats in the U.S. Congress to aid the rebellion, (5) all who resigned commissions in the army or navy and thereafter aided the rebellion, and (6) all persons who treated colored persons, or white persons in charge of such, otherwise than lawfully as prisoners of war. Persons who fell into the excepted categories could make and receive pardons on an individual basis.

An important issue that arose in administering the oath concerned the status of those in the seceded states who had remained loyal to the Union. Despite protests, Lincoln determined that all persons, "loyal as well as disloyal," had to take the oath because "it does not hurt them, clears all questions as to right to vote, and swells the aggregate number who take it, which is an important object."

President Johnson issued his first proclamation of general amnesty on May 24, 1865 in which he excepted seven classes in addition to those specified by Lincoln. The additonal excepted classes were (1) persons who were absent from the United States for the purpose of aiding the rebellion, (2) all Confederate officers who were educated at West Point or Annapolis, (3) persons who held the office of governor in the states of the Confederacy, (4) all persons who left their homes within the jurisdiction of the United States to aid the Confederacy, (5) all persons who were engaged in the destruction of the commerce of the United States and who made raids into the United States from Canada, (6) all voluntary participants in the rebellion whose taxable property was worth over $20,000, and (7) all who had taken and subsequently violated the previous amnesty oath. Persons in the excepted classes could apply individually for pardons. After the war former soldiers, with the exception of those in the excepted classes, could take the general amnesty oath.

CHARACTERISTICS OF THE SAMPLE

Approximately 200,000 amnesty oaths for the non-excepted classes are housed in the National Archives (Record Group 59). These oaths were taken under the first three presidential proclamations (December 8, 1863; March 26, 1864; and May 29, 1865) and are described in Preliminary Inventory No. 157 (National Archives 1963) under entries 466 and 467. Several forms for the oaths were apparently printed throughout the South; all included space for the name, date, and county and state of residence, and many provided for a physical description, including age, height, eyes, hair, and complexion, and the occupation of the individual. Many oaths were taken under later presidential proclamations, but these do not include a physical description of the individual.

A sample of 6,738 oath takers was drawn for analysis. The oaths are arranged alphabetically by state and thereunder alphabetically by name of the oath taker. The sampling procedure drew observations in proportion to the white population of fifteen southern states as reported in the 1860 census. This procedure exhausted the age-height information available for Virginia, Kentucky, Missouri, Tennessee, and Florida. The age-height data are abundant for North Carolina, South Carolina, Georgia, Alabama, Mississippi, Louisiana, Texas, and Arkansas.

Apparently there were no age restrictions for taking the oath. The youngest oath taker recorded in the sample was age thirteen and the oldest was age ninety-seven. Clearly most of those who took the oath were capable of managing property or voting. More than 98 percent were age eighteen or above and nearly 25 percent were age fifty or above.

The sample of adults aged twenty-five to forty-nine comprises 3,937 individuals and covers a considerable part of the South, including 418 countries in thirteen southern states. These oaths span the time period from June 1863 to August 1866; about 84 percent of the oaths were taken in 1865, and within that year about 77 percent were taken from June through October. About 68 percent of the records include the individual's occupation. Of those that reported occupation, 161 different occupations were listed, of which 55.3 percent were farmers, 8.3 percent were merchants, and 5.5 percent were lawyers. The sample is concentrated in these 3 occupations relative to the occupational distribution reported by the 1860 census. Based on census data for thirteen southern states, 42.6 percent were farmers, 1.7 percent were merchants, and 0.5 percent were lawyers.

ANALYSIS

Table 24.3 displays the profile of height by age.[5] Southern white adults in this sample averaged 69.15 inches, which falls in approximately the 56th centile of modern height standards. Based on the 98 percent criterion, southern whites attained adult height at approximately age nineteen, which is slightly more than three years behind modern standards. At age eighteen, for example, southern whites reached the 24th centile. Thus average heights in excess of modern standards were achieved through prolonged growth.

It should be emphasized that the height profiles from the amnesty records may not reflect conditions in the southern white population as a whole. Recovery of property seized during the war was a motive for signing an oath and, other things being equal, height tends to increase with income or wealth (Steckel 1983). The amnesty records are probably weighted toward wealthier and therefore taller Southerners, although little can be said about the extent of bias until more is known about the socioeconomic backgrounds of people in the sample. It should be noted, however, that at the time of the American Revolution Southerners were 0.3 to 0.5 inches taller than recruits born in the North (Sokoloff and Villaflor 1982) and that a height advantage prevailed for Southerners during the Civil War (Gould [1869] 1969) and during World War II (Karpinos 1958).

Plausible determinants of height available from the amnesty records include state of residence, occupation, and year of birth.[6] State of residence may capture systematic differences in diet and in the disease environment as influenced by climate and the frequency and type of exposure to outside sources of disease. Occupation may measure two separate influences. First, to the extent that fathers' and sons' occupations were correlated and that occupation determined income, occupation may reflect the nutrition and health that were available during an individual's growing years. Second, size may have influenced comparative advantage and therefore occupational choice. Year of birth may have been correlated with the disease environment as influenced by epidemics, by per capita income growth, or by changes in the distribution of income or wealth.[7]

Table 24.4 reports the regression results. The coefficients for each group of variables (state, occupation, and year of birth) are significantly different from zero at 0.01. The coefficients of the state of residence variables show that, other things being equal, taller people were usually found in the interior and most-northern states in the South. With the exception of Florida, heights were generally small in the coastal states from North Carolina to Texas, and were particularly small in South Carolina and Texas. The lower coastal states may have been unhealthy for

Table 24.3. Southern White Heights Compared to Modern Height Standards

Age	Mean	N	Standard Deviation	Centile of Modern
18	66.95	121	2.83	24.2
19	68.11	122	2.58	39.7
20	67.71	132	3.12	27.1
21	68.63	209	2.63	47.6
22	68.95	166	2.95	52.4
23	68.58	176	2.71	46.8
24	69.22	161	2.53	56.4
25–49	69.15	3,925	2.63	55.6

Source: Civil War amnesty records and calculated from Tanner et al. (1966).

reasons of exposure to disease. In addition to a warmer climate, which promoted food spoilage and insect vectors of disease, the coastal areas had a larger urban population and the region functioned as a collection point for products and diseases shipped to and from the interior. In addition, diet may have been superior in the border states because agriculture in these areas emphasized small grains and livestock (Gray [1933] 1958).

Net nutritional conditions (as measured by adult heights) for the southern white population exceeded those in the North, where the average height of enlistees was 68.5 inches (Margo and Steckel 1983). The southern advantage also prevailed in subregional comparisons. The heights of adult oath takers from Tennessee, Kentucky, and Missouri, for example, were approximately 69.3 inches, which exceeded those from the Midwest (Ohio, Indiana, Michigan, Illinois, and Wisconsin) by approximately 0.5 inches (Gould [1869] 1969, 104). The concluding section discusses possible explanations for the southern height advantage.

Table 24.4. Regression of Height on State of Residence, Occupation, and Year of Birth, Southern White Males Aged 23–49

Variable	Coefficient	t-Value	Sample Mean
State of Residence			
Arkansas	−0.308	−1.61	0.082
Alabama	−0.466	−2.61	0.121
Florida	−0.005	−0.01	0.019
Georgia	−0.283	−1.61	0.134
Kentucky or Missouri	0.057	0.17	0.018
Louisiana	−0.471	−2.72	0.107
Mississippi	−0.320	−1.55	0.084
North Carolina	−0.485	−2.64	0.142
South Carolina	−0.717	−3.25	0.064
Texas	−0.632	−3.31	0.120
Virginia	0.713	0.89	0.003
Occupation			
Artisan (physical)	−0.576	−3.02	0.059
Artisan (non-physical)	−1.135	−3.83	0.020
Clerical	−0.465	−1.76	0.026
Farmer	0.314	2.77	0.380
Laborer	−1.370	−4.21	0.016
Merchant	−0.479	−2.41	0.054
Professional	0.370	1.92	0.057
Year of Birth			
Before 1820	0.418	2.71	0.152
1820–1824	0.357	2.30	0.145
1825–1829	0.142	0.97	0.190
1830–1834	0.331	2.26	0.193
1835–1839	0.009	0.06	0.198
Intercept	69.279	422.15	—
N	4,261		
R-Square	0.03		

Note: Dependent variable equals height in inches. The omitted variables are Tennessee, occupation not given, and born 1840–1844.
Source: Civil War amnesty records.

In an attempt to test the influence of diet and climate on height, the coefficients of the state of residence variables were regressed on measures of per capita pork and beef production in 1840, 1850, and 1860 (from Hutchinson and Williamson 1971 and Hilliard 1972) and mean annual temperature at the state capital. Pork and beef production per capita proxy the quality of the diet while mean annual temperature at the state capital represents the severity of the disease environment within the South. The coefficients have the expected sign (positive for meat production and negative for temperature) but the overall regression is statistically insignificant. The results are inconclusive, possibly because meat production per capita and average temperature may be poor measures of diet and climate or because migration made conditions in the state of residence a poor measure of actual conditions during growth.

The results by occupation show that farmers and professionals were relatively tall, laborers were relatively short, and that artisans, clerical workers, and merchants fell between these groups.[8] While it is possible that height influenced the productivity of professionals and therefore affected occupational choice, it is entirely plausible that the environment in which professionals grew up was favorable to growth. Farmers may have been tall because they had good diets during the growing years and because height probably increased productivity in this occupation. Laborers were small despite the advantages that height may have furnished in this occupation, which suggests that family poverty during the growing years impeded both physical growth and skill acquisition for these people. The artisans were separated into groups requiring heavy physical labor such as blacksmith, carpenter, and mason and those requiring light physical labor such as jeweler, photographer, and watchmaker. Because both types of artisan required training and therefore family support (or savings), it is possible that conditions of nutrition and health were similar for both groups during the growing years and that much of the difference in average height of nearly 0.6 inches was attributable to the effect of size on occupational choice.

With the exception of the slight rise for birth cohorts in 1830–1834, height tended to decline from earlier to later birth cohorts. The differences across cohorts are moderate, however, because the coefficients differ by no more than approximately 0.4 of an inch.[9]

COMPARISONS OF SLAVES AND WHITES

It is clear from examination of Tables 24.1 and 24.3 that as adults southern whites were nearly 2 inches taller than ex-slaves. Thus southern white adults reached the 56th centile of modern standards while ex-slaves attained the 25th centile. Although both groups attained adult height at approximately the same age (roughly nineteen according to the 98 percent criterion) it is clear that southern whites had a substantial advantage by the late teens. At age eighteen, for example, southern whites reached the 24th centile of modern standards but slaves attained only the 9th centile. One cannot tell from these data at what age the southern white height advantage appeared. However, an examination of slave height profiles in early childhood combined with an analysis of seasonal patterns of slave infant mortality suggest that stress on slave growth—possibly arising from seasonal patterns of work and diet—occurred during pregnancy (Steckel 1986c). To the extent that seasonal patterns of women's work and diet favored southern whites, the advantage of whites may have appeared as early as the fetal period.

Tables 24.2 and 24.4 show interesting similarities and contrasts among determinants of heights for ex-slaves and southern whites. In both groups heights were generally lower among those born or living in the lower coastal states and were lowest in South Carolina.[10] Climate obviously may have contributed to the regional pattern, and to the extent that diets within regions were similar for slaves and whites, patterns of food production and consumption may also have contributed.

The occupational classifications were sufficiently different for slaves and southern whites that direct comparisons are difficult. Nevertheless it appears that comparative advantage according to size influenced occupational choice (or allocation) in both populations. Field hands were tall because size and strength increased output while slave servants were relatively short, despite likely access to a good diet, because size was unimportant for their performance. Similarily, it was noted earlier that white artisans, especially those in jobs not requiring physical strength, were relatively short despite the likelihood that the environment for growth was favorable among those who became artisans.

Although the average nutritional status was higher among southern whites, comparison of the overall mean alone masks the greater diversity within the southern white population. Among slaves, field hands were about 0.53 inches taller than servants while southern white professionals exceeded laborers by approximately 1.3 inches. The slave-white contrasts were largest at the upper end of the spectrum. Laborers, for example, at 67.91 inches, were only 0.5 inches taller than field hands (67.22 inches) and artisans (physical), who attained 69.22 inches, exceeded slave artisans (67.16) by more than 2 inches. Thus, conditions surrounding freedom substantially improved the relative nutritional status of middle- and upper-class whites.

The year of birth coefficients in Tables 24.2 and 24.4 show that height declined by 0.33 to 0.47 inches for those born after 1830–1834. Among births before 1830 the patterns differ: Southern white heights declined but slave heights rose after cohorts of 1820 and maintained a relatively high plateau. Separate regressions for farmers and non-farmers demonstrate that the southern white height decline was concentrated among farmers. Among northern whites the height decline was concentrated among the non-farm urban born (Margo and Steckel 1983). Thus time trends within broad occupational groups differed across the North and the South, and within the South the major rural populations (slaves and southern white farmers) had opposite trends. Determinants of height that may have influenced these trends include income, the disease environment, diet, work effort, breast-feeding practices, ethnic origin, and the distribution of income of wealth. Until more is known about the time profiles of these variables and their importance to height, little can be said about their relative contribution.

Composition effects involving time period of birth, or region of birth or residence cannot explain the 2-inch height advantage enjoyed by southern white adults compared with ex-slaves. Relatively more of the ex-slaves were drawn from the interior or upper states where heights were tall, but relatively more whites were born in years in which adult heights were tall. The regression coefficients by state of birth or residence and time period of birth can be used to estimate the size of these effects. If the relevant sample weights are applied to southern white regression coefficients, the region effect widens the height difference between slaves and whites by 0.23 inches, but the time period effect narrows it by 0.11 inches. The net effect of 0.12 inches (0.23–0.11) suggests that the difference in sample means of 2 inches slightly understates the difference that would have been observed if the samples had the same region of birth or residence and year of birth weights. If the ex-slave regression coefficients are used the net of the region and time period effects is approximately zero.

CONCLUDING REMARKS

Records for ex-slaves who fought in the Union Army and for southern whites who took amnesty oaths show that adult male slaves approached and adult male southern whites exceeded modern height standards. The 2-inch height advantage enjoyed by southern white adults over slaves may have been influenced by selectivity bias in the amnesty records. The typical oath taker may have had living standards that were relatively high for the antebellum South. Nevertheless the advantages which higher incomes or wealth or lower work effort may have been able to furnish for these southern whites apparently failed to insulate them from some adverse conditions. Slaves and whites born or residing in the lower coastal states were shorter than natives or residents of the interior and Upper South states, and the heights for slaves and whites declined for births after 1830. Thus diverse conditions of health and nutrition prevailed within the antebellum South across regions and over time.

It remains to be established whether the adverse conditions that influenced health and nutrition were similar for slaves and whites. It is plausible that the disease environment, operating through climate and rates of migration, and regional patterns of food production and consumption were among the common influences on health and nutrition. Analysis of state-level data is inconclusive on these matters. However, county-level data from the censuses of agriculture suggests that food production systematically influenced height among slaves (Margo and Steckel 1982).

The height advantage enjoyed by southern whites over slaves was not an artifact of sample composition by year of birth, or region of birth or residence. Analysis of data from slave manifests and plantation records suggests that patterns of diet and work during pregnancy and shortly after birth retarded slave growth and development (Steckel 1986c). To the extent that maternal diets and work routines favored whites, the height (or size) advantage may have appeared as early as the fetal period. The decline of slave heights with plantation size (Margo and Steckel 1982) is consistent with the hypothesis that work effort in relation to diet was an important determinant of growth and development.

The amnesty records indicate that Southern whites were nearly 1 inch taller than northern whites serving in the Union Army (Fogel et al. 1983, 463). At the time of the Revolution, southern whites averaged 68.3 inches as adults, an advantage of 0.3 to 0.4 inches over their northern counterparts (Sokoloff and Villaflor 1982, 457). If the available data accurately portray the underlying populations then southern white heights increased faster than northern white heights; the precise timing of these changes, however, is difficult to identify with the evidence at hand. The antebellum rise in southern white heights also suggests that improving nutrition may help explain the reduction in crude death rates in the South over the same period (Fogel et al. 1978, 77).

Given the positive relationship between height and per capita income and the negative relationship of height with inequality in the distribution of income discovered for modern populations (Steckel 1983) the southern white height advantage is paradoxical. Per capita income estimates are higher for the North (Easterlin 1961), income and wealth were probably less evenly distributed in the South (Yang 1984a), and the disease environment was probably less favorable in the South. These adverse influences on height appear to have been counteracted by higher meat consumption in the South (Vinovskis 1972; Fogel et al. 1978; Sokoloff and Villaflor 1982; Gray [1933] 1958), by higher death rates that selected taller Southerners, and by lower urbanization (Margo and Steckel 1983).

Understanding the differing time profiles of height is a topic for future research. The first step in this endeavor is to distinguish composition effects from genuine time-related influences. It is well established that heights differ at a point in time by socioeconomic class and other categories. Thus heights may have changed over time simply by changing weights of categories in the sample. Disaggregation of time trends by categories such as wealth, ethnicity, literacy, places of birth and residence, and occupation would shed light on genuine time-related influences. Increasing the sample size would permit further disaggregation, and linking the amnesty records to the census manuscripts would provide information on socioeconomic determinants of height such as wealth, literacy, and ethnicity.

NOTES

1. For a detailed discussion of the Olson sample, see Margo and Steckel (1982), Margo (#9, *TP*, Vol. I), or Metzer (1981).
2. The estimated heights are the sample means; quantile bend estimates (see Wachter 1981) indicate that the bias due to shortfall is very small (0.1 to 0.15 inches at any age). The quantile bend estimates of the standard deviations, however, increase by 2.8 to 3.0 inches, which is consistent with the figures reported by Eveleth and Tanner (1976) for modern day African Americans.

   Europeans, Americans of European descent, and Americans of African descent who grew up under good nutritional circumstances have approximately the same patterns of growth and final heights (Eveleth and Tanner 1976, App.), which suggests that British standards reported by Tanner et al. (1966) are suitable as a standard of comparison.

3. See Margo and Steckel (1982) for evidence that taller (and heavier) slaves commanded significantly higher prices.

4. This result contrasts with our findings for northern whites (Margo and Steckel 1983), which show a significant negative association between height and year of enlistment. The lack of any such association among ex-slave recruits is important, since it suggests that the fall in height observed among ex-slave recruits born after 1835 was not due to an influx of individuals of inferior stock enlisting at the end of the war.

5. The raw data displayed evidence of age and height rounding and heaping (preference for ages ending in zero and heights ending in even-numbered inches, especially whole feet), characteristics also shared by modern data (see National Center for Health Statistics 1965). Simulations and sensitivity analyses show, however, that heaping and rounding observed in these data did not seriously distort secular trends or cross-sectional differences (see Fogel et al. 1983, 455–456).

6. As pointed out in our earlier paper (Margo and Steckel 1982), ex-slave recruits born between 1820 and 1824 in the South Atlantic region were unusually tall, and recruits born in 1835 unusually short. If these observations are excluded from the adult regression, the data show an increase in adult height from the early 1820s to mid-1830s cohorts. Also, recruits born after 1835 may still have experienced further growth due to cartilage expansion (see Tanner 1978, 18–19) which may account for some of their relative shortness. Friedman (1982) demonstrates that shorter slaves (in Trinidad) had higher death rates, which suggests that our estimated time profile of adult height may be biased downward, although Tanner (1982) argues and simulations (discussed in note 9) suggest that such an effect would be relatively minor.

7. Regressions on heights of persons aged eighteen to twenty-two at the time of the oath are not discussed because none of the region or occupation variables are statistically significant for this group in regressions similar to those reported in Table 24.4. Persons aged eighteen to twenty-two were growing during the war years, and wartime hardships and dislocations may have disrupted the systematic growth patterns observed for older southern whites. For these reasons the average heights reported for this group in Table 24.3 should be viewed cautiously as an indicator of antebellum conditions. The older southern whites in the sample may have achieved adult heights at a lower age than suggested by the figures in Table 24.3.

8. The occupational groupings follow those suggested in Thernstrom (1973), App. B. Clerical included bookkeeper and clerk; professional included primarily dentist, doctor, engineer, and lawyer; artisan (physically demanding) included primarily blacksmith, bricklayer, carpenter, mechanic, painter, and wheelwright; artisan (not physically demanding) included primarily bookbinder, conductor, jeweler, miller, pilot, printer, tailor, and watchmaker; and farmer also included planter and rancher. Given the imprecision of the raw data and the debate over appropriate groupings, the results provide no more than a general indication of height by occupation.

9. Friedman (1982, 500) reports that survivors were taller than non-survivors among slaves in Trinidad. Over a 1-year period the average difference in heights was about 0.63 inches among nonadults. This phenomenon contaminates comparisons of heights to a small degree. If the difference in mortality rates between two populations was 10 per thousand at each age, for example, then over an eighteen year period of growth the difference in heights attributable to selective survival would have been only $18 \times 0.01 \times 0.63 = 0.11$ inches.

10. The small sizes for ex-slave recruits in certain states did not permit us to disaggregate place of birth further than the regional dummies given in Table 24.2. As a result the state of birth or residence effects are not directly comparable for ex-slaves and southern whites. Nevertheless the general pattern in which heights were larger in the interior and upper states is clear for both populations.

TWENTY-FIVE

A Linear-Programming Solution to the Slave Diet

Charles Kahn

Quantitative examination by Fogel and Engerman has rekindled debate on the adequacy of the slave diet. "The belief that the typical slave was poorly fed is without foundation in fact," they claim (1974a, 1:109–110), going on to emphasize the variety of foods and the quantity of meat and general nutritional adequacy of the typical diet.

Critics such as Sutch (1976, 234) have objected that

> economic incentive . . . if not human kindness, would rule out serious food depriva-
> tion as a characteristic of slave life. . . . The issue then is not whether the slaves were
> typically starved. They clearly were not. Rather Fogel and Engerman join the debate
> with the historians who precede them over the issue of the variety and quality of the
> slave's diet.

Sutch goes on to argue that the same considerations of economics would impose a "monotonous and barely adequate" diet.

We propose therefore to examine the problem from the opposite direction, by asking the following question: What would have been the least costly diet that would have given a slave adequate nutrition? We calculate such a diet by solving a linear-programming problem. In this problem, from a potential menu of ten foods we calculate the least-cost menu that meets or exceeds minimum nutritional standards in protein, calories, vitamins, and minerals.

The exercise serves two purposes. In the narrow sense it provides a check on the reasonableness of the Fogel and Engerman and Sutch estimates and a baseline—the lowest possible baseline—against which to discuss the adequacy or inadequacy of the actual diet. The tenor of the Sutch argument is that the observed diet should have approximated this least-cost estimate; the tenor of the Fogel and Engerman thesis is that it would lie well above.

The exercise also serves in the investigation of several broader questions. Our understanding of the diet of the mass of population in the nineteenth century is still rudimentary. We have much data on the price of foodstuffs, and at macro levels there are data on the supply of foodstuffs. However, the data are of insufficient detail for many of the questions that we are interested in examining, and we are very quickly reduced to speculation. For example, there is great interest in the effect of changing standards of nutrition on the health of various social classes. The understanding we have at present of the diet is just not sufficient to tackle these problems.

Consider foods prices in particular: It has been argued that by 1860 wholesale prices throughout the country had gone much of the distance toward convergence and it had become legitimate to speak of a "national market" (Cole 1938). Nonetheless if we examine different estimates of particular relative prices of foodstuffs enormous variation remains—so much so that national averages may be misleading representations of relative costs in various areas.

In calculating U.S. farm product, Towne and Rasmussen (1960) compiled prices from several sources into weightings meant to represent a national average. Among the sources used were the wholesale prices collected by Cole and an index of local prices throughout Virginia collected by Peterson (1929). In some respects the national averages and the southern prices are in close agreement (Table 25.1); all estimates, for example, show wheat as twice as expensive as corn. On the other hand, some of the differences are striking, and with present knowledge there is simply no way to determine whether this represents differences in the quality of the foodstuffs described or true differences in relative costs. And if relative costs in various areas are still uncertain, even less is known about relative quantities produced or consumed.

In such a situation it should not be surprising that, in general, historians have hesitated to go on to the investigation of the more interesting set of issues of *why* a particular mix of foods was chosen by a particular set of people at a particular time. This is obviously a complicated question. Economists, with the prejudices of their discipline, would emphasize the effect of relative costs in the determination of the diet. Social historians with other backgrounds might emphasize "folkways." These two sets of explanations are certainly mutually reinforcing and, in general, impossible to disentangle. "Taste" can be a datum in the short run and a variable in the longer run; its influence on human action is pervasive and complex.

Table 25.1. Three Reports of Prices of Foods in 1860 (Cents Per Pound)

	New Orleans (Cole)	Virginia (Peterson)	U.S. Average (Towne and Rasmussen)
Pork	9.54	4.50–6.34–11.00	6.52
Beef	6.60	6.78	6.98
Mutton	—	9.44	8.75
Butter	23.88	16.00	8.30
Milk	—	—	0.83
Sweet Potatoes	—	0.62–1.38	0.96
Irish Potatoes	—	1.46–0.95	0.62
Cowpeas	—	1.82	1.46
Corn	1.28	1.27	0.82
Wheat	2.36	2.33	1.70

For the slave, if for anybody, individual tastes and preferences would be subordinated by the master to the plantation's profitability. Thus, in examining the diet of the slave we should be observing the maximal influence that economic factors will ever assert on choice of diet. Should the results be small in this case, they can be expected to be even smaller in other cases. The relative abundance of data from previous investigations of the slave diet, the relative simplicity of the objectives of those in control, and the relative simplicity of the foods themselves make the slave diet an ideal starting point for investigating the economic determinants of diet.

THE LIMITS TO COST MINIMIZATION

In pursuing this approach we must take as a maintained assumption that slaveowners were profit maximizers. Although some historians have emphasized other motivations (Genovese 1974), there seems to be ample evidence of the "economic rationality" of the running of southern plantations for this assumption to be taken as a fruitful working hypothesis.

Homo economicus in the guise of a plantation owner would indeed be interested in minimizing the cost of the food provided to slaves. After all, there are repeated references by slaveholders to the care that was to be taken in allocating food and avoiding waste. The ration was weighed carefully and generally allocated under the supervision of the foreman or the owner himself (Postell 1951, 36). Nonetheless, there are several reasons that a minimum cost estimate as derived here might not mimic the actions of a rational slaveholder.

First of all, man does not live by calories and vitamins alone. By sticking to the bare minimum diet, a planter might destroy morale and lose more in production than any savings made in food costs. It could be the constraints of morale rather than nutrition which are the relevant ones.[1]

This argument is an appeal to "tastes." Two aspects of tastes may be at issue: a taste for (or against) particular staples[2] and a taste for variety (or other forms of quality) in general. It could be the case that the observed slave diet represented an implicit bargain between slave and master for higher quality rations in return for greater effort. The mechanism by which such agreements might occur is not obvious, and its working out would require examination of the costs to masters of enforcement of discipline by other means—in short it will be a hefty undertaking.[3] Nonetheless such bargains may certainly form one of the wedges between observed and least-cost diets.

An appeal to tastes for this or that individual food is on shakier ground. If slaves disliked a particular food, a planter might be induced for a time to keep it out of the ration. But planters were involved in long-term investments and would have therefore engaged in long-term planning. If the food were indeed healthy and sufficiently cheap, the incentive would be there to "make the slave like it"—by introducing it gradually, or, if all else failed, then by raising the young on the new food.[4]

A second wedge is due to the very cost or difficulty of making the least-cost calculations. We need not worry that in 1860 solution of linear programs by the simplex method and related procedures was still nearly a century away.[5] We do not claim that any individual planter actually sat down with pencil and paper to calculate the constrained optimum; the actions of the group of planters as a whole could have duplicated the simplex procedure by trial and error. One planter tries a diet, sees that his slaves thrive on it and then looks around for one adjustment or another that "cuts corners." Through agricultural journals or more informal means, communication of successes and failures or of proposals for further experimentation speeds up the process of innovation.

For this process to take place, the planter need not even have theoretical information on factors involved in nutrition. The health of the slaves is of considerable concern and closely observed. The planter may not know the scientific name for the disease he observes, and formal science may have no knowledge of the specific nutritional factor involved. The forces pushing his actions are simply the necessity of making some drastic change if his slaves fall ill and the pressure of the costs of their food, if the slaves are healthy.

Viewed in this light, our linear programming problem is a stylized summary of a complicated dynamic process. However, in real time the process is always incomplete; as costs and requirements change there will always be a lag in innovation leaving the planter somewhere within the cost frontier. This lag is the second component of the wedge between the observed cost of the diet and the cost we will calculate.

This view of the process is also useful for illustrating the limits beyond which the cost-minimizing approach cannot be pushed. Planters are rational, but their information is imperfect. The modifications that might be contemplated are boundless and the planter's imagination is limited. Moreover the planter is risk-averse; he will avoid experiments that appear too drastic, and instead stick to modifications that are close to the observed standards.[6]

If we hope to model the process successfully, we must keep our sights equally limited. We cannot hope to include as possibilities foods not known in the region, or processes of cooking not yet invented. Nor can we hope to account for improved strains of existing foods. Indeed part of the exercise that follows will be an examination of constraints that might have been perceived as binding at the time without actually having been so. We will indicate one such perceived constraint which actually accounts for a large part of the observed discrepancy between the cost minimization and actual diet.

THE INITIAL CALCULATION

For the initial calculation we have based minimum nutritional requirements on estimates by the World Health Organization (WHO), prices of foods on estimates for Virginia by Peterson (1929), and nutritive content of foods on tables by Watt and Merrill (1950). The following sections outline the details of these estimations.

NUTRITIONAL REQUIREMENTS

The WHO estimates may be found in Beaton and Bengoa (1976). We used the energy requirements for the "reference man with very heavy work" (459) or 4,000 calories per day.[7] Other requirements (Table 25.2) are also based on Beaton and Patwardhan's (1976, 455–456) with the following modifications: Vitamin D, folic acid, and vitamin B_{12} requirements were not included in our calculation. Given adequate exposure to the sun, vitamin D is synthesized in the skin.[8] Data on the amount of B_{12} in various foods are not readily available. In any event deficiencies of B_{12} appear to be very rare: Although B_{12} is produced only by animal sources even strict vegetarians seem typically to acquire sufficient amounts, perhaps through contamination of water or vegetable products by microorganisms (Layrisse, et al. 1976, 75; also National Research Council 1980, 117). Folate deficiency is more common and some data on the folic acid content of foods are available (To-epfer 1951, Table 9), but the estimates show extremely wide variation and thus are not easily used in a linear program. However, for all the diets described in this paper, with the exception of the "standard ration," calculations of lower bounds on total folic acid demonstrated that all had considerably more than the 400 μ recommendation.

The WHO requirements of thiamine, niacin, and riboflavin are initially calculated per 1,000 kcal of diet (Beaton and Patwardhan 1976, 475). For niacin and thiamine, we have multiplied these estimates by four to obtain our requirements. However we have retained the "reference man" estimate for riboflavin because "while it has been customary to describe riboflavine requirements in terms of energy requirements . . . there is no evidence that the requirements are closely linked" (Beaton 1976, 148).

Estimates of recommended nutritional requirements, recommended dietary allowances (RDAs), are also made by the National Research Council of the United States (National Research Council 1980). In Britain, the Department of Health and Social Security makes estimations (see Davidson et al. 1975, 184, for tables). The differences between the three are not great although the RDAs for many nutrients are somewhat higher than WHO estimates. The WHO estimates were used because they were somewhat more closely linked to actual deficiency estimates than to such factors as body saturation.[9] The most important differences between the RDA and

Table 25.2. Minimum Daily Nutritional Requirements

Calories	4,000 kcal
Protein	62 g
Vitamin A	3,750 IU
Vitamin C	30 mg
Thiamine	1.6 mg
Riboflavin	1.8 mg
Niacin	26.4 mg
Calcium	500 mg
Iron	9 mg

Source: See text.

WHO estimates are for vitamin C and for calcium. In each case, the National Research Council recommendations are approximately double the WHO recommendations.

For iron and protein, recommendations vary with the composition of the diet. We have taken the recommendations under the worst case. Since these constraints turned out not to be binding, no further modifications were necessary.

FOODS

The ten foods included in this estimate are beef, pork, mutton, milk, butter, potatoes, sweet potatoes, cowpeas, wheat, and corn. With the exception of small grains, this list represents those foods listed in the 1860 census of agriculture, from which estimates of the actual slave diet have been made by Fogel and Engerman (1983, 5) and Sutch (1976, 262–263). These items probably accounted for the bulk of the diet.[10]

For these ten foods, nutritional values were taken from Watt and Merrill (1950, Table 2) under the following assumptions. All meats consumed were of the "thin" class. Given descriptions of the haphazard management of southern livestock (Hilliard 1972, 95–101, 125–130), this assumption seems the most reasonable. It was assumed that the entire dressed carcass was consumed by slaves. Altough it is true that choicest cuts would have been reserved for the master's table, the error caused by this simplification should be minor (Hilliard 1972, 57). It was assumed that the dressed weights were the following percentages of live weights of the animal: beef, 55 percent; pork, 75 percent; and mutton, 48 percent.[11]

All corn was consumed as whole ground unbolted corn meal; all wheat was consumed as whole wheat flour from hard wheat. All cowpeas were consumed as mature dried seeds. All milk was whole (not skimmed or buttermilk).[12]

The vitamin A content of many vegetables varies with their color. In particular, yellow varieties of corn have an abundance of vitamin A and white varieties have virtually none. The variance is also important in sweet potatoes. Thus the nutritional value of these two foods turns on the question of which variety was typically grown. It was arbitrarily assumed that half of the sweet potatoes had vitamin A at modern levels while half had none. In fact, many varieties of each vegetable were grown and there appears to be no way at present to estimate the proportions, although Sutch gives evidence from Patent Office reports that white varieties of corn were more common than yellow in most (but not all) of the southern states (U.S. Patent Office 1849). Nonetheless, it turns out that yellow corn is so rich in vitamin A, that even if only 7 percent of the corn consumed were yellow, the vitamin A requirement could be satisfied by corn alone in the least-cost diets calculated below.

Since there is no indication of yellow corn being so rare, it would appear fairly safe to assume that the least-cost diet proposed using the *average* mixture of corn would indeed exceed requirements for vitamin A. Of course in any one location or at any one time it could be that only white corn was used in the diet, in which case, these estimates would no longer apply and a more detailed analysis would be required, subject to the various varieties of corn and sweet potatoes actually available.

Since tryptophan can be converted into niacin in the body at an average ratio of 60 mg of tryptophan to 1 mg of niacin,[13] tryptophan contents of food were also calculated from the estimates of Orr and Watt (1951) and added in to form "niacin equivalents."

Some niacin occurs in food in a bound form unavailable to the digestive system. There are at present no satisfactory estimates of available (as opposed to total) niacin. Nonetheless it appears that corn in particular has large amounts of bound niacin because of the long-observed relation between pellagra (a niacin-deficiency disease) and diets dominated by corn. We have therefore made estimates under two assumptions: one, that all niacin in corn was available for nutrition, and two, that none was (but that all niacin in all other foods was fully available). These assumptions thus represent the extreme possibilities as to the usefulness or uselessness of corn to the diet.

It must be emphasized that the evidence on niacin in particular is preliminary and very unsatisfactory. However, the problem appears to be a most difficult one from the nutritional standpoint as well (Nutrition Reviews 1974; Darby et al. 1975). The niacin content depends on the coarseness of the grain used: Pellagra in the South seems to have increased with extra refining of cornmeal (Davies 1964; but see Kiple and Kiple 1977b). It is further complicated by the fact that treatment of grains with alkalis seems to release extra amounts of the niacin.[14] Hominy was made by a process that used lye, an alkali.[15] Thus, a more complete estimation will have to take into account the details of the processing of hominy, and the proportion of hominy in the diet.[16]

PRICES

Weighted prices for 1860 were taken from Peterson (1929, Table 85) for wheat, corn, beef cattle, sheep, and butter. Milk was assumed to have a price one-tenth of that of butter (Towne and Rasmussen 1960, 288). Peterson's price series for Irish potatoes only begins after the Civil War. Therefore the average price for the 1870s of early potatoes was deflated to an 1860 figure by using the 1870s average of Peterson's price index for Virginia agricultural goods. Sweet potato prices were available only for selected years in the 1870s. For these years the average price relative to potatoes was calculated and then these prices were again deflated to the 1860 level.[17]

Hog prices are not available for 1860. Therefore three estimates were used: The highest was simply to take the 1860 price of bacon and the lowest was to use the average 1870s price of hogs relative to beef deflated by the 1860 price of beef. These two estimates are also widely separated; in fact they bound the relative price estimates of Towne and Rasmussen and of Cole for New Orleans. An intermediate estimate of hog prices was derived by multiplying the Peterson beef price by the Towne-Rasmussen relative price.

RESULTS

Under the above assumptions, the least-cost diet consists of 0.5 pound of milk, 0.25 pound of sweet potatoes, 0.5 pound of cowpeas, and 1.75 pounds of cornmeal per day.[18] The limiting nutrients in the diet are calories, riboflavin, niacin, and vitamin C. That is, for these nutrients, this diet provides exactly the minimum requirements, while for other nutrients amounts are provided in excess of the minimum.

Note that corn is in the diet despite the assumption of the lowest niacin availability; and no meat is in the diet despite the lowest assumption on the cost of pork. Altering these assumptions therefore has no effect on the composition of the diet. The reason for the inclusion of the corn is quite simple: It supplies the greatest calories per dollar. The amount of corn and milk is about the same as Fogel and Engerman's estimate (corn is somewhat less than and milk somewhat greater than in Sutch's estimate). Only cowpeas appear in the diet in greater quantities than in Fogel and Engerman's estimate (Table 25.3).

The Fogel and Engerman diet is 5 percent cheaper than the Sutch diet. The crucial difference is the amount of meat: Fogel and Engerman's diet gives 0.459 pound per day and Sutch's gives 0.628 pound per day. However, the difference in cost between these two estimates is small compared with the difference between either estimate and the least-cost diet. The least-cost diet is 46 percent cheaper than Fogel and Engerman's and 50 percent cheaper than Sutch's; it is even 15 percent cheaper than the unsupplemented "standard ration" of 2 pounds of corn and 0.5 pound of pork.[19] In each case the crucial difference is the absence of meat.

The first and most important puzzle then is "Where did the pork go?" The more that this question is considered, the more troubling it becomes. Meat was not as common a part of the slave diet in the rest of the Americas; Kiple and Kiple (1980, 202) claim that for the Caribbean slave 0.5 pound of meat a day would be an

Table 25.3. Comparison of Diets (pounds per day)

	Least-Cost Diet	Fogel and Engerman Estimate	Sutch Estimate	Standard Ration
Pork	—	0.31	0.53	0.50
Beef	—	0.15	0.10	—
Mutton	—	0.01	—	—
Butter	—	0.01	0.01	—
Milk	0.60	0.60	0.41	—
Sweet Potatoes	0.25	1.12	0.72	—
Irish Potatoes	—	0.08	0.06	—
Cowpeas	0.58	0.35	0.12	—
Corn	1.74	1.78	2.23	2.00
Wheat	—	0.12	0.12	—
Cost (cents/day)	4.4	8.2	8.7	5.2

Notes: The estimates by Fogel and Engerman and Sutch have been multiplied by 1.28 to convert to an adult ration (Fogel and Engerman 1974a), 2:97. The least-cost estimate and the costs themselves are derived using the Peterson prices in Table 25.1. For this particular estimate we used the intermediate price of pork and the first of the two prices listed for sweet potatoes and Irish potatoes. The price of milk is assumed to be one-tenth the price of butter.

overestimate. Meat was not even such a common portion of the diet in working-class England at the time (Oddy 1976, 214–231; Burnett 1966, 96, 122–130, 148–157). Nor can we appeal to the argument that it was actually necessary to the health of the slave—no matter what nutrient we consider, there was readily available a cheaper, meatless way of supplying it.

It might be assumed that a cost-minimizing plantation owner would actually have to replace milk with meat in this proposed diet, because of lactase deficiency among adult blacks. Cardell and Hopkins (*EM*, #45) have argued that the relatively small amounts of milk consumed by slaves can be explained by lactase deficiency. They cite evidence that most of the milk consumed by blacks was consumed by children. Young children are typically not affected by lactase deficiency (Woodruff 1976).

However, this line of reasoning will not eliminate as infeasible the least-cost diet we have estimated, because lactase deficiency is asymptomatic for small doses of milk. In fact, some adults do not realize they have the deficiency until some special circumstance (such as an ulcer) puts them on a high milk content diet. The deficiency is tested for with a dose of 50 g of lactose (Davidson et al. 1975, 154). The diet proposed would only give 13 g of lactose a day. Another indication of the feasibility of such a diet even for lactase-deficient individuals is the work of Zaal who showed that lactase-deficient schoolboys could thrive on diets supplemented with 250 ml of milk—that is, approximately 0.5 pound, and thus comparable to our figure for adults (Nutrition Reviews 1978).

Nutritional recommendations for vitamins and nutrients are typically made to be two standard deviations above "true" average requirements, in order to leave some measure of assurance that almost all of the population receives adequate amounts of the nutrients. For instance, it is known that clinical signs of scurvy can be cured with only 10 mg/day of vitamin C; and pellagra can be prevented with as little as 4.4 mg/1,000 kcal of niacin. The dosage of riboflavin actually necessary is fairly uncertain partly since the symptoms of riboflavin deficiency are not nearly so dramatic as those for the other vitamins. Estimates for the minimum requirement range from 1 to 2 mg per day.[20] If for any of these nutrients we decreased the requirement in our linear-programming problem, the net result would be an increase in the importance of the calorie constraint, and thus corn would remain in the diet, and probably increase in importance. Meats would never be brought in by any of these adjustments.

One possibility is that the opportunity costs on the plantation are not being adequately represented. Perhaps transportation costs rather than being constant percentage markups on price are more closely represented by constant amounts per weight of the food. Unfortunately this would mean that the expensive foods in the market are even more expensive, relatively speaking, on the farm. The same holds if we assume that animals are cheaper to transport on the hoof.

The price of milk in the equation is the subject of greater uncertainty than the other prices. However, even if the milk price is varied we will not be able to bring meat into the diet or throw corn out. In these diets milk supplies riboflavin and (in some variations) calcium, neither of which are particularly prevalent in meats.

ADDING A FAT CONSTRAINT

It thus becomes apparent that the observed diet cannot be explained solely in terms of nutritional levels and costs. The next step in the explanation is to include extra constraints and to see which minimal set of constraints makes the diet begin to mirror reality. Then we have a prima facie case for the importance of those considerations.

The constraint we want to examine is the addition of a fat requirement. Strictly speaking, fat is necessary to a diet only for supplying small amounts of essential fatty acids and for transport of fat-soluble vitamins. These needs can be met with 15–25 g of fat daily (National Research Council 1980, 33), an amount well below that supplied by any of these diets (Table 25.4). In addition, fats make some desirable, as opposed to necessary, contributions to a diet: They make foods more palatable, partly by lubricating, and they contribute to a feeling of satiety because they are more slowly absorbed (Davidson et al. 1975, 89). In high-calorie diets, fat may be of practical importance as a concentrated means of acquiring the calories. Otherwise individuals may spend much of their day eating.

Table 25.4. Fat in the Diet (grams)

	Least-Cost Diet	Fogel and Engerman Estimate	Sutch Estimate	Standard Ration
Total Fat	45.8	100.7	128.3	100.4
Fat From Meat	0	48.6	74.1	65.0

Whatever the actual needs in the diet, there is no doubt that at the time the average planter believed that fat was a necessary part of the diet, particularly for hard-working slaves. Meat allowances were typically adjusted to the level of fat: The leaner the meat, the more was given. A typical ration was to give 3.5 pounds of bacon if middlings and 4 pounds if shoulder. Beef, being leaner than pork in general, was fed in larger rations.[21]

Much of contemporary nutritional theory argued otherwise, dividing foods into "fibrinous" (i.e., proteins, used in building tissues) and "heat producing" (fats, starches, and the like) (Hollingsworth 1976; *Southern Cultivator* 1847, 69). Those engaged in heavy labor would require more meat, to build muscle, but fat as such would be undesirable. One doctor decried the "Erroneous belief that pork—and the fatter the better—is the only proper substance of animal food for Negroes," arguing that fats and oils built fatty tissue rather than muscle, and were in fact harmful for the human body. "It follows therefore that *Beef,* or any article which affords a lessened quantity of oil or the injurious element *Carbon,* entering so largely into its composition and more of nitrogen, &c, is the more appropriate substance" (Draughon 1850; emphasis in original).

The response to this suggestion by a planter was telling:

One of your correspondents has endeavored to prove that lean meat is more nutritious than fat. It is, however, a well known fact that the more exhausting the labor, the fatter the meat which the negroe's appetite craves, and it agrees well with him.

This I regard as one of the instincts of nature; and think experience is opposed to your correspondent's theory (Tattler 1850).

The first problem then, is the proper level of the constraint. Strictly speaking the argument would set the constraint at the observed level: We are then looking for the least costly way of providing the level of fat actually observed in the diet. We have chosen a slightly different level—that provided by the standard ration. The differences between the two approaches are minor.

Two versions of the fat constraint were considered: one considering only meat fat, the other allowing the fat to be from any source. The linear programs were then run under two extreme assumptions for the price of pork (Table 25.5). At the low extreme of pork prices, either version of the fat constraint brings in pork as the right food for meeting the constraint. Introducing pork to the diet has little effect on the other foods, except to reduce the requirement of cowpeas. Because of this reduction, calcium becomes a binding constraint, and either niacin or riboflavin ceases to be one. Using the meat constraint, pork of course is used to meet the constraint exactly; except for peas little else in the diet is changed.

Even if we increase the pork price to the extreme of bacon, it is still the cheapest means of obtaining meat fat, since pork is so much fatter than other meats. However, then butter is a cheaper means of obtaining fat in general, and in the problem where we allow the constraint to be satisfied by non-meat products as well butter becomes the cheapest source. (Butter has very little carbohydrate and thus very little lactose so again the question of the lactase deficiency is irrelevant.)

CONCLUSION

If we examine costs per unit of nutrient, we will see that corn is the cheapest way of consuming calories and pork is the cheapest way of consuming fat. These facts are

Table 25.5. Least-Cost Diet with Minimum Fat Requirements

	100.4 g of Fat from All Sources		65.0 g of Meat Fats
	Assuming Lowest Price of Pork	Assuming Highest Price of Pork	Assuming Either Price of Pork
Pork	0.43	—	0.50
Beef	—	—	—
Mutton	—	—	—
Butter	—	0.14	—
Milk	0.65	0.31	0.63
Sweet Potatoes	0.29	0.28	0.30
Irish Potatoes	—	—	—
Cowpeas	0.11	0.53	0.09
Corn	1.79	2.22	1.75
Wheat	—	—	—
Cost (under medium price of pork in cents/day)	6.42	6.70	6.75

not sufficient for the two staples to be included in a linear-programming solution. For cost minimization, what counts is not the food's contribution in any single nutrient, but its marginal contribution in all limiting nutrients. But because of the particular needs met by these particular foods and their relationship to the others included in the diet the two-clause summary: "Corn was for calories; pork was for fat" turns out to be a fair mnemonic.

This two-clause conclusion is robust, and it accounts for the basic facts about the slave diet. Even though the diets described in the last estimations begin to bear resemblance to actual average slave diet, there remains a fair discrepancy between estimated minimum costs and observed costs. The first diet in Table 25.5, for example, still costs 22 percent less than Fogel and Engerman's and 26 percent less than Sutch's.[22]

Of course, in many respects these results are preliminary, since a linear program with only ten foods and nine constraints is certainly simpler than the true cost minimization involved. There are numerous possibilities for improvements in these estimates, and some of the following complications may be worth considering.

First of all, the ten prices we consider may be an inadequate representation of the opportunity costs to the plantation, since plantation production involves considerable complementarity. For example, one of the advantages of producing corn is that its cultivation and harvest can be adjusted around the cultivation of cash crops. Cowpeas are useful because they can be planted among the corn rows, and hogs can be let loose to fatten on the remaining plants (Hilliard 1972). Then there are minor vegetables and game that slaves can obtain in their own time—foods which planters might regard as essentially free goods.

Furthermore, the nutritional requirements vary by age or sex of the individual (notably for iron) and even by season of the year (in the case of vitamin D). The nutrition derivable from foods may be a complex function of the conditions of their storage and preparation or the mix eaten at one time (Kiple and Kiple 1977a; Sutch, 1976).

Finally, and most importantly, it must be emphasized that this paper has only examined one side of the decision to provide a particular diet, namely the costs. An alternative explanation of the decision to provide meat to slaves may lie in the demand side. Thus it is also important to investigate the use by planters of variety and quality of food as a technique for controlling the slave population.

NOTES

1. Closely related are the arguments cited by contributors to agricultural journals at the time that slaves would steal food if not adequately fed. See the citations in Sutch (1976), 282, n. 144.
2. For specific examples of this sort of argument, see Hilliard (1972), 49, 59, 62.
3. Recent theoretical work in the economics of principals and agents and in implicit contracts could usefully be incorporated into an examination of the complications of such relations between masters and slaves.
4. Just such a proposal for introducing beef rather than pork into the diet was made by one doctor at the time (See Draughon 1850).
5. Of course linear programs were solved by trial and error long before the simplex method. For an

interesting example of an early text explaining the use of trial and error to solve the least-cost problem for animal feeds, see Henry (1910), 110–115.

6. It was an abolitionist charge that such experiments were made with exotic "foods" such as cotton-seed, although no firsthand accounts were cited (see Sydnor [1933] 1966, 30).

7. Durnin and Passmore (1967) record higher expenditures for forestry workers (6,550 in Germany, 5,700 in Sweden) and rickshaw pullers in Calcutta (4,880) but emphasize that these are short-run figures, not yearly averages. Studies of coal miners, whose work is steadier show daily energy expenditures between 2,970 and 4,560 with 3,660 as the mean (Durnin and Passmore 1967), 126).

8. Heavy pigmentation reduces synthesis of vitamin D (Layrisse, et al. 1976, 61). However, the effect is serious only in children not exposed to the sun. Since Kiple and Kiple (1977a) among others argue that childhood rickets were extremely common among slaves, vitamin D requirements will have to be taken into account in recalculating least-cost diets for children.

9. Compare, for example, National Research Council (1980), 128–129, and Beaton and Patwardhan (1976), 469–470.

10. Rice was not included in the estimate because it could not be grown on the typical plantation. For most foods, prices, even though representing prices in the city market, may reasonably be taken as proxies for the opportunity cost of producing the food: Essentially we assume that transportation costs of bringing produced food to the market were always proportional markups on the observed price. But if the food must be transported in the other direction, then the true opportunity cost is market price *plus* rather than minus the markup. Rather than try to calculate these transportation costs, we simply ruled rice out *ab initio.*

11. For pork, see the discussion in Sutch (1976), 243–245, and in Fogel and Engerman (1983), 21. For beef, see Sutch (1976), 249, n. 40. The ratio for sheep was taken from Watt and Merrill (1950).

12. *Milk:* Most was buttermilk (Hilliard 1972, 61; Kiple and Kiple, 1977a), but since the fat content of milk is not what makes it useful in the diets estimated the assumption makes little difference. Even in the subsequent section of this paper, where fat content is a consideration, milk never turns out to be the best source. *Wheat:* The tables do not carry figures for whole wheat flour from soft wheat. However, when hard and soft whole grain wheat are compared, soft has lower nutritional value on every factor except iron. Since iron turns out not to be limiting factor and whole wheat flour from hard wheat is excluded from the least-cost diet, we conclude that the diet would exclude soft wheat flour as well.

13. See Beaton and Patwardhan (1976), 456, and National Research Council (1980), 92. However, the variance with which this conversion takes place is high and depends on the other uses to which the body is putting tryptophan.

14. See Davidson et al. (1975), 168, and Barakat (1976), 129. However, see also Goldsmith (1964), 2:181–182.

15. Sutch (1976), 280, n. 140, citing U.S. Patent Office (1849), 153.

16. Hilliard (1972), 50–56, argues hominy was subordinate.

17. Milling losses were ignored. According to Sutch (1976), 261, such losses for corn should be small. The following conversions were used for bushels:

Sweet Potatoes	50 lb
Irish Potatoes	60 lb
Cowpeas	50 lb
Corn	56 lb
Wheat	60 lb

For discussions of these standards, see Sutch (1976), Peterson (1929), and Homans and Homans (1858). A second method of calculating potato prices from Peterson's data (1929), 175–180, was to use the December 1 prices of late potatoes, which were also available for the 1870s. According to Peterson (1929), 52, since late potatoes were commonly stored for resale, the price did not vary greatly during the year; nonetheless this seems a less acceptable procedure. Since it yielded such different prices from the initial estimate it was felt desirable to use this estimate as well, as a check on the robustness of the results. December 1 prices of sweet potatoes were also available for several years in the 1870s; these formed the basis of a second estimate of sweet potato prices.

18. Using the alternate price for sweet potatoes (note 17) and the reduced price for Irish potatoes brings Irish potatoes into the diet but does not knock any other food out.

19. The standard ration is the basic allotment to slaves cited in most traditional histories. See Sutch (1976), 235, for references.

20. *Vitamin C:* Hodges (1976), 121, National Research Council (1980), 73. *Niacin:* Barakat (1976), 128, National Research Council (1980), 93. *Riboflavin:* Davidson et al. (1975), 170, Beaton (1976), 148.

21. Hilliard (1972), 56–59, Postell (1951), 32, 34. Peas, too, were valued for their oil (Postell 1951, 34).

22. Even though the discrepancies are large, they are nowhere near the magnitude of the discrepancies between modern least-cost estimates and modern diets (see Stigler 1945; Dantzig 1963). Although this difference may be in part due to the difference in the situation of the slave, it is largely due to the more limited menu we allow in estimates of the least-cost diet.

TWENTY-SIX

Punishments and Rewards

Stephen C. Crawford

Slavery presents the slaveowner with the problem of both controlling and motivating his chattel. If the slave narratives are indeed a true indication of the lives of southern slaves, the use and threat of physical punishment were an important part of the plantation social system. Most of the interviews which provide an in-depth look at the informant's experience as a slave confront the issue of physical punishment either in terms of the slave's firsthand experience or of his knowledge of practices on nearby plantations. Restricting the discussion to the firsthand experience of the ex-slaves and their parents allows a systematic investigation of both the use of physical punishment and the trade-off between physical punishment and positive incentives. While the discussion may not resolve the presently hotly debated issues on the use of physical punishment, it should allow a fuller examination of the experience of slaves under the different systems within the late antebellum South.

The most important information for the examination of physical punishment is the ex-slave's characterization of the frequency of physical punishment on his last plantation. Of the 444 ex-slaves providing information on the frequency of punishment, 18.9 percent resided on plantations without physical punishment, 42.6 percent resided on plantations characterized by infrequent physical punishment, and the remainder, 38.5 percent, characterized their plantation as high frequency of punishment. There are two major problems with this distribution. First, black and white interviewers report a different distribution of frequency of punishment. Table 26.1 cross-tabulates the frequency of punishment by the race of the interviewer. Black interviewers relate a harsher view of slavery. In particular the relative importance of the infrequent- and frequent-punishment plantations reverses from white to black interviewers. Using the white and black interviewer distributions as lower and upper bounds allows a preliminary estimate that from roughly 36 to 45 percent of southern slaves lived on plantations of frequent physical punishment.

The other major problem with the overall distribution of frequency of physical punishment stems from the overrepresentation of young slaves in the narrative sample. Although dealt with empirically below, it is worth noting that the sources strongly suggest that young children knew about and reacted to incidents of punishment, especially within their own families. The awareness of young slaves coupled

Table 26.1. The Frequency of Punishment Distribution Reported by Black and White
        Interviewers

Race	White	Black
Frequency		
No Physical Punishment	23	15
	(16.4)	(16.7)
Infrequent Physical Punishment	67	35
	(47.9)	(38.9)
Frequent Physical Punishment	50	40
	(35.7)	(44.4)

Notes: Because of the small sample size (230) the chi-square value (2.06) of the difference between black and white interviewers is significant only at the 0.35 level. However, the consistency between the harsher view reported by black interviewers on this issue with those on other issues (where the difference was statistically significant), suggests that a larger sample size would confirm the impression. For a further discussion of this issue see *EM,* #51.

  Of the five other tables in this paper in which formal tests of significance are relevant, the significance levels for chi-square are 0.01 for Table 26.4, 0.01 for Table 26.5, 0.00 for Table 26.6, 0.03 for Table 26.7, and 0.30 for Table 26.8. In my discussion of the quantitative evidence I have taken account not only of the formal tests but of the consistency of the findings with other evidence, both quantitative and non-quantitative.

with the ability of slave parents to communicate their own experiences leaves little reason to believe that the skewed age distribution biases the information toward a more favorable view of slavery.

  Plantations characterized by infrequent and frequent punishment differed not only in the basic frequency but, also in the type of punishment and the reasons for its use. In general, physical punishment meant whipping on both infrequent- and frequent-punishment plantations. Whipping was not, however, a homogenous category. A whipping could be either mild or severe and on particularly bad plantations was accompanied by practices such as washing the cuts with salt. From the standpoint of the slave the most important distinction between the two types of plantation was in his ability to alter his personal probability of punishment. Frequent-punishment plantations were generally characterized both by more strenuous rules and by the more capricious application of punishment. The ex-slaves clearly distinguished between whippings which were "deserved" and those which were unavoidable. Charlie Morriss grew up on a plantation where whipping was rare and clearly made this distinction in presenting his personal story of punishment. "Old man Tom Murphy raised me up to a big nigger and never did whip me but twice and that was cause I got drunk on tobacco and turned out his horse" (Rawick 1972, 10:220, Pt. 5). Whippings such as these were avoidable. As Tom McAlpin, whipped only once for letting pigs into the master's corn, stated, "Boss, dat was de onlies' lesson I ever needed in my life. It done de wuk" (Rawick 1972, 6:269).

  The fundamental difference between Charlie Morriss and Tom McAlpin and the slaves on frequent-punishment plantations was the inability of the latter to significantly control their personal probability of punishment. Sarah Craves lived on such a plantation and related, "I've had many a whippin', some I deserved, an' some I got for being blamed for doin' things the master's children did. My master whipped his slaves with a cat-o-nine tails. H'd say to me, 'you ain't had a curryin' down for some time. Come here!!! Then he whipped me with the cat" (Rawick 1972, 11:131–132). Mrs. Lou Griffin put the problem of the slave on such plantations more directly, "Dey lash you till you was forced to pray den dey whip you like anything for prayin" (Rawick 1972, 11:143).

A more systematic view of the difference between infrequent- and frequent-punishment plantations can be had from looking at the information on actual incidents of punishment described by the ex-slaves. Close to 400 ex-slaves, roughly 22 percent of the sample, mentioned an actual incident of physical punishment involving either himself or a family member. The actual incidents differed considerably, with most being full-fledged adult whippings of varying severity such as those described in the previous quotations. A small minority, however, were little more than normal childhood discipline administered by the slaveowner rather than the parent.[1] All but the most trivial of the latter are included in the analysis. The inclusion of minor incidents in the overall analysis should introduce a small bias in favor of overemphasizing the level of punishment.

The percentage of people on frequent- and infrequent-punishment plantations actually reporting a punishment incident is presented in Table 26.2. Living on a frequent-punishment plantation clearly increased the probability of punishment. The probability of an ex-slave from a frequent-punishment plantation being punished was 50 percent greater than for his counterpart on the infrequent-punishment plantation. The probability of his parents being punished increased by over 200 percent from one plantation type to the next. The relatively small increase in the ex-slave's probability of punishment compared to that for his parents is open to two interpretations. Either the ex-slave characterized the punishment frequency of the plantation on the basis of the experience of his parents or a small increase in the probability of the slave himself being punished elicited a categorization of the plantation as high frequency of punishment. Under the latter interpretation it took a significantly greater increase in the probability of a parent being punished to elicit the same response.

An indication of the proper interpretation of the ratios of the probability of punishment on infrequent- and frequent-punishment plantations can be gleaned from looking at the same information controlled for the age of the ex-slave. Table 26.3 presents this information for the ex-slave and his mother, and the computations for the father are dropped because of the lack of information. The movement in the ratio indicates that the youngest ex-slaves based their characterization of the

Table 26.2. Actual Punishment Incidents Involving the Ex-Slave and His Parents

	Infrequent-Punishment Plantation		Frequent-Punishment Plantation		
	Number Punished	Percent Punished	Number Punished	Percent Punished	Ratio[a]
Ex-Slaves	38	20.1	53	31.0	1.54
Mothers	10	5.3	25	14.6	2.75
Fathers	3	1.6	6	3.5	2.19

[a]The ratio is the percentage punished on frequent-punishment plantations divided by the percentage whipped on infrequent-punishment plantations.

frequency of punishment on their mother's rather than their own experience. These youngest ex-slaves actually reported more specific incidents on infrequent-punishment plantations than on frequent-punishment plantations. The experience of their mothers is quite different, however, with almost eight times as many incidents on frequent-punishment plantations compared to infrequent-punishment plantations. Ex-slaves in the middle age group from frequent-punishment plantations mentioned slightly more personal incidents than their infrequent-punishment plantation counterparts and almost three times as many incidents involving their mothers. With the oldest ex-slaves, the relationship reverses completely with the ratio higher for the ex-slave than for his mother. The proper interpretation of Table 26.3 seems to be that the overall sample was weighted toward ex-slaves still quite young in 1865 who tended to base their interpretation of punishment frequency on their parent's rather than their own experience.

Frequent- and infrequent-punishment plantations differed in both the probability of physical punishment and in the reasons for its application. Table 26.4 presents the reported reasons for punishment on both infrequent- and frequent-punishment plantations. The information is not restricted to the reasons for actual incidents of punishment but, rather, covers the ex-slave's statement of the possible punishable offenses. The most dramatic increases on the different plantation types are in the categories for unauthorized prayer service and inadequate production. Clearly these offenses loomed larger for slaves whose owners frequently resorted to physical punishment. Punishment on infrequent-punishment plantations was based more heavily on what might be called major offenses such as stealing, harming another slave, destroying property, learning to read (an offense considered important by wary slaveowners), and being off the plantation without a pass. The higher observed probability of punishment on frequent-punishment plantations was undoubtedly in part due to the administration of punishment for more unavoidable

Table 26.3. Actual Punishment Incidents Involving the Ex-Slave and His Mother Controlling for Age of Ex-Slave

Plantation Type	Ex-Slaves Punished (Percent and Number)	Ratio	Mothers Punished (Percent and Number)	Ratio
Ex-Slaves Older Than 17				
Infrequent Punishment	25.0 (9)		5.6 (2)	
		1.89		1.48
Frequent Punishment	47.2 (17)		8.3 (3)	
Ex-Slaves 9–17				
Infrequent Punishment	18.8 (13)		7.3 (2)	
		1.30		2.79
Frequent Punishment	24.5 (12)		20.4 (10)	
Ex-Slaves 0–8				
Infrequent Punishment	19.4 (7)		2.8 (1)	
		0.70		8.11
Frequent Punishment	13.6 (3)		22.7 (5)	

Table 26.4. Reasons for Punishment on Infrequent- and Frequent-Punishment
          Plantations

Reason	Infrequent Punishment	Frequent Punishment
Inadequate Production	19	41
	(16.1)	(23.6)
Stealing	9	7
	(7.9)	(4.0)
Running Away	16	30
	(13.6)	(17.2)
Harming Another Slave	3	2
	(2.5)	(1.1)
Destroying Property	5	5
	(4.2)	(2.9)
Learning to Read	12	13
	(10.2)	(7.5)
Off Plantation without Pass	33	30
	(28.0)	(17.2)
Attending Unauthorized Prayer Service	2	9
	(1.7)	(5.2)
Unclassified Offense	19	37
	(16.1)	(21.3)

Note: Column percentages in parentheses.

offenses such as inadequate production and attending prayer services. The increase
in the category for offenses that do not fit into the major categories also indicates
that on these plantations punishment was more capricious and consequently unavoidable.

The primary difference between infrequent- and frequent-punishment plantations boils down to the interrelationship between the individual probability of
punishment and the differing reasons for which punishment was administered.
Most slaves tried to minimize their personal probability of punishment. The ability
to alter this probability was intimately affected by the actions of the master. If the
master set a heavy work load and then punished slaves for not completing tasks,
there was little that the slave could do to avoid the whip. If plantation rules im-
pinged on such slave rights as religious services, the probability of punishment
could only be minimized at considerable psychic cost. On many plantations, however, punishment was administered for offenses that the slaves were willing to
accept as constraints on their activity. Under these conditions, where punishment
was not capricious and rules were explicit, each slave controlled his own destiny. As
Emma Howard said, "Massa would only whip a slave for two things, one thing if
things warn't done up jes' right at hog killin' time and de other was iffen a nigger
warn't clean when he 'ported for work on Monday mornin's" (Rawick 1972,
6:212).

Since the frequency of punishment was primarily set by the master, it is interesting to see if the overall punishment distribution is affected by such factors as the
size and the location of the plantation. There is no indication of any regional effect

on the frequency of punishment. Ex-slaves who grew up in either the new or the old South report a quite similar distribution of punishment frequency. The same cannot be said for those on different size plantations. Table 26.5 presents the cross-tabulation of the frequency of punishment by the size of the plantation. As the size of the plantation increased, the likelihood of the ex-slave characterizing the plantation as one with frequent physical punishment also increased. This increase in frequent punishment was most marked for the largest plantations and was counterbalanced primarily by a drop in the infrequent-punishment category rather than in the no-punishment category. The statistically unusual master who employed no physical punishment was somewhat randomly distributed across plantation sizes. The real trade-off affected by plantation size was between frequent and infrequent punishment.

There are at least two possible explanations of the observed effect of plantation size on the frequency of punishment. The most obvious is that large slaveowners were on average harsher and more likely to resort to the whip. This could have been due to any number of size-related tendencies. The infrequent contact between the master and the ordinary slave on the large plantation undoubtedly led to a more impersonal regime of social control. The master who did not know his slaves well could not hope to control by persuasion and positive incentives alone. The gang-labor system, more prevalent on the larger plantations, could also have required increased physical punishment to enforce the more intense labor. Any number of reasons including a simple preponderance of cruel men could have led to the higher percentage of large slaveowners who resorted frequently to the whip. An alternative explanation is that plantation size did not affect the personal probability of punishment but, rather, the frequency with which a punishment incident took place. The larger plantation had more people at risk of being whipped. Thus the size effect might not have been in terms of a change in the probability of an average slave being whipped but, rather, in the probability of an on-plantation whipping incident. More incidents led to an unfavorable characterization of the frequency of punishment on the plantation.

The ability of slaves to affect their probability of punishment implies that these probabilities changed over the life cycle of the slave. Table 26.3 can be used to examine this question. For the purposes of this table, the mother is assumed to be thirty years older than the ex-slave. On infrequent-punishment plantations, the

Table 26.5. The Frequency of Punishment on Different Size Plantations

	Size			
	1–15	16–49	50–99	100–More
No Punishment	9	10	2	11
	(16.4)	(27.0)	(7.1)	(15.3)
Infrequent Punishment	34	20	18	28
	(61.8)	(54.1)	(64.3)	(38.9)
Frequent Punishment	12	7	8	33
	(21.8)	(18.9)	(28.6)	(45.8)

Note: Column percentages in parentheses.

probability of being punished remains roughly 0.19 through age seventeen before rising to 0.25 for those aged seventeen to twenty-five. After age thirty the probability of punishment drops significantly to 0.06 or 0.07. The small rise in the probability from age thirty to age fifty-five is probably due more to the young slaves increasing knowledge of the situation of his parents rather than any real rise in the probability of punishment. The cycle on infrequent-punishment plantations thus shows a somewhat constant probability of punishment during childhood and early adolescence with an increase in late adolescence and early adulthood preceding the dramatic drop during the slaves' middle and later years.

The life-cycle experience of slaves on frequent-punishment plantations shows a clearer progression through late adolescence where, as on the infrequent-punishment plantations, the punishment probability peaks. In addition to the peak in early adulthood, there is the same dramatic drop in the probability of being punished in the later years. It is likely that this dramatic increase in late adolescence would be accentuated by restricting the analysis to incidents of strong physical punishment rather than including those cases which differed insignificantly from family discipline.

The life-cycle probabilities of punishment suggest that slaveowners most often resorted to the whip during the slave's late teens and early twenties. The higher probability of punishment undoubtedly reflects the rebelliousness of this age group in both free and slave societies. This rebelliousness is borne out by the reasons for punishment reported by different age groups. Age is positively correlated with punishment for inadequate production, running away, and harming another slave. It is negatively correlated with punishment for being off the plantation without a pass and attending an unauthorized prayer service. Clearly, the late teens and early twenties were the time when the ex-slave was most likely to run away, most likely to fight with his peers, and most likely to rebel against the master-defined work load. Slaveowners resorted to the whip at the point when young slaves began to establish their own identity in the adult world.

The kind of information available in the narratives allows a preliminary investigation of the meaning of physical punishment to the slave population. Table 26.6, which cross-tabulates the frequency of punishment by the ex-slave's attitude toward his last master, clearly demonstrates the importance of physical punishment to the slave. All the very bad masters punished frequently, none of the very good masters did. Only 13 percent of the good masters punished frequently compared to almost 95 percent of the bad masters. While the frequency of punishment does not perfectly predict the ex-slave's attitude toward his master, it provides a strong indication. The reasons for punishment also have some bearing on the ex-slave's conception of his master. Bad and very bad masters are more likely to punish for inadequate production and attending unauthorized prayer services. Good and very good masters more often punished for being off the plantation without a pass, harming another slave, and stealing. The other categories move either randomly or show no dramatic differences. The ex-slaves strongly disliked physical punishment but distinguished between the reasons for its administration. Punishment for work-related offenses and attending church were more heavily condemned than punish-

Table 26.6. Frequency of Punishment Under Different Types of Master

	Master				
	Very Bad	Bad	Ambivalent	Good	Very Good
No Punishment	0	1	10	48	11
	(0.0)	(1.8)	(16.1)	(27.9)	(34.4)
Infrequent Punishment	0	2	28	101	21
	(0.0)	(3.6)	(45.2)	(58.7)	(65.6)
Frequent Punishment	37	53	24	23	0
	(100)	(94.6)	(38.7)	(13.4)	(0.0)

Note: Column percentages in parentheses.

ment for such major offenses as stealing and harming another slave. The latter could be avoided. Punishment for non-fulfillment of a master-established work routine or for attending a religious service were more capricious and potentially unavoidable.

The major controversy over the extent of physical punishment revolves around its use as a labor incentive. The information already examined suggests, however, that physical punishment was not primarily used for work-related offenses. Of the ex-slaves providing information, between 10 and 20 percent gave inadequate production as a reason for punishment.[2] The remaining 80 to 90 percent stressed offenses that related to social rather than work-related control of the slave population. While social control was undoubtedly linked to the efficient use of the slave labor force, punishment remained primarily non-work related.

That the frequency of punishment was closely related to infraction of the social code rather than the production code meant that slaves could more easily minimize their personal probability of punishment. The exceptional slave might gain freedom from physical punishment through his ability as a worker as in the story told by Jake Green (Rawick 1972, 6:168–169).

> Sometimes us got whupped but Massa had fo' men he didn't 'low nobody to hit, white or black. Dey was Unker Arch, he was de main carriage driver, my father, he was de house servant; Unker Julius, de fo'man of de plow han's an' Unker Ed'eards, de fo'man of de hoe han's. When ever anybody wanted to hire anybody to work for 'em, de Massa send dem fo' out and' hire 'em by de day to chop cotton or pick . . . dey could pick five hundred pounds apiece an' leave de sun still runnin'.

For the normal slave, however, avoiding punishment meant performing one's job as well as possible and not breaking any of the social rules that governed the slave community and the slave's relationship with his master.

Physical punishment was effective because it both punished the offender and had a strong demonstration effect on the potential offender. As Mrs. Esther Easter so clearly stated (Rawick 1972, 7:89), "I done see one whipping and that enough." A minority of slaveowners chose not to employ the whip. Most, however, resorted to it to a greater or lesser degree. It is doubtful if negative incentives alone could have been sufficient to motivate slaves to both perform their tasks and abide by the social rules of the master. Most slaveowners realized this and coupled physical punishment and the threat of physical punishment with positive incentives. To disobey the rules meant punishment, to obey the rules meant both the lack of punishment and a chance at improved material conditions.

Slaveowners used physical punishment as an integral part of their system for maintaining social discipline and regulating work activity. It was not, however, the only important component of the system of motivation. Slaveowners combined physical punishment with both long- and short-run positive rewards. The most important of the long-run rewards was the potential for occupational advancement documented in Crawford (1980, Ch. 2). The interrelationship between punishment and rewards is clearly demonstrated by the period of rapid occupational turnover during the twenties also being the time when the slave faced the highest probability of punishment. Thus this period of difficult socialization into the adult slave system was traversed with both the stick of physical punishment and the carrot of occupational advancement.[3]

Occupational advancement could not have acted as a long-run incentive unless it carried with it some real short-run rewards. It is possible that these rewards were, at least in part, psychic. But, psychic rewards alone seem insufficient to differentiate skilled positions from regular field hand positions to the extent that the former were an important part of a system of positive rewards. Nor is there any indication that the rewards to skilled and household workers were in the form of increased leisure. Skilled fathers worked insignificantly less hours per week, but there is an indication that house servants were required to work longer than field hands. Additionally, both house servants and skilled workers worked closely with the slaveowners, a task many historians consider a significant burden.

While there is no specific information in the narratives, skilled and household positions could have been sought because of a different intensity of work rather than different actual hours of work. The gang system, especially on the larger plantations, required a high level of intensity during the working hours. The interdependence of the gang also restrained the common field hand from either setting his own task or his own pace. Skilled and household positions brought both a greater diversity of tasks and the ability to define, within limits, the pace at which tasks were performed. It is also likely that skilled workers and house servants were more capable of defining their own work hours. This possibility is partially confirmed by information presented in Crawford (1980, Ch. 2). Although the length of the workweek was roughly constant across occupational categories, there is an indication that house servants and skilled workers traded more hours of work per day for less days of work per week. Whether or not the ability to work more hours per day was related to a different level of work intensity compared to field work, the resulting trade-off probably freed more time for family and other non-working activities.

The lure of skilled and household positions, especially if the sole advantage was in the intensity of the labor or the ability to define the trade-off between hours per day and days per week, could not have been sufficient to motivate the slave labor force. At the most basic level, slaveowners needed a system of motivation for those slaves who were not chosen in the initial selection for preferred positions. Skilled workers were chosen for training in their late twenties, leaving a majority of the labor force in need of continued motivation to perform their field tasks when there was little hope for substantial occupational advancement. More importantly, there needed to be some system of rewards which provided a higher level of real income to workers who performed well in either preferred or ordinary positions. Motivating work and social performance by tying the slave's level of income to performance was possible either through monetary payments or regulating such master supplied goods as food, clothing, and housing. The latter possibility is examined in detail in Crawford (1980). Monetary payments need to be examined separately, however, since they are the most obvious direct reward for satisfactory performance. If physical punishment was counterbalanced by material rewards, it would seem most efficient to use monetary payments which the slave could use at his own discretion.

Using the narratives to examine the role of money in slave society is complicated by a number of problems. The first problem is that the sample is weighted toward young children who even in a free society would not be expected to have money on a regular basis. As previously mentioned, the older the ex-slave, the more likely was he to have had money as a slave. Equally as important, the circumstances under which the ex-slaves received money changed with age. Young children were most likely to receive a small gift from the master or a white visitor and to use the money for such childhood luxuries as candy or firecrackers. While some older slaves received monetary gifts, it was more likely that the money was earned through extra work. This age bias can be partially circumvented by concentrating on the ex-slave's parent's possession of money. While potentially incomplete, this information allows a firmer analysis of the degree to which different groups within the slave population had access to money.

Establishing the proper categories for the analysis of monetary payments creates additional problems. All the ex-slaves reporting monetary payments were grouped together. This categorization was necessary because it is not always possible to differentiate between those who earned money on a regular basis and those who received it only as a gift. In the cases where the source of money is known a fuller analysis is possible. Generally, however, the category of ex-slaves who had money includes both those who earned it and those who received it as a gift. The ex-slaves who mentioned money are compared to all those who did not mention having money. Some of these informants specifically stated that they never received money while others simply failed to touch on the subject. Comparing those ex-slaves who had money to those who mentioned nothing about money should provide a lower-bound estimate of the actual percentage of slaves who had money. The final problem with the information on monetary payments is the very strong interviewer bias. Black interviewers report a much higher percentage of people with money. The difference persists when controlling for other variables and remains one of the most important cases of interviewer bias. If it is assumed that the informants withheld information on monetary payments from white interviewers, the reported percentage can once again be seen as a lower bound of the real level of money among the slaves. If, however, ex-slaves exaggerated monetary payments to black interviewers, a small upward bias would be introduced into the analysis. The only way to handle the problem is to remember the interviewer bias and control for it whenever possible.

Roughly 10 percent of the ex-slaves said that they personally had money during slavery. About the same percentage of people indicated that their parents received money. Although the figures reflect a considerable downward bias, they strongly suggest that monetary payments affected a small minority of the slave population. An upper-bound estimate of the extent of monetary payments can be had by comparing those ex-slaves with money or whose parents had money to those who specifically stated that they never had money. With this method of estimation, roughly 24 percent of the ex-slaves and 30 percent of their parents received money. While these figures indicate a wider use of monetary payments, it still appears that the use of direct monetary incentives was restricted to less than one-third of the slave population.

A close look at the reports of monetary payments suggests that roughly half of the ex-slaves who personally received money earned it on a regular basis while the remainder received it as an either one time or infrequent gift. Roughly two-thirds of the parents who received monetary payments earned it on a regular basis. Earned money generally came from the performance of extra work after the completion of the normal workday. In a majority of the cases, slaves worked the extra hours on their own patch of land. For instance, the father of Matthew Hume "was allowed to raise for himself one acre of tobacco, one acre of corn, garden stuff, chickens and have milk and butter from one cow" (Rawick 1972, 6:107). Other slaves raised cotton or foodstuffs or kept chickens and hogs and sold the produce to the master (Rawick 1972, 6:148, 3:272, Pt. 3). Slaves also made money through such after work tasks as splitting rails, making charcoal, or weaving baskets (Rawick 1972, 10:155, Pt. 5, 10:106, Pt. 6, 11:321). Although rare, some people mention payments for extra work at a normal task as in the case of Issam Morgan (Rawick 1972, 6:282).

> Massa Morgan sol' wood to de steam boats, an' us slave hands cut wood, an' split it up into smaller pieces. Anytime a slave worked overtime or cut mo' wood dan he s'pose to, Massa pay him money for it, caze whenever one of us slaves seen somp'n we lak, we did jus' lak de white folks does now. Us bought it.

Almost never were slaves rewarded monetarily for work during the normal workday. In fact, a number of ex-slaves explicitly stated that their wages were the normal provisions of food, clothing, and housing (Rawick 1972, 3:157, 172, Pt. 3). Money to be spent at the slave's own discretion was generally only available with extra work.

The percentage of slaves receiving monetary payments was unaffected by either the region or the size of the plantation.[4] This is somewhat surprising since it seems plausible to posit a positive relationship between monetary payments and the integration of the plantation into the market. On largely self-sufficient plantations there would be little reason to pay slaves when they had few opportunities to exchange money for goods. Large plantations, especially in the more settled Old South, were more integrated into the market although there is no indication that slaves under these conditions received more monetary payments. In part this could be due to the small amounts of money involved which required only an itinerant salesman or small store to allow slaves to purchase goods. Whatever the explanation, slaves in different regions and on different size plantations were about equally likely to receive money.

If preferred occupations carried with them higher real income, there should be a positive correlation between monetary payments and skill level. This correlation is evident looking at the relationship between the father's occupation and monetary payments. Only 6.4 percent of the ex-slaves with field hand fathers reported money in the family compared with 16.3 percent with house servant fathers and 17.2 percent with skilled fathers.[5] Thus a skilled or house servant father increased the likelihood of the slave family having money by two and a half to three times. Curiously, the relationship between the occupation of the mother and the possession of money is just the opposite with field hand mothers being more than one and one half times as likely to have money.[6] The information on the ex-slave's father's occupation supports the contention that preferred occupations included a greater access to monetary rewards. The percentage of slaves receiving money remains quite small indicating that while slaveowners used money as a positive incentive it was not a practice which affected a large percentage of the slave population.

It is doubtful that many slaves earned money to save for the future. The long-run security of the slave was in the hands of his master. Monetary payments were an effective incentive because they allowed the slave to decide how to improve his own immediate situation. Money was generally spent on such small luxury items as tobacco, candy, firecrackers, extra clothing, and whiskey (Rawick 1972, 3:51, Pt. 4, 6:168). A more systematic analysis of how money was spent is available by looking at the reported adequacy of the ex-slave's diet and clothing for those with and without money. Roughly 7 percent of the ex-slaves with money reported inadequate diets compared with 12.5 percent of those without money.[7] This difference probably does not reflect food purchases but, rather, the fact that many people made money from the sale of produce from their garden plots which would be eaten rather than sold under conditions of potential diet inadequacy. Roughly 10 percent of those who said their parents had money reported inadequate clothing compared with 17.5 percent of those without money. The comparison is even more dramatic looking at the ex-slave's personal possession of money. Only 8.5 percent of the ex-slaves with money reported inadequate clothing compared with 17.7 percent of those without money. More importantly, close to 28 percent of those with money mentioned store-bought clothing compared with 14.3 percent of those who did not mention having money.[8] Thus both the qualitative and quantitative information point toward the use of money either for special treats or to supplement the clothing allowance.

The narrative sample suggests that less than one-third of the slaves were involved in monetary transactions of any kind. Of this number, roughly half earned money on a regular basis while the remainder received money as a special, if not unique, gift. Additionally, money was rarely earned during the normal workday, requiring either extra work for the master or on the slave's own land. Nor is there any direct information that monetary gifts were for the satisfactory completion of regular tasks. Thus if monetary payments were used as a positive incentive, it was indirectly, through a system which gave slaves who performed well and obeyed plantation rules access to tasks that earned money. Unfortunately, there is no information to either confirm or dismiss such indirect methods of payment.

Just as the importance of physical punishment as a negative incentive is not solely based on the personal probability of punishment, the importance of monetary payments is not defined by the probability of a given slave receiving money. Additionally, given that many plantations strived for self-sufficiency, it is natural that rewards often came not in money, which had to be exchanged for goods, but, rather, in real goods such as better food and clothing. It is nonetheless instructive to examine the information on positive and negative incentives to see if there is any trade off in their use or any relationship between the conditions of work and the kind of incentives used by the slaveowner.

The analysis of the trade-off between short-run incentives and plantation conditions is complicated by two factors. First, the only direct information is on the relationship between punishment, monetary payments, and the conditions of work. As previously stressed, motivating work was less important than enforcing social regulations as a cause for punishment and by analogy as a reason for monetary payments. Second, the information is on the relationship between incentives and conditions on the plantation as a whole. The desired information is whether on a given plantation, a hard-working slave was less likely to be whipped and more likely to be rewarded monetarily than a lazy slave. Unfortunately, the information in the narratives can only show if a slave who received money or was punished frequently was more likely to be on a plantation characterized by longer hours of work or whether the slave who earned money was on a plantation characterized by frequent or infrequent physical punishment. The answers can be used only tentatively to examine the real trade-off between punishment, rewards, and conditions of work.

There is a clear positive correlation between the frequency of punishment and the length of the workweek based primarily on the relationship between days worked per week and punishment. Table 26.7 clearly demonstrates that slaves pushed to work more days per week were more likely to be on plantations characterized as high frequency of punishment. Eighty percent of those who performed Sunday work reported frequent punishment compared with 36.7 percent of those working six days per week and 0 percent of those working five days per week. There is also a fairly clear correlation between the length of the workweek and the probability of a slave receiving money. Twenty percent of the ex-slaves who worked less than dawn to dusk received money compared with 7.1 percent of those who worked dawn to dusk and 9.9 percent of those who worked more than dawn to dusk.[9] The same relationship is suggested by Table 26.8, which reports monetary payments by the number of days in the workweek. Those without Sunday work were two and a half to three times as likely to have had money, suggesting that the time needed to earn money was extended by the slaveowner. Slaves working long hours were rarely given money and rarely had the extra time needed to earn it.

There is no clear relationship between the frequency of punishment and the probability of receiving money. While the ex-slaves from frequent-punishment plantations report the lowest level of monetary payments, the difference is not dramatic (7.0 percent to roughly 13 percent) or highly significant.[10] In all but roughly 19 percent of the cases where the ex-slave's parents either earned or were given money, physical punishment was used on the plantation and in close to 27 percent of these cases punishment was frequent. The latter figure is roughly 30 percent less than the frequent-punishment percentage within the sample as a whole, 38.5 percent, indicating an apparent trade-off between punishment and rewards at least at the plantation level.

Physical punishment clearly outweighed short-run positive incentives at least as reflected in monetary payments. But, both the extent and the purpose of physical punishment have been misunderstood. Physical punishment was used more to maintain social control than to motivate labor. Because of this focus, slaves were able to minimize their personal probability of punishment by restricting actions which slaveowners considered unlawful. In the case of restricting interplantation visits there was a real loss in welfare but other activities such as fighting, breaking equipment, and stealing could be avoided without serious problems. The extent of actual physical punishment has also been exaggerated primarily because of the strong demonstration effect which a whipping had on other slaves. As previously

Table 26.7. The Relationship between the Number of Days Worked per Week and the Frequency of Punishment

	Working Days		
	7.0–6.5	6.0–5.5	5.0
No Punishment	0	17	2
	(0.0)	(21.5)	(40.0)
Infrequent Punishment	2	33	3
	(20.0)	(41.8)	(60.0)
Frequent Punishment	8	29	0
	(80.0)	(36.7)	(0.0)

Note: Column percentages in parentheses.

Table 26.8. The Relationship between Monetary Payments and the Length of the Workweek

	Working Days		
	7.0–6.5	6.0–5.5	5.0
Parents Had Money	2	25	3
	(5.0)	(13.4)	(15.8)
No Mention of Money	38	162	16
	(95.0)	(86.6)	(84.2)

Note: Column percentages in parentheses.

pointed out, 30 percent of the ex-slaves from frequent-punishment plantations were actually whipped. Because of the age bias this figure understates the true figure in the population as a whole. Looking at the age group at greatest risk of physical punishment, those seventeen to twenty-five years of age, leads to the conclusion that roughly half of all slaves on frequent-punishment plantation were ever whipped.[11] On infrequent-punishment plantations roughly one-quarter of the slaves were ever whipped. A best estimate of the percentage of people in the slave population as a whole ever whipped is 30 percent.[12] Curiously, this is roughly the same percentage as people with money. While physical punishment and monetary payments existed side by side, the former was significantly more important because of its much stronger demonstration effect.

NOTES

1. See, for example, Rawick (1972), 6:156. William M. Quinn worked with the master's son. When they didn't work they were whipped "and that meant his own boy would get a licking too."
2. The higher and lower estimates are based respectively on the black and white interviewer samples. The reasons for punishment is another issue where the interviewer bias enters.
3. The fact that the period of highest probability of punishment came during the early twenties when slaves were nearing peak production and in a period of occupational transition significantly increases the problems of interpreting the effect of positive and negative incentives on productivity.
4. Based on a sample of 596 ex-slaves.
5. Based on a sample of 337 ex-slaves.
6. Based on a sample of 583 ex-slaves.
7. Based on a sample of 730 ex-slaves.
8. Based on a sample of 544 ex-slaves.
9. Based on a sample of 327 ex-slaves.
10. Based on a sample of forty-four ex-slaves.
11. This estimate assumes that those adults punished after age thirty-five were previously punished during the years of highest risk. Assuming the opposite, that all cases of adult punishment were additions to the total percentage of people punished would raise the estimates by roughly 50 percent.
12. The estimate is the weighted average of the probability of being punished on different plantation types using weights based on both the white and black interviewer samples. White interviewer sample: $0.189(0) + 0.426(0.25) + 0.385(0.50) = 0.299$. Black interviewer sample: $0.67(0) + 0.388(0.25) + 0.44(0.50) = 0.317$.

TWENTY-SEVEN

An Agency Theory Approach to Slave Punishments and Rewards

Charles Kahn

It seems to be the case that American slaves were not held at the base subsistence level by their masters. Fogel and Engerman (1974a) argue that in terms of food, clothing and shelter the lot of the slave was not the marginal existence it had sometimes been caricatured as being; at the level of material comfort it indeed was comparable to the lot of free working-class Americans. Critics such as Sutch (1976) have argued that the Fogel and Engerman view overstates the material well-being of slaves. Although they have in certain cases provided lower estimates of slaves' welfare, in the case of food, at least, Kahn (#25, in this volume) has shown that even these adjustments lie well above cost-minimizing subsistence.

This paper is an attempt to illustrate why profit maximizing, non-altruistic plantation masters might find it in their self-interest to stray from the apparently least-cost means of maintaining their chattel. The argument uses the techniques of agency theory (e.g., Ross 1973) to develop an incentive structure in which a master controls his slaves through several tools at his disposal—in particular, both positive and negative incentives.

The agency approach provides several theoretical advantages over previous approaches to the examination of incentives imposed on slaves. It is less *ad hoc,* in that it explicitly takes into account the slave's capacity for rational decision making. It makes a distinction between simply examining levels of punishments or rewards and the examination of the linkages between punishments or rewards and actions. Thus it permits the investigator to explore the relationship between rewards or punishments and ease or difficulty of supervising workers.

We will briefly compare the predictions of our model with two sets of accounts. The first is a set of essays written by slaveowners on the principles of slave management and published in various southern agricultural journals in the early nineteenth century. The second is Crawford's (1980) analysis of the narratives of ex-slaves collected by the Writers Project of the 1930s. Both accounts provide support for our approach.

THE FRAMEWORK AND PREVIOUS ACCOUNTS

In this section, we develop a framework in which we can describe the results of three previous theoretical accounts of slave incentives: Fogel and Engerman (1974a), Canarella and Tomaske (1975), and Fenoaltea (1984). We will subsequently add an agency structure to this same framework so as to be able to compare the predictions of an agency model with those of these earlier models.

We assume the plantation master has two sources of wealth: the value of the slaves he owns and the value of the crops they produce. The output of the plantation depends on how hard the slaves work and, possibly, on unobservable chance circumstances such as the weather.

The plantation master has three relevant costs: the cost of enforcing discipline, the costs of "essentials," and the costs of "rewards." Of course, the latter two are summaries of a large set of goods needed or desired by the slave population. Food is an essential for the health of the slave but special items of food—"delicacies"— might be rewarded for good behavior. For our purposes we will divide the two classes in the following way—an expense is an essential if it maintains or increases the resale value of the slave directly—that is, if its omission would debilitate the slave in any way; it is a "reward" if the expense cannot be justified on such direct grounds.[1] One goal of this paper, then, is to determine conditions under which the use of rewards is a profit-maximizing strategy.

Formally we may write the profits of the master as

$$\pi = v(f, p, e) + Ey(e) - pc_p - f - c_r r$$

where v is the value of his slaves, a concave function; $Ey(e)$ is the expected value of output if the slave expends effort e, an increasing, concave function; f is the expenditure on essentials ("food"); p is the level of discipline ("punishment"); e is the effort the slave put in; r is the expenditure on rewards; and c_p and c_r are the costs of punishment and rewards, measured relative to the cost of food.[2]

We assume the following derivatives:

$$v_f \geq 0$$

$$v_p \leq 0$$

$$v_e \leq 0$$

These should generate little objection: In regions of interest, reduction in food should lower the health and thus the value of the slave,[3] similarly, overworking him or beating him will damage him and his capital value.[4]

This logic was well known by slaveholders and writers on slave management:

> it is the law of nature which imperatively associates the true interest of the owner with the good treatment and comfort of the slave. Hence abuses and harsh treatment carry their own antidote, as all such cases recoil upon the head of the owner. . . . It being, therefore, so manifestly against the interest of all parties, as well as opposed

to the natural feelings of humanity, and refinement, and civilization of the age, a case of cruelty or abuse of a slave by his owner is seldom known, and universally condemned (Collins 1854, 422).

If we consider only direct effects, there is never cause for the use of reward and punishment. The argument, both in Fogel and Engerman and in Canarella and Tomaske, is that effort of the slave can be affected by punishment and reward. Fogel and Engerman emphasize that a slave's effort is—in at least some regions—an increasing function of rewards and a decreasing function of punishment. If so, then masters will use rewards to increase the effort of slaves to the optimal level—namely the level where the marginal productivity equals the wear and tear on the slave's health. But "excessive" punishment—meaning punishment severe enough to cause the effort level to decrease—serves no useful purpose and will simply not be used.[5]

Again, this position is often stated by slaveowners. The following comments are typical. "Every attempt to force the slave beyond the limits of reasonable service, by cruelty or hard treatment, so far from exacting more work, only tends to make him unprofitable, unmanageable; a vexation and a curse" (Collins 1854, 422). "Punishments are rarely required and when inflicted are generally of a mild character. Negroes are capable of gratitude and love and it is not only more agreeable but more profitable to govern them by kindness, than the *Bull Whip*" (Foby 1853, 228).

Canarella and Tomaske, on the other hand, emphasize that at sufficiently moderate levels, effort is increased *either* by increasing punishment *or* increasing rewards. In general both instruments are used in pushing a slave to the optimum level of work. This attitude is also exemplified in the articles on slave management: "At times through the year, they have given to them extra flour, rice, molasses, and coffee, by way of reward and encouragement. The fear of punishment and the hope of reward, however, must act conjointly with them as motives to exertion; of which the former is by far the most effective" (Southron 1857, 379). Since excessive punishment is irrational, we will never observe levels of punishment in the region whose effort is a declining function of punishment. Instead, all masters will confine themselves to the region where effort is an increasing function of punishment. If we assume this function is concave then we will find the following potentially testable implications:

1. The relative use of rewards and punishment varies with the relative cost of the two measures. (For example, if punishment is labor intensive relative to rewards, then cross sections with variations in relative prices might yield tests of the hypothesis.)

2. The absolute use of both rewards and punishment varies with the value of the work of the slave relative to his resale value. Children might be both rewarded less and punished less; the oldest slaves, who ought to be pushed to work harshly, will be rewarded and punished more.[6]

Fenoaltea derives additional testable implications by positing that the relation between rewards, punishments and effort will vary from job to job. Citing studies in the managerial and psychological literature, he argues that for certain types of job, which he calls "care-intensive," the effort-maximizing level of punishment is lower than for other types of job, which he calls "effort-intensive." He posits that effort intensity corresponds to physical rather than mental exertion and to land-intensive rather than capital-intensive (human or physical) production. Thus field hands incur higher levels of punishment than do artisans or other skilled workers.

Although these three accounts do yield testable implications, they remain unsatisfactory in that they ignore the slave's capacity for rational decision making. So far the explanation of the slave's actions is purely mechanical. There is no logical reason why he *should* work harder or less hard in response to external stimuli.

THE INCENTIVE STRUCTURE APPROACH

Describing the master's behavior in terms of profit maximization is only the starting point for a satisfactory economic theory. Additional mileage can be gained by describing the slave's actions in terms of utility maximization as well. The slave's utility

$$u(f, r, p) - e$$

is an increasing function of essential food and rewards, and a decreasing function of punishment and harshness of work.

$$u_f > 0$$
$$u_r > 0$$
$$u_p < 0$$

Slavery is lack of control over one's life. Yet, such control can never be absolute. The slave is in principle free to rebel, to attempt to steal, or to attempt to run away. His choices are determined by the effect these will have on the part of his environment that he does not control. Thus he must have expectations as to the links between his actions and those of his master.

The models described above take the *levels* of rewards or punishment as the variables of interest. But from the slave's point of view it is the *functional relationship* between reward and action which is crucial. The master controls the environment in which the slave acts. He not only picks levels of goods and bads that affect the slave's welfare, he chooses how these will relate to the actions the slave takes. A master who employed the whip at random would elicit very different behavior from a master who employed the whip when shirking was observed—even if both masters employed the whip with equal frequency. That is, a master chooses an "incentive structure," relating reward and punishment to the slave's actions. The slave responds to the incentive structure imposed on him.

What evidence is there that this more complicated perspective is of use in analyzing the relationship between slaves and masters? To begin with, the testimony of slaveholders and writers on managing slaves indicates that incentive structures were a major consideration for the master; although their prescriptions are couched in the language of law and justice, it is explicit that the objective of the law of the plantation is deterrence of the slave from repetition of an offense and the demonstration to other slaves of the consequences of such behavior.

A recurrent theme is the need for clear and consistent linkage between behavior and punishment: "It is the *certainty*, more than the *severity*, of punishment that prevents crime. Never fail, therefore, to notice the breach of an established rule, and be equally unfailing in punishing the offender justly" (Acklen 1857, 376). "[I]t is of great consequence to have perfect system and regularity, and a strict adherence to the rules that may be adopted for the government of the place. Each hand should know his duty, and be required to perform it" (Collins 1854, 424–425).

Furthermore, the rules and their linkage to punishment must be clearly known to the slaves, "they [the Negroes] must be kept under strict discipline, which can be accomplished by talking to them, and punishing moderately, but promptly and certainly. The rules and regulations in regard to the negroes, stock, implements, etc., must be read to the negroes every three months by the managers on the various places" (Acklen 1857, 379). "No person should ever be allowed to break a law without being punished, or any person punished who has not broken a well known law. Every person should be made perfectly to understand what they are punished for, and should be made to perceive that they are not punished in anger, or through caprice" (Weston 1857, 44).

For the incentive structure to work, for the linkage between behavior and punishment to be clear, the slaves must harbor no doubts that the system will be maintained. Particular harshness is therefore reserved for insubordination: "If the negro is humble and appears duly sensible of the impropriety of his conduct, a very moderate chastisement will answer better than a severe one. If, however, he is stubborn or impertinent, or perseveres in what you *know* to be a falsehood, a slight punishment will only make bad worse" (Agricola 1855, 362).

> The basis of this discipline must consist in accustoming your negroes to an absolute submission to orders; for if you suffer them to disobey in one instance, they will do so in another; and thus an independence of spirit will be acquired, that will demand repeated punishment to suppress it, and to re-establish your relaxed authority. You should, therefore, lay it down as a rule, never to suffer your commands to be disputed" (Professional Planter [1803] 1969), 130.

In short, several themes noted by the slave management essayists are most readily interpretable in terms of incentive structures.

SIGNALS AND UNCERTAINTY

If the master had complete information about the slave's actions he could effectively wield complete control. With complete control, the master's task is very simply stated: Give the slave the profit-maximizing levels of necessities. Determine the profit-maximizing level of effort to demand from the slave. Punish him severely if he deviates from the optimal level of effort; however, if he does not deviate, neither punish nor reward him.

If the slave is convinced that this is the structure that the master is imposing, he will find it in his own interest to work at the level the master demands.

There are two problems in accepting this as a reasonable description of the situation on a plantation: It implies that neither punishments nor rewards occur. Of the two, the lack of punishment is less damaging to the theory: The effectiveness of the master's strategy depends on slaves' believing that punishment will be carried out if necessary. A bold slave may very occasionally test the rules to see if they indeed apply, and to demonstrate that the threat is still credible, punishment will then be imposed.

Thus occasional, severe punishment can be accounted for with minor modifications, but there is no way that the model can yet account for rewards. It makes no sense for a master to bribe a slave if the threat of whipping is a cheaper alternative—all the more so since the threat will almost never have to be carried out.

In order for it to be sensible for the master to bribe his slaves and to impose regular rather than exceptional punishment, slaves must have some residual source of power. It is not difficult to find the source of such power; it lies in the difficulty the master has in monitoring the actions of the slaves.

This informational advantage of the slave appears in many forms. In the course of his daily work a slave has opportunities for sabotage, for shirking, and for running away. Each instance is small in itself but in the aggregate they are sufficient to impose significant costs on a master. If the master cannot be sure he will catch the slave in any of these acts, he may have to find himself a more sophisticated means of control.

Thus in a sense, we may be able to explain the difference between subsistence and the observed material receipts of the slave as a return to the informational advantage the slave possesses.[7]

To see how this process works, we will consider a fairly straightforward agency problem. We will begin by presenting the problem in a general form, superimposed on the framework outlined above. We will then derive comparative statics conclusions from a specialized example.

Assume the master would like to link punishment of the slave to the level of effort the slave expends, but he can only observe some imperfect proxy for effort. (If some random event, like the weather, can be observed then the rewards and punishment are adjusted to take account of that consideration. A slave is not punished for a bad crop which the master in fact knows to be due to a drought. Nonetheless, as long as some random events are not observable by the master, the basic point remains intact.)

Let the slave be an expected utility maximizer; let the master be an expected profit maximizer. The task before the master, then, is to link rewards and punishments to output in such a way as to encourage the slave to work hard enough. (It will turn out that the slave working too hard is never a problem.)

He does so by choosing an *incentive structure*. Let s be a "signal," a proxy for effort which can be observed by the master (for example, s could be the observed level of output). The master will choose, not a single level of punishment ("five lashes") but a schedule stating the relationship between signals and the punishment to be meted out—for example, five lashes if the output is more than 50 percent below the quota, extra rations if the output exceeds the quota by more than 50 percent.

In mathematical terminology, the master chooses *functions F, R*, and *P*, mapping from the set of possible signals into the set of necessities, rewards, and punishments. Treat these as a set of rules posted for the slave; if the signal turns out to be *s*, then slave and master look at the rules to find the mandated values of necessity, reward, and punishment. Given the functions *F, R*, and *P*, we denote the values that result in the event that the signal turns out to be *s*, by $F(s)$, $R(s)$, and $P(s)$, respectively. Let $\phi\ (s|e)$ represent the probability density function for *s* when the slave expends effort *e*. Given the incentives imposed by the master, the slave picks *e* to maximize

$$\int u(F(s),R(s),P(s))\phi\ (s|e)\ ds - e \tag{1}$$

The master's problem is to pick functions *F, R*, and *P* to maximize

$$\int [v(F(s),P(s),e^*) - P(s)c_p - F(s) - R(s)c_r]\phi(s|e^*)ds + Ey(e^*) \tag{2}$$

where e^* maximizes equation 1.

The problem is best handled by splitting it into two subproblems. Given a choice e^*, there are various ways to give a slave utility level $\bar{u}$. Let the triple $f(\bar{u}, e^*), p(\bar{u}, e^*), r(\bar{u}, e^*)$ be the way which is cost minimizing, i.e., let these values be the levels which satisfy problem A:

$$\min_{f, p, r} v(f, p, e^*) - f - pc_p - rc_r$$

such that

$$u(f, p, r) - e^* = \bar{u}$$

where $r \geq 0$ and $p \geq 0$.

Under standard assumptions about the *u* and *v* function, there is a level of utility $\bar{u}_0$ such that the cost minimizing way for the master to impose $\bar{u}_0$ on the slave involves neither reward nor punishment. Higher levels of $\bar{u}$ will be imposed with rewards but no punishment. Lower levels of $\bar{u}$ will be imposed with punishment but no rewards. For higher levels of $\bar{u}$, expenditure on necessities will also exceed the level that the master would choose in the absence of concern for incentives. For lower levels of $\bar{u}$, expenditure on necessities will fall short of levels that the master would choose in the absence of concern for incentives.

In other words, if the master is interested in increasing the slave's utility he will do so by omitting punishments and raising the expenditure on necessities and rewards. If he is interested in reducing the slave's utility he will do so by omitting rewards, reducing the expenditures on necessities and increasing punishment. In general, since all the margins are useful for discipline, we would expect all would be used. Nevertheless, we would still expect that changes in the level of necessities would have such a large effect on the capital value of the slave that the changes actually observed in the levels of necessities would be small. Most of the observed variability would be in the levels of rewards and punishments.

Now let $A(e^*, u)$ be the profits to the master when problem A is solved in the cost-minimizing manner. The master's overall problem is to pick a function which states the degree of linkage between the slave's utility level and various possible signals. In other words, he picks a function U which maps from signals to slave's utility. Again, given such a function, $U(s)$ will denote the slave's utility after the master observes the signal s. Using problem A, we can rewrite the general problem as follows: Given the function U, the slave picks e^* to maximize

$$\int U(s)\phi(s|e^*)ds - e^*$$

and the master picks the function U to maximize

$$\int A(e^*, U(s))\phi(s|e^*)ds$$

Under appropriate assumptions regarding the distributions $\phi(s|e)$, the solution entails a *sharing* rule: If effort involves disutility and if effort increases the likelihood of high production, then the incentive scheme will yield a positive correlation between payoff and output.[8]

This result yields the following prediction. Consider a cross section or time series of output on plantations. Adjust for all the known factors affecting productivity (plantation size, regional variables, and the like). There should be a positive correlation between rewards and the residual output, and a negative correlation between punishment and the residual output.

Although the predictions are the same as Fogel and Engerman's, the causality is different: It was not the level of punishment and reward that caused the difference in output. Instead, the incentive structure caused the slaves to expend effort, and the rewards and punishments were meted out on the basis of results.

A SIMPLE MODEL AND ITS IMPLICATIONS

In order to investigate the predictions of models with incentive structures, we will consider a highly specialized version of the above agency model. In this version of the model, the level of necessities will be assumed fixed; therefore they can be omitted from the analysis. The slave's utility will be

$$Ar - Bp - e$$

so that A is the marginal benefit to the slave of a unit of rewards, and B is the marginal cost to the slave of a unit of punishment. The master's profits will be

$$Ey(e) - c_p\, p - c_r\, r \tag{3}$$

where c_p is the cost of punishments (the loss of the slave's capital value because of excessive punishment has been consolidated with any direct cost of punishments) and c_r is the cost of rewards. As before, increases in effort increase expected output.[9]

The signaling structure is extremely simple. The signal takes one of two values: "good" and "bad." The probability that the good realization occurs is $\pi(e)$, an increasing, strictly concave function of the level of effort expended by the slave.

$$\pi'(e) > 0$$

$$\pi''(e) < 0$$

In this case the incentive structure that the master imposes will consist of values for rewards and punishments as a function of the signal the master receives. As in the general model, it never makes sense for a master simultaneously to reward and punish. It is easy to show that the incentive structure will not have positive levels of punishment if the good signal is received, nor positive levels of rewards if the bad signal is received. Thus an incentive structure is a pair of values (r, p), where r is the reward (possibly zero) the slave receives if the good signal occurs, and p is the punishment (again, possibly zero) the slave receives if the bad signal occurs. Thus the master's expected profits from the slave and his work are

$$-\pi(e)rc_r - (1 - \pi(e))pc_p + Ey(e) \tag{4}$$

The slave's choice of effort given the incentives imposed on him is determined by the first-order conditions for maximization of the following problem:

$$\pi(e)Ar - (1 - \pi(e))Bp - e$$

The first-order conditions are

$$\pi'(e)\,(Ar + Bp) - 1 = 0 \tag{5}$$

which we can regard as an equation implicitly defining e as a function of r and p.

The master's problem is to pick the incentive scheme that at the same time minimizes his direct costs of the scheme and induces the optimal level of effort on the part of the slave. More precisely the master chooses r and p to maximize equation 3 subject to equation 5.

As before, we divide the problem into two portions. First we consider, for a given level of e, the cost-minimizing incentive scheme which will induce e. The following results are derived by solving problem A above for the particular set of utility and profit functions. If

$$\pi(e)c_r/A > (1 - \pi(e))c_p/B \tag{6}$$

the cost-minimizing incentive scheme involves a punishment of

$$1 \,/\, \pi'B$$

in the bad state, and no reward or punishment in the good state. If the inequality is reversed, the cost-minimizing incentive scheme involves a reward of

$$1 \,/\, \pi'A$$

in the good state, and no reward or punishment in the bad state. This calculation leads to the following conclusion.

Theorem 1: A master is more likely to use punishments rather than rewards to extract a given level of effort from his slaves (1) the higher the cost of punishment relative to rewards, (2) the higher the disutility to the slave of punishments relative to the utility of rewards, and (3) the more common the occurrence of the good signal relative to the occurrence of the bad signal.

The first of these conclusions is analogous to the conclusion of Canarella and Tomaske: As the relative cost of one technique increases, the other technique is substituted for it. This result will hold for much more general distributions, and for more general utility functions for slaves. The effects of allowing effort to vary as well will be noted below.

The second conclusion is similar: If a particular slave has a great fear of punishment, then the threat of relatively low and inexpensive levels of punishments will be adequate to keep him in line. As for the boldest slaves, those for whom the punishments will have to be extreme to keep them obedient, a master may find it in the end cheaper to "co-opt" them—placing them into positions in which they receive rewards for good outcomes rather than punishments for bad outcomes. In this context it is worth noting that drivers and other slaves in privileged positions were often exempted from physical punishment by the overseer, and more likely to share in the rewards of the plantation.[10]

The final conclusion is also intuitive: Rewards or punishments, by their nature, should be given only in exceptional circumstances. The least-cost outcome, that is, neither reward nor punishment, should be the most common outcome. In a situation in which it is very common for the master to receive the good signal, but rare to receive the bad signal, it will be cheaper for the master to keep slaves in line by punishing when the occasional bad signal arises. If it is the good signal that is rare, and the bad signal that is common, it will be cheapest for the master to keep slaves in line by handing out the occasional reward when the good signal arises. Similar results can be obtained when effort is treated as endogenous.

This observation suggests that any "rewards" which are in fact the norm cannot be explained as the outcome of an incentive mechanism. It also predicts a general bias toward punishment rather than reward. If the desired behavior makes it unlikely that some signal is observed and the undesired behavior makes it more likely, then punishment should be attached to that signal. Rewards should be attached only to signals which are unlikely if the desired behavior is followed, and even more unlikely if the undesired behavior is followed.

Next we consider the general problem of the master's choice of the level of effort he will induce in the slave. For a given level of effort the profit of the master is

$$Ey(e) - \min\left[\frac{\pi(e)c_r}{\pi'(e)A}, \frac{(1 - \pi(e))c_p}{\pi'(e)B}\right]$$

where the first term in the brackets is the cost of the incentive structure when a reward is chosen and the second is the cost of an incentive structure when a punishment is chosen. The master chooses e to maximize this expression.

As e varies, the optimal scheme varies as follows: For low values of e the optimal scheme is a reward scheme. As e increases, $\pi'(e)$ falls and it becomes necessary to increase the levels of reward to induce the increasing levels of effort. Moreover, as effort increases, the odds of the reward actually being received also increase. Beyond some critical level of effort it becomes cheaper to use punishment schemes rather than reward schemes. As effort continues to increase, the punishments become harsher, inducing the slave to work harder in order to make the punishment less likely to occur.

These considerations lend to the following theorems. The first extends the Canarella and Tomaske results.

Theorem 2: As the cost of rewards falls there is a tendency to substitute reward structures for punishment structures. In addition, there is a tendency to induce greater effort by increasing the levels of rewards.

The results are analogous if the cost of punishments falls.[11]

Theorem 3: As the marginal return to effort increases, the master will wish to induce higher levels of effort, which will imply a tendency toward greater rewards and greater punishments, but also a tendency to switch from reward structures to punishment structures.

Crawford's (#26, in this volume) analysis gives interesting confirmation for the predictions of theorem 3. He tabulates the relationship between length of the workweek on a plantation, frequency of punishment on the plantation, and frequency of monetary payments. If we take length of workweek as an independent measure of effort, and monetary payments as a proxy for the use of positive incentives, then Crawford's results imply a positive correlation between frequent punishments and level of effort demanded, and a negative correlation between use of rewards and level of effort demanded. Moreover there is negative correlation between the use of rewards and punishments, although the difference is not great.

Next we consider the effects of ease or difficulty of supervision on the incentive structures chosen by the master. As noted before, it is the difficulty of determining whether the slave has complied with commands which makes the incentive problem a non-trivial one. The identical problem is faced in all management positions, and slaveowners were well aware that the ability to determine whether slaves were or were not working the proper amount was a major aspect of being a qualified overseer: "In nothing does a good manager so much excel a bad, as in being able to discern what a hand is capable of doing, and in never attempting to make him do more" (Weston 1857, 40).

In our simple model, ease or difficulty of supervision corresponds to high or low levels of π'. When π' is high, then very small changes in the slave's activities yield great changes in the signals that the master is likely to receive. On the other hand, if π' is small, then the master is likely to receive the same signal no matter which of numerous actions the slave takes. Thus we can identify high levels of π' with very informative signals, and so with the master possessing very good information about the slave's actions.

Under a given incentive structure, as $\pi'(e)$ increases, the marginal benefit to the slave of an extra unit of effort also increases. Payoffs change more in response to the slave's actions, since it becomes more likely that the good outcome will arise from an increase in the slave's effort. Thus, the same incentive structure induces higher levels of effort as $\pi'(e)$ increases. Equivalently, the same level of effort can then be induced with lower rewards or lower punishments. Changes in $\pi'(e)$ do not change the relative likelihood of rewards or punishments, except through any induced changes in the level of effort demanded of the slave.

In the case of a reward incentive structure, the first-order conditions describing the choice of the optimal level of e are as follows:

$$Ey'(e) = [1 - \pi''(e)\,\pi(e)/\,(\pi'(e))^2]\,c_r\,/\,A$$

In the case of a punishment incentive structure they are

$$Ey'(e) = [\,-\,1 - \pi''(e)\,(1 - \pi(e))\,/\,(\pi'(e))^2]\,c_p\,/\,B$$

In each case the second-order conditions require that the marginal cost of the incentive structure (the right side of each condition) increase at least as rapidly as the marginal benefit of the additional effort obtained. An increase in π' in the neighborhood of e (with no change in π or π'') reduces the marginal cost of eliciting additional effort, and therefore increases the amount of effort that will be observed in the optimal incentive structure.

To summarize, the following are the effects that result from a local increase in π'. The severity of the punishment or the lavishness of the reward necessary to induce a given level of effort is reduced. Since the marginal cost of maintaining a level of effort is also reduced, the level of effort demanded of the slave increases, offsetting the reduction in severity or lavishness of the incentive structure. If we regard the induced change in effort as a second-order effect (as it would be for example if the marginal return to effort declines sharply in the neighborhood of observed effort levels) then we would predict

Theorem 4: High levels of π' correspond to higher levels of effort, less-extreme punishments, less-extreme rewards, and a slight tendency to use punishment rather than reward.

This last effect comes through the inducement to higher levels of effort, which tend to correspond to punishment rather than reward structures. Thus we expect that slaves who can be closely supervised will work harder, be subject to less severe threats of punishment, be promised less lucrative rewards, and be somewhat more likely to have punishments than rewards in their incentives.

There are two types of situation in which we may expect to find systematic variation in the ease of supervision of the slave: The first is the variation that occurs with type of job and the second is the variation that occurs with the size of the plantation.

Simple, routine jobs tend to be easy to supervise: There will be little doubt whether the slave is doing his job. The more complex the job, and/or the greater the isolation in which it is done, the more likely the slave will be able to conceal his true actions. Fenoaltea's "effort intensive" types of work—field work and construction—stand at one extreme; skilled jobs, particularly jobs off the plantation, stand at the other extreme. The above results yield the following four predictions.

1. More extreme effort will be demanded in the easily supervised jobs.
2. More punishment relative to rewards will be used in the easily supervised jobs.
3. If rewards are used, they will be smaller in the easily supervised jobs.
4. If punishments are used, they will be more extreme in the hard-to-supervise jobs.

The first three predictions seem clearly to be borne out. As Fenoaltea notes, a slave artisan was likely to pay a fixed amount to his master, and bear the entire brunt of the success or failure of his enterprise himself.

Similar considerations operate in comparing the incentive structure under a gang system and under a task system. Since the gang system requires coordination the supervisor is already at hand, and the cost of supervision is low. On a task system the slave is charged a fixed amount of "output" in terms of a specific chore. The slave bore the entirety of the risk for any attendant complications which impeded the performance of his task. If the task took longer than anticipated, the slave lost whatever time he might have devoted to his own plot.

The prediction which does not seem to correspond to observation is the prediction that the more severe punishments should correspond to the difficult-to-supervise jobs—for example, skilled artisans and foremen. However, this too may be consistent, if we take the threat of a return to an unskilled occupation as the threatened punishment.

There is likely to be a limit to our ability to analyze the difference across occupations with such a simple model, since, in particular, the skilled occupations were such a small proportion of the total slave population and likely to be populated by a very exceptional set of individuals.

A second comparison less subject to this objection is the examination of incentive structures across plantations of different sizes.

There are two systematic ways in which large plantations should be expected to be different from small plantations. First, because of the ability to employ slaves in specialized techniques, and to coordinate their work, we would expect large plantations to have advantage in productivity, making a slave's effort more valuable on a large plantation than on a small one. Thus one systematic source of difference would likely be a greater marginal value of productivity of effort and a higher level of work on a large plantation. On the other hand, because of the difficulties of supervising a large work force, the managerial problems should increase. In particular, we would expect the master to have less control over the work of the individual slave on a large than on a small plantation, in the sense of greater imperfections in his ability to monitor slaves' effort. In the language of our model, the master of a large plantation receives noisier signals—that is, they face lower values of π'.

These two considerations, greater productivity and noisier signals, should have offsetting effects on the level of effort demanded. However the effects should be reinforcing in terms of differences observed in incentive structures. Larger plantations would be expected to use more stringent punishments, both because higher effort is more productive and because the inability to monitor effectively means that more extreme measures are necessary for the same level of deterence. (Similarly, when rewards are used, they should be more lucrative on larger plantations.)[12]

Crawford indeed finds a positive correlation between the size of the plantation and the frequency of the punishment. This is consistent with our hypothesized decline in the accuracy of monitoring as the plantation becomes larger. In addition, Crawford finds a difference in the grounds for punishment on high-punishment plantations. On low-punishment plantations, the slave had better control over his ability to avoid punishments, which tended to be imposed for breaking specific rules. On high-punishment plantations punishment was more often due to circumstances less in the slave's control—notably, inadequate production.

Again, the pattern is consistent with masters on larger plantations possessing less-complete information on the slave's activities and thus being less able to distinguish between malingering and bad luck. On small plantations, however, the masters could still observe activity sufficiently well to control with threat of punishment rather than the punishment itself. Nonetheless, it should be noted that only a minority of instances of punishments recounted in the slave narratives were due to inadequate production—less than one-fourth even on frequent-punishment plantations (Crawford, #26, in this volume).

CONCLUSION

In this paper we have compared an agency model with several previous theoretical accounts of the determinants of the use of rewards and punishments in controlling slaves. Among the theoretical advantages of the agency model and its attendant incentive structure account are the following: (1) it explicitly takes into account the capacity of the slave for rational decision making, (2) it makes a distinction between a simple level of punishments or rewards and the linkage of punishment or reward to behavior, (3) it makes a distinction between the threat of the punishment and the frequency with which the threat is carried out, and (4) it permits us to analyze the effect of ease or difficulty of supervision on rewards and punishments.

We have found that the agency model generates insights consistent with several themes observable in essays written by slaveholders on slave management. We also found that several of the predictions of our simple model conform to observations in the accounts of former slaves as summarized by Crawford.

We must also note one serious disadvantage of the agency model: the potential lack of generality of the results. In particular, as we build more complicated signaling structures, it becomes difficult even to calculate the optimal incentive structure, much less to determine how it varies with exogenous parameters such as ease or difficulty of supervision. Given the complexity of the problem of managing a real plantation compared with even the most complicated economic model imaginable, it is hard to believe that a slaveowner would have been able to determine the optimal structure and to enforce it.

On the other hand, at the level of generality which we have been considering, it is easy to believe that plantation masters were conscious of the importance of incentives and attempted to take them into account. Thus it could very well be the case that our simplified model yields more insight into the determinants of a slave's rewards and punishments than would a more accurate and detailed model of the circumstances of production and information flows on any particular plantation.

NOTES

1. The division is not free from ambiguity: If we take account of the fact that people are creatures of habit and if rewards induce docile behavior, it may be the case that offering rewards will have direct effects on the resale value of slaves through indirect means. We could extend the framework to include direct effects of essentials on current output, but it is simpler, and nothing in exposition is lost, to include all direct effects in the capital value.
2. In what follows we will include the possibility that c_p is zero.
3. Note, however, that these values must always be relative to the scientific information available at the time. If plantation owners (mistakenly) believed that fat slaves were healthy slaves, there would be a direct incentive to "overfeed" relative to modern standards of health.
4. We are again speaking only of direct effects: Indirect effects will be discussed below.
5. Necessities can be made an argument of the effort function as well: Feeding a slave more increases not only his willingness, but also his ability to work hard. However, for our purposes this extension is not necessary, for our problem is to explain provisions of food beyond the point useful for keeping even extremely hard working slaves healthy.
6. Again, if there is an investment component to rewards and punishments—that is, if they ensure future docility and hard work—then children should be rewarded and punished *more*. Crawford finds that the incidence of punishment peaked for slaves in their late teens and early twenties; he concludes that punishment was primarily used for social control.
7. Indeed, strictly speaking, this informational advantage is his *sole* possession.
8. For conditions under which this result holds, see Grossman and Hart (1983) or Rogerson (1985).
9. For simplicity we have not included the possibility that excessive effort by the slave directly damages his capital value. That consideration can be added with no significant complications.
10. A more complete analysis would also consider the effects of relative risk aversion of slave and master. If the slave is more risk averse, there will be a pronounced tendency to the use of extreme punishments with very small probabilities.
11. The results become much more complicated under risk aversion.
12. Crawford (#26, in this volume) lists a number of reasons besides incentives that masters on large plantations should treat punishment as lower cost, and therefore punish more. However many of these reasons (for instance, remoteness of the master from the slave and attendant lack of concern) would also imply that rewards are higher cost, so that rewards should be observed less.

PART SIX

THE TRANSITION
TO FREEDOM

Introduction

The transition to freedom occurred for some slaves by the process of manumission while slavery as a system persisted. For most slaves, however, the transition to freedom occurred as a result of legally imposed emancipation, which ended the legal basis of slavery. Debates about the nature and terms of emancipation were prominent in all slave societies, and differences in the particular circumstances by which emancipation was achieved and in the amount and form of compensation allowed to slaveowners existed. The principal questions related to slave emancipation that have been studied include: Why was such legislation passed and to which of the voters was it of direct interest? What were the costs of emancipation? And what was the nature of the new labor system that emerged when the controls of the slave economy were terminated? Studies of manumissions in slave societies have dealt with the magnitude of manumission and the characteristics of those manumitted as well as of those doing the manumitting. Examinations of both transitions to freedom are important for their bearing on the political and economic characteristics of the societies involved, and for their revelations of the patterns of belief of slaveowners, free members of slave society, and slaves. Furthermore, the examination of the adjustments to the end of slavery can provide understanding of the conditions of the ex-slaves under freedom and the opportunities they had to pursue their own interests in the future.

The papers in this section include analyses of the nature and outcome of slave emancipation in the United States, Great Britain's West Indian colonies, and Brazil as well as of manumission in New Orleans. New data are drawn from sources such as the petitions for emancipation recorded by the police jury for New Orleans, voting statistics taken from British Parliamentary sources, the labor contracts recorded by the Freedmen's Bureau in the aftermath of the Civil War, plantation sharecropping contracts, postbellum newspapers and magazines, and various sources of data on prices and hire rates of slaves. Several of the essays include theoretical discussions of the economic costs to the planters; of various emancipation schemes; and the role of risk, non-pecuniary factors, and economic returns in explaining the new agricultural system in the postbellum South.

Steven B. Webb provides a study of the voting for emancipation in Britain in 1833, using personal and constituency information to examine the classic debate on the relative importance of economic and humanitarian factors in the successful ending of slavery in the British colonies. Robert W. Fogel and Stanley L. Engerman use information based on the prices of slaves to examine the distribution of the burdens of the emancipation schemes legislated in Great Britain in 1833 and those in the northern states of the United States in the late eighteenth century. For Great Britain, there were cash payments to slaveowners as well as a period of required labor by ex-slaves for their former owners, whereas most of the northern states freed children born after a certain date to slave mothers, but then required a period of compulsory labor by the free born for the owner of their mother. Therefore, the costs were borne in various parts by slaveowners, ex-slaves, and the free population, and it is this allocation that Fogel and Engerman attempt to determine. Laurence J. Kotlikoff and Anton J. Rupert analyze petitions for emancipation in New Orleans from 1827 to 1846, to examine the gender and age patterns of those manumitted and the social and racial characteristics of those freeing their slaves. Claudia D. Goldin analyzes the economics of various proposed emancipation schemes, estimating costs for alternative proposed schemes for the United States on the eve of the Civil War. Using data on price and hire rates for Brazil, Pedro C. de Mello studies the reactions of planters to the legislation, such as the Rio Branco Law (Free Womb Law) of 1871, and subsequent legislative debates influencing the legal status of slavery in Brazil. By looking at trends in the level and structure of slave prices, he demonstrates the changes in planter expectations as to the timing of the ending of slavery.

The final two papers are concerned with the adjustments to a new system of agricultural organization after the emancipation of slaves in the United States. Joseph D. Reid, Jr., with the use of sharecropping contracts, utilizes the economic analysis of tenure choice to examine the importance of attitudes toward risk and race in explaining the postbellum rise of sharecropping. Here, again, the analysis has important implications for the behavior of ex-slaves as well as of ex-planters. By examining the Freedmen's Bureau labor contracts and contemporary newspapers and magazines, Ralph Shlomowitz also studies the factors in the rise of sharecropping and the emergence of small farms for the production of cotton by ex-slaves. Using these sources he describes the relative importance of coercive and market factors in influencing ex-slave behavior and the impact of the preferences of the ex-slaves on the new agricultural order. (For information on the economic productivity of this new form of southern agricultural organization in comparison with that of the antebellum South, see the essay by Jon Moen, #15, *TP*, Vol. I.)

TWENTY-EIGHT

Saints or Cynics: A Statistical Analysis of Parliament's Decision for Emancipation in 1833

Steven B. Webb

In 1833 the British Parliament passed a bill to end slavery throughout the empire—chiefly in the West Indies. The bill promised the planters monetary compensation equal to half the value of their slaves as of a few years earlier. It stipulated that in 1834 the slaves would begin a four- to six-year apprenticeship in the custody of their masters, in order to prepare them for complete freedom. In 1838, Parliament cut the apprenticeship short, largely because of the brutality with which many planters tried to squeeze the last few pounds of profit out of their former chattel. Through statistical analysis of indicators of Members of Parliament's positions on slavery, their positions on other issues, and their personal and constituency characteristics, this paper seeks to improve our understanding of what motivated the Members of the House of Commons in 1833 to pass emancipation.

While this paper approaches the issue of motivations within the context of the historiography described in the next section, it is worth keeping in mind the perceptions of emancipation held by participants in the 1833 debate. Members of Parliament (MPs) generally shared the view that the measure entailed a *limited* redefinition of property rights and a *limited* change in labor discipline. The slaveholders' property rights could not be legally abridged without compensation, even if that required increasing the national debt by £20 million. The planters, as employers, retained the rights to set the conditions of work, to use corporal punishment, and to have indentured servants. The Anti-Slavery Society defined emancipation as a measure "to substitute judicial for the Private and Irresponsible Authority now exercised over 830,000 of their fellow-creatures [the slaves], and to obtain for them an equal enjoyment of civil rights with free-born subjects of Great Britain."[1] The same Parliament that freed the slaves revealed its views on the legal rights of free-born British workers. The New Poor Law of 1834 laid down the principle that the workers should have the right to choose only between the horrors of the poorhouse and whatever gainful employment was available.

The parliamentary debate over emancipation centered around its moral and economic significance.[2] Those sympathizing with the planters emphasized the minimal if not negative moral impact of emancipation and its catastrophic economic implications. Radical Tories usually favored freedom for all West Indians, but worried more about the enormous cost (£20 million) of the proposed compensation to the planters. Radical antislavery forces attached monumental moral significance to the measure, yet maintained that the West Indian planters and Great Britain would benefit or at least not suffer economically by emancipation, because the freedmen would produce more working for wages than they had as slaves. The Whig government in 1833 took the position, shared by a plurality if not a majority of the MPs, that the emancipation would have substantial economic, social, political, and moral effects.

Subsequent events showed that all sides had seen a part of the truth. Whatever moral improvement emancipation brought to the West Indian slaves was not along the lines envisioned by the Evangelical and humanitarian reformers in Britain. The Afro-West Indians probably preferred a life of impoverished peasantry to slavery, but they rarely used their freedom to seek the "spiritual elevation" of wage labor and English Christianity. The Emancipation Bill of 1833 had its greatest moral impact within Britain. If slavery epitomized the sinful and irrational aspects of the nation's political economy, as David Davis (1975, 386–402) claims, then emancipation must have brought a sense of relief and moral accomplishment to many Britons.

Emancipation in the British West Indies brought no great economic difficulties to the mother country, but had a heavy economic impact in the islands, as those with economic interests there had warned. Still, continued transformation, not sudden destruction, would best describe the economic events in the West Indies after 1834 (Adamson 1972; Mathieson 1932; Burn 1937). Many plantations went out of business in the late 1830s and early 1840s as slaves left them to become independent small holders, but the decline of the older plantations had gone on for decades before, weakening the West Indian resistance to emancipation. Indeed, the slave uprisings of 1831 may have forewarned of an end to slavery much less favorable to the planters than the compensated emancipation which came in 1834–1836.[3] In the 1840s planters, in areas with soil still suited to plantation cultivation, replaced African slaves with indentured Asian laborers.

The first section of this paper sketches the historiography of British antislavery. The second section describes the regression analysis of the role of the personal and constituency characteristics of the MPs in determining their positions on emancipation. The third section discusses the relationships between emancipation and other issues dealt with by the Parliament of 1833–1834. The concluding section summarizes the contribution of the statistical analyses to the historical debate.

HISTORIOGRAPHY

The traditional Whig interpretation holds that the humanistic arguments of the antislavery leaders reflected their true motivations and were largely responsible for persuading Parliament to legislate abolition of the slave trade in 1806–1807 and emancipation in 1833. Coupland (1923, [1933] 1964) took this view unself-consciously in his biography of Wilberforce and in his history of the antislavery movement. Against the attacks it has received over the last thirty years, the humanitarian thesis has been defended by Anstey and Drescher, at least insofar as it relates to the abolition of the slave trade. Anstey (1975, 408) writes,

> because one is so conditioned to expect interest to masquerade as altruism . . . one may miss altruism when concealed beneath the cloak of interest—the mass of independent members of Parliament were ready, against all the evidence of the West Indies' importance to the nation, to act as the children of the later eighteenth century, with its manifest anti-slavery convictions, that they really were. In other words, the religiously motivated abolitionist leadership, whose unselfish impulses one need not question, used arguments of economic and national interest to further their cause.

Anstey implies that the MPs upon whom this tactic worked (bringing them to vote for abolition) also knew that the economic interest arguments for abolition were basically wrong and, like the abolitionist leadership, used them chiefly as a front for their true humanitarian, religious, or philosophical motivations.

Drescher (1977) applies a different mode of analysis to the same question and comes to essentially the same conclusions as Anstey. After looking seriously but unsuccessfully, Drescher contends that one cannot find any significant group who could expect to benefit economically from abolition. Largely by process of elimination, therefore, he vindicates the traditional interpretation.[4] At the risk of unfairly putting words in their mouths, Anstey's and Drescher's revival of the religious, humanitarian thesis seems to be a general statement about the motivation for parliamentary action against slavery, whether in 1806–1807 or in 1833.

Reacting to Coupland's sentimental portrayal of the saintly abolitionists, Williams (1944) made the classic presentation of the argument that chiefly economic self-interest motivated the decision for abolition. "The capitalists had first encouraged West Indian slavery and then helped to destroy it. When British capitalism depended on the West Indies, they ignored slavery or defended it. When British capitalism found the West Indian monopoly a nuisance, they destroyed West Indian slavery as the first step in the destruction of West Indian monopoly" (Williams 1944, 169). Specifically, British merchants and manufacturers wanted free trade legislation to end the West Indian sugar monopoly in order to facilitate trade with Brazil, and industrial employers wanted cheaper sugar to lower the subsistence wage bill. Abolition and emancipation also solved problems of short-run overproduction of sugar. Specific details of Williams's thesis have been attacked and refuted, but the basic idea that chiefly economic interests motivated the anti-slavery movement has not ceased to spark controversy and scholarly debate (Drescher 1977; Anstey 1968; Dixon 1971).[5]

Davis (1975, Chs. 8, 9), like Williams, argues for the importance of capitalist interests in the antislavery movement, but he posits no direct, deterministic connection between the two. Davis (1975, 384–385) says the British antislavery movement

helped ensure stability while accommodating society to political and economic
change; it merged Utilitarianism with an ethic of benevolence, reinforcing faith that
a progressive policy of laissez faire would reveal men's natural identity of interests.
It opened new sources of moral prestige for the dominant social class, helped to
define a participatory role for middle-class activism, and looked forward to the
universal goal of compliant, loyal, and self-disciplined workers.

Using laissez-faire and utilitarian economic philosophies to indict slavery helped
legitimize these ideologies, which were often accused of being coldhearted. The
depiction of slavery as the absolutely intolerable, immoral, and irrational form of
exploitation and labor discipline allowed the newly emerging disciplines of the
factory to appear moderate and reasonable by comparison. Davis's point is not that,
as Williams maintained, capitalists supported the antislavery crusade with the
expectation of direct material gain through the rearrangement of world trade patterns, but rather that the antislavery philosophies developed in a way that helped
resolve domestic problems associated with the emergence of industrial capitalism.

The debate on British antislavery has come to focus on whether the motivations
of the protagonists were material or ideal or some merger of the two—on whether
we can better understand the advocates of abolition and emancipation as saints or
as cynics.[6] The question is clearly not whether opponents of slavery believed it was
immoral and inhumane. Both MPs in favor of and MPs opposed to emancipation
presumably convinced themselves of the morality and humanity of their positions.
The question is, what factors can explain why some MPs concluded that slavery was
immoral and others did not and why those conclusions elicited stronger responses
from some MPs than from others? The debate has been waged largely with literary
evidence on what the antislavery leaders believed and with quantitative evidence on
the profitability of slavery and its relation to capitalist development. Although
further research with these methods will surely prove fruitful, this study takes a
different approach.

THE REGRESSION ANALYSIS

This study employs two types of statistical procedure to test hypotheses about the
motivation of MPs in their decision for emancipation. The first procedure uses
regressions to determine the ability of characteristics of MPs and their constituencies to explain variation in measures of the MPs' antislavery sentiment. The second
procedure tests how the antislavery sentiment of MPs related to their positions
(votes) on other issues that seem relevant to the hypotheses about antislavery
motivations. Neither the profits and losses of slavery and emancipation nor MPs'
affiliations with political parties, which began to emerge at this time, enter directly
into the analysis. All MPs are treated as individuals rather than as members of
coalitions that shared the professed desires of their leaders. MPs' public and parliamentary positions on slavery enter the analysis as dependent variables to be explained, not as part of the explanation.

Understanding the regression model requires a detailed description of the variables. The calculation of dependent variables, the measures of each MP's anti-slavery sentiment, presented substantial difficulties and remains largely subjective. Support for the emancipation bill as a whole was so nearly universal that no roll call vote ("division") was taken on any of the three readings of the bill in its entirety. The bill, furthermore, not only emancipated the slaves, but also stipulated a mandatory "apprenticeship" of the ex-slaves and £20 million in compensation to the planters. (The latter two provisions increased the bill's attractions to West Indian interests and decreased its attractiveness to some antislavery MPs.) What an MP said in the parliamentary debates, how he voted in divisions on certain amendments to the emancipation bill, whether he belonged to the Anti-Slavery Society, and how he fared in two ratings of the MPs on the emancipation issue, in total, give enough basis for estimating his position on emancipation.

In the course of debate, the Commons took fourteen divisions on amendments to the bill. For four of the divisions no record remains; for the other divisions only the minority votes were recorded. Of these ten, only six related directly to the desirability of emancipation. Most of the others concerned the planters' compensation. Some MPs opposed monetary compensation as recognizing the legality of slavery, while others mainly opposed the cost. Some MPs favored doing whatever necessary, including compensation, in order to pass emancipation, while opponents of emancipation favored compensation to protect planter's interests. Thus compensation had an ambiguous relationship to the central issue of emancipation. The remaining six antislavery amendments would have (1) limited apprenticeship to the minimum necessary for the welfare of the Negro and not used it as part of the compensation to the planters, (2) terminated apprenticeship for agricultural laborers in 1836 instead of 1840, (3) withheld one-half of the compensation until emancipation was complete, (4) limited female indenture to the age of eighteen instead of twenty-one, (5) prohibited flogging of apprentices, except for treason or mutiny, and (6) removed the apprenticeship requirement for young children. All these amendments were defeated, and the Division Index equals the number of times an MP appeared in the minority favoring them.

Members' speeches in the debates were rated (-3 to $+3$) by me on four issues: the entire bill, immediate emancipation, shortened apprenticeship, and concern for the physical well-being of the slaves. The Debate Index equals the sum of these ratings, with a potential range from $+12$ to -12.

Two sources give systematic surveys of the MPs' reputations on emancipation, which entered into an index called Ratings. *Dod's Parliamentary Companion* of 1833 tells whether an MP favored immediate emancipation, favored gradual emancipation, or opposed immediate emancipation, which added $+2$, $+1$, or -2, respectively, to the Ratings Index. During the 1832 election campaign, the Agency Anti-Slavery Committee, an executive committee of the Anti-Slavery Society, published lists of candidates certainly in favor of immediate emancipation and of those certainly opposed.[7] Appearing on these lists added $+2$ or -2 to an MP's Ratings Index. Participation in the Anti-Slavery Society also contributed to an MP's Rating Index. MPs who attended society meetings received $+2$ on their Ratings Index, $+3$ if Dixon considered them particularly active. Non-attending subscribers received +1 (Dixon 1971, 234). I chose the above values to give each part of the index roughly equal weight and to give the whole Ratings Index a magnitude comparable with the other indexes. The Ratings Index seemed an important, if *ad hoc,* way to take account of the broad-based support for emancipation.

The simple sum of the Division, Debate, and Ratings indexes equals the Composite Index. Summing the indicators to create an index for each MP seemed to be the best way to use all the available information. The Division Index had non-zero values for 33 percent of the MPs, the Ratings Index for 31 percent, and the Debate Index for only 13 percent. The Composite Index was non-zero for 52 percent of the MPs.

The independent variables, the characteristics of the MPs and their constituencies which may explain their positions on emancipation, fall into four substantive categories. Since religion and economic interest are the major competing explanations for the antislavery movement, the dependent variables include religious and economic characteristics. The effects of the Reform Bill of 1832 and a combination of regionalism and demography provide two other dimensions.

Information on the religious characteristics of constituencies comes from the 1851 census of England, Wales, and Scotland and the 1861 census of Ireland.[8] The 1851 census recorded for each county and for the larger cities the number of persons attending worship services of each denomination on March 30, 1851. From this information I calculated the share of the total population attending morning services and the share of attenders of the five most popular demoninations—Church of England, Church of Scotland, Roman Catholic, Wesleyan Methodist, and Independent (Congregationalist). Because of their legendary status as abolitionists, I also included the Society of Friends (Quakers). The residual, baseline category was a miscellany of dissenting denominations—non-Wesleyan Methodists, various Presbyterian groups, etc. For Ireland the 1861 census recorded religious confession rather than attendance. The shares professing allegiance to each denomination were treated the same as the denomination attendance shares for the rest of Britain. I assumed that the aggregate share of the population attending the morning worship was the same for Ireland as the average for the constituencies in the rest of Britain, 27 percent. So in the statistical analysis, this variable mattered only for the non-Irish constituencies, where it showed variation from its mean.

Information on the MPs' religious orientation came from *Dod's Parliamentary Companion* of 1833. For MPs described as favoring church reform, the MP-Religion variable took a value of +1. For MPs who were themselves dissenters, it was +2; presumably they also favored reform of the Established Church.

Four variables measure the extent to which constituencies were economically dependent on textiles, coal and iron, banking, and shipping. A survey in 1835 recorded the number of power looms in each county of England, Wales, and Scotland (Smith 1968, 127). The Constituency-Textiles variable equals the number of power looms in 1835 divided by the county population of 1831. Although the textile industry included more than power weaving, the power looms per capita is probably a good proxy. The Constituency-Textiles variable took the same value for all MPs from the same county and its boroughs. Coal and iron production were closely related, both statistically and functionally. So the Constituency-Coal-Iron variable equaled the sum of the per capita coal and per capita iron output for each county (Smith 1968, 148; Clapham 1964, 1:236; Leser 1954, 111–113; Carr and Taplin 1962, 6; Birch 1967, 145–177). Because it resulted in slightly stronger statistical relationships, the Coal-Iron variable was not zero only for boroughs with a population over 10,000. Based on its reputation as a center for banking and commerce, London and the adjacent boroughs had a special dummy variable called Constituency-London. Another dummy variable, Constituency-Port Borough, equaled 1 for boroughs with a population over 10,000 in counties with a major seaport.

The MP-Economic variables were, with one exception, dummy variables that registered whether an MP had a personal involvement in any one of six economic activities—manufacturing, commerce (as a merchant), banking, shipping (owner or builder), East Indies trade, and West Indies trade or plantations. The data mostly came from *Dod's* (1833) or Judd (1955), with supplementary data on East and West Indian involvement from Dixon (1971, App. A, B). The MP-West Indian variable was an index equal to the sum of dummies for being a West Indian planter, a West Indian merchant, and an attender at meetings of the West Indian Committee. Most MPs were agricultural landowners, which had no dummy variable and, therefore, was the baseline category.

The five Reform Bill variables seek to test the hypotheses that link liberal political reform with the passage of emancipation. The Reform Bill of 1832 culminated three years of political crisis and social unrest, expanded the franchise, eliminated or reduced the seats of many pocket boroughs, and added seats for many heavily populated towns. The first Parliament elected under the new law, although not much different from its predecessor in terms of personnel or social origin, felt compelled to make some dramatic reforms (Halévy 1950, 3, 67–69). Emancipation may have seemed like thicker ice on which to tread than the hot domestic issues like poor-law reform, factory regulation, church reform, or further electoral reform. Or perhaps the reformers just wanted emancipation to weaken the antireform camp. In any case, emancipation was the first major reform enacted by the first reformed Parliament (Halévy 1950, 3, 80–85; Davis 1975, 349). The Constituency-New 1832 variable is a dummy equal to 1 for districts created by the Reform Bill. The Constituency-Reform Bill Seats variable equals the number of seats gained or lost by previously existing districts and ranges from −2 to +2 in value. The Constituency-Reform Bill Influence variable is +2 if *Dod's* said that the Reform Bill totally eliminated the ability of a noble or rich commoner to determine the MP for the district and equals +1 if this influence was partially reduced. The Constituency-Old Influence variable equals +2 if the Reform Bill did not reduce the corrupting influence of a noble or rich commoner and equals +1 if the Reform Bill only partially reduced the influence.[9] I expected this last variable to have a negative coefficient and all the other Reform Bill variables to have a positive ones. The variable MP-New 1832, a dummy that equaled 1 for MPs elected for the first time in December 1832, also reflected, among other things, the effects of the Reform Bill.

Aydelotte (1977) found that classifying constituencies into one of three types helped explain the parliamentary voting patterns of MPs in the 1840s. The three types of constituency are (1) counties and universities in England, Scotland, and Wales and all of Ulster, (2) English and Welsh boroughs with under 1,760 electors, and (3) English and Welsh boroughs with over 1,770 electors, all Scottish boroughs, and all of southern Ireland. Dummy variables were entered for types 2 and 3, making type 1 the baseline. The issue is whether these variables can add anything to the explanations provided by the religious, economic, and Reform Bill variables.

Many of the variables described above could have been handled in a number of defensible ways. So the choice of method had to be to some extent arbitrary. Resisting the temptation to experiment with a lot of variable forms, preserved, I believe, the validity of the measures of statistical significance.

The purpose of the regression analysis was not to estimate the coefficients of the independent variables (except their sign), but rather to determine which made statistically significant contributions to explaining the variation of the dependent variables, the measures of antislavery sentiment. The regressions were ordinary least squares.

Table 28.1 reports regressions that included all independent variables with an F-statistic of at least 2.5. In order to be significant at the 0.05 level, the F-statistic for an individual variable must be over 3.85 and over 6.7 for significance at the 0.01 level. Each measure of antislavery sentiment has a different list of significant independent variables, but there are some similarities between the lists. Two variables, MP-Manufacturer and Constituency-Old Influence, are significant in three of the four equations, and the MP-Religion variable is significant in all four. This result lends credence to the first three explanations for emancipation—religion, economic interest, and the Reform Bill.

The signs on the beta coefficients are mostly what one would expect.[10] MP-Shipping is the only variable with significant coefficients of opposite signs in different regressions, positive with the Division Index and negative with the Ratings Index. The negative sign supports Drescher's contention that the antislavery movement imposed sacrifices on the nation's commerce, and the positive sign supports Williams's contention that the international trading interests had turned against slavery. The positive coefficients for the Port Borough variable also supports Williams. The negative coefficient for the MP-East Indian variable, on the other hand, goes against Williams's suggestion that the East Indians aligned themselves with the antislavery movement in order to break the West Indian monopoly on the British sugar market (Williams 1944, 137, 183–188).

Of the constituency religion variables, only Methodists and Independents have significant coefficients in more than one equation. This surprised me, because they would seem most similar to the baseline group, miscellaneous dissenters. Roman Catholic was the only other religious constituency variable with a significant coefficient in any equation. Its positive sign probably reflected not so much the effect of Catholicism as the anti-colonialism of southern Ireland and the liberalism of industrial districts, which had many Irish immigrants.

Table 28.1. Regressions Testing the Significance of Individual Independent Variables with Different Measures of Antislavery Sentiment as Dependent Variables

Dependent Variable	Significant Independent Variables	F-Statistic of Independent Variable[a]	Beta Coefficient	R-Square of Equation (Adjusted)
Division Index				0.163
	MP-Religion	27.6	0.194	
	MP-New 1832	25.4	0.184	
	MP-Manufacturer	12.5	0.131	
	Constituency-Old Influence	12.9	−0.144	
	Constituency-Aydelotte 2	11.7	0.139	
	MP-Shipping	4.0	0.074	
	MP-East Indian[b]	3.4	−0.067	
	MP-Merchant[b]	3.2	0.067	
Debate Index				0.045
	Constituency-Reform Bill Influence	11.6	0.131	
	MP-Manufacturer	5.8	0.094	
	MP-Religion	4.4	0.082	
	Constituency-Religious Attendance[b]	2.9	−0.066	
	Constituency-Port Borough[b]	2.8	0.064	
	Constituency-Roman Catholic	5.0	0.100	
	Constituency-Independent Religion[b]	2.5	0.071	
Ratings Index				0.156
	MP-West Indian	30.3	−0.202	
	Constituency-Independent Religion	12.7	0.140	
	Constituency-Old Influence	9.7	−0.123	
	MP-Religion	8.7	0.109	
	Constituency-Methodist	9.5	0.124	
	Constituency-Aydelotte 3	3.9	0.086	
	MP-Shipping	8.6	−0.109	
	MP-Merchant	4.0	0.076	
	Constituency-New 1832	5.4	0.096	
	Constituency-Reform Bill Seats	5.2	0.090	
	Constituency-Port Borough	5.0	0.084	
	Constituency-Textiles	4.6	−0.082	
	MP-Manufacturer[b]	3.4	0.072	
Composite Antislavery Index				0.161
	MP-Religion	25.1	0.184	
	MP-Manufacturer	14.6	0.142	
	Constituency-Old Influence	17.2	−0.154	
	Constituency-Methodist	11.2	0.132	
	MP-West Indian	13.0	−0.131	
	Constituency-Port Borough	5.5	0.087	
	Constituency-Independent Religion	10.2	0.121	

Table 28.1 (continued)

Dependent Variable	Significant Independent Variables	F-Statistic of Independent Variable[a]	Beta Coefficient	R-Square of Equation (Adjusted)
	MP-New 1832[b]	3.4	0.068	
	Constituency-Aydelotte 3	4.2	0.085	
	Constituency-Reform Bill Influence[b]	3.5	0.068	

[a] For the variable to be significant at the 0.05 level, F must be at least 3.85.
[b] F is between 2.5 and 3.85.

While the experiments reported in Table 28.1 show which individual variables were most important, they do not systematically test the major hypotheses about antislavery. To do this, one must test the significance of groups of variables, a procedure whose results appear in Table 28.2. The base case includes all twenty-five independent variables described earlier. The amount that the R-Square declines when a group of variables is omitted indicates the explanatory significance of the omitted variables. The F-statistic for the omitted variables as a group equals the proportional change in the sum of squared errors (or in one minus R-square) times the degrees of freedom in the original regression divided by the number of omitted variables. I performed these tests only with the Composite Antislavery Index as the dependent variable.

The economic variables were significant as a whole group and also when broken down into the constituency and MP subgroups. The significance of the MP subgroup is greater, probably because two of its components, manufacturers and West Indian, are individually significant. Only one constituency economic variable, Port Borough, is significant by itself (see Table 28.1).

The religious variables are significant as a group because of the great significance of the MP-Religious variable. The subgroup of constituency religious variables are not significant. The significance of the Methodist and Independent religious variables does not suffice to make the subgroup significant. In view of the relatively poor quality of information going into it, the strong showing of the MP-Religious variable is surprising. I also tried using separate dummy variables for *Dod's* rating of MPs as favoring church reform and being dissenters. This brought only an insignificant rise in the R-square. Both dummy variables were significant, but the dissenter one was surprisingly less significant ($F = 6.5$) than the church reform variable ($F = 17.5$). Perhaps better data on the religious convictions of MPs—more accurate and covering all religions—would reverse the apparent implication that a general reform orientation was more important than personal involvement in pious dissent.

The two Aydelotte constituency variables were not statistically significant as a group. This does not refute Aydelotte's findings, but indicates rather that, at least with respect to the Emancipation Bill, his variables do not tell much that is not more accurately told by the economic, religious, and Reform Bill variables.

The Reform Bill variables are significant as a group because of the significance of the constituency subgroup. The Constituency-Old Influence variable is the main

Table 28.2. Regressions Testing the Significance of Groups of Independent Variables Using the Composite Index as the Dependent Variable Measuring MPs' Antislavery Sentiment

Variables Omitted	Number of Omitted Variables	R-Square	F of Omitted Group of Variables	Minimum F for Significance[a]	
				0.05	0.01
None (base case)[b]	0	0.19455	—	—	—
Economic Variables					
All	10	0.14600	3.81	1.85	2.37
Constituency	4	0.17998	2.84	2.39	3.36
MP	6	0.15630	4.98	2.12	2.85
Religious Variables					
All	8	0.14714	4.63	1.96	2.55
Constituency	7	0.17746	1.91	2.03	2.69
MP	1	0.16576	22.48	3.86	6.70
Aydelotte Constituency					
Types	2	0.19112	1.34	3.02	4.66
1838 Changes (Reform Bill, etc.)					
All	5	0.15169	6.69	2.23	3.06
Constituency	4	0.15965	6.81	2.39	3.36
MP (New 1832)	1	0.19221	1.83	3.86	6.70
All Constituency					
Variables	17	0.12257	3.31	1.67	2.04
All MP Variables	8	0.11142	8.11	1.96	2.55

[a]With 400 degrees of freedom in the denominator.
[b]With 629 degrees of freedom.

explainer here. The MP-New 1832 variable is less significant in Table 28.2 than in Table 28.1, probably because of its correlation with the Constituency-New 1832 variable (correlation coefficient = 0.25), which was not significant enough to be included in the regression with the Composite Index in Table 28.1.

Both the constituency variables and the MP variables were significant as entire groups. The lower F-statistic (lower significance) of the constituency variables supports the notion that MPs did not feel rigidly bound to uphold the interests of their district (Gash 1953, xviii–xix). Regressions with the subset of MPs who were reelected by the same district in 1835 showed, to my surprise, a slightly *lower* F-statistic for the group of constituency variables. This supports Aydelotte's conclusion that, although constituency characteristics exert a significant influence on MPs' votes, electoral contests do not seem to be the avenue of that influence (Aydelotte 1977, 244–245).

The R-squares of the regressions, mostly under 0.20, indicate that the independent variables explain a low proportion of the variation in the dependent variables—the measures of antislavery sentiment. While R-squares this low are not unusual in cross-sectional analyses, they do show that much remains unknown about antislavery motivations. Contrary to the views of many writers, the issue need not be whether morality or self-interest explains most of the antislavery phenomenon. Even if better data doubled the explanatory power of the religious and economic variables, over half of the variation in antislavery sentiment would remain unexplained.

THE LINKS TO OTHER ISSUES

The hypotheses to explain antislavery sentiment in Parliament not only posit relationships with characteristics of MPs and their constituencies but also imply relationships between emancipation and other issues. On five such issues Parliament took divisions that Hansard (1833) recorded. Two related to religious freedom, one to free trade, and one to general humanitarianism. The fifth (the amendment of the poor laws) concerned both economic and humanitarian issues.

The statistical methodology is straightforward. For three of the divisions Hansard (1833) lists both the ayes and the noes; for the others he lists only the minorities. The average antislavery index is calculated for the MPs in each of the two or three categories, including a category for those not voting. For this test, I used the Composite Index and, because it also measured MPs' voting, the Division Index. The test is whether the index averages differ in the expected way and whether the differences were significant.[11]

The interpretation of antislavery as an unselfish religious and humanitarian movement implies that MPs voting to allow unlicensed laymen to preach, to allow dissenters into the universities, and to prohibit flogging in the army would have above average scores on the antislavery indexes. The results in Table 28.3 almost unanimously bear out this hypothesis. The average antislavery indexes of MPs favoring these measures are always higher than the other categories of MPs and, except for one case, significantly so (t-statistics greater than 2). The exception is that those opposed to freedom of religious worship had antislavery scores higher than those not voting and not significantly different from those in favor. This anomaly may reflect the obscurity of the division. The bill itself only extended to layman of the Church of England a right that dissenters already enjoyed, and the division was technically not on the entire bill but rather on an amendment from the opposition to delay by six months the enactment of the bill.

The hypothesis that the antislavery movement somehow furthered the material interests of the industrial capitalists implies that the MPs voting to lower the grain duties would have above average antislavery scores. Table 28.3 bears out this prediction, with the t-statistic for the difference in means being around 6. While this shows that the free traders tended to be avid opponents of slavery, one must bear in mind that the overwhelming majority that opposed free trade must have had many MPs in common with the overwhelming majority that passed emancipation.

Predicting the relationship between emancipation and the Poor Law of 1834 depends as much on one's opinion of the New Poor Law as on one's theory of antislavery motivations. Both measures fundamentally revised the means by which property owners could exert control over the labor force. Both intended to have labor allocated through as nearly a free market as possible. The difference was that

Table 28.3. Antislavery Measures Compared with MPs' Votes on Other, Hypothetically Related Issues

Issue	Statistic	Measure of Antislavery Sentiment	
		Composite Index	Division Index
Freedom of	Mean Index of MPs		
Religious	79 voting for	3.65	1.33
Worship	539 not voting	1.43	0.65
	29 voting against	1.52	0.79
	t-Statistic for Difference in Means		
	MPs for and against	2.27	1.52
	MPs for and not voting	7.00	4.21
Dissenters'	Mean Index of MPs		
Admission to	180 voting for	2.93	1.23
Universities	425 not voting	1.40	0.60
	42 voting against	−0.36	0.10
	t-Statistic for Difference in Means		
	MPs for and against	5.38	4.43
	MPs for and not voting	5.53	5.22
Abolish	Mean Index of MPs		
Flogging in	140 voting for	3.79	1.77
the Army	362 not voting	1.29	0.54
	142 voting against	0.68	0.24
	t-Statistic for Difference in Means		
	MPs for and against	7.97	9.44
	MPs for and not voting	7.96	9.21
Fix and Lower	Mean Index of MPs		
Duties on Grain	98 voting for	3.49	1.45
Imports	553 voting against or not voting	1.33	0.59
	t-Statistic for Difference in Means	6.33	5.90
New Poor Law	Mean Index of MPs		
(third reading)	41 voting against	3.12	1.27
	614 voting for or not voting	1.60	0.70
	t-Statistic for Difference in Means	2.99	2.63
Amendment to	Mean Index of MPs		
Poor Law to	30 voting for	3.50	1.53
Continue	625 voting against or not voting	1.60	0.70
Allowing Out-of-Doors Relief			
	t-Statistic for Difference in Means	3.20	3.30

Source: Division lists from Hansard (1833).

emancipation meant a less harsh labor discipline for West Indian blacks, both in fact and in the minds of most MPs. The Poor Law of 1834, on the other hand, abolished a generous, if inefficient, system that usually amounted to a guaranteed subsistence income for the working population (McCloskey 1973; Blaug 1963). The New Poor Law would provide relief only to men willing to give up all possessions and regular employment and move, with their families, into a poorhouse or workhouse. Supporters of the new law expected it to restore the efficiency and dignity of the English worker. Opponents thought it was inhumane and in violation of the English workers' right to life.

Most writers on the antislavery movement do not consider the possibility of a connection between the New Poor Law and emancipation. Davis, however, does discuss the "striking . . . parallels between the rise of anti-slavery and a profound transformation in attitudes toward the English poor." He acknowledges that the connection between them was not consistent or inevitable; abolitionist leaders took both sides on the Poor Law questions. Yet, "the chief figures who helped to revise the traditional paternalism toward the 'laboring poor' were all outspoken opponents of Negro slavery" (Davis 1975, 356–358).

Those who opposed slavery out of concern for the physical welfare of their fellow beings should have also opposed the New Poor Law. On the other hand, those who sought to destroy slavery chiefly in order to advance the interests of capitalism and free enterprise should have favored the New Poor Law. The evidence in Table 28.3 shows that opponents of the New Poor Law, both in the division on the entire bill and in a division to amend one of its harshest provisions, had significantly above average antislavery indexes.[12] This evidence supports the humanitarian interpretation of antislavery. It does not, however, refute the economic interest explanation.

Analysis of voting on two bills that allegedly represented the interests of the bourgeois classes—lowering the grain tariffs and revising the Poor Law—appears to give mixed evidence on the economic interest interpretations of antislavery. The MPs who favored freer trade had higher than average antislavery indexes, but they were a small minority in the Parliament that passed emancipation. On the other hand, overwhelming majorities of the same Parliament (i.e., largely overlapping sets of MPs) passed both the Poor Law amendment and emancipation, but the minority opposing the New Poor Law had above average antislavery indexes. The apparent contradiction resolves itself, however, when one remembers that most MPs in 1833 were aristocratic or gentry landowners, not bourgeois capitalists. The division on the Corn Laws fits with an eclectic hypothesis that free trade was one but not the only motivation for antislavery. The divisions of the Poor Law fit with an hypothesis that agricultural landlords as well as bourgeois capitalists had an economic interest in the Poor Law amendment. (Most of the poor were, after all, in agricultural areas, and taxes were paid there for their relief.) That this coalition as a whole had below average antislavery indexes does not prove that the bourgeois portion of it did.

The analysis of the relationships between emancipation and other issues facing the Parliament of 1832–1834 confirms, for the most part, the regression results indicating that both religious humanitarianism and economic interests motivated MPs to oppose slavery.

CONCLUSIONS

The statistical results described above reveal a great deal about the motives for emancipation but also show that even more remains unknown.

The results recommend an eclectic rather than a monocausal explanation of the antislavery movement. The regressions give about equally strong support to the religious, economic interest, and Reform Bill hypotheses. Being a religious dissenter or reformer or a manufacturer or from a constituency with a seaport or a large proportion of Methodists and Congregationalists increased the likelihood that an MP would favor emancipation. Being a West Indian or from a corrupt borough increased the likelihood of an MP's opposing emancipation. On the other hand, some variables that implicitly loom large in the traditional accounts of antislavery do not have statistically significant coefficients—notably, being a merchant, banker, or East Indian, and being from a constituency with a large share of Quakers or strong indicators of industrialization.

The idea of an eclectic explanation for emancipation and antislavery in general is not new. Most writers make some concession to it (Williams 1944, 178–196; Coupland [1933] 1964, xxi, 62, 123; Klingberg 1926, 305). As Engerman and Eltis (1980, 274–275) point out in their review of the abolition debate,

> there seems little basis with which to distinguish economic from humanitarian, and other political and social influences. It is precisely the purpose of an ideology to merge divergent strands into one world-view. . . . One striking aspect of the anti-slavery creed was the belief that economics, religion, and humanitarianism, indeed all aspects of the anti-slavery argument, came to point to the same outcome. There was no reason for the motivations to be separated, and it would be difficult to believe that any individual could convincingly make the sharp categorization implied by either Coupland or Williams.

One can never know what MPs actually believed about their moral obligations and economic interests, and this study does not attempt to show whether emancipation actually fulfilled a moral obligation or served any economic interest. This study does show that religious affiliation and economic activities of MPs and their constituencies, which can be objectively measured, both contribute to an explanation of the attitudes of MPs toward slavery. This implies but does not prove that both morality and self-interest motivated British MPs to pass emancipation. The relationship of antislavery sentiment to votes on other issues also supports this eclectic hypothesis.

NOTES

1. "The Agency Society List of Acceptable and Unacceptable Candidates," (1832).
2. United Kingdom, Parliament, 1833 (1834). Hansard (1833) provides an abridged version of the debates.
3. Fogel and Engerman (#29, in this volume), 599–600, estimate "that the compensation package offered to slaveowners amounted to about 96 percent of the value of their slaves . . . with the slaves themselves 'contributing' close to half of the payment" through their apprenticeship.
4. For two other versions of the humanitarian interpretation, see Klingberg (1926) and Mellor (1951).
5. Many of Williams's ideas appeared earlier in Hochstetter (1905). This work attracted little attention outside Germany.
6. For a more detailed review of the debate, see Engerman and Eltis (1980).
7. "The Agency Society List of Acceptable and Unacceptable Candidates," (1832).

8. United Kingdom, House of Commons (1852–1853), 89:199–238; (1854), 59:319–332; (1863), 59:16–19.

9. In other words, if Reform Bill Influence equals 1, so does Old Influence, and vice versa. There seemed to be no a priori way to determine whether the corruption that was eliminated or the corruption that remained was more important.

10. The beta coefficient equals the standard regression coefficient times the ratio of standard deviations of the independent and dependent variables. In other words, the beta coefficient tells how much of a standard deviation the dependent variable will change in response to a one standard deviation change in the independent variable. Because the units of the variables are arbitrary, beta coefficients allow greater comparability than ordinary regression coefficients.

11. Some MPs had to be omitted from the analysis; the numbers reported on each side in Table 28.3 therefore differ from the actual number on each side in Hansard's lists. Some were omitted because they were not in Parliament at the time it debated and passed the emancipation bill. A few were omitted because Hansard's list did not sufficiently identify them.

12. Analysis of the division on the second reading of the bill gave the same results.

TWENTY-NINE

Philanthropy at Bargain Prices: Notes on the Economics of Gradual Emancipation*

Robert W. Fogel and Stanley L. Engerman

In recent years there has been much discussion of the "reparations bill" to be paid to American blacks as compensation for their exploitation under slavery.[1] "Reparations" was also a subject of debate during the slave era. During slavery times, however, the point at issue was the amount of the compensation that should be paid to slaveholders. For even those legislators who were most passionate in their attack on the institution of slavery generally respected the legal and moral rights of owners of property, including property rights in human beings. The central economic issue of emancipation, then, was not whether owners of slaves should be compensated, but rather who should bear the costs of such compensations.

There were three groups who could have been forced to finance the direct cost of emancipation.[2] Slaveowners constituted one of these groups; non-slaveowning free men made up the second. The third group consisted of slaves. To modern minds it may seem fatuous to suggest that a class as poor as slaves could have possessed, or somehow have acquired, the capital needed to make a significant contribution to the compensation bill. But to the free men who participated in the political councils during slavery times this possibility was not only real but eminently practical.

Still the question remains: How could a class as impoverished as slaves be made to shoulder the heavy burden of compensation? The answer to this problem was found in "gradual emancipation." In this paper we consider two general variants of schemes for gradual emancipation. The first is the one which was implemented in the northern United States.[3] The special feature of this scheme is that it succeeded in relieving non-slaveholding free Northerners of almost the entire direct financial burden of emancipation.[4] The second is the scheme implemented in the British colonies. In the British case, non-slaveholding free men did pay something for their

---

*Reprinted, with revisions and additions, and with permission from *The Journal of Legal Studies* 3(1974):377–401. © 1974 by The University of Chicago.

principles, for a significant share of the cost of compensation was borne by British taxpayers.[5]

We do not mean to give the impression that slaveholders escaped scot-free. To the extent that the compensation made to slaveholders was less than 100 percent of the value of their slaves they too were forced to bear some of the direct cost of emancipation.[6] What is surprising, however, is how close to 100 percent of market value they were promised. This discovery helps to explain why so many of the affected slaveholders eventually acquiesced in gradual emancipation. While they may not have liked the new order of things that was being forced upon them, at least they were not being required to underwrite financially the principles of the abolitionists. That burden was, for the most part, shifted to the slaves themselves. Indeed, the overarching characteristic of most schemes for gradual emancipation is that slaves were to bear the lion's share of the direct financial cost of their freedom. However, not all of the schemes worked out as promised and in the British case the actual cost to the planters was significantly higher than the advertised cost.

Between 1777 and 1804 each of the eight states of the northeastern region of the United States took legal measures to provide for the emancipation of the resident slave population.[7] Little is known about the process of emancipation in Vermont, Massachusetts, and New Hampshire. In these three states vague constitutional clauses provided the legal basis for emancipation, and the conditions of emancipation are still to be determined.[8]

In the other five states, slavery was ended by legislative enactments which provided for gradual emancipation. Under these enactments all persons enslaved at the date of the passage of the enactment were to remain in bondage. Emancipation was thus limited to the unborn children of the slaves. And emancipation was not immediate even for them. The "free born" were required to continue in servitude— under conditions similar to indentured servitude—for between eighteen and twenty-eight years (see Table 29.1).[9] The ownership right to the free born during their period of servitude was generally salable, but such sales were restricted in various ways. In New Jersey, for example, a free-born person could not be sold out of state without his permission.

Despite a significant expansion of research on the process of emancipation, published work to date has yet to produce clear definitions of the blocs which formed over the various political, economic, and social issues related to the struggle over northern emancipation. Little is known about the motivation of particular groups with respect to particular legislative proposals or the ways in which economic or social class, political objectives, and ideological commitments interacted to produce one or another coalition.[10]

The form which the legislation took—the freeing not of present slaves but of a future generation of potential slaves—suggests that those who were politically dominant in the process of emancipation were less concerned with slaves themselves than with the burden of the issue of slavery. For the legislation appears to have been designed to relieve the states of this divisive issue rather than to relieve slaves of the economic and social burden imposed on them. This impression is

Table 29.1. Age of Emancipation for the Free Born

State	Date of Enactment	Age of Emancipation	
		Male	Female
Pennsylvania	1780[a]	28	28
Rhode Island	1784[b]	21	18
Connecticut	1784[c]	25	25
New York	1799[d]	28	25
New Jersey	1804[e]	25	21

[a]The last census which enumerated any slaves in Pennsylvania was that of 1840.
[b]All slavery was abolished in 1842.
[c]The age of emancipation was changed in 1797 to age twenty-one. In 1848, all slavery was abolished.
[d]In 1817, a law was passed freeing all slaves as of July 4, 1827.
[e]In 1846 all slaves were emancipated, but apprenticeships continued for the children of slave mothers and were introduced for freed slaves.

enhanced by what little is known about the way in which the enactments were carried out. What is at issue here is not merely the absence of effective enforcement procedures (in no state was there a separate agency to enforce the enactments). Various loopholes were created—either by legislative design, by judicial interpretation, or by executive toleration—which allowed slaveowners to perpetuate slavery, as long as such perpetuation was carried on in another political jurisdiction. The chief loophole, of course, was the sale of slaves to buyers in states which continued to countenance slavery. Other abuses of slaves that were tolerated included increased intensity of labor imposed on the free born, the abandonment of the aged and other non-productive slaves, and the deterioration of the maintenance of slaves.

The provisions of the enactments, as well as the debates over them, also indicate that those who dominated the legislatures believed that slaveowners had a property right that had to be protected or, at least, that should not be confiscated. This respect for property was reinforced by a widely held fear over "premature" release of slaves from bondage before they could be "educated" into appropriate habits toward work and life.

Perhaps the greatest fear expressed by the dominant group was that the burden of emancipation might be shifted to the non-slaveholder. That such taxpayers should be kept free from the burden was emphasized over and over in the debates both inside and outside of the legislatures. Unlike the British, the majority of these antislavery critics do not appear to have had a sense of responsibility for the perpetuation of human bondage nor a feeling of guilt for having benefited from it. Quite the contrary, they emphasized that they had not personally gained from the existence of slavery. For unlike the South, slaves were not a significant fraction of their labor supply. And unlike Britain, the northern states were a minor market for slave-produced products. Of course some Northerners had been implicated in, and had profited from, the slave trade; but most had not.

Consequently much attention was given to provisions that would keep the burden of emancipation from falling on the general taxpayer. Individual manumissions could not, therefore, be effected unless "the master posted a security that the slave would not become a public charge."[11] With one exception—Rhode Island—the expense of raising and educating the free born until they reached maturity was placed on the master; and the Rhode Island law that permitted this cost to be placed on the township was repealed at the end of one year. New York and New Jersey also repealed provisions that had allowed slaveowners to abandon free-born children who were more than one year old when state expenditures on such children rose to significant levels.

The circumstances surrounding British legislation on emancipation differed from those in the northern United States in several respects.[12] First, the basic British legislation was enacted more than a quarter of a century later than in the northern states. The protracted ideological and political struggle against slavery in Britain appears to have had a far-reaching influence on all politically active classes in Britain and made emancipation a more acute issue than in the northern United States. Second, non-slaveholders, both inside and outside of Parliament, exhibited a substantial sense of British involvement in, and responsibility for, the horrors of slavery. For it was generally acknowledged that the demand of Britons for cheap sugar, as well as a long series of parliamentary enactments and governmental actions, had promoted slavery in the British colonies. Third, the political influence of slaveholders within the Parliament was substantially greater than in the legislatures of the northern states. Indeed, so powerful was their influence that the government, through the Colonial Office, while identifying itself with the desirability of emancipation as a long-range goal, in practice pursued reforms aimed merely at ameliorating the circumstances of servitude—reforms that had at least the begrudging approval of the legislatures of the slave colonies.

These, of course, were not the only factors that influenced the timing or the content of British legislation on emancipation. Parliamentary action was also influenced by such matters as the rising concern over the condition of the English industrial classes, especially the children and women employed in the factories and mines (cf. Drescher 1986). However, we believe that the factors we have singled out are relevant to an explanation not only of what was common to the British and northern cases, but also to certain important differences regarding the distribution of the financial burden of emancipation.

What was common to the two cases, of course, was agreement that the title of slaveholders to their chattel was a valid property right that had to be respected. There were some in the British antislavery movement who held that the claims of slaves to their freedom represented a higher morality than the claims of owners of property. But they were a small minority among the British public and were virtually without voice in Parliament. Those who dominated the antislavery bloc within Parliament showed no desire to bring into question so fundamental a tenet of their own social order. Forced emancipation, of course, even with full compensation to slaveholders, represented some degree of tampering with property rights. But taxes and governmental regulation of commerce were also intrusions. And so the parliamentary struggle for emancipation was generally confined to proposals that involved only degrees of interference consistent with the prevailing practices. This viewpoint was so widely accepted and deeply held that the proslavery bloc continually invoked the specter of an attack on property rights to stave off legislation that moved in the direction of emancipation.

The primary difference between the British and northern cases was the staunch opposition of abolitionists to any solution that put the entire financial burden of emancipation on the slaves. By 1833 the antislavery bloc within Parliament had swung strongly to the view that freedom must be granted not only to the future children of slaves but also to those who were currently in bondage. The government attempted to steer between the demands of the antislavery bloc and the commitment to the property rights of the slaveholders by proposing that all slaves be emancipated twelve years after the enactment of legislation directed toward the end. For reasons to be explained below, such a postponement would have put 71 percent of the cost of emancipation on the slaves. The government left open the possibility that the remainder of the value of slaves could be obtained either by a subsidy from the British taxpayers or by loopholes which permitted slaveowners to recover all or part of the balance of the value of their titles through increasing the intensity of the labor of their slaves or reducing the expenditure on slave maintenance. The proposal for the involvement of British taxpayers took the form of a loan. The subsidy to the slaveowners could have been of any magnitude up to the face value of that loan depending on what interest rate was attached to the loan and what share of the principal the slaveowners were required to repay.

Parliamentary leaders of the abolitionist bloc rejected the proposal of a twelve-year extension of slavery as being too onerous. They had sufficient strength to force the government to agree that the continuation of slavery would be limited to a six-year period, euphemistically titled "apprenticeship." Another provision of the plan called for the immediate emancipation of all slave children under six as well as all those born during the period of apprenticeship. All slaves age six and over were required to labor for their masters during the period of apprenticeship. Assuming an average work week of sixty hours, Parliament ruled that only forty-five hours were to be expended on behalf of the master; the product of the remaining fifteen hours was to go to the slaves. Other issues regarding the conditions of work and maintenance were to be governed by legislation enacted by the various colonial legislatures.

Since it was anticipated that these provisions would be insufficient to compensate masters adequately for the loss of their slaves, Parliament voted a subsidy to slaveowners of £20 million. This sum, which it was assumed would equal roughly 40 percent of the market value of the slave population, was to be allocated among owners according to the number of their slaves, taking account of age, sex, skill, health, and other factors affecting their value. This subsidy was to be paid in each colony when legislative action on apprenticeship was completed. As far as we can presently determine, 80 percent of the subsidy was paid in 1836—roughly two years after the emancipation decree took effect—and the rest was paid during 1837.[13]

In order to estimate the distribution of the cost of emancipation between slaves and slaveholders it is necessary to make use of equations which relate the price of male and female slaves at any given age to the net income that owners could have expected to have derived from ownership of them over the balance of their lives (see Table 29.2 for definitions of symbols). The equation for males is

$$P_{sx} = (R_f) \sum_{t=1}^{n} \frac{\psi_t \lambda_t}{(1 + i)^t} \tag{1}$$

This equation states that the price of male slaves at any age was determined by the net earnings from field production over the life cycle, the probability that the slave would survive to any given year, and the rate of discount of future income. The profile of net earnings for males in the United States at each age from zero to seventy in about 1800 is shown in Figure 29.1. The corresponding price-age profile is shown in Figure 29.2.

While the price of a male was usually based on net earnings from production in the fields alone, the price of the female reflected not only her productive capacity in the fields but also her childbearing capacity. Consequently, the equation for the price of a female slave is of the form

$$P_{swx} = (R_{wf}) \sum_{t=1}^{n} \frac{\psi_{wt} \lambda_{wt}}{(1 + i)^t} + (B) \sum_{t=1}^{n} \frac{\phi_t \lambda_{wt}}{(1 + i)^t} \tag{2}$$

In equation 2, the first term on the right-hand side gives the present value of the female field productive capacity at age x, while the second term represents the present value of her childbearing capacity at age x. Figure 29.3 shows the division

Table 29.2. Definitions of Symbols

Symbol	Definition
P_s	The price of a slave.
R	The annual net revenue derived from a slave.
ψ_t	The ratio of annual net earnings of a slave during a given year to the peak-age net earnings of slaves.
λ	The probability that a slave will live through a given age.
B	The value of a "birthright" (the zero-age price of a slave).
ϕ	The probability of a live birth in a given year.
V	The ratio of the value of the childbearing capacity of a woman of a given age to her price at that age.
$\bar{C}$	The average compensation per slave.
$\bar{S}$	The average cash payment per slave by the British government.
$\bar{Y}$	The average gross revenue derived from a slave.
$\bar{M}$	The average maintenance expenditure per slave.
$\bar{P}_s$	The average market value of a slave.
i	The rate of return or rate of discount.
n	The expected number of years that a slave will be held; the expected number of years between age x and death.
x	A subscript indicating the age of a slave.
f	A subscript which indicates that the value of the variable pertains to a prime-aged hand.
t	A subscript or exponent designating a year.
w	A subscript which indicates that the variable pertains to females.

Figure 29.1. Annual net earnings from male slaves by age, about 1800.

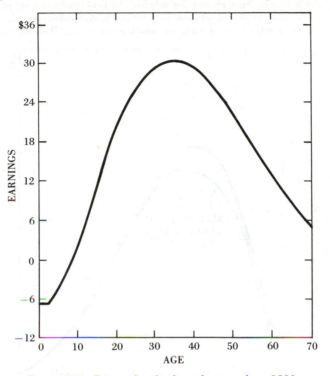

Figure 29.2. Prices of male slaves by age, about 1800.

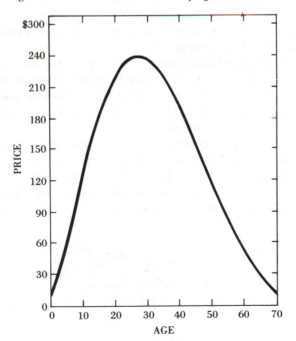

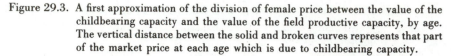

Figure 29.3. A first approximation of the division of female price between the value of the childbearing capacity and the value of the field productive capacity, by age. The vertical distance between the solid and broken curves represents that part of the market price at each age which is due to childbearing capacity.

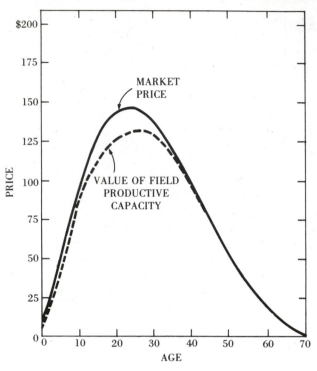

of a female's price at each age between these two components. Figure 29.4 shows how the average annual net earnings derived from females was divided between her activities in production and childbearing at each age of her life.[14] In comparing Figures 29.3 and 29.4, it is worth noting that the childbearing capacity represented a significant element of a female's price even at ages in which she was too young to bear children, although, of course, it had no effect on her value at older ages, when the probability of childbearing returned to zero.

Emancipation laws of the type instituted by the three large slaveholding states in the North—New York, New Jersey, and Pennsylvania—involved no *direct* loss for owners of male slaves, since no slave alive at the time of the enactment of the emancipation law was freed. There was, however, a capital loss suffered by owners of female slaves since, as equation 2 shows, a share of the price of a female slave equal to

$$V = \frac{(B) \sum_{t=1}^{n} \frac{\phi_t \, \lambda_{wt}}{(1 + i)^t}}{P_{swx}} \tag{3}$$

Figure 29.4. A first approximation of the division of annual net earnings from females between childbearing capacity and field earnings, by age. The vertical distance between the solid and broken curves represents the expected annual value of the childbearing capacity at each age.

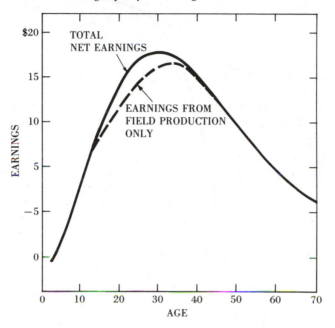

was due to her childbearing capacity. Figure 29.3 shows that the value of V rose from 10 percent at age nine to a peak of 13 percent at age twenty and then fell gradually to zero at age fifty. On average, the ratio of the value of the childbearing capacity of a woman to her price was 10.1 percent.

The exact amount of the loss imposed on owners of women depended on the age of emancipation. Figure 29.5 indicates that the break-even age for rearing males in the Old South in about 1850 was twenty-six years. If that break-even age also applies to the period 1780–1804, an emancipation law which freed newly born slave children at age twenty-six would reduce the value of the birthright (B) of those children to zero.[15] When the effect of an emancipation law is to reduce B from a positive value to zero, the capital loss imposed on the owner of a female, expressed as a percentage of the original price of the female, is exactly V. Emancipation laws that freed children before the break-even age would make the value of B negative and would have imposed a capital loss greater than V. Emancipation laws that freed children at ages greater than the break-even age would have left B positive and, hence, imposed a capital loss of less than V.

In the case of a law that freed children at the break-even age, then, the average capital loss imposed on owners of female slaves would be about 10 percent. Since female slaves represented about 37 percent of the value of all slaves, the average loss to all owners of emancipated slaves would be 3.7 percent (10×0.37).

The preceding discussion was based on the assumption that slaveowners con-

Figure 29.5. The average accumulated value (expected present value) of the income expropriated from slaves over the course of the life cycle (in dollars of 1850).

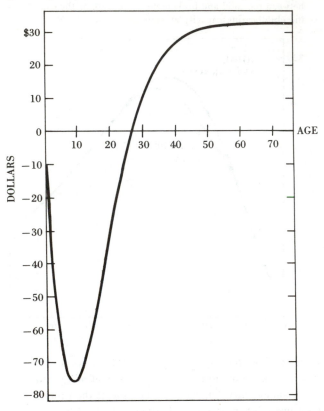

tinued to provide the same treatment to slaves scheduled to be freed as had been
true before the emancipation laws. This is a dubious assumption. The immediacy of
emancipation would have given owners an incentive to work slaves harder and to
provide poorer maintenance for them, since these owners would no longer bear the
consequence of any deterioration in the health of slaves that showed up after the
age of emancipation. To the extent that this incentive became operative, the capital
loss to slaveholders would have been reduced below 3.7 percent.

The various emancipation schemes debated and enacted in the North are described in detail by Zilversmit.[16] The development of the age-price profiles has
made it possible to evaluate the cost to slaveholders of various schemes. Table 29.3
presents estimates of the capital losses implicit in several of the emancipation
schemes enacted by northern states, on the assumption that slaveholders could find
no loopholes. Since available evidence suggests that many slaveholders did take
advantage of the loopholes, these estimates are probably upper bounds.[17]

In this connection it is worth noting that in the states with emancipation laws
there was a sharp decline in the rate of increase of the black populations after the
closing of the international slave trade in 1807.[18] Table 29.4 gives the rates of

Table 29.3. Probable Upper Bounds on Capital Losses Imposed on Slaveholders in Three States

State	Year of Enactment of the Law	Age of Emancipation for Free Born	Capital Loss as a Percentage of the Original Capital Value of the Slaves
Pennsylvania	1780	28	2.7
New York	1799	25[a] 28[b]	3.2
New Jersey	1804	21[a] 25[b]	4.7

[a]Female.
[b]Male.

growth of the black population in three emancipation states between 1810 and 1820 and compares these with the rates of growth of the black population in the same states between 1790 and 1810 as well as the growth rates of the southern slave population and the total U.S. black population.

The entries in Table 29.4 strongly suggest that slaveholders in New York and New Jersey were selling their slaves to the South, especially between 1810 and 1820. These sales were probably motivated by the sharp rise in slave prices after the closing of the slave trade which permitted slaveowners to obtain capital gains in excess of the transactions costs involved in slave sales. Thus it is probable that, to a substantial degree, the decline of slavery in the North was due not to emancipation but to the actions of northern slaveholders who were cashing in on capital gains by selling their chattel in southern markets.

The data on the age-sex structure of the black population provide further support for our conjecture regarding interstate sales. The shortfall of males in 1820 (the first census with age and sex breakdowns for blacks) was greatest in the northern states in the age category fourteen to twenty-six.[19] Such a shortfall is consistent with slave-trading patterns. As we have noted elsewhere, the economics

Table 29.4. The Relative Rates of Growth of the Black Population in Emancipated States between 1810 and 1820 Compared with Those of Other Populations (percent)

	Decade Rates of Change Black Population (Slave and Free)		Decade Rates of Change in the Slave Population	
	1790–1810	1810–1820	1790–1810	1810–1820
New York	+24.6	−2.4	−16.1	−32.8
New Jersey	+14.8	+7.1	−2.5	−30.4
Pennsylvania	+50.6	+30.6	−53.9	−73.5
North	+25.2	+12.0	−17.5	−30.5
South	+33.5	+30.0	+31.0	+30.5
United States	+32.8	+28.6	+28.7	+29.1

of interstate trading resulted in a concentration of slave exports from "selling states" in the age category fifteen to twenty-five.[20]

There is a further factor that reduced the cost of emancipation to the slaveowners. Both the New York and New Jersey laws included a legal loophole under which owners could technically abandon their free born and then obtain sums of money for them from the state during the period of apprenticeship. Zilversmit (1967) suggests that these sums paid by the state exceeded the annual costs, and argues that this was a device meant to provide compensation to the owners. The costs of these programs were apparently high, however, and New York terminated theirs in five years, while New Jersey ended its application to the newborn after 1805, and repealed the legislation in 1811.

It is more difficult to estimate the distribution of the costs of emancipation among the three classes—slaves, slaveowners, and non-slaveowning taxpayers—in the British than in the northern case. The increased difficulty does not stem from conceptual considerations. While the equation that must be applied to the British case is somewhat different from that employed in the northern calculation, it represents only a minor variation of the standard equation for the capitalization of an income stream.

The British case is more difficult because far less is known about economic developments in the British West Indies between 1820 and 1850 than in the United States between 1790 and 1860. Consequently, the data needed for reliable estimation of the effect of certain specific provisions of the British emancipation law, as well as the response of both slaves and slaveowners to these provisions, are not presently available—at least not in the detail that is required. A key variable in the discussion that follows is the average annual price of the land and equipment on slave plantations, but only scattered prices of a handful of estates are currently available, together with some impressions of general movements in estate values. Other important points on which available evidence is (at best) quite sketchy are the effect of the immediate emancipation of children under six on the maintenance expenditures of slaveowners, the magnitude of the income loss imposed on slaveowners by the provision that apprentices could not be required to labor on the account of slaveholders for more than forty-five hours per week, and the cost saving that slaveowners were able to effect by reducing the quality of slave maintenance.

In order to extract maximum information from that evidence which is available, we first consider only the effect of the limitation of slavery to six years. To do so we initially assume that during these six years slaveowners earned exactly the same average net revenue per slave that they would have earned in the absence of apprenticeship. For convenience we refer to this computation as the "theoretical" value of the compensation package. We then consider how actual experience may have departed from this theoretical value.

Given adequate data, the average theoretical compensation per slave paid to British slaveholders can be computed from equation 4.

$$\overline{C} = \sum_{t=1}^{6} \frac{\overline{Y}_t - \overline{M}_t}{(1 + i)^t} + \sum_{t=1}^{6} \frac{\overline{S}_t}{(1 + i)^t} \tag{4}$$

In this equation the first right-hand term is the average value of compensation paid by the slaves themselves as a result of the continuation of slavery for six years. The second right-hand term is the average value of the payment made by British taxpayers.

Dividing both sides of equation 4 by the average market value of a slave yields

$$\frac{\overline{C}}{\overline{P}_s} = \frac{\displaystyle\sum_{t=1}^{6} \frac{\overline{Y}_t - \overline{M}_t}{(1+i)^t}}{\overline{P}_s} + \frac{\displaystyle\sum_{t=1}^{6} \frac{\overline{S}_t}{(1+i)^t}}{\overline{P}_s} \tag{5}$$

This division transforms absolute values into shares. The three terms of equation 5 are thus the share of the value of slaves for which slaveowners were compensated, the share of that value paid by the slaves, and the share paid by taxpayers.

Under the assumption that the emancipation law did not change the average annual net revenue per slave, the first right-hand term of equation 5 may be interpreted as the ratio of the value of an annuity for six years to the value of the same annuity in perpetuity. Then the evaluation of this term depends only on the discount rate. Given the discount rates that appear to have prevailed in the West Indies during the first third of the nineteenth century, perpetuation of slavery for six years was equivalent to the recovery of approximately 47 percent of the original value of the slave population.[21]

The evaluation of the last term of equation 5 is a little more complex than is usually supposed. In working out the distribution of the total British subsidy among individual slaveholders British officials developed an elaborate formula which involved the division of the slave population into eighteen categories, each with a different valuation.[22] Owners of slaves of any particular category received 44 percent of the appraised value of slaves in that category. Actual selling prices of slaves during the years 1823–1830 were used as the basis of the appraisal.[23] Scholars who have studied the elaborate formula under which particular awards were made have thus come to the conclusion that the British subsidy amounted to 44 percent of the appraised value of the slaves.[24]

While the manner in which the total subsidy was divided among individuals bears on the fortunes of particular slaveholders, it is irrelevant in evaluating the compensation to the slaveowning class as a whole.[25] For the latter task, the relevant considerations, indicated by the third term of equation 5, are the stream of total cash payments per slave (i.e., the present value of the total cash payments divided by the slave population in 1834) and the average actual value of slaves. Since the British government made payment of £16.7 million in 1836 and £4.1 million in 1837, the discounted value of the cash subsidy in 1834 was £16.6 million or £21.3 per slave (16,600,000 ÷ 780,993). Using the average of the 1823–1830 selling prices to value the slave population in 1834, and adjusting for the departure of the age-sex structure of marketed slaves from the age-sex structure of the overall slave population, the estimated average value of a slave was £43.2. Thus the compensation paid to slaveowners by British taxpayers accounted for 49 percent of the estimated actual value of their slaves (21.3 ÷ 43.2).[26]

From the foregoing it appears that the theoretical value of the compensation package offered to the West Indian slaveowners amounted to about 96 percent of the value of their slaves (47 + 49), with the slaves themselves "contributing" close to half of the payment. How, or in what direction, will this theoretical valuation have to be altered in order to estimate the actual loss of the West Indian planters?

The analytical apparatus developed in the preceding section also applies to the estimation of the actual capital loss suffered by West Indian planters as a consequence of emancipation. However, it is now necessary to drop certain assumptions maintained in the theoretical computation and look at what actually happened. The chief point at issue is the assumption that the average net revenue per slave remained constant after 1834. As is indicated by Table 29.5, sugar production fell off by 10 percent during the first four years of apprenticeship.[27] Despite the loss in output the revenue from sugar (in constant British pounds) actually increased, by 13 percent, because the British demand for sugar was inelastic (see *EM*, #19). Thus it was British consumers who bore the main burden of the decline in productivity associated with apprenticeship, not the planters.

However, matters soon turned sharply against the West Indian planters. First, agitation by the antislavery forces in Parliament became so threatening that the West Indian legislatures, in order to head off potential slave uprisings, voluntarily terminated apprenticeship in 1838 (Green 1976). Second, the further decline in labor productivity and, consequently, in the total output of West Indian sugar, forced the British price of sugar still higher. However, at these higher prices the extra duty on sugar produced outside of the West Indies was no longer as prohibitive as it had been and foreign sugar began to flow into the British market in greater volume. Because foreign sugar replaced about 80 percent of the decline in the West Indian supply between 1839 and 1846, price rise in British sugar was kept in check.[28] The total sugar revenue of West Indian planters during 1839–1846 fell off sharply from the level of the apprenticeship years, now averaging about 14 percent less than revenues during the decade that preceded emancipation (see Table 29.5).

Caught between increased labor costs and declining revenues, planters began to suffer capital losses on the value of their land and equipment, which had accounted for between 50 and 60 percent of the investment in plantations before 1834 (Ward 1978). Capital losses on land, buildings and equipment were not taken into account in the parliamentary compensation package nor in the "theoretical" valuation of the capital loss suffered by planters under the parliamentary compensation scheme presented above. To adjust the theoretical valuation to take account of the total capital loss of the planters requires better data on the course of estate prices than is

Table 29.5. Indexes of Sugar Production, Price, and Total Revenue from Sugar in the British West Indies, 1824–1846

Period	(1) Production	(2) Price	(3) Total Revenue
1824–1833	100	100	100
1834–1838	89.9	126	113
1839–1846	64.1	134	85.6

currently available. The data which are available suggest that although estate prices plunged immediately before the enactment of emancipation, they recovered or exceeded their previous values during 1835–1837 (see *EM,* #18). After 1838, however, they declined again.

Declining estate prices during 1840s not only reflected the increased cost of labor and the increased share of foreign sugar in the British market, but the growing fear that the tariff preference for West Indian sugar would be eliminated. A head-on assault on these preferences was launched in Parliament, spurred by forces more concerned with the effect of rising sugar prices at home than with either parliamentary assurances to West Indian planters or the struggle against slavery in Cuba, Brazil, and its other outposts. In 1840 a private motion to eliminate the protection of West Indian sugar lost by twenty-seven votes. In 1841, a new motion to eliminate the preference, now sponsored by the government, was beaten by the antislavery forces, but the handwriting was on the wall. The pressure for the elimination of the protection of West Indian sugar mounted, and in 1846 Parliament voted to do so. With that act, English sugar prices went into a steep decline and so did the economic fortunes of West Indian planters (Deerr 1949–1950, 2:430–441, 531; Green 1976; Hall 1959; Moohr 1972; Eisner 1961; Engerman 1982, *EM,* #18).

The legislative struggles over gradual emancipation in the northern United States and in Great Britain can be interpreted as attempts to bring about a *limited* redefinition of the scope of property rights. Considered from this viewpoint, the movement to end slavery was an effort to exclude from the domain of freely traded assets one particular form of property rights—namely, long-term property rights in human beings.

The reform desired by the legislative majorities was limited in two respects. First, it involved only a relatively small proportion of the total stock of negotiable real capital—less than 1 percent in the United States and less than 2 percent in Great Britain.[29] Second, the reform was specifically designed to leave unencumbered the negotiability of non-human forms of capital such as land, structures, and equipment—which represented by far the greatest part of long-term, traded real assets.

The effort to confine strictly the scope of reform gave rise to a new issue. If future transactions in titles to human capital were to be precluded without threatening the title to other forms of property, or encumbering their negotiability, owners of slaves would have to be compensated. Thus it was the desire to limit the assault on property rights to one, and only one, type of property that set the stage for the protracted struggle over how the economic burden of emancipation would be distributed among the classes.

It has been argued that the property owners who supported the antislavery movement did so in order to ensure the enhancement and perpetuation of the types of property right on which their wealth and power depended. These scions of wealth were, the argument states, motivated to embrace the antislavery banner because, consciously or subconsciously, they recognized it as a device for directing discontent into benign protests, for magnifying the moral stature of the non-slaveholding sectors of the ruling class, and for promoting free trade and other commercial policies which would enlarge their profits. No doubt some reformers were moved to take up the antislavery cause for such reasons. Yet no evidence has been brought forth so far which shows that more than a handful of the opponents of slavery were, consciously or subconsciously, impelled *primarily* by these considerations (see Webb, #28, in this volume). Indeed, there is considerable evidence that many of those who embraced antislavery legislation recognized, and were troubled by, the possibility that the attempt to encumber property rights in human beings might be extended into a far-reaching attack on the entire system of property rights. Nor was this fear misplaced. It is striking how much of the rhetoric of the abolitionists was taken over by the critics of capitalism who forged it into a weapon of attack on private rights to physical capital.[30]

Why, then, did so many of those property owners who recognized this threat nevertheless align themselves with the antislavery movement? We suggest that it was because, in varying degrees, they were the intellectual offspring of an age of political and social revolution who had imbibed the new moral values of that age. Such men were forced to balance their penchant for the new morality against their other desires and interests. To the question, "What price, the new morality?" some of these men replied: virtually any price. But to many, the desire for this form of philanthropy seems to have been much more limited. Freedom for slaves was a commodity they were prepared to purchase if it could be obtained at a very moderate cost. Gradual emancipation appears to have offered them at least in theory, the opportunity to engage in philanthropy at bargain prices. The theory appears to have worked out in the northern case. But in the British case British taxpayers, British consumers, and West Indian planters probably bore the principal economic costs of emancipation.

NOTES

1. See Bittker (1973) for a discussion of such proposals based not only on the slave experience but also on discrimination suffered in the subsequent period.
2. The term "direct cost" refers to the market value of a slave—the expected discounted present value of the excess of the marginal value product of the slave above maintenance costs, over the balance of the slave's life. See Fogel and Engerman (1974a), 2:54–75, 119–125.

   Since slaves did not receive the full value of their marginal product, some part of the income that they produced was expropriated. In Fogel and Engerman (1974a), 1:244–246, 2:155–162, we estimated that other forms of exploitation reduced the real income of slaves by amounts substantially greater than were involved in expropriation. We have estimated that the non-pecuniary cost to slaves of working in gangs, at an extremely intense pace, was roughly ten times larger than the amount of the expropriation. On these and related issues see *EM*, #53, #54.

   Indirect recognition of types of exploitation other than expropriation was given by planters when they argued that the cost of emancipation to them exceeded the market value of a slave, since emancipation, by reducing the level of labor inputs, would lead to a decline in land values. Planter fear of the decline in the effective labor supply was, of course, behind various vagrancy and apprenticeship laws which were imposed upon labor in most postslavery societies. Thus until the last section of this paper when we refer to the level of compensation we have in mind only the market value of slaves and not the indirect losses imposed on slaveowners because of a decline in the value of land or other assets. The last section considers losses associated with declining land values. For discussions of the cost of emancipating U.S. slaves in 1860 that have pointed to the possible decline in land values, see Goldin (31, in this volume), Weintraub (1973), and West (1972). See also Moen (#15, *TP*, Vol. I) and *EM*, #56.

3. Limitation of emancipation to those born after a specified date, with a period of labor due owners, was a procedure initially adopted also in upper Canada, Chile, Gran Columbia, Venezuela, Cuba, Puerto Rico, and Brazil. In several of these cases the laws were subsequently changed to provide for freeing of all slaves. On upper Canada, see Riddell (1920) and Winks (1971), 96–99. On Gran Colombia and Venezuela, see Bierck (1953), 365, and Lombardi (1971), 46–53, 135–144. On Chile, see Galdames (1941), 169, 224. On Cuba and Puerto Rico, see Knight (1970), 169–178; Scott (1985); and Corwin (1967). For the most recent studies of the Brazilian case, see Conrad (1972), Toplin (1972), de Mello (1977), and Correa do Lago (1978).

4. This paper deals primarily with the cost of compensation. Another cost was the rise in the price of slave-produced goods which was borne by the consumers of these goods. Under slavery planters were able to achieve economies of scale and other productive efficiencies that could not be realized in a free labor market. For a fuller discussion of this issue see Fogel and Engerman (1974a), 1:232–246; 2:155–162; #16, *TP*, Vol. I; #32, in this volume; and *EM*, #18, #19.

5. Payment by taxpayers to slaveowners, in the form of either cash or bonds, was also an aspect of emancipation procedures in Venezuela, the French West Indies, and the Dutch West Indies. On Venezuela, see Lombardi (1971). On the French West Indies, see Priestley (1938), 63–69, and McCloy (1966), 148–152. On the Dutch colonies, see Hiss (1943), 106–109, 207.

6. We should note an important similarity between the issue of compensation of slaveowners and a frequent barrier to the effective implementation of anti-trust policy. One reason often given for the failure to pursue policies which would impose capital losses on stockholders of firms held in violation of anti-trust laws (and a justification for the introduction of measures to reduce these) is that the affected stockholders might not be the ones who received the financial benefits of monopolization. Current stockholders might be earning only normal profits since the original beneficiaries sold out at a price that capitalized the expected monopoly profits of the corporation. In such cases those who captured the monopoly rent are beyond the range of the government's legal authority to exact financial retribution. To the extent that the owners of slaves at the time of emancipation were not the ones who captured the rent from slave ownership, the analogy holds. Thus it is possible that unwillingness to impose capital losses on "innocent" slaveholders affected the position of some antislavery critics. See Fogel and Engerman (1974a), 2:123–124, and the literature cited there.

7. The best summary of northern emancipation is contained in Zilversmit (1967). See also McManus (1973) and Farnam (1938), 211–215, 415–474. For discussions of emancipation in specific states, see Moore (1866), Steiner (1893), McManus (1966), Cooley (1896), and Turner (1911). Some of the laws are published in Hurd (1858–1862). For a discussion of various cases relating to northern emancipation, see Catterall (1936).

8. In 1780 the eight states contained 9.3 percent of the black population of the American colonies. Of these, the New England states had 26.8 percent, more than one-half being in Rhode Island and Connecticut. Thus the relative number of slaves in those states for which there was little information was quite small (U.S. Bureau of the Census 1960, 746).

9. The 1796 proposal of the Virginia jurist, St. George Tucker, would have been even more gradual, and imposed even lower costs, than the northern schemes that were actually adopted. Only females born after the adoption of his plan would have been freed; moreover they and all their descendants would owe service to their owners for twenty-eight years. Tucker held that "the loss of the mother's labour for nine months, and the maintenance of a child for a dozen or fourteen years, is amply compensated by the services of that child for as many years more, as he has been an expense to them" (Tucker 1796, 89–102).

10. Davis (1975, 1984) provides much important background to the debate on emancipation in both the United States and in England. See also Locke (1901), Jordan (1969), MacLeod (1974), Anstey (1975), Green (1976), Drescher (1986), and *RF*, Pt. II, esp. 238–254.

11. Klebaner (1955), 443, 445.

12. On British emancipation the principal secondary sources include Burn (1937), Klingberg (1926), Mathieson (1926), Ragatz (1928), and Williams (1944), Davis (1975, 1984), Anstey (1975, 1980, 1981), Green (1976), Engerman and Eltis (1980), Engerman (1982, 1984, 1986a, 1986b), Turner (1982), and Drescher (1986); cf. *RF*, Ch. 7.

13. See Mitchell (1962), 396–399.

14. For a fuller discussion of the method of constructing Figures 29.1–29.5 see Fogel and Engerman (1974a), 2:79–85, 119–125. The prices used in Figures 29.2 and 29.3 were obtained from a sample of probate records in Maryland. Although it is possible that slave prices in New York, New Jersey, and Pennsylvania were slightly lower than those which prevailed in Maryland (see Zilversmit 1967, 231–241) this would not affect the estimate of the loss as long as the estimate is presented as a percentage of the peak-age price of slaves or of the overall value of the slave labor force. This conclusion follows because the shape of the age-price profile of slaves is independent of its level (Fogel and Engerman 1974a, 2:79).

     Figures 29.3 and 29.4 are presented as first approximations because we may have overestimated both the value of the female childbearing capacity and the earnings attributable to this capacity. Since the international slave trade was still legal in 1800, it is probable that importation of slaves kept the part of the value of the birthright that was a capitalized rent close to zero. Of course, overestimation of the rental component of the birthright affects only the dashed lines in Figures 29.3 and 29.4. In other words, total value and total net earnings are unaffected. The error is in the division of value and of net earnings between field work and childbearing capacity. For a further discussion of this issue see *EM*, #49.

     The earnings shown in Figures 29.1 and 29.4 are the averages for an entire cohort, including those who become unproductive because of illness or infirmity. Thus these curves decline more rapidly at later ages than would curves constructed exclusively on the basis of the earnings of healthy, full-time workers.

15. The "value of the birthright" is the term we use for the price of a slave at age zero. The significance of this price is discussed in Fogel and Engerman (1974a), 2:119–125; cf. *EM*, #49. In Figures 29.2 and 29.3, it is the price at the point where the profile intersects the price axis.

16. Zilversmit (1967).

17. Related estimates prepared by Fielding (1973), when properly adjusted, provide estimated capital losses 3.2, 3.7, and 5.4 percent of the original capital value of slaves in Pennsylvania, New York, and New Jersey, respectively. Fielding's estimates were adjusted because his procedures underestimated the total value at birth of the infants born to each female, but overstated the proportion that the value of female slaves was of the value of all slaves.

     In Fogel and Engerman (1974a), 2:33–35, we argued that if the birthright had been zero, our assumption of a positive birthright necessarily biased upward the estimate of the capital loss imposed on slaveowners by emancipation at age twenty-six. That argument was erroneous. We failed to recognize that a zero birthright meant that slaveowners would not recover rearing costs by the age of emancipation. For a discussion of the share of the birthright that is a capitalized rent see *EM*, #49.

18. For an unsubstantiated claim that some part of this demographic pattern was due to census underreporting of free blacks see McManus (1973), Ch. 11.

19. Whereas the ratio of males to females in this age group was 0.99 in the South, for the northeastern states the ratio was only 0.87. In the Northeast the ratio for children under fourteen was 1.05.

20. See Fogel and Engerman (1974a), 1:49–50, 2:53.

21. A discount rate of 11 percent was used, based on data presented in Sheridan (1965), 292, and Sheridan (1968), 46.

22. The average payment per slave in each West Indian colony was based upon the average selling price during 1823–1830, but the division did vary among the colonies. For example, whereas in Jamaica the payments for children under six averaged 20.7 percent of those on predial (agricultural) field laborers, in British Guiana the ratio was 29.5 percent. Accounts of compensation claims are reprinted in Martin (1843). Prices of 1823–1830 may already have been depressed by the anticipation of emancipation (see Engerman 1984, *EM*, #18).

23. The amount of compensation available to slaveowners in each colony was based upon the average

selling prices in that particular colony in the period 1823–1830. Thus differentials in the average compensation were determined by differentials in selling prices. These differences have apparently puzzled some scholars. See Deerr (1949–1950), 2:305. For a discussion of the limited inter-island trade in slaves in this period, consistent with the pattern of relative prices, see Eltis (1972), 55.

24. Sugar prices were lower in 1831–1833 than in 1823–1830, so some fall in slave prices, even without the threat of emancipation, might have occurred. We should note also that the price of slaves would reflect anticipations about the persistence of slavery, but these presumably did not have a major impact on prices in the years chosen as the base for slave compensation.

25. There was some speculation in compensation claims, so that the time and amount of effective receipt of funds by any one slaveowner is not certain.

26. The age structure of the overall slave population was based upon that of British Guiana in 1832, presented in Roberts (1952), 238. Cf. data on age structure in Higman (1984), 138–141, 462–470. The age pattern of marketed slaves was based upon that which prevailed in the notarial records of New Orleans during 1804–1861, as reported in Fogel and Engerman (1974a), 1:49–50. The relative prices at each age are from Fogel and Engerman (1974a), 1:76, Fig. 18.

27. The figures for production and sugar prices are from Deerr (1949–1950), 2:377, 531. The sugar prices were deflated by the Gayer, Rostow, and Schwartz index of British commodity prices in Mitchell (1962), 470.

28. British per capita consumption of sugar declined by only 8 percent although the West Indian supply declined by 36 percent (Table 29.5 and Deerr 1949–1950, 2:532).

29. Blodget (1806) estimated the total valuation of "all the real and personal property in the United States" in 1805 at $2.5 billion of which $1.3 billion (based on the 1798 distribution in Pitkin 1835, 336) was in the northern states that instituted emancipation programs. He placed the value of the 1 million slaves at $200 million, or just 8 percent of total national wealth. The slave population was 893,041 in 1800 and 1,191,364 in 1810, so Blodget's estimate (which excludes Louisiana) of the number of slaves is reasonable. However, he noted that whereas all other varieties of property are "below the mark," "slaves . . . are rated too high." Data which we have collected indicate that Blodget's estimate of the average value of a slave in 1805 should be reduced by about 25 percent. Using a value of $200 per slave, slaves accounted for less than 1 percent of wealth in the northern states that instituted emancipation programs. Pitkin (1835), 336, indicates that slaves in the North in 1798 accounted for 0.7 percent of the value of that region's land, houses, and slaves.

There was an estimate of the total wealth of Great Britain and its colonies published in 1833 by Pebrer (1833). The total value for Great Britain and Ireland was £3.68 billion, with the value of dependencies, colonies, and possessions elsewhere, exclusive of India, raising the total to £3.94 billion. These estimates were extrapolations from the earlier (1811) estimates of Colquhoun (1814). Pebrer merely increased Colquhoun's estimates of the capital value of all areas except the West Indies by one-third. The West Indies value was left at the 1811 level. Pebrer argues that he might have raised the West Indies by one-fifth, but "to ensure moderation" he didn't. Pebrer did observe, however, that the figure used by Colquhoun as the average value of a slave was too high. For 1811 Colquhoun estimated the value of property in Great Britain plus Ireland at £2.76 billion; adding the value of the property in the rest of the empire (except India and those conquered West Indian possessions not retained) raises this to £2.95 billion. The value of West Indian slaves in these calculations was £42.36 million; including the slaves in Mauritius and the the Cape of Good Hope raises the sum to £48.31 million. Thus, in the early nineteenth century, the value of slaves was only about 1.6 percent of British wealth, and the actual ratio in the early 1830s was no doubt lower. See *EM*, #56.

30. For an interesting discussion of the relationship between slavery and the movement for factory reform in England, see Hartwell (1971), 390–408.

The question of the distribution of the economic burden of emancipation also arises with respect to European serfs. There is some evidence that at least part of the cost of the emancipation of Russian and German serfs was shifted from landlords to serfs by legislation delaying the times at which dues were terminated, and the amounts and terms under which land was transferred to the ex-serfs. The circumstances of Russian emancipation are discussed by Blum (1961), Ch. 26, and Gershenkron (1965). The German case is discussed in Clapham (1936), 41–46.

THIRTY

The Manumission of Slaves in New Orleans, 1827-1846*

Laurence J. Kotlikoff and Anton J. Rupert

From 1827 through 1846 the police jury of New Orleans was responsible for hearing all petitions requesting permission to manumit a slave. The police jury minutes from this period record these petitions: They constitute a body of data rich enough to explore a number of issues concerning the extent and nature of the emancipation of slaves in the antebellum South. One issue that appears to have been greatly overlooked in the literature on slave emancipation is the role played by the free black community in securing freedom for slaves. The most significant finding of this study is the major role played by free blacks in emancipating slaves. Of the 1,159 successful petitions for emancipation presented to the police jury from 1827 to 1846, 435 or 37.5 percent were presented by free blacks accounting for 646 or 36.5 percent of the 1,770 slaves manumitted. These figures are even more striking when one considers the number of free black households living in New Orleans at this time. Roughly one in every eight households was engaged in the emancipation of one or more slaves during this period.[1] In addition to detailing the roles of free blacks and whites in freeing slaves this paper discusses the characteristics of the slaves emancipated: By comparing the characteristics of slaves freed with those of the general slave population one may distinguish economic from non-economic factors influencing the emancipation decision. This paper proceeds with a brief history of legislation pertaining to manumissions in New Orleans. This section is followed by a description of the data and the presentation of general findings. The final section considers the role of economic and non-economic factors motivating emancipation and ends with a summary of the paper.

THE LEGISLATIVE HISTORY OF MANUMISSION IN NEW ORLEANS

Louisiana was acquired from France in 1803 through the Louisiana Purchase and on April 30, 1812, Louisiana was admitted as a state to the Union. In the interim

*Reprinted from *Southern Studies* 19(1980):172–181, with permission by The Southern Studies Institute.

the only federal law regulating slavery in the territory of Louisiana was simply the embargo on slave imports from foreign countries. During this period the Superior Council of the colony enacted legislation pertaining to slavery. Any master twenty-five years of age or older could manumit his slaves with the permission of the Superior Council. In 1807 an act was passed forbidding the manumission of slaves under thirty years old as well as any slave found guilty of bad conduct within the preceding four years. Any variance from this law required approval from the Superior Council, and, after statehood, from the state legislature. Eventually this became too burdensome for the legislature, and in 1827 it ruled that a master could manumit a slave under thirty provided he petition the police jury of his parish and get the approval of three-quarters of its members.

In 1830 the first in a series of attempts was made to reduce the number of free Negroes in Louisiana with an act that required anyone who manumitted a slave to post a $1,000 bond to ensure that the slave would leave the state within thirty days unless the police jury ruled that the slave was not required to do so. This act may have had little affect on manumissions since no slave in the study years was ever required to leave the state. Each minute entry ended with the clause "without being compelled to leave the state."

In 1846 the responsibility for hearing the manumission was transferred from the police jury to the Emancipation Court. (The records of the Emancipation Court are available only in French and include only the name of the petitioner, and the name, age, and sex of the slave.)

The 1840s and 1850s witnessed an influx of white immigrants into the cities of the South. This influx coupled with a growing apprehension that free Negroes would be agents of revolt led to stricter legislation regarding the manumission of slaves (Genovese 1974, 400–401; Reinders 1962). In 1852 the legislature ruled that no slave could be freed unless the master were to post $150 which would be used to ship the slave back to Africa. This effectively ended the manumission of slaves in Louisiana: Between 1852 and 1855 only thirty slaves were freed in the entire state. In 1857 the legislature simply outlawed the manumission of slaves.[2]

DESCRIPTION OF THE DATA AND GENERAL FINDINGS

The petitions of emancipation recorded in the police jury minutes indicate the name and race of the emancipator and the name, age, sex, and often color of slaves to be manumitted. The petitions frequently provide information about the relationship that existed between the owner and the slaves and between the slaves themselves. In addition they stipulate whether the emancipated slave was required to leave the state. An example of a petition of manumission is provided below.

In several of the 1,166 petitions examined information is provided detailing the previous purchase of the slave or slaves to be freed. For example, in the petition presented, the free man of color Frans Larche provides the police jury with his title to the mulatto boy Valcin and the mulatto girl Charlotte. The title indicates that Larche purchased the two slaves under the expressed condition that he would emancipate them. Unfortunately the price at which the previous owner sold the two slaves is unknown, hence the previous owner's contribution to the emancipation cannot be determined. This example cautions against attributing the emancipation solely to the generosity of the last owner mentioned on the petition. Indeed white or free black slaveowners may have received side payments from whites or free blacks or from the slaves themselves leading to the emancipation. An example of the latter is found in this 1831 petition: "On the petition of Zelma Row, f.w.c., praying that the consent of the police jury be granted to emancipate her slave Laure, a Negro woman aged 42 years, in consideration of her faithful services and good conduct, and whereas said Laure has reimbursed the sum that the petitioner had paid for her to B. Doubler of whom she had bought her in 1827." Regrettably information of this kind detailing the exact circumstances of the emancipation is rarely provided on the petitions.

During the period from 1827 to 1846, a total of 1,166 petitions were filed in New Orleans to manumit 1,780 slaves. Only 10 slaves in 7 petitions were actually denied freedom. Four of these petitions involved manumitting children too young to support themselves, 1 was a petition brought by a non-resident of New Orleans, and in the remaining 2 cases no reason was given for rejection.

Table 30.1 presents the yearly breakdown of emancipations together with the real and nominal prices of slaves in New Orleans.[3] The table indicates no systematic relationship between the number of emancipations and the real price of slaves. Even ignoring the fact that implicit or explicit commitments to emancipate a slave in a given year may have been made many years earlier, economic theory has no unambiguous prediction relating the real price of slaves to emancipation. On the one hand the rise in the real slave price increases the wealth of slaveholders and presumably increases charitable contributions of all kinds including emancipations; on the other hand the higher real slave price raises the price of emancipation relative to other charitable acts.

The data detail the age of emancipated slaves for 92 percent of observations and the sex for 97 percent. The race and the sex of the emancipator is always indicated. In addition the color of the emancipated slaves is reported in 48.1 percent of the cases. In 1830, 1840, and 1850, females represented respectively 58.0 percent, 48.4 percent, and 58.1 percent of the New Orleans slave population.[4] Females are clearly overrepresented among emancipated slaves accounting for 68 percent of all manumissions. This overrepresentation of females occurs, however, only for slaves above the age of fifteen. Emancipated male and female are distributed in proportion to the sex ratio of the slave child population.

Of the slaves 9.15 percent received their freedom through the death and subsequent will of their owner. In this tabulation we include all manumissions where a will was mentioned or where the petition was brought by a woman referred to as "the widow of" which seems to imply the recent death of her husband and there is a possibility that a will is not being mentioned. This excludes all petitions presented by a woman referred to simply as "widow," i.e., the Widow Avert as opposed to the Widow of Louis Avert.

An examination of Tables 30.2 and 30.3 reveals that male children below age

Table 30.1. Number of Slaves Manumitted per Year in New Orleans and the Real and
Nominal Prices of Prime-Aged Male Slaves in New Orleans

Year	Number of Slaves	Real Price in 1850 Dollars	Nominal Price in Dollars
1827	24	631	568
1828	30	526	479
1829	39	662	596
1830	8	673	579
1831	75	815	652
1832	103	796	701
1833	30	805	797
1834	163	744	714
1835	119	716	881
1836	138	810	1,069
1837	121	1,169	1,263
1838	140	838	897
1839	129	709	823
1840	65	879	800
1841	125	802	746
1842	91	832	624
1843	94	781	547
1844	109	729	547
1845	106	822	608
1846	71	909	709

ten are overrepresented among emancipated males. Older females (above forty) are overrepresented in the female emancipation distribution, although the same does not appear true for males above age forty. One factor accounting for the pattern of these age-sex distributions is the joint emancipation of mothers with their children. Fewer than 15 percent of emancipated children under age sixteen were emancipated without their mothers. Mothers and children emancipated together represent 35.5 percent of white manumissions and 30.5 percent of free black manumissions.

THE MANUMISSIONS OF SLAVES BY FREE BLACKS

In order to manumit a slave a free black had to first own the slave. The substantial number of slaves emancipated by free blacks points, therefore, to a substantial ownership of slaves by free blacks.[5] This was indeed the case. In 1830, one of every seven New Orleans slave was owned by a free black. The average holdings of the 752 black owners in 1830 was 3.1 slaves. Since the daily wage of laborers in New Orleans was probably less than the $1 daily wage of laborers in Philadelphia in 1830, the expenditure of $579 (see Table 30.1) for a prime-aged male slave would entail perhaps two years of work by the average laborer with no consumption![6] Of course, the prime-aged males were the most expensive, but even a twelve-year-old male slave would cost about $300.[7] How then did the free blacks of New Orleans, themselves presumably former slaves, acquire the financial position to own and

Table 30.2. Age Distribution of Emancipated Males and Male Slave Population

Male Slaves						Emancipated Males		Males Emancipated by Whites	
1830		1840		1850					
Age	Percent	Age	Percent	Age	Percent	Age	Percent	Age	Percent
0–10	24.6	0–10	24.3	0–10	23.0	0–10	30.5	0–10	33.8
10–24	30.8	10–24	26.7	10–20	20.3	10–20	18.4	10–20	16.0
24–36	27.6	24–36	31.5	20–30	23.4	20–30	15.4	20–30	11.2
36–55	12.8	36–55	13.7	30–40	17.5	30–40	20.0	30–40	23.2
55+	4.2	55+	3.8	40–50	9.9	40–50	8.7	40–50	7.5
				50–60	4.1	50–60	5.2	50–60	6.0
				60–70	1.4	60–70	1.6	60–70	2.0
				70+	0.4	70+	0.2	70+	0.3

Table 30.3. Age Distribution of Emancipated Females and the Female Slave Population

Female Slaves						Emancipated Females		Females Emancipated by Whites	
1830		1840		1850					
Age	Percent	Age	Percent	Age	Percent	Age	Percent	Age	Percent
0–10	20.6	0–10	20.4	0–10	16.2	0–10	19.5	0–10	20.2
10–24	32.2	10–24	29.6	10–20	19.6	10–20	11.8	10–20	9.9
24–36	30.8	24–36	33.9	20–30	23.3	20–30	15.2	20–30	15.2
36–55	12.8	36–55	13.0	30–40	21.3	30–40	29.1	30–40	30.7
55+	3.6	55+	3.1	40–50	12.0	40–50	15.2	40–50	14.3
				50–60	5.3	50–60	7.4	50–60	7.7
				60–70	2.0	60–70	1.4	60–70	1.6
				70+	0.6	70+	0.4	70+	0.4

then free such large numbers of slaves? The answer is that a large proportion of the New Orleans free black population had been free for generations. The 1789 New Orleans census lists 1,147 free people of color. During the French and Spanish occupations of New Orleans, concubinary relationships between the slaves and the French and Spanish settlers were commonplace. It was the custom that any Frenchman or Spaniard who fathered a child by a black slave should free that child. Substantial numbers of adult slaves were freed as well. As the free black population grew rich, Frenchmen and Spaniards entered into unofficial marriage relationships with free black women called placages. The children of these relationships were well educated; occasionally they were educated in Europe. Under the Code Noir, the French guaranteed freed slaves the rights, privileges, and immunities enjoyed by free-born persons. This law was enforced with respect to property as well as personal rights. This legal protection permitted large numbers of the free blacks to become wealthy merchants, artisans, and real estate brokers (Haskin 1975).

Assuming the ratio of slaves owned by free blacks to slaves owned by whites remained constant during the 1827–1846 period at the 1830 level of 0.164, the probability that a slave owned by a free black would be emancipated was three and one-half times greater than the corresponding probabilities for slaves owned by whites.[8] The assumption of a fixed ratio of relative slaveownership during this period is probably incorrect. The ratio of the adult white population to the adult free black population was about 2.5 for 1 in 1830, rose to almost 4 by 1840, and continued sharply upward until 1850. Hence the 3.5 ratio of relative emancipation frequencies is probably biased downward. If slaveownership was proportionate to the adult population the calculation using the 1840 ratios of slaveownership would rise to 5.5. Relative to their slaveholdings free blacks made a substantial contribution to the emancipation of slaves. Nor was this contribution simply in terms of the numbers of slaves freed. As Tables 30.2 and 30.3 indicate the age structure of slaves emancipated by free blacks is virtually identical to the overall age distribution of emancipated slaves. In addition the female percentage of emancipations by free blacks is 65, quite close to the overall 68 percentage. Since the manumissions performed by free blacks occurred somewhat more frequently in the later years when the real price of slaves was higher, the average cost per slave emancipated was if anything higher for slaves freed by blacks than for slaves freed by whites.

KIN RELATIONSHIPS BETWEEN FREE BLACKS AND THEIR EMANCIPATED SLAVES

The first 8 years of petitions from 1827 through 1834 provide detailed information concerning familial ties between the free blacks and their emancipated slaves. After these first 8 years little extraneous information of any kind is provided; rather the entries in the police minutes are perfunctory and include only the basic facts of the case. It appears that in 1835 there was a change in the amount of information deemed worthy of recording as well as in the individuals recording the information. This latter fact is apparent from an examination of the handwriting styles prior to and after 1835. Considering then only the pre-1835 years we find the emancipation of 194 slaves by free blacks; 122 of these slaves are stated to be related to the petitioner and in the remaining 72 cases no mention of familial ties is made. Hence at least 63 percent of the slaves freed by free blacks were family members. Some free blacks emancipated a number of their family members at the same time, others presented petitions for emancipation over a period of years. Fifty-five free blacks presented more than one petition and were responsible for freeing 191 slaves during this period. The average duration between petitions was 3.3 years.

MISCEGENATION, CONCUBINAGE, AND THE MANUMISSION OF SLAVES

While questions of miscegenation and concubinage have generally been raised with reference to white ownership of slaves, these issues are pertinent to black ownership as well. The 1860 census which designated all mulattoes, quadroons, quarteroons, and octoroons as "mulatto" reports that 81 percent of free people of color were mulatto. Concubinage and the resulting blood relationships of masters to slaves may have played a role in the emancipation of slaves by both whites and blacks.

For white emancipations one indirect piece of evidence concerning these potential slave-owner relationships is the percentage of emancipated children of mixed blood compared with the percentage for the overall slave population. Unfortunately the census reports show color only for 1860. In that year 24.8 percent of the slave population was classified as mulatto. One further piece of information is Kotlikoff's calculation that 21 percent of the Louisiana slaves sold in the New Orleans market from 1804 to 1862 were light colored.[9] Among the total population of emancipated slaves color is reported in only 48.1 percent of the cases; this 48.1 percent can be broken down into 24.4 percent mixed blood and 23.7 percent black. A large proportion of the cases in which color is not reported involves the color of children emancipated with their mother. If we consider only children under sixteen emancipated by whites separately from their mothers, we find that of the 79 percent with a color reported 88.8 percent are of mixed blood. Whether this apparent overrepresentation of light colored children is explained by white parentage, the intercession of a free black relative of mixed blood or simply the greater potential conflict with one's conscience in enslaving people so similar to oneself, is unknown. The police jury minutes give us little indication of the real motivation of the white emancipator. Some petitions state that the slaves were freed as a reward for faithful service; others were freed as a reward to the parents of the slave. Some petitions claim the slave was bought with the express purpose of emancipation as soon as possible. In no case was any mention of white parentage made.

FREEDOM FOR NON-PRODUCTIVE SLAVES

While the sex and age distributions of the emancipated slaves are somewhat skewed toward the less-expensive slaves the data appears to rule out negative net productivity as the major factor in generating emancipation by either free blacks or whites. Although the data neither indicate physical defects nor state slave prices from which such defects could be inferred, one would expect to see substantially more elderly slaves among those emancipated if negative productivity were the major determinant of emancipations. The police jury would presumably have been loath to free a slave who could become a charge on the state; the fear that the police jury would require the $1,000 bond to ensure that the slave leave the state may have deterred some would-be emancipators, i.e., the expected costs from emancipating a non-productive slave may have exceeded the costs of keeping the slave.

SUMMARY

While the New Orleans data on emancipations from 1827 to 1846 raise a number of questions which remain unresolved, they do indicate that a major role was played by the free black community in emancipating slaves. This contribution by the free black community appears to have been overlooked by previous writers on this subject.

The exact extent to which these New Orleans emancipations reflect the generosity of the owner, concubinary relations with the slaves, the freeing of non-productive slaves, and the efforts of the slaves themselves to work their way to freedom remains unresolved. Certainly no single factor dominates the data. It is hoped that additional data will emerge which are capable of attaching precise relative weights to each of the economic and non-economic factors involved in the emancipation of slaves.

NOTES

1. Woodson (1925) lists 1,830 free Negro heads of households for the year 1830. The adult population of free blacks in New Orleans roughly doubled from 1830 to 1840. By 1850 the free black adult population had declined to approximately the 1830 level (see U.S. Census Office 1832, 1841, 1853). We take 2,700 as the (probably too high) average number of free black households in New Orleans during the period 1827–1846. During these years 361 different free blacks presented petitions to free one or more slaves.
2. The material in this section draws extensively from Taylor (1963).
3. Kotlikoff (#3, TP, Vol. I) developed a price series for prime-aged male field hands sold in New Orleans between 1804 and 1862. This series is then deflated by Taylor's wholesale price index for New Orleans.
4. U.S. Census Office (1832, 1841, 1853).
5. See Woodson (1925), 6015 and U.S. Census Office (1832). Woodson cautions that a few of the free blacks counted as slaveowners were really plantation managers for absentee owners.
6. U.S. Bureau of the Census (1975), 163. Unfortunately, there is no available wage information for New Orleans for 1830.
7. See Kotlikoff (#3, TP, Vol. I).
8. The ratio of slaves emancipated by free blacks to slaves emancipated by whites is 0.575. Dividing 0.575 by 0.164 gives the relative probabilities of emancipation by free blacks as opposed to whites.
9. See Kotlikoff (#3, TP, Vol. I).

THIRTY-ONE

The Economics of Emancipation*

Claudia Goldin

INTRODUCTION

This paper deals with various emancipation plans: those actually enacted in various slave societies, those discussed by legislators who debated slave and antislave proposals, and those which, being purely fictional, have become part of counterfactual history.

The form that emancipation took in different slavocracies reflected their view of property rights in man. In many societies slaves were recognized as property, and the freeing of bondsmen without full compensation to their owners was illegal. In others, slavery was immoral, and payment to manumit slaves was considered de facto recognition of the institution of slavery. Some forms of compensated emancipation have been viewed as early precedents for the doctrine of eminent domain. The type of emancipation also reflected the relative political strengths of the slave and non-slaveholding classes, making property rights an endogenous variable. Empirical evidence suggests that the smaller the percentage of slaveowners relative to the electorate, the less the degree of compensation. Many gradual abolition schemes can be viewed as attempts to lessen the strength of the slaveholding class so that non-compensated, immediate abolition could be instituted.

Almost every slave society in the Western Hemisphere terminated slavery with some form of legislative emancipation. The schemes varied in many respects. Under certain plans slaves were emancipated at once, although others were gradual, either providing for the creation of apprenticeships or stipulating that children of slaves be freed after a period of service. Many schemes gave full monetary compensation to owners of slaves, some had partial compensation, and still others entailed outright expropriation. For many slavocracies emancipation was the direct result of abolitionist sentiment; in others it was the culmination of years of slave unrest. This paper will briefly review the emancipation schemes enacted in the

*Reprinted, with revisions, from *The Journal of Economic History* 33(1973):66–85. © The Economic History Association. Reprinted with permission of Cambridge University Press.

Western Hemisphere prior to the adoption of the Thirteenth Amendment in the
United States as background for a discussion of the American slave South. The
schemes represent alternatives available to the Union prior to the outbreak of the
Civil War.

A BRIEF REVIEW OF EMANCIPATION SCHEMES

The American North led emancipation in the Western Hemisphere with Vermont's
proclamation of abolition in 1777.[1] Massachusetts (including Maine) followed close
behind and, unwittingly, wrote emancipation into its state constitution. This constitution, as well as the Declaration of Independence, were interpreted by the Massachusetts courts as freeing that state's slaves. Although the slave trade in Massachusetts was declared illegal in 1788, confusion surrounding court decisions enabled
many Massachusetts owners to sell their slaves in the South, thereby avoiding
capital loss from abolition.[2]

Those northern states with the largest numbers of slaves, Pennsylvania, New
York, and New Jersey, all adopted gradual abolition with Pennsylvania leading the
group in 1780. The Pennsylvania law stipulated that all children of slaves be freed
at age twenty-eight. The state supreme court later interpreted the law as implying
that slavery would last but one more generation in Pennsylvania. The children of
emancipated slave children would automatically be freed even if both parents were
slaves.[3]

The New York law provided that all Negro children born after 1799 be freed
after serving their mothers' masters for twenty-eight years if male and twenty-five if
female. New Jersey's law had similar provisions and declared that males would be
freed after twenty-five and females after twenty-one years of service if born after
1804. The difference in age for the freeing of male and female slaves in New York
and New Jersey legislation can be rationalized in two ways. First, it could represent
the desires of legislators to free slave children at the age they would begin their own
families, if females married at an earlier average age than did males.

Another interpretation of the emancipation age is to minimize the number of
abandoned children. One objective of the legislators may have been to free slave
children at the earliest possible age under the constraint that there be few orphaned
slave babies. If so, they would choose an age such that the birth price would be, on
average, zero.[4] Using data for another region I find that the years in the New York
and New Jersey laws are in agreement with this theory. The emancipation years
stipulated in the New York act imply prices at birth of between $1 and $3 for male
and female infants, instead of the previously prevailing rate of about $25 per
newborn.[5] Because female slaves were more productive in their teens than their
male counterparts[6] the earlier emancipation age for females is consistent with this
rationalization of the gradual abolition schemes.

Both hypotheses arrive at the same conclusion concerning the approximate ages
for emancipating male and female slaves. Direct evidence supports the latter view.
New York legislators were greatly concerned about the social problem of orphaned

slave children. The 1799 act provided for the public care of abandoned youths, reimbursing masters up to $3.50 per month for the support of children who would otherwise be abandoned. In some sense, this provision made gradual abolition more palatable to slaveowners by enabling some compensation in disguised form.

The costs to slaveowners[7] of the gradual abolition programs outlined above were small, compared with those of immediate emancipation. The loss to slaveowners from gradual emancipation is the reduction in the price of female slaves. If the birth price of children becomes zero by the choice of the age at which freedom is granted, the entire rents from the breeding capabilities of females also become zero. The breeding portion of a female slave's price varied with her age. It was between one-half and one-quarter the price of a slave girl under ten years of age, and between two-tenths and one-tenth the price of a grown female between twenty and thirty years old.[8]

Gradual abolition had many beneficial aspects. The cost to slaveowners was low, and it appeared to foster a slow and easy transition for society. But gradual abolition had many drawbacks. It was effective in achieving the abolitionists' goal only if it was not anticipated and if the slave trade between the North and South was closed. If the bill was anticipated, owners could sell their bondsmen to slave areas before an embargo on trade could be declared. In New York, for example, data suggest that the 1799 abolition plan was anticipated by some slaveowners, but that many more took advantage of loopholes in the gradual abolition law to sell their slaves in the South. It is entirely possible that only 12,000 New York State slaves were freed by abolition legislation, whereas 24,000 were sold to slave states farther south.[9]

In addition to the smuggling problem, gradual abolition in any area would encourage more intensive use of slaves during their productive period. In the New York, New Jersey, and Pennsylvania cases, gradual abolition involved the emancipation of slave children after a period of service. These children were probably worked harder than if their owners had had property rights to their lifetime earnings streams. In 1817 a bill was passed in New York providing for the freedom of all slaves born before 1799 as of 1827. This must surely have encouraged masters to work their slaves more intensively during the ten years of remaining service. Announced or anticipated gradual abolition of this type certainly would be against the interests of abolitionists, and, of course, the slaves.

It is perhaps due to smuggling and the "working of slaves to death" that gradual abolition was almost always closely followed by immediate emancipation.[10] As suggested in the introduction to this paper, gradual abolition may also have been used as a way of diluting the slaveowning class so that full emancipation could be enacted with less resistance. New York passed its total emancipation bill in 1817, although the act freed slaves ten years hence. Pennsylvania abolitionists tried to pass a similar piece of legislation, but failed, and slavery was terminated more gradually in that state. New Jersey, in 1846, ended slavery by changing the status of all slaves to that of apprentice.

Emancipation in the British West Indies was sparked by British abolitionists, although slave revolts in Jamaica contributed to the freeing of West Indian bondsmen. The 1820s marked the beginning of a full-scale antislavery campaign in Parliament, and legislation in 1824 was passed prohibiting the transportation of slaves from one British colony to another. In 1834, after much debate, the British government put into effect an emancipation plan stipulating that field hands would be completely free in six years and non-field hands in four. During the interim they were to work as apprentices to their former masters for forty-five hours a week. They were to be given their customary allowances, and any money earned in overtime could be used to purchase their remaining years of service.[11] Twenty million pounds were allocated by the Parliament from the public funds of the United Kingdom as an indemnity grant to the slaveowners.[12]

The abolition of slavery in Venezuela was a by-product of the wars for independence of that nation. After independence, in 1821, the Cúcuta Slave Law was passed which provided for the free birth of all slave children, although minors had to serve their mothers' masters for eighteen years. In 1830 the age was increased to twenty-one, and later the government further extended servitude to age twenty-five. Specific taxes were collected by the government for the manumission of a number of slaves every year, and this together with gradual abolition served to decrease the slave population in Venezuela. In 1854, after depression, discontent, and revolution, an abolition law was passed providing for the freedom of all slaves and full compensation to their owners.[13]

The emancipation schemes outlined above were all effected prior to the American Civil War and all represent possible avenues of solution to the slave problem in the American South. Among all Western Hemisphere countries only Cuba and Brazil freed their slaves after the passage of the Thirteenth Amendment. In both, gradual emancipation was instituted and was followed about twenty years later by complete abolition. In both countries, slaveowners had the opportunity of working their chattel harder during the remaining years of servitude.

All the emancipation schemes described involved balancing abolitionist and slaveowning interests. Even in the American North, where slaveowners were clearly in a minority, emancipation did not involve the complete confiscation of property. Full abolition bills were passed in all these areas only after years of trying gradual abolition. A slow eroding of the slaveowning forces may have made complete freedom easier to push through the legislature. If, then, the American Civil War was caused in part by slavery, why didn't the Union choose one of the options suggested by the comparative analysis?

The next section outlines the options available to the Union prior to 1861 and analyzes the costs associated with each. These options are viewed in light of the previous comparative discussion and in terms of the debate on emancipation during the Thirty-seventh (Civil War) Congress.

THE OPTIONS AVAILABLE TO THE UNION IN 1860

Many of the options discussed below may not have been politically feasible in the years preceding the Civil War. Further, there may be some skepticism that the

schemes were alternatives to battle. These issues are difficult to resolve. Nevertheless, a measurement of the effects of various abolition plans and a comparison of
them with the realized costs of the Civil War provides useful information. In particular, such an exercise might add credence to the hypothesis that the costs of the war
were poorly anticipated and that emancipation was rejected by both sides in favor of
what appeared to be a better alternative. Alternatively, this research might serve to
substantiate the thesis that the North was rational in fighting the Civil War because
its net benefits from winning were positive.[14]

The first option to consider is that of immediate emancipation with full compensation. Full compensation is required for this and the other schemes because it
reflects a view of property rights held by the majority of the populace in 1860.
Other than certain radical Republicans, few members of the Thirty-seventh Congress condoned the expropriation of slave property; most were in agreement that
slaveowners must be fully compensated for their losses.[15] Lincoln, for one, felt
strongly about the issue of compensation, and he doubted the constitutionality of
the Emancipation Proclamation because it did not provide compensation. Under
this hypothetical emancipation scheme, the federal government would issue to the
states, and then the states to slaveowners, bonds with principal equal to the value of
the slaves.[16] The initial cost of such a program would be the capital value of all
slaves in the United States in 1860.[17] I have estimated the capital value of all slaves
in 1860 to have been 2.7 billion 1860 dollars. This number was calculated using
age-specific slave price data recently collected from southern probate records and
slave bills of sale.[18]

The financing of so great a venture as the purchase of $2.7 billion worth of
capital, when gross national product was only $4.2 billion, would have required
borrowing. In the emancipation schemes outlined by Congress during the years
1861 to 1863, thirty-year bonds, yielding from 5 to 6 percent were to be offered
states fulfilling various criteria.[19] Similarly, I shall assume that the government
buys slaves from their owners with bonds that pay 6 percent[20] and are refunded, an
equal amount each year, over a period of thirty years. If I assume that all persons,
except ex-slaves, pay taxes to finance the bonds, refunding the bonds at a constant
rate over the thirty-year period implies a per capita tax of $7.25 in 1860. This
represents about 5 percent of per capita income for that year, with the percentage
declining during the thirty-year period because of growth in both per capita income
and population. If Southerners are to be compensated for their tax burden too, the
per capita cost would be $9.66 in 1860, with Southerners receiving a transfer.
Certainly, the slaves themselves may have been willing to contribute to their own
freedom. If they too are assumed to pay taxes, the per capita cost is reduced to
$6.30 and is $8.40 if Southerners are compensated for the tax.[21]

These bonds would be given to the slaveowners in return for the freedom of
their slaves, each bond having a principal value equal to that of a slave. The
transfer of income in the first part of this analysis is essentially from all whites to
slaves. The net wealth position of slaveholders remains exactly the same, and they
should be indifferent between holding slaves or bonds. Slaves are the only gainers
in this analysis, because they are, in essence, given money to purchase their free-

dom. The entire real wealth position of the United States is assumed not to change.[22]

Had the reference point been 1850 instead of 1860, the debt produced by immediate and fully compensated emancipation would have been smaller because of the smaller number of slaves in 1850 and the rapid increase in slave prices from 1850 to 1860.[23] The capitalized value of slaves in 1850 was 1.3 billion 1850 dollars. The scheme outlined above would have involved a per capita payment of $4.80 in 1850 and less per year thereafter. Per capita income in 1850 (in 1850 prices) was $110; therefore the first payment would have been 4 percent of per capita income. This, too, would decline over the thirty-year refunding period.

Another emancipation scheme, suggested by the review above, was gradual abolition with eventual immediate emancipation. This would lower the costs of compensation considerably. The gradual abolition scheme I have considered would free slave children at an age that made their birth price zero. This would reduce the probability that slave children would be abandoned. Using a 10 percent discount rate, male children would have been freed at age twenty-five in the lower South and twenty-six in the upper South. Female slave children would be completely emancipated at an earlier age on average, at twenty-five in the lower South but at twenty-two in the upper South. Given that all children are freed so that their birth price is zero, the rent on the breeding capacity of female slaves is zero. Only the returns to field and household labor now comprise a female slave's price. The entire capital loss from this portion of gradual abolition would have been $210 million in 1860, or only 8 percent of the total capitalized value of all slaves in 1860.

Gradual abolition was almost always closely followed by full emancipation. The legislation proposed during the Thirty-seventh Congress recognized that complete and immediate emancipation would be a difficult social transition. Therefore, most of the bills dealing with abolition provided for complete freedom after a period of time. One proposed measure, which would have freed the border state slaves, allowed for a twenty-year transition period. That for Missouri specified complete freedom within thirteen years. If a gradual abolition bill was passed specifying total emancipation after a given period of time, the costs of fully compensating slaveowners would have increased. For instance, if all slaves were freed by 1890 there would have been approximately 5.3 million bondsmen emancipated at that date[24] at an 1860 value of about $340 million.[25] To this sum would have to be added the 1860 capitalized value of the loss in breeding rights of females; therefore, the total loss from this form of gradual abolition would have been $550 million in 1860.

One problem with the hypothetical compensated emancipation schemes developed above is that many Northerners and Southerners believed that colonization of ex-slaves was a necessary part of abolition plans. According to one historian, Lincoln "doubted that whites and free Negroes could live together in peace, and this led him to advocate colonization" (Franklin 1963, 21). Colonization never became an issue in the Latin American and Caribbean emancipation debates because preabolition race relations in these areas made freedom more acceptable than in the United States. One author has noted that in Cuba "there was no fear of emancipation . . . for the Cubans had long since accepted both racial miscegenation and an open-class system of social stratification" (Klein 1967, 258).

If compensated emancipation in the United States were followed by complete colonization of the ex-slaves, the costs of resettlement would have to be added to the amount of debt created for compensation. In the legislation proposed and passed during the Thirty-seventh Congress, about one-tenth of the total amount allotted to compensation and colonization was to be spent on the latter.[26] This would imply, in the above case of immediate and fully compensated abolition, an average of $78 to be allocated for the colonization of each slave. This figure can be compared with actual values spent by the Colonization Society. During the period 1816 to 1860 this organization colonized 10,498 free blacks at a cost of $1,806,705, or about $172 per person (Staudenraus 1961, 15). The Colonization Society probably spent more per slave that would have been allotted by Congress, and $100 per slave appears reasonable in view of the costs involved and the willingness of the elector-ate to allocate funds. This would add $384 million to the costs of compensated emancipation, if colonization were a necessary step in the passage of an abolition bill.

Southerners, too, viewed colonization as a necessary adjunct to emancipation. The colonization issue arose during debates in the Virginia Legislature from 1831 to 1832. In summarizing the consensus, Dew (1963, 21) stated that "all seemed to be perfectly agreed in the necessity of removal in case of emancipation." In view of this southern opinion, it is interesting to derive the effects of colonization on total factor returns in the South, to see if some factors could have gained from the removal of ex-slaves. It can be shown[27] that under the assumption of a Cobb-Douglas production function for agricultural goods in the South, capitalists would have lost from compensated emancipation and colonization of slaves if the elasticity of demand for agricultural goods were greater that one. They would have gained if it were less than one. Free laborers would always gain. Other models may produce different results, and to the extent that Southerners consumed cotton textiles and staple crops, they would lose from price increases. Northerners would also lose from increases in price.

The colonization schemes discussed during the Thirty-seventh Congress and the 1831–1832 Virginia state legislature involved groups of slaves much smaller in number than the 4 million I am considering here. Certainly the speedy removal of 4 million ex-slaves would have been virtually impossible. Nevertheless, the abun-dance of debate on colonization makes the issue a necessary corollary to hypotheti-cal emancipation schemes.

THE *EX POST* COSTS OF THE CIVIL WAR

But to what can the costs of these emancipation schemes be compared? To deter-mine whether legislators in 1860 were rational it is necessary to ascertain the anticipated costs and gains of the Civil War to the North and the South. Because this is not possible, I will outline the *ex post* costs of the Civil War.[28] Although this does not shed much light on the anticipated costs, it allows one to ask whether an emancipation scheme would have been acceptable had the true costs of the war been known.

Direct estimates of the costs of the Civil War involve only scraps of evidence. It is known that the Union and the Confederacy borrowed about $3 billion (1860 dollars) to finance the war and that about 600,000 soldiers died in battle or from battle wounds.[29] But we do not have reliable direct estimates of all losses, such as capital destruction and political instability. Therefore, I suggest that these costs be measured indirectly.

The costs measured are those to persons alive in 1860,[30] because these individuals determined the course of events culminating in the war. I assume that the cost of the war to those alive in 1860 is the discounted value of the difference in consumption between that achieved without the war and that actually observed. The technique for computing these costs involves the construction of a hypothetical consumption stream for the period following 1860—a consumption stream in the absence of the war. The difference between this consumption stream and that actually observed, discounted to 1860, is construed to be the cost of the War Between the States. Therefore, the cost is given by:

$$C = \sum_{j=1860}^{n} [(C'_j - C_j)/(1 + i)^{j - 1860}]$$

where C'_j is hypothetical consumption in year j and C_j is actual consumption in that year. The discount rate, i, is taken to be 0.07. The calculation described below takes n as 1909, for after that date the costs, C, are trivially incremented. Given certain assumptions concerning the hypothetical consumption stream, C is calculated to be about $10 billion (1860 dollars).

The hypothetical consumption stream for the period 1860 to 1869 was constructed by assuming that per capita real income would have grown at the average 1839 to 1859 rate had the Civil War not occurred. It also assumes that the real and hypothetical worlds are equal by 1885. After that year per capita growth for both streams is taken to have been the same. One million people are assumed to have died directly from the war.[31] There are 1 million more persons in the hypothetical than in the actual world in 1869, and these persons die at rates according to data for 1900. Immigration is subtracted from the population increase, because the costs of the war are only to those living in 1860.

To compare the costs of emancipation to the costs of the Civil War it is necessary to assume that the hypothetical world of emancipation without the Civil War would not have involved political instability. One might convincingly argue that had the states underwent some form of fully compensated, voluntary emancipation, rather than an imposed settlement after battle, the process of change would have been much smoother. This will be my assumption in the analysis.

The costs of the Civil War, measured by various means, were much above the costs of any of the compensated emancipation plans. Of course, the burden of the costs for the two alternatives is different. The war involved "dead-weight" losses and a redistribution of income from slaveowning persons to slaves, whereas the emancipation schemes are only income-redistribution plans. But to free persons who could vote in 1860 these costs are both weighed equally in their decisions. Southerners decide on their strategy by assessing the probability of winning the war times the expected net costs or benefits of the war. If they weigh this against a fully compensated emancipation scheme,[32] they should choose battle only if the expected net gains of the war are positive. The Northerners also make the same calculation, but they weigh the expected net gains from the war against the costs of financing the compensation scheme.

From a casual glance at the data summarized in Table 31.1 it seems clear that an incorrect choice was made. Was this a function of a stalemated political process? Are there reasons to believe that the emancipation schemes were not feasible as political solutions? Are the costs of the alternatives being measured incorrectly? One cannot ignore the fact that the costs of the Civil War were very imperfectly anticipated, and that the expected gains from winning appeared large. In addition, there is still the possibility that the war would have been fought even had one of the emancipation schemes been adopted.

Table 31.1. The Costs of Fully Compensated Immediate and Gradual Abolition in 1860 and the *Ex Post* Costs of the Civil War

The Costs of Fully Compensated Abolition in 1860[a]			
(1) Capital Value of 1860 Stock of Slaves		2.7	billion
(2) Breeding Rights of Female Slaves in 1860		210	million
(3) Capital Value of 1890 Stock of Slaves in 1860 after Gradual Abolition[b]		340	million
(4) Colonization Costs in 1860[c]		384	million

	Per Capita Cost[d]		
	All Free Persons Pay (in Dollars)	Only Northerners Pay (in Dollars)	Slaves Plus Free Persons Pay (in Dollars)
Immediate Abolition, row 1	7.25 (5)[e]	9.66 (7)	6.30 (4)
Immediate Abolition, row 1 + row 4	8.00 (6)	10.70 (8)	6.90 (5)
Gradual Abolition, row 2 + row 3[f]	1.50 (1)	2.00 (1.5)	1.30 (1)

The *Ex Post* Costs of the Civil War	
Direct Outlays	$3 billion
Deaths, Military	635,000
Ex Post Cost Defined as the Difference in Two Consumption Streams	$10 billion

[a]All costs are expressed in 1860 dollars.
[b]Gradual abolition is defined as the freeing of all children of slaves after a period of twenty-five years of service. This is followed by total abolition as of 1890; therefore, the costs of the remaining stock of slaves must be added to the decline in the capitalized value of the females.
[c]Colonization costs for 3.84 million slaves at $100 per slave.
[d]The bonds used to finance these schemes are refunded such that an equal amount of principal and interest is paid each year.
[e]The numbers in parentheses are the percentage of 1860 per capita income represented by the tax transfer in 1860. The percentage would decline during the thirty-year refunding period.
[f]The costs of gradual abolition involve both the losses of breeding rights to females, row 2, and the loss of the capital stock of males and females (not including breeding rights) as of 1890, discounted back to 1860, row 3.
Source: See text.

WHY EMANCIPATION SCHEMES WERE NOT PROPOSED AND ENACTED BEFORE 1861

The previous analysis took the sum of all slave rents to equal the amount necessary fully to compensate all slaveholders. If the method of purchasing back slaves were non-political, that is if each slave were bought back individually, then this assessment is correct. But because the slaveowning region would have to decide on the amount necessary for compensation, there are reasons to believe that the figures given above are underestimates.[33] More correct figures can be obtained if one takes into account rents accruing to other productive factors in the South due to the existence of slavery.

If slaves were emancipated, with or without colonization taking place, factors specific to the slave economy would lose. For example, if the scale of farms were reduced with large living quarters broken down, additional transition costs would have to be paid. White overseers and other specific factors would lose by the abolition schemes, and these factors would also have to be compensated for emancipation to be amenable to the South as a whole. There is no evidence bearing on the magnitude of these losses, although they probably were trivial in comparison with the capital value of slaves.

Another loss might be the positive externalities the slave system conferred on certain persons in the South. With emancipation, these positive external benefits would be removed. If the abolition scheme were voted on by the entire slaveowning region, these losses would have to be compensated. One possible external benefit was the satisfaction Southerners received from the institution of slavery as a racist device; another is that the slave system might have represented a "way of life" to Southerners as a group. Although each master valued his slave at the market price, which reflected only the productive (and breeding) capabilities of the slave, the slave system as a whole may have been worth more than the sum of these prices.

Even though Lincoln and many influential Northerners and Southerners wanted colonization, it is possible that Southerners as a whole did not. In that case there may have been additional costs to factors in the South had ex-slaves moved North. Because the relative magnitude of free labor in the South prior to 1861 was small, it is likely that wages did not equalize between the northern and southern regions. Because slaves could not migrate, factor prices did not have to equalize. Therefore, emancipation could induce a massive migration to the North, with losses of inframarginal products to certain productive factors remaining in the South. This can only be counted as a loss if Southerners did not want the removal of ex-slaves. On the other hand, had Southerners chosen colonization as part of an emancipation scheme, the federal government would not have to pay for the inframarginal losses.

It is possible, therefore, that the capitalized value of slaves was less than the required amount of compensation. Specific factors in the South may have lost, positive external benefits would have been curtailed, and the decline in inframarginal products would have to be compensated. Although it is impossible to assess these amounts, it seems reasonable to assume that they were not double or triple the value of slaves in 1860. Therefore, the required compensation costs still appear to be smaller than the realized costs of the Civil War.

In all probability, the major reason war was declared and political settlement avoided was that the costs of war were incorrectly anticipated. The North was surprised by the tenacity of the South, and the South had counted on more support from Great Britain. Neither side thought the war would last more than one or two years. As the war dragged on, Lincoln expressed the opinion that the costs of the war were dreadfully and surprisingly high and that slavery could be "bought out" at a cheaper price. In a letter to J. A. McDougall of California in 1862, Lincoln stated that "[l]ess than one half-day's cost of this war would pay for all the slaves in Delaware at $400 per head . . . [and] less than 87 days cost of the war would pay for all in Delaware, Maryland, District of Columbia, Kentucky and Missouri" (Franklin 1963, 22).

The "Beard-Hacker" thesis also can serve to explain the apparent northern apathy toward political resolution of the problem.[34] The settlement imposed on the South after the war may have redistributed income to Northerners. Persons in the North need not have weighed the costs of the war against the cost of compensated emancipation. Rather, they should have compared the net costs or gains of the war with the costs of compensated emancipation.

A final reason for the lack of legislative discussion of abolition prior to 1861 is that slavery may not have been a major cause of the Civil War. The war may have been fought with or without the institution of slavery. As a corollary, the Civil War and emancipation may not have been exclusive events. Even had a fully compensated emancipation scheme been passed prior to the firing on Fort Sumter, the political balance of power would have remained delicate. The Civil War might still have been fought, and both the costs of redistribution from non-slaveowning to slave and the costs of the war would have been incurred.

CONCLUDING REMARKS

Although the Union was able to view in historical perspective emancipation schemes of all types, none was seriously considered before 1861. After that date abolition plans were discussed only as part of the Union's war effort. It appears from a summary of the data in this paper, given in Table 31.1, that the Union erred. It did not look to other slavocracies for advice in solving its slave problem, for the realized costs of the Civil War were far greater that those of various emancipation schemes. Of course, the Union's winning the war may have given the northern states a greater market basket of goods than just the abolition of slavery. It is possible that it more carefully weighed the costs and benefits of the war than has been apparent from this analysis.

The South lost doubly from fighting the Civil War. It paid large amounts for the machinery of war and incurred the destruction of lives and property. In addition, its slaveowners had their property expropriated after the battles were over. However, the gains to the South of winning the war have not been assessed, and the expected losses of its entering into battle may have been small.

I have reviewed various emancipation schemes which were adopted by certain slavocracies. These and the discussions during the Thirty-seventh Congress have suggested various counterfactuals concerning the antebellum United States. Given the *ex post* costs of the Civil War it is surprising that so few persons considered emancipation in any form prior to the war.

NOTES

1. See Zilversmit (1967) for an excellent discussion of the antislavery movement in the North and the slave legislation, proposed and enacted, which it furthered.
2. See Moore (1866) for a summary of the events culminating in the emancipation of Massachusetts's slaves.
3. The Pennsylvania Supreme Court in *Miller v. Dwilling* (1826) declared that "no child can be held to servitude till the age of twenty-eight . . . but one whose mother was . . . a slave at the time of its birth . . . [implies that] the legislature of Pennsylvania though it abolished slavery for life, established . . . a servitude . . . which may continue . . . to the end of the world." The state supreme court, therefore, decided that "the child of one bound to serve to the age of twenty-eight, was not bound . . . for the same period; but was absolutely free" (see Catterall 1936, IV: 282).
4. If the price at birth were less than zero, the owner should choose to abandon the child, as the maintenance costs during the early period of development are greater than the stream of benefits from the later working stage. A positive price would ensure a low rate of abandonment, but would also involve a later age for freedom. Therefore, a zero price would accomplish both a minimal number of orphans and an early age at which freedom would be guaranteed.
5. The calculations were performed using Maryland slave price data for the same period. The prices at age twenty-five and twenty-eight were discounted to year zero (birth) and these were subtracted from the prices at birth. The resulting figure is the price at birth of a slave whose services are guaranteed for twenty-five years (for a female) or twenty-eight years (for a male). A 10 percent discount rate is used because this appears to have been the internal rate of return on slaveowning.
6. See Fogel and Engerman (1972) for a discussion of the differences in slave male and female age-net hire-rate profiles. They find that female children begin to earn a positive yearly net hire at age 7.5, whereas male children produce positive net earnings at age 8.5. Females continue to be more productive than males until they are 19 years of age. After that point, male slaves produce substantially more net income than do females.
7. If the schemes were compensated, this would refer to the costs to the taxpayers.
8. The division of female price between the value of the childbearing capacity and the value of field productive capacity has been computed by Fogel and Engerman (1972), Charts V, VI.
9. The U.S. population census reveals that in 1790 there were 21,324 slaves in New York state and 20,343 in 1800. This indicates a drop of about 5,000 slaves, if a 20 percent rate of net increase is allowed for during the ten-year period. This decline in the slave population was partially due to slaveowner anticipation of the 1799 act. The decline in the slave population during the period 1800 to 1820 is even more dramatic. The gradual abolition bill was not actually effective in freeing slaves during this period, although it may have engendered the manumission of certain slaves due to mounting social pressure. The 1800 slave population in New York was 20,343, but the 1820 figure is 10,088. Using again a 20 percent net rate of increase yields 19,205 slaves who were either manumitted, abandoned children, or smuggled South to slave states. One student of New York slave history believes that independent evidence substantiates the latter hypothesis. He cites as evidence that the gains to be made in smuggling an able-bodied slave South were £40 "after commissions, insurance costs and shipping charges were paid" (McManus 1966, 170). Certainly after 1817, when the immediate abolition of slaves was guaranteed in ten years, the gains to be made by circumventing the antislave trade laws were great.
10. This would, of course, increase the costs to slaveowners of gradual emancipation. The increased

cost would be the discounted value of all remaining productive services from male and female (not including breeding rights as these have been subtracted out before) slaves.

11. The details of these provisions, as well as the personnel which the British sent to secure them legally for the slaves, indicate that Parliament knew that gradual abolition could involve the working of slaves more intensively. This law was obviously designed to accomplish the abolitionists' goals without the hardship which the northern gradual abolition laws may have entailed.

12. This sum was probably not sufficient to compensate the owners fully, and represented about one-twentieth of British total national product in the 1830s.

13. It is difficult to state whether or not there was full compensation, since payment was based on a schedule of prices set by law. See Lombardi (1971), App. 1, for information concerning the number of slaves emancipated from 1830 to 1854 and the compensation awards to slaveowners through the 1854 Abolition Law. Emancipation in Venezuela is interesting because the slave population was very small and the slaveowning class was rather minor compared to the free population, but compensation was awarded to slaveowners.

14. See, for example, Hacker (1947), for a complete discussion of this notion. This paper, though, does not attempt to assess the North's gains from victory in terms of redistributing income from the South to the North. Therefore, this work alone cannot lead to a rejection or acceptance of the "Beard-Hacker" thesis (see n. 34).

15. Some might challenge this statement because most emancipation schemes discussed and enacted during the Thirty-seventh Congress provided for less than full compensation. For example, the District of Columbia bill appropriated $1 million for compensation to masters or an average of about $300 per slave. The border state bill also allotted $300 for each slave freed. Although this was slightly less than one-half the price of slaves during 1860 for these areas, it must be remembered that these acts were wartime measures. District of Columbia slaveowners readily sold their slaves at these "low" prices, probably because they feared expropriation if the South won. In addition, many of the bills passed and debated provided for gradual abolition of slaves. Therefore, although the monetary compensation was less than the total value of the slave, the owner had a longer period of service than if emancipation was immediate.

16. Because slavery was a state issue, the states would have to purchase the rights to the slaves with the federal bonds.

17. Because the slave region can be identified with a specific economic and regional group, there may be reasons that a political settlement would result in a compensation transfer greater than the sum of slave prices. This is considered below. In addition, all slaves are freed at once; therefore one does not have to consider the effects on price of an increasingly smaller stock of slaves. The federal government does not have to pay slaveowners the area under the demand curve for slaves, but merely their price as slaves in 1860. This becomes clearer if one considers slaves as free men to be equivalent to slaves as slaves. As slaves are freed they become free laborers; therefore the supply function for slaves moves to the left but that for free laborers moves equally in the opposite direction. Thus the price of workers does not change as slaves are freed.

18. This capital value is about $1 billion (1860 dollars) less that that computed by Rose (1964). The prices for slaves used in the Rose estimate were partially based on those collected by Phillips. The lower price series which I have used resulted from a sample collected by Fogel and Engerman from the identical collection of New Orleans bills of sale which Phillips used. The Fogel and Engerman prices are about 20 percent lower for a "prime field hand" (a slave between the ages eighteen and thirty) than those given by Phillips. Phillips's sample is biased upward for an unknown reason.

19. For example, the House version of Lincoln's border state bill provided that " 'whenever the President of the United States shall be satisfied that any one of the states of Delaware, Maryland, Virginia, Kentucky, Tennessee or Missouri shall have emancipated [their] slaves . . .' he should cause to be delivered to such state 5 percent, 30 year bonds in an amount equal to $300 for each slave freed" (Curry 1968, 47–48). In addition, the House Select Committee on Gradual Emancipation reported a bill in January 1863 which also authorized the president to issue thirty-year, 5 percent bonds to Missouri when that state adopted immediate abolition (Curry 1968, 53). Other bills provided for 6 percent, thirty-year bonds. I have chosen the 6 percent figure to bias my costs upward slightly.

20. One may wonder why the interest rate on the bonds is 6 percent when the internal rate of return on slaves was somewhat higher. The bonds are far less risky assets than the slaves, and if persons are risk averse a smaller rate of interest would be necessary to induce them to hold bonds instead of slaves in their portfolios.

21. These calculations were computed as follows. At 6 percent, $2.7 billion could be refunded at a constant rate by the taxation of $195,480,000 per year for thirty years. In 1860 there were 26,923,000 whites in the United States; therefore, the per capita tax in 1860 would have been $7.25. Per capita income in 1860 was $141; therefore the tax represented about 5 percent of per capita income. The southern population (that is, the Confederate population) was about 20 percent of the entire nation; therefore the per capita tax would be $9.66 if a refund was to be given the Southerners to compensate them not only for their slaves but also for their tax burden. Taxation in this example is assumed to have an equal effect on all. If revenue were raised by a tariff, this might not be the case, and one region could bear a greater percentage of the burden.

22. The possible exceptions to this statement will be raised in a later section of this paper. Hall (n.d.) discusses the possibility of changes in the interest rate due to the existence of slavery, in the same way that the creation of debt can result in a real burden (see Sutch 1967, 540–541, for a summary of the Hall paper). But the perfection of a market for human capital, like the creation of a mortgage market, does not change anything real except the lowering of transaction costs of borrowing or lending. This paper does not consider the issue of transaction cost changes but does implicitly reject the hypothesis in the Hall manuscript. For a discussion of the real differences between a slave and non-slave economy see Engerman (1973).

23. Slave prices, deflated by the Warren and Pearson wholesale price index, rose approximately 5 percent on an average annual basis from 1850 to 1860.

24. This computation involves several assumptions. The slave population is assumed to grow at a decadal rate of 22 percent. Survivor information (that is, the percent of any cohort that survives to the next decade) from the period 1850 to 1860 was used to get the hypothetical number of slaves in each cohort that would have been in the population in 1890. The first effects of gradual emancipation are felt in 1885 when a cohort of twenty-five year olds is emancipated. By 1890 there are no slaves between the ages of twenty and twenty-five. I also assume that childbearing is deferred by these female slaves, so that no children are born into slavery after 1885. An equivalent assumption would be to invoke the Pennsylvania Supreme Court's decision in *Miller v. Dwilling* (1826), which stated that the children of emancipated slave children were free at birth. If this held, and if those children were cared for by their mothers' masters, the costs of gradual abolition would be slightly higher than that calculated here.

25. I assume here that by 1890 the percentage of slaves in the Old (upper) South equaled that in the New (lower) South. In addition, the peak prices for male and female slaves in 1860 are increased at an average annual rate of 1.3 percent to 1890. Therefore, the peak price for an average of the upper and lower South would have been $1,772 for males in 1860. That for females would have been $1,275; this does not include the birthrights to the children, because they have been subtracted by the previous exercise. For a justification of the average annual rate of increase in slave prices from 1860 to 1890 see Fogel and Engerman (1971a), 331.

26. The emancipation bill for the District of Columbia appropriated $100,000 for the colonization of about 3,000 slaves. The border state proposal allotted $20 million for this deportation, and that for Missouri "pledged federal support for voluntary colonization" (see Curry 1968).

27. The supply function for southern agricultural products can be characterized as Cobb-Douglas and of the form $Q_a = AK^{(1-\alpha)} [L_w + L_b]^\alpha$, where L_w is free and L_b is slave labor. If the wage rates for these two labor groups are the same, the total factor returns to either w or b can be expressed quite simply. For example, the total return to w is: $\lambda_w = [L_w/(L_w + L_b)] \cdot \alpha \cdot P_a \cdot Q_a$, where P_a is the price of agricultural goods deflated by the price of all other goods in the economy. The total return to capital can be expressed similarly as: $\lambda_k = (1 - \alpha)P_a \cdot Q_a$. In this analysis L_w is identified with free laborers and K with slaveowners. To see the effects of compensated emancipation and colonization on λ_w and λ_k, designate two time periods, 0 and 1, the latter corresponding to the colonization case. That is, in time period 1 the only labor is L_w. If the demand function for agricultural products takes the simple form: $Q_a = D_a P_a^{-\eta}$, the gains or losses from colonization can be easily derived.

The ratio of the return to free labor in the two time periods is: $\lambda_{w_1}/\lambda_{w_0} = [(L_w + L_b)/L_w]$ $[1 - \alpha(1 - 1/\eta)]$. Since $0 < \alpha < 1$ and $\eta > 0$, this ratio is always > 1. The corresponding ratio for the capitalists is: $\lambda_{k_1}/\lambda_{k_0} = [L_w/(L_w + L_b)]^{[\alpha(1 - 1/\eta)]}$, which is $\gtrless 1$ as $\eta \lessgtr 1$. Therefore, capitalists gain if the demand for agricultural products is inelastic. In addition, capitalists are compensated fully for their slaves; therefore they are not losing the annual net hire rate of their now-freed bondsmen.

28. Much of this section is taken from Goldin and Lewis (1975).
29. See Wright (1943), for a discussion of war deaths, and Beard and Beard (1933), 2:107, for an estimate of the northern debt created during the Civil War. The burden of the war expenditures was less than the amount given because much of the money was spent on items such as food and clothing which would have been purchased by civilians in the absence of the war.
30. Persons alive in 1860 are assumed to value the consumption stream of their children and grandchildren, and to discount it at the rate at which they would their own. The loss of consumption to immigrants who enter after 1860 is not counted in the calculation described below.
31. Although this is probably an upwardly biased estimate of Civil War–related deaths, the analysis does not take into consideration some of the losses due to war wounds not resulting in death.
32. I assume here that the bonds are financed in such a way that Southerners are compensated for their tax burden as well as for their slave property.
33. This argument will not involve bargaining problems. That is, if all costs were known, the South could "hold out" for a much larger sum. In addition, factors such as economies of scale and conspicuous consumption have already been included in the above figures. That is, if slaves afforded economies of scale in staple crop production, whereas free labor did not, then the price of slaves would reflect this advantage. The same argument applies to the possible existence of conspicuous consumption in slaveowning.
34. Hacker's statement of this proposition can be found in the following passage (1947, 373).

> The American Civil War turned out to be a revolution indeed. But its striking achievement was the triumph of industrial capitalism. The industrial capitalists, through their political spokesmen, the Republicans, had succeeded in capturing the state and using it as an instrument to strengthen their economic position. It was no accident, therefore, that while the war was waged on the field and through Negro emancipation, in Congress' halls the victory was made secure by the passage of tariff, banking, public-land, railroad, and contract-labor legislation.

THIRTY-TWO

Expectation of Abolition and Sanguinity of Coffee Planters in Brazil, 1871-1881

Pedro C. de Mello

This paper argues that, given existing characteristics and legal constraints, the declining demand for slaves in Brazil during the period 1882–1888 indicates that Brazilian slavery was moribund in the 1880s. It will also be argued that the reason for the declining demand for slaves in the 1880s was not the inherent unprofitability of slavery in coffee plantations, but the effect of the increasing "abolitionist pressure"—or the cumulative impact of an antislavery ideology—on the optimism of coffee planters regarding the political viability of slavery.

First one must define what one means by a "moribund institution." As economists use the term "moribund institution," slavery would be moribund if the market price of a prime field hand slave was tending to be, or actually was, below the costs of rearing this slave (Yasuba 1961). Was Brazilian slavery moribund in this sense?

Since the "Free Womb Law" of 1871, which gave freedom to children born of slave mothers after that date, slavery could not be perpetuated by the self-growth of its population. To be sure, slavery was doomed to disappear. Since the stock of slaves could not be replenished, death would put an end to it after a span of time. But abolition occurred well before slavery's natural death. Had the final Abolition Law of 1888 not been passed, the twenty-one- to sixty-year-old slave population could have been estimated at 835,000 in 1892 and 544,000 in 1902 (de Mello 1977, 94). A population of this size could have provided an adequate supply of slaves to meet the actual coffee production of the 1880s and 1890s by an internal shift of the slave population toward the coffee plantations. The question is whether slavery would have remained economically viable, in the absence of political pressure during the span of time from the 1871 Free Womb Law until the hypothetical date in which the country's shrinking stock of slaves would be inadequate to meet the slave labor requirements in coffee plantations. More specifically, this paper is concerned with devising an operational test that would indicate whether slavery was moribund in the economic sense by 1888.

A good indicator of a moribund institution in a particular region or economic activity, such as coffee plantations, is the steady decline of vested interest in the institution of slavery measured by the wealth in slaves (their number times their average price) owned by slaveowners.[1] To be made formal, all cases of domestically promoted pacific abolition required legal sanction or parliamentary measures, and most historical evidence will show that laws sanctioning abolition were passed after the importance of a country's vested economic interest in slavery had dwindled. Thus for an institution to be moribund, it is not necessary that the extreme case of zero wealth in slaves be reached, only that a strong trend in that direction be present.

Although the relationship between economic interest and political sentiment is very complex, it seems safe to suppose that the reactions of slaveowners (those being principally coffee planters, who constituted the most influential group in the political decision-making process during this period) to abolition would be less severe within a context of falling slave values, than in a case of a sudden abolition at a time when both prices and quantities of slaves were rising.

Since the short-run supply curve of slaves in the purchase market was completely inelastic, slave prices were determined by short-run changes in the demand schedule. Thus, when treating an institution (or industry) like slavery in coffee plantations after 1871, the characteristic that would suggest its becoming nonviable (or moribund) is a continuous decline in the demand for the specialized capital (slaves) used in the production of the industry's product (slave labor services).

Figure 32.1 illustrates this for the entire slave population. Suppose that in 1871 the price of a prime field hand was just equal to the present value of his rearing costs (RC). Suppose now that the demand was increasing from D_{71} to D_{88} in Figure 32.1A and declining from D_{71} to D'_{88} in Figure 32.1B. The same forces

Figure 32.1. Hypothetical effects of changes in the demand schedules on slave prices.

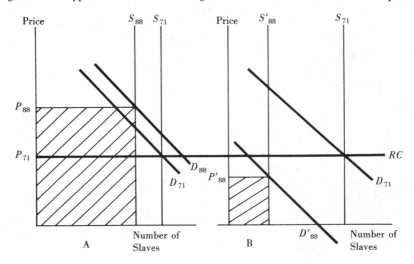

compensating for a rising or falling demand also affected the number of manumissions. Suppose then that supply decreased only for reasons of mortality, as in Figure 32.1A, from S_{71} to S_{88}. In Figure 32.1B the number of slaves, in addition to the mortality reasons, also decreased because of manumissions, the joint effect being a shift from S_{71} to S'_{88}.

One can see that not only would the aggregate value of slaves be different in both cases (area marked), but that in Figure 32.1A dynamic forces were working to increase the value and give incentive to increase the supply of slaves ($P_{88} > RC$), either by lobbying for non-enforcement of the Free Womb Law or by any scheme to have the *ingenuos* (children born of slave mothers) as de facto slaves after they completed their twenty-first birthday, or by making the alternative cost of manumissions very high and putting the economic stakes involved in the passing of the Sexagenarian Law and the Final Abolition Law in a different situation. In Figure 32.1B, however, since the demand for slaves would be continuously falling, no such economic incentives would be present. Thus the continuously declining demand for slaves after 1881 indicates that the institution of slavery was moribund. What caused this falling demand? What are the competitive hypothesis to explain it? How do we test them?

In order to explain the decline in the demand for slaves on coffee plantations I put stress on exogenous factors, which will be termed the "abolitionist pressure." The relatively sudden growth of a powerful antislavery movement both inside and outside Brazil has been amply documented. Although both the idea and the institution of slavery existed in virtually the entire Western world for 3,000 years, its ethical legitimacy seldom disputed, in less than 100 years, beginning in the last decades of the eighteenth century, slavery disappeared from the scene, condemned by all but a few (Davis 1966).

According to this study, the increasingly dynamic political and ideological abolitionist movement, involving both domestic and foreign influence on Brazilian public opinion—in sum, the constant erosion of society's support for the institution and the political acceleration of the movement after 1885—was the central factor causing the decline in the demand for slaves on coffee plantations.

Among the causes of the abolitionist pressure, it is important to stress the influence which other slave societies of the New World had on the Brazilian experience. It is generally agreed that the late 1860s and the mid-1880s were characterized by abolitionist agitation (although of admittedly different natures). It is also no coincidence that the first period occurred just after the U.S. Civil War and the death of North American slavery, and that the second coincided with the 1884 abolition in Cuba (Laerne 1885),[2] leaving Brazil as the last bastion of slavery in the Americas. Although I think most interpretations would note the importance of the decline of society's support of the institution of slavery, the point I want to make is that this erosion was happening in spite of the economic interests of coffee planters, those being based on profitability considerations.

The competitive hypothesis that I want to investigate is based on arguments very similar in content to those raised by Phillips (1905, [1918] 1966) in his explanation for the non-profitability of slavery in the United States. According to

Phillips, slavery was condemned on technical grounds, since it lacked flexibility and efficiency and was a riskier application of capital than were other activities—that is, slavery was a non-profitable investment.[3] With the onset of Brazilian modernization and the beginnings of the experiment with capitalism in the second half of the nineteenth century, slavery, a pre-capitalist institution, had to be given up due to the gradual decline in the demand for slave labor services, a decline caused by gradual modernization.

In addition, there was a split in coffee planters' interest and attitudes regarding slavery. One group, the Paraíba Valley planters, was bound by traditional social values and attitudes: Its demand for slaves was based more on reasons of tradition, social prestige, and paternalism than on profitability considerations (Genovese 1971, 84–85). This group can be contrasted with the coffee planters of central and west São Paulo, who were of a more dynamic capitalist mentality, open to new ideas, trying new forms of labor organization (such as European immigration), and increasingly dissatisfied with slaves as a solution to their labor problems (Genovese 1971, 85–88). As the coffee-planted area was rapidly expanding to the west of São Paulo, both economic and political power were shifting to this region, where a new kind of planter was ready to innovate by substituting free labor for slave labor. It can therefore be argued that the non-profitability of slavery, together with the regional shift in coffee production to the west of São Paulo, would cause a gradual decline in the demand for slave labor services (a process which was happening with an increasing pace in the 1870s and 1880s). As a result the demand for slaves would gradually fall during this period.

I have shown elsewhere, however, that the process of selective concentration of slaves was well under way in west São Paulo in the 1870s, more than in any other part of the coffee region (de Mello 1977, Ch. 2). Furthermore, between 1871 and 1881 the ownership of slavery by the Paraíba Valley planters could be well explained by profitability considerations.[4] Nevertheless, since the demand for slaves was indeed falling during the 1880s, the above hypothesis does seem to offer a plausible interpretation of this fact. Let us therefore test the two hypotheses—mine and the one above—in order to discover which best describes the circumstances.

Let us consider slavery as an industry in which firms owned or rented capital goods (slaves) and used them as factors of production to produce a marketable commodity (labor services). One must make a distinction between the rental market, where slave services were transacted, and the purchase market, where slaves themselves (capital goods) were transacted.

Assuming competition, all firms faced a single hire rate. In the short run, the revenue of the fixed factor (slaves) was a residually determined quasi-rent. Assuming long-run equilibrium for the industry and all slaves homogeneous in age, skill, and physical strength, the price of the capital good (slaves) was then the capitalized value of these quasi-rents during the life span of a slave.

The hypothesis outlined above focuses implicitly on the interplay between the rental and purchase markets for slaves, since the society's increasing knowledge of the inefficiency and non-profitability of slavery, translated into market behavior, would produce a falling demand for slave labor services and thus (with a short-run totally inelastic supply) a fall in the price of slave labor services (i.e., in the hire rate). Assuming constant maintenance costs, the capitalization of this falling net hire rate would then produce a falling price for slaves. According to this interpretation, the falling price for slaves in the purchase market would be caused by the falling net hire rates in the rental market.

My interpretation, in contrast, focuses exclusively on the purchase market. The abolitionist pressure created uncertainty, defined as the holding of anticipations which are not unanimous or universal but constitute a probability distribution under which the parameters of the distribution are themselves varied (Lutz and Lutz 1951, 182). This uncertainty acted in the purchase market through the capitalization of the net hire rate, and not in the rental market—assuming, quite plausibly, that the abolitionist movement did not produce non-pecuniary costs for the rental of slaves in coffee plantations.

Since we are not directly interested in the *ex ante* investment decision per se, the manner in which the uncertainty is formally introduced is irrelevant. By knowing the *ex post* price of slaves, we already know how the market performs this capitalization.

To facilitate the analysis, a simple formula is used to express the price of a prime field hand:

$$P_{sf} = \frac{H_f}{i} \left[1 - \frac{1}{(1+i)^n} \right] \qquad (1)$$

in which P_{sf} = price of prime slave field hand, H_f = annual net revenue derived from a slave, equal to the net hire rate, i = rate of discount, n = expected economic life of a slave, in which the upper bound would be the biological life of the slave, as given by the slave life tables (de Mello 1977, 123), and $x = 1 - 1/(1 + i)^n$.

In order to choose between the two competing hypotheses, I propose to use four tests, using information about the rental and purchase market for slaves: (1) the "sanguinity index," (2) an index of the real hire rate of slaves, (3) the change in the shape of the slave age-price profiles, (4) an index of the "political death" of slavery.[5] Although obtaining the data required extensive research using primary sources, the indexes in themselves are simple. However, together they constitute a strong test which enables one to decide among the two hypotheses.

SANGUINITY INDEX

The first test involves constructing Fogel and Engerman's "sanguinity index." Although used by these authors to answer a different question, this index can also be used in our case if we change its interpretation.[6]

This index is a ratio of two series: (1) the annual price over hire rate for the period 1871 to 1887 and (2) the average price over hire rate for a period in which there exists an "average" or "normal" state of expectations.

It is difficult to define series 2. In the discussion of the behavior of slave prices during this period, we saw that during the 1850s slave prices were forced to adjust to changes occurring in the supply of slaves provided by the African slave trade and by internal sources. The 1880s were characterized by the growing importance of the abolitionist movement. Thus I will take the period 1860–1879 as representative of the "average" state of expectations.

Formally, the sanguinity index can be defined as:[7]

$$I_s = \left[\frac{\dfrac{P_i}{H_i}}{\dfrac{\displaystyle\sum_{j=1}^{n} \left(\dfrac{P_j}{H_j} \right)}{n}} - 1 \right] 100$$

where P_i = price of slaves in year i, H_i = hire rate of slaves in year i, j = years of the period characterized as of "normal" or "average" expectations, and n = number of years of the "normal" expectation period. The annual hire rate reflects the market appraisal of the productive value of slave labor services in a particular year. The purchase price reflects this market's appraisal in this year and the following years, during the life time of slaves.

The sanguinity index, being the ratio of the two series, can therefore test the relative optimism or pessimism about the future prospects of the institution of slavery. By totally differentiating equation 1, we obtain

$$\overset{*}{P}_{sf} = \overset{*}{H}_f - \overset{*}{i} + \overset{*}{x} \tag{2}$$

where an asterisk (*) over any variable represents it in rate-of-change form. Suppose the interest rates do not change during this period ($\overset{*}{i} = 0$). According to the competitive hypothesis, the n in equation 1 would be equal to the biological life of a prime slave field hand, since the uncertainty element in the economic life of slavery, if existent, would not change during this period. Assuming that the slave mortality conditions do not change during this period, $\overset{*}{n} = 0$. Therefore, since $\overset{*}{i}$ and $\overset{*}{n}$ can be interpreted as equal to zero in this interpretation, $\overset{*}{x}$ would also be equal to zero (that is, the capitalization factor would not change during this period). One would expect that slave prices and hire rates would change at the same rate ($\overset{*}{P} = \overset{*}{H}$) and that I_s would either be a straight line or would present only a few fluctuations during this time.[8]

In my interpretation, however, the n in equation 1 is the expected economic life of slavery, which because of the increasing uncertainty caused by the "abolitionist pressure," was declining at an increasing rate. Since one would expect that the capitalization factor x, would be declining, $\overset{*}{x}$ would be negative. Thus in this interpretation I_s would fall continuously in the last years of slavery.

Using the information on the price and hire rates of "all slaves" presented in Tables 32.1 and 32.2, I present in Figure 32.2 the sanguinity index for the period 1871–1888.

Although it can be observed that slaveowners were pessimistic in the two years

Table 32.1. Rio de Janeiro All Slave Prices, 1835–1887 Mean Price (Milréis)

Year	Mean Price (Nominal)	Standard Deviation	Sample Size[a]	Coefficient of Variation	Real Prices[b]
1835	272$100[c]	59.9	57	0.22	627$000
1837	310$700	57.5	55	0.19	616$500
1839	294$500	73.6	51	0.25	551$500
1841	359$800	84.5	40	0.23	700$000
1844	378$500	95.9	40	0.25	716$900
1845	369$700	95.2	35	0.26	683$400
1847	366$400	98.6	55	0.27	646$200
1849	338$800	93.2	60	0.28	614$900
1850	320$000	150.2	16	0.47	589$300
1851	448$600	202.7	80	0.45	780$200
1852	694$000	269.7	72	0.39	1,139$600
1853	806$500	349.6	69	0.43	1,250$400
1854	668$800	368.5	43	0.55	973$500
1855	811$100	379.4	62	0.47	1,111$100
1856	874$400	399.9	80	0.46	1,126$800
1857	1,006$400	553.0	66	0.55	1,290$300
1858	1,151$500	390.6	73	0.34	1,470$600
1859	1,090$300	485.6	78	0.45	1,387$200
1860	1,016$500	379.6	111	0.37	1,288$300
1861	938$500	394.0	92	0.42	1,185$000
1862	1,007$200	405.4	81	0.40	1,266$900
1863	900$000	343.1	116	0.38	1,100$200
1864	1,031$900	353.7	126	0.34	1,227$000
1865	896$600	408.3	97	0.45	1,035$300
1866	797$100	309.3	82	0.39	894$600
1867	768$500	337.4	66	0.44	838$100
1868	859$500	326.3	113	0.38	910$500
1869	931$600	420.9	103	0.45	958$400
1870	1,007$900	326.8	177	0.32	1,007$900
1871	815$800	292.2	99	0.36	816$600
1872	859$200	347.0	254	0.40	860$900
1873	975$700	305.0	297	0.31	977$700
1874	958$500	354.3	105	0.37	961$400
1875	1,028$300	304.3	184	0.30	1,032$400
1876	1,025$700	325.9	111	0.32	1,016$600
1877	1,093$500	339.0	124	0.31	1,070$000
1878	932$400	368.3	83	0.40	900$900
1879	1,035$100	371.9	154	0.36	986$700
1880	893$200	342.0	73	0.38	840$300
1881	917$800	325.0	45	0.35	850$600
1882	607$900	252.6	42	0.42	555$200
1883	550$000	178.0	10	0.32	495$000
1884	584$400	286.8	16	0.49	536$600
1885	796$700	279.8	6	0.35	746$700
1886	325$000	106.1	2	0.33	311$300
1887	450$000	44.7	6	0.10	439$900

[a]Sample size is the number of individual slaves advertised.
[b]Deflated by Buescu price index, 1870:100.
[c]In the nineteenth century, the official unit of currency was the *milréis*, which was divided into 1,000 *reis*. Many commercial and financial transactions involved a larger unit, the *conto*, worth 1,000 *milréis*. Amounts were written with a dollar sign between the *milréis* and *reis*. From 1850 to 1888, the *conto* averaged approximately $500 in U.S. money.

Table 32.2. Rio de Janeiro All Slaves Monthly Hire Rates, 1835–1888 (Milréis)

Year	Mean Hire Rate (Nominal)	Standard Deviation	Sample Size	Coefficient of Variation	Real Hire Rates[a]
1835	15$000[b]	1.41	2	0.09	18$800
1837	18$000	6.93	3	0.39	19$400
1841	11$000	1.16	4	0.11	11$600
1844	13$700	1.53	3	0.11	14$100
1845	12$300	3.74	9	0.30	12$400
1847	10$500	0.90	12	0.09	10$100
1849	13$700	3.25	18	0.24	13$500
1851	13$000	3.90	108	0.30	12$300
1852	18$600	5.20	122	0.28	16$600
1853	18$400	6.66	110	0.36	15$500
1854	19$600	5.82	137	0.30	15$500
1855	19$100	5.18	117	0.27	14$200
1856	20$800	5.93	109	0.29	14$600
1857	23$700	6.23	109	0.26	16$500
1858	23$400	6.22	117	0.27	16$300
1859	25$100	7.24	96	0.29	17$400
1860	25$000	6.75	70	0.27	16$700
1861	26$100	8.37	97	0.32	17$900
1862	26$400	5.17	77	0.20	18$000
1863	24$000	6.34	85	0.26	15$900
1864	24$200	7.01	63	0.29	15$600
1865	24$300	5.05	86	0.21	15$200
1866	24$500	6.51	80	0.27	14$900
1867	23$900	5.46	88	0.23	14$200
1868	24$000	5.72	65	0.24	13$800
1869	24$500	6.33	52	0.26	13$700
1870	26$900	5.28	130	0.20	14$600
1871	25$900	6.18	42	0.24	14$100
1872	24$200	4.34	46	0.18	13$200
1873	31$000	8.87	102	0.29	16$900
1874	32$700	7.35	117	0.22	17$800
1875	32$000	8.03	102	0.25	17$500
1876	30$500	8.00	99	0.26	16$400
1877	29$500	6.89	85	0.23	15$700
1878	29$700	7.83	89	0.26	15$600
1879	28$400	8.22	89	0.29	14$700
1880	29$000	8.12	82	0.28	14$800
1881	26$600	8.70	172	0.33	13$400
1882	27$200	8.22	189	0.30	13$500
1883	27$200	8.89	235	0.33	13$300
1884	26$600	8.71	242	0.33	13$300
1885	26$900	11.50	237	0.43	13$700
1886	26$700	10.10	235	0.38	13$900
1887	27$900	10.80	229	0.39	14$800
1888	28$700	10.30	99	0.36	15$200

[a]Buescu Price Index, 1850:100.
[b]Please see Table 32.1, n. c, for explanation of *milréis* notation.
Source: Advertisements in *Jornal do Comercio* (Rio de Janeiro) (1835–1888).

Figure 32.2. Sanguinity index, 1871–1888.

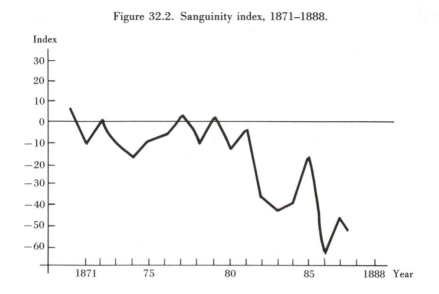

following the Free Womb Law, their optimism increased and oscillated throughout this period up until 1881. In the years immediately following, optimism lessened significantly, rising again in 1885 in the hope that with the passage of the Sexagenarian Law, thought to be a concession to the abolitionist forces, abolitionist pressure would decrease. However, since the abolitionist movement reached full power in 1886, its pressure continued to be felt and hopes were drastically diminished until the very end.[9]

It is clear that sanguinity declined rapidly in the 1880s, showing that the abolitionist pressure was acting in the purchase market through the capitalization of the net hire rate. This is even more apparent in Figure 32.3, which, while presenting the sanguinity index based on the prices and hire rates of male and female adult urban slaves and of male rural slaves aged twenty to twenty-nine, uses the 1860–1879 period as the "average" period of expectations.

Two features of the urban and rural sanguinity indexes are noteworthy. The first is the fact that the sanguinity index falls rapidly in the 1880s for both urban and rural slaveowners; the second is the fact that, by comparing the 1870s rural and urban sanguinity indexes, the expectations of rural slaveowners, although volatile, conform with the trend of "normal" or "average" expectations. Urban slaveowners, however, were consistently more pessimistic during this period than were rural ones, which supports the interpretation that the Brazilian abolitionist movement was mainly an urban phenomenon (da Costa 1966; Graham 1966).

REAL HIRE RATE INDEX

This index further supports the interpretation that it is the purchase market, and not the rental market, which is relevant to the decline of demand for slaves during this period.

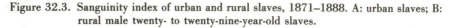

Figure 32.3. Sanguinity index of urban and rural slaves, 1871–1888. A: urban slaves; B: rural male twenty- to twenty-nine-year-old slaves.

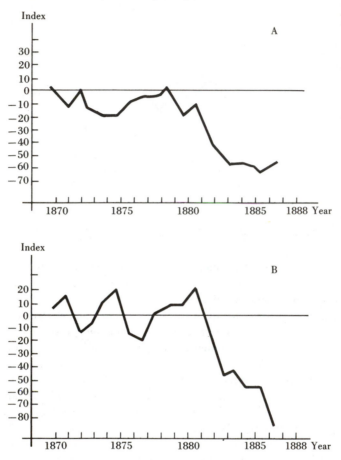

For the construction of the index I used the evolution of the real annual hire rate for male rural slaves in the period 1871–1888 (1871 = 100), based on data presented elsewhere (see #5, *TP*, Vol. I, Table 5.3).

According to the theory that the decline in the demand for slaves was caused by both the non-profitability of slaves and the increasing importance of modern planters in coffee production, the real hire rate should have been gradually and steadily falling during this period, reflecting the declining demand for slave labor services.[10]

Figure 32.4 shows that real hire rates increased from 1871 to 1876 at the average geometric annual growth rate of 2.4 percent, fell in the period of 1876 to 1883 at the rate of 3.15 percent per annum, increased again between 1883 and 1887 at the growth rate of 2.9 percent per annum, and fell again only in the last year of slavery. Although growth rate was slightly negative in the overall period of 1871–1888 (−0.76 percent per annum), in the critical 1882–1887 period the

Figure 32.4. Index of real net hire rate for rural male slaves (1871 = 100).

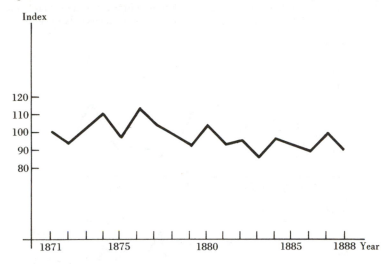

trend was positive.[11] The validity of these results would not be compromised if other series of slave real monthly hire rates by sex or occupation were included.[12]

The cyclical movements in the real net annual hire rate for male rural slaves during 1871–1888, rather than supporting an interpretation of a continuous and steady falling in the demand for slave labor services, seem to reflect the fluctuations and trends in coffee exports and revenues during this period, as can be seen in Figure 32.5.

CHANGES IN THE SLAVE AGE-PRICE PROFILE

My intention is to examine the purchase market of slaves, with the objective of exploring the competing hypothesis regarding this market—specifically, uncertainty regarding price or output of coffee as compared with uncertainty over the future of the institution of slavery. Since expectations other than the "abolitionist pressure" like falling coffee prices, depressions in the world coffee market, etc., could have been acting in the purchase market for slaves, the presentation of the age-price profiles for slaves in different time periods intends to examine these possibilities. As we will see below, the result reinforces the interpretation developed in the sanguinity index.

But first of all it is useful to examine the situation of coffee prices and output during this period, since most economic studies agree that the formation of expectations about price and output is generally based on a weighted average of current and past experience of those magnitudes (e.g., the adaptive expectation model), with lower weights placed on the more distant past than on recent experience.

Figure 32.5 presents the course of real coffee prices and revenues, and coffee exports during the 1871–1888 commercial years. As can be observed, although the trend of real coffee prices was slightly negative in this period,[13] there was a high

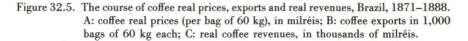

Figure 32.5. The course of coffee real prices, exports and real revenues, Brazil, 1871–1888.
A: coffee real prices (per bag of 60 kg), in milréis; B: coffee exports in 1,000
bags of 60 kg each; C: real coffee revenues, in thousands of milréis.

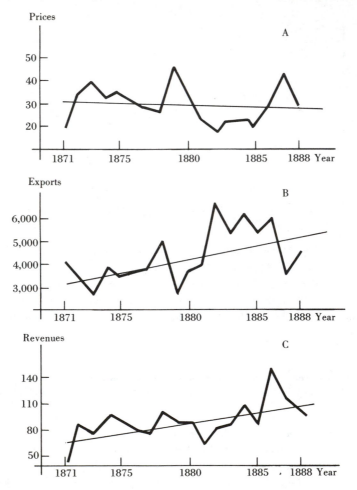

positive trend in coffee exports[14] and an almost perfect matching of falling real
prices and rising exports, so that the real coffee revenues also showed a positive
trend during this period.[15] It should be noted that the period from 1871 to 1888
was a booming one for exports within the longer period 1821–1889 and was
characterized by high coffee prices and revenues. In addition, if one focuses only on
the subperiod of the commercial years of 1882 to 1888, then the trends of real
coffee prices, coffee exports, and real coffee revenues are all positive.[16] The evidence presented above suggests that there was no sustained basis for the pessimism
of coffee planters about the long-range future of the coffee market which could
explain such a huge decline in the demand for slaves in the period from 1882 to
1887.

Slave age-price profiles can be used to support the interpretation that the principal reason for this falling demand was fear of abolition and not expectations about the prospects of the coffee market.

The basic shape of the age-price profiles was resistent to differences in the trend of slave prices. That is, the shape would not change during the ups and downs of average slave prices, although the whole curve would shift up and down. This can be seen in Figure 32.6 which compares the age-price profiles of coffee plantation slaves in 1858 and 1875.[17]

Although economic factors affecting the expectations of coffee planters (such as the coffee market's business cycles) could have affected the average price of slaves by causing changes in the demand for slaves, they would probably have tended to have had little impact on the age cohorts. In other words, they would not have significantly affected the distribution according to age. The abolitionist pressure, however, by creating expectations about abolition with less than full indemnification (or even none) according to market values, would have had a greater impact on the shape of the age-price profile. One would therefore expect a change in the shape

Figure 32.6. Changes in the shape of age-price profiles of male and female slaves, sixteen to sixty years old.

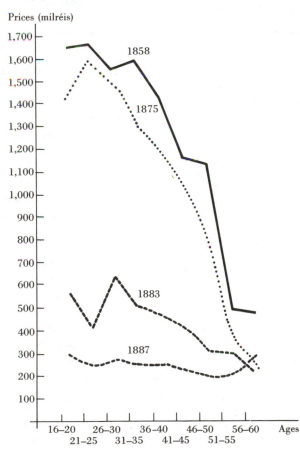

of the age-price profile, probably with a flattening in the younger ages. Since the price of slaves was the capitalized value of the net stream of future labor services, prices of younger slaves (aged fifteen to thirty-five, for example) would have had a relatively higher decline when compared with middle-aged or old slaves (aged forty-five to sixty, for example).

Figure 32.6 presents the age-price profiles of male and female slaves between the ages of sixteen and sixty for the years 1858, 1875, 1883, and 1887. They are expressed in absolute values and as averages of slave prices for five-year age cohorts.[18] By comparing 1858 with 1875, we see that the age-price profile was resistant to differences in the trend of average prices. In addition, there was no abolitionist pressure during the period 1850–1880 similar to the one prevailing in the 1880s according to which slavery was expected to be abolished with no indemnification. The age-price profiles of 1858 and 1875 can be interpreted, therefore, as typical of the period before the abolitionist pressure of the 1880s. However, looking to the age-price profiles for 1883 and 1887, a different picture emerges: These profiles became increasingly flat in the 1880s and in 1887 the profile is virtually flat.

THE "POLITICAL DEATH" OF SLAVERY

The term "abolitionist pressure" needs some clarification.[19] Although in a broad sense there was some sort of abolitionist pressure throughout the entire period beginning in the years preceding the closing of the African slave trade and ending in 1888, one can distinguish three different periods, each with its specific effects on the expectations among coffee planters about the future of slavery.

The period stretching from 1831, when the African slave trade was declared illegal in Brazil,[20] to the early 1850s, when it was finally abolished after considerable pressure from Great Britain, can be considered the first period for our classification of coffee planters' expectations.[21] Given the 300-year-long planters' reliance on the importation of African slaves, the realization in the 1840s that the end of the trade was approaching and the period of price adjustment following the trade's effective termination in 1851 created a spurt of expectation that slave labor would become scarce and more expensive and that a substitute for the cheap African slave was therefore needed. Although the first attempts to bring European and Chinese workers to coffee plantations were made during this period (Prado 1889), there was neither expectation nor mention of an immediate end to the slavery institution among coffee planters. This relative lack of concern can be seen in the sentiments of contemporary Brazilian society where little evidence can be found that the legitimacy of the institution was being challenged at this time.

With the development of the internal slave trade and the completion of the adjustment period of slave prices to the new supply conditions, these expectations were dissipated.

With the debate of the Free Womb Law, beginning in 1867 and lasting until the early 1870s, there was another spurt of expectations of coffee planters about slavery. This time, however, it became evident that the inevitable demographic shrink-ing of slavery would require a discussion of the alternatives for slave labor. A consensus gradually emerged among coffee planters that the deaths and manumis-sions of slaves would produce a natural end to slavery, and that meanwhile a permanent (i.e., European immigration) or transitory (i.e., Chinese immigration) substitute for slave labor had to be found. Although during the late 1860s and early 1870s coffee planters felt that slavery was doomed, neither they nor the Brazilian social body at large expected involuntary manumissions or an abrupt end to slavery without full indemnification according to market prices. Slavery was still legitimate in society's eyes.

Coffee planters therefore viewed the gradual abolition of slavery by natural causes, together with the search for suitable substitutes, as a reasonable way to achieve the transition to free labor while sparing agricultural production. This position, called "Emancipacionismo," was sharply attacked by the "Abolicionis-tas," who pointed out that slave longevity and concentration of slaves in coffee plantations would unacceptably prolong the institution in Brazil.

However, it was only in the 1880s that the abolitionist pressure increased and that coffee planters' expectations acquired a new nature. This time they expected slavery to end for political, as opposed to natural, reasons (as would happen as a consequence of demographic decline). Moreover, after 1882, when the abolitionist movement gained momentum and became widespread, coffee planters became in-creasingly aware that there would probably be no indemnification whatsoever. Their main concern, therefore, was no longer their financial loss but the urgent solution to the labor crisis they felt would occur along with abrupt abolition. As the London-based *South American Journal*, quoting government sources, noted in 1885, it is fair enough to admit "that advocates of slavery open and avowed there are none in Brazil," and that "those who are not abolitionists assume the title of emancipators."[22]

The coffee planters' attitude was to accept the political death of slavery while trying to prolong it as much as possible, pegging its end to the discovery of a temporary or permanent solution to the expected labor problem. Indemnification became only a secondary concern, the major issue being a smooth transition from slave labor to a suitable substitute for work in coffee plantations. It is in this last sense that the term "abolitionist pressure" was used in this study, emphasizing the connections between the political and ideological movement to abolish slavery in the 1830s and the demand for slaves by coffee planters.

That by the mid-1880s coffee planters were pessimistic is well documented by observers. Laerne (1885, 86, 95), in a survey of coffee plantations in late 1883 and early 1884, noticed that planters did not expect slavery to last beyond 1890. In 1885 the *South American Journal* commented that Premier Saraiva, assuming the government of the empire and taking into account all those elements of acceleration of the abolitionist movement, ventured to express his conviction that by 1892 Brazilian slavery would finally be extinct.[23]

Neither did the effect of abolitionist pressure on slave prices escape the atten-tion of some observers. As a member of the cabinet of the empire remarked in

1884, the institution of slavery created an economic anomaly, for its value is determined in direct proportion to the number of slaves: As slave labor becomes scarce, the value of the remaining slaves decreases as well.[24] Ruy Barboza, a great Brazilian statesman, argued along the same lines and maintained that the reason for this anomaly is the "spontaneous action" of the abolitionist movement (Barboza 1884, 16).

Indeed, one can obtain in a more formal way, via slave prices, the number of years coffee planters expected slavery to last for each year of the period 1881–1887 and then to translate this into the date they expected the political death of slavery. With the information on the prices of the twenty- to twenty-nine-year-old male rural slaves (see #5, TP, Vol. I, Table 5.4) and the estimates of interest rate (de Mello 1977, Ch. 5), it is possible to measure the unnatural "death" of slavery, by the use of equation 1. In this case, however, n only represents the expected "economic life" of the slave, and not the expected average life of male slaves represented by the life table. Using the information on slave prices and hire rates presented in columns 1 and 2 of Table 32.3, and using the 10 percent point estimates for the alternative rate of return,[25] we can solve for n in equation 1.

The results are shown in column 3 of Table 32.3, and they indicate, for each year of the period 1881–1887, for how many years coffee planters expected slavery to last. The year 1881, as argued before, was typical of the period in which abolitionist pressure was not yet present, so the n for this year (29 years) is very close to the estimated boundaries (26.76 and 29.18) of the life expectancy of a twenty-year-old male slave.[26] From this year until 1883 there was a dramatic fall in the value of n to a very low magnitude (6 years), a trend which continued at this level until 1887, when there is another intense decline (n becomes 1 year), showing that months before the final Abolition Law of May 13, 1888, slavery was already virtually extinct in Brazil.

The information presented in column 4 of Table 32.3, representing the dates slavery was expected to end, also bears upon the above analysis. If 1881 can be considered typical of the expectations prevailing in the years before the abolitionist pressure of the 1880s, coffee planters in the 1870s expected slavery to be in

Table 32.3. The "Political Death" of Slavery

Years	(1) Prices[a]	(2) Hire Rates[a]	(3) n^b	(4) Expected Year of Abolition
1881	1,700$000	181$720	29	1910
1882	1,341$000	188$470	13	1895
1883	723$500	170$530	6	1889
1884	800$000	186$210	6	1890
1885	715$900	178$710	5	1890
1886	647$800	169$010	5	1891
1887	255$700	187$810	1	1888

[a]Nominal values in milréis. Please see Table 32.1, n. c, for explanation of milréis notation.
[b]The value of n measures the expected "economic life" of slaves, in years, and was obtained by solving the equation $P_s = (H/i) \{1 - [1/(1 + i)^n]\}$, in which P_s is the slave prices; H, the annual net hire rates; and i, the rate of discount.

existence after the turn of the nineteenth century. With the acceleration of aboli-tionist pressure, however, those expectations were rapidly reassessed. Slavery, which in 1881 was expected to last until at least 1910, was subjected to a remark-able change of expectations in less than two years. As early as 1883, coffee planters correctly perceived that slavery would end at a date close to 1890. Although opti-mism increased in the years surrounding passage of the Sexagenarian Law, 1887 marked the coffee growers' realization that the political death of slavery would occur the following year. Thus slaveowners quite perceptively foresaw this occur-rence five years before the 1888 final abolition. This means that since the slave purchase market had translated those expectations into gradually falling prices, the capital losses of slaveowners occurred more intensely in the years of 1882 and 1883, and again in 1887, and *not* in 1888.

In conclusion, the evidence presented by the sanguinity index, the evolution of the real hire rates, the change in slave age-price profiles, and the political death of slavery, all suggest the need to consider more than purely economic factors in order to understand the process of abolition in coffee plantations. As Engerman (1973, 65) wrote, "more complicated models, drawing upon social, political, and moral, in addition to economic considerations are necessary before we can develop a more complete explanation of the . . . fall of slavery."

Although a full explanation for the abolition path in Brazilian coffee plantations would require more than a command of economics, I hope the economic analysis and quantitative evidence I have used can illuminate some of the issues involved in the debate.

NOTES

1. For a similar view, see Goldin (#31, in this volume) and Gunderson (1974).
2. The Emancipation Act of May 8, 1884 decreed that slavery in Cuba should be abolished by degrees, but in practice virtually abolished slavery.
3. See, as an example, Ianni (1969), 298, 304, 316–317, 319.
4. See de Mello (#5, *TP*, Vol. I).
5. The profitability test, although not inappropriate if the yearly rate of capital losses are included in the calculation of the internal rate of return, does not yield adequate insight here.
6. For an explanation of the construction and interpretation of the index, see Fogel and Engerman (1971b), 331–332.
7. The formula is based on an interpretation of Fogel and Engerman (1974a), 2:104, Fig. 32.
8. Presumably, $\overset{*}{H} < 0$, $\overset{*}{P} < 0$, but $\overset{*}{H} = \overset{*}{P}$.
9. As Conrad (1972), 211, remarked, the Sexagenarian law "was a change in the status quo and so broke the forward momentum of the liberation movement, causing it to mark time in late 1885 and early 1886, before the final rush for triumph."
10. Even assuming a constant or falling supply of slaves services during this period, reflecting the "demographic shrinking" of the stock of slaves.
11. $\text{Log}\, H_t = 5.072 + 0.01371t$; R-square = 0.15.
12. See de Mello (1977), Ch. 2, Figs. 8, 9, 10.
13. The trend line for coffee prices in 1871–1888 is $P_c = 31.2 - 0.183t$; R-square = 0.014.
14. For coffee exports, $E_c = 3.178 + 121.2t$; R-square = 0.29.
15. For coffee revenues, $R_c = 97{,}046 + 2{,}468t$; R-square = 0.36.
16. For the real coffee prices in 1882–1888; $P_c = 14.17 + 3.02t$; R-square = 0.58. For coffee

exports, $E_c = 3,504.8 + 25.8t$; R-square $= 0.019$. For real coffee revenues, $R_c = 112,988 + 5,369.4t$; R-square $= 0.24$.

17. Real slave prices (three years moving average) for 1858, 1,382$700, were 37.8 percent higher than 1875 prices, 1,003$460, as can be seen in de Mello (1977), Table 16.

18. The total sample consisted of 1,004 male and female slaves from ages sixteen to sixty. For the year 1887, prices from 363 slaves in the Rio de Janeiro (city) *Cartas de Libertação dos Escravos* were used; for the other years, Rio de Janeiro (province) coffee plantation inventories: 226 slave prices (1858), 277 (1875), and 138 (1883). For list of sources see de Mello (1977), App. B.

19. The three best sources for a description and analytical interpretation of the abolitionist movement are Da Costa (1966), Conrad (1972), and Beiguelman (1966).

20. Law of November 7, 1831, prohibiting the African slave trade, which was never enforced.

21. For the abolition of the African slave trade, see Bethell (1970).

22. *South American Journal and Brazil and River Plate Mail* (1885), 305.

23. *South American Journal and Brazil and River Plate Mail* (1885), 306.

24. Conselheiro Martim Francisco, Acta da Conferencia de Estado, June 25, 1884, quoted in Barboza (1884), 17.

25. The use of the estimated 13 percent rate of return on the investment of slaves (as presented in #5, *TP*, Vol. I). This volume would not alter the results.

26. For data on the life expectancy of slaves see de Mello (1977), Ch. 3, 123, Table 31.

THIRTY-THREE

Sharecropping as an Understandable Market Response: The Postbellum South[*]

Joseph D. Reid, Jr.

On the eve of the Civil War southern per capita real income was 80 percent of northern. Treating slaves as property, real income per free Southerner was 4 percent greater and growing at the same rate as its northern counterpart. Southern per capita income was but 51 percent of the national average in 1880 and only slowly began to relatively advance after 1900.

Hypotheses advanced to explain the postbellum South's poor relative per capita income performance typically fall into two classes: (1) explanations which identify the postbellum stagnation as a continuation of the South's alleged antebellum stagnation and (2) explanations which attribute the postbellum stagnation to agricultural inefficiencies stemming from the fall in average farm size, the rise of sharecropping, or the monopolistic exploitation of southern agriculture by ubiquitous country stores. The South's antebellum relative income record casts immediate doubt on type 1 explanations. One may debate whether the slave-inclusive or slave-exclusive antebellum income relative is more relevant, but each is high and growing relative to its postbellum counterpart. Non-existent antebellum stagnation seems a poor direct precedent for postbellum stagnation. Indirectly, however, racism may have been an antebellum heritage. Racism clearly was a characteristic of antebellum southern society which remained a virulent force in the postbellum period; but racism must have market ramifications to affect the rate and direction of economic development.[1] Hence, these potentially competing explanations are often merged, with racism cited as the underlying motivation behind *inefficient* postbellum developments in southern agriculture; the fall in average farm size, the rise of sharecropping, and the transfer of crop liens to country stores.

*Reprinted, with revisions, from the *Journal of Economic History* 33(1973):106–130. © The Economic History Association. Reprinted with the permission of Cambridge University Press.

The remainder of this paper cites postbellum agricultural contracts supporting the applicability of a new theory of agricultural tenancy choice. Evidence and theory combined imply that the rise of tenancy should have *increased* southern agricultural productivity, *ceteris paribus*. Thus the postbellum fall in southern agricultural productivity cannot be directly attributed to the rise of tenancy. Space limitations prevent consideration of the efficiency implications of country stores within this paper, but the extensive competition among stores for the southern rural trade makes an appeal to their alleged monopolistic depredations of questionable fruitfulness.[2] By elimination, the fall in available supplies of agricultural capital (occasioned by the Civil War) and labor (occasioned by emancipation) emerges as the likely explanation of the precipitous fall in southern relative income between 1860 and 1880.[3]

THE IMMEDIATE POSTBELLUM PERIOD

Effective emancipation in the cotton South forced a hasty reorganization of the black labor force to secure the harvest. Planters generally reinstituted antebellum financing arrangements with surviving factors and offered money wages or crop shares plus specified rations and garden rights to freedmen for resumption of slave-style work-gang employment in the cotton fields. Alonzo T. Mial's 1866 contract with twenty-seven blacks to work his Wake County, North Carolina, plantation is typical in its specification of the length of the working day, from sunrise to sunset "and when ever necessary even after sunset to secure the crop from frost, or taking up fodder or housing cotton in picking season after the days work is over, or any other small jobs liable to loss by not being attended to the night before." Mial specified the summer dinner period to be from 12:00 to 1:30; in other seasons 12:00 to 1:00 was allotted for dinner. Farther south, the dinner period lengthened. Mial followed his fellow planters in pledging his laborers to

> do our work faithfully and in good order, and . . . be respectful in our deportment to the said Mial & family or superintendent. That we will work under the directions and management of the said Mial or any superintendent. . . . That we will attend to the plantation on Sundays, and will be responsible for the loss or damage from neglect . . . of all tools placed in our possession.

Mial's laborers followed custom in agreeing that "all loss of time from sickness or absence with leave will not be paid for [by Mial]," and that unexcused lost time would be paid for (to Mial) at double wages. Mial's laborers were representative in agreeing "one half of our monthly wages shall be retained by the said Mial till the end of the year, and the amount so retained shall be forfeited by a violation of this contract on our part." In return, Mial agreed to pay each laborer at the stipulated rate of $10 plus 15 pounds of bacon and 1 bushel of meal per month per full-hand (women and children received less money and bacon), to sell additional provisions "as I may have to spare at the retail shop price in the City of Raleigh," and to give them half of every other Saturday outside the cotton-planting or -picking season for their own time as well as use of animals and tools "for a small crop."[4]

Peter B. Bascot went into even more detail contracting with forty-one freedmen to work his South Carolina plantation during 1866. After requiring the freedmen "to conduct themselves faithfully, honestly, civilly: & diligently to perform all labor," he defined daily work measures: "The said servants agree to perform the daily tasks hitherto usually allotted on said plantation, to wit: 125 to 150 rails; cutting grain, 3 to 6 acres; ditching and banking, 300 to 600 feet; hoeing cotton, 70 to 300 rows, an acre long; corn, 4000 to 6000 hills. In all cases where tasks cannot be assigned, they agree to labor dilligently ten hours a day." After proclaiming fines for missed work (50 cents per excused day, $2 per unexcused day) which accrued "to the benefit of the employer & employees in proportion to their relative shares" and charging the hands to "take good care of all utensils, tools & implements" and "keep their houses, lots & persons in neat condition," Bascot agreed

> to furnish each family with quarters on his plantation, with a fourth of an acre of land for a garden, & the privilege of getting firewood . . . & to divide the crop with them in the following proportions, viz: to the hirelings one third of the corn, peas & potatoes gathered & prepared for market; one third *net* proceeds of the ginned cotton, or its market value at the time which it may be sold; & when practicable to furnish the usual bread & meat rations to be accounted for at the market price out of their share of the crop.

Bascot further agreed to furnish necessary tools and furnish and feed the work animals. He closed with the stipulation that the record of fines and advances would be binding upon the laborers and granting his permission for each laborer "to keep two hogs, & ten head of fowls, but at his own expense." The agreeing laborers were rated full-hand, three-quarter-hand, half-hand, or quarter-hand. Three signers were designated "foreman," "stockman," and "nurse."[5]

Thomas Johnston likewise contracted with laborers to work a Marengo County, Alabama, plantation in his charge for 1866. At each laborer's option, he could work for a monthly money wage or a proportional share of one-fourth of the crop.[6]

THE RISE OF TENANCY

Work-gang agriculture under similar contracts continued throughout the South during Reconstruction and beyond,[7] but its importance in total agricultural production was greatly reduced. The relative abandonment of work-gang labor is commonly attributed to planters' disenchantment with intraseason competition for labor and laborers' disappointment with the received fruit. High expectations for cotton prices and initially auspicious growing conditions led planters to entice one another's labor with rising wage promises. The Black Codes' stern penalties for "vagrancy" and "enticing" and recurrent attempts to organize planter cartels were insufficient to stifle the upward pressure on wages. Labor often migrated in midseason and the planters spent much time trying to secure their work forces. Falling cotton prices (often joined with army-worm depredations) evaporated a large portion of the planters' and freedmen's expected earnings.[8] Perhaps an additional motivation for the freedmen to make their working terms more desirable was the dying out of their hope to receive 40 acres and a mule from the U.S. government. President Johnson thwarted the radical Republicans' land confiscation measure by wholesale amnesty of ex-Confederates. Efforts to forfeit southern railway grants were blocked by their northern owners. Hence, congressional land acts to aid the freedmen were confined to extending the Homestead Act to the 46 million acres of public domain in the South—land heavily forested or of poor soil quality (Pope 1962; Gates 1940).

By 1867 a majority of planters and laborers were ready to explore alternative crop-making arrangements. The emergent solution was renting (usually for a fixed crop payment) and sharecropping (for a specified share of the total crop, generally one-half). When (in November 1867) the editor of the *Southern Cultivator* stated that "experience of the past two seasons has demonstrated that plantations on an extended scale, with free labor, cannot be made profitable," and urged, "the first change that must occur . . . is the subdivision of landed estates,"[9] the called-for subdivision was already occurring throughout the South.

One result of substituting renting or sharecropping for work-gang labor was a fall in average farm size. In 1870 average farm size in the cotton South was 60 percent of its 1860 level; in 1880 average farm size was 39 percent of its 1860 level.[10] Whether this fall in farm size directly occasioned agricultural inefficiency is still a hotly disputed question. Gavin Wright's (1969, Ch. 4) regressions of antebellum cotton output per laborer against scale variables found no indication of economies of scale. Wright's results may just reflect proportionality between cotton harvested and the labor force harvesting or biases in his sample selection procedure.[11] Historians arguing a priori for economies of scale in antebellum agriculture, however, have generally made much of the slaveowners' power to coerce labor, a foundation unavailable for postbellum analysis. Postbellum planters seemingly felt the work-gang system more conducive to effective direction of the labor force, but apparently not worth the requisite wage premium.[12] Hence, it seems safe to conclude that postbellum economies of scale, if any, were small and couldn't directly account for a significant portion of the decline in southern agricultural income.

In 1880 17 percent of farms in the cotton South were rented and 28 percent were sharecropped. The corresponding percentages were 12 percent rented and 26 percent sharecropped in the former Confederacy. At the same time, 8 percent of all United States farms were rented and 18 percent sharecropped (Ransom and Sutch 1970a, Table 7).[13]

Whatever tenancy's initial reception, commentators rapidly came to be highly critical, especially of sharecropping. Contemporary arguments against tenancy were essentially two: (1) tenancy is inherently inefficient, for it removes the laborer from the control and direction of knowledgeable planter management and encourages his laziness and (2) tenancy unfortunately leads to agriculture's thralldom to a merchant class with resultant overproduction of cotton. The arguments were often joined.[14]

Contemporary southern criticism of inherent inefficiencies in tenancy rested on the supposed ignorance and sloth of Negro labor not directly supervised by whites. Georgia's commissioner of agriculture believed that "it is not reasonable to suppose that men, naturally indolent, ignorant and superstitious, mere muscular automata by habit, having been accustomed to direction even in the minutia of their work, could, by a presidential proclamation, be converted into intelligent and reliable business managers."[15] To this general indictment, more sophisticated critics appended a presumed implication of tenants' short-term interest in the land—wasteful cultivation practices (Hilgard 1884, 78–79). Economists have generally supported this contention that divorce of land cultivation from landownership will lead to inefficiency, and, in the specific case of sharecropping, have suggested this inefficiency will be compounded by the laborer's reluctance to fully apply himself to the soil. Alfred Marshall (1920, 642–644), noting the landlord's interest in preserving his soil's fertility and presuming his greater capability to finance permanent improvements, downplayed the possibility of *renting* leading to wasteful cultivation. Marshall felt the landlord would guard his land from tenant misuse. However, Marshall employed the (then) recently elaborated marginal analysis to show that an unrestrained sharecropper would pace his application of labor so as to equate his marginal product to a multiple of his opportunity wage rate and consequently supply less labor per unit of sharecropped land than a renter or owner would. Marshall noted that this inefficiency of sharecropping would not occur if the landlord could regulate his tenants' labor, and speculated that impermanence of tenure might be a sufficient landlord guarantee of an optimal rate of labor supply to sharecropped land.[16] Except for a recent deviation, economists have largely ignored Marshall's speculation and condemned absentee renting and sharecropping as inherently inefficient.[17]

The deviant, Stephen N. S. Cheung, founded his generally misunderstood critique of economists' traditional sharecropping analysis by noting that the simultaneous existence of alternative tenure arrangements combining homogeneous land with homogeneous labor in a competitive regime without transactions costs and uncertainty *should* equalize factor reward across tenures. Competition among tenants for land should ensure that landlords get at least the opportunity product of their land in (equivalent) rent; competition among landlords for tenants should ensure that tenants receive at least the opportunity wage for their effort; the coexistence of owning, renting, and sharecropping should equate respective factor rewards regardless of tenure. By constraining the landlord's objective function to (equivalently) pay sharecrop labor its opportunity wage, Cheung (1969, Ch. 2) derived first-order conditions for a landlord optimum which indeed implied the above results. As Marshall (1920) and D. Gale Johnson (1950) previously noted, in a two-factor (land and labor) model, this required that labor's input rate be contractually stipulated. In another paper (Reid 1976) I derive Cheung's constraint that landlords pay laborers their opportunity wage as a first-order condition of a general equilibrium model simultaneously embracing landlords and tenants. I also show that contractual stipulation of labor's supply rate is a prerequisite *in a two-factor model,* but is not necessary if there is a third factor whose variable supply rate is under the landlord's control, for example, managerial assistance.[18]

This model implies that sharecropping and renting were not inherent sources of agricultural inefficiency in the postbellum South. The postbellum planter's participation in tenancy contracts did not require him to be lazy, contrary to the allegations of his contemporary scientific agriculturalists, nor a racist willing to forgo money for control over tenants.[19] A necessary (but not, of course, sufficient) condition for viewing the southern landlord as an income maximizer is that he took active steps to guard his land's fertility and ensure the proper application of labor. Additional supporting evidence would record changes in tenancy contracts in response to fluctuations in factors' opportunity wages or crop price or yield conditions.

Brooks (1914, 440) reported that Georgia landlords didn't abandon their land to sharecroppers: "The supervision of his [tenants'] operations is as close as the planter can make it." And later he says, "Instead of standing over the gang of laborers constantly, the owner or his representative now rides from farm to farm, watching the state of the crop, deciding on the method of cultivation, requiring the tenant to keep up his property, and above all enforcing regularity of work" (1914, 458). Rupert Vance (1929, 163) found that "Sunday is occasion for the vigilant landlord to visit his farm, walk over his acres, and inspect the crop. The tour often ends with a visit to the tenant's shack and much good advice." David Harris of Spartanburg, South Carolina, subdivided his plantation in 1867. Like many postbellum landowners, Harris farmed a portion with hired help under his direction and rented or went shares on the remainder. His journal records him diligently watching his tenants—some renting for a fixed amount of crop, some on shares and one freedman renting one field for a fixed rent and another for two-thirds of its yield plus a bale of cotton. After surveying his various tenants' preparations, Harris concluded his March 25 entry by writing, "I think I have rented my land for about as much as I usually made with my negroes and mules."[20] However, at the end of the year, Harris refused to renew a disappointing renter's contract and only after much debate renewed a contract with another share tenant. The remaining tenants' leases he apparently renewed without change.[21]

In 1872 Charles H. Rice of St. Paul's Parish, South Carolina, let land to T. G. Smith and agreed to furnish Smith a mule and half its feed in return for one-half of the yield secured employing Rice's mule and one-quarter of the remainder. Smith agreed to "plant and cultivate the same in corn cotton Rice Pease & potatoes in sutch proportions as the said parties may agree upon, work the same in due time and keep it in good order." At the same time Rice renewed a contract with B. Kelley. Their original contract gave Kelley the right to two years of rent-free use of land he agreed to clear and three-fourths of the agreed-upon produce from previously cleared land. An 1872 amendment to their original contract ordered Kelley "to plant all the new land he has cleared . . . that is two years old as well as the old land he planted last year." Rice also converted J. Smith's part money, part shares contract of 1871 into an all for shares contract, as usual, subject to the proviso of cultivation "in sutch proportions as the parties concerned may agree upon." In 1873 Rice and J. Smith continued sharecropping together and went halves in turpentine gathering on part of Rice's land. And in 1872 Rice renewed a one-fourth share lease with Henry Daniels, but reduced from twenty-five to twenty-three the acres allotted Daniels.[22]

In 1870, B. T. Blake shared his house and furnished J. A. Hundley with necessary implements and animals (as well as two milk cows) to specifically grow fifteen acres of cotton "around the stubly," sufficient "acres in the low ground of Poplar meadows . . . to make a crop for one horse and also lots for Potatoes Melons and other vegetables." In return Hundley agreed to grow at least six acres of lowlands in corn, to pay for all the wheat seed and guano used thereupon, and to give half the total crop to Blake. At the same time Blake "sold" P. Bryand a mare in return for a note due in one year and Bryant's promise to "clear, plant, and give one-fourth the yield from the lot of land known as the slave house." B. Price secured from Blake "thirty-five acres . . . which half he is to cultivate in Corn peas and Oats, punkkins" and ten acres of uplands "to be planted in cotton" in return for one-third of the crop. (In 1877 Price was renting land from R. Terrell for one bale of cotton.) I. Parr signed a similar contract with Blake, securing a mule and its feed in addition, for half the crop.[23] Blake assigned liens on all these crops to Alonzo Mial, who had opened up a general store in Raleigh that year.

Although now a storekeeper, Mial kept his own land in cultivation under a variety of contracts. For 1877 Mial gave N. Gunter use of the Scott Place plus implements, a mule with feed, seed, and half the guano in return for Gunter's promise "to cultivate the crop, to repair the fencing around the place, making it eleven rails high, to clean out the hillside ditches and cut new ones wherever required" and half of Gunter's crop. Mial also agreed to advance Gunter monthly supplies during the year up to $125. J. Phipps and T. Earp owned a horse, so Mial let "the burn mill pond field" to them and paid them $30 and animal feed in return for half their crop. Phipps and Earp were ordered to ditch and build a twelve-rail fence, as well as to cultivate all the land in "any . . . crops they may wish."

In 1866 Mial rented land and mule to A. Blake for 1,000 pounds of cotton and $20. Mial charged Blake "to feed and keep the mule in good work conditions and not to abuse the same nor to lend . . . the said mule to anyone." Blake also pledged to keep hillsides ditched where deemed necessary by Mial "to keep the same from washing." Mial further agreed to advance Blake 45 pounds of bacon, 3.5 bushels of meal, and the mule's feed per month—to be paid at harvest. A similar rental contract with P. Williams added "Williams agreed to do all things forre the preservation of said farm."

Mial's 1886 half-share contract renewal with Ira Richardson required Richardson's agreement "to work faithfully and dilligently without any unnecessary loss of time, to do all manner of work on said farm as may be decided by said Mial." Besides land, Mial furnished Richardson with mule and feed, implements, and seed; Mial agreed to advance Richardson 40 pounds of bacon and 3 bushels of meal per month up till harvest. Mial's similar sharecropping contracts with C. Pearce, G. Mial, H. Mial, A. Fostno, and F. Powell awarded all the cotton seed to the landlord and had the tenant pay for half of the fertilizers used. Mial's half-share contract with J. Pool for thirty acres directed Pool to plant six acres of cotton and the remainder in corn. Pool was also required to "labor on the construction & building of the Tobacco barnes"; specifically, Pool and his family were required "to cut the barn poles, to assist in raising the same, and do the dobbies" as well as put on the roof.[24]

In 1869 John Devereux let his farm, Old Quarter, to J. W. Newsome for three years in return for a quarter of the crop and Newsome's agreement to diligently guard the harvest and conduct the business in a "farmer like manner." Newsome also agreed that "[t]he cotton land shall be well manured at least one year in two," to employ a specified number of hands and mules in cultivation of the crop, and to "keep the ditches and fences . . . in good order." They further agreed that "[a]ll hogs sheep cattle horses or mules raised or fattened on the said farm shall belong absolutely" to the tenants and not be shared. Any irresolvable disputes between landlord and tenant were to be bindingly arbitrated by "three men one of whom shall be chosen by each party the two thus chosen to select a third" Devereux reserved the right to inspect the farm at any time. In 1872 Devereux attached similar conditions in renting Old Quarter to E. Smith for 15 bales of cotton.[25]

A. H. Arrington employed twenty-four freedmen on his Alabama plantation under his overseer's direction in 1867. In return for their labor, they received half the crop, less rations (at Mongomery prices), and a deduction of 75 bushels of corn and 2,000 pounds of fodder for each mule furnished by Arrington. At the same time another former slave, Richard, chose to work Arrington's adjoining Coleman and Eubanks' places for two-thirds of the crop (buying necessary mules from Arrington to be paid for at harvest). In 1868 Arrington continued his work-gang cultivation (with his share increased to two-thirds and the deduction for work animals ended), and expanded his sharecropping operations, that year taking one-third of the corn and fodder and one-fourth of the cotton.[26]

In 1872 E. Dromgoole furnished land, mules and feed, and tools to four tenants who promised "to work faithfully and diligently . . . and to cultivate the land properly" in return for half the crop. Apparently satisfied, Dromgoole renewed their contract in 1873 for $225 and one-third of the balance of the crop. For 1873 Dromgoole specified 1 ton of fertilizer (selected by him) should be applied, with expenses proportionately shared, tools expense would be split fifty-fifty, seed corn would be advanced at 50 percent interest, and that a crop of spring oats would be planted. He reserved the right to hire (at the tenants' expense) additional labor or penalize the original tenants if they were tardy in performance of their duties. Finally, Dromgoole required that he receive additional rent of 20 percent of the excess value of the crop if over $1,000.[27]

The appendix to this paper contains in its entirety an 1882 sharecropping contract, showing in detail what one North Carolina landlord required of his tenants. The contracts described are representative of many more postbellum tenancy contracts held in the cited archives. Since the archives' holdings are biased toward big landowners, they are probably a representative sample of the typical tenancy contract. Many contracts were very detailed, as Grimes's (in the Appendix to this paper) or Mial's, although many were less so. A typical share contract would require the tenant to diligently farm *and* perform specific non-crop related tasks, for example, fencing, clearing, or barn maintenance. Less frequently, the share contract would require the cropper to accept the advice given by the landlord, to plant specific crops in specific areas, or apply a unilaterally determined minimum amount of fertilizer. Ancillary expenses were most often shared in proportion to the parties' shares, but important exceptions were animal feed, seed, fertilizer, and other land improvement materials. Expense for the first was generally borne by the landlord where he supplied the work animals; the remainder were either supplied by the landlord or their application intensity was unilaterally decided by him regardless of contractual expense shares. When the depreciation-investment nature of these expenditures is noted, it is economically appealing that landlords took extraordinary steps to ensure their assets' survival. Although "fifty-fifty" or "third and fourth" are good general summaries of standard sharecropping contracts, they are incomplete. The specific expense allocations and duties (and therefore the true share rates) varied over time and across regions of the South contrary to the tenor of uniformity in share terms received from Hilgard's survey and repeated by subsequent historians. The impression of much variation in individual terms revealed by these sample contracts is supported by other independent investigations. For example, Harry Hammond's 1880 summary of South Carolina sharecropping terms reported the landlord generally received half the crop when he furnished tenants with tools, stock, and stock feed besides, but that "[i]n Greenville and in portions of [Fairfield and Spartanburgh counties] the laborer takes one-third and the landlord two-thirds under the above conditions" (Hilgard 1884, 2:522). Wharton ([1947] 1965, 69–70) found tenants' shares varied inversely with land quality in postbellum Mississippi. Brooks (1914, 484–493) observed that rising cotton prices in Georgia were accompanied by modifications in share contracts. Variations in side-payment terms among the three South Carolina sharecropping contracts cited by Rosser H. Taylor (1943, 125–127) imply a 9 percent change in the cropper's average gross income.[28] As illustrated above, land per cropper also varied and length of tenure correlated with satisfaction given.

Fixed-rent contracts similarly varied with time, location, and tenant duties (Banks 1905, 87). Landlords often placed specific contractual restraints upon tenants to guard against deterioration of land and capital (instructions regarding drainage, type of plowing permissible, number and type of crops allowed, maintenance of fences and buildings, prohibitions upon stock grazing in clover or fallow, and instructions regarding manures and commercial fertilizer).

The picture of the postbellum agricultural labor market gleaned from rental and sharecrop contracts reveals much economically intelligible variation. It is variation about a mean, to be sure: fifty-fifty sharecropping or 1,000 pounds of lint cotton for a "one-horse" farm. However, much truth of the postbellum South is not revealed by this mean, but by the nature and scope of variation about it. Of course, written tenancy contracts at best imperfectly record the true relations between landlords and tenants. Custom seems, if anything, a more powerful constraint upon postbellum contracts than upon current contracts. But the custom evidenced is one of *greater* landlord control over tenants than typically contractually indicated, not less. The story of close landlord-tenant interaction told by Banks, Brooks, Range, Vance, and Williamson is convincingly supported by the journals and letters in southern archives. As will shortly be evident, I believe the nature of landlord-tenant interaction under different contracts was an important determinant of tenure choice. Johnson's (1950, 118) assertion that "there is no evidence that the rental share varies with the intensity of cultivation" is probably invalid for post–World War II Iowa, and is certainly invalid for the postbellum South where contract terms clearly changed and land migrated among tenures and tenants.

TENURE CHOICE

In his attack on economists' traditional analysis of sharecropping, Cheung (1969, 62–72) observed that agricultural production is subject to much price and yield uncertainty which is differently distributed between landlord and labor under alternative contractual arrangements. Owner cultivation with fixed-wage work gangs distributes all income uncertainty to the tenant; sharecropping distributes income uncertainty between landlord and tenant in proportion to their respective shares.[29] Cheung speculated that contractual negotiation and enforcement costs (transaction costs) would be higher for sharecropping contracts than for rental or owner-cultivation contracts. Assuming all parties to be risk averse (such that a certain income would be preferred to an uncertain income of equal average size), he hypothesized "the choice of contractual arrangement is made so as to maximize the gain from risk dispersion subject to the constraint of transaction costs" (1969, 64). Assuming that transaction costs were highest for sharecropping contracts, he reasoned share tenancy would only be preferred if agricultural income variance were high and other risk dispersal means (such as futures markets in contemporary agriculture) were even more costly.[30]

Risk sharing restrained by higher transaction costs seems at best a partial explanation for sharecropping's prevalence in the postbellum South. Dividing the standard deviation of corn and cotton annual per acre yields by their respective mean yields as an index of crop uncertainty, Table 33.1 shows that the ranking by

Table 33.1. Yield Variation and Extent of Sharecropping by Race, 1910

State	Corn			Cotton		
	Yield Variance[a]	Percent Black Share-cropping[b]	Percent White Share-cropping[b]	Yield Variance[a]	Percent Black Share-cropping[b]	Percent White Share-cropping[b]
North Carolina	0.095	49.5	23.2	0.096	55.1	28.6
South Carolina	0.237	34.6	16.5	0.158	41.6	20.6
Georgia	0.099	39.3	22.7	0.125	42.5	27.2
Florida	0.100	12.5	6.3	0.120	16.7	9.9
Tennessee	0.159	38.7	23.8	0.143	34.3	26.3
Alabama	0.173	25.8	21.6	0.133	23.9	23.9
Mississippi	0.204	38.2	16.9	0.125	41.5	19.6
Arkansas	0.230	32.9	23.6	0.145	40.0	28.4
Louisiana	0.150	58.3	16.7	0.248	61.2	18.6

[a]Coefficient of variation computed from average yields, 1900–1909, in Higgs (1973), Table 2.
[b]Percentage of specific crop acreage sharecropped, by race, from U.S. Bureau of the Census (1918), 623–624.

proportion of each crop sharecropped was the *opposite* of the relative uncertainty ranking in half of the considered cases. This should not be a surprising result, even though postbellum participants were clearly aware of the risk-distribution implications of the alternative contracts.[31] In general equilibrium the supply of southern land and labor interact with the degree of landlords' and labor's risk aversion to uniquely determine total expected agricultural income and income's total standard deviation, the unique aggregate distribution of both between landlords and labor, labor's certain wage rate, land's certain rental rate, and society's risk premium.[32] Taking these rates as parameters and assuming equal per acre contracting (transaction) costs regardless of tenure, any individual laborer or landlord maximizes his utility by choosing his optimal expected income and standard deviation, constrained only by his endowment of land and labor. This process is illustrated for a southern laborer in Figure 33.1, where expected income is measured along the vertical axis and income uncertainty along the horizontal axis. With an endowment of L labor units, the laborer could work for wages and receive certain income W equal to the established wage rate multiplied by his labor endowment L. Alternatively the laborer could allot all his labor to sharecropping, raising his expected income to I_s, but at the expense of raising his income uncertainty to V_s. If he decided to allot all his labor to renting, he would have an expected income of I_R and income uncertainty of V_R. The triangle OWR comprises the set of possible expected income-uncertainty pairs for a laborer with this endowment. Because the laborer is assumed to be averse to risk, his constant utility (indifference) curves are everywhere upward sloping. He will maximize his utility by equating his marginal rate of

Figure 33.1. Graphical representation of laborer's allocation of time among alternative tenures to maximize utility

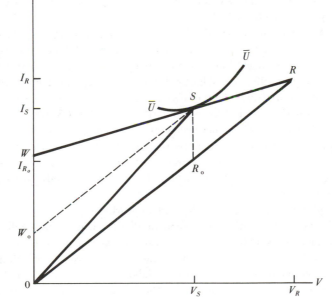

substitution between expected income and income uncertainty to the societal rate (given by the slope of line WR) along the WR ray.

For exposition, assume that this utility maximizing tangency occurred at S. The laborer could secure his utility maximizing expected income-uncertainty pair by allotting all his time to sharecropping (moving along the ray OS). Alternatively, he could allow OW_0/OW of his labor to work gang labor (thereby receiving income W_0 for certain) and W_0/OW of his labor to renting (receiving expected income I_{R_0} therefrom at the cost of uncertainty V_S) to achieve the same expected income-income uncertainty pair. These results hold equally for a landlord.

Neither at the aggregate nor individual level is there a unique relation between the extent of sharecropping and the degree of risk aversion. Clearly, if sharecropping's transaction costs were *higher* and risk shedding was its principal impetus, sharecropping would be seldom observed. Risk aversion and equal per acre contracting costs imply tenancy, but no determinate distribution of tenants between renters and sharecroppers. Risk aversion is an insufficient impetus for sharecropping.

The assumption of sufficient competition among landlords for tenants and among tenants for landlords to ensure against exploitation of either factor in the postbellum South seems more defensible. Brooks (1914, 407–408) reports substantial immigration of Negroes to regions of greater cotton productivity in immediate postbellum Georgia, with attendant pressure on landlords in less favored regions to increase labor's compensation. Wharton ([1947] 1965, 51, 104–112) cites similar evidence for Mississippi. And Vance (1929, 152) describes how "the last of December is for the cropper and [fixed rent] tenant a time for deals," with "[t]he landlord's questions . . . likely to deal with the crop made under the renter's former landlord, his reasons for leaving, the number in the family able to work, the acreage to be planted in cotton. The tenant wants to know the kind of house on the farm and the details of supplies to be furnished."

One reason often cited by landlords for abandoning for-wages work gangs was the difficulty of securing harvest labor. Tenancy supporters felt giving the laborer a stake in the crop encouraged him to labor diligently through the harvest (Hilgard 1884, passim; Banks 1905, 79; Wharton [1947] 1965, Ch. 3). The Negro is typically represented as desiring to rent or own land, so as to escape any vestiges of his antebellum status (Brooks 1914, 452; Wharton [1947] 1965, 63). The implied conclusion is that the rise of tenancy was totally induced by the changed conditions of labor supply, and sharecropping, in particular, was perhaps a racist compromise between landowners' and Negroes' desires. The latter conclusion seems especially questionable in light of the high proportion of southern whites also sharecropping (revealed by Table 33.1).

Labor's preference for tenancy instead of work-gang employment need not reflect an irrational land thirst, nor need landlords' acquiescence reflect impotence—and for reasons additional to risk aversion. As was noted by many of the respondents to Hilgard's survey, tenancy's incentive assured labor's diligence in farming and secured at lower cost a variable labor force (the tenant family) with a minimum of search or contractual negotiation. That cost may have been lower because of tenants' land thirst, but was certainly lower because the family (including the head) had a multiplicity of employment possibilities (housekeeping, children's education, hunting and fishing, livestock, raising, leisure, and crop tending) which could be pursued with varying relative intensity as the expected payoffs varied over the crop year. (Indeed, subsequent historians of the antebellum period may find that the slave work gangs were instituted to guard against runaways, not to enhance productivity.)

A major impetus for the coexistence of renting, sharecropping, and owner cultivation with fixed-wage labor may be sharecropping's *lower* transaction costs over the life of the contract. Agricultural production and deviation from expectation occur *over* the growing season. As the contracts cited earlier illustrated, the typical postbellum tenancy contract often specified many non-crop related duties and restraints to guard against deterioration of land or farm capital; some contracts specified crop proportions. As deviation from the prior expectation increased, so would the profitability of contract renegotiation between tenant and landlord. For example, if unexpectedly favorable weather over the first part of the growing season increased anticipated yield, the profitability of more intensive cultivation of the enhanced crops—to the neglect of less-favored crops and negotiated land maintenance or improvement duties—would rise. To efficiently take advantage of this unexpected situation, contractual renegotiation is required. Land maintenance duties and crop restrictions must be relaxed under a fixed-rent contract. Labor limitations on hours supplied or the variety of acceptable work must be relaxed under a fixed-wage contract. In the former case, such renegotiation might be restrained by disagreement between renter and landlord over their respective shares of the windfall. In the latter case, laborers and landlord would no doubt similarly contend over their respective shares. Landlord-labor strife might be sufficiently large to limit or eliminate productivity-enhancing contractual renegotiation within the crop year.

Under a share contract, both landlord and tenant have an immediate incentive to alter previously agreed upon production plans in response to deviations from initial expectation occurring over the contracts life.[33] Such renegotiation could occur informally and cheaply. The typical postbellum sharecropper pledged to perform his agreed duties to the satisfaction of his landlord. Merely by lowering the requisite level for accomplishment for "satisfaction" on relatively non-enhanced duties, advantage could be taken of the accumulating deviation from the initial expectation, mean income raised, and total income variance decreased.

On an *inverted* foundation, then, risk is an impetus for sharecropping. Sharecropping is not (necessarily) used to facilitate risk sharing, but to facilitate aggregate risk reduction. By encouraging both parties to the tenure arrangement to similarly respond to revisions in expectation over the crop season and by providing a cheap avenue for such response, sharecropping minimizes expected total risk from agricultural production.

While a sharecropping contract's incentive for profitable renegotiation over the crop year seems the cornerstone for understanding the relationship between agricultural uncertainty and sharecropping, this is not the only (and probably not even the main) impetus for sharecropping. *The central feature of a sharecropping contract is the continuing interest of both landlord and tenant in the efficiency of agricultural production.* The above theory requires such landlord-tenant interaction. Postbellum contracts and landlord's letters and journals record such interaction. Postbellum historians report such interaction.

This evidence clearly supports the contention that the sharecropping landlord supplied managerial expertise as well as land to his tenants. A sharecropping contract's commonality of factors' interests ensures the tenant of increased managerial direction when most profitable to both, while ensuring the landlord-manager that his exhortations won't fall on deaf ears nor need much repeating (in contrast to for-wages labor, for example). Such an arrangement economizes on required management time and, because of the strong incentive for self-management by the sharecropping tenant, permits greater flexibility in the delivery timing of the managerial input. Consequently, when the rewards from landlord supervision are high and/or landlords' alternative earnings fluctuate, sharecropping's guarantee of the tenants' attention may make it the preferred tenure.[34] This analysis implies that lesser skilled tenants and higher skilled landlord-managers would relatively prefer sharecropping. Similarly, as the managerial complexity of the crop increases (from the possibility of fruitfully applying fertilizer, for example), sharecropping should become increasingly preferred.

The cojoining of factors' interests under sharecropping emphasized above suggest additional reasons for the preference of sharecropping over renting. If tenants are poorer or less well known than landlords to purveyors of agricultural credit, lenders may supplement their investigation of tenants' credit worthiness with the landlord's evaluations. That a tenant has entered a sharecropping arrangement evidences his landlord's favorable evaluation of the tenant's productivity and guarantees the landlord's assistance in helping the tenant succeed. Such supplementation of the tenant's credit worthiness may partly explain the country stores' reported preference for sharecroppers in the postbellum South.

CONCLUSION

In this paper I have suggested the desirability of redistributing risk between landlords and labor, the possible increase in agricultural productivity from varying the intensity of managerial attention to labor (lowest with renting, intermediate with sharecropping, highest with work gangs), and increased competition for landlords' attention as important explanatory factors underlying the rise of agricultural tenancy (renting and sharecropping) in the postbellum South.

In particular, the cojoining of tenant-landlord interests under a sharecropping contract was identified as the distinguishing feature of sharecropping and as a determinant of the choice among tenure forms. Evidence of this cojoining in actual contracts and citations of landlords' journals and correspondence in southern archives, along with references to supporting historians, were presented. The choice of sharecropping over renting was explained by reference to sharecroppings' aggregate risk *reduction* (as opposed to distribution) potential. Its sharing features motivated the propitious cooperation over time of the interacting factors of land, labor, and (often) management; in addition, its information-enhancing effect made it attractive to agricultural creditors.

The analysis clearly reduced (if it did not eliminate entirely) the role of "land thirst" and "racism" in explaining the postbellum rise of tenancy. Further, no theoretical rationale for agricultural inefficiency was found in the analysis of tenure choice. Indeed, by permitting a more optimum distribution of management talent among tenants and a preferable distribution of agricultural risk between laborers and landlords, as well as facilitating risk reduction, the rise of tenancy should have increased southern agricultural productivity.

APPENDIX

GRIMES'S SHARECROP CONTRACT, 1882

To every one applying to rent land upon shares, the following conditions must be read, and *agreed to.*

To every 30 or 35 acres, I agree to furnish the team, plow, and farming implements, except cotton planters, and I *do not* agree to furnish a cart to every cropper. The croppers are to have half of the cotton, corn and fodder (and peas and pumpkins and potatoes if any are planted) if the following conditions are complied with, but—if not—they are to have only two fifths (2/5). Croppers are to have no part or interest in the cotton seed raised from the crop planted and worked by them. No vine crops of any description, that is, no watermelons, muskmelons, c——— or squashes or anything of that kind, except peas and pumpkins, and potatoes, are to be planted in the cotton or corn. All must work under my direction. All plantation work to be done by the croppers. My part of the crop to be *housed* by them, and the fodder and oats to be hauled and put in the house. All the cotton must be topped about 1st August. If any cropper fails from any cause to save all the fodder from his crop, I am to have enough fodder to make it equal to one half of the whole if the whole amount of fodder had been saved.

For every mule or horse furnished by me there must be 1000 *good sized* rails m———, hauled, and the fence repaired as far as they will go, the fence to be torn down and put up from the bottom if I so direct. All croppers to haul rails and work on fence wherever I may order. Rails to be split when I may say. Each cropper to clean out every ditch in his crop, and where a ditch runs between two croppers, the cleaning out of that ditch is to be divided equally between them. Every ditch bank in the crop must be shrubbed down and cleaned off before the crop is planted and must be cut down every time the land is worked with his hoe and when the crop is "laid by," the ditch banks must be left clean of bushes, weeds, and seeds. The cleaning out of all ditches must be done by the first of October. The rails must be split and the fence repaired before corn is planted.

Each cropper must keep in good repair all bridges in his crop or over ditches that he has to clean out and when a bridge needs repairing that is outside of all their crops, then any one that I call on must repair it.

Fence jams to be done as ditch banks. If any cotton is planted on the land outside of the plantation fence, I am to have *three fourths* of all the cotton made in those patches, that is to say, no cotton must be planted by croppers in their home patches.

All croppers must clean out stables and fill them with straw, and haul straw in front of stables whenever I direct. All the cotton must be manured, and enough fertilizer must be brought to manure each crop highly, the croppers to pay for one half of all manure bought, the quantity to be purchased for each crop must be left to me.

No cropper to work off the plantation when there is any work to be done on the land he has rented, or when his work is needed by me or other croppers. Trees to be cut down on Orchard, House field & Evanson fences, leaving such as I may designate.

Road field to be planted from the *very edge of the ditch to the fence,* and all the land to be planted close up to the ditches and fences. *No stock of any kind* belonging to croppers to run in the plantation after crops are gathered.

If the fence should be blown down, or if trees should fall on the fence outside of the land planted by any of the croppers, any one or all that I may call upon must put it up and repair it. Every cropper must feed, or have fed, the team he works, Saturday nights, Sundays, and every morning before going to work, beginning to feed his team (morning, noon, and night *every day* in the week) on the day he rents and feeding it to and including the 31st day of December. If any cropper shall from any cause fail to repair his fence as far as 1000 rails will go, or shall fail to clean out any part of his ditches, or shall fail to leave his ditch banks, any part of them, well shrubbed and clean when his crop is laid by, or shall fail to clean out stables, fill them and haul straw in front of them whenever he is told, he shall have only two-fifths ($2/5$) of the cotton, corn, fodder, peas and pumpkins made on the land he cultivates.

If any cropper shall fail to feed his team Saturday nights, all day Sunday and all the rest of the week, morning/noon, and night, for every time he so fails he must pay me five cents.

No corn nor cotton stalks must be burned, but must be cut down, cut up and plowed in. Nothing must be burned off the land except when it is *impossible* to plow it in.

Every cropper must be responsible for all gear and farming implements placed in his hands, and if not returned must be paid for unless it is worn out by use.

Croppers must sow & plow in oats and haul them to the crib, but *must have no part of them.* Nothing to be sold from their crops, nor fodder nor corn to be carried out of the fields until my rent is all paid, and all amounts they owe me and for which I am responsible are paid in full.

I am to gin & pack all the cotton and charge every cropper an eighteenth of his part, the cropper to furnish his part of the bagging, ties, and twine.

The sale of every cropper's part of the cotton to be made by me when and where I choose to sell, and after deducting all they may owe me and all sums that I may be responsible for on their accounts, to pay them their half of the net proceeds. Work of every description, particularly the work on fences and ditches, to be done to my satisfaction, and must be done over until I am satisfied that it is done as it should be.

No wood to burn, nor light wood, nor poles, nor timber for boards, nor wood for any purpose whatever must be gotten above the house occupied by Henry Beasely—nor must any trees be cut down nor any wood used for any purpose, except for firewood, without my permission.[35]

NOTES

1. Cf. Wharton ([1947] 1965), Stampp (1966), and Williamson (1965). C. Vann Woodward (1966) deemphasizes racism's virulence in the immediate postbellum period. In his view bourbon and mercantile factions were naturally competing for postredemption control. Both were neutral toward the Negro until the rise of serious agrarian protest in the 1880s made Negro disfranchisement mutually desirable to forestall future third-party movements.
2. The major historical treatments of southern country stores are united in finding an absence of evidence of monopoly profits or of monopolistic control in the stores' records. See Bull (1952); Clark (1964); and Woodman (1968).
3. Employing a Cobb-Douglas agricultural production function, however, Engerman (1971b) concluded that increased inefficiency in southern farming contributed at least as much to the relative income decline as wartime destruction.
4. Contract of January 29, 1866, from the Alonzo T. and Millard Mial Papers.
5. Contract of January 1, 1866, at Darlington District, South Carolina, from the Bascot Papers (#916).
6. Contract of January 1, 1866, from the Johnston-McFaddin Papers (#2489).
7. See I. F. Lewis's contracts for 1874 and 1884 in the Lewis Plantation Records (#2528).
8. See Wharton's ([1947] 1965) description of the immediate postbellum in Mississippi and Williamson's (1965) parallel description of South Carolina.
9. Quoted in Brooks (1914), 45.
10. See Ransom and Sutch (1970a).
11. Robert Fogel and Stanley Engerman (1971c) have criticized Wright's exclusion of farms with extremely high or low corn/cotton ratios from his sample. If, as they believe, economies of scale encouraged relatively high cotton (low cotton) production on large (small) farms, Wright's sample band would bias inclusion toward super efficient small farms and super inefficient large farms with a consequent downward bias of estimated scale economies. A good review of prior debate over the existence of antebellum economies in cotton production is Woodman (1966). See especially the selections authored by J. E. Cairnes ([1863] 1966), Lewis C. Gray ([1933] 1966a; 1966b), Ulrich B. Phillips ([1903] 1966; [1905] 1966), and Robert R. Russel ([1938] 1966; [1941] 1966).
12. See responses to the question, "Does the share system give satisfaction?" at the end of each state's "Report on the Cotton Production" in Hilgard (1884).
13. See also U.S. Census Office (1897) 3:590.
14. See Hilgard's (1884), 78, description of Mississippi's labor system; Hammond (1897), 179, 187; Range (1955); Brooks (1914); and Stampp (1966).
15. Janes (1875), quoted in Ransom and Sutch (1970b), 75–76.
16. For the first economist's reservations about agricultural tenancy and sharecropping, in particular, see Smith ([1776] 1937), 367–368.
17. A representative sample of condemnation is Adams and Rask (1968); Bardhan and Srinivisan (1971); Bhagwati (1966), 152–157; Schultz (1965), 118–121, 167–168; and references cited in Cheung (1969) Chs. 1, 3. Post-Marshall tenancy condemnations ironically often cite his analysis to support their reverse contention that landlords are exploiting tenants.
18. This is an important generalization; Bardhan and Srinivisan (1971), 52, reject Cheung's model because Cheung maximizes "only from the landlord's point of view."
19. For such allegations see Banks (1905); Brooks (1914); Stampp (1966); and Taylor (1970).
20. From the David Golightly Harris Books (1867), M-982.
21. *Ibid.*, entries of December 14 and 25, 1867.

22. From the indicated contracts of Charles H. Rice in the John D. Bivens Papers (1871, 1872, 1873).
23. From the indicated contracts of B. T. Blake in the Mial Papers (1870).
24. *Ibid.*, from the indicated contracts of Alonzo T. Mial.
25. From the indicated contracts of John Devereux in the Devereux Family Papers (1869; 1872).
26. From the indicated contracts of A. H. Arrington in the A. H. Arrington Papers (1867; 1868) #3240.
27. From the indicated contracts of E. Dromgoole in the George C. Dromgoole Papers (1872; 1873).
28. South Carolina's average cotton yield, 1870–1890, was 158 pounds per acre. Multiplying this by thirty acres (the size of a "one-horse" farm) gives an average yield of 4,740 pounds of cotton, of which the sharecropper retained half or 2,370 pounds. At 10 cents per pound his average crop was worth $237. The reported side payment varied by $22, from $70 to $48.
29. Where contracts stipulate a fixed compensation in crop units rather than money, price uncertainty is always proportionately borne by each party.
30. Banks's prescient study of Georgia agriculture (1905), 92–100, also recognized the important risk and supervision dimensions of alternative tenures.
31. Cf. responses to Hilgard's (1884) survey about the desirability of sharecropping.
32. These results and those following are illustrated and proved in Reid (1976).
33. Parallel reasoning is extremely suggestive for the analysis of why firms give stock options to top management and the growth pattern of franchisers.
34. During southern Reconstruction the antebellum landowners' opportunities to regain their lost political hegemony by responding swiftly to fluctuations in federal policy may have put a high implicit value on their political participation and led landlords to sharecrop so as to minimize income fluctuations occasioned by their (politically prompted) frequent inattention to agriculture.
35. From the Grimes Family Papers (1882), #3357.

THIRTY-FOUR

"Bound" or "Free"? Black Labor in Cotton and Sugar Cane Farming, 1865–1880

Ralph Shlomowitz

Whether it is more accurate to describe black labor in cotton farming areas of the postbellum South as "bound" or as "free" and a related question—whether sharecropping had its origins in class conflict or in the free operation of market forces—have been among the focal points of debate in recent scholarship on the early postbellum period. According to Jonathan M. Wiener (1978), the operation of the labor market in cotton farming was restricted: Employers colluded to limit the competition for labor and placed restraints on the mobility of the freedmen, thereby curbing their access to alternative employment. Hence, he argues, sharecropping was "bound" labor (70), "coercive" (36), and "repressive" (53) labor control, which had its origins in class conflict. In contrast, according to Robert Higgs, Harold D. Woodman, and other scholars, a free market for labor in cotton farming was created: Employers competed freely for labor, and the freedmen were free to move in response to better job offers. Hence, they argue, sharecropping arose in response to market forces.[1]

Despite the importance of this set of topics for the study of southern history, relatively little historical evidence has been used to study the differences between these competing hypotheses.[2] This paper will attempt to contribute to the debate by assembling such evidence for the early postbellum period, 1865–1880, in which sharecropping had its origins.

Evidence on southern planters combining to set maximum wage levels and maximum shares of the crop to be paid to the freedmen consists primarily of reports by contemporary observers on the initial establishment of such combinations. An example is the report, published in 1868, that "planters of Talladega county [Ala-

*Reprinted, with revisions and additions, from the *Journal of Southern History* 50 (1984):569–596.
© 1984 by the Southern Historical Association. Reprinted by permission of the Managing Editor.

bama] organized a Farmers' Club for that county," one of whose objectives was "to regulate labor and make it uniform and profitable."[3] However, the significance of this evidence can be evaluated only in conjunction with further related evidence on whether these combinations were effective, whether the effective combinations persisted over time, and whether the influence of these combinations was more widespread than reports from isolated localities suggest. Such related evidence as does exist and a variety of other types of evidence, which will be presented below, suggest that both the overt and the covert arrangements made by employers probably were nothing more than fleeting experiments on a local scale. This was also the conclusion reached by the editor of a southern agricultural journal in reviewing the post–Civil War history of employers' combinations from the vantage point of the 1880s: "Co-operation among farmers has often been attempted but has never achieved any decided success."[4]

Contemporary commentators often observed with regret that there was no concerted action by planters who employed black labor.[5] They acknowledged, however, that such an objective was impractical because combinations were difficult if not almost impossible to effect.[6] A correspondent of a southern agricultural journal, for example, bemoaned that "it is proverbial that farmers cannot unite on 'anything.' "[7] The reasons for the lack of unity and for the difficulty in establishing and maintaining effective combinations are clear. Combinations were difficult to establish because organizing large numbers of widely dispersed farmers was expensive and because the interests of farmers in different localities, usually dissimilar with respect to soils, climates, and distances from transport networks and markets, diverged. These themes are succinctly brought out in the following report: "It is impracticable to control the operations of individual farmers by any sort of resolutions or covenants or pledges. There are too many of them; they are too widely separated; they cannot meet in mass conventions; their circumstances and surroundings are too varied and diverse."[8]

However, even in cases where these problems were surmountable and combinations could be established, their continued viability was precarious. Because individual members of a combination had the incentive to attract labor by secretly making offers in excess of the rates set by the combination, the behavior of the members of the combination had to be monitored and the rate provisions enforced. Such policing was difficult, and with reliance placed on "social pressure" as the sole disciplinary device, enforcement may not have been effective. Furthermore, the viability of combinations in particular districts depended on farmers in other districts following suit; otherwise, to the extent that freedmen were mobile, they were able to leave districts where low rates were set and seek jobs in other districts.

Despite such difficulties, contemporary observers repeatedly advocated the establishment of combinations that would effect "A well regulated . . . system of labor" with a "general plan of hiring" and so thwart the operation of free market forces.[9] These calls for cooperation would have been unnecessary had effective combinations been in existence; they are, accordingly, good supportive evidence for the hypothesis that competitive market forces were ascendant.[10]

A variety of other types of evidence can also be taken as indications of the dominance of competitive forces in the market for labor in the farming of cotton. In constructing a typology of these kinds of evidence, it will be useful to make a distinction between two broad classes of evidence: Direct evidence on the competitive behavior of employers consists of reports of employers bidding for labor by offers of higher remuneration and/or preferred working conditions; indirect evidence on the existence of competition consists of, among other things, reports of labor turnover and of the variety in the terms of labor contracts entered into by employers and employees.[11]

It should be noted that, whereas the relationship between the category of direct evidence and the degree of competition in the labor market is straightforward, the relationships between the types of evidence that make up the category of indirect evidence and the degree of competition in the labor market are often many, diverse, and complex. Accordingly, the validity and importance of some of the types of evidence that make up the category of indirect evidence must be treated with caution.

A considerable body of direct evidence on the existence of competition in the postbellum labor market in the farming of cotton can be reported. Contemporary articles and letters use such evocative expressions as employers were "tampering" with each other's labor, employers were "enticing" other employers' labor from them by better offers, employers were "outbidding" one another, employers were "pulling against" each other, there was a "lively competition" for labor, and there was a "scramble" for labor.[12] The following two overviews of developments in the post–Civil War agricultural labor market, made from the vantage point of the mid-1870s, are vivid illustrations of the competitive process at work. In 1874 a Georgia correspondent of a southern agricultural journal reported

> When the negroes were set free, many agriculturists . . . found themselves without laborers. . . . Each one said to himself . . . I must get laborers by some hook or crook, or I shall be ruined in a short time. —Under the circumstances, it is not at all strange, that the negroes have had things their own way to an alarming extent, and have been flattered and cajoled, and begged and implored, and whiskied and allowed latitude.[13]

In 1877 the editor of the same agricultural journal described the behavior of employers "during the past ten years" in the following terms: "Every one seemed to fear that everybody else would get ahead of him and that he would have no labor at all. Hence a universal rush at the negro—each out bidding the other, the negro in the mean time feeling like a maiden with a dozen suitors at her feet—entire master of the situation."[14]

The following are various types of indirect evidence on competition in the postbellum labor market in cotton farming areas. First, it appears that the freedmen changed jobs frequently.[15] The evidence suggests that these job changes were primarily voluntary resignations by the freedmen rather than discharges or layoffs over which the freedmen had little control. Unfortunately, little is known of the motivation of the freedmen making such job changes. Some planters and contemporary observers attributed the behavior of the freedmen to wanderlust, a love of change for its own sake.[16] Others said that job change was the result of the freedmen's search for the employers who offered the best terms.[17]

High job turnover rates are good evidence that the freedmen were not bound labor; they show that attempts to restrict the mobility of the freedmen were not effective. In addition, attributing job turnover to the search for better job offers is good evidence for the existence of competition for labor. However, most of the evidence on job turnover either attributes it to the love of change for its own sake or does not specify the cause; accordingly, for the purpose of ascertaining the degree of competition in the labor market, this subset of the body of evidence on job change should be discounted as it is consistent with the presence of either collective or competitive forces in the labor market.

A second type of indirect evidence relates to the freedmen's acquisition of information about various jobs (such as the offers made by various employers and on their reputation as fair employers), to their ability to bargain over terms of employment, and to their collective efforts in transmitting this market information and in pressing their demands.[18] These themes are well illustrated in the following newspaper report written in late 1866 by a correspondent from Georgia.

> Planters who have failed to pay their hands this year, or who have earned a reputation among the freedmen as hard and unjust task-masters, by the manner in which they have treated them during the past year, cannot secure labor for the future at any price. On the contrary, those who have paid well, fed well, and behaved well generally toward their employes [sic], find but little difficulty in obtaining the best of labor. Involuntarily and without premeditation, the freedmen have organized themselves into a protective association, prompted by mutual interest, which is as effective as any mechanics' union in the North, and already the South has commenced to feel the power of labor over capital. Slowly but surely, and by such indirect influences as this general protective combination, the freedmen are working a revolution in sentiment here which will finally result in their obtaining enlarged privileges from the hands of those who are not most violently opposed to them.[19]

A third type of indirect evidence relates to the variety of contracts negotiated by planters and labor in the farming of cotton and to the variety in the rates of remuneration paid to labor.[20] This variety can be interpreted, as has been pointed out by William N. Parker (1980), in a number of different ways. It could reflect "how well tailored were the market devices to the matching of individual situations and preferences," "the perfectness of the exploitation, where landlords acted as a discriminating monopolist," or, more simply, the existence of a poorly arbitraged labor market (Parker 1980, 1030–1031).[21]

However, it is possible to distinguish in part among these interpretations. Contemporary observers acknowledged that economic factors were associated with the systematic variation in the shares going to labor under the share form of contract; other things being equal, a higher share would be given to labor working on relatively less fertile land; to labor who were more skillful and/or who were expected to work harder; on farms where relatively fewer horses or mules were in use and so relatively more of the labor had to be done by hand; in contracts that stipulated that labor was to perform, in addition to their work on the crop, relatively more general farm work, such as subsoiling, underdraining, collecting and spreading manure, erecting buildings and fences, and opening up new lands; and in contracts that stipulated that labor would receive relatively fewer special privileges in the way of clothing, the use of a few rent-free acres of land to grow their own crops, the use of the planter's work animals during their own time for working their own patches and for recreational purposes such as visiting a nearby village or town, and the permission to keep and pasture their own hogs, cattle, and cows on the property.[22] That the variation in shares is associated with economic factors is consistent with the view that, to an important extent, these shares were the outcome of the free interaction of market forces.

A fourth type of indirect evidence relates to year-to-year increases in the remuneration of labor. Unfortunately, statistical information on such year-to-year changes in the remuneration of labor under the fixed-wage or under the share system is very limited. However, there are some fragments of evidence that suggest that, in some instances, the share of the crop received by labor did increase in the first few years after emancipation, but caution should be used in generalizing on the basis of this evidence.[23]

A fifth and final type of indirect evidence relates to the complementary rewards to collusion in the product and labor markets in which southern planters operated. The South produced a substantial part of the world's cotton; accordingly, if southern planters had combined effectively they would have been able to not only set the level of labor's remuneration but also the world price of cotton. That southern planters were unable collectively to set prices in world markets for cotton is further support for the view that they were also unable to set the level of labor's remuneration.

A review of the above evidence suggests that a strong case can be made for the viewpoint that competitive forces in the postbellum market for cotton-farming labor were triumphant.[24] In contrast, successful combinations of employers in some sugar cane parishes of Louisiana can be documented. During much of the 1870s agreements were intermittently introduced by sugar cane planters in particular parishes, and they were reasonably effective in reducing wage levels over limited periods of time.[25]

The alternating periods of the ascendancy of competitive and collective forces in the labor market for sugar cane farming in these parishes can be briefly set out as follows: Initially, from 1865 to 1873, competitive forces were given free rein and wage rates appear to have increased steadily.[26] By 1873 adult male freedmen on annual contracts received between $18 and $20 per month with rations for their labor.[27] Through combinations these wage levels were reduced to $15 per month in Saint Mary and the other Attakapas parishes and to $13 per month with rations in the parishes of Saint James and Terrebonne for the 1874 crop year.[28] These lower wage levels persisted through 1875 and 1876.[29] At the end of 1876 this agreement broke down, and wage rates in 1877 returned to their 1873 competitive level of

$20 per month with rations.[30] In the parish of Saint Mary, the planters' combination was reestablished for the 1878 crop year, with the wage level being reduced to $15 per month with rations.[31] Although attempts were made to extend the geographical coverage of the Saint Mary combination, these efforts do not seem to have been successful, at least in the parishes of Saint James and West Baton Rouge.[32] However, the coverage of the Saint Mary arrangement appears to have been more widespread in 1879.[33] By 1881 wage rates were once again being determined by competitive forces.[34]

Thus it appears that during the 1870s collective activity by planters was localized to a subset of parishes in the sugar cane growing region of Louisiana, and even in those parishes its effectiveness was limited to a couple of specific time periods, namely, 1874–1876 and 1878–1879.[35] Many freedmen did not remain passive onlookers in the face of this concerted activity on the part of sugar cane planters. Their immediate reaction was to forge their own institutions and collectively withhold their labor from the marketplace. In the parish of Terrebonne, for example, "about two hundred plantation laborers . . . organized an association. . . . Binding themselves not to work for any planter for less that $20 per month, rations etc., the payments to be made monthly in cash."[36] In another locality such an association was called a "Laborer's Constitution."[37] An alternative strategy employed by some freedmen was simply to leave the plantation on which they had been working and seek out work in other parishes in which planters' combinations were not in force.[38]

The above discussion suggests that the competitive model is the appropriate framework for analyzing the position of black labor for the period from 1865 to 1880, the bounds set by this paper, in the farming of cotton and for the period from 1865 to 1873 in the farming of sugar cane.[39] Thus, from 1865 to 1873, the period when the major changes in southern agricultural work institutions were being crystallized, labor markets in both cotton and sugar cane farming were dominated by competitive forces. An important consequence from this depiction of these labor markets follows; namely, that freedmen were able to influence some non-pecuniary aspects of their well-being through market processes. By having the opportunity to express their preferences on some non-pecuniary aspects of their employment in the marketplace, the freedmen had the means to determine some facets of how they worked and lived. This had an important effect on the choices available to the freedmen and on the circumstances molding their culture and life-style.[40]

The following work preferences were attributed to the freedmen. First, their desire for a degree of autonomy in the workplace is well documented in the literature. This was particularly reflected in their aversion to working in gangs that were closely monitored by the employer or his agent (an overseer, for example). An illustration of this distaste is the report by a newspaper correspondent in 1870 that the freedman does not "like the discipline, the working in gangs, the sharp, curt orders of the plantation system. It savors too much of Slavery."[41]

Second, the slaves and freedmen expressed a preference for some types of work over other types. Their rankings of these activities was such that, according to some commentators, the gathering of turpentine was one of the most-preferred activities while cultivating rice and sugar cane were among the least-preferred activities.

Turpentine is the crude sap of pine trees. To obtain it, various operations had to be performed: "boxing," chopping a cavity or "box" into the trunk of the tree for receiving the sap that flowed from the face of the trunk above it; "cornering," shaping the face of the box so that the sap is channeled into a corner of the box; "hacking" or "chipping," cutting off the bark and a few of the outer rings of wood above the box to stimulate the flow of sap; and "dipping," removal of sap from the box.[42]

The only two extant fragments of evidence on the attitudes of the slaves toward working on turpentine plantations contrast sharply with each other. Frederick Law Olmsted ([1861] 1953, 146) considered that the slaves "employed in the turpentine business . . . seem to me to be unusually intelligent and cheerful." Edmund Ruffin considered that this type of "labor they dislike very much, because it is solitary. The work is light & healthy, & the task easily performed. But each laborer is alone on his separate allotment of 10,000 trees. A negro cannot abide being alone—& will prefer work of much exposure & severe toil, in company, to any lighter work, without any company. Hence their aversion to the turpentine business" (Ruffin in Scarborough 1972, 52). After emancipation, two commentators argued that the freedmen had a preference for turpentine gathering over crop farming. The first, a newspaper correspondent, reported in 1866 from South Carolina,

A negro laborer's first choice is generally turpentine-making. It is singular, too; for while traveling through those pine woods, and seeing nothing but the few huts and the turpentine still amid such wilderness, I often wondered how man could thus content himself. I suppose the reason the negro's liking the turpentine the best is because the work is easy. The land is dry; there is little or no dust, and they are not exposed to the sun so much as in cotton and rice growing. All these combine to make turpentine-gathering pleasant and healthy labor.[43]

The second commentator, a traveler, also reported in 1866 from South Carolina,

I infer from all I saw and heard while in the northeastern section [of South Caro-lina], that the negroes at work in the pines are more generally contented than those on plantations anywhere in the State. There is more variety in the turpentine and rosin business than in cotton-growing; and though the work may be harder for one or two days in any given week, there are other days in which there is little to do."[44]

Some distasteful aspects of turpentine gathering were mentioned by another com-mentator in 1867. He suggested that "hacking" was a "tedious sort of labor, little relished by the hands" and that with regard to "dipping," it was "very difficult now to find any hands willing to execute this branch of the business. Their hands and clothing became smeared with the gum, and even two dollars per diem will not now induce a piny woodsman or freed man to dip much turpentine."[45]

Contemporary perceptions of the freedmen's attitudes to rice and sugar cane farming were that they were widely considered to be among the most irksome of all branches of field labor and, accordingly, to be more dependent on the compulsion of

the slave labor system than any other type of agriculture.[46] Despite the fishing and
hunting that accompanied work in the rice swamps, the freedmen had to contend
with working in water, a most unhealthful environment, and summer harvesting.[47]
In sugar cane farming, the two-month harvesting-cum-milling season was particularly onerous; the manual harvesting of sugar cane and the loading of the cut cane
on punts or carts were among the most physically exhausting and punishing tasks in
agriculture, and milling involved long hours of labor, including night work.

A third type of work preference relates to the freedmen's attitudes toward
collective versus individual work patterns. It has been shown above that according
to the perceptions of contemporary commentators, slaves and freedmen disliked the
individual and solitary nature of work in turpentine making. It appears that they
rather preferred working with others (Stearns [1872] 1969, 517). This is clearly
seen in their enjoyment of the social interaction that accompanied special collective
tasks, such as logrolling, corn shucking, threshing jousts, and quilting bees.[48]
These became social events, festive occasions that had elements of a frolic with
singing and plenty to eat and drink. Rivalry between carefully selected work groups
and the excitement of the work song elicited exceptionally hard work from slaves or
freedmen.

Slaveowners, accordingly, fostered such work institutions. Sugar cane planters
realized, for example, that by making the sugar cane harvesting-cum-milling season
a prolonged festive occasion, the harshness of working conditions during this season could be made more palatable. Some contemporary commentators actually
argued that the slaves preferred the harvesting-cum-milling of sugar cane to other
tasks involved in sugar cane culture and also to the picking of cotton. For instance,
Frederick Law Olmsted ([1861] 1953, 255) reported,

> Mr. R. said that his negroes were as glad as he was himself to have the time for
> grinding arrive, and they worked with greater cheerfulness than at any other season
> . . . the reason of it evidently is, that they are then better paid; they have better and
> more varied food and stimulants than usual, but especially they have a degree of
> freedom, and of social pleasure, and a variety of occupation which brings a recrea-
> tion of the mind, and to a certain degree gives them strength for, and pleasure in,
> their labour.

Olmsted went on to report that a slave in Louisiana told him that they like the
milling season "because it's merry and lively" (263). Immediately after the Civil
War, a correspondent of the Franklin *Banner* reiterated this viewpoint. He argued
that slaves

> who were employed on both cotton and sugar plantations preferred making sugar.
> . . . The picking of cotton is a constant monotonous business, employing from three
> to four months of the year, while sugar making takes only about two months or less,
> and is like a frolic. The hands were singing all the time, were well fed and cared for,
> and had syrup and molasses to eat at discretion, and on many plantations had coffee
> to drink at the proper times; and the sugar-making season was generally, too the
> most delightful weather of the whole year, as good as could be wished.[49]

The above reports suggest that the slaves based their preference for sugar cane harvesting on both material and non-material considerations. It is not clear, however, if these non-material work preferences of slaves would have been carried over to freedom.

In making their choices among various jobs, the freedmen would have taken into account both the non-pecuniary characteristics of these jobs and the rates of remuneration offered by employers.[50] It is important to recognize, however, that these rates of remuneration were not determined independently and without reference to the non-pecuniary characteristics of the jobs. In fact, these rates of remuneration were directly affected by the process in which the freedmen expressed their non-pecuniary preferences in the marketplace. In particular, it can be argued that the freedmen were prepared to trade pecuniary gain for various non-pecuniary amenities of the jobs.

It is possible to confront the logic of the above line of reasoning with historical evidence. Two types of evidence can be presented. First, it has been shown that the freedmen considered labor in rice and sugar cane farming relatively more onerous than labor in cotton farming; accordingly, Louisiana rice and sugar cane planters, in order to attract the freedmen from labor in cotton farming, had to, and did, offer them rates of remuneration considerably higher than what they could have earned in cotton farming.[51] In addition, there is some evidence to suggest that the freedmen found having to contend with working in water in the farming of rice particularly onerous, and this is reflected in wage rates paid to workers in rice farming in Louisiana exceeding those received by the corresponding class of workers in sugar cane and cotton farming.[52] It should also be noted that the systematic difference in remuneration to labor in rice and sugar cane farming in Louisiana as compared to cotton farming more generally in the South, which can be explained by the existence and importance of non-pecuniary factors, is further evidence, albeit of an indirect kind, in support of the hypothesis that the labor market for the farming of these crops was characterized more by competitive that coercive forces.

Second, it has been shown that the freedmen generally desired autonomy and that they could obtain it under the sharecropping system. Each family worked a separate parcel of land in return for a share of the crop, and neither the property owner nor his agent monitored labor performance on a day-to-day basis. However, such autonomy could not be obtained under the fixed-wage system, which on plantations, was associated with closely monitored gang labor.[53] Accordingly, if property owners desired to induce the freedmen to sign fixed-wage rather than sharecropping contracts, they had to offer an income premium; similarly, the freedmen were prepared to receive a lower pecuniary income under the sharecropping as compared to the fixed-wage system in order to satisfy this non-pecuniary objective. This proposition is supported by the following qualitative evidence drawn from reports published in a southern agricultural journal.[54] The first report, in 1871, was from an Arkansas planter:

Our usual manner of hiring them or taking them as partners [under the share system], encourages their natural propensity to idleness. . . .

Now the remedy for this is to hire for wages, and let the laborer have no interest but that of *doing his duty or else get no pay.* But says one, how can I hire for wages when everybody hires on shares? Unless all hire for wages I cannot obtain labor. This seems to be a clencher [*sic*], as it is proverbial that farmers cannot unite on "anything." But is this in reality a barrier to hiring for wages? I think not. The law of "self-interest" generally governs the world—This is not so to any great extent with the indolent negro, the majority of them prefer "little work and little pay" to "big work and big pay." Yet there are a few of them that are governed by self-interest in the matter of hiring—Now let those "few" farmers who wish to hire hands for wages, make it to the "self-interest" of those "few" negroes to hire to *them* for *wages* instead of *cropping* with others. Of course they must do this by paying them more than said negroes can make under the cropping-system.[55]

The second report, in 1880, was from a Georgia planter:

In my section of the county, debating clubs are being, and have been, organized by the colored people, in which are discussed the propriety of working only upon the tenant system or for part of the crop raised. . . . The writer heard one of the speakers say that "the privilege which a cropper has over and above that allowed one working for stated wages, was worth $50 a year."

Now, this one word "privilege," this glorious word "privilege," which, properly analyzed by the colored man, means to work only when he feels like it, sums up the whole secret for this great rush among them from the wages into the cropping system of farming.[56]

It will be shown below that although the old plantation system was restructured in the farming of cotton, with sharecropping becoming the primary mode of organizing and paying for labor, it was retained using hired wage labor, in the farming of rice and sugar cane in Louisiana. The previously mentioned income differential between employment in rice and sugar cane farming, in Louisiana on the one hand, and cotton farming, more generally in the South on the other, can, accordingly, be considered compensation to labor for bearing the burden of two sets of negative non-pecuniary factors, namely, the backbreaking and unpleasant work in rice and sugar cane farming and the lack of autonomy under the wage system that was adopted in rice and sugar cane farming in Louisiana.

In the 1870s a number of surveys of cotton planters were made to discover what they considered the most profitable system, shares or fixed wages, for hiring the freedmen. The results of surveys of cotton planters in Georgia conducted from 1875 to 1877 showed that while fewer than one-third of the freedmen were hired under the fixed-wage system, two-thirds or more of the planters reported that the fixed-wage system was deemed the most profitable system to them.[57] However, in surveys of cotton planters conducted in 1879 as part of the tenth census, the advocates of the two systems were much more evenly matched in number, and in many regions of the South the share system was reported as giving general satisfaction to the employers.[58]

In contrast to this division of opinion among cotton planters as to the relative merits of the share and fixed-wage systems, it appears that the freedmen over-whelmingly preferred the share system. The body of evidence that documents the freedmen's preference for the share over the fixed wage system can be divided into two categories. The first category consists of contemporary reports that simply state that the freedmen had a preference for the share over the fixed-wage system,[59] while the second category consists of contemporary reports of the freedmen actually insisting on the adoption of the share system over the opposition of planters. Contemporary commentators used such expressions as the freedmen were "unwill-ing" or "refused" to work under the fixed-wage system, planters had to "yield" to the "demands" of the freedmen or not be able to secure labor, and the share system was a "concession" to the freedmen.[60] The following two reports are clear examples of the viewpoint that the freedmen were instrumental in bringing about the share system. In 1869 it was reported that "a share in the crops is the universal plan; negroes prefer it and I am forced to adopt it. Can't choose your system. Have to do what negroes want. They control the matter entirely" (Loring and Atkinson 1869, 32), and in 1870 a government report commented on the share system in the following terms: "It is not a voluntary association from similarity of aims and interests but an unwilling concession to the freedman's desire to become a proprie-tor."[61] More recently, Ronald L. F. Davis has also argued that the freedmen alone effected the share system. In the Natchez district, according to Davis (1981, 158), "Planters were dragged kicking and screaming into the [share] system because blacks refused to work in any other system of labor."

These sets of arguments can be conceptualized in terms of the framework that has previously been developed. The freedmen had a choice between employment at a fixed wage and employment for a share of the crop, and they would have based their decision on both pecuniary and non-pecuniary considerations. That the freed-men chose the share system in the farming of cotton implies that the income differential between what they could have earned under the wage system, at the current wage rate, and the share system, at the current share of the crop to be received by labor, was insufficient to compensate them for the harsh working condi-tions that accompanied the wage system. The logic of this line of reasoning implies that if working conditions were tolerable or if the wage rate was sufficiently high as, for example, what was being offered in rice and sugar cane farming, the freedmen would have been quite willing to work under the wage system. That southern cotton planters were not prepared to offer an income premium over what the croppers could earn under the share system implies that planters were not necessarily wed-ded to the wage system in the farming of cotton even though this system appeared to offer them control over the freedmen and their labor. To resolve this apparent paradox it is necessary to consider the special features of running a cotton farm under slave or free labor regimes.

The requirements of cotton farming were such that an assured labor force had to be on hand for the entire year so that the labor would be available to harvest what had been planted, and this labor force had to be depended upon to pay continuous and constant attention to the crop. The requirement for steady and diligent labor was particularly important during the so-called critical periods in the growth and maturing of the crop. One of these critical periods was when, after a heavy rainfall in the growing season, the cotton plant was engulfed in weeds and grass, and the entire labor force had to be mustered into service to save the plant by removing weeds and grass. Another of these critical periods was when, during the maturing season, the bolls had to be picked as soon as they opened; otherwise, they might be bleached by the sun or stained and soiled by rain, spoiling the color and quality and reducing their market value. Labor had to be performed promptly at these critical periods because neglect or suspension of work at such times could not be redeemed by additional work at a later stage. After a heavy rainfall in the growing season, for example, weeding the fields a few weeks later was futile; by that time the crop had already been lost.[62]

Accordingly, it was argued by a correspondent to a southern agricultural journal,

> On account of the pressure of work at these critical periods, a cotton plantation is obliged to be a despotism. Every one employed on it must yield to the urgency of the occasion, and submit implicitly to the will of the controlling mind; and he must have such a hold upon his hands, that he may retain them, and secure their labor at these critical periods.[63]

Such control was ensured under the slave system, and it was to be expected that after the Civil War planters would have been anxious to fashion a new labor system that would preserve as much as possible of this control. The problem of retaining the freedmen for the entire year was solved by instituting a system of annual contracts in which either a part or the entire payment to labor was postponed until the completion of the contract.[64] This could be effected by paying the freedmen a share of the crop, to be presented after the harvest, or by paying a fixed monthly wage, to be presented partly at the end of each month and partly at the conclusion of the contract. This "holdback" acted as a security deposit for the faithful performance of the contract and was forfeited when the contract was not honored. A further inducement to "localize" the freedmen was the provision of a few rent-free acres for their exclusive benefit; if the freedmen did not complete the contract, they forfeited all benefits accruing from these acres of land.[65]

The problem of getting the freedmen employed on annual contracts to pay constant attention to the crop throughout the year proved to be much more difficult. Planters found that they were unable to control their workers as formerly, in the old slave days. The labor supply had become uncertain.[66]

The fixed-wage system did not offer the planter enough control over the freedmen to secure their labor throughout the year and to provide sufficient labor at the most critical periods of the crop cycle.[67] The wage system was unable to provide this control because its disciplinary powers were insufficient. The system of annual labor contracts prevented a midseason reservoir of unemployed workers from which planters could replace workers who had been fired for shirking their tasks. Accordingly, the rate of dismissal from a plantation for neglect of work was much reduced. Instead of dismissing workers, planters levied fines, to be subtracted from their wages, for any neglect of work. Consequently the performance of labor had to be monitored, and this was costly because the workers were usually widely dispersed on the plantation. In addition, planters had to resolve disputes with their employees over fines for lost time.

The fine schedule was important. One contemporary commentator suggested the following schedule for loss of time:

> 1st. Time lost by actual sickness or other causes unavoidable on part of hireling, time to be charged at same rate of wages. . . . 2d. Voluntary loss of time, without consent of proprietor, this, as it often happens, at a time when their services are worth much more than at other times, should be charged for at much higher rates, always high enough to deter hands from such loss of time.[68]

It appears that fines for "voluntary loss of time" were not set at the prohibitive rate recommended above and seldom varied with the changing value of labor over the crop cycle; consequently their effectiveness as a deterrent was minimal.[69]

Thus despite their eagerness to control the labor of the freedmen, planters were deterred from embracing the system that would have given them the most control. The wage system was more costly than other systems and was also less effective than other systems in ensuring a supply of labor during the entire crop year.

The solution to the problem was the sharecropping system. Under this system, supervision costs could be reduced because the freedmen were allowed to manage their own time, and, by harnessing their self-interest, a supply of labor over the entire year could be ensured.[70] There is a wealth of evidence that planters and their spokesmen were aware of and spoke favorably of the incentive aspects of the share system and that their approval of the share system was not clouded by a recognition that to a substantial degree the system had emerged as a result of actions by the freedmen.[71] Other factors were also suggested by contemporaries as contributing to the popularity of the sharecropping system. They included, among other things, the disinclination of some planters to have anything to do with free labor[72] and the belief that, under the sharecropping system, labor would be available from women and children, who, perhaps for social reasons, had withdrawn from the plantation labor force.[73]

Hence it can be suggested that the adoption of the sharecropping system represented a convergence of the interests of most planters and freedmen, and many scholars of the postbellum South have concurred in this conclusion.[74] However, it is also recognized that there were planters and freedmen who did not support the adoption of the share system. Some planters tried to make the fixed-wage system work, and some freedmen preferred the fixed-wage system with monthly wages being paid in full at the end of the month's work.[75] These freedmen desired "immediate" and "certain" payment for their labor. This was a reflection of their preference for "ready money" over "delayed" payment, which was contingent on the success of the crop and the willingness of the planter to honor the terms of the contract.[76]

It would be incorrect to infer from the above analysis that the sharecropping

solution was instantaneously arrived at by planters and freedmen. Rather, it was
the result of an extensive period of experimentation that subsided a decade or more
after the end of the Civil War. A wide variety of contracts were initially tried by
planters and freedmen, and during this period they learned about the economic and
social advantages and disadvantages of each. Planters debated which type of contract would best suit their ends, and this issue was not settled early on. The protracted course of this debate can be illustrated by making reference to the reports of
the Georgia correspondent of *The New York Times* over a period from 1866 to 1870.
Initially, he reported that planters were enthusiastic in their support for the share
system. By January 1869, however, this support was wavering. Although it was
concluded that the share system was "the safest and best," he did point out that
"the long-mooted case of money-wages versus a share of the crop is still undecided"
and that the fixed-wage system "would be the best mode of compensation in the
interest of the planter if the negro would work." Thereafter, he reported that
planters had abandoned their support for the share system. In May 1869 he reported their support for one variant of the fixed-wage system, with wages being paid
in cash each quarter, while in January 1870 he reported their support for another
variant of the fixed-wage system, with wages being paid half at the end of each
month and the balance in cash at the end of the year. However, it appears that the
freedmen were unwilling to accept this, preferring the share system.[77]

There is considerable evidence to suggest that from the first year of labor
contracts immediately after the Civil War, the share system was the most popular
mode of contracting, and it was widely adopted throughout the South.[78] It is important to note that initially under this system all the freedmen on the plantation
contracted as a group with the planter for a share of the crop. This form of the share
system can be called the "collective" share arrangement and can be distinguished
from the "individual" share arrangement (the institution known as "sharecropping") whereby each family operated a separate parcel of land for a share of the
crop produced on that land. This distinction has been recognized in recent literature on the postbellum South.[79] Its non-recognition in earlier scholarship is quite
understandable as contemporary observers, to describe these arrangements, did not
use the term "the collective share arrangement" or, initially, the term "sharecropping." Rather, they used such terms as "the share system," "working on shares,"
and "contracts for a share of the crop," which applied to collective and individual
arrangements alike. Occasionally, they used the term "the cropping system," which
gave emphasis to the custom that the freedmen, under either the collective or the
individual share arrangement, worked exclusively on the crop and were not expected to work outside the crop by doing general farm work.[80]

Under the collective share arrangement it was intended that the division of the
proceeds of the freedmen's share of the crop among the members of the collective
would be made in proportion to the value of the respective work performed by each
member, so as to match the reward to the performance. It appears that the proceeds
were distributed among the freedmen by the planter, by the freedmen themselves,
or by the freedmen with the assistance of the planter.[81]

Planters thought of the collective share arrangement as a group incentive scheme that encouraged self-policing and reciprocal monitoring, among the members of the group, of each other's performance. By applying group pressure, contemporaries hoped that "it is made the interest of the hand to work faithfully, and to induce those about him to do the same" and that it would "stimulate each other to action"; however, "if you find occasional exceptions among your employees, whose industry is not quickened by the dictates of self-interest, you have but to convince the industrious that they are working for the benefit of the sluggard . . . and they will soon make it too uncomfortable for the laggard to continue in his idleness."[82]

The collective share arrangement did not prove to be a stable solution. The hopes of planters that group pressure would counter the so-called free rider problem of group payment schemes were not realized. This was clearly recognized by contemporary observers who reported that, under this arrangement, the freedmen became discontented with each other, "saying that this one will not do as much work as the other" or "accusing each other of loosing (sic) time unnecessarily and of not working well enough to be entitled to an equal share in the crop."[83] The non-viability of the collective share arrangement was perhaps most clearly shown in the comment of Charles Stearns ([1872] 1969, 515–517),

> We found that a large portion of those engaged in this [collective share] enterprise, would inevitably shirk their portion of the work, leaving it to be performed by those more honest; and yet would claim an equal share in the profits with others. This, of course, created dissatisfaction among the industrious ones, and jangling and disputes followed; until it was apparent that those most needed in such an enterprise, preferred working for themselves.

The mechanism of transition from this collective share arrangement for the entire plantation labor force to the individual share arrangement has been the subject of recent research. It has been shown that scaling down the size of the collective sharing in the crop was made either directly or via an intermediate stage, which was called by contemporaries "the squad system." Squads were self-selecting, semi-autonomous worker peer groups that were formed as subgroups of the plantation labor force working assigned parcels of land for a share of the crop. For at least a decade after the end of the Civil War this was a clearly defined system, distinguishable from family tenantry.[84]

In the world cotton and sugar cane economies of the late nineteenth century, cotton was generally considered a smallholding crop while sugar cane was generally considered a plantation crop. The interesting issue to pose, accordingly, is not so much why collective arrangements in cotton farming gave way to individual family arrangements, but why the demise of these collective arrangements took so long. Perhaps it can be explained in terms of the initial interest of many freedmen in trying group work arrangements and/or the difficulty that many farmers had in shedding views about the importance of group farming that were part of the old slave days. In contrast to the transformation of the cotton plantation, gang labor persisted on sugar cane plantations. Although there was an initial experimentation with the collective share arrangement on sugar cane plantations after the Civil War, this was soon discontinued, and by the late 1870s planters and freedmen had largely settled down to individual wage payments.[85] Later in the nineteenth and in the early twentieth century many sugar cane plantations were subdivided into tenant farms, but these tenants were almost invariably white, operating their tenant farms with hired black labor.[86] It has been shown elsewhere that the supremacy of the plantation system in cultivating sugar cane was due to its technical advantages over the smallholding system. The advantages offered by the centralized plantation in the farming and milling of sugar cane included the more efficient coordination of the harvesting and milling activities so that a regular supply of cut cane could be fed to the mill, the reduction in the risks of running a mill by having an ensured supply of cane to crush, and, perhaps, the provision of superior management skills.[87]

This paper addresses a number of issues relating to the nature of the transition from slavery to freedom in the postbellum South and the arguments that have been put forward can now be drawn together. The slave system can be thought of as a legally enforced employer cartel to control and exploit labor, and in the aftermath of the Civil War and emancipation planters hoped to fashion a new labor system that would contain many of the features of the old slave system. In particular, they wished to limit the rights of the freedmen to choose among employers. By binding freedmen to particular employers, planters could dictate the freedmen's working conditions. To this end, the so-called Black Codes were enacted, planters strove to act in concert through the establishment of employer cartels, and intimidation and intermittent violence were used to coerce the freedmen to accept the type of labor system that planters hoped to engineer.

The planters, however, were not able to reimpose slave-type labor relations because they failed to establish the controls required to sustain their program. In particular, their repressive legislation was set aside, and their employer combinations were not viable. The freedmen did not become bound to particular employers, and their ability to change employers was not constrained. That the freedmen had the freedom to choose among employers and their job offers meant that planters had to compete for labor. Accordingly, planters, to obtain and hold their labor force, had to abide by the rules of a free labor market.

Thus a free labor market was created in which the freedmen were free to change jobs, and planters were required to bid against each other for labor. The freedmen took advantage of the existence of this free labor market to obtain better working conditions. These conditions related both to the pecuniary remuneration for their labor and to various non-pecuniary amenities. In particular, they desired autonomy, and in the farming of cotton, but not of sugar cane, they achieved it through the sharecropping system. The adoption of the sharecropping system had the support of planters too because they saw advantages for themselves in the system.

Hence it can be concluded that the institution known as sharecropping was not a form of bound labor, a coercive mode of labor control, that had its origins in class conflict. Rather, the sharecropping system represented, in large measure, a convergence of the interests of planters and freedmen that arose from the free interplay of market forces.

NOTES

1. On this debate, see Wiener, Higgs, and Woodman (1979); Wiener (1978), 35–73; Reid (#33, in this volume); Higgs (1977), 47–49; Sutch and Ransom (1978); Wayne (1983), 116–132; Powell (1980), 60–61; Wright (1982).
2. This lacuna in the literature has been acknowledged by Parker (1980), 1020.
3. *New Orleans Daily Picayune,* October 29, 1868. For other examples see Wiener (1978), 40–41; Higgs (1977), 47.
4. "Thoughts for the Month," (1888), 46:1.
5. See Lightfoot (1869), 152–153; Edmondston (1869), 25–26; Aiken (1871–1872), 113–115; Aiken (1874–1875), 455; Sam Postlewaite to James A. Gillespie, March 27, 1867, March 14, 1869, and January 20, 1860; James A. Gillespie to A. K. Farrar, April 26, 1876, Gillespie Papers.
6. Aiken (1871–1872), 113–115; Lightfoot (1869), 152–153; Ex-Confed. (1870), 141.
7. O. J. (1871), 370–371.
8. "Thoughts for the Month," (1888), 46:1.
9. An Occasional Contributor (1870–1871), 572–574 (first quotation); Southerner (1871), 339 (second quotation). See also *New Orleans Daily Crescent,* May 21, 1866; Cosmopolitan (1868), 12–13; "Treatment and Pay of Freedmen," (1868), 212–213; Edmondston (1869), 25–26; Ex-Confed. (1870), 141; Aiken (1871–1872), 113–115; *Tuskaloosa Blade,* November 20, 1873.
10. See Higgs (1977), 47; DeCanio (1974), 38–39. During the first few years after the Civil War, a further obstacle to the establishment of combinations was the policy of the Freedmen's Bureau. There is evidence that officers of the bureau were active in breaking up such combinations; see testimony of Major General Clinton B. Fisk in U.S. Congress (1865–1866), 3:29.
11. The classificatory scheme presented in this paper builds upon and extends the frameworks developed by Higgs (1977), 47–49, and DeCanio (1974), 16–17, 51.
12. Wilmer Shields to William N. Mercer, January 1, 1867, William Newton Mercer Papers (first quotation); Southerner (1871), 339 (second quotation); "Thoughts for the Month," (1877), 35:1 (third quotation); Aiken (1874–1875), 455 (fourth quotation); *New York Tribune,* January 10, 1868 (fifth quotation); Loring and Atkinson (1869), 17 (sixth quotation). See also Reid (1866), 561; *New York Tribune,* February 6, 1866; *The New York Times,* February 12, 1866; Wilmer Shields to William N. Mercer, December 1, 12 1866 and January 6, 1867, William Newton Mercer Papers; *New Orleans Daily Picayune,* January 27, 1869; Lightfoot (1869), 152–153; Aiken (1869–1870a), 476; *The New York Times,* January 21, 31, 1870; Southerner (1871), 339; "Thoughts for the Month," (1871), 29:444; U.S. Department of Agriculture (1877), 130; *The New York Times,* February 23, 1880; "Thoughts for the Month," (1883), 41:1.
13. J. A. Oliphant (1874), 125–126.
14. "Thoughts for the Month" (1874), 32:125–126.
15. In addition to the evidence cited in notes 16 and 17, of this paper, see Monthly Report of the Subassistant Commissioner for Unionville, South Carolina, February 1867, Reports of Conditions and Operations, Bureau of Refugees, Freedmen, and Abandoned Lands, (National Archives, Record Group 105); "Large Farms and Associated Capital," (1867–1868), 8; Vox (1868), 33; *New Orleans Daily Crescent,* January 22, 29, 1869; *Natchez Weekly Democrat,* March 15, 1871; De Leon (1874), 301; A South Carolinian (1877), 675, 677; *New Orleans Daily Picayune,* January 14, 1878; Campbell (1879), 151, 364, 379, 389, 390; Bruce ([1889] 1970), 177–178; Willets (1903) 2:701; Fleming (1905), 731 (Fleming's account is based on planters' recollections of the early postbellum period); Testimony of James Barrett, a farmer from Georgia, O. B. Stevens, Commissioner of Agriculture for Georgia, and Robert R. Poole, Commissioner of Agriculture for Alabama, in U.S. Congress (1901), 10:46, 908–909, 921; Cance (1908), Ch. 8, p. 7; Brannen (1924), 44. This body of evidence documents job change behavior at the conclusion of the annual employment contract. Job changes were also made during the period of employment contracts. However, this was, to a large extent, a reflection of ill-treatment and coercion. That this type of job change usually gave the mere semblance of freedom is well documented in the records of the Freedmen's Bureau, which

present cases in which employers evicted freedmen before the conclusion of their contracts without compensation and freedmen broke their contracts because of ill-treatment. There were, of course, other causes of job change during the term of employment contracts, such as freedmen being enticed to break their contracts by the offer of higher remuneration from other planters and employers. See Monthly Reports of the Subassistant Commissioners for Aiken, July, September, November, 1866; August 1867; Charleston, November 1866; Darlington, March, April, May, June, 1867; Edisto Island, June 1867; Sumter, August 1867; Union, August 1867; Unionville, March 1867; Williamsburg, June 1868, Report of Conditions and Operations for South Carolina, Bureau of Refugees, Freedmen and Abandoned Lands (National Archives, Record Group 105); Loring and Atkinson (1869), 4; *The New York Times*, January 21, 31, 1870; Magdol (1977), 150–152, 272.

16. See Loring and Atkinson (1869), 4–5; Southerner (1871), 329; Fleming (1905), 724.
17. See *New Orleans Daily Crescent*, January 18, 1866; *New Orleans Daily Picayune*, January 14, 1869.
18. In addition to the evidence cited in note 19, of this paper, see *The New York Times*, November 30, 1866; January 7, 1867; *New York Tribune*, April 2, 1867; *New Orleans Daily Picayune*, February 5, 1869; Aiken (1871–1872) 113–115.
19. *The New York Times*, November 19, 1866.
20. See Dennett ([1865–1866] 1965), 51, 281; Trowbridge (1866), 391; *New York Tribune*, March 31, 1866; *The New York Times*, December 23, 1866; Gregory (1866), Testimony of J. S. Brisbin, in U.S. Congress (1865–1866), 3:70; Kiddoo (1866), 146; U.S. Department of Agriculture (1866), 81; U.S. Department of Agriculture (1867), 416–417; H (1867), 511; "Labor Contracts," (1869), 85–86; Edmondston (1869), 25–26; *New Orleans Daily Picayune*, January 27, 1869; Southerner (1871), 330; Aiken (1871–1872), 113–115; De Leon (1873–1874), 272, 276; King (1875), 273; U.S. Department of Agriculture (1876), 131–135, 152; U.S. Department of Agriculture (1890), 313; Willets (1903), 2:715.
21. A discriminating monopolist, in this context, refers to an employer combination that exploits individual workers differentially, according to the separate and distinct characteristics, preferences, and situations of each worker.
22. See "Contracts with Laborers," (1865), 180; Marcel (1865), 237–239; "Form of Contract with Plantation Hands," (1866), 4; Andrews (1866), 99, 128–29; U.S. Department of Agriculture (1867), 416–417; Aiken (1869–1870b), 141; De Leon (1873–1874), 276; U.S. Department of Agriculture (1876), 152; "Croppers—Equitable Division of Crops," (1886), 468; Bruce ([1889] 1970), 213; Gilman (1893), 14; U.S. Congress (1901), xvi; Shlomowitz (1979), 565–566.
23. See Lightfoot (1869), 152–153, and Norwood (1876), 210–211. For additional citations to this evidence, see DeCanio (1974), 59–60, and Higgs (1977), 49.
24. Wayne (1983), 52. This free labor market was accompanied by arrangements that unmistakably reflected coercion by planters and others. Convicts, for example, were excluded from this free labor market. Their quantitative significance, however, was slight.
25. The greater success of employers' combinations in sugar cane than in cotton farming was probably due to the relatively small number of sugar cane employers and their geographic concentration in the Louisiana Delta. It should also be noted that the 1870s was a period of declining cotton and sugar cane prices; this reduced the monetary incomes earned by the freedmen employed on share-cropping contracts in cotton farming, and it also put downward pressure on money wage rates in sugar cane farming, thereby helping sugar cane employers. More generally, the 1870s was a period of deflation in prices in the country as a whole, and this was associated with a marked countrywide decline in money, but not necessarily in real, farm wage rates. See U.S. Department of Agriculture (1885), 381–382.
26. For direct evidence on competition, see Bouchereau (1870), ix; *New Orleans Daily Picayune*, August 24, 1873, January 14, 1874. On high turnover rates, see *New Orleans Daily Picayune*, September 4, 1873.
27. See *New Orleans Daily Picayune*, January 11, 15, February 13, 1874.
28. *New Orleans Daily Picayune*, January 10, 11, 14, 15, 1874; *The New York Times*, January 14, 1874.
29. *New Orleans Daily Picayune*, December 28, 1874; September 1, 1875.
30. *New Orleans Daily Picayune*, December 28, 1874; September 1, 1875.
31. *New Orleans Daily Picayune*, December 21, 1877.

32. *New Orleans Daily Picayune,* January 19, 29, 1878.

33. *New Orleans Daily Picayune,* June 2, 1879; *The New York Times,* August 6, 1879.

34. See *Weekly Louisianian,* January 15, April 2, 1881.

35. For an overview of the extent and effectiveness of employer combinations in the labor market for sugar cane farming in Louisiana during this period, see Sitterson (1953), 245–247.

36. *New Orleans Daily Picayune,* January 20, 1874.

37. *New Orleans Daily Picayune,* January 20, 1874.

38. See *New Orleans Daily Picayune,* January 14, February 13, 1874; January 29, 1878.

39. This paper does not address the issue of the relative strengths of competitive and coercive forces in the labor markets for the farming of the South's other staple crops, such as rice and tobacco and for the production of the South's forestry products, such as turpentine. It is noted, however, that there is evidence to suggest that during the period from 1865 to 1873 the labor market for rice farming in Louisiana was also dominated by competitive forces. In 1873, for example, a newspaper correspondent reported that in rice farming the "price of labor has been continually rising since 1865" (see *New Orleans Daily Picayune,* October 7, 1873). There is also evidence that wages in rice farming on the South Atlantic coast were increasing during this period; see Clifton (1978), 148.

40. It is acknowledged, however, that many important circumstances molding their culture and life-style were beyond their control. These circumstances included the legacy of slavery, their poverty, and southern specialization in cotton production.

41. *New York Tribune,* June 4, 1870.

42. For a discussion of these tasks, see "Turpentine," (1869), 171–174.

43. *New York Tribune,* March 17, 1866.

44. Andrews (1866), 205. Further documentation of the freedmen's preference for turpentine gathering can be found in Dennett ([1865–1866] 1965), 174; Reid (1866), 335–336.

45. "The Pine Forests of the South," (1867), 196–198.

46. See Reid (1866), 31, 473; *The New York Times,* November 11, 1866; *New Orleans Daily Picayune,* July 6, 1873; De Leon (1873–1874), 275. In contrast to the arduous and distasteful labor in rice and sugar cane farming, work in cotton and tobacco farming was relatively light. See "Cotton and Tobacco," (1868–1869), 283.

47. See testimony of H. S. Welles, in U.S. Congress (1865–1866), 3:110; Reid (1866), 94; *New York Tribune,* March 17, 1866; *The New York Times,* July 4, 1874; *The New York Times,* December 18, 1879; Harris (1881), 184; Testimony of Milton Whitney, Chief, Soils Division, United States Department of Agriculture, in U.S. Congress (1901), 864–865.

48. See "Thoughts for the Month," (1873), 31:283; Grady (1881), 725; Barrow (1882), 8.

49. Reprinted in *DeBow's Review* (1866), 1:659.

50. For an example of this recognition, see Loring and Atkinson (1869), 8.

51. See *New Orleans Daily Picayune,* October 7, 1873; April 28, 1877; June 15, 1879; Harris (1881), 149, 167; Anderson (1981), 16–17. This proposition does not necessarily also apply to rice farming in Georgia and South Carolina. There the task system was viewed favorably by the freedmen, and the advantages of this mode of labor organization may have offset the drawbacks of rice cultivation.

52. See *New Orleans Daily Picayune,* October 7, 1873; Harris (1881), 184. Unfortunately, these sources do not specify the size of the wage differentials.

53. That the freedmen had substantially more work autonomy under the share system than under the fixed wage system is well documented in the primary literature. See Roberts (1866), 211; *The New York Times,* February 4, 1866; Letters of Wilmer Shields to Dr. Mercer, December 1, 1866; January 6, May 23, 1867, William Newton Mercer Papers; *New York Tribune,* January 14, 1867; *New Orleans Daily Picayune,* October 19, 1867; S. W. (1868), 133; "The Industrial Condition of the South," (1869), 164–165; Dennis (1869), 58–59; Evans (1867), 54–55; Loring and Atkinson (1869), 31; "Department of Labor and Immigration: Labor and Wages," (1869–1870), 570–571; *Natchez Weekly Democrat,* March 29, 1871; Southerner (1871), 332; *New York Tribune,* June 8, 1871; B (1872–1873), 64; *The New York Times,* November 14, 1874; "Thoughts for the Month," (1874), 32:293; Aiken (1874–1875), 455; U.S. Department of Agriculture (1876), 131, 182; J. W. O. (1880), 444; Hilgard (1884), 1:186, 476, 640, 819, 2:250–251, 522; Barrow (1881), 831; U.S. Department of Agriculture (1888), 586–587. On occasion, however, there were cases where freed-

men employed under the share system lacked such work autonomy and were summoned to work by a bell ring and had their hours of work regulated by the employer. For example, see Montgomery (1879), 445. These cases of employer control over sharecropper labor appear to have become much more widespread after the turn of the century; see Brannen (1924), 43; Cance (1908), Ch. 8, pp. 5, 10.

54. A quantitative test of this proposition would require data on the expected earnings of groups of freedmen under each labor system, where the labor input of each group had been standardized for differences in their age and sex composition. Such a test would allow for the possibility, for example, that married workers were more often employed under the sharecropping system and unattached young men more under the wage system. However, comparative data on earnings for this period, 1865–1880, whether expected or realized, do not appear to be available.

55. O. J. (1871), 370–371, emphasis in the original.

56. J. W. O. (1880), 444.

57. Janes (1875), 1:2–3; Janes (1876), 2:7; Janes (1877), 3:16.

58. Hilgard (1884), 1:185–186, 356, 476, 640–641, 819; 2:165–166, 251, 438–439, 609.

59. See *New York Tribune,* September 5, 1865; May 25, June 8, 1871; *The New York Times,* November 30, 1866; *New Orleans Daily Picayune,* January 23, 1869; *The Independent,* January 25, 1866; Southerner (1871), 330; U.S. Department of Agriculture (1876), 131.

60. *The New York Times,* January 7, 1870 (first quotation); *New Orleans Daily Picayune,* January 23, 1869 (second quotation); Aiken (1870–1871), 323–324 (third quotation); *New Orleans Daily Picayune,* January 5, 1867 (fourth quotation); Evans (1867), 54 (fifth quotation). See also Dennett ([1865–1866] 1965), 202–203; Osborn (1866), 278, 39; *New York Tribune,* January 14, 1867; Oconee (1872), 57–58; U.S. Department of Agriculture (1888), 586; Fleming (1905), 722.

61. "Department of Labor and Immigration: Labor and Wages," (1869–1870), 570–571.

62. See "Contracts with Laborers," (1865), 180–181; Hansen (1866–1867a), 138–139; Hansen (1866–1867b), 341–342; Moore (1974), 145; Testimony of Harry Hammond, cotton planter, in U.S. Congress (1901), 819.

63. "Contracts with Laborers," (1865), 180.

64. There were many reasons why planters feared that, in the absence of the postharvest payment system, some freedmen would leave before the harvest. One recurring concern in this regard was the "enticement" activities of other planters or their agents; see *The New York Times,* January 21, 31, 1870.

65. See *New Orleans Daily Picayune,* February 7, 1867; J. S. J. (1871), 10; Brannen (1924), 26.

66. See *The New York Times,* November 5, 1866; Loring and Atkinson (1869), 7; *New York Tribune,* September 28, 1872.

67. See *New Orleans Daily Crescent,* July 14, 1866; U.S. Department of Agriculture (1867), 416–417; "Labor in the South," (1869), 272.

68. W. M. R. (1870–1871), 118.

69. In a survey of over 700 bureau-supervised labor contracts, only 2 contracts were found that specified a forfeiture schedule for lost time making allowance for a variable fine. These 2 contracts were entered into in 1866 in Newberry district, South Carolina, and their forfeiture schedule for lost time was $1 per day from March 15 to August 1 and 50 cents per day for the other times during the year. See contracts of A. M. Smith with fourteen freedmen and D. V. Scurry with thirteen freedmen, in *Records of the Assistant Commissioner* (National Archives, Record Group 105).

70. It may be thought that a piece-rate system, which allowed for higher rates during the "critical" periods of the crop cycle, would also be a viable solution as it would reduce monitoring costs and give the worker an incentive to effort. Monitoring costs would be reduced because performance is monitored only at the completion of the task rather than continually during its operation; an incentive to effort is given because the worker would be paid according to the amount of work performed. There are, however, problems of quality control with the use of this system—as payment is related only to the quantity of work performed, the worker would have little incentive to perform the task well.

71. See *New Orleans Daily Crescent,* January 31, February 8, July 14, 1866; *New Orleans Daily Picayune,* January 12, 1868; September 1, 1873; *New York Tribune,* September 5, 1865; July 10,

1866; Monthly Reports of the Subassistant Commissioner for Union, South Carolina, for June and September 1867, Reports of the Conditions and Operations, Bureau of Refugees, Freedmen, and Abandoned Lands, (National Archives, Record Group 105); Trowbridge (1866), 392; Loring and Atkinson (1869), 31; "Labor in the South," (1869), 272; "The Industrial Condition of the South," (1869), 164; Somers (1871), 60, 146–147; De Leon (1873–1874), 272; "Thoughts for the Month," (1877), 35:1; Fleming (1905), 722. *The New York Times* correspondent from Georgia, who used the nom de plume "Quondam," emphasized in successive reports that these incentives were the main impetus to the adoption of the share system (see *The New York Times*, March 18, June 8, November 5, 1866; April 2, 1867; January 18, 1869; January 7, 1870).

72. See U.S. Department of Agriculture (1876), 131.

73. See "Labor in the South," (1869), 273. Some contemporary observers suggested that the impetus to the widespread adoption of the sharecropping system was due to a shortage of currency in the South after the Civil War. This argument is, however, of secondary importance because under both the fixed-wage and the sharecropping systems planters needed almost the same amount of currency. Under the fixed-wage system, a portion of the monthly wage was usually retained by the planter until the completion of the contract and under both systems the planter usually supplied rations and other items and services such as clothing, medical expenses, and credit facilities. In addition, the normal response to a lack of currency, in the absence of other considerations, is fixed wages in kind rather than the sharecropping system. Other contemporary observers suggested that the rationale for the adoption of the sharecropping system was the desire of planters to shift part of the incidence of risk in cotton farming onto the freedmen. This argument is also of secondary importance as planters were in a much better financial position than the freedmen to bear risk, and they also had alternative ways of effecting risk dispersion.

74. For example, see Thompson (1915), 81; Wharton, ([1947] 1965), 68; Kolchin (1972), 41–42.

75. Systematic quantitative evidence on the extent of the use of the fixed-wage system is available for the period when the Freedmen's Bureau supervised labor contracting, 1865–1868, but not for the remainder of the nineteenth century. However, its continued use is shown by drawing upon data from the 1910 census. In that year, 28.5 per cent of the improved land on cotton plantations was worked by wage labor; see Brannen (1924), 19–21.

76. Report of Commissioner Howard in U.S. Congress (1865), 25 (first and fourth quotations); Ferguson (1866), 230–231 (second quotation); Rev. C. W. Howard (1867), 473 (third quotation). See also Report of Commissioner Howard in U.S. Congress (1865), 28; E. Whittlesey (1865–1866), 391; Testimony of J. W. Turner, E. W. Whittlesey, and J. W. Alvord, in U.S. Congress (1865–1866), 30:5, 182, 189, 260; *The New York Tribune*, January 14, 1867; *New Orleans Daily Picayune*, September 4, 1868; *The New York Times*, May 30, 1869. Agents of the Freedmen's Bureau spoke well of this system; this could have reflected their concern to avoid friction between planters and freedmen over the division of the crop under the share system and over the size of the holdback, after the deduction of fines for lost time, under the fixed-wage system.

77. See *The New York Times*, January 18, 1869 for the quotations; see also *The New York Times*, March 18, June 8, November 5, 1866; April 2, 1867; May 30, 1869; January 7, 1870.

78. For evidence on the extensive use of the share system in the early postbellum years, 1865–1867, see *New York Tribune*, October 6, 1865; August 11, 20, 1866; *The New York Times*, February 12, March 11, June 8, December 11, 1866; April 2, December 23, 1867; January 7, 1870; July 4, 1874; *New Orleans Daily Crescent*, January 31, 1866; U.S. Department of Agriculture (1867), 416–417; Wagener (1867), 359; Andrews (1866), 99; Foster (1866), 43; Lewis (1866), 130; and Kiddoo (1866), 146; Shlomowitz (1979), 563.

79. For instance, see Williamson (1965), 128; Ransom and Sutch (1977), 60–61, 90, 74; Shlomowitz (1979), 566–567.

80. See Aiken (1869–1870b), 141; Evans (1867), 51–52; J. S. J. (1871), 10; Waternook (1870), 44–45; Dickson (1870), 87. For examples, however, where the terms "cropper" and "crop-er" did relate to the sharecropping system, see Roberts (1866), 211; "Thoughts for the Month," (1874), 32:293. In the latter case, the terms "croppers" and "share men" were distinguished.

81. See "Contracts with Laborers," (1865), 181; *The Independent*, February 1, 1866; "Labor Contracts," (1867–1868), 218–220; Monthly Report of the Subassistant Commissioner for Charleston,

James M. Johnston, for December 1866, Reports of Conditions and Operations (National Archives, Record Group 105).

82. "Contracts with Laborers," (1865), 181 (first quotation); Report of Subassistant Commissioner for Luna Landing, Arkansas, Thomas Abel, for September 1866, cited in Bentley (1955), 150 (second quotation); Rawlins (1866), 422 (third quotation).

83. Testimony of Major General Lorenzo Thomas of Concordia Parish, Louisiana, in U.S. Congress (1865–1866), 4:141 (first quotation); Report of Subassistant Commissioner for Cuthbert, Georgia, Charles Raushenberg, November 14, 1867, cited in Cox and Cox (1973), 341–342 (second quotation).

84. See Shlomowitz (1982b); Cance (1908), Ch. 3, p. 21; Ch. 4, pp. 11, 24–25; Davis (1982), 89, 95, 102—103, 105; Engerrand (1981), 72, 76–77, 80–81; Thompson (1915), 293–294; Wayne (1983), 124–125, 129, 132. Gerald D. Jaynes of Yale University is currently assembling what should be the most extensive documentation on the squad system to date.

85. See *New York Tribune,* August 31, 1873; De Leon (1873–1874), 272, 273; *New Orleans Daily Picayune,* July 18, 1877; Sitterson (1953), 240.

86. See U.S. Department of Commerce (1913) 30; Sitterson (1953), 314–315.

87. See Shlomowitz (1982a), 329–331; Shlomowitz (1984).

Appendix:
Contents of Companion Volumes

WITHOUT CONSENT OR CONTRACT: THE RISE AND FALL OF AMERICAN SLAVERY BY ROBERT WILLIAM FOGEL

Foreword: Discoveries and Dilemmas   9

Part I. Slavery as an Economic and Social System

 1. Slavery in the New World   17
 2. Occupational Patterns   41
 3. Unraveling Some Economic Riddles   60
 4. The Development of the Southern Economy   81
 5. The Population Question   114
 6. Changing Interpretations of Slave Culture   154

Part II. The Ideological and Political Campaign Against Slavery

 7. The British Campaign   201
 8. The American Campaign: From the Revolution to the Abolitionist Crusade   238
 9. The American Campaign: Breaching the Barriers to Antislavery Politics   281
10. The American Campaign: Forging a Victorious Antislavery Coalition   320

Afterword: The Moral Problem of Slavery   388

Acknowledgments   418
Notes   423
References   487
Index   525

EVIDENCE AND METHODS.

Editors: Robert William Fogel, Ralph A. Galantine, and Richard L Manning. *Contributors:* N. Scott Cardell, Stephen C. Crawford, Stanley L. Engerman, Robert W. Fogel, Gerald Friedman, Ralph A. Galantine, Randall B. Grossman, Martha K. Hoffman, Mark M. Hopkins, Laurence Kotlikoff, Barbara McCutcheon, Richard L Manning, John F. Olson, Sebastian Pinera, Richard Robb, Jr., Barbara J. Stufflebeem, Nathaniel Wilcox, and Donghyu Yang

Preface   xiii
Initials and Names of Contributors   xv
Conventions Followed in Referencing   xvii

Introduction: Notes on the Art of Empirical Research in the Social Sciences during an Age of
Plunging Costs in Data Processing   1

Part I. Notes on Recent Slavery Research and on the Rise of Slavery in the New World

1. The Long Reach of the Ideological Issues That Produced the Civil War   45
2. Risks and Rewards of Planters in the New World   47
3. Problems in Measuring the Extent of Slave Smuggling   50
4. Revised Estimates of the U.S. Slave Trade and of the Native-Born Share of the Black
   Population   53
5. The Slave Labor Force before the American Revolution   58
6. An Estimate of the Generational Distribution of U.S. Blacks, 1640–1860   62

Part II. Evidence on the Structure of Slave Occupations

7. Sources of Data on Slave Occupations: Their Uses and Limitations   69
8. The Rent and Hire of Slaves   77
9. Slaves and Free Blacks in Urban Crafts, Rural Crafts, and Managerial Occupations   78
10. The Overseer Problem: A New Data Set and Method   84
11. The Gang System and the Structure of Slave Employment   109
12. Occupational Determination in Slave Societies   119
13. Labor-Force Participation and Life Cycles in Slave Occupations   140

**Part III. Characteristics of Markets for Slaves and Slave Products, the Profitability of
Slavery, and the Technical Efficiency of Slave Plantations**

14. Some Economic Aspects of the British Slavery Debate   153
15. The Origin and History of Economic Issues in the American Slavery Debate   154
16. The "Decline" Theory of West Indian Emancipation   163
17. The Profitability of West Indian Properties   165
18. The Profitability of Sugar Production under Apprenticeship   166
19. British Sugar Demand, West Indian Production, and the "Decline" Theory of West Indian
    Emancipation, 1790–1850   168
20. Fluctuations in the U.S. Production and Prices of Indigo, Rice, and Tobacco   190
21. The Rise of the New South and the Geographic Regions of Cotton, Rice, and Sugar   192
22. Regional Markets for Slaves and the Interregional Slave Trade   195
23. The Debate over the Economic Viability of Slavery   199
24. Basic Procedures for the Computation of Outputs and Inputs from the Parker-Gallman
    Sample, Including a Procedure for the Elimination of Defective Observations   205
25. An Alternative Procedure for Eliminating Incomplete Data and Outliers from the Parker-
    Gallman Sample   210
26. A Note on the Danger of Introducing Biases Through Cleaning Procedures   212
27. Problems and Implications for the Measurement of Productivity Stemming from the Use of
    Indirect Procedures to Estimate Omitted Labor, Omitted Activities, and the Distribution of
    Labor Inputs Across Farm Products   214
28. An Alternative Approach to the Valuation of Farm Output   223
29. An Alternative Procedure for the Aggregation of Farm Outputs and Inputs for the Purpose of
    Comparing the Total Factor Productivity of Classes of Farms   228
30. Notes on the Sensitivity of Regional Comparisons of Total Factor Productivity to Alternative
    Procedures   233
31. Notes on Some Aspects of the Measurement of Inputs and Outputs in the Computation of
    Productivity Measures from the Parker-Gallman Sample   237

**Part IV. The Distribution of Wealth, Economic Growth, and Economic Structure in the
South, 1840–1880**

32. Recent Findings on the Distribution of Wealth, on Social Structure, and on Economic Mobil-
    ity among Free Southerners during the Late Antebellum Era   243

33. Notes on the Wealth Distribution of Farm Households in the United States, 1860: A New
    Look at Two Manuscript Census Samples   245
34. Some Notes on the Apparent Aversion to the Separate Sale of Children under Age Ten in the
    New Orleans Slave Market   256
35. Some Economic Aspects of the Southern Interregional Migration, 1850–1860   259
36. The Debate on the Elasticity of the Cotton Supply   264
37. The Debate over the Growth in the Demand for Cotton   269
38. Explanations for the Decline in Southern Per Capita Income 1860–1880   273
39. Reclassifying Manufacturing to Explain the "Southern Lag" in Industrialization   277
40. Notes on the Explanation of the Growth of Southern Per Capita Income 1840–1860   278

Part V. The Vital Rates, Health, and Nutritional Status of Slaves

41. The Life Expectation of U.S. Slaves c.1830   285
42. Estimating the Undercount of Births and Deaths below Age Three   286
43. The Slave Diet on Large Plantations in 1860   291
44. A Note on the Relationship between Plantation Size and Diet Adequacy   304
45. The Effect of Milk Intolerance on the Consumption of Milk by Slaves in 1860   306
46. The Relation Between the Cost of Calories for Suckling Babies and for Nursing Mothers 310
47. The Body Mass Index of Adult Male Slaves in the U.S. c.1863 and Its Bearing on Mortality
    Rates   311
48. The Effect of Non-Random Censoring on the Distribution of Final Heights   318
49. Was the Overwork of Pregnant Slaves Profit Maximizing?   321
50. A Production Function Framework for Questioning the Existence of Slave Breeding   326

Part VI. Problems in the Study of Slave Culture

51. Problems in the Quantitative Analysis of the Data Contained in WPA and Fisk University
    Narratives of Ex-Slaves   331
52. A Method of Estimating the Income Distribution of Slaves c.1860 from the Available Patchy
    Evidence   371
53. A Correction to the Computation in *Time on the Cross* of the Value of Freedom at Low Income
    Levels   379
54. The Exploitation-Expropriation Debate   383
55. The Distribution of U.S. Slaves by Size of Slaveholding in 1850 and 1860   387

Part VII. Aspects of the British Struggle against Slavery

56. A Comparison between the Value of Slave Capital in the Share of Total British Wealth
    (c.1811) and in the Share of Total Southern Wealth (c.1860)   397
57. The Cost of British Slave Trade Suppression   398
58. The Relationship of the Abolition of the Slave Trade to Parliamentary Reform and the
    Repeal of Religious Restriction   401

**Part VIII. Sources and Consequences of Population Growth, Labor Force Growth, and
Rapid Urbanization in the North, 1820–1860**

59. An Estimate of the Proportion of the Northern Population outside of New England in 1820
    That Was Yankee or of Yankee Origin   405
60. An Analysis of the Growth of the Northern Population 1820–1860; Part A: Estimates of the
    Actual and Natural Rates of Growth of the Northern Labor Force   406
61. The Problem of Measuring the Cost of Housing to Northern Urban Workers and the Share of
    Rent in their Expenditures, 1830–1855   415

Part IX. Factors Affecting Political Realignments in the North, 1840–1860

62. Understanding the Distribution of Urban Wealth: The United States in 1860   419
63. A Note on the Occupational Distribution of the Urban United States in 1860   458

64. A Note on Coping with Sample Selection Bias: The Moen Sample of Urban Households　473
65. An Estimate of the Distribution of Northern Non-Farm Labor between Natives and the Foreign Born in 1860　479
66. The End of the Railroad Construction Boom and Its Effect on the Competition for Jobs among Nonagricultural Workers in the Midwest 1849–1856　480
67. Problems in Measuring the Real Wages of Native Non-Farm Workers in the North, 1848–1855　482
68. An Exploration into the Causes of the Growth of Per Capita Income in the North, 1840–1860　485
69. The Change in Voter Alignments in the North between 1852 and 1860: An Exploratory Analysis　496

Part X. Issues in the Interpretation of the Moral Problem of Slavery

70. A Note on the Effect of Moral Issues on the Debates among Cliometricians　589
71. Channing on the Place of Material Treatment in the Moral Indictment of Slavery　591
72. Moral Aspects of the Debate over the "Extra Income" of Slaves　593
73. A Skeptical Note on Sexual Exploitation, Slavery and Cliometry　596
74. Thoughts on the Treatment of Moral Issues in *Time on the Cross*　599

Appendix: Contents of Companion Volumes　605
Acknowledgments　609
References　611
Index　635

MARKETS AND PRODUCTION: TECHNICAL PAPERS (VOLUME I):

Editors: Robert William Fogel and Stanley L. Engerman. *Contributors:* Stanley L. Engerman, Robert W. Fogel, David W. Galenson, Claudia D. Goldin, Thomas F. Huertas, Laurence J. Kotlikoff, Robert A. Margo, Pedro C. de Mello, Jacob Metzer, Jon R. Moen, John F. Olson, Sebastian E. Pinera, Andrew M. Rosenfield, Donghyu Yang.

Publisher's Note　ix
Conventions Followed in Referencing　xi
General Introduction　xv

Part I. Markets for Human Capital
Introduction　3
1. White Servitude and the Growth of Black Slavery in Colonial America by David W. Galenson　5
2. The Market Evaluation of Human Capital: The Case of Indentured Servitude by David W. Galenson　14
3. Quantitative Description of the New Orleans Slave Market, 1804 to 1862 by Laurence J. Kotlikoff　31
4. The Taxonomy of Horizontal and Vertical Addition of Demand Curves: An Historical Approach by Andrew M. Rosenfield　54
5. Rates of Return on Slave Capital in Brazilian Coffee Plantations, 1871–1881 by Pedro C. DeMello　63
6. The Old South's Stake in the Interregional Movement of Slaves, 1850–1860 by Laurence J. Kotlikoff and Sebastian E. Pinera　80
7. An Explanation for the Relative Decline of Urban Slavery: 1820–1860 by Claudia D. Goldin　95

Part II. Skill Formation under Slavery
   Introduction   135
  8. The Occupational Structure of Southern Plantations during the Late Antebellum Era by John F. Olson   137
  9. Civilian Occupations of Ex-Slaves in the Union Army, 1862–1865 by Robert A. Margo   170

Part III. The Productivity of Slave Agriculture and Southern Economic Growth
   Introduction   189

10. Rational Management, Modern Business Practices, and Economies of Scale in Antebellum Southern Plantations by Jacob Metzer   191
11. Clock Time versus Real Time: A Comparison of the Lengths of the Northern and Southern Agricultural Work Years by John F. Olson   216
12. Explaining the Relative Efficiency of Slave Agriculture in the Antebellum South by Robert W. Fogel and Stanley L. Engerman   241
13. Explaining the Relative Efficiency of Slave Agriculture in the Antebellum South: Reply by Robert W. Fogel and Stanley L. Engerman   266
14. Agricultural Productivity in the Northern United States, 1860 by Donghyu Yang   304
15. Changes in the Productivity of Southern Agriculture between 1860 and 1880 by John R. Moen   320
16. Damnifying Growth in the South by Thomas F. Huertas   351

   Appendix: Contents of Companion Volumes   A1
   Acknowledgments   A7
   References   A9
   About the Contributors   A25
   Index   A29

Acknowledgments

In addition to the acknowledgments made in the primary volume and in the individual papers of this volume, the editors wish to express their appreciation to Martha K. Hoffman, Barbara J. Stufflebeem, Susan E. Jones, and Katherine A. Chavigny for their editorial assistance. They bore the principal burden of checking citations, integrating the system of referencing and cross-referencing, and of responding to the numerous queries of the copy editor. The various drafts were quickly and efficiently typed by Carol Miterko, Regina Strug, Anthony May, Cynthia Davis, and Kimberly Lee.

References

Acklen, A.S. 1857. Rules in the management of a Southern estate: Concluded. *DeBow's Review* 22:376–381.

Adams, Dale W., and Norman Rask. 1968. Economics of cost-share leases in less developed countries. *American Journal of Agricultural Economics* 50:935–942.

Adamson, Alan H. 1972. *Sugar without slaves: The political economy of British Guiana, 1838–1904.* New Haven, CT: Yale University Press.

Affleck, T. 1851. On the hygiene of cotton plantations and the management of Negro slaves. *Southern Medical Reports* 2:429–436.

African Institution. 1815. *A review of the reasons given for establishing a registry of slaves in the British colonies.* London: Hatchard.

The agency society list of acceptable and unacceptable candidates. 1832. British Museum, document BM 8052 il (74), London.

Agricola. 1855. *DeBow's Review* 19:362.

Aiken, D. Wyatt. 1869–1870a. Agriculture in Mississippi. *Rural Carolinian* 1:476.

———. 1869–1870b. Southern farming and farm labor. *Rural Carolinian* 1:141.

———. 1870–1871. Does farming pay in the South? *Rural Carolinian* 2:323–324.

———. 1871–1872. Labor contracts. *Rural Carolinian* 3:113–115.

———. 1874–1875. A few words on the labor question. *Rural Carolinian* 6:455.

Anderson, Eric. 1981. *Race and politics in North Carolina, 1872–1901: The black second.* Baton Rouge: Louisiana State University Press.

Andrews, Sidney. 1866. *The South since the war.* Boston: Ticknor and Fields.

Anstey, Roger T. 1968. Capitalism and slavery: A critique. *Economic History Review* 21:307–320.

———. 1972. A reinterpretation of the abolition of the British slave trade, 1806–1807. *English Historical Review* 87:304–332.

———. 1975. *The Atlantic slave trade and British abolition, 1760–1810.* London: Macmillan.

———. 1980. The pattern of British abolitionism in the eighteenth and nineteenth centuries. In Christine Bolt and Seymour Drescher, eds., *Anti-slavery, religion, and reform.* Folkestone, UK: W. Dawson.

———. 1981. Religion and British slave emancipation. In David Eltis and James Walvin, eds. *The abolition of the Atlantic slave trade.* Madison: University of Wisconsin Press.

Arrington, A.H. 1867–1868. Papers. Southern Historical Collection, University of North Carolina, Chapel Hill.

Ashby, H.T. 1915. *Infant mortality.* Cambridge, UK: Cambridge University Press.

Ashworth, A. 1982. International differences in infant mortality and the impact of malnutrition: A review. *Human Nutrition: Clinical Nutrition* 36c:7–23.

Aydelotte, William O. 1977. Constituency influence on the British House of Commons, 1841–1847. In W.O. Aydelotte, ed., *The history of parliamentary behavior.* Princeton, NJ: Princeton University Press.

B. 1872–1873. Notes by a Florida planter. Rural Carolinian 4:64.

Bai, K. Indira, and B. Vijayalakshmi. 1973. Sexual maturation of Indian girls in Andhra Pradesh. *Human Biology* 45:695–707.

Ball Family. 1786–1825. Papers. South Carolina Library, University of South Carolina, Columbia.

Ball, John and Keating S. 1803–1833. Papers. Southern Historical Collection, University of North Carolina, Chapel Hill.

Bancroft, Frederic. [1931] 1959. *Slave trading in the old South.* New York: Frederick Ungar.

Banks, Enoch M. 1905. The economics of land tenure in Georgia. *Studies in History, Economics and Public Law* 23:1–142.

Barakat, M.R. 1976. Pellagra. In G. H. Beaton and J. M. Bengoa, eds., *Nutrition in preventative medicine: The major deficiency syndromes, epidemiology, and approaches to control.* Geneva: World Health Organization.

Barboza, Ruy. 1884. *Emancipação dos escravos.* Rio de Janeiro: Typographia Nacional.

Bardhan, P.K., and T.N. Srinivisan. 1971. Cropsharing tenancy in agriculture: A theoretical and empirical analysis. *American Economic Review* 61:48–64.

Barrow, David C., Jr. 1881. A Georgia plantation. *Scribner's Monthly* 21:830–836.

———. 1882. Plantation Life: Autumn scenes on a Georgia plantation. *Southern Cultivator* 40:8–9.

Bascot. 1866. Papers. Contract at Darlington District, SC, Jan. 1. #1916. Southern Historical Collection, University of North Carolina, Chapel Hill.

Bauer, R.A., and A.H. Bauer. 1942. Day to day resistance to slavery. *Journal of Negro History* 27:388–419.

Beard, Charles A., and Mary R. Beard. 1933. *The rise of American civilization.* New York: Macmillan.

Beaton, G.H. 1976. Some other nutritional deficiencies. In G. H. Beaton and J. M. Bengoa, eds., *Nutrition in preventative medicine: The major deficiency syndromes, epidemiology and approaches to control.* Geneva: World Health Organization.

Beaton, G.H., and Bengoa, J.M., eds. 1976. *Nutrition in preventative medicine: The major deficiency syndromes, epidemiology and approaches to control.* Geneva: World Health Organization.

Beaton, G.H., and V.N. Patwardhan. 1976. Physiological and practical considerations of nutrient function and requirements. In G. H. Beaton and J. M. Bengoa, eds., *Nutrition in preventative medicine: The major deficiency syndromes, epidemiology, and approaches to control.* Geneva: World Health Organization.

Beiguelman, Paula. 1966. *A formação do povo no complexo cafeeiro: Aspectos politicos.* São Paulo: Livraria Pioneira Editora.

Bentley, George R. 1955. *A history of the Freedman's Bureau.* Philadelphia: University of Pennsylvania.

Bethell, Leslie. 1970. *The abolition of the Brazilian slave trade.* Cambridge, UK: Cambridge University Press.

Bhagwati, J. 1966. *The economics of underdeveloped countries.* New York: McGraw-Hill.

Bierck, Harold A. 1953. The struggle for abolition in Gran Columbia. *Hispanic American Historical Review* 33:365–386.

Birch, Alan. 1967. *The economic history of the British iron and steel industry, 1784–1879.* London: Cass.

Bittker, Boris I. 1973. *The case for black reparations.* New York: Vintage Books.

Bivens, John D. 1871–1873. Papers. Perkins Library Archives, Duke University, Durham, N.C.

Blaug, Mark. 1963. The myth of the old Poor Law and the making of the new. *Journal of Economic History* 23:151–179.

Blodget, Samuel. 1806. *Economica: A statistical manual for the United States of America.* Washington, D.C.: By author.

Blum, Jerome. 1961. *Lord and peasant in Russia from the ninth to the nineteenth century.* Princeton, NJ: Princeton University Press.

Bogue, Donald J., and James A. Palmore. 1964. Some empirical and analytic relations among demographic fertility measures, with regression models for fertility estimation. *Demography* 1:316–338.

Bojlen, K., and M.W. Bentzon. 1968. The influence of climate and nutrition on age at menarche: A historical review and modern hypothesis. *Human Biology* 40:69–85.

Bolt, Christine, and Seymour Drescher, eds. 1980. *Antislavery, religion, and reform.* Folkestone, UK: W. Dawson.

Bongaarts, J., and M. Cain. 1982. Demographic responses to famine. In K.M. Cahill, ed., *Famine.* Maryknoll, NY: Orbis Books.

Botkin, B.A., ed. 1945. *Lay my burden down: A folk history of slavery.* Chicago: University of Chicago Press.

Bouchereau, Louis. 1870. *Statement of the sugar and rice crops made in Louisiana, 1869–1870.* New Orleans: M.F. Dunn and Bro.

Bouvier, L.F., and J. van der Tak. 1976. Infant mortality: Progress and problems. *Population Bulletin* 31:3–33.

Brannen, C.O. 1924. *Relation of land tenure to plantation organization.* United States Department of Agriculture, *Bulletin* No. 1269. Washington, D.C.

Brass, W., A.J. Coale, P. Demeny, D.F. Heisel, F. Lorimer, A. Romaniuk and E. van de Walle. 1968. *The Demography of Tropical Africa.* Princeton, NJ: Princeton University Press.

Brathwaite, E.K. 1981. *The folk culture of the slaves in Jamaica.* London: New Beacon Books.

Breeden, J.D. 1980. *Advice among masters: The ideal in slave management in the Old South.* Westport, CT: Greenwood.

Brozek, J., and B. Schurch, eds. 1984. *Malnutrition and behavior: Critical assessment of key issues.* Lausanne, Switzerland: Nestle Foundation.

British Solomon Islands. Census Office. 1970. *Report of the census of population, 1970.* By K. Groenewegen. Honiara, British Solomon Islands Protectorate: Western Pacific High Commission.

Brooks, Robert P. 1914. The agrarian revolution in Georgia, 1865–1912. *Bulletin of the University of Wisconsin, History Ser.* No. 3.

Bruce, Philip A. [1889] 1970. *The plantation Negro as a freeman.* Williamstown, MA: Corner House.

Brundtland, G.H., and Lars Walløe. 1976. Menarcheal age in Norway in the 19th century: A reevaluation of historical sources. *Annals of Human Biology* 3:363–374.

Bull, Jacqueline P. 1952. The general merchant in the economic history of the New South. *Journal of Southern History* 28:37–59.

Burn, W.L. 1937. *Emancipation and apprenticeship in the British West Indies.* London: Jonathan Cape.

Burnett, John. 1966. *Plenty and want: A social history of diet in England from 1815 to the present day.* Harmondsworth, UK: Penguin Books.

Burrell, R.J.W., M.J.R. Healy, and J.M Tanner. 1961. Age at menarche in South African Bantu schoolgirls living in the Transkei reserve. *Human Biology* 33:250–261.

Cairnes, John Elliot. [1862] 1969. *The slave power: Its character, career, and probable designs: Being an attempt to explain the real issues involved in the American contest.* Introduction by Harold D. Woodman. New York: Harper & Row.

———. [1863] 1966. Excerpt from *The slave power: Its character, career and probable designs: Being an attempt to explain the real issues involved in the American contest,* rev. ed. In Harold D. Woodman, ed., *Slavery and the southern economy: Sources and readings,* 2nd ed. New York: Harcourt Brace & World.

Campbell, George. 1879. *White and black: The outcome of a visit to the United States.* London: Chatto and Windus.

Campbell, J. 1984. Work, pregnancy, and infant mortality among southern slaves. *Journal of Interdisciplinary History* 14:793–812.

Canarella, Giorgio, and John A. Tomaske. 1975. The optimal utilization of slaves. *Journal of Economic History* 35:621–629.

Cance, Alexander E. 1908. Economics and land tenure in Mississippi. Ph.D. dissertation, University of Wisconsin.

Cantrelle, P., and H. Leridon. 1971. Breast feeding, mortality in childhood and fertility in a rural zone of Senegal. *Population Studies* 25:505–533.

Carr, J.C., and W. Taplin. 1962. *A history of the British steel industry.* Cambridge, MA: Harvard University Press.

Catterall, Helen T., ed. 1936. *Judicial cases concerning American slavery and the Negro. Vol. IV: Cases from the courts of New England, the middle states, and the District of Columbia.* Washington, D.C.: Carnegie Institution of Washington.

Chavez, Adolfo, and Martinez, Celia. 1982. *Growing up in a developing community.* Mexico: Institute of Nutrition of Central America and Panama.

Cheung, Stephen N.S. 1969. *The theory of share tenancy.* Chicago: University of Chicago Press.

Christianson, R.E., B.J. Van den Berg, L. Milkovich, and F.W. Oechsli. 1981. Incidence of congenital anomalies among white and black births with long-term follow-up. *American Journal of Public Health* 71:1333–1341.

Clapham, John H. 1936. *The economic development of France and Germany, 1815–1904,* 3 vols. Cambridge, UK: Cambridge University Press.

———. 1964. *An economic history of modern Britain.* Cambridge, UK: Cambridge University Press.

Clark, Thomas D. 1964. *Pills, petticoats, and plows: The southern country store.* Norman: University of Oklahoma Press.

Clifton, James M. 1978. Twilight comes to the rice kingdom: Postbellum rice culture on the South Atlantic Coast. *Georgia Historical Quarterly* 62:146–154.

Cole, Arthur H. 1938. *Wholesale commodity prices in the United States, 1700–1861,* 2 vols. Cambridge, MA: Harvard University Press.

Coale, Ansley J., and Paul Demeny. 1966. *Regional model life tables and stable populations.* Princeton, NJ: Princeton University Press.

———. 1983. *Regional model life tables and stable populations,* 2nd ed. New York: Academic Press.

Collins, Dr. [1811] 1971. *Practical rules for the management and medical treatment of Negro slaves in the sugar colonies, by a professional planter.* Freeport, NY: Books for Libraries Press.

Collins, Robert. 1854. Essay on the management of slaves. *Debow's Review* 17:421–426.

Colquhoun, P. 1814. *Treatise on the wealth, power, and resources of the British Empire.* London: Joseph Mawman.

Conrad, Robert. 1972. *The destruction of Brazilian slavery, 1850–1888.* Austin: University of Texas Press.

Contracts with laborers. 1865. *Southern Cultivator* 23:180.

Cooley, Henry S. 1896. *A study of slavery in New Jersey.* Baltimore, MD: Johns Hopkins University Press.

Correa do Lago, Luiz Aranha. 1978. The transition from slave to free labor labor in agriculture in the southern and coffee regions of Brazil: A global and theoretical approach and regional case studies. Ph.D. dissertation, Harvard University.

Corwin, Arthur F. 1967. *Spain and the abolition of slavery in Cuba, 1817–1886.* Austin: University of Texas Press.

Cosmopolitan. 1868. The question of labor. *Southern Cultivator* 26:12–13.

da Costa, Emilia Viotti. 1966. *Da senzala à colonia.* São Paulo: Difusão Européio do Livro.

Cotton and Tobacco. 1868–1869. *The American Farmer* 3:282–284.

Coupland, Reginald. 1923. *Wilberforce: A narrative.* Oxford, UK: Clarendon Press.

———. [1933] 1964. *The British anti-slavery movement.* London: T. Butterworth.

Covert, James. 1912. *Seedtime and harvest.* U.S. Department of Agriculture, Bureau of Statistics, *Bulletin* No. 85. Washington, D.C.: Government Printing Office.

Cox, La Wanda and John H. Cox, eds. 1973. *Reconstruction, the Negro, and the New South.* Columbia: University of South Carolina Press.

Crawford, Stephen C. 1980. Quantified memory: A study of the WPA and Fisk University slave narrative collections. Ph.D. dissertation, University of Chicago.

Croppers—Equitable division of crops. 1886. *Southern Cultivator* 44:468.

Curry, Leonard P. 1968. *Blueprint for modern America.* Nashville, TN: Vanderbilt University Press.

Curtin, Philip D. 1955. *Two Jamaicas: The role of ideas in a tropical colony.* Cambridge, MA: Harvard University Press.

———. 1968. Epidemiology and the slave trade. *Political Science Quarterly* 83:190–216.

———. 1969. *The Atlantic slave trade, A census.* Madison: University of Wisconsin Press.

———. 1975. Measuring the Atlantic slave trade. In Stanley L. Engerman and Eugene D. Genovese, eds., *Race and slavery in the Western Hemisphere.* Princeton, NJ: Princeton University Press.

Daget, Serge. 1971. L'abolition de la traité des noirs en France de 1814 à 1831. *Cahiers d'études africaines* 11:14–58.

———. 1973. Catalogue des navires . . . de participation au trafic négrier Atlantique entre 1814 et 1833. Manuscript. Abidjan.

Damon, Albert. 1974. Larger body size and earlier menarche: The end may be in sight. *Social Biology* 21:8–11.

Dantzig, George B. 1963. *Linear programming and extensions.* Princeton, NJ: Princeton University Press.

Darby, William J., M.D., Kristen W. McNutt, and E. Niege Todhunter. 1975. Niacin. *Nutrition Reviews* 33:289–297.

Davidson, Leybourne S.P., Sir, R. Passmore, J.F. Brack, and A.F. Truswell. 1975. *Human nutrition and dietetics,* 6th ed. Edinburgh, UK: Churchill Livingstone.

Davies, J.N.P. 1964. The decline of pellagra in the southern United States. *Lancet* 2:195–196.

Davis, David Brion. 1966. *The problem of slavery in Western culture.* Ithaca, NY: Cornell University Press.

———. 1975. *The problem of slavery in the age of revolution, 1760–1823.* Ithaca, NY: Cornell University Press.

———. 1984. *Slavery and Human Progress.* New York: Oxford University Press.

Davis, Edwin A., ed. 1943. *Plantation life in the Florida parishes of Louisiana 1836–1844 as reflected in the diary of Bennet H. Barrow.* New York: Columbia University Press.

Davis, Ronald L.F. 1981. Labor dependency among freedmen, 1865–1880. In Walter J. Frazer and Winifred B. Moore, eds., *From the Old South to the New South: Essays on the transitional South.* Westport, CT: Greenwood Press.

———. 1982. *Good and faithful labor: From slavery to sharecropping in the Natchez District, 1860–1890.* Westport, CT: Greenwood Press.

DeBow's Review. Vol. 2, 1846; Vol. 3, 1847; Vol. 10, 1851; Vol. 11, 1851; Vol. 12, 1852; Vol. 17, 1854; Vol. 1, 2nd ser., 1866.

DeCanio, Stephen J. 1974. *Agriculture in the postbellum South: The economics of production and supply.* Cambridge, MA: MIT Press.

Deerr, Noel. 1949–1950. *The history of sugar,* 2 vols. London: Chapman Hall.

De Leon, Edwin. 1873–1874. The new South. *Harper's New Monthly Magazine* 48:270–180, 406–422.

————. 1874. Ruin and reconstruction of the southern states. *Southern Magazine* 14:17–41, 287–309.

Dennett, John R. [1865–1866] 1965. *The South as it is: 1865–1866.* New York: Viking Press.

Dennis. 1869. A visit to Mr. Dickson's plantation. *Southern Cultivator* 27:58–59.

Department of Labor and Immigration: Labor and wages. 1869–1870. *Rural Carolinian* 1:570–571.

Devereux Family. 1869, 1872. Papers. Perkins Library Archives. Duke University, Durham, North Carolina.

Dew, Thomas R. 1963. Review of the debate in the Virginia legislature of 1831 and 1832. In Eric L. McKitrick, ed., *Slavery defended: The views of the Old South.* Englewood, NJ: Prentice-Hall.

Dickson, David. 1870. *A practical treatise on agriculture.* Macon, GA: J.W. Burke.

Dixon, Peter F. 1971. The politics of emancipation: The movement for the abolition of slavery in the British West Indies, 1807–1833. Ph.D. dissertation, Oxford University.

Dod's parliamentary pocket companion for 1833, including a compendious peerage. 1833. London: Whittaker, Treacher and Arnot.

Doring, Gerhard K. 1969. The incidence of anovular cycles in women. *Journal of Reproduction and Fertility* 18:77–82.

Dorris, J.T. 1953. *Pardon and amnesty under Lincoln and Johnson: The restoration of the Confederates to their rights and privileges, 1861–1898.* Chapel Hill: University of North Carolina Press.

Draper, N.R., and H. Smith. 1966. *Applied regression analysis.* New York: John Wiley & Sons.

Draughon, Robert J., M.D. 1850. Provisions for field hands. *Southern Cultivator* 8:4.

Dreizen, S., C.N. Spirakis, and R.E. Stone. 1967. A comparison of skeletal growth and maturation in undernourished and well-nourished girls before and after menarche. *Journal of Pediatrics* 70:256–263.

Drescher, Seymour. 1977. *Econocide: British slavery in the era of abolition.* Pittsburgh: University of Pittsburgh Press.

————. 1982. Public opinion and the destruction of British colonial slavery. In J. Walvin, ed., *Slavery and British society 1776–1846.* Baton Rouge: Louisiana State University Press.

————. 1986. *Capitalism and antislavery.* London: Macmillan.

Dromgoole, George C. 1872, 1873. Papers. Perkins Library Archives. Duke University, Durham, North Carolina.

Durnin, J.V.G.A., and R. Passmore. 1967. *Energy, work, and leisure.* London: Heinemann Educational Books.

Easterlin, Richard A. 1961. Regional income trends, 1840–1850. In Seymour Harris, ed., *American economic history.* New York: McGraw-Hill.

————. 1971. Does human fertility adjust to the environment? *American Economic Review: Papers and Proceedings* 61:399–407.

————. 1976a. Factors in the decline of farm family fertility in the United States: Some preliminary research results. *Journal of American History* 63:600–614.

————. 1976b. Population change and farm settlement in the northern United States. *Journal of Economic History* 36:45–83.

————. 1977. Population issues in American economic history: A survey and critique. In R.E. Gallman, ed., *Research in economic history, Suppl. 1.* Greenwich, CT: JAI Press.

Easterlin, Richard A., George Alter, and Gretchen A. Condran. 1978. Farms and farm families in old and new areas: The northern United States in 1860. In Tamara K. Hareven and Maris A. Vinovskis, eds., *Family and population in nineteenth-century America.* Princeton, NJ: Princeton University Press.

Eaton, Joseph W. and Albert J. Mayer. 1953. The social biology of very high fertility among the Hutterites: The demography of a unique population. *Human Biology* 25:206–264.

Eblen, J.E. 1972. Growth of the black population in antebellum America. *Population Studies* 26:273–289.

————. 1974. New estimates of the vital rates of the United States black population during the nineteenth century. *Demography* 11:301–319.

————. 1975. On the natural increase of slave populations: The example of the Cuban black population, 1775–1900. In Stanley L. Engerman and Eugene D. Genovese, eds., *Race and slavery in the Western hemisphere: Quantitative studies.* Princeton, NJ: Princeton University Press.

Editor. 1851. Special report on the fevers of New Orleans in the year 1850. *Southern Medical Reports* 2:79–99.

Edmondston, P.M. 1969. Labor, etc. in the South. *The American Farmer* 4:25–26.

Eisner, Gisela. 1961. *Jamaica, 1830–1930: A study in economic growth.* Manchester, UK: Manchester University Press.

Elkins, S.M. 1976. *Slavery: A problem in American institutional and intellectual life,* 2nd ed. Chicago: University of Chicago Press.

Ellis, R.W.B. 1945. Growth and health of Belgian children. *Archives of the Diseases of Childhood* 20:97–109.

Eltis, D. 1972. The traffic in slaves between the British West Indian Colonies, 1807–1833. *Economic History Review* 25:55–64.

Engerman, Stanley L. 1966. The economic impact of the Civil War. *Explorations in Economic History* 3:176–199.

———. 1967. The effect of slavery on the southern economy. *Explorations in Economic History* 4:71–97.

———. 1971a. The economic impact of the Civil War. In Robert W. Fogel and Stanley L. Engerman, eds., *The reinterpretation of American economic history.* New York: Harper & Row.

———. 1971b. Some economic factors in southern backwardness in the nineteenth century. In John Kain and John Meyer, eds., *Essays in regional economics.* Cambridge, MA: Harvard University Press.

———. 1973. Some considerations relating to property rights in man. *Journal of Economic History* 33:43–65.

———. 1982. Economic adjustments to emancipation in the United States and British West Indies. *Journal of Interdisciplinary History* 12:191–220.

———. 1984. Economic change and contract labor in the British Caribbean: The end of slavery and the adjustment to emancipation. *Explorations in Economic History* 21:133–150.

———. 1986a. Slavery and emancipation in comparative perspective: A look at some recent debates. *Journal of Economic History* 46:317–339.

———. 1986b. Servants to slaves to servants: Contract labour and European expansion. In P.C. Emmer, ed., *Colonialism and migration: Indentured labor before and after slavery.* Dordrecht, The Netherlands: Martinus Nijhoff.

Engerman, Stanley L., and David Eltis. 1980. Economic aspects of the abolition debate. In Christine Bolt and Seymour Drescher, eds., *Antislavery, religion and reform.* Folkestone, UK: W. Dawson.

Engerman, Stanley L., Robert W. Fogel, Eugene D. Genovese, and Herbert G. Gutman. 1972. New directions in black history. *Forum: A Journal of Social Commentary and the Arts* 1:22–41.

Engerman, Stanley L., and Eugene D. Genovese, eds. 1975. *Race and slavery in the Western Hemisphere.* Princeton, NJ: Princeton University Press.

Engerrand, Steven William. 1981. "Now scratch or die": The genesis of capitalist agricultural labor in Georgia, 1865–1880. Ph.D. dissertation, University of Georgia.

Evans, Robert, Jr. 1962. The economics of American Negro slavery. In *Aspects of Labor Economics.* Universities-National Bureau Committee for Economic Research. Princeton, NJ: Princeton University Press (for NBER).

Evans, W.H. 1867. The labor question: Communicated from the transactions of the pomological and farmer's club of Society Hill, South Carolina. *Southern Cultivator* 27:54–55.

Eveleth, P.B., and Tanner, J.M. 1976. *Worldwide variation in human growth.* New York: Cambridge University Press.

Everaert, J. 1963. Les fluctuations du trafic négrier Nantais (1763–1792). *Les cahiers de tunisie* 11:37–62.

Ex-Confed. 1870. To manage laborers. *Southern Cultivator* 28:141.

Falconbridge, Alexander. 1788. *An account of the slave trade on the coast of Africa.* London: J. Phillips.

Farley, Reynolds. 1965. The demographic rates and social institutions of the nineteenth-century negro population: A stable population analysis. *Demography* 2:386–398.

———. 1970. *Growth of the black population.* Chicago: Markham.

Farnam, Henry W. 1938. *Chapters in the history of social legislation in the United States to 1860.* Washington, D.C.: Carnegie Institution of Washington.

Fenoaltea, Stefano. 1984. Slavery and supervision in comparative perspective: A model. *Journal of Economic History* 44:635–668.

Ferguson, Robert. 1866. *America during and after the war.* London: Longmans.

Fielding, Ronald H. 1973. American slave emancipation: The costs in the South, the District of Columbia, and the North. Typescript.

Fiji. 1958. *Report on the census of the population, 1956.* By Norma McArthur. Suva, Fiji: Government Press.

———. 1968. *Report on the census of the population, 1966.* By F.H.A.G. Zwart. Suva, Fiji: Government Press.

Finney, D.J. 1952. Probit analysis. Cambridge, UK: Cambridge University Press.

Fitzhardinge, P.M., and E.M. Steven. 1972. The small-for-date infant, I. Later growth patterns. *Pediatrics* 49:671–681.

Fleming, Walter L. 1905. *Civil War and reconstruction in Alabama.* New York: P. Smith.

Foby. 1853. Management of servants. *Southern Cultivator* 11:226–228.

Fogel, Robert William. 1986. Nutrition and the decline in mortality since 1700: Some preliminary findings. In Stanley L. Engerman and Robert E. Gallman, eds., *Long-term factors in American economic growth.* Conference on Research in Income and Wealth, Vol. 51. Chicago: University of Chicago Press (for NBER).

Fogel, Robert W., and Stanley L. Engerman eds. 1971a. *The reinterpretation of American economic history.* New York: Harper & Row.

———. 1971b. The economics of slavery. In Robert W. Fogel and Stanley L. Engerman, eds., *The reinterpretation of American economic history.* New York: Harper & Row.

———. 1971c. The relative efficiency of slavery: A comparison of northern and southern agriculture in 1860. *Explorations in Economic History* 8:353–367.

———. 1972. The market evaluation of human capital: The case of slavery. Paper presented to the Annual Cliometrics Conference, Madison, WI.

———. 1974a. *Time on the cross: The economics of American Negro slavery,* 2 vols. Boston: Little, Brown.

———. 1974b. Further evidence on the nutritional adequacy of the slave diet. Typescript.

———. 1975. The relative efficiency of slave and free agriculture in 1860 and 1850. Typescript.

———. 1979. Recent findings in the study of slave demography and family structure. *Sociology and Social Research* 63:566–589.

———. 1983. Further evidence on the economics of American Negro slavery. Typescript.

Fogel, Robert W., Stanley L. Engerman, R. Floud, G. Friedman, R.A. Margo, K. Sokoloff, R.H. Steckel, J.T. Trussell, K.W. Wachter, and G. Villaflor. 1983. Secular changes in American and British stature and nutrition. *Journal of Interdisciplinary History* 14:445–481.

Fogel, Robert W., Stanley L. Engerman, and J. Trussell. 1982. Exploring the uses of data on height: The analysis of long-term trends in nutrition, labor welfare, and labor productivity. *Social Science History* 6:401–421.

Fogel, Robert W., Stanley L. Engerman, J. Trussell, R. Floud, C.L. Pope, and L.T. Wimmer. 1978. The economics of mortality in North America, 1650–1910: A description of a research project. *Historical Methods* 11:75–108.

Form of contract with plantation hands. 1866. *Southern Cultivator* 24:4.

Forster, Colin, and G.S.L. Tucker. 1972. *Economic opportunity and white American fertility ratios, 1800–1860.* New Haven, CT: Yale University Press.

Foster, J.G. 1866. *Report of the assistant commissioner for Florida.* Reports of the Assistant Commissioner, S. Doc. 6. 39th Cong., 2d sess., 1866–1867.

Franklin, John Hope. 1963. *The Emancipation Proclamation.* New York: Doubleday and Co.

Frazier, E. Franklin. 1966. *The Negro family in the United States.* Chicago: University of Chicago Press.

Friedman, G.C. 1982. The heights of slaves in Trinidad. *Social Science History* 6:482–515.

Frisch, Rose E. 1975. Demographic implications of the biological determinants of female fecundity. *Social Biology* 22:17–22.

Frisch, Rose, D.M. Hegsted, and K. Yoshinaga. 1975. Body weight and food intake at early estrus of rats on a high-fat diet. *Proceedings of the National Academy of Science* 72:4172–4176.

Frisch, Rose, and J.W. McArthur. 1974. Menstrual cycles: Fatness as a determinant of minimum weight for height necessary for their maintenance or onset. *Science* 185:949–951.

Frisch, Rose, and Roger Revelle. 1969. The height and weight of adolescent boys and girls at the time of peak velocity of growth in height and weight: Longitudinal data. *Human Biology* 41:536–559.

Gaillard, Peter. 1840–1863. Plantations Records. Microfilm. Southern Historical Collection, University of North Carolina, Chapel Hill and Southern Carolina Historical Society, Charleston.

Gaillard, Samuel Porcher. 1786–1825. Papers. South Caroliniana Library, University of South Carolina, Columbia.

Galdames, Luis. 1941. *A history of Chile.* Trans. and ed. by Isaac Joslin Cox. Chapel Hill: University of North Carolina Press.

Gash, Norman. 1953. *Politics in the age of Peel: A study of the technique of parliamentary representation, 1830–1850.* London: Longmans Green.

Gates, Paul W. 1940. Federal land policy in the South. *Journal of Southern History* 6:303–330.

Genovese, Eugene D. 1971. *The world the slaveowners made.* New York: Vintage Books.

———. 1974. *Roll, Jordan, roll: The world the slaves made.* New York: Pantheon.

Gershenkron, Alexander. 1965. Agrarian policies and industrialization: Russia 1861–1917, Vol. 6 of *Cambridge economic history of Europe.* Edited by H.J. Habakkuk and M. Postan. Cambridge, UK: Cambridge University Press.

Gilbert and Ellice Islands Colony. 1970. *A report on the results of the census of the population, 1968.* By F. H. A. G. Zwart and K. Groenewegen. Sidney, Australia: New South Wales Government Printer.

———. 1975. *Report on the 1973 census of population: Gilbert and Ellice Islands.* Bairiki, Tarawa, Gilbert Islands: Office of the Chief Minister.

Gillespie Papers. n.d. Louisiana State University Library. Baton Rouge, Louisiana.

Gilman, Nicholas P. 1893. *Profit sharing between employer and employees: A study in the evolution of the wage system.* Boston: Houghton Miflin.

Gini, C. 1924. Premières recherches sur la fécundabilitée de la femme. *Proceedings of the International Mathematics Congress* 2:889–892.

Glass, D.V., and Grebenik, E. 1965. World population, 1800–1950, Vol. 6 of *The Cambridge economic history of Europe.* Edited by H.J. Habakkuk and M. Postan. Cambridge, UK: Cambridge University Press.

Goldin, Claudia Dale. 1976. *Urban slavery in the American South: A quantitative history.* Chicago: University of Chicago Press.

Goldin, Claudia Dale, and Frank Lewis. 1975. The economic cost of the American Civil War: Estimates and implications. *Journal of Economic History* 35:299–326.

Goldsmith, Grace A. 1964. The B vitamins: Thiamine, riboflavin, niacin. In George H. Beaton and Earle W. McHenry, eds., *Nutrition: A comprehensive treatise,* Vol. 2 of *Vitamins, requirements and food selection.* New York: Academic Press.

Good Hope Plantation. 1835–1856. Accounts. South Carolina Historical Society, Charleston.

Goubert, Pierre. 1968. Legitimate fecundity and infant mortality in France during the eighteenth century: A comparison. *Daedalus* 97:593–603.

Gould, Benjamin Anthorp. [1869] 1969. *Investigations in the military and anthropological statistics of American soldiers,* Vol. 2, reprint. New York: Arno Press.

Grady, Henry W. 1881. Cotton and its kingdom. *Harper's Magazine* 63:725.

Graham, Richard. 1966. Causes for the abolition of Negro slavery in Brazil: An interpretative essay. *Hispanic American Review* 46:123–127.

Gray, Lewis Cecil. [1933] 1958. *History of agriculture in the southern United States to 1860,* 2 vols. Gloucester, MA: Peter Smith.

Gray, Lewis Cecil. [1933] 1966a. Competitive advantages of Negro slavery under the plantation system. Excerpt from *History of agriculture in the southern United States to 1860.* In Harold D. Woodman, ed., *Slavery and the southern economy: Sources and readings,* 2nd ed. New York: Harcourt, Brace & World.

———. [1933] 1966b. Farmer unable to compete with slaveowning planter. Excerpt from *History of agriculture in the southern United States to 1860.* In Harold D. Woodman, ed., *Slavery and the southern economy: Sources and readings,* 2nd ed. New York: Harcourt, Brace & World.

Green, William A. 1976. *British slave emancipation: The sugar colonies and the great experiment 1830–1865.* Oxford, UK: Clarendon Press.

Green-Pedersen, Sv. E. 1973. Om forholdene pa danske slaveskibe med søerlig henblik pa dødeligheden, 1777–89. In Henning Henningson, ed., *Handels-og Søfartsmuseet på Kronborg.* Elsinore, Denmark: Selskabet Handels-og Søfartsmuseets Venner.

Gregory, E.M. 1866. *Report of the assistant commissioner for Texas.* Papers of the Freedmen's Bureau, H. Doc. 70. 39th Cong., 1st sess., 1865–1866.

Grimes Family. 1882. Papers. Southern Historical Collection, University of North Carolina, Chapel Hill.

Grossman, Sanford, and Oliver Hart. 1983. An analysis of the principal-agent problem. *Econometrica* 51:7–45.

Grunfeld, Y., and Zvi Griliches. 1960. Is aggregation necessarily bad? *Review of Economics and Statistics* 42:1–13.

Gunderson, Gerald. 1974. The origin of the American Civil War. *Journal of Economic History* 34:915–950.

Gutman, Herbert G. 1975. *Slavery and the numbers game.* Urbana: The University of Illinois Press.

Gutman, Herbert G., and Richard Sutch. 1976a. Victorians all? The sexual mores and conduct of slaves and their masters. In Paul A. David, Herbert G. Gutman, Richard Sutch, Peter Temin, and Gavin Wright, eds., *Reckoning with slavery.* New York: Oxford University Press.

———. 1976b. Sambo makes good, or were slaves imbued with the protestant work ethic. In Paul A. David, Herbert G. Gutman, Richard Sutch, Peter Temin, and Gavin Wright, eds., *Reckoning with slavery.* New York: Oxford University Press.

H. 1867. Hints on the labor question. *Southern Planter* 1:511.

Habicht, J.-P., Julie Davanzo, W. P. Butz, and Linda Meyers. 1985. The contraceptive role of breastfeeding. *Population Studies* 39:213–232.

Hacker, Louis. 1947. *The triumph of American capitalism.* New York: Columbia University Press.

Haines, M.R., and R.C. Avery. 1980. The American life table of 1830–1860: An evaluation. *Journal of Interdisciplinary History* 11:73–95.

Hajnal, J. 1953. Age at marriage and proportions marrying. *Population Studies* 7:111–132.

Halévy, Élie. 1950. *A history of the English people in the nineteenth century.* 6 vols. in 7. Trans. by E.I. Watkin. London: T.F. Unwin.

Hall, Douglas. 1959. *Free Jamaica, 1838–1865: An economic history.* New Haven, CT: Yale University Press.

Hall, Robert. n.d. The Burden of Slavery. Manuscript.

Hammond, James H. Papers. 1832–1863. South Carolina Library, University of South Carolina, 1832–1863. Columbia.

———. 1844. Plantation manual. Manuscript. South Carolina Library, University of South Carolina, Columbia.

Hammond, Matthew B. 1897. *The cotton industry: An essay in American economic history.* New York: Macmillan.

Handler, J.S., and R.S. Corruccini. 1986. Weaning among West Indian slaves: Historical and bioanthropological evidence from Barbados. *William and Mary Quarterly* 48:111–117.

Hansard's Parliamentary Debates. 1833. Third ser., Vols. 15, 16, 17, 18, 19, 20. London: T.J. Hansard.

———. 1834. Third ser., Vols. 21, 22, 23, 24, 25. London: T.J. Hansard.

Hansen, L. A. 1866–1867a. Farming prospects in the South. *The American Farmer* 1:138–139.

———. 1866–1867b. Large farms and associated capital. *The American Farmer* 1:341–342.

Harris, David Golightly. Books. 1867. Southern Historical Collection, University of North Carolina, Chapel Hill.

Hartwell, R.M. 1971. Children as slaves. In R.M. Hartwell, *The industrial revolution and economic growth.* London: Methuen.

Haskin, James. 1975. *The creoles of color of New Orleans.* New York: Thomas Y. Crowell Co.

Henripin, Jacques. 1954. *La population Canadienne au début du XVIIe Siècle,* cahier no. 22. Paris: I.N.E.D.

Henry, Louis. 1956. *Anciennes familles Genevoises,* cahier no. 26. Paris: I.N.E.D.

———. 1965. French statistical research in natural fertility. In M.C. Sheps and J.C. Ridley, eds., *Public health and population change.* Pittsburgh: University of Pittsburgh Press.

———. 1968. The verification of data in historical demography. *Population Studies* 22:61–81.

Henry, W.A. 1910. *Feeds and feeding: A handbook for the student and stockman,* 10th ed. Madison: By author.

Hiernaux, Jean. 1968. Ethnic differences in growth and development. *Eugenics Quarterly* 15:12–21.

Higgs, Robert. 1973. Race, tenure, and resource allocation in southern agriculture, 1910. *Journal of Economic History* 33:149–169.

———. 1977. *Competition and coercion: Blacks in the American economy, 1865–1914.* Cambridge, UK: Cambridge University Press.

Higman, B.W. 1976. *Slave population and economy in Jamaica, 1807–1834.* Cambridge, MA: Cambridge University Press.

———. 1984. *Slave populations of the British Caribbean, 1807–1834.* Baltimore, MD: Johns Hopkins University Press.

Hilgard, Eugene W., ed. 1884. *Report on cotton production in the United States,* 2 vols. Washington, D.C.: Government Printing Office.

Hill, K., and J. Trussell. 1977. Further developments in indirect mortality estimation. *Population Studies* 31:313–314.

Hilliard, Sam Bowles. 1972. *Hog meat and hoecake: Food supply in the old South, 1840–1860.* Carbondale: Southern Illinois University Press.

Hiss, Philip Hanson. 1945. *Netherlands America: The Dutch territories in the West.* New York: Duell, Sloane, and Pearce.

Hochstetter, Franz. 1905. *Die wirtschaftlischen und politischen motive für die abschaffung des Britischen Sklavenhandels im Jahre 1806–7.* Leipzig, Germany: Duncker & Humblot.

Hodges, R.E. 1976. Scurvy. In G.H. Beaton and J.M. Bengoa, eds., *Nutrition in preventative medicine: The major deficiency syndromes, epidemiology, and approaches to control.* Geneva: World Health Organization.

Hollingsworth, Dorothy F. 1976. Developments leading to present day nutritional knowledge. In Derek J. Oddy and Derek S. Miller, eds., *The making of the modern British diet.* London: Croom Helm.

Homans, J. Smith, and J. Smith Homans, Jr. 1858. *A cyclopedia of commerce and commercial navigation.* New York: Harper & Brothers.

House, Albert V, ed. 1954. *Planter management and capitalism in ante-bellum Georgia.* New York: Columbia University Press.

Howard, Charles Wallace. 1867. *Conditions and resources* of Georgia, 1866 report. U.S. Department of Agriculture, Washington, D.C.: n.p.

Hurd, John C. 1858–1862. *The law of freedom and bondage in the United States.* Boston: Little, Brown.

Hurley, L.S. 1980. *Developmental nutrition.* Englewood Cliffs, NJ: Prentice-Hall.

Hutchinson, W.K., and S.H. Williamson. 1971. The self-sufficiency of the antebellum South: Estimates of the food supply. *Journal of Economic History* 31:491–612.

Hutson, J.B. 1927. Working day of farmers a high average. In United States Department of Agriculture *Yearbook of Agriculture, 1926.* Washington, D.C.: Government Printing Office.

Hytten, F.E., and G. Chamberlain, eds. 1980. *Clinical physiology in obstetrics.* London: Blackwell.

Hytten, F.E., and I. Leitch. 1971. *The physiology of human pregnancy.* Oxford: Blackwell.

Ianni, Otavio. 1969. O progresso econômico e o trabalhador livre. In Sergio B. de Hollanda, ed., *História Geral da Civilazacão Brasileira,* vol. 3, tomo 2. São Paulo: Difusão Européia do livro.

The Independent. January 25, 1866.

The industrial condition of the South. 1869. *Nation* 9:164–165.

Jain, Anrudh. 1969. Fecundability and its relation to age in a sample of Taiwanese women. *Population Studies* 23:69–85.

James, John A. 1978. The welfare effects of the antebellum tariff: A general equilibrium analysis. *Explorations in Economic History* 15:231–256.

Janes, Thomas P. 1875. *Statistical farm reports.* Georgia Department of Agriculture *Annual Reports,* Vol. 1. Atlanta.

———. 1876. *Statistical farm reports.* Georgia Department of Agriculture *Annual Reports,* Vol 2. Atlanta.

———. 1877. *Statistical farm reports.* Georgia Department of Agriculture *Annual Reports,* Vol. 3. Atlanta.

Jelliffe, E.F.P. 1968. Low birth-weight and malarial infection of the placenta. *Bulletin of the World Health Organization* 33:69–78.

John, A. Meredith 1984. The slave population of nineteenth century Trinidad: A demographic analysis. Ph.D. dissertation, Princeton University.

———. 1988. *The plantation slave population of Trinidad, 1783–1816: A mathematical and demographic enquiry.* New York: Cambridge University Press.

Johnson, D. Gale. 1950. Resource allocation under share contracts. *Journal of Political Economy* 58: 111–123.

Johnson, M. P. 1981. Smothered slave infants: Were slave mothers at fault? *Journal of Southern History* 47:493–520.

Johnston, Francis E. 1974. Control of age at menarche. *Human Biology* 46:159–171.

Johnston-McFaddin. 1866. Papers. Contract, Jan. 1. # 2489. Southern Historical Collection, University of North Carolina, Chapel Hill.

Jones, Jacqueline. 1985. *Labor of love, labor of sorrow: Black women, work and the family from slavery to the present.* New York: Basic Books.

Jordan. 1972. *Human fertility in Jordan: Findings and conclusions of the National Fertility Sample Survey.* By Hannah Rizk. Amman, Jordan: Department of Statistics of the Hashemite Kingdom of Jordan.

Jordan, Winthrop D. 1969. *White over black: American attitudes toward the Negro, 1550–1812.* Baltimore: Penguin Books.

Jornal do Comercio. (Rio de Janeiro, Brazil) 1835–1888.

Joseph, E.L. [1838] 1970. *History of Trinidad.* London: Frank Cass and Co.

Joy, J. Leonard, and Philip R. Payne. 1975. *Nutrition and national development planning: Three papers.* Brighton, UK: Institute of Development Studies, University of Sussex.

J.S.J. 1871. Labor contract. *Southern Cultivator* 29:10.

Judd, Gerrit P. 1955. *Members of parliament 1734–1832.* New Haven, CT: Yale University Press.

J.W.O. 1880. Labor contracts for 1881. *Southern Cultivator.* 38:444.

Karpinos, B.D. 1958. Height and weight of selective service registrants processed for military service during World War II. *Human Biology* 40:292–321.

Kemble, Frances Anne. 1961. *Journal of a residence on a Georgia plantation in 1838–1839,* edited and with an introduction by John A. Scott. New York: Knopf.

Kiddoo, J.B. 1866. *Report of the assistant commissioner for Texas.* Reports of the Assistant Commissioner, S. Doc. 6. 39th Cong., 2d sess., 1866–1867.

King, Edward. 1875. *The southern states of North America.* London: Blackie and Son.

Kiple, Kenneth F., and V.H. King. 1981. *Another dimension to the black diaspora: Diet, disease, and racism.* Cambridge, MA: Cambridge University Press.

Kiple, Kenneth F., and Virginia H. Kiple. 1977a. Slave child mortality: Some nutritional answers to a perennial puzzle. *Journal of Social History* 10:284–309.

———. 1977b. Black tongue and black men: Pellagra and slavery in the antebellum South. *Journal of Southern History* 43:411–428.

———. 1980. Deficiency diseases in the Caribbean. *Journal of Interdisciplinary History* 51:197–215.

Klebaner, Benjamin Joseph. 1955. American manumission laws and the responsibility for supporting slaves. *Virginia Magazine of History and Biography* 63:443–453.

Klein, Herbert S. 1967. *Slavery in the Americas: A comparative study of Virginia and Cuba.* Chicago: University of Chicago Press.

———. 1969. The trade in African slaves to Rio de Janeiro, 1795–1811: Estimates of mortality and patterns of voyages. *Journal of African History* 10:533–549.

———. 1972. The Portuguese slave trade from Angola in the eighteenth century. *Journal of Economic History* 32:894–918.

Klein, Herbert S., and Stanley L. Engerman. 1975. Shipping patterns and mortality in the African slave trade to Rio de Janeiro. *Cahiers d'études Africaines* 15:381–398.

———. 1978. Fertility differentials between slaves in the United States and the British West Indies: A note on lactation practices and their possible implications. *William and Mary Quarterly* 35:357–374.

Klingberg, Frank J. 1926. *The anti-slavery movement in England: A study in English humanitarianism.* New Haven, CT: Yale University Press.

Kloosterboer, W. 1960. *Involuntary labor since the abolition of slavery.* Leiden: E.J. Brill.

Knight, Franklin W. 1970. *Slave society in Cuba during the nineteenth century.* Madison: University of Wisconsin Press.

Knodel, J., and H. Kinter. 1977. The impact of breast feeding patterns on the biometric analysis of infant mortality. *Demography* 14:391–409.

Kolchin, Peter. 1972. *First freedom: The responses of Alabama's blacks to emancipation and reconstruction.* Boston: A. Williams and Co.

Komlos, John. 1987. The height and weight of West Point Cadets: Dietary change in antebellum America. *Journal of Economic History* 47:897–927.

Kralj-Cercek, Lea. 1956. The influence of food, body build and social origin on the age of menarche. *Human Biology* 28:393–406.

Labor contracts. 1867–1868. *The American Farmer* 2:218–220.

Labor contracts. 1869. *Southern Cultivator* 27:85–86.

Labor in the South. 1869. *Merchants' Magazine and Commercial Review* 61:272.

Laerne, C.F. Van Delden. 1885. *Brazil and Java: Report on coffee culture in America, Asia, and Africa.* London: W.H. Alden.

LaPorte, M. 1946. The effect of war imposed dietary limitations on growth of Paris school children. *American Journal of Diseases of Childhood* 71:244–247.

Large farms and associated capital. 1867–1868. *The American Farmer* 2:8.

Layrisse, M., M. Roche, and S.J. Baker. 1976. Nutritional anemias. In G.H. Beaton and J.M. Bengoa, eds., *Nutrition in preventative medicine: The major deficiency syndromes, epidemiology, and approaches to control.* Geneva: World Health Organization.

Leet, Don R. 1976. The determinants of the fertility transition in antebellum Ohio. *Journal of Economic History* 36:359–378.

Leser, C.E.V. 1954. Coal mining. In A.K. Cairncross, ed., *The Scottish economy.* Cambridge, UK: Cambridge University Press.

Lewis, J.R. 1866. *Report of the assistant commissioner for Tennessee.* Reports of the Assistant Commissioner, S. Doc. 6. 39th Cong., 2d sess., 1866–1867.

Lewis Plantation. Records. Southern Historical Collection, University of North Carolina, Chapel Hill.

Lightfoot, A. R. 1969. Conditions and wants of the cotton states. *DeBow's Review* 6:152–153.

Lithel, U.B. 1981. Breast-feeding habits and their relation to infant mortality and marital fertility. *Journal of Family History* 6:182–194.

Litwack, L. 1979. *Been in the storm so long: The aftermath of slavery.* New York: Alfred A. Knopf.

Lobo, Eulalia Maria Lahmyer, Oclavio Canavarros, Zakia Feres, Sonia Gonçalves, and Lucena Barbosa Madureira. 1971. Evulção doe precos e do padrão de vida no Rio de Janeiro, 1820–1930: Resultados preliminares. *Revista Brasileira de Economia* 25:235–266.

Locke, Mary Stoughton. 1901. *Slavery in America from the introduction of African slaves to the prohibition of the slave trade, (1619–1808).* Boston: Ginn.

Lockridge, Kenneth A. 1966. The population of Dedham, Massachusetts, 1636–1736. *Economic History Review* 19:318–344.

Lombardi, John V. 1971. *The decline and abolition of Negro slavery in Venezuela, 1820–1854.* Westport, CT: Greenwood Publishing Co.

Loring, F.W., and C.F. Atkinson. 1869. *Cotton culture in the South considered with reference to emigration.* Boston: A. Williams and Co.

Lutz, Friedrich, and Vera Lutz. 1951. *The theory of investment of the firm.* Princeton, NJ: Princeton University Press.

Mackay and Stiles Family. 1814–1860. Papers. Southern Historical Collection, University of North Carolina, Chapel Hill.

MacLeod, Duncan J. 1974. *Slavery, race and the American revolution.* London: Cambridge University Press.

McCloskey, Donald N. 1973. New perspectives on the old Poor Law. *Explorations in Economic History* 10:419–436.

McCloy, Shelby T. 1966. *The Negro in the French West Indies.* Lexington: University of Kentucky Press.

McCormick, M.C. 1985. The contribution of low birth weight to infant mortality and childhood morbidity. *New England Journal of Medicine* 312:82–90.

McCutcheon, Samuel. 1832–1861. Papers. Louisiana State University, Baton Rouge.

———. 1840. Papers. Manuscript. Department of Archives, Louisiana State University, Baton Rouge.

McManus, Edgar J. 1966. *A history of Negro slavery in New York.* Syracuse, NY: Syracuse University Press.

———. 1973. *Black bondage in the North.* Syracuse, NY: Syracuse University Press.

McMillen, S. 1985. Mother's sacred duty: Breast-feeding patterns among middle- and upper-class women in the antebellum South. *Journal of Southern History* 51:333–356.

Madhavan, Shantha. 1965. Age at menarche of South Indian girls belonging to the states of Madras and Kerala. *Indian Journal of Medical Research* 53:660–673.

Magdol, Edward. 1977. *A right to the land: Essays on the freedmen's community.* Westport, CT: Greenwood Press.

Malcolm, L.A. 1969. Growth and development of the Kaiapit children of the Markham Valley, New Guinea. *American Journal of Physical Anthropology* 31:39–51.

———. 1970. *Growth and development in New Guinea—A study of the Bundi people of the Madang district.* Madang, New Guinea: Institute of Human Biology.

Mallet, F. [1797] 1964. Descriptive account of the island of Trinidad. In R.V. Tooley, ed., *Some early printed maps of Trinidad and Tobago,* No. 10 of *Map collectors' series.* London: Map Collectors' Circle.

Mandle, Jay R. 1978. *The roots of black poverty: The southern plantation economy after the Civil War.* Durham, NC: Duke University Press.

Mannix, Daniel P., and Malcolm Cowley. 1962. *Black cargoes: A history of the Atlantic slave trade, 1518–1864.* New York: Viking Press.

Marcel. 1865. Feeling of the South Carolinians. *Nation* 1:237–239.

Margo, Robert A. 1986. Educational Achievement in segregated school systems: The effects of "separate-but-equal." *The American Economic Review* 76:794–801.

Margo, Robert A., and Richard H. Steckel. 1982. The heights of American slaves: New evidence on slave nutrition and health. *Social Science History* 6:516–538.

———. 1983. Heights of northern whites during the antebellum period. *Journal of Economic History* 43:167–174.

Marshall, Alfred. 1920. *Principles of economics*, 8th ed. New York: Macmillan.

Martin, Bernard, and Mark Spurrell, eds. 1962. *Journal of a slave trader (John Newton): 1750–1754*. London: Epworth Press.

Martin, Robert Montgomery. 1843. *History of the colonies of the British empire*. London: W.H. Allen.

Martorell, R. 1980. Interrelationships between diet, infectious disease, and nutritional status. In L.S. Green and F.E. Johnston, eds., *Social and biological predictors of nutritional status, physical growth, and neurological development*. New York: Academic Press.

Mata, L.J. 1978. *The children of Santa Maria Cauque: A prospective field study of health and growth*. Cambridge, MA: MIT Press.

Mathieson, William Law. 1926. *British slavery and its abolition, 1823–1838*. London: Longmans, Green.

––––––. 1932. *British slave emancipation 1838–1849*. London: Longmans, Green and Co.

Meeker, E. 1972. The improving health of the United States, 1850–1915. *Explorations in Economic History* 9:353–373.

––––––. 1976. Mortality trends of southern blacks, 1850–1915. *Explorations in Economic History* 13:13–43.

de Mello, Pedro C. 1977. The economics of labor in Brazilian coffee plantations, 1850–1888. Ph.D. dissertation, University of Chicago.

Mellor, George R. 1951. *British Imperial trusteeship, 1783–1850*. London: Faber and Faber.

Menken, Jane. 1975. Estimating fecundability. Ph.D. dissertation, Princeton University.

Mercer, William Newton. n.d. Papers. Louisiana State University Library, Baton Rouge.

Mettas, Jean. 1973. Honfleur et la traité des noirs au XVIIIe siècle. *Revue Française d'histoire d'outre-mer* 60:5–26.

Metzer, Jacob. 1981. The records of U.S. colored troops as a historical source: An exploratory examination. *Historical Methods* 3:123–132.

Meyer, Jean. 1960. Le commerce négrier nantais. *Annales: Economies, sociétés, civilisations* 15:120–129.

Mial, Alonzo T. and Millard. 1866, 1870, 1877. Papers. North Carolina Department of Archives and History, Raleigh.

Millette, J. 1970. *The genesis of crown colony government: Trinidad 1783–1813*. Curepe, Trinidad: Moko Enterprises, Ltd.

Minor, William J. and Family. 1849–1864. Papers. Louisiana State University, Baton Rouge.

Mitchell, B.R. 1962. *Abstract of British historical statistics*. Cambridge, UK: Cambridge University Press.

Montgomery. 1879. Rates and conditions for labor contracts. *Southern Cultivator* 37:445.

Moohr, Michael. 1972. The economic impact of slave emancipation in British Guiana, 1832–1852. *Economic History Review* 25:588–607.

Moore, George H. 1866. *Notes on the history of slavery in Massachusetts*. New York: Appleton.

Moore, John H. ed. 1974. *The Juhl letters to the Charleston Courier: A view of the South, 1865–1871*. Athens: University of Georgia Press.

Moore, W.M.O. 1983. Prenatal factors influencing intrauterine growth: Clinical implications. In R. Boyd and F.C. Battaglia, eds. *Perinatal medicine*. London, UK: Butterworths.

Morgan, Edmund S. 1975. *American slavery, American freedom: The ordeal of colonial Virginia*. New York: W.W. Norton.

Mosley, W.H., and L.C. Chen. 1983. An analytical framework for the study of child survival in developing countries. Mimeograph.

Murray, D.J. 1965. *The West Indies and the development of colonial government, 1801–1834*. Oxford, UK: Clarendon Press.

Naeye, R.L. 1980. Sudden infant death. *Scientific American* 242:56–62.

Naeye, R.L., and E.C. Peters. 1982. Working during pregnancy: Effects on the fetus. *Pediatrics* 69:724–727.

Naeye, R.L., and N. Tafari. 1983. *Risk factors in pregnancy and diseases of the fetus and newborn*. Baltimore, MD: Williams and Wilkins.

Natchez Weekly Democrat. January 18, 1866 to March 29, 1871.

National Archives. *General records of the Department of State*. Record Group 59.

––––––. 1963. *Preliminary inventory of the genral records of the Department of State (Record Group 59)*. Publication no. 64–65, preliminary inventory no. 157. Compiled by Daniel T. Goggin and H. Stephen Helton. Washington, D.C.

––––––. *Monthly reports of the subassistant commissioners*. Record Group 105.

―――. 1877. *The Negro in the military service of the United States,* 8 vols. Prepared by the Adjutant General's Office. Microfilm.

―――. *Records of the assistant commissioner for the state of South Carolina.* Bureau of Refugees, Freedmen, and Abandoned Lands. Record Group 105.

―――. *Records of the Bureau of Customs.* Record Group 36.

―――. *Records of the office of the quartermaster general.* Consolidated correspondence file, Box 199, Record Group 92.

―――. *Reports of conditions and operations.* Bureau of Refugees, Freedmen, and Abandoned Lands. Record Group 105.

National Center for Health Statistics. 1965. *Heights and weights and and selected body dimensions of adults, United States, 1960–1962,* No. 8, Ser. 11. Washington D.C.: U.S. Department of Health, Education, and Welfare, Public Health Service.

―――. 1970. *Height and weight of children, United States,* No. 104, Ser. 11. Rockville, MD: U.S. Department of Health, Education, and Welfare, Public Health Service.

―――. 1973a. *Age at menarche, United States,* No. 133 of DHEW publication (HRA) 75–165, Ser. 11. Rockville, MD: U.S. Department of Health, Education, and Welfare.

―――. 1973b. *Body weight, stature, and sitting height: White and Negro youths 12–17 years, United States,* No. 126 of *DHEW publication* (HRA) 74-1608, Ser. 11. Rockville, MD: U.S. Department of Health, Education, and Welfare.

―――. 1977. *NCHS growth curves for children, birth–18 years, United States,* No. 165 of *DHEW publication* (PHS) 78-1650, Ser. 11. Hyattsville, MD: U.S. Department of Health, Education, and Welfare.

National Research Council. Committee on Maternal Nutrition/Food and Nutrition Board. 1970. *Maternal nutrition and the course of pregnancy.* Washington, D.C.: National Academy of Sciences.

―――. Food and Nutrition Board. 1980. *Recommended Dietary Allowances,* 9th rev. ed. Washington, D.C.: National Academy of Sciences.

Nerlove, M., and S.J. Press. 1973. Univariate and multivariate log-linear and logistic models. Rand Paper R-1306-EDA/NIH. Santa Monica, CA: Rand Corporation.

New Hebrides. 1968. *Condominium of the New Hebrides: A report on the first census of the Population, 1967.* By Norma McArthur and J. F. Yaxley. Sydney, Australia: V. C. N. Blight, Government Printer.

New Orleans Daily Crescent. January 31, 1866 to January 14, 1878.

New Orleans Daily Picayune. January 5, 1867 to June 5, 1878.

The New York Times. February 12, 1866 to February 23, 1880.

New York Tribune. September 5, 1865 to August 31, 1873.

Northup, Solomon. 1853. *Twelve years a slave.* Auburn, NY: Derby & Miller.

Norwood, J.H. 1876. A decade in cotton planting. *Southern Cultivator* 34:210–211.

Nutrition Reviews. 1974. Forms of bound niacin in wheat. *Nutritional Reviews* 32:124–125.

―――. 1978. Nutritional significance of milk intolerance. *Nutritional Reviews* 36:133–134.

An Occasional Contributor. 1870–1871. The question of labor in the South. *Rural Carolinian* 2:572–574.

Oconee. 1872. Share System of labor. *Southern Cultivator* 30:57–58.

Oddy, Derek J. 1976. A nutritional analysis of historical evidence: The working class diet, 1880–1914. In Derek J. Oddy and Derek S. Miller, eds., *The making of the modern British diet.* London: Croom Helm.

O.J. 1871. Labor question. *Southern Cultivator* 29:370–371.

Oliphant, J.A. 1874. Letter to the editor. *Southern Cultivator* 32:125–126.

Olmsted, Frederick L. 1856. *A journey in the seaboard slave states.* New York: Dix and Edwards.

―――. 1860. *A journey in the back country.* New York: Mason Brothers.

―――. [1861] 1953. *The cotton kingdom,* 2 vols. in 1. New York: Knopf.

Orr, Martha L., and Bernice K. Watt. 1951. *Amino acid content of foods.* United States Department of Agriculture, Home Economics Research Report No. 4. Washington, D.C.: Government Printing Office.

Osborn, T.W. 1866. *Report of the assistant commissioner for Florida.* Papers of the Freedmen's Bureau, H. Doc. 70. 39th Cong., 1st sess., 1856–1866.

Parker, William N. 1980. The South in the national economy, 1865–1970. *Southern Economic Journal,* 46:1019–1048.

Patterson, H.O. 1967. *The sociology of slavery: An analysis of the origins, development and structure of Negro slave society in Jamaica.* Rutherford, NJ: Fairleigh-Dickinson University Press.

Pebrer, Pablo. 1833. *Taxation, revenue, expenditure, power, statistics, and debt of the whole British empire.* London: Baldwin and Cradock.

Peterson, Arthur G. 1929. Historical study of prices received by producers of farm products in Virginia, 1801–1927. Virginia Agricultural Experiment Station, *Tech. Bulletin* No. 37. Blacksburg, VA: n.p.

Phillips, Ulrich B. [1903] 1966. The economics of the plantation. Excerpt. In Harold D. Woodman, ed. *Slavery and the southern economy: Sources and readings,* 2nd ed. New York: Harcourt, Brace & World.

———. [1905] 1966. The economic cost of slaveholding in the cotton belt. Excerpt. In Harold D. Woodman, ed. *Slavery and the southern economy: Sources and readings,* 2nd ed. New York: Harcourt, Brace & World.

———. 1905. The economic cost of slaveholding in the cotton belt. *Political Science Quarterly* 20:257–275.

———. [1918] 1966. *American Negro slavery: A survey of the supply employment and control of Negro labor as determined by the plantation regime.* New York: D. Appleton and Company.

The pine forests of the South. 1867. *DeBow's Review* 3:196–198.

Pitkin, Timothy. 1835. *A statistical view of the commerce of the United States of America.* New Haven, CT: Durrie and Peck.

Pope, Christine F. 1962. The Southern Homestead Act: A punitive measure. M.A. thesis, University of Chicago.

Postell, William D. 1951. *The health of slaves on southern plantations,* No. 1 of Louisiana State University Studies, Social Sciences Series. Baton Rouge: Louisiana State University Press.

Potter, J. 1965. The growth of population in America, 1700–1860. In D.V. Glass and D.E.C. Eversley, eds., *Population in history.* Chicago: Aldine Publishing Co.

Powell, Lawrence N. 1980. *New masters: Northern planters during the Civil War and reconstruction.* New Haven, CT: Yale University Press.

Prabhakar, A.K., K.R. Sundaram, T.K.T.S. Ramanujacharyuhi, and A.D. Taskai. 1972. Influence of socio-economic factors on the age at the appearance of different puberty signs. *Indian Journal of Medical Research* 60: 789–792.

Prado, Eduardo da Silva. 1889. Immigration. In Frederico José de Santa-Ana Nery, ed., *Le Brésil en 1889.* Paris: C. Delagrave.

Preece, R.L., and M.J. Baines. 1978. A new family of mathematical models describing the human growth curve. *Annals of Human Biology* 5:1–24.

Priestly, Herbert Ingram. 1938. *France overseas: A study of modern imperialism.* New York: Appleton-Century.

Professional Planter. [1803] 1969. Practical rules for the management and medical treatment of Negro slaves in the sugar colonies. In Ulrich B. Phillips, ed., *Plantation and frontier, 1649–1863,* Vol. 1. New York: Burt Franklin.

Ragatz, Lowell Joseph. 1928. *The fall of the planter class in the British Caribbean, 1763–1833: A study in social and economic history.* New York: Century.

Range, Willard. 1955. *A century of Georgia Agriculture, 1850–1950.* Athens: University of Georgia Press.

Ransom, Roger, and Richard Sutch. 1970a. Debt peonage as a cause of economic stagnation in the Deep South following the Civil War. Institute of Business and Economic Research, University of California, Berkeley: Southern Economic History Project Working Paper 9.

———. 1970b. Tenancy, farm size, self-sufficiency, and racism: Four problems in the economic history of southern agriculture. Southern Economic History Project. Working Paper 8. University of California, Berkeley: Institute of Business and Economic Research.

———. 1977. *One kind of freedom: The economic consequences of emancipation.* New York: Cambridge University Press.

Rawick, George P., ed. 1972. *The American slave: A composite autobiography,* 19 vols. Westport, CT: Greenwood Publishing Co.

Rawlins, E.A. 1866. Treatment of the freedman—Management of a large farm, etc., etc. *The Farmer* 1:422.

Rees, Gareth. 1971. Copper sheathing, an example of technical diffusion in the English merchant fleet. *Journal of Transportation History* N.S. 1:85–94.

Reid, Joseph D., Jr. 1971. Some risk is an impetus to sharecropping. Manuscript. University of Chicago.

Reid, Whitelaw. 1866. *After the war: A tour of the southern states, 1865–1866.* London: S. Low, Son and Marson.

Reinders, Robert C. 1962. The decline of the New Orleans free Negro in the decade before the Civil War. *Journal of Mississippi History* 24:88–98.

Riddell, William R. 1920. The slave in Canada. *Journal of Negro History* 5:261–377.

Riley, F.L. 1909. Diary of a Mississippi planter, January 1, 1840 to April, 1863. *Publications of the Mississippi Historical Society* 10:305–481.

Rinchon, Dieudonné. 1938. *Le trafic négrier, Vol. 1, L'organisation commerciale de la traité des noirs.* Brussels: Atlas.

———. 1964. *Pierre Ignace Liévin van Alstein, captain négrier.* Dakar, Senegal: Memoires of IFAN, No. 71.

Roberts, D.F. 1969. Race, genetics, and growth. *Journal of Biosocial Science* 1:43–67.

Roberts, Derek, and T.C. Dann. 1967. Influence of menarcheal age in girls in a Welsh college. *British Journal of Preventive and Social Medicine* 21:170–176.

Roberts, G.W. 1952. A life-table for a West Indian slave population. *Population Studies* 5:238–243.

———. 1957. *The population of Jamaica.* Cambridge, UK: Cambridge University Press.

Roberts, Percy. 1866. The southern cotton crops—Mississippi. *DeBow's Review* 2:211.

Rochester, A. 1923. *Infant mortality: Results of a field study in Baltimore, Md. based on births in one year.* Children's Bureau Publication No. 119. Washington, D.C.: U.S. Government Printing Office.

Rogerson, William P. 1985. The first-order approach to principal-agent problems. *Econometrica* 53: 1357–1368.

Rose, W.L. 1964. *Rehearsal for Reconstruction: The Port Royal experiment.* Indianapolis: Bobbs-Merrill.

Rosenberg, Charles E. 1962. *The cholera years.* Chicago: University of Chicago Press.

Rosenwaike, I. 1966. Seasonal variation of deaths in the United States, 1951–1960. *Journal of the American Statistical Association* 61:706–719.

Ross, S. 1973. The economics theory of agency: The principal's problem. *American Economic Review* 63:134–139.

Rules for Overseers. 1840. *Farmers Register* 8:230.

Russel, Robert R. [1938] 1966. The general effects of slavery upon southern economic progress. Excerpt. In Harold D. Woodman, ed., *Slavery and the southern economy: Sources and readings,* 2nd ed. New York: Harcourt, Brace & World.

———. [1941] 1966. The effects of slavery upon nonslaveholders in the Ante-bellum South. Excerpt. In Harold D. Woodman, ed., *Slavery and the southern economy: Sources and readings,* 2nd ed. New York: Harcourt, Brace & World.

Russell, Robert. 1857. *North America: Its agriculture and climate.* Edinburgh, UK: Adam and Charles Black.

Rutman, D.B., and A.H. Rutman. 1976. Of agues and fevers: Malaria in the early Chesapeake. *William and Mary Quarterly* 38:31–60.

Savitt, Todd L. 1978. *Medicine and slavery: The diseases and health care of blacks in antebellum Virginia.* Urbana: University of Illinois Press.

Scarborough, William K., ed. 1972. *The diary of Edmund Ruffin.* Baton Rouge: Louisiana State University Press.

Schultz, T.W. 1965. Transforming traditional agriculture. New Haven, CT: Yale University Press.

Scott, Rebecca J. 1985. *Slave emancipation in Cuba: The transition to free labor, 1860–1899.* Princeton, NJ: Princeton University Press.

Scrimshaw, N.S. 1975. Interactions of malnutrition and infection: Advances in understanding. In R.E. Olson, ed., *Protein-calorie malnutrition.* New York: Academic Press.

Sheridan, Richard B. 1961. The West India sugar crisis and British slave emancipation, 1830–1833. *Journal of Economic History* 21:539–551.

———. 1965. The wealth of Jamaica in the eighteenth century. *Economic History Review* 18:292–311.

———. 1968. The wealth of Jamaica in the eighteenth century: A rejoinder. *Economic History Review* 21:46–61.

———. 1974. *Sugar and slavery: An economic history of the British West Indies, 1623–1775.* Barbados: Caribbean University Press.

Shlomowitz, Ralph. 1979. The origins of southern sharecropping. *Agricultural History* 53:557–575.

———. 1982a. Melanesian labor and the development of the Queensland sugar industry, 1863–1906. *Research in Economic History: A Research Annual,* Vol. 7. Greenwich, CT: JAI Press.

———. 1982b. The squad system on postbellum cotton plantations. In Orville V. Burton and Robert C. McMath, eds., *Toward a New South? Studies in post–Civil War southern communities.* Westport, CT: Greenwood Press.

————. 1984. Plantations and smallholdings: Comparative perspectives from the world cotton and sugar cane economies, 1865–1939. *Agricultural History* 58:1–16.

Shuttleworth, Frank. 1939. *The physical and mental growth of girls and boys age 6 to 19 in relation to age at maximum growth,* Vol. 4 of *Monographs of the Society for Research in Child Development.*

Siampos, Georje S. 1968. *The population of Cambodia, 1945–1968.* Phnom Penh, Cambodia.

Sitterson, Joseph C. 1953. *Sugar country: The cane sugar industry in the South, 1753–1950.* Lexington: University of Kentucky Press.

Smith, Adam. [1776] 1937. *The wealth of nations.* New York: Modern Library.

Smith, D.B. 1978. Mortality and family in the colonial Chesapeake. *Journal of Interdisciplinary History* 8:403–427.

Smith, Daniel Scott. 1972. The demographic history of colonial New England. *Journal of Economic History* 32:165–183.

————. 1973. Parental power and marriage patterns: An analysis of historical trends in Hingham, Massachusetts. *Journal of Marriage and the Family* 35:419–428.

————. 1977. A homeo-static demographic regime: Patterns in Western European family reconstitution studies. In Ronald Demos Lee, ed., *Population patterns in the past.* New York: Academic Press.

Smith, T.E. 1960. The Cocos Islands: A demographic laboratory. *Population Studies* 14:94–130.

Smith, Wilfred. 1968. *An historical introduction to the economic geography of Great Britain.* New York: Praeger.

Sokoloff, Kenneth L., and Georgia C. Villaflor. 1982. The early achievement of modern stature in America. *Social Science History* 16:453–480.

Somers, Robert. 1871. *The southern states since the war, 1870–1871.* London: Macmillan.

South American Journal and Brazil and River Plate Mail, 1879–1889. London: Latin American Trade.

A South Carolinian. 1877. South Carolina society. *Atlantic Monthly* 39:670–684.

Southern Cultivator. 1847. On the nature and the process of nourishment. *Southern Cultivator* 5:69.

Southerner. 1871. Agricultural labor at the South. *The Galaxy* 12:328–340.

Southron. 1857. The policy of the southern planter. *Cotton Planter and Soil* 1:292–296.

Stampp, Kenneth M. 1956. *The peculiar institution: Slavery in the ante-bellum South.* New York: Alfred A. Knopf.

————. 1966. *The era of reconstruction, 1865–1877.* New York: Alfred Knopf.

Staudenraus, P.J. 1961. *The African colonization movement 1816–1865.* New York: Columbia University Press.

Stearns, Charles. [1872] 1969. *The black man of the South and the rebels.* New York: Negro Universities Press.

Steckel, Richard H. 1977. The economics of U.S. slave and southern white fertility. Ph.D. dissertation, University of Chicago.

————. 1979. Slave height profiles from coastwise manifests. *Explorations in Economic History* 16: 363–380.

————. 1980a. Antebellum southern white fertility: A demographic and economic analysis. *Journal of Economic History* 40:331–350.

————. 1980b. Slave marriage and the family. *Journal of Family History* 5:406–421.

————. 1982. The fertility of American slaves. *Research in Economic History* 7:239–286.

————. 1983. Height and per capita income. *Historical Methods* 16:1–7.

————. 1985. *The economics of U.S. slave and southern white fertility.* New York: Garland Press.

————. 1986a. Birth weights and infant mortality among American slaves. *Explorations in Economic History* 23:173–198.

————. 1986b. A peculiar population: The nutrition, health and mortality of American slaves from childhood to maturity. *Journal of Economic History* 46:721–741.

————. 1986c. A dreadful childhood: The excess mortality of American slaves. *Social Science History* 10:427–465.

————. 1987. Growth depression and recovery: The remarkable case of American slaves. *Annals of Human Biology* 14:111–132.

Stein, Z., M. Susser, G. Saenger, and F. Marolla. 1975. *Famine and human development: The Dutch hunger winter of 1944–45.* New York: Oxford.

Steiner, Bernard. 1893. *History of slavery in Connecticut.* Baltimore, MD: Johns Hopkins University Press.

Stephenson, Wendell Holmes. 1936. A quarter century of a Mississippi Plantation, Eli Capell of "Pleasant Hill." *Mississippi Valley Historical Review* 33:355–374.

Stigler, George J. 1945. The cost of subsistence. *Journal of Farm Economics* 27:303–314.

Sturge, Joseph, and Thomas Harvey. 1838. *The West Indies in 1837*. London: Hamilton, Adams.

Sutch, Richard. 1967. Discussion of slavery and economic growth. *Journal of Economic History* 27:540–541.

———. 1972. The breeding of slaves for sale and the westward expansion of slavery, 1850–1860. Institute of Business and Economic Research. University of California, Berkeley: Southern Economic History Project, Working Paper 10.

———. 1975a. The breeding of slaves for sale and the westward expansion of slavery 1850–1860. In Stanley L. Engerman and Eugene D. Genovese, eds., *Race and slavery in the Western Hemisphere*. Princeton, NJ: Princeton University Press.

———. 1975b. The treatment received by American slaves: A critical review of the evidence presented in *Time on the Cross*. *Explorations in Economic History* 12:335–438.

———. 1976. The care and feeding of slaves. In Paul A. David, Herbert G. Gutman, Richard Sutch, Peter Temin, and Gavin Wright, eds., *Reckoning with slavery*. New York: Oxford University Press.

Sutch, Richard, and Roger Ransom. 1978. Sharecropping: market response or mechanism of race control? In D.G. Sansing, ed., *What was freedom's price?* Jackson: University Press of Mississippi.

S.W. 1868. The labor question. *Southern Cultivator* 26:133.

Sydnor, Charles S. 1930. The life span of Mississippi slaves. *American Historical Review* 35:566–574.

———. [1933] 1966. *Slavery in Mississippi*. New York: Appleton-Century.

Tafari, N., R.L. Naeye, and A. Gobezie. 1980. Effects of maternal undernutrition and heavy physical work during pregnancy on birth weight. *British Journal of Obstetrics and Gynecology* 87:222–226.

Talwar, P.P. 1965. Adolescent sterility in an Indian population. *Human Biology* 37:256–261.

Tannenbaum, Frank. 1946. *Slave and Citizen: The Negro in the Americas*. New York: Vintage.

Tanner, J.M. 1962. *Growth at Adolescence*. Oxford, UK: Blackwell.

———. 1965. The trend toward earlier physical maturation. In A.S. Parker and J.D. Meade, eds., *Biological aspects of social problems*. London: Oliver & Boyd.

———. 1973a. Trend toward earlier menarche in London, Oslo, Copenhagen, the Netherlands, and Hungary. *Nature* 243:95–96.

———. 1973b. Growing up. *Scientific American* 229(3):35–43.

———. 1975. Age at menarche: Evidence on the rate of human maturation. Paper presented at the 2nd Annual General Meeting of the British Society for Population Studies, London.

———. 1978. *Fetus into man: Physical growth from conception to maturity*. London: Open Books.

———. 1981a. *The history of the study of human growth*. New York: Cambridge University Press.

———. 1981b. Menarcheal age (letter). *Science* 214:604.

———. 1982. The potential of auxological data for monitoring economic and social well-being. *Social Science History* 6:571–581.

———. 1990. *Foetus into man: Physical growth from conception to maturity*, rev. ed. Cambridge, MA: Harvard University Press.

Tanner, J.M., and P.B. Eveleth. 1975. Variability between populations in growth and development at puberty. In S.R. Berenberg, ed., *Puberty, biological and psychological components*. Leiden: Stenfert Kroese.

Tanner, J.M., and B. O'Keeffe. 1962. Age at menarche in Nigerian schoolgirls and weights and heights from age 12 to 19. *Human Biology*. 34:187–196.

Tanner, J.M., R.H. Whitehouse, E. Marubini, and L.F. Resele. 1976. The adolescent growth spurt of boys and girls of the Harpenden Growth Study. *Annales of Human Biology* 3:109–126.

Tanner, J.M., R.H. Whitehouse, and M. Takaishi. 1966. Standards from birth to maturity for height, weight, height velocity, and weight velocity: British children, Parts I and II. *Archives of Disease in Childhood* 41:454–471; 41:613–635.

Tattler. 1850. Management of Negroes. *Southern Cultivator* 8:162.

Taylor, Joe Gray. 1963. *Negro slavery in Louisiana*. Baton Rouge: Louisiana Historical Association.

Taylor, Paul S. 1970. Slave to freedman. University of California, Berkeley: Southern Economic History Project, Working Paper 7.

Taylor, Rosser H. 1943. Post-bellum southern rental contracts. *Agricultural History* 17:121–128.

Thernstrom, S. 1973. *The other Bostonians: Poverty and progress in the American metropolis, 1880–1970*. Cambridge, MA: Harvard University Press.

Thompson, Clara Mildred. 1915. *Reconstruction in Georgia: Economic, social, political, 1865–1872*. New York: Columbia University Press.

Thompson, W.S., and P.K. Whepton. 1933. *Population trends in the United States*. New York: McGraw-Hill.

Thoughts for the month. *Southern Cultivator* 1871, 29:444; 1873, 31:283; 1874, 32:125–126, 293; 1877, 35:1; 1883, 41:1; 1888, 46:1.

Toepfer, E.W., Elizabeth Gates Zook, Martha Louise Orr, and L. R. Richardson. 1951. *Folic acid content in foods: Microbiological assay by standarized methods and compilation of data from the literature.* United States Department of Agriculture, Table 9. Washington, D.C.: Government Printing Office.

Toplin, Robert Brent. 1972. *The abolition of slavery in Brazil.* New York: Atheneum.

Towne, M.W., and W.D. Rasmussen. 1960. Farm gross product and gross investment in the nineteenth century. In *Trends in the American economy in the nineteenth century.* Conference on Research in Income and Wealth, Vol. 24. Princeton, NJ: Princeton University Press (for NBER).

Treatment and pay of freedmen. 1868. *DeBow's Review* 5:212–213.

Trowbridge, John T. 1866. *The South: A tour of its battlefields and ruined cities.* Hartford, CT: L. Stebbins.

Trussell, James. 1975. A re-estimation of the multiplying factors for the Brass technique for determining childhood survivor rates. *Population Studies* 29:97–107.

Trussell, J., and S. Preston. 1982. Estimating the covariates of childhood mortality with retrospective reports of mothers. *Health Policy and Education* 3:1–36.

Tuchfeld, Barry S., Leverett L. Guess, and Donald W. Hastings. 1974. The Bogue-Palmore technique for estimating direct fertility measures from indirect indicators as applied to Tennessee counties, 1960–1970. *Demography* 11:195–205.

Tucker, G.S.L. 1974. A note on the reliability of fertility ratios. *Australian Economic History Review* 2:160–167.

Tucker, R.C. 1958. James Henry Hammond: South Carolinian. Ph.D. dissertation, University of North Carolina.

Tucker, St. George. 1796. *A dissertation on slavery.* Philadelphia: Mathew Carey.

Turner, Edward R. 1911. *The Negro in Pennsylvania: Slavery-servitude-freedom, 1639–1861.* Washington, D.C.: American Historical Association.

Turner, Mary. 1982. *Slaves and missions: The disintegration of Jamaican slave society, 1787–1834.* Urbana: University of Illinois Press.

Turpentine. 1869. *DeBow's Review* 6:171–174.

Tuscaloosa Blade. November 20, 1873.

United Kingdom. 1788. Accounts and Papers. Parliamentary Papers, xxii (565).

————. 1790. Accounts and papers. Parliamentary Papers, xxix (698).

————. Colonial Office. 1812. Order-in-Council of March 26, 1812. 295/28.

————. House of Commons. *Sessional Papers,* sessions 1852–1853, paper no. 1690; 1854, paper no. 1764; 1863, paper no. 3204III.

————. House of Lords. 1788. An act to regulate for a limited time the shipping and carrying of slaves in British vessels from the coast of Africa. Public General Acts, 28 George III.

————. House of Lords. 1792. An account of the number of troops sent to the West Indies from the year 1775 to the year 1782, December 14, 1972. Records Office, Papers.

————. House of Lords. 1799. Copies of log books and surgeon's journals. Record Office, Papers, June 19, 1799.

————. Parliament, 1833. 1834. The debates in Parliament, Session 1833, on the resolutions and bill for the abolition of slavery in the British Colonies. London: Maurice.

United Nations. 1954. *Foetal, infant and early childhood mortality, Vol. 2. Biological, social, and economic factors,* No. 13, Ser. A of *Population Studies,* Add. 1. New York, United Nations.

————. Department of Economic and Social Affairs, Population Studies. 1967. *Methods of estimating basic demographic measures from incomplete data.* No. 42 of *Population Studies.* New York: United Nations.

————. Statistical Office. 1964. *Demographic yearbook, 1963.* New York: United Nations.

————. Statistical Office. 1974. *Demographic yearbook, 1973.* New York: United Nations.

————. Statistical Office. 1976. *Demographic yearbook, 1975.* New York: United Nations.

United States Bureau of the Census. 1909. *A century of population growth.* Washington, D.C.: Government Printing Office.

————. 1918. *Negro population, 1790–1915.* Washington, D.C.: Government Printing Office.

————. 1922. *U.S. census, 1920, agriculture,* Vol. 5. Washington, D.C.: Government Printing Office.

————. 1960. *Historical statistics of the United States, colonial times to 1957.* Washington, D.C.: Government Printing Office.

————. 1973. *1970 census of population, subject report PC(2)-3A: Women by number of children ever born.* Washington, D.C.: Government Printing Office.

———. 1975. *Historical statistics of the United States, colonial times to 1970*, bicentennial ed., parts I and II. Washington, D.C.: Government Printing Office.

United States Bureau of Labor Statistics. 1934. *History of wages in the United States from colonial times to 1928. Bulletin* No. 604. Washington, D.C.: Government Printing Office.

United States Census Office. 1802. *Return of the whole numbers of persons within the several districts of the United States*, 2nd census, 1800. Washington, D.C.: Apollo Press.

———. 1811. *Aggregate amount of the description of persons within the United States in the year 1810*, 3rd census, 1810. n.c.: n.p.

———. 1821. *Census for 1820*, 4th census, 1820. Washington, D.C.: Gales and Seaton.

———. 1832. *Fifth census or enumeration of inhabitants of the United States*, 5th census, 1830. Washington, D.C.: Duff Green.

———. 1841. *Statistics of the United States of America: The sixth census*, 6th census, 1840. Washington, D.C.: Blair and Rives.

———. 1853. *The seventh census of the United States, 1850*, 7th census. Washington, D.C.: Robert Armstrong.

———. 1854. *Statistical view of the United States.* Washington, D.C.: Beverly Tucker, Senate Printer.

———. 1862. *Preliminary report of the eighth census, 1860.* Washington, D.C.: Government Printing Office.

———. 1864a. *Agriculture of the United States in 1860.* Prepared by Joseph G.C. Kennedy. Washington D.C.: Government Printing Office.

———. 1864b. *Population of the United States in 1860*, 8th census, 1860. Washington, D.C.: Government Printing Office.

———. 1883a. *Statistics of the population of the United States (June 1, 1880).* Washington, D.C.: Government Printing Office.

———. 1883b. *Report on the production of agriculture (June 1, 1880).* Washington, D.C.: Government Printing Office.

———. 1884. *Report on cotton production in the United States, 1880*, 2 parts. Washington, D.C.: Government Printing Office.

———. 1895. *Eleventh census of the United States: 1890; Report on the statistics of agriculture in the United States.* Washington, D.C.: Government Printing Office.

———. 1897. *Compendium of the eleventh census, 1890*, 3 parts. Washington, D.C.: Government Printing Office.

United States Congress. House. 1865. *Report of the Commissioner of the Bureau of Refugees, Freedmen, and Abandoned Lands* H.R. 11. 39th Cong., 1st sess., 1865.

———. House. 1865–1866. *Report of the joint committee on Reconstruction H.R. 30.* 39th Cong., 1st sess., 1865–1866.

———. House. The Industrial Commission. 1901. *Report of the Industrial Commission on agriculture and agricultural labor H. Doc. 179.* 57th Cong., 1st sess., 1901.

United States Department of Agriculture. 1863. *Report of the commissioner of agriculture, 1862.* Washington, D.C.: Government Printing Office.

———. 1866. *Wages of farm labor.* Washington, D.C.: Government Printing Office.

———. 1867. *Southern agriculture.* Washington, D.C.: Government Printing Office.

———. 1868. *Report of the commissioner of agriculture, 1867.* Washington, D.C.: Government Printing Office.

———. 1876. *Annual report of the statistician: Cotton investigation.* Washington, D.C.: Government Printing Office.

———. 1877. *Report of the commissioner of agriculture, 1876.* Washington, D.C.: Government Printing Office.: Government Printing Office.

———. 1885. *Report of the statistician: Wage of farm labor.* Washington, D.C.: Government Printing Office.

———. 1888. *Report of the statistician.* Washington, D.C.: Government Printing Office.

———. 1890. *Annual report of the division of statistics.* Washington, D.C.: Government Printing Office.

———. 1912. *Seedtime and harvest.* Prepared by James Covert. *Bulletin* 85. Washington, D.C.: Bureau of Statistics.

United States Department of Commerce. 1913. *Sugar industry.* Bureau of Foreign and Domestic Commerce, *Misc. Ser. 9.* Washington, D.C.

United States Patent Office. 1849. *Annual report of the commissioner of patents for the year 1848. H. Doc. 59.* Washington, D.C.: Wendell and Van Benthuysen.

Urrutia, J.J., L.J. Mata, F. Trent, J.R. Cruz, E. Villatoro, and R.E. Alexander. 1975. Infection and low birth weight in a developing country: A study in an Indian village of Guatemala. *American Journal of Diseases in Childhood* 129:558–561.

Valdes-Dapena, M.A. 1980. Sudden infant death syndrome: A review of the medical literature, 1974–1979. *Pediatrics* 66:597–614.

Vance, Rupert. 1929. *Human factors in cotton culture.* Chapel Hill: University of North Carolina Press.

Vinovskis, Maris A. 1972. Mortality rates and trends in Massachusetts before 1860. *Journal of Interdisciplinary History* 32:184–213.

———. 1975. The demography of the slave population in antebellum America. *Journal of Interdisciplinary History* 5:459–467.

———. 1978. Recent trends in American historical demography: Some methodological and conceptual considerations. *Annual Review of Sociology* 4:603–627.

———. 1979. *Demographic changes in America from the Revolution to the Civil War: An analysis of the socio-economic determinants of fertility differentials and trends in Massachusetts from 1765 to 1860.* New York: Academic Press.

Vollman, R.F. 1967. The length of the premenstrual phase by age of woman. In Bjorn Westin and Nils Wiqvist, eds., *Fertility and sterility: Proceedings of the fifth world congress.* Amsterdam, NY: Excerpta Medica Foundation.

Vox. 1868. The labor question. *Southern Cultivator* 26:33.

Wachter, K. W. 1981. Graphical estimation of historical heights. *Historical Methods* 14:31–42.

Wagener, John A. 1867. Report of the state commissioner of immigration for South Carolina. *DeBow's Review* 4:359.

Walsh, L.S., and R.R. Menard. 1974. Death in the Chesapeake: Two Life tables for men in early colonial Maryland. *Maryland Historical Magazine* 69:211–227.

Walvin, J., ed. 1982. *Slavery and British society 1776–1846.* Baton Rouge: Louisiana State University Press.

Ward, J.R. 1978. The profitability of sugar planting in the British West Indies, 1650–1834. *Economic History Review* 31:197–213.

Wark, Lynette, and L.A. Malcolm. 1969. Growth and development of the Lumi child in the Sepiti district of New Guinea. *The Medical Journal of Australia* 2:129–136.

Waternook. 1870. Labor, fertilizers, etc. *Southern Cultivator* 28:44–45.

Watson, Henry, Jr. 1843–1860. Papers. Duke University Library, Durham, North Carolina.

Watt, Bernice K., and Annabel L. Merrill. 1950. *Composition of foods: Raw, processed, prepared.* United States Department of Agriculture, Agricultural Handbook No. 8, rev. ed., 1963. Washington, D.C.: Government Printing Office.

Wayne, Michael S. 1983. *The reshaping of plantation society: The Natchez District, 1860–1880.* Baton Rouge: Louisiana State University Press.

Weekly Louisianan. January 15, 1881 to April 2, 1881.

Weintraub, Andrew. 1973. The economics of Lincoln's proposal for compensated emancipation. *American Journal of Economics and Sociology* 32:171–177.

Wesley, Charles H. 1942. The manifests of slave shipments along the waterways, 1808–1864. *Journal of Negro History* 27:155–174.

West, Robert Craig. 1972. Social, political, and economic factors concerning the feasibility of compensated emancipation during the 1860s. Typescript.

Weston, P.C. 1857. Management of a southern plantation: Rules enforced on the rice estate of P.C. Weston. *DeBow's Review* 22:38–44.

Wharton, Vernon L. [1947] 1965. *The Negro in Mississippi, 1865–1890.* New York: Harper & Row.

Whittlesey, E. 1865–1866. *Report of the assistant commissioner for North Carolina.* Papers of the Freedmen's Bureau, H. Doc. 70. 39th Cong., 1st sess., 1865–1866.

Wickes, I.G. 1953. A history of infant feeding, parts I–V. *Archives of Diseases in Childhood* 28:151–158, 232–240, 332–340, 416–422, 495–502.

Wiener, Jonathan M. 1978. *Social origins of the new South: Alabama, 1860–1880.* Baton Rouge: Louisiana State University Press.

Wiener, Jonathan M., Robert Higgs, and Harold D. Woodman. 1979. AHR forum: Class structure and economic development in the American South, 1865–1955. *American Historical Review* 84:970–1006.

Willets, Gilson. 1903. *Workers of the nation: An encyclopedia of the occupations of the American people and a record of business, professional, and industrial achievement at the beginning of the twentieth century,* 2 vols. New York: P.F. Collier and Son.

Williams, Eric. 1944. *Capitalism and slavery.* Chapel Hill: University of North Carolina Press.

Williamson, Joel. 1965. *After slavery: The Negro in South Carolina during reconstruction, 1865–1877.* Chapel Hill: University of North Carolina Press.

Wilson, D.C. and I. Sutherland. 1950. Age at menarche. *British Medical Journal* 1:1267.

———. 1960. The present age of menarche in southern England. *Journal of Obstetrics and Gynecology of the British Commonwealth* 67:320–332.

Winks, Robin W. 1971. *The blacks in Canada: A history.* New Haven, CT: Yale University Press.

Wirth, John D. 1970. *The politics of Brazilian economic development, 1930–1954.* Stanford, CA: Stanford University Press.

Wolff, G. 1940. A study in the trend of White school children from 1933–1936, material based on the examination of pupils of elementary schools in Hagerstown, Maryland. *Child Development* 11:159–180.

Woodbury, R.M. 1925. *Causal factors in infant mortality.* United States, Department of Labor, Children's Bureau Publication No. 142. Washington, D.C.: Government Printing Office.

Woodman, Harold, ed. 1966. *Slavery and the southern economy: Sources and readings.* New York: Harcourt, Brace, and World.

———. 1968. *King cotton and his retainers.* Lexington: University of Kentucky Press.

———. 1974. The Old South and the new history. Paper presented to the MSSB-University of Rochester conference on *Time on the Cross,* Rochester, NY.

———. 1977. Comment to Claudia Goldin's paper. *Journal of Economic History* 67:109–112.

W.M.R. 1870–1871. The wages question. *Rural Carolinian* 2:118.

Woodruff, Calvin W., M.D. 1976. Milk intolerances. *Nutritional Reviews* 34:33–37.

Woodson, Carter. 1925. *Free Negro heads of families in the U.S. in 1830 together with a brief treatment of the free Negro.* Washington D.C.: The Association for the Study of Negro Life and History.

Woodward, C. Vann. 1966. *Reunion and reaction.* Boston: Little, Brown.

———. 1970. Emancipations and reconstructions: A comparative study. Paper presented to the 13th International Congress of Historical Sciences, Moscow.

Wray, J.D. 1978. Maternal nutrition, breast-feeding and infant survival. In W.H. Mosley, ed., *Nutrition and human reproduction.* New York: Plenum Press.

Wright, Chester W. 1943. The more enduring consequences of America's wars. *Journal of Economic History* 3:9–26.

Wright, Gavin. 1969. The economics of cotton in the antebellum South. Ph.D. dissertation, Yale University.

———. 1982. The strange career of the new southern economic history. *Reviews in American History* 10:164–180.

Wrigley, E.A. 1966. Family limitation in pre-industrial England. *Economic History Review,* 2nd ser., 20:82–109.

———. 1969. *Population and world history.* New York: McGraw-Hill.

———. 1977. Birth and baptisms: The use of Anglican baptism registers as a source of information about the numbers of births in England before the beginning of civil registration. *Population Studies* 31:281–312.

Yang, Donghyu. 1984a. Notes on the wealth distribution of farms households in the United States, 1860: A new look at two manuscript census samples. *Explorations in Economic History* 21:88–102.

———. 1984b. Aspects of United States agriculture circa 1860. Ph.D. dissertation, Harvard University.

Yasuba, Yasukichi. 1961. The profitability and viability of plantation slavery in the United States. *The Economic Studies Quarterly* 12:60–67.

———. 1962. *Birth rates of the white population in the United States, 1800–1860,* Ser. 79, No. 2 of *The Johns Hopkins University Studies in Historical and Political Science.* Baltimore, MD: Johns Hopkins Press.

Yetman, Norman R. 1970. *Life under the peculiar institution: Selections from the slave narrative collection.* New York: Holt, Rinehart and Winston.

Zelnik, M. 1966. The fertility of the American Negro in 1830 and 1850. *Population Studies* 20:77–83.

Zilversmit, Arthur. 1967. *The first emancipation: The abolition of slavery in the North.* Chicago: University of Chicago Press.

Some Unpublished Memorandums

Individuals who desire copies of these unpublished memorandums should write to Marilyn Coopersmith, Center for Population Economics, 1101 East Fifty-eighth Street, Chicago, IL 60637. Documents will be supplied at the cost of reproduction, postage, and handling.

Crump, Marjorie. 1974a. The distribution of slaves in the Parker-Gallman sample.
————. 1974b. The distribution of slaves in the sample of probate records.
Ericksen, G. 1973. Problems and prospects in quantifying the W.P.A. slave narratives. University of Chicago: Workshop in Economic History, Report #7273-18.
Fogel, Robert W. 1971a. Holdings of the Southern Historical Collection of the University of North Carolina.
————. 1971b. Holdings of the State Archives in Atlanta, GA.
Fogel, Robert W., and Stanley L. Engerman. 1968. The economics of slavery. Report 6803. University of Chicago.
————. 1972. The market evaluation of human capital: The case of slavery. University of Chicago.
————. 1973. The role of force in the determination of the labor supply in slave, free, and semi-free societies. University of Chicago: Applications Workshop.
————. 1975a. The relative efficiency of slave and free agriculture in 1850 and 1860: The status of research. Harvard University.
————. 1975b. Further evidence on the economics of American Negro slavery. Why the U.S. slave population grew so rapidly: Fertility, mortality, and household structure. University of Chicago.
————. 1977. Explaining the disparity in rates of natural increase: Fertility vs. mortality. Harvard University.
Furet, Francois, and Emmanuel LeRoy Ladurie. 1974. An interview on the historiographic and political implications of *Time on the Cross*. Mimeograph. Department of Economics, University of Rochester.
Foote, Thelma. 1982. Bibliography of recent quantitative studies of slavery. Harvard University.
Friedman, Gerald. 1980. The demography of Trinidad slavery. Harvard University: Workshop in Economic History.
Gardener, Grant. 1979. Program to edit and aggregate the Bateman-Foust sample.
Gore (Coopersmith) Marilyn. 1972a. Notes on the slave manifests at the National Archives in Washington, D.C. (July 10).
————. 1972b. Notes on the southern manuscript collection at the Library of Congress, Washington, D.C.
————. 1972c. Notes on the holdings of the National Archives, Washington, D.C., and the Virginia State Library, Richmond, VA.
Hopkins, Mark M., and N. Scott Cardell. 1974. The cost of freedom. University of Rochester.
Huertas, Thomas F. 1978. Technical Appendix to "Damnifying growth in the antebellum South," *Journal of Economic History* 39 (1979).
Kotlikoff, L. J. 1975. Toward a quantitative description of the New Orleans slave market. University of Chicago: Workshop in Economic History, Report 7475-24.
Petzel, Todd E. 1974. A description of the New Orleans slave sales sample. University of Rochester.
Reid, Joseph D., Jr. 1974. Discussion of Professors Davis, Sutch, and Wright on *Time on the Cross*.
————. 1987. Reconstruction in the American South. George Mason University.
Shlomowitz, Ralph. 1973. The transition from slave to freedman: Property arrangements in southern agriculture, 1860–1880. University of Chicago: Workshop in Economic History, Report 7273-16.
————. 1974a. Citations for Quotations in volume I and Appendix A of *Time on the Cross*.

————. 1974b. A description of samples of freedmen labor contracts and payrolls, 1863–1868.

————. 1974c. The effect of the emancipation of slaves on southern agricultural land values. University of Chicago: Workshop in Economic History, Report 7374-2.

————. 1974d. Gangs, squads and postbellum cotton plantations. University of Chicago: Workshop in Economic History.

————. 1975. The search for institutional equilibrium in southern agriculture after the Civil War. University of Chicago: Workshop in Economic History, Report 7475-12.

Steckel, Richard H. 1971. Negro slavery in the Western Hemisphere. University of Chicago.

————. 1972a. Holdings at the Southern Historical Collection of the University of North Carolina.

————. 1972b. Holdings at Emory University, Atlanta, Ga., South Caroliniana Library, Columbia, S.C., and Perkins Library, Duke University, Durham, N.C.

————. 1973a. Notes on the Louisiana State Archives, Baton Rouge, and the Alabama State Archives, Montgomery. University of Chicago.

————. 1973b. The economics of U.S. slave and southern free white fertility. University of Chicago: Workshop in Economic History, Report 7273-17.

————. 1973c. Notes on the manuscript collections at the University of Virginia (Charlottesville), Virginia State Library (Richmond), and the Virginia Historical Society (Richmond). University of Chicago.

————. 1973d. Holdings at the Mississippi Department of Archives and History. University of Chicago.

————. 1973e. Slave marriage, fertility, and society. University of Chicago: Workshop in Economic History, Report 7374-4.

————. 1974. A list of 54 plantations containing systematic data on the demographic characteristics of the slave population.

————. 1981. Nineteenth century migration patterns and their implications. University of Chicago: Workshop in Economic History, Report 8081-15.

Additional Works on Slavery and Related Topics by the Contributors

This list does not include papers presented in either volume of *Without Consent or Contract: Technical Papers* or sources that are listed in the references to these volumes, nor does it include contributions to *Without Consent or Contract: Evidence and Methods.*

Engerman, Stanley L. 1970. The antebellum South: What probably was and what should have been. In William N. Parker, ed., *The structure of the cotton economy in the antebellum South.* Washington, D.C.: The Agricultural History Society.

———. 1971. The effects of slavery upon the southern economy. In Hugh G.J. Aitken, ed., *Did slavery pay?* Boston: Houghton Mifflin.

———. 1972. The slave trade and capital formation in the industrial revolution. *Business History Review:* 46:430–443.

———. 1976. Comments on Richardson and Boulle and the Williams thesis. In *The Atlantic slave trade: New approaches.* Paris: Societé Française d'Histoire d'Outre Mer. Librairie Orientaliste Paul Genthner SA.

———. 1976. The height of slaves in the United States. *Local Population Studies* 16:45–49.

———. 1976. The southern slave economy. In Harry P. Owens, ed., *Perspectives and irony in American slavery.* Jackson: University of Mississippi.

———. 1977. Changes in black fertility and family structure, 1880–1940. In Tamara K. Hareven and Maris Vinovskis, eds., *Family and population in nineteenth-century America.* Princeton, NJ: Princeton University Press.

———. 1977. Introduction. *Southern Studies* 16:347–354.

———. 1977. Quantitative and economic analysis of West Indian slave societies: Research problems. In Vera Rubin and Arthur Tuden, eds., *Comparative perspectives on slavery in new world plantation societies.* New York: New York Academy of Sciences.

———. 1977. Studying the black family: A review of *The Black Family in Slavery and Freedom, 1750–1925. Journal of Family History* 2:117–138.

———. 1978. Marxist economic studies of the slave South. *Marxist Perspectives* 1:148–165.

———. 1978. Relooking at *The Slave Community.* In Al-Tony Gilmore, ed., *Revisiting John Blassingame's slave community.* Westport, CT: Greenwood Press.

———. 1979. The realities of slavery: A review of recent evidence. *International Journal of Comparative Sociology* 20:46–66.

———. 1981. Notes on the patterns of economic growth in the British North American colonies in the seventeenth, eighteenth, and nineteenth centuries. In P. Bairoch and M. Levy-Leboyer, eds., *Disparities in economic development since the industrial revolution.* New York: St. Martin's Press.

———. 1981. Some implications of the abolition of the slave trade. In David Eltis and James Walvin, eds., *Abolition of the Atlantic slave trade.* Madison: University of Wisconsin Press.

———. 1983. Contract labor, sugar, and technology in the nineteenth century. *Journal of Economic History* 43:635–659.

———. 1985. Economic change and contract labor in the British Caribbean: The end of slavery and the adjustment to emancipation. In David Richardson, ed., *Abolition and its aftermath: The historical context, 1790–1916.* London: Frank Cass and Company.

———. Coerced and free labor: Property rights and the development of the labor force. *Annales: Economies, sociétés, civilisations* Forthcoming.

Engerman, Stanley L., Manuel Moreno Fraginals, and Herbert S. Klein. 1983. The level and structure of slave prices on Cuban plantations in the middle of the nineteenth century: Some comparative perspectives. *American Historical Review* 88:1201–1218.

Engerman, Stanley L., Manuel Moreno Fraginals, and Frank Moya Pons. 1985. *Between slavery and free labor: The Spanish-speaking Caribbean in the nineteenth century.* Baltimore, MD: Johns Hopkins University Press.

Engerman, Stanley L., Katia M. de Queiros Mattoso, and Herbert Klein. 1986. Trends and patterns in the prices of manumitted slaves, Bahia, 1819–1888. *Slavery and Abolition* 7:59–67.

Engerman, Stanley L., David Dowd, and Eli Ginzberg. 1970. Slavery as an obstacle to economic growth in the United States: A panel discussion. In Irwin Unger and David Reimer, eds., *The slavery experience in the United States.* New York: Holt, Rinehart, and Winston.

Engerman, Stanley L., and Barbara L. Solow, eds. 1987. British capitalism and Caribbean slavery. *Journal of Interdisciplinary History* 17:707–870.

Fogel, Robert W. 1968. Econometrics and southern economic history: A comment. In Ralph Adreano, ed., *The new economic history.* New York: John Wiley & Sons.

———. 1975. Three phases of cliometric research on slavery and its aftermath. *American Economic Review* 65:37–46.

———. 1977. Cliometrics and culture: Some recent developments in the historiography of slavery. *Journal of Social History* 11:34–51.

———. 1977. *Ten lectures on the new economic history.* [In Japanese]. Tokyo, Japan: Nan-un-do.

Fogel, Robert W., and Stanley L. Engerman. 1970. A comparison of the efficiency of slave and free agricultural labor in the United States during 1860. In *Papers and proceedings of the Fifth International Economic History Conference,* Vol. 7. Leningrad, USSR: NAUKA.

Fogel, Robert W., Stanley L. Engerman, Roderick Floud, Gerald Friedman, Robert A. Margo, Kenneth Sokoloff, Richard H. Steckel, James Trussell, Georgia Villaflor, and Kenneth W. Wachter. 1983. Secular changes in American and British stature and nutrition. *Journal of Interdisciplinary History* 14:445–482.

Galenson, David W. 1978. "Middling people" or "common sort"?: The social origins of some early Americans reexamined. *William and Mary Quarterly* 35:499–524.

———. 1979. The slave trade to the English West Indies, 1673–1724. *Economic History Review* 32:241–249.

———. 1979. The social origins of some early Americans: Rejoinder. *William and Mary Quarterly.* 36:264–277.

———. 1980. British servants and the colonial indenture system in the eighteenth century. In Gerald D. Nash, ed., *Issues in American economic history: Selected readings,* 3rd ed. Lexington, MA: D.C. Health and Co.

———. 1980. Demographic aspects of white servitude in colonial British America. *Annales de demographie historique* 1980:239–252.

———. 1981. Literacy and age in preindustrial England: Quantitative evidence and implications. *Economic Development and Cultural Change* 29:813–829.

———. 1982. The Atlantic slave trade and the Barbados market, 1673–1723. *Journal of Economic History* 42:491–511.

———. 1984. The rise and fall of indentured servitude in the Americas: An economic analysis. *Journal of Economic History* 44:1–26.

———. 1985. Population turnover in the English West Indies in the late seventeenth century: A comparative perspective. *Journal of Economic History* 45:277–235; errata 45:719.

———. 1986. *Traders, planters and slaves: Market behavior in early English America.* Cambridge, UK: Cambridge University Press.

———. 1987. Economic aspects of the growth of slavery in the southern colonies. Typescript.

———. 1988. Indentured servitude and slavery. In Randall Miller and John David Smith, eds., *Dictionary of afro-American slavery.* Westport, CT: Greenwood Press.

Galenson, ed., *Markets in history: Economic studies of the past.* Cambridge, UK: Cambridge University Press, 1989.

Galenson, David W., and Russell Menard. 1977. Economics and early American history. *Newberry papers in family and community history,* paper 77-4E.

———. 1980. Approaches to the analysis of economic growth in colonial British America. *Historical Methods* 13:3–18.

Goldin, Claudia D. 1975. Cities and slavery: The issue of compatibility. In Leo Schnore, ed., *The new urban history.* Princeton, NJ: Princeton University Press.

———. 1977. Female labor force participation: The origin of black and white differences, 1870–1880.

Journal of Economic History 37:87–108. To be reprinted in Darlene Clark Hine, et al., eds., *Black women in United States history.* New York: Carlson. Forthcoming.

———. 1979. "N" kinds of freedom: An introduction to the reprinted as Credit merchandising in the New South: The role of competition and risk, in Gary M. Walton and James F. Shepherd, eds., *Market institutions and economic progress in the New South, 1865–1900.* New York: Academic Press, 1981.

Goldin, Claudia D., and Frank Lewis. 1978. The post-bellum recovery of the South and the cost of the Civil War: Comment. *Journal of Economic History* 38:487–492.

John, A. Meredith. 1988. Plantation slave mortality in Trinidad. *Population Studies* 42:161–182.

———. 1988. The smuggled slaves of Trinidad, 1813. *The Historical Journal* 31:365–375.

Klein, Herbert S. 1966. The colored militia of Cuba, 1568–1868. *Caribbean Studies* 6:17–27.

———. 1966. Sociedades esclavistas en las Americas: Un estudio comparativo. *Desarrollo económomico* (Buenos Aires) 6:227–245.

———. 1969. Anglicanism, Catholicism and the Negro slave. In E. Genovese and L. Foner, eds., *Slavery in the New World: A reader in comparative history.* Englewood Cliffs, NJ: Prentice Hall.

———. 1970. North American competition and the characteristics of the African slave trade to Cuba, 1790–1794. *William and Mary Quarterly* 28:86–106.

———. 1971. The internal slave trade in nineteenth century Brazil: A study of slave importations into Rio de Janeiro in 1852. *Hispanic American Historical Review,* 51:567–568.

———. 1971. The settlement pattern for the afro-American population in the new world. In Nathan Huggins and Martin Kilson, eds., *Key issues in the afro-American experience,* 2 vols. New York: Harcourt, Brace, Jovanovich.

———. 1972. Nineteenth century Brazil. In D.W. Cohen and Jack Greene, eds., *Neither slave nor free: The freedmen of African descent in slave societies of the new world.* Baltimore, MD: Johns Hopkins University Press.

———. 1973. Consideraciones sobre la viabilidad de la esclavitud y las causas de la abolición en Cuba del siglo xix. *La Torre* (PR) 21:307–318.

———. 1973. O tráfico de escravos africanos para o porto do Rio de Janeiro, 1825–1830. *Anais de História* (São Paulo) 5:85–101.

———. 1973. Slavery in Latin America. In Joseph Tulchin, ed., *Problems in Latin American history,* New York: Harper & Row.

———. 1975. The Cuban slave trade in a period of transition, 1790–1840. *Revue Française d'histoire d'outre-mer* 67:67–88.

———. 1975. Slaves and shipping in eighteenth century Virginia. *Journal of Interdisciplinary History* 5:383–411.

———. 1978. The English slave trade to Jamaica, 1782–1808. *Economic History Review,* 31:25–45.

———. 1978. *The middle passage: Comparative studies in the Atlantic slave trade.* Princeton, NJ: Princeton University Press.

———. 1978. Schiavitù. In Marcello Carmagnani, ed., *Storia dell'America Latina.* Florence: La Nuova Italia.

———. 1983. African women in the Atlantic slave trade. In Claire Robertson and Martin A. Klein, eds., *Women and slavery in Africa.* Madison: University of Wisconsin Press.

———. 1984. The population of Minas Gerais: New research on colonial Brazil. *Latin American Population History Newsletter* 4:3–7.

———. 1986. *African slavery in Latin America and the Caribbean.* New York: Oxford University Press.

———. 1987. African slavery in Latin America in the 18th century. In Valerio Castronovo and Enrico Castelnuovo, eds., *Europa Moderna.* Milan: Banca Nazionale del Lavoro.

———. 1987. Demografia do tráfico Atlantico de escravos para ao Brasil. *Estudos Econômicos* (São Paulo) 17:129–150.

———. 1987. Tráfico de Escravos. IBGE *Estatísticas históricas do Brasil.* Rio de Janeiro: Instituto Brasileiro de Geografia e Estatística.

———. 1988. Recent trends in the study of the Atlantic slave trade. *Revista historica* (UPR, Rio Piedras) 1:123–142.

———. 1990. Economic aspects of the eighteenth century Atlantic slave trade. In J. Tracy, ed., *The rise of merchant empires.* Cambridge, UK: Cambridge University Press.

Klein, Herbert S., and Stanley L. Engerman. 1976. The English slave trade in the 1790's. In Roger Anstey and P.E.H. Hair, eds., *Liverpool, the Aftrican slave trade and abolition.* Liverpool, UK: Historical Society of Lancashire and Cheshire.

————. 1976. Shipping patterns and mortality in the African slave trade to Rio de Janeiro. *Cahiers d'etudes Africaines* 59:381–398.

————. 1979. *A note on mortality in the French slave trade in the eighteenth century.* In Henry Gemery and Jan Hogendorn, eds., *The uncommon market.* New York: Academic Press.

————. 1984. The demographic study of the American slave population. In Mario Luiza Marcilio, ed., *Populacão e sociedade. Evolucão das sociedades pre-industriais.* Petropolis, Brazil: Vozes.

————. 1985. The transition from slave to free labor: Notes on a comparative economic model. In Manuel Moreno Fraginals, Frank Moya Pons, and Stanley L. Engerman, eds., *Between slavery and free labor: The Spanish-speaking Caribbean in the nineteenth century.* Baltimore, MD: Johns Hopkins University Press.

Klein, Herbert S., and Charles Garland. 1985. The allotment of space for African slaves aboard eighteenth century British slave ships. *William and Mary Quarterly* 42:238–248.

Klein, Herbert S., and Nathaniel Leff. 1974. Demographic-economic theory and the rate of population increase in 19th century Brazil. *Research Papers,* No. 31. Columbia University, Graduate School of Business.

Margo, Robert A. 1982. Race differences in public school expenditures: Disfranchisement and school finance in Louisian, 1890–1910. *Social Science History* 6:9–34.

————. 1984. Accumulation of property by southern blacks before World War I: Comment and further evidence. *American Economic Review* 74:768–776.

————. 1984. Teacher salaries in black and white: The South in 1910. *Explorations in Economic History* 21:306–326.

————. 1985. *Disfranchisement, school finance, and the economics of segregated schools in the U.S. South, 1890–1910.* New York: Garland Press.

————. 1986. Educational achievement in segregated school systems: The effects of "separate-but-equal." *American Economic Review* 76:794–801.

————. 1986. Race, educational attainment, and the 1940 census. *Journal of Economic History* 46:189–198.

————. 1986. Race and human capital: Comment. *American Economic Review* 76:1221–1224.

————. 1987. Accounting for racial differences in school attendance in the American South, 1900: The role of "separate-but-equal." *Review of Economics and Statistics* 69:661–666.

————. 1989. The effect of migration on black incomes: Evidence from the 1940 census. *Economics Letters* 31:403–406.

————. *Race and schooling in the American South: A quantitative history.* Chicago: University of Chicago Press, forthcoming.

Margo, Robert A., and Claudia D. Goldin. 1982. Education and the earnings of black males during the great depression: A research note. Unpublished Working Paper, Department of Economics, University of Pennsylvania.

Margo, Robert A., and G. Villaflor. 1987. The growth of wages in antebellum America: New evidence. *Journal of Economic History* 47:873–895.

de Mello, Pedro C. 1978. Aspectos ecônomicos da organizacão do trabalho na economia cafeeira do Rio de Janeiro, 1850–1888. *Revista Brasileira de economia* 32:19–67.

————. 1983. Estimativa da longevidade dos escravos no Brasil na segunde metade do seculo XIX. *Revista de estudos econômicos* 13:151–179.

————. 1984. Oz fazendeiros de café e o mercado financeiro de capitais, 1871–1888. *Revista de estudos econômicos* 14:145–161.

de Mello, Pedro C., and Robert W. Slenes. 1980. Analise econômica da escravidão do Brasil. In Paulo Neuhaus, ed., *Economia Brasileira: Uma visão histórica.* Rio de Janeiro: Editora Campus.

————. 1982. Slavery in the coffee regions of Brazil, 1850–1888: Labor systems, social institutions and slave accomodation, resistance. In *Typology of Colonial Economic Development (B6),* Eighth International Economic History Congress. Budapest, Hungary: Akademiai Kiado.

Metzer, Jacob. 1977. Institutional change and economic analysis: Some issues related to American slavery. *Louisiana Studies: An Interdisciplinary Journal of the South.* Winter:321–343.

Reid, Joseph D., Jr. 1976. Progress on credit: Comment. *Agricultural History* 50:117–124.

————. 1976. Sharecropping and agricultural uncertainty. *Economic Development and Cultural Change* 24:549–576.

————. 1977. The theory of sharecropping revisited—Again. *Journal of Political Economy* 85:403–407.

————. 1979. The evaluation and implications of southern tenancy. *Agricultural History* 53:153–169.

————. 1979. Tenancy in American history. In James Roumasset, ed., *Risk, Uncertainty, and agricul-*

tural development. College Laguana, Philippines: Southeast Asian Regional Center for Graduate Study & Research in Agriculture.

———. 1981. White land, black labor, and agricultural stagnation: The causes and effects of sharecropping in the post-bellum South. In Gary M. Walton and James F. Shepherd, eds., *Market institutions and economic progress in the New South, 1865–1900.* New York: Academic Press.

———. 1983. Notes toward a geography of farm tenure choice. In J. Peter DeBraal and Gene Wunderlick, eds., *Rents and rental practices in U.S. agriculture.* Farm foundation in cooperation with the Economic Research Service, U.S. Department of Agriculture.

———. 1987. The theory of sharecropping: Occam's razor and economic analysis. *History of Political Economy* 19:551–570.

———. Economic development: Lessons from the Past. In Michael M. Kurth, ed., *Private initiative for economic development,* Forthcoming.

Shlomowitz, Ralph. 1979. The search for institutional equilibrium in Queensland's sugar industry, 1884–1913. *Australian Economic History Review* 19:91–122.

———. 1979. Teamwork and incentive: The origins and development of the butty gang system in Queensland's sugar industry, 1891–1913. *Journal of Comparative Economics* 3:41–55.

———. 1979. The transition from slave to freedman labor arrangements in southern agriculture, 1865–1870. *Journal of Economic History* 39:333–336.

———. 1981. Indentured Melanesians in Queensland: A statistical investigation of recruiting voyages, 1871–1903. *Journal of Pacific History* 16:203–208.

———. 1981. Markets for indentured and time-expired Melanesian labour in Queensland, 1863–1906: An economic analysis. *Journal of Pacific History* 16:70–91.

———. 1982. Labor and the development of the Queensland sugar industry, 1863–1906, in Vol. 7 of P. Uselding, ed., *Research in Economic History, a Research Annual.* Greenwich, CT: JAI Press.

———. 1982. The profitability of indentured Melanesian labor in Queensland. *Australian Economic History Review* 22:49–67.

———. 1983. New and old views on the rural economy of the post-bellum South: A review article. *Australian Economic History Review* 22:258–275.

———. 1985. Time expired Melanesian labor in Queensland: An investigation of job turnover, 1884–1906. *Journal of Pacific History* 20:55–56.

———. 1986. The Fiji labor trade in comparative perspective, 1864–1914. *Pacific Studies* 9:107–152.

———. 1986. Indian and Pacific Islander migrants in Fiji: A comparative analysis. *Journal of Pacific Studies* 12:59–86.

———. 1986. Infant mortality and Fiji's Indian Migrants. *Indian Economic and Social History Review* 23:289–302.

———. 1987. Fertility and Fiji's Indian migrants, 1879–1919. *Indian Economic and Social History Review* 24:205–213.

———. 1987. The internal labor trade in Papua (1884–1941) and New Guinea (1920–1941): An economic analysis. *Journal de la société des Océanistes.*

———. 1987. Mortality and the Pacific labor trade. *Journal of Pacific History* 22:34–55.

Steckel, Richard H., 1978. The economics of U.S. slave and southern white fertility. *Journal of Economic History* 38:289–291.

———. 1983. A deplorable scarcity: *The failure of Industrialization in the Economy* by Fred Bateman and Thomas Weiss. Review. *American Journal of Sociology* 5:998–1000.

———. 1985. Dimensions and determinants of early childhood health and mortality among American slaves. National Bureau of Economic Research Working Paper 1662.

———. 1985. Estimating neonatal mortality rates from the heights of children: The case of American slaves. National Bureau of Economic Research Working Paper 1628.

———. 1985. *Virginia Slave Trade Statistics* by Walter Minchinton, Celia King, and Peter Waite. Review. *Journal of Economic History* 45:999.

———. 1986. Birthweights and infant mortality among American slaves. *Explorations in Economic History* 23:173–198.

———. 1986. *The Caribbean slave: A biological history* by Kenneth F. Kiple. Review. *Agricultural History* 60:96–97.

———. 1986. Mortality and indentured labour in Papua (1884–1941) and New Guinea (1920–1941). *Journal of Pacific History* 82–83:177–178.

———. 1987. *Traders, planters, and slaves: Market behavior in early English America* by David W. Galenson. Review. *Journal of Economic History* 47:550–552.

Steckel, Richard H., and Richard A. Jensen. 1986. Evidence on the causes of slave and crew mortality in the Atlantic slave trade. *Journal of Economic History* 46:57–77.

About the Contributors

Stephen C. Crawford received his B.A. in History from Princeton University and his M.A. in Latin American studies from the University of Texas at Austin. In 1980, he was awarded a Ph.D. in History from the University of Chicago. Since 1976, he has worked for Leo Burnett Advertising in Chicago, where he is currently an account director.

Stanley L. Engerman is John H. Munro Professor of economics and professor of history at the University of Rochester and a research associate of the National Bureau of Economic Research.

Robert W. Fogel is the Charles R. Walgreen Professor of American institutions in the graduate school of business at the University of Chicago, where he directs the Center for Population Economics. He was also the director of the program Development of the American Economy at the National Bureau of Economic Research from 1977 to 1991. He has previously taught both history and economics at the University of Rochester, Harvard University, and Cambridge University. His Ph.D. was awarded by Johns Hopkins University in 1963 and he received a D.Sc. from the University of Rochester in 1986. He was elected to the National Academy of Sciences in 1973 and to the Royal Historical Society in 1975. The author or editor of twelve volumes and of numerous professional papers in history, economics, demography, and epidemiology, he is currently completing *The escape from hunger and high mortality: Europe and America 1750–2050* and is also engaged in a collaborative project titled The Aging of Union Army Men: A Longitudinal Study, 1830–1940.

Claudia Goldin is professor of economics at Harvard University. After graduating from Cornell University, she received a Ph.D in economics from the University of Chicago. Her second book is *Understanding the gender gap: An economic history of women and work in America* (Oxford University Press, 1990) and she is the author of numerous papers on the economic history of slavery, the postbellum South, the family economy, the female labor force, and the evolution of modern labor market institutions. She was recently editor of the *Journal of Economic History* and is the director of the program Development of the American Economy at the National Bureau of Economic Research.

A. Meredith John is a research demographer at the Office of Population Research, Princeton University, and an associate of the research division of the Population Council, New York. She has also taught mathematical demography, epidemiology, and human biology at Stanford University and demography at the Graduate Group in Demography at the University of California at Berkeley. The author of *The plantation slave population of Trinidad, 1783–1816: A mathematical and demographic enquiry*, she currently works on population biology, epidemiology, and mathematical demography.

Charles M. Kahn is associate professor of economics at the University of Illinois, Urbana-Champaign. He received his Ph.D. from Harvard University and subsequently taught at the University of Chicago. In 1985–1986 he was a national fellow at the Hoover Institution, Stanford University. He specializes in mathematical economics and the economics of information and uncertainty, with occasional forays into economic history. He is currently combining these interests in an examination of nineteenth-century banking systems from the perspective of information economics and mechanism design.

Herbert S. Klein is professor of history at Columbia University. He is the author of three comparative studies of slavery—*Slavery in the Americas, A comparative study of Cuba and Virginia* (1967), *The Middle Passage: Comparative studies of the Atlantic slave trade* (1978), and *African slavery in Latin America and the Caribbean* (1987). He has also written three works on various aspects of Bolivian history—*Parties and political change in Bolivia, 1880–1952* (1969), *Revolution and the rebirth of inequality* (with J. Kelley, 1980), and *Bolivia, the evolution of a multi-ethnic society* (1982). Most recently he has published, with John TePaske, a collection of primary materials, *The Royal treasuries of Spanish America* (1982), and *Ingresos e Egresos de la Real Hacienda en Nueva Espana* (1986). He studied Latin American history and anthropology at the University of Chicago with J. Fred Rippy and Eric Wolf and U.S. history with Stanley Elkins and Eric McKitrick. His current work on immigration forms part of his long-term interests in comparative economic and social history.

Laurence J. Kotlikoff is professor of economics at Boston University and a research associate of the National Bureau of Economic Research. He received his Ph.D. in economics from Harvard University in 1977 and subsequently taught at the University of California, Los Angeles, and at Yale University. In 1981–1982 he served as a senior economist with the President's Council of Economic Advisors. Professor Kotlikoff is a consultant to the International Monetary Fund, the World Bank, and the Organization for Economic Cooperation and Development. He is author of *What determines savings?* (forthcoming), coauthor (with Alan Auerbach) of *Dynamic fiscal policy*, coauthor (with Daniel Smith) of *Pensions in the American economy*, and coauthor (with David Wise) of *Pension backloading and retirement incentives: The wage carrot and the pension stick*, and has published extensively in professional journals, newspapers, and magazines on issues of deficits, the tax structure, social security, pensions, saving, and insurance.

Robert A. Margo is professor of economics at Vanderbilt University and a research associate at the National Bureau of Economic Research. He received his Ph.D. in economics from Harvard University in 1982 and taught at the University of Pennsylvania from 1981 to 1986. From 1986 to 1988 he held the Banfi Vintner's Chair in American Economic History at Colgate University. Author of numerous papers on the economic history of segregated schools, slavery, and labor, his current research interests are the history of wages in nineteenth-century America and the economic and social history of the teaching profession.

Pedro Carvalho de Mello is professor of economic history in the department of economics at The University of São Paulo, Brazil, and an economist working in the financial sector. As an economic historian he has published articles on the economics of slavery in Brazilian economic history and is working on maritime economic history.

Joseph D. Reid, Jr., is associate professor of economics at George Mason University. Concerned with economic history and development, he has published many articles on the impact of economic and political institutions.

Anton J. Rupert's contribution to this volume was made while working on his senior honors thesis at Harvard University. Laurence Kotlikoff, his coauthor, was his faculty adviser there. Mr. Rupert graduated from Harvard *magna cum laude* in economics and received his Juris Doctor from Stanford. He is a practicing trial lawyer in Oklahoma City, Oklahoma.

Ralph Shlomowitz is senior lecturer in economic history at the Flinders University of South Australia, Adelaide, Australia. He has published articles on the postbellum southern economy and on economic and demographic aspects of the Pacific labor trade from 1863 to 1941. Currently, he is researching a population history of Australia.

Richard H. Steckel is professor of economics at Ohio State University and a research associate at the National Bureau of Economic Research. With research interests in historical demography, he has published numerous articles on migration, fertility, mortality, and health, and a book, *The economics of U.S. slave and southern white fertility*.

James Trussell is a professor of economics and public affairs and faculty associate, Office of Population Research, Princeton University. A demographer, he has published books and articles on the in direct estimation of demographic parameters from incomplete and inaccurate data and on the statistical analysis of demographic data.

Steven B. Webb is senior economist at the World Bank, in the policy, planning and research department. As an economic historian he has published articles on economic development in nineteenth-century Germany and the book, *Hyperinflation and stabilization in Weimar Germany*.

Index

Italicized page numbers refer to figures and tables.

abandonment of slaves, 615–16, 619, 625n4
abolition of slave trade: *see* abolitionism;
    abolition of slavery; slave trade
abolition of slavery:
    in Brazil, 624–49
    British, 571, 572–82
    U.S. Civil War and, 621–22, *622,* 623–24
    see also abolitionism; emancipation of slaves;
        gradual emancipation of slaves
abolitionism:
    Brazil and, 629, 631, 633–45, *641*
    in Britain, 413, 572–82, 584–85, 591, 616,
        617
    and critiques of capitalism, 602
    slave mortality and, 393
    slave registration and, 413
adolescence:
    "adolescent sterility," 446
    growth spurt, among slaves, 501
    nutrition and, 497
adoption, among slave populations,
    452–53n2
"adult fertility": *see* child productivity
Africa:
    slave customs originating in, 505
    slave trade and, 473, 474, 477, 479–80
African Institution (Britain), 413
age at first birth:
    infant mortality and, 497
    masters' incentive to alter, 468–71,
        469
    maternal mortality and, 443
    schedules of, 436–39, 441–43, *442*
    of slave women, 497
    white vs. slave, 496, 497
    see also age at last surviving birth; birth
        interval, surviving; child-spacing interval;
        first birth, mean age at

age at last surviving birth:
    from probate records, *379,* 380
    slave vs. white, 385–86
age-specific mortality rates: *see* mortality, slave
age-price profiles of slaves (Brazil), 639, 640–42,
    641
age-net-hire rates of slaves, 625n6
agency theory:
    disadvantages of, 564–65
    modeling motivation of slaves with, 551,
        556–64
    see also incentive structures
agriculture:
    inefficiency of, in postbellum South 651–52,
        661
    infant and child mortality and, *406,* 407
    postbellum southern stagnation and,
        647–48
    seasonal death patterns and, 408
    see also specific crops
Alabama, 649, 654
amnesty records (U.S. Civil War), 508, 513–14,
    519
Angola, 477, 480
Anstey, Roger T., 573
antislavery index, 575–76, 584
Anti-Slavery Society (British), 571, 575–76
apprenticeship (of slaves):
    in British colonies, 571, 600
    emancipation of slaves by Parliament and,
        591, 617
    failure of, in northern U.S., 616
    see also gradual emancipation of slaves
Arawak Indians, 414
Aydelotte, William O., 578, 580

Banks, Enoch M., 665
Barboza, Ruy (Brazilian statesman), 664

Bauer, A. H., 504
Bauer, R. A., 504
"Beard-Hacker" thesis, 624, 628n34
Beaton, G. H., 526
Bengoa, J. M., 526
Bentzon, M. S., 447
binary response model, 417–18
biological adaptation thesis and health of slave
    children, 502
birth interval, surviving:
    approximations of, 390–91n8
    fertility and, 382
    slave vs. white, 386–88, *388*
    see also child-spacing interval
birth lists, plantation, 490–91
birth order, 386, 412
birth outcome, 493
birth price: *see* prices of slaves
births, underreporting of, 400–403
    see also underreporting of infant death
birth weight, 493–94
birthing practices, 414
Black codes, southern postbellum, 649, 680
    see also Code Noir
black labor: *see* labor in the postbellum South;
    freedmen; gang-labor system;
    sharecropping; slave labor; tenancy,
    agricultural
black population:
    age-sex structure of antebellum, 597–98
    in early national period, 603n8
    malnutrition, effects of, 503–4
    rate of growth, North vs. South, *597*, 596–97
black regiments (Union army), 509
Bojlen, K., 447
Brass logit relationship, 416, 417
Brazil, 479, 617
    abolition of slavery by, 624–49
    antislavery movement and, 629, 631
    labor alternatives in, 643
    market for slaves, 631, 639–42
    planter mentality, 632
breast feeding, 411n8
    among Caribbean slaves, 505
    among slaves and whites (U.S.), 386, 399,
        495, 505
    contraceptive effects of, 403, 411n9
    infant mortality and, 398, 506n9
    work and, 496, 503
Britain:
    abolition of slave trade by, 573–75, 584
    antislavery sentiment in Parliament, 574–77,
        584
    House of Commons, constituencies of, 577–78
    slaveholders' influence in Parliament, 590

British colonies:
    abolition of slave trade in, 413
    compensation to slaveowners in, 590,
        599–600, 604n22n23
    emancipation of slaves in, 616–17
    West Indies, 598, 600–601
Brookes (slave ship), 473, 480
Brooks, Robert P., 652, 655, 658
Bundi of New Guinea, 501

caloric expenditures of laborers, 526, 534n7
Canarella, Giorgio, 552, 553, 560, 561
Cardell, N. Scott, 530
Caribbean slaves:
    African customs of, 505
    birthing practices of, 414
Catholic Church and treatment of slaves, 415–16
census data, antebellum:
    age-specific mortality rates, 397
    child-spacing interval, 373
    fertility studies and, 369, 370, 372, *376*
Cheung, Stephen N.S., 651, 656
childbearing (slave):
    delay of, and slave-breeding hypothesis,
        467–68
    menarche and, 444–46, 448–52
    patterns of, vs. southern whites, 390
    value of slave women and, 592, 594, 595, 616
childless women, antebellum, 443–44, *445*
child mortality (slave), *399*, 407, 410
    age at first birth schedule and, 438–39
    diseases causing, 415
    gender differences in, 434
    migration and, 400
    profit motive of slaveowners and, 502–3
    seasonal patterns of, 408–9, *409*, 410
    time pattern of, 496, 399–400, *400*, 401
    in Trinidad, 414–16, 423–29, 434
    variables influencing, 398, *406*
    weaning and, 399
    see also survival probability; infant mortality;
        neonatal mortality; postneonatal mortality;
        underreporting of infant death
child productivity:
    as fertility measure, 456, 457
    sex ratios and, 456, 457, 458
    slave-breeding hypothesis and, 458
children, slave: *see* slave children
child-spacing interval:
    change of slave partner, 388
    child mortality rate and, 373
    factors related to, 386, *387*, 388
    plantation records and, 379
    synthetic total fertility rate and, 373
    see also birth interval, surviving

child-woman ratio, 369–70
  direct measures of fertility and, 374
  migration and, 388–89
  mortality and, 370
  regional differences in, 370, 388–89
  sex-ratio and, 459, *460*
  slave-breeding hypothesis and, 456, 457
  of slaves (U.S.), *463, 460*
  synthetic total fertility rate and, 374
  of various populations, *463*
  time trend of, 370, *371*
China, 447
cholera, 400, 496
Civil War (U.S.), 631
  alternatives to, 617–20
  amnesty records from, 508, 513–14, 519
  cost of, 620–22, *622*, 623–24
  ex-slave recruits (Union Army), data on,
    509–13
  losses incurred during, 624
  treason, as defined by North, 5113–14
climate:
  child mortality and, 407
  heights of southerners and, 517
Coale, Ansley J., 393–94, 399, 409, 417
Coale and Demeny life tables: see model life
    tables
coastal regions (U.S.):
  health and nutrition in, 516
  height and, 515, 518
coastwise manifests of U.S. slave trade,
    491
  height-age data from, 449–59
Cobb-Douglas production function, 620
Cocos Island women, fertility of, 462, *463*
Code Noir (Louisiana), 611
coffee, 415
  Brazilian planters of, 632
  revenues from (Brazil), 641–42
  slavery and production of, 631, 643–44
Cole, Arthur H., 523, 528
colonization of ex-slaves, 619–20, 627*n*26
  American attitudes toward, 623
Colonization Society (U.S.), 620
The Concept of Stable Populations (UN Study),
    394
concubinage and manumission of slaves, 611,
    612, 613
Confederacy, 508, 621
Confiscation Act (1862), 513
Congo, 479, 480
corn, in slave diet, 527–28, 532
Corn Laws (Britain), 584
cotton, cultivation of:
  mortality rates and, 494–95

seasonal patterns of work, 492–93
  by slave women, pregnant and postpartum,
    493, 495
cotton farming, postbellum:
  collective tenancy vs. sharecropping, 679–80
  competition for labor, 666–69, 673
  freedmen's attitudes toward, 673
  share system and, 675–76
Coupland, Reginald, 573
Crawford, Stephen C., 544, 545, 551, 561,
    564
crop:
  distribution of slaves by, 411*n*7
  height of slaves by, 512
  see also specific crops
crowding on slave ships, 475–77, *475, 476*, 480
  see also provisioning of slave ships; slave
    trade, mortality in
Cuba, 617, 619–20, 631
Cúcuta Slave Law (Venezuela), 617

Dann, T. C., 447
David, Ronald L. F., 675
Davis, David Brion, 573–74, 584
death: *see* mortality; child mortality; infant
    mortality; mortality; mortality, slave;
    neonatal mortality; postneonatal mortality;
    slave trade, mortality in; survival
    probability
Declaration of Independence, 615
Demeny, Paul, 393–94, 399, 409, 417
demography of slavery:
  birth and mortality time series, 395
  prices of slaves and, *465*
  and tobacco, 389, 390, 398
  transatlantic slave trade and, 474–83
  see also age at first birth; birth interval,
    surviving; black population, antebellum;
    census data, antebellum; child mortality;
    child productivity; child-spacing interval;
    child-woman ratio; crop; fecundability;
    fertility; fertility rate, synthetic total; first
    birth, mean age at; height of slaves; height
    velocity; infant mortality; marriage;
    menarche, age of; migration; model life
    tables; mortality, slave; neonatal mortality;
    plantation records; probate records;
    sex-ratios; slave-breeding hypothesis;
    survival probability
developing countries:
  height data for, 499–500
  seasonal patterns of health in, 492
Dew, Thomas R., 620
direct cost, of slave, 602*n*2
  see also price of slave

diet:
  evaluation of historical diets, 515, 517
  and height of southerners, 517
  meat in working class diet, 530
  of mother, and child growth profile, 519–20
  state of residence and, 515
  see also diet of slaves; malnutrition; nutrition
diet of slaves:
  adults, 500–501
  children, 500–501
  cost of various diets, 502–3, 522–23, 524–25,
    529, 529–30, 532, 532–33, 535
  fat in, 531, 531–32
  foods in, 527–29
  growth profile and, 503
  menarche and, 449
  milk vs. meat in, 530
  rice in, 534n 10
  seasonal fluctuation in, 494
  taste and, 523–24
  work routine and, 501, 520
dichotomous dependent variables and regression
    analysis, 404
disappearance method of estimating food
    consumption, 503
disciplining of slaves: see incentive structures;
    management of slaves; punishment of
    slaves; whipping of slaves
disease:
  age at menarche and, 448
  child mortality and, 415
  seasonal death patterns and, 408, 409
  slave children and, 415, 500, 502
  slave mortality and, 400
  on slave ships, 477, 482
  see also disease environment; specific diseases
disease environment:
  height of slaves and, 510
  of plantations, 407, 415, 423, 425
  regional variation in, 515–16
  slave mortality profiles and, 496
  southern, 501
  variables indicating, 515
  see also disease, specific diseases
District of Columbia, 626n 15, 626n 26
Dod's Parliamentary Companion, 575, 576, 577
Doring, Gerhard K., 446
dose response model: see binary response model
Drescher, Seymour, 473
dysentery, 482, 484n 22

earnings of slaves:
  expropriated by slaveowner, 596
  female, 506n 188, 595

  male, 593
  see also money
Easterlin, Richard A., 496
Eblen, J. E., 393–94
effective fertility: see child-woman ratio
Elkins, Stanley M., 504
Emancipation Court of Louisiana, 607
emancipation of slaves:
  age of, in U.S. North, 615–16
  apprenticeship and, 571
  in British West Indies, 616–17
  during Civil War (U.S.), 626n 19
  and colonization schemes, 619–20
  conditions of, non-American, 603n 3
  forms of, 614–15
  free-born, age of, 589
  gradual abolition and, 616
  in northern U.S., 588–90, 615–16
  Parliamentary issues linked with, 582–84, 583
  postbellum southern labor force and, 643
  property rights and, 601–2
  slaveowners' losses, 595, 623, 602–3n 2,
  in South America, 616
  see also abolition of slavery; emancipation of
    slaves, cost of; manumission of slaves,
    gradual emancipation of slaves
emancipation of slaves, cost of:
  Britain vs. U.S. North, 591
  compensation to slaveholders, 587, 603n 4
  distribution of cost, 591–602
  emancipation legislation and, 589–90
  for Britain, 598–601
  to slaveowners, 595, 602–3n 2, 623
  in U.S., 618–22
  vs. European serfs, 605n 30
  see also emancipation of slaves, gradual
    emancipation of slaves
emancipation petitions, 607–8
Emancipation Proclamation (U.S.), 618
employer's combinations, postbellum South, 666,
    682n 25
Engerman, Stanley L., 438, 440, 645
  on age at first birth, 436, 438–39, 444
  on capital value of slaves, 626n 18
  on disappearance method of estimating food
    consumption, 503
  on farm size, 19th century South, 663n 11
  on intrusion by slaveowners into sexual mores
    of slaves, 435
  on punishment and rewards of slaves, 553,
    554, 558
  sanguinity index, 633
  on slave diet, 522, 529, 529, 527, 522
  on slave incentives, 552

on slave mobility, 400
on standard of living of slaves, 551
on work ethic of slaves, 504
Eskimos, 645
Evans Robert Jr., 393
Eveleth, P. B., 449
expropriation versus exploitation of slave labor,
  602n2

family-formation decisions, antebellum, 383,
  385, 389
family limitation, antebellum, 380, 385–86, 497
family tenantry: *see* sharecropping; tenancy,
  agricultural
Farley, Reynolds, 393
farms:
  rented vs. sharecropped, U.S., 650
  size, southern postbellum, 650
  see also plantations
fat in slave diet, 531–32, *531*
fecundability, 446–47
"female fertility": see child-woman ratio
Fenoaltea, Stefano, 552, 553–54, 563
fertility:
  age-specific rates and reproductive behavior,
    436
  birth interval and, 382
  breastfeeding and, 507n21
  child mortality and, 504–5
  child-woman ratio and, 370
  data on slave, quality of, 374–79
  manipulation of slave fertility, 451–52, 455
  plantation characteristics and, 374, *375*, 389
  migration and, 389, 390
  sex ratio and, 459
  slave and white women, *375, 376*, 380–82,
    389, 462, *463*
  slave-breeding hypothesis and, 456–64
  slave prices and, 465–66
  socioeconomic factors affecting, 383, 385
  tobacco plantations and, 389, 390
  see also fertility rate, synthetic total; fertility
    studies
fertility rate, synthetic total, 370
  advantages of, 374
  behavior effecting, 380, *381*
  biases in, 372, 373
  child spacing and, 386
  child-woman ratio and, 372, 373, 374
  components of, 370, *381*
  definition of, 372
  last surviving birth and, 380, *381*
  in Louisiana 377, *377*
  predicted vs. computed values of, 377, *378*

singulate mean and, 373
time trend of, 380–82
true total fertility rate and, 372
fertility studies:
  antebellum data for, 370, 372, 380
  comparative analysis in, 369, 389
first birth, mean age at:
  as measure of behavior, 439
  childless women effects on, 443–44
  in a growing population, *437*, 437–38
  mortality and, 436–37, *437*
  truncation bias and, 438, *438*
  see also age at first birth
Fogel, Robert W., 438, 440
  on age at first birth, 436, 438–39, 444
  on capital value of slaves, 626n18
  on disappearance method of estimating food
    consumption, 503
  on farm size, 19th century southern, 663n11
  on intrusion by slaveowners into sexual mores
    of slaves, 435
  on punishment and rewards of slaves, 553,
    554, 558
  sanguinity index, 633
  on slave diet, 522, 529, *529,* 527, 522
  on slave incentives, 552
  on slave mobility, 400
  on standard of living of slaves, 551
  on work ethic of slaves, 504
foods:
  prices of, 19th century, 528
  regional vs. national markets in 1860, 523, *523*
free blacks (antebellum):
  efforts to reduce number of (Louisiana),
    607
  kin relationships to emancipated slaves,
    611–12
  manumission of slaves by, 606, 609–11
  mixed blood of, 612
freedmen:
  associations of, 670
  bargaining with employers, 668
  job turnover among, 667–68
  and share-system, attitude toward, 667, 675
  in southern agricultural labor force, 648,
    649–51
  work preferences of, 670–73
Free Womb Law of 1871 (Brazil), 629, 631, 637,
  642
French-Canada, fertility rates of, *382*

gang-labor system:
  physical punishment in, 541
  vs. skilled and household work, 544

gang-labor system *(continued)*
 vs. task system, 563
 see also work-gang agriculture
gender:
 and age at emancipation, northern U.S.,
  615–16
 height-by-sex data, slave and modern, 497–98,
  498
 survival probability of slave children and,
  423–29, 434
 see also age at first birth; earnings of slaves;
  fertility; birth interval, surviving;
  breast-feeding; child-spacing interval;
  child-woman ration; first birth, mean age at;
  marriage; sex-ratios; slave labor;
  slave-breeding hypothesis; slave women
Genovese, Eugene D., 504
Georgia, 377, *377*, 658
Germany, 499, *499*
Goldin, Claudia, 464, *465*
Gould, Benjamin Apthorp, 509
gradual abolition of slavery: *see* gradual
 emancipation of slaves
gradual emancipation of slaves:
 in northern U.S., 587, 588–90, 615–16
 in Brazil, 642–43
 by Britain, 571, 591
 in British colonies, 587, 590–91
 cost of, vs. cost of Civil War, 621–22, *622*
 drawbacks of, 616
 full abolition vs., 616–17
 property rights and, 601
 treatment of slaves under, 595–96
 see also abolition of slavery; apprenticeship;
  emancipation of slaves
growth profiles:
 factors affecting, 601
 as index of health and nutrition, 502, 508
 height-by-age data, various populations,
  499
 height-by-age data, 19th century, 491, 509,
  509, 514, 515, 508
 of slaves, 491, 500, 518, 503
 time trends, 520
 see also height velocity; growth studies
growth spurt, adolescent: *see* height velocity
growth studies:
 modern vs. slave, 477
 longitudinal, 449
Gutman, Herbert, 455

Hajnal, J. 439–40
Hajnal formula: *see* singulate mean
Hansard's Parliamentary Debates, 582

health:
 indexes of, 491, 502
 nineteenth century, cycles vs. trends, 496
 nutrition and, 19th century, 519
 regional differences in, 515, 516, 518
 seasonal patterns of, 492
 slavery and, 501–3, 505
 of slaves, antebellum debate over, 489
 see also disease; disease environment; specific
  diseases
height:
 demographic uses of data on, 449
 health and, 491, 502
 income and, 520
 job choice and, 518
 modern standards of, 506*n* 12
 of northern whites, 496
 nutrition and, 500
 regional U.S. differences in, 515, 519
 of southern whites, 501–2, 514–15, *515*, *516*,
  516–17
 southerners vs. northerners, 501–2, 515, 520
 time trends and, 520
 see also growth profile; growth studies; heights
  of slaves; height velocity
heights of slaves:
 by gender, 497–98, *498*
 vs. height of whites, 517–19
 occupation and, 518
 plantation size and, 520
 vs. other populations, *498*, 498–99, 517
 regional variation of, 510
 skin color and, 510
 of slave children, 496, 500, 518
 time pattern of, 512, 518
 variables influencing, 509–13, *511–12*,
  519–20
 see also height
height profiles: *see* growth profiles
height-by-age data: *see* growth profiles
height velocity:
 adolescent growth spurt, 497, 501
 of females, *451*
 of female slaves, *450*
 peak, and age at menarche, 449–51
 profiles of, modern vs. slave, 497, *498*
Henry, Louis, 403
Henry's hypothesis, 446 *see also* fecundability
heterosis, theory of, 510
Higgs, Robert, 665
Higman, B. W., 407, 414–15, 496
Hilgard, Eugene W., 655, 658
hire-rate indexes of slaves (Brazil), 637–39, *639*
Homestead Act, 650

Homo economicus as plantation owner, 524
hookworm, 408
Hopkins, Mark M., 530
House of Commons (Britain), 571, 574–78

immigration as alternative to slavery in Brazil, 643
income of slaves: *see* earnings of slaves; money
income, per capita (19th century), 647
incentive structures:
   conditions for effective, 555
   function of, in slave management, 554–55
   mathematical formulation of, 557–58
   punishment and rewards in, 552–55
   supervision of slaves and, 561
   theoretical accounts of slave, 522–24, 552–54
India, 447
infant mortality (slave), 410
   age of mother and, 368, 388, 405
   birth order and, 386, 412
   breast-feeding practices and, 398
   child-spacing and, 386, 388
   diseases and, 400, 415
   height and, 518
   marriage patterns and, 385, 412
   maternal care and, 415
   migration and, 400
   by plantation, *402*
   probability of, 405–7, *406*, 410
   profit motive of slaveowners and, 502–3
   rates of, *403*
   seasonal patterns of, 409
   by time period, *401*
   time trend of, 399–400, *400*, 401
   in Trinidad, 414–16, 423–24
   see also child mortality; underrepporting of
      infant death; mortality, slave; neonatal
      mortality; postneonatal mortality; stillbirth;
      survival probability
infectious disease on slave ships, 482
   see also disease, specific diseases
inoculation of slaves:
   against smallpox, 415, 482, 484*n*18
   against yaws, 415
Ireland, 440

Jain, Anrudh, 446
Jamaica, 407, 616–17
   slave infant mortality in, 415
Johnson, Andrew, 513, 650
Johnson, D. Gale, 651, 655–56

Kiple, Kenneth F., 398, 502, 529–30
Kiple, Virginia H., 398, 502, 529–30

Kotlikoff, Laurence J., 612
Kralj-Cercek, Lea, 447

labor in the postbellum South, 678–79
   black, 650–51, 665–80
   competition for, 666–69, 673
   daily wage for, vs. the North, 609
   market for, 670, 668–69
   wage-labor system and, 648–49, 673–74,
      676–77
   see also sharecropping; tenancy, agricultural;
      work-gang agriculture
lactase deficiency in black populations, 530
Laerne, C. F. Van Delden, 643
life expectation: see mortality, slave
life table (1850), 393
   see also model life tables
Lincoln, Abraham, 513, 618, 619, 623, 624
linear programming models:
   diets of slaves and, 522–33
   as summaries of complex processes, 524
Liverpool, Lord (Secretary of State for War and
   Colonies), 413
Lockridge, Kenneth A., 394
logistic models of survivorship, 429, 434
logistic regression models in mortality studies,
   420–21
logit regression model:
   postneonatal mortality and, 495
   probability of early death and, 491
   slave mortality and, 415
Louisiana, 377, *377*, 669, 670
   rice and sugar cane farming in, 672, 673, 674
   laws regulating slavery in territory of, 606–7
Louisiana Purchase (1803), 606

Maine, 615
malaria, 408, 493, 495
malnutrition:
   among slave children, 501
   infection and, 505
   role of protein in, 453–55*n*11
   see also diet; diet of slaves; nutrition
management of slaves, principles of, 552–53,
   554, 555, 561
   see also incentive structures; punishment of
      slaves; whipping of slaves
manumission of slaves:
   age-sex distribution in New Orleans, 608–9,
      610
   concubinary relationships and, 611, 612
   conditions of, 589–90
   by free blacks, 609–11
   legislative history of (New Orleans), 606–7

manumission of slaves *(continued)*
  price of slaves and, 607, *609*
  termination of, in Louisiana, 607
"marital fertility," 461
  Richard Sutch's definition, 471n7
marriage:
  definition of slave marriage, 391n10
  infant mortality rates and, 385, 412
  remarriage among slaves and whites, 385–86, 390
  slaves' patterns of, 383, 462
Marshal, Alfred, 651
Massachusetts, 588, 615
master:
  as profit maximizer, 556–58
  slaves' perception of, 542–43, *543*
  see also slaveowner; planter
maturation, physical, time trend of, 447–48
  see also menarche, age of; height velocity
maximum likelihood logistic probability model, 404–5
menarche, age of:
  adolescent growth spurt and, 497
  "adolescent sterility" and, 446
  age at first birth, 446–48
  calculation of, from direct data, 453n8
  factors influencing, 446–48
  malnutrition and, 454–55n11
  slave, estimation of, 448–50, *450*
  in various populations, 447–48
measles:
  and child mortality, 415
  on slave ships, 482
meat:
  in slave diets, 500–501, 502–3, 529–30
  in working class diets, 529–30
Meeker, E., 496
Merrill, Annabel L., 525, 527
"middle passage" *see* slave trade; slave trade, mortality in; crowding on slave ships
migration:
  child-woman ratio and, 391–92n15
  fertility rates and, 388–89, 390
  height of slaves and, 510
  singulate mean age at first birth and, 439, 440
  slave mortality rates and, 400, 496
Miller vs. Dwilling, 625n3, 627n24
miscegenation, of free blacks and slaves, 612
Mississippi, 655
Missouri, 619, 627n26
model life tables, 393–94
  age patterns of slave mortality and, 398
  binary response models and, 417–18
  Brass logit relationship and, 416, 417

logistic regression models and, 417, 418
  of slave populations, 398, 399
money:
  payments of, as incentive to slaves, 547, 548, 549, *549*
  slaves' uses of, 547
  sources of, in slave society, 545–47
  workweek of slaves and, 546
  see also earnings of slaves
mortality:
  age dependency of models of, 416–17
  child-woman ratio and, 370
  logistic models of, 416
  maternal, and mean age at first birth, 443
  singulate mean and, 439, 440
  see also mortality, slave; neonatal mortality; postneonatal mortality; stillbirth; survival probability
mortality, slave:
  age pattern of, 398–99, 501
  age specific rates, 397, *397*
  antebellum concern over, 393
  binary response models of, 416
  in Jamaica, 407
  life expectation of slaves, 399
  model life table approximating, 394–95
  modern studies of, 393–94
  regression analysis of, 403–7
  seasonal variation in, 493, 494, 408–9, *409*, 410
  slave prices and, 466
  survival functions and, 422
  time patterns of, 399–403
  in Trinidad, 414–16, 423–24
  tobacco plantations and, 398
  underreporting of, 409–10
  vital registration data and, 387
  vs. white mortality, *490*, 520
  work vs. crop effects on, 494–95
  see also child mortality; infant mortality; neonatal mortality; postneonatal mortality; slave trade, mortality in; stillbirth; survival probability
Mozambique, 480

Nantes slave trade survey, 474, 483n6, 483n7
  death rates, vs. Portuguese slave trade, 560
narratives of slaves (WPA and Fisk University), 551
  biases of, 536–37, 545–46
  punishment in, 536
National Research Council of the United States, 526, 527

neonatal mortality, 490
    factors influencing, 491–95
    modern studies of, 491
    slave and white, 505n3
    see also child mortality; infant mortality;
        postneonatal mortality; stillbirth
New Guinea, 447
New Hampshire, 588
New Jersey, 588, 590, 597–98, 615, 616
    emancipation law of, 594
New Orleans, 606–7, 609, 611, 612, 613
    slave sales in, 472n9
New York (state), 590, 597, 598
    emancipation in, 594, 615, 616
    slave population of, 625n9
niacin content of foods, 528
North Carolina, 648, 654
nuptiality schedule, 439–40
nutrition, 500
    age of menarche and, 447–48, 449
    behavior and, 504
    caloric requirements of laborers, 526,
        534n7
    child development and, 503–4
    growth patterns and, 500–501, 508
    health and, 519
    minimum requirements, 526–27, 529, 530
    theories of, 19th century, 531–32
    see also diet; diet of slaves; malnutrition

occupations of slaves:
    categories of, 521n8
    child slave mortality and, 423
    as incentive for slaves, 562–63, 544–45
    nutrition and health and, 547
    physical size and, 510, 515, 517
    monetary payments to slaves and, 547
    vs. southern whites, 517
    workweek and, 544
    see also slave labor
Olmsted, Frederick Law, 671, 672
Olson, John F., 509
ordinary least squares linear probability model,
    404
Orr, Martha L., 528
overcrowding, index of: see crowding, on slave
    ships

parasitic infection, 408
Parker-Gallman sample, 459
    fertility rates and, 460, 462, 463
Parker, William N., 668
Parliament (British), 573–76, 584, 590
Patterson, Orlando H., 415

pellagra, 528, 530
Pennsylvania, 609, 615, 616
    emancipation in, 594, 625
Philadelphia, 609
Phillips, Ulrich Bonnell, 631–32
Peterson, Arthur G., 523, 525, 528
pork in slave diet, 532
placage, 611
plantations (slave):
    child-woman ratios of, 460
    disease environment of, 407, 415
    fertility on, 389, 390
    height of slaves on, 512, 520
    incentive structures on, 562, 563–64
    monetary payments to slaves, 546–47
    mortality, 397–98, 407, 496
    punishment on, 537–43, 538, 540–41,
        541
    sex ratios of, 460
    see also farms, southern; plantation records
plantation records, 395, 394, 490–91
    birth history and, 395
    child-spacing intervals and, 373
    cross-sectional and time series data from, 395
    fertility studies and, 370, 376, 379
    life expectation and, 399
    location of, 396
    singulate mean age at first birth and, 444
    slave mortality and, 396
    underreporting of infant death, 402
planters:
    Brazilian, views on abolition, 643
    contracts with labor, 648–59, 652–53, 655,
        668
    as Homo economicus, 524
    labor, attempts to control, 670, 665–66,
        676–77
    as managers, 651–54, 659–60
    as utility maximizers, 657–58
    wage vs. share systems and, 665–66, 674–75,
        677, 678–79
    work-gangs and, 649–50
    see also masters; slaveowners
Poor Law of 1834 (Britain), 571, 582–84
population growth, 19th century, 369
Portugal, 477, 479
Postell, William D., 394
postneonatal mortality:
    definition of, 490
    factors influencing slave, 495–97
    time pattern of slave, 496
    see also infant mortality; neonatal mortality;
        stillbirth; survival probability
pregnancy, 492, 493

prices: *see* specific commodities, prices of slaves
prices of slaves:
    age-specific data on, 618
    birth price, 615–16, 625*n*4
    in Brazil, *635*, 644, *644*, 645,
    change in, *466*, 627*n*23
    childbearing capacity and, 592–94, *594*
    of children, 472*n*9
    closing of transatlantic slave trade and, 597
    demand schedule and, *630*
    determined by, 592–94
    male and female, *593, 594*
    manumission and, 608, *609*
    slave breeding and, 464–71, 469
    slave demographics and, 464, *465*, 465–66
    sugar prices and, 605*n*24
probate data:
    first birth schedules and, 436, 438–39, 444
    recording practices of, 377
    slave adoption practices and, 452*n*2
    slave fertility studies and, 370, 373, *375, 376,
        377*, 377, 379
probit models, 416
profit-motive of slaveowners:
    diet of slaves and, 502, 503, 524
    health of slaves and, 502–3, 505
    slavebreeding and, 465–71
property rights of slaveowners:
    British attitudes about, 590–91
    emancipation and, 571, 589, 601–2
    U.S. attitudes toward, 1860, 618
protein, 506*n*17
Protestantism and slavery, 415–16
provisioning of slave ships:
    costs of, 482
    factors affecting, 482
    minimum requirements for, 480, 481
    mortality and, 477
    see also slave trade; slave trade, mortality in
punishment and reward: *see* incentive structures;
    punishment of slaves; whipping of slaves
punishment of slaves:
    frequency of, *537*, 537–43, *538*, 550
    gang-labor system and, 541
    life cycle of slaves and, 541–42, 550
    offenses eliciting, 539–40, *540*
    perception of master colored by, 542–43, *543*
    rewards vs., 544, 549, 550, 554–55
    slave narratives as information on, 536, *537*,
        538–39
    social control vs. labor incentive motives for,
        543–44, 549–48, *549*
    workweek and, 548–49, *549*
    see also whipping of slaves

racism in the postbellum South, 647, 661,
    663*n*1
Range, Willard, 655
Rasmussen, W. D., 523, 528
Reconstruction (U.S.), 649–50, 664*n*34
Reform Bill of 1832 (Britain), 576, 585
regression analysis:
    of British emancipation Bill, 574–82
    slave mortality and, 403–7
registration of slaves, British West Indies,
    413–14
religious ideology and treatment of slaves,
    415–16
reproductive behavior of slaves, manipulation of,
    435
    see also slave-breeding hypothesis
revolts of slaves, 616–17
    fear of, 607
rewarding of slaves: *see* incentive structures;
    punishment of slaves
Rhode Island, 589–90
Rinchon, Dieudonné, 474, 480, 483*n*7
    see also Nantes slave trade survey
rice in slave diet, 534*n*10
rice, cultivation of:
    freedmen's attitude toward, 670, 671–72, 673
    slave mortality and, 398, 407, 410, 494, 495
    wage-system in Louisiana and, 674
Roberts, Derek, 447

sanguinity index, 633–34
    Brazilian, 634–37, *637*
    urban vs. rural slaves, *638*
São Paulo, 632
scurvy, 530
Sexagenarian Law (Brazil), 631, 637, 645,
    645*n*9
sex-ratio:
    fertility and, 455–58, 459–62
    of slave plantations, *460*
sharecroppers, as utility maximizers, 657–58
    see also sharecropping
sharecropping, 680
    autonomy of freedmen under, 673
    vs. 'collective' share system, 678–79
    contemporary criticism of, 650–51
    contracts, terms of, 652–57, 661–63
    control of labor, 676–77
    country stores and, 663*n*2
    credit and, 660
    determination of shares under, 668–69
    economic advantages of, 659, 660
    freedmen's preference for, 660, 675
    landlord as manager, 660

origins of, 665, 668–69
planters and freedmen, convergence of
    interests, 677
renting and, 660
race and, *656*, 658
risk-sharing in, 656–57, 658, 659, 660
see also tenancy, agricultural
"sickly season", 493, 494
singulate mean, 339–443, 444, 452
    age at first birth, slaves vs. whites, 383, *384,*
        444
    synthetic total fertility rate and, 373
    see also childless women
skin color and height of slaves, 510
slave-breeding hypothesis, 455–71
    breeding farms, identification of, 462–64
    demographic case for, 456–64
    economic case for, 464–71
    fertility measures and, 455–65
    price fluctuations and, 465–66
    profitability and, 465–71
    slave marriage patterns and, 383–85
slave children:
    abandonment of, 625*n*4
    diet of, 502–3
    gradual emancipation's effect on, 615–16,
        619
    health of, 502–3
    heights of, 496, 498–500, 519–20
    labor of, 500, 519–20
    prices of, 472*n*9
    survival of, rewards for, 414
    transporting of, 389
    work done by, 500
slave labor:
    children and, 500, 519–20
    collective, slave preference for, 672
    money paid for, 546, 548
    pregnant and postpartum women and, 493,
        493
    regulation of, 544
    routines of, various crops, 495
    work-week, 548–49, *549*
    see also gang-labor system; occupations of
        slaves
slaveowners:
    Brazilian, 636–37
    compensation to, for emancipation, 591, 588,
        599–601, 614–15, 604–5*n*22*n*23, 617,
        618–21
    free blacks as, 609–11
    gradual emancipation and, 595, 596–97, *597,*
        616
    influence of, in British Parliament, 590

management of slaves, 552–53
    as profit maximizers, 524
    slave fertility, manipulation of, 455,
        469–71
    see also masters; planters; profit motive of
        slaveowners; property rights of slaveowners
slavery:
    autonomy and resistance of slaves, 505
    in Brazil, gradual abolition of, 629–33,
        642–45
    British opposition to, character of, 584–85
    caloric needs of laboring slaves, 526
    decline of, in northern U.S., 597–98
    end of, in U.S., 623–24
    as industry, model describing, 632–33
    manumission of non-productive slaves,
        612–13
    non-profitability in U.S. thesis, 631–32
    responsibility for, Britain and U.S., 590
    slaves as utility maximizers, 554, 556, 557–58
    transition to freedom, labor supply, 680
    value of slaves in U.S., 618, 619
    see also demography of slavery; mortality,
        slave; management of slaves; prices of
        slaves; punishment of slaves; slave children;
        slave labor; slave trade; slave trade,
        mortality in; slaveowners; slave women;
        whipping of slaves
slave trade:
    Brazil and abolition of, 642
    Britain and abolition of, 413, 573, 617
    in British colonies, 617
    gradual abolition of slavery and, 616
    historiography of transatlantic, 473–74
    Massachusetts abolishes, 615
    Portuguese, 477, 580
    sailing times, various ports of exit, 480
    tonnage regulations, 477
    U.S., abolishes transatlantic, 491, 596–97
    U.S., internal, 449, 450–51, *451,* 596–97
    see also Nantes slave trade survey;
        provisioning of slave ships; slave trade,
        mortality in
slave trade, mortality in, 473–83
    of crews, 477–79, *479,* 483*n*9
    crowding on ships and, 475–77, *475, 476,*
        480
    declining trend of, 474–75, *475,* 480
    of slaves, 474–77
    and time at sea, 477, 479–81, *481*
slave women:
    child-bearing capacity and value of, 592, 594,
        595
    earnings of, U.S., 506*n*18

slave women *(continued)*
  height velocities of, *450*
  pregnancies of, 492–97
Spanish colonies, 414
  see also specific colonies
*South American Journal and Brazil and River
    Plate Mail*, 643
South Carolina, 512–13, 518, 649, 671
  sharecropping in, 652, 655
Southern Cultivator, 650
southern postbellum stagnation, 647–48
smallpox, 415, 482, 484n 18
"smothering" deaths of slave infants, 494
Stampp, Kenneth M., 504
stature: *see* height
Stephen, James (British abolitionist), 413
stillbirth:
  factors associated with, 491, 492
  seasonal fluctuations in, 494
  among slaves, 491
sugar:
  British tariffs on, 601
  English prices of, 601
  slave prices and, 605n 24
  West Indian revenues from, 600, *600*
  see also sugar cane cultivation
sugar cane cultivation, 415
  employers' combinations, 682n 25
  freedmen's distaste for, 670, 671–72, 673
  infant and child slave mortality and, 407, 494,
      495, 496
  plantation system and, 680
  postbellum labor markets for, 669–70
  wage labor vs. collective share system, 679–80
  wage system and, 674
  white tenantry and, 680
  work effort required in, 495
sudden infant death syndrome (SIDS), 494
survival probability:
  covariate analysis of, 418–19, 420–23
  factors influencing, 418–19
  gender differences and, 423–29, 434
  of slave children, 423, *424, 425*, 427, *430,
      431*
surviving birth interval: *see* birth interval,
    surviving
Sutch, Richard:
  on cost of slave diet, 533, 529, *529*
  on fertility measures, 456–58
  on slave-breeding, 455–71
  on slave diet, 503, 522, 527
  on standard of living of slaves, 551
Sweden, 440
Sydnor, Charles J., 393

Taiwan, *446*
Talwar, T. T., 447
Tanner, J. M., 447–48, 449
Taylor, Rosser H. 655
tenancy, agricultural, 650
  criticism of, 650–51
  economists view of, 651–52
  efficiency of, 651–52
  "land-thirst" theory of, 658–60, 661
  postbellum agriculture and, 648
  preference of laborers for, 658–59, 660
  rise of, in the South, 649–51
  risk aversion and, 656–58
  tenants' choice of tenure, 656–60
  terms of, 654–56
  vs. work-gang labor, 650
  see also sharecropping
tetanus, neonatal, 414–15
Thirteenth Amendment, 615, 617
"tight-packing:" *see* crowding, on slave ships
Time on the Cross (Fogel and Engerman), 435,
    394
tobacco, 389, 390, 398
Tomaske, John A., 552, 553, 560, 561
Towne, M. W., 523, 528
treason, defined as, after U.S. Civil War, 513–14
Trinidad, 414
  disease environments of, 415
  heights of slaves in, *499*, 499, 521n 6, 521n 9
  mortality of slave children, 423–34
  mortality of slaves in, 521n 6, 521n 9
  registration of slaves in, 413–14
typhoid, 408

underenumeration of infant death: see
    underreporting
underreporting of infant death, 410
  in slave records, 400–403, *401*, 398
  successive confinement method of estimating,
      403, *404*
United States:
  non-profitability of slavery thesis, 631–32
  see also Civil War (U.S.), Union, Confederacy
Union army:
  ex-slave recruits, 508, 509–13
  financing of war effort, 621
urbanization, 512

value of slave, 618, 619, 602–3n 2
  see also prices of slaves
Vance, Rupert, 652, 655, 658
Venezuela, 617, 626n 13
Vermont, 588, 615
Vinovskis, Maris A., 394, 496

Virginia, 377, *377*, 620
vital registration data, 397
vitamins:
    content of foods, 527–28
    deficiency and disease, 397
    minimum requirements of, 525, 526–27,
      526
Vollman, R. F., 446

Watt, Bernice K., 525, 528, 527
wealth:
    fertility and, 383, 389
    of Britain and U.S. (19th century), 605*n*29
weaning, 398, 399
West Africa: see Africa
West Indies: see British colonies
Wharton, Vernon L., 655, 658
whipping of slaves:
    demonstration effect of, 543–44, 549,
      550
    perceptions of, 537–38
    see also punishment of slaves
Wiener, Jonathan M., 665

Wilberforce, William, 413
Williams, Eric, 572, 573
Williamson, Joel, 655
Woodman, Harold D., 665
Woodward, C. Vann, 663*n*1
women, with surviving children, 383, 384
    see also slave women; gender
work ethic of slaves, 504
work-gang agriculture, 654
    freedmen's attitude toward, 670, 658–59
    in postbellum South, 648, 656
    vs. tenancy, 649–50
    see also freedmen; gang-labor system; labor in
      the postbellum South; sharecropping
World Health Organization (WHO), 525,
    526–27, *526*
Wright, Gavin, 650
Wrigley, E. A., 401

yaws, 415
yellow fever, 408

Zilversmit, Arthur, 596, 598